ADULT LEARNING AND EDUCATION

ADULT LEARNING AND EDUCATION

EDITOR

KJELL RUBENSON
University of British Columbia
Department of Educational Studies
Vancouver, BC
Canada

ELSEVIER

AMSTERDAM • BOSTON • HEIDELBERG • LONDON • NEW YORK • OXFORD
PARIS • SAN DIEGO • SAN FRANCISCO • SINGAPORE • SYDNEY • TOKYO
Academic Press is an imprint of Elsevier

ACADEMIC
PRESS

Academic Press is an imprint of Elsevier
The Boulevard Langford Lane, Kidlington, Oxford OX5 1GB, UK

British Library Cataloguing in Publication Data
A catalogue record for this book is available from the British Library

Library of Congress Catalog Number
A catalogue record for this book is available from the Library of Congress

ISBN: 9780123814890

For information on all Elsevier publications
visit our website at books.elsevier.com

Printed and bound by CPI Group (UK) Ltd, Croydon, CR0 4YY

Transferred to Digital Print 2012

PREFACE

In the introduction to the second edition of the *International Encyclopedia of Adult Education and Training*, the editor points out that adult education is heuristic, multidisciplinary, and eclectic in orientation, and that its knowledge base is diffuse and incomplete (Tuijnman, 1996, p. xv). If anything, this is even truer a decade or so later. Other fields of study (such as economics, political science, psychology, sociology, and organizational sciences) take an increasing interest in adult learning and contribute crucial knowledge to its theoretical and empirical knowledge base. So it becomes increasingly difficult to precisely define what constitutes the core of adult education and learning. With this in mind, this book attempts to present an overview of the still emerging field of adult education. The 46 articles included provide insight into the historical development of the field, its conceptual controversies, domains and provision, perspectives on adult learning, instruction and program planning, outcomes, relationship to economy and society, and its status as a field of scholarly study and practice. However, it should be recognized that with a diverse field like this, it is of course impossible to fully represent the many nuances of adult learning.

The entries in this book were originally commissioned for inclusion in *The International Encyclopedia of Education*, 3rd edition, which was published in May 2010. The proposed contributors were selected on the strength of their reputation and in an attempt to get an international representation.

The 46 entries are grouped into four main sections. The three entries included in Section I provide a general overview of the field of adult education, including its historical development, and looks at the recent shift from adult education to adult and lifelong learning. Section II comprises 11 entries dealing with a broad array of perspectives on adult learning, instruction, and program planning with an emphasis on the former. Section III, with 19 entries, looks at adult learning from the point of the rich array of domains and providers of adult learning, and takes account of recent developments in prior learning assessment and portfolio assessment. In addition, the second part of this section also includes overviews of participation and barriers to adult learning as well the financing of adult learning. Adult education as a field of study is the focus of the four entries in Section IV and is addressed the way gender, class, and race and ethnicity have been addressed in adult education scholarship. Further, the section contains an overview of trends in workplace learning research, a growing field in adult education scholarship. Finally, Section V comprises nine entries devoted to broader social and economic issues of adult learning. It looks at the impact of the modernization process and political economy on adult learning, the role adult learning is playing in civil society, nation building, and health as well as the impact of globalization. Finally economic and wider benefits to adult learning are reviewed.

The preparation of this volume required an enormous amount of work. A special debt of gratitude is due to Penelope Peterson, Eva Baker, and Barry McGaw, the Editors-in-Chief of the parent Encyclopedia, who carefully reviewed the incoming entries and to the many people at Elsevier who worked so attentively throughout the production of the original Encyclopedia.

June 15, 2010
Kjell Rubenson
Vancouver, Canada
(© 2011, Elsevier Limited. All rights reserved.)

CONTENTS

DOMAINS PROVISIONS AND PARTICIPATION

PERSPECTIVES IN ADULT EDUCATION RESEARCH

ADULT LEARNING, ECONOMY, AND SOCIETY

CONTRIBUTORS

M Ahmed
Brac University, Dhaka, Bangladesh

P Andersson
Linköping University, Linköping, Sweden

D Beckett
The University of Melbourne, Melbourne, VIC,
Australia

S Billett
Griffith University, Brisbane, QLD, Australia

P Bélanger
UNESCO Institute for Education, Hamburg, Germany

R M Cervero
University of Georgia, Athens, GA, USA

R M Cervero
The University of Georgia, Athens, GA, USA

B Connolly
National University of Ireland, Maynooth, Republic of
Ireland

P Cranton
Penn State University at Harrisburg, Middletown, PA,
USA

J Crowther
University of Edinburgh, Edinburgh, UK

C H O Daeyeon
Sookmyung Women's University, Seoul, Republic of
Korea

B J Daley
University of Wisconsin – Milwaukee, Milwaukee,
WI, USA

R Desjardins
Danish University of Education, Copenhagen, Denmark

D Drake-Clark
The University of Georgia, Athens, GA, USA

C Duke
University of Leicester, Leicester, UK; University of
Stirling, Scotland, UK; RMIT University, Melbourne, VIC,
Australia

P-E Ellström
Linköping University, Linköping, Sweden

T Fenwick
University of Alberta, Edmonton, AB, Canada

A Ferrer
University of Calgary, Calgary, AB, Canada

J Field
University of Stirling, Stirling, UK

K Forrester
University of Leeds, Leeds, UK

R S Grenier
University of Connecticut, Storrs, CT, USA

B J Hake
University of Leiden, Leiden, The Netherlands

N Z Haniff
University of Michigan, Ann Arbor, MI, USA

P Hodkinson
University of Leeds, Leeds, UK

R Höghielm
Stockholm University, Stockholm, Sweden

K Illeris
Danish University of Education, Copenhagen,
Denmark

P Jarvis
University of Surrey, Guildford, UK

J Johnson-Bailey
The University of Georgia, Athens, GA, USA

V Klenowski
Queensland University of Technology, Brisbane, QLD,
Australia

B Kriechel
ROA – Maastricht University, Maastricht,
The Netherlands; IZA, Bonn, Germany

D-B Kwon
Sookmyung Women's University, Seoul, Republic of
Korea

P Loveder
National Centre for Vocational Education Research,
Adelaide, SA, Australia

I Martin
University of Edinburgh, Edinburgh, UK

P Mayo
University of Malta, Msida, Malta

S B Merriam
University of Georgia, Athens, GA, USA

T Nesbit
Simon Fraser University, Vancouver, BC, Canada

H S Olesen
Roskilde University, Roskilde, Denmark

J M Parisi
University of Illinois at Urbana–Champaign, Champaign, IL, USA

G Rees
Cardiff University, Cardiff, UK

W C Riddell
University of British Columbia, Vancouver, BC, Canada

M Robitaille
University of Quebec in Montreal, Montreal, QC, Canada

K Rubenson
University of British Columbia, Vancouver, BC, Canada

D Schugurensky
University of Toronto, Toronto, ON, Canada

T Schuller
OECD, Paris, France

M Slowey
Dublin City University, Dublin, Republic of Ireland

Å Sohlman
Ministry of Employment, Stockholm, Sweden

J Stalker
University of Waikato, Hamilton, New Zealand

R St.Clair
University of Glasgow, Glasgow, UK

E A L Stine-Morrow
University of Illinois at Urbana–Champaign, Champaign, IL, USA

L Tett
University of Edinburgh, Edinburgh, UK

S Tøsse
Norwegian University of Science and Technology, Trondheim, Norway

S Walters
University of Western Cape, Bellville, South Africa

L West
Canterbury Christ Church University, Canterbury, UK

A L Wilson
Cornell University, Ithaca, NY, USA

INTRODUCTION

The Field of Adult Education: An Overview

Rewriting the History of Adult Education: The Search for Narrative Structures

Lifelong Learning

The Field of Adult Education: An Overview

K Rubenson, University of British Columbia, Vancouver, BC, Canada

This entry provides a brief introduction to the field of adult education, presenting its historical roots, issues around its definition, structure of the field, perspectives on learning, the field of scholarship, and issues of broader economic factors that have framed the field.

Toward a Field of Adult Education

Although J. H. Hudson's 1851 *The History of Adult Education* identified it as a unique field, only in the last 1960s has adult education been recognized as a distinct field of practice and study. Organized forms of education serving very limited elite groups of adults have been noted since ancient time. Plato's *Republic* presents a well-laid-out structure of what we today would call lifelong learning for the ruling class and outlines in detail what kind of education would be required at various stages in life from childhood up to middle age. Similar examples are available from early civilizations in Egypt, China, and India, in which the technological advancements and complex administrative systems relied on education and training of a small leading segment of the adult population (Kidd and Titmus, 1989, p. xxiv). A different and later form of adult education has its roots in the Protestant reformation in Northern and Central Europe during the later part of the sixteenth century and the first-half of the seventeenth century. During this period, adult education was influenced by translations of the Bible and the invention of the printing press that among other things supported Bible-study groups and a reading public. The modern forms of adult education and learning have their roots in the modernization of industrial processes and the resulting far-reaching changes to society that took place in the late nineteenth and early twentieth century. Thus, the historical evolution of educational movements, the rise and fall of celebrated adult-education institutions, as well as policies and reforms have to be seen in the context of the broader dynamics of social change and conflict. Currently, we can observe how regionally different models of lifelong learning policies are emerging as a response to changes in relatively unique cultural, economic, and political contexts.

The second part of the nineteenth and the first part of the twentieth century saw a marked increase in educational activities for adults in Europe and North America. However, as Kidd and Titmus (1989, p. xxiv) note, these were perceived as discrete activities rather than part of a coherent field of adult education. By the early twentieth century, adult education had become the fastest-growing educational sector in the United States. This highlighted the urgency to form national associations of adult education and saw a gradual move to a professionalization of the field. The first study of adult education in the United States, initiated by the Carnegie Corporation in 1924, resulted in the formation of the American Association for Adult Education (AAAE), in 1926. The purpose of AAAE was to advance lifelong learning; serve as a central forum for a variety of adult-education interest groups; influence local, state, and regional adult-education efforts; monitor legislation; conduct special studies; and maintain a speakers' bureau. One of the first activities of the AAAE was to start the publication of a *Handbook of Adult Education* series, the first being released in 1928. Since then, nine handbooks have been published, including the latest edition that is to be published in 2010.

In Europe, the formation of adult-education associations originally had less to do with developing a professional orientation but was instead aimed at bringing adult education to the working class and others, for example, women previously denied access to education. The primary examples of this are the mechanics institutes and the Association for the Higher Education of Working Men formed in 1903, and renamed as the Workers' Educational Association (WEA) in 1905. The WEA movement quickly spread to Australia, Canada, and New Zealand, where adult education became seen as an essential tool for encouraging new immigrants to contribute to their new society. Folk high schools and study associations tightly connected to the labor movement and other social movements appeared in the Nordic countries. Germany and some other continental and Eastern European countries saw the development of various forms of *Volksbildung*. However, it was not before the later part of the 1960s that a more discernable and cohesive academic field of adult education started to take shape.

One sign of a maturing field of adult education has been the mushrooming of local, national, regional, and world organizations. From its early beginnings, a defining character of the evolving field has been its strong international dimension built around shared values and aspirations. This has positioned adult education as an international movement promoting adult education as a way to combat inequalities, support democracy, and promote cultural and social, democratic development (Duke, 1994). The first

United Nations Educational Scientific and Cultural Organization (UNESCO) International Conference of Adult Education (CONFITEA) took place in 1949, and was followed by additional conferences in 1960, 1972, 1985, 1997, and 2009. The growth of the field can be illustrated by the attendance at these conferences. In 1949, at the conference in Montreal, there was attendance from 25 countries, and in 1997, in Hamburg, the figure had increased to 130 and is expected to reach 175 at the 2009 conference.

Concepts

Since adult education began to emerge as a field, there have been constant discussions about what terminology to use to describe the enterprise as well as about its definition and boundaries. The understanding of what constitutes adult education has not only changed over time, but also varied depending on cultural and institutional context. Until the 1920s, the tradition had been to talk about specific aspects such as literacy for immigrants, university extension, mechanic institutes, workers' education, but not to group these under an overall umbrella labeled adult education. As part of the professionalization of adult education that took place in the United States, in the first two decades, the term adult education came to be commonly used as a composite term to denote different activities relating to the education of adults. However, in most other parts of the world, the professionalization process came later and it was not until the 1960s that the generic term adult education was more broadly used. In many European countries, it had up until then been customary not to refer specifically to the education of adults but more generally to popular enlightenment as in France or the Nordic countries or *Volksbildung* as in Germany.

While the term adult education steadily won ground, there remained a lack of agreement on its definition and boundaries. Selman and Dampier (1991, p. 2) note that different terms are used for the same thing and people doing similar work may refer to this as community education, continuing education, adult training, literacy, extension, or adult education. Similarly, the terminology differs from country to country depending on historical circumstances. In fact, the organization of articles in this encyclopedia reflects the idiosyncrasies of what to include or not to include under the term adult education. Thus, to many in the field, several entries that are now presented in the volume on vocational education and training ought to have been included in the adult-education section and similar argument could be made for moving entries from the adult-education section to the one on vocational education and training.

Over the years, different definitions of the term adult education have appeared (see e.g., Bryson, 1936;

Houle, 1972; Verner, 1962). The most commonly used definition is presently the one adopted by UNESCO (1976, p. 2) and reads in abbreviated form:

> The term 'adult education' denotes the entire body of organized educational processes, whatever the content, level and method, whether formal or otherwise, whether they prolong or replace initial education in schools, colleges, and universities as well as in apprenticeship, whereby persons regarded as adult by the society to which they belong develop their abilities, enrich their knowledge, improve their technical or professional qualifications or turn them in a new direction and bring about changes in their attitudes or behavior in the twofold perspective of full personal development and participation in balanced and independent social, economic, and cultural development; adult education, however, must not be considered as an entity in itself, it is a sub-division, and an integral part of, a global scheme for lifelong education and learning.

Critical in the UNESCO definition, as in most other attempts to outline adult education, is how the term adult is best understood. Building on (human-development) stage theory, Darkenwald and Merriam (1982, p. 9) state: "adult education is a process whereby persons whose major social roles are characteristic of adult status undertake systematic and sustained learning activities for the purpose of bringing about changes in knowledge, attitudes, values and skills." Thus, adult education refers to "activities intentionally designed for the purpose of bringing about learning among those whose age, social roles, or self-perception define them as adults" (Merriam and Brockett, 1997, p. 8). According to this view, it is not age as such that defines someone as an adult, but the social roles that the person is carrying out. The second key dimension in the UNESCO definition relates to the special educational organization of the education for adults. It is in this context that adult education refers to "its own peculiar organization, methods and curriculum, which distinguishes adult education from any other field of education." In the words of Verner (1964, p. 1), "...the term adult education is used to designate all those educational activities that are designed specifically for adults." However, it has become increasingly difficult to maintain this kind of definition. First, not all adults taking part in adult education are adults in the terms of social roles and functioning. Second, it is commonly pointed out that participation in adult education is not always a volunteer act but it is more commonly becoming something an adult has to do to keep their work or become eligible for certain benefits like unemployment insurance. Third, attempts to separate adult learners from first-time students attending regular school or university are also becoming more blurred. The traditional pattern of study has changed and with an increasing number of students moving in and out of the educational system and the labor market, it is difficult to identify who is in the first cycle of studies and who is a recurrent learner.

While recognizing the problems of defining who is an adult learner, various pragmatic solutions are being sought. So, for example, recent studies like the International Adult Literacy Survey and the Adult Literacy and Life Skills Survey (OECD, 2003, 2005) allow for the exclusion of all regular, full-time students, except the following: full-time students subsidized by employers; full-time students over 19 enrolled in elementary or secondary programs; and full-time students over 24 enrolled in postsecondary programs. While this approach may be pragmatic, it is evident that in the emergent learning society, the traditional distinctions between initial education, particularly higher education, and adult education are becoming increasingly blurred.

The 1976 UNESCO definition reflects the strong and growing calls to see adult education as a segment within an overall principle of lifelong learning. Today Ideas of lifelong learning are having strong influence over adult-education policy and different regional models are developing UNESCO (1976). In this perspective, it is of interest to note that the UNESCO Institute of Education has changed its name to UNESCO Institute of Lifelong Learning. This use of the concept departs from the fundamental principle of lifelong learning as put forth by transnational organizations such as the European Union (EU), the OECD, and the UNESCO which proclaim that the concept of lifelong learning is based on three fundamental attributes:

- it is lifelong and therefore concerns everything from cradle to grave;
- it is life-wide recognizing that learning occurs in many different settings; and
- it focuses on learning rather than limit itself to education.

In adult-education circles, particularly in the Anglo Saxon countries, lifelong learning is given a more restrictive understanding and has increasingly come to be used interchangeably with just one segment of lifelong learning, namely adult learning. This is, for example, the case in the United Kingdom, where departments of adult education have been renamed departments of lifelong learning. Similarly, one of the leading scholarly journals in adult education is named *International Journal of Lifelong Education* focusing almost exclusively on adult learning.

The embracement of lifelong learning, in its broad or restrictive meaning, results in a shift from the concept of adult education to adult learning, resulting in a further proliferation of the terminology in use. So, for example, today a distinction is being made between three basic categories of settings where purposeful learning activity takes place (European Commission, 2000):

1. *Formal learning.* This learning typically takes place in an education or training institution; it is structured (in terms of learning objectives, learning time, or learning support) and leads to certification. Formal learning is intentional from the learner's perspective.

2. *Nonformal learning.* It is learning that is not provided by an education or training institution and typically does not lead to certification. It is, however, structured (in terms of learning objectives, learning time, or learning support). Nonformal learning may be provided in the workplace and through the activities of civil-society organizations and groups. It can also be provided by organizations or through services that have been set up to complement formal systems, for example, arts, music, and sports classes. Nonformal learning is intentional from the learner's perspective.

3. *Informal learning.* It is learning resulting from daily life activities related to work, family, or leisure. It is not structured (in terms of learning objectives, learning time, or learning support) and typically does not lead to certification. Informal learning may be intentional but in most cases it is nonintentional (or incidental/random).

While policy documents overwhelmingly subscribe to definitions of adult learning that broadly correspond to those presented by the European Communities' policy documents, the scholarly literature contains many different and competing definitions and questions the advisability of trying to seek clear definitional distinctions between the three concepts. Others warn that the tendency to substitute learning for education can de-politicize the field and move the focus away from broader issues such as equity, the role of the state, policy, and resources that are central when addressing issues of democracy and equality (Duke, 1994; Rubenson, 2006). In this respect, it is of interest to note that the CONFINTEA VI meeting in 2009 used the label adult learning and education (ALE), a concept that may become prevalent in the years to come.

As the debate over how to delimit education continues, many students of the field will likely agree with Duke (1994, p. 8) when he states:

> The important point about the concept field and scope of adult education is that it is necessarily broad, diffuse, multilocational in terms of research sites and academic identities. It reflects the diffuseness and weakly bounded nature of adult education (and learning) itself.

To some, the concerns over a breakdown of the traditional boundaries of adult education and adult education as a profession are misplaced. Instead, they recommend that the focus be on practitioners working professionally with adults, whoever and wherever they may be (Usher *et al.*, 1997, p. 27).

Adult Education Domains and Provision

While the structure and provision of adult education vary considerably from country to country, some main sectors are discernable:

- adult basic education including adult literacy and numeracy;
- immigrant and citizenship education;
- adult higher education;
- workplace education and training (see section on vocational education and training);
- community education;
- popular adult education; and
- museums, radio, and TV and libraries.

When the AAAE was formed in 1926, adult education was generally understood in a narrow sense and expected to fulfill two main purposes. First, was to teach English to immigrants and to prepare them for American citizenship, and second, to provide a second chance for those that had been deprived of education in their earlier years. These two purposes have remained central to adult education. As immigration spread more and more, countries started to devote significant human and material resources to citizenship and immigrant education. Focusing almost exclusively on preparing the new immigrants for the labor market and assimilating into the prevailing culture, there have been increasing number of programs having the dual purpose of stimulating unity and diversity. In the 1960s and 1970s, the expansion of educational opportunities for the young, in combination with rising skill demands in the economy, brought basic adult education and literacy onto the policy agenda. With the emerging knowledge economy, functional adult literacy, and the national pool of human competencies have gained a renewed interest by policymakers (OECD, 2005). In the developing world, adult literacy is considered central to development as well as to addressing issues of human immunovirus/acquired immunodeficiency syndrome (HIV/AIDS). Adult basic education and particularly adult literacy education display a great variation in terms of structure, provider, and philosophy. It can be found in churches, schools, colleges, community settings, workplaces, and libraries and offered by professional or unqualified staff.

The structure of the current university adult and continuing-education programs reflects their historical roots. In the United Kingdom and the Commonwealth, these are to be found in the adult and extra-mural tradition with its special centers or departments dedicated to offering university courses to adults. In the United States, on the other hand, the tradition emanated from the Land Grant universities with their explicit mission to support the local community and rural development. Reflecting an acceptance of the principle of lifelong learning, adult learners now make up a large proportion of students in higher education – in some countries, they even constitute a majority. A large number of these are enrolled in regular courses or programs, while others take a continuing-education course. Among the latter, an increasing number is found in continuing professional education which has increased dramatically with rising demands for mandatory continuing education in several professions. As with any educational system, continuing professional education has many stakeholders with multiple agendas that are being shaped by professional and social, institutional, and educational considerations (OECD, 2005). A new growing clientele for the university are older adults who take advantage of courses offered by continuing-education departments or specialized programs like Elder-hostel or the University of the Third Age.

Information on enrolment in different forms of adult education reveals a dramatic shift in provision over the last three decades. In the OECD countries, this is primarily caused by a remarkable increase in employer-supported activities that have radically altered the landscape of adult education (Bélanger and Valdivieso, 1997; Desjardins et al., 2006). The data reflect the broader changes that have occurred in the labor market, which, among other things, forces people to participate because they are ordered or feel pressurized to undergo some form of adult education and training linked to their work (Carré, 2000). This education and training is being offered by a multiplicity of providers from different sectors, including formal educational institutions, commercial schools/private training providers, and employers and suppliers of equipment. The range and diversity of providers of workplace-related education contributes to the uncertainties about the reach and impact of public policy decisions on the structure of adult education and training.

Another distinct sector involves popular adult education in which today we can find two dominant traditions: one Nordic and one Latin American, though each has some followers in other parts of the world. Folk high schools and adult-education associations with roots in the classical social movements are a vital part of the adult-education sector particularly in the Nordic countries. In the latter countries, it is free and voluntary, despite considerable state and municipal subsidies; it lies at the crossroads between civil society and the state and has three major roles: it acts as an agency of popular movements, it is an adult educator, and it is a supporter of culture. It does not primarily cater to individuals' careers and job needs, but broadly responds to their role as citizens, parents, and/or personal development. In many parts of the world, popular adult education, while less structured than in the Nordic countries and lacking state subsidy, plays an important role in the life of various social movements. The Latin American tradition is closely associated with the work and pedagogy of Paulo Freire. Because of working closely with oppressed groups, the focus is often on improving their literacy and consciousness raising with an aim to inspire solidarity and collective political awareness and action. This tradition of popular adult education draws heavily on popular culture traditions, dance, song, drama, and storytelling. Its vitality can be seen in other areas of educational activity as well. For example, labor education, which can take many different forms, is sometimes an important avenue for popular education. Community education is a form of locally funded educational and recreationally program that can be seen to occupy a space between the formal educational system and popular adult education. This form of provision is particularly well developed in the United Kingdom, Ireland, Australia, and parts of the United States and also in several African countries, for example, South Africa. Traditions and structure of community education vary between countries and at times the role of the state in setting direction is more direct while in other traditions, for example, the so-called Wisconsin model, it follows a hands-off approach.

However, a common denominator is the rootedness in the community and the focus on preparing the community and its inhabitants to respond to structural and educational disadvantage.

The section on domains and provision has addressed actual structures of adult education, but in addition to these, it is worth mentioning a recent idea that focuses not on specific providers but considers a city or region as a learning entity. The concept can be seen as a political and social utopia that expresses what a city or region wants to become in the emerging knowledge society. Another current development is the general idea of prior learning assessment (PLA), which is about acknowledging and giving formal recognition to prior learning, irrespective of when, where, and how learning has taken place. PLA can be seen as a natural consequence of the acceptance of the principle of lifelong learning and breaks with the tradition of defining adult-education activities in terms of provider and instead recognizes learning in whatever form it takes.

Adult Learning, Instruction, and Program Planning

The literature on adult education has primarily focused on what and how adults learn, instructional methods appropriate when working with adults, and how to design and organize educational activities for adults.

A hotly debated issue has been whether or not adult learning should be understood as a distinctive process that significantly differs from how children learn. In *The Modern Practice of Adult Education: Andragogy Versus Pedagogy*, Knowles (1970) argues that adult learning differs fundamentally from how children learn. The book, which contains a set of principles that should guide adult learning practices, quickly became somewhat of a Bible for practitioners. Facing extensive criticism for the sharp division he had drawn between how adults and children learn, Knowles changed his position and suggested that rather than see a dichotomy between andragogy and pedagogy, they constituted a continuum. Consequently, in the 1980 edition of *The Modern Practice of Adult Education*, the subtitle was changed to read *From Pedagogy to Andragogy*. To many, even this softening of the original position does not go far enough and they challenge the idea of trying to build an academic field focusing distinctly on adult learning. This is the case among scholars working in the biographic perspective on adult learning who stress the continuities between early life and adult experience (Knowles, 1970). Others, while recognizing that adults' and children's learning from the point of psychological functioning may not differ, maintain that this position holds only for some very basic features of learning. Their key point is that in the planning of adult-education practices, one has to recognize that adult learning, in contrast to children's learning, is principally selective and self-directed.

Andragogy, like two other dominant perspectives on adult learning, self-directed learning and transformative learning, is informed by humanistic psychology and focuses on the individual adult learner. Following the general developments in learning research, scholars in adult education have become more skeptical to the traditional strong individual orientation and have increasingly adopted a situated-cognition orientation. This is particularly noticeable in writings on workplace learning, an area that is prominent in recent adult education learning literature. The research on the situated nature of learning at work has helped shed light on why there is often less of a transfer between what has been learned in a school situation and the application of this knowledge and experiences at the workplace. The focus on workplace learning has stimulated an interest to understand not only how individuals learn but also how organizations themselves might hinder or encourage learning. A learning organization is being promoted as an ideal form of organization that fosters continuous organizational renewal through encouraging the learning of its members (Knowles, 1970). With the interest in organizational learning and situated-cognition workplace learning, scholars have embraced a network and community of practice traditions, more recently a co-participation model that encourages combined micro- and macrolevel analysis of workplaces.

Outcomes of Adult Education

With increased public and private investment in adult education, there is a growing interest in developing a more comprehensive understanding of how adult education and learning can contribute economically and socially to the well-being of the individual and society. The two central questions are "who is participating in what kind of adult education and learning?" and "what benefits does this learning have for the individual and society?"

Current research shows that participation rates vary substantially across countries and that there are marked differences between countries with quite similar economies too. Regardless of the overall participation rate, participation patterns are very similar. In all countries, older adults, the poor, and unemployed, low-skilled workers, migrants, ethnic minorities, and rural inhabitants report a reduced tendency to participate (Desjardins *et al.*, 2006). Gender inequalities vary between countries with some reporting a higher rate of participation among women and the others a lower. However, despite similar patterns of exclusion, the degree of inequality varies substantially among countries. Comparative findings suggest that policy does matter and that political commitment to high standards of equity, and willingness to address market failures through sustained public policy efforts affect participation patterns. Thus, government intervention can affect a person's capability to participate through fostering broad structural conditions relevant to participation and construct targeted policy measures that are aimed at overcoming both structurally and individually based barriers (Rubenson and Desjardins, 2009).

The main individual outcomes of participation in adult education that have been examined are labor-market outcomes such as wages, employment, and earnings. For employers, the key outcome of adult education and training is worker productivity (OECD, 2003). The literature suggests that while there may be unaccounted-for factors, returns to training, particularly employer training and off-the-job training, are generally positive.

Further, there seem to be interesting differences between countries (Desjardins, Rubenson and Milana, 2006). Most studies tend to focus solely on skills and competencies for economic outcomes and neglect the relationships between various forms of adult learning and quality of life as well as overlook the synergy between formal, nonformal, and informal learning. Naturally, the impacts of adult education and learning extend beyond various economic outcomes and during recent years, there has been a growing interest in the wider benefits of adult learning, particularly health and civic engagement.

The work carried out so far suggests a positive impact on health and civic and political participation, but it has also identified a range of difficult methodological issues. One general problem is that situating outcomes of adult learning in the broader context of lifelong learning requires measures that allow comparisons across formal, nonformal, and informal learning settings, so that substitution and complementarity between the various forms of adult learning can be assessed. While participation in organized learning is quite restricted, almost everyone seems to be engaged in purposeful informal learning activities – but so what? What consequences flow from being involved in particular forms of adult learning? The shift in focus from adult education to lifelong learning has moved the attention away from inputs toward outputs.

As part of the professionalization process of adult education, scholars and practitioners began to pay serious attention to designing and organizing adult educational activities. Over time, the program planning literature in adult education, predominantly from the United States, has come to provide a rich body of competing models and theories on decisions and actions about what is to be learned, how the learning is to take place, who the learners and the teachers are, and what the education is for. Despite the great number of models developed for specific programs over the years, there seems to be more uniformity than could be expected, which has made some scholars suggest the existence of a generic model (Sork and Cafarella, 1989). These reviews have also identified a sense of a growing gap between what is prescribed in the theories and what practitioners actually do when planning programs. The explanation for this is to be found in the fact that the proposed planning theories are limited in their understanding of what actual planning practice is required, and instead are rooted in a form of instrumental rationality that privileges normative prescriptions of what planners should do.

Adult Education, Economy, and Society

A full appreciation of adult education and learning requires that they be seen in their socioeconomic, political, and cultural contexts. In a historical perspective, the idea of modernization provides an insight into the changing institutional realities and conceptual meanings of adult education and learning. For example, literacy education was needed to enable modern societies and a condition for socioeconomic development, while popular and community education has had a perspective on social, cultural, and political self-articulation as well as social and political struggle (Sork and Cafarella, 1989). Further, recent stress on continuing-skills upgrading reflects changes in the reproduction of labor. Traditionally, skills upgrading occurred when younger more skilled workers replaced retiring workers. In the new economy, this is no longer a sufficient process to secure economic survival. Thus, contemporary policies on and approaches to adult education are driven by the expected role of adult learning in human-capital formation, particularly for the so-called knowledge economy.

While considering how different societies are responding to the stress of a globalized knowledge economy, we should remember Martin Carnoy's point that there are crucial differences in what adult education attempts to do and can do in different social–political structures. He states (Carnoy, 1995, p. 3):

> Ultimately, these differences depend heavily on the possibilities and limits of the state, since it is the state that defines adult education and is the principal beneficiary of its effective implementation. These possibilities and limits of the state are, then, a key issue understanding the form and content of adult education.

Carnoy's point helps understand the importance of situating the present discussion of skills in the political economy of adult education and to take account of the social construction of skills. It also foregrounds the political purpose of adult education, which becomes evident when juxtaposing adult education and nation building. The region of the Southern African development community provides an illustrative example of how adult education and nation building is influenced by local regional and global developments (Carnoy, 1995).

The political will of government is reflected in the extent to which, as well as how, adult education gets funding, the balance between public and market-driven funding mechanisms, and how this reflects on the social justice and distributional aspects of adult education and learning. Concerned about the latter, adult educators have critiqued the dominance of a strong market approach and governments' reluctance to address market failures in the learning market. In response to the dominant political economy, driving adult education, there has been a revival of adult education for civil society which further illustrates how socioeconomic, political, and cultural context informs the formation of adult education. Adult education, for civil society, can in Gramscian terms (Adamson, 1980; Boggs, 1976), be understood as a struggle to build a counter hegemony to the dominant discourse on adult education and learning. In countries affected by the collapse of the totalitarian communist states, or being freed from other forms of dictatorship, it is also a response to the need for a new form of citizenship.

There are particularly three aspects of justice with regard to adult education that concern adult-education scholars, class, gender, and race and ethnicity. Understandings of class have been central in explaining inequalities of opportunities, standards of living, and widening disparities between the rich and the poor. From an adult-education perspective, two issues stand out. First, how are adult education and learning practices linked to the globalized nature of capitalism and second, the operation of a distinctive working-class learning style (Boggs, 1976). Similar questions are asked by feminist scholars engaged in gender analysis. Gender analysis that can reflect different theoretical perspectives is shaped by its history and provides a strategy for research process and strategic initiatives to address inequalities (Boggs, 1976). Like class and gender, race and ethnicity play a major role in structuring society and the opportunities it provides. Reviews of the literature reveal somewhat surprisingly that the way race has been socially constructed has remained stable over the last 50 years. Further, it is noted that it was not until 15 years ago that the issue of race was taken for an in-depth analysis in the adult-education literature (Boggs, 1976).

Field of Study

Since adult education began to emerge as a field of study in the late 1920s, it has undergone three quite distinctive phases. These phases are most noticeable in the United States, which to a large extent has come to define the nature of the scholarly field, but they are also clearly discernible in Europe and to a lesser extent in some other parts of the world.

As the demand for trained instructors to teach the large number of immigrants grew, a few U.S. universities began offering specific courses on how to teach adults, starting with the University of Columbia in 1922 (Milton *et al.*, 2003). Quite soon, graduate programs began to emerge. The first began at Teachers College at Columbia University in 1930, and by 1964, 16 universities in the United States offered master and doctoral programs in adult education (Houle, 1991). A similar development took place in the United Kingdom, in departments of extra-mural studies offering university courses, where adults developed an interest in adult-education research, and in 1926, the first chair in adult education was established at the University of Nottingham (Hake, 1994).

With a small but growing number of adult-education programs, universities started to focus on how to generate a body of knowledge that would help in the growth of the evolving field. Guided by funding from the W. K. Kellogg Foundation, the Commission of Professors in the United States set out to define the conceptual foundations of adult education (Jensen *et al.*, 1964). Officially titled, *Adult Education: Outlines of an Emerging Field of University Study* and published in 1964, their work has come to be known as the Black Book. This publication can be seen as ushering in the second phase of adult education, characterized by a major expansion of graduate programs and the coming of age of adult education as a field of study. Between the release of the Black Book and the publication of its follow up, *Adult Education: Evolution and Achievements in a Developing Field of Study*, in 1991, the number of adult-education graduate programs in the United States increased from 16 to 124 (Houle, 1991). Another indication of the growing knowledge base of adult education was the launch in 1969 of the yearly American Adult Education Research Conference (AERC) and the development of *Adult Education Quarterly* – arguably, the preeminent journal in the field.

Similar developments took place in Canada and in parts of Europe. In the former, the first graduate program was established at the University of British Columbia in 1957 and by the late 1980s, there were ten graduate programs in the country (Selman and Dampier, 1991, p. 255). In the United Kingdom and Germany, the number of departments of adult education increased, first slowly in the 1950s and 1960s, and thereafter faster in the 1970s and 1980s. Sweden, with a very long tradition of adult education, introduced special funding for adult-education research at the end of the 1960s, and university programs and chairs sprang up in Finland, the Netherlands, Germany, France, Poland, the former Yugoslavia, and somewhat later in several other European countries. In 1991, the European Society for the study of adult education was formed.

In other parts of the world, particularly in the developing countries, the process began later and many countries are in what can be seen as the first phase. This is the case in several African and Latin American countries. In some instances, like in Brazil, there is an acceleration of programs and departments specializing in adult education. In China, the first MA program was launched at East China Normal University in 1993 and a Ph.D. program in 2004. In 2008, China reports to have some 100 specialized institutions for adult-education research and is moving into what can be seen as the second phase.

The 1991 review of the evolution and achievements in the developing field of adult education (Peters and Jarvis, 1991) can be read as a summary of situation in North America and Northern Europe at the end of phase 2. The book paints a very positive picture depicting the significant expansion in the knowledge base, lessened dependency on related disciplines, broadening of research methodologies, exponential growth of graduate programs, and that the field has become more internationalized. Based on the achievements so far, the book ends on a positive outlook and with expectations of continuous growth and solidification of the field of adult education over the coming 25 years. While there does not exist any comprehensive review of what has happened, since the 1991 book, there are several indications that the field of study has not progressed as anticipated and that it has entered into a new phase in its development. In North America and those parts of Europe where the field had expanded and matured during the second phase, the last two decades have not seen a continuing growth in specialized adult-education departments. Instead, the trend has been to amalgamate adult-education programs with other areas into larger departments or in some instances to close them down. These developments have been driven by a combination of forces external and internal to the field of adult education. First, the amalgamations have been part of a general restructuring of university departments into larger structures, which tends to hamper the building of a field of adult education as foreseen under phase 2. Second, the embracement of the principle of lifelong learning also weakens the ambition of building a separate field of adult education. Third, with workplace learning being by far the fastest-growing area of adult-education practice, adult-education researchers have increasingly come to be engaged in research on workplace learning. Over the last decade, workplace learning has increasingly taken on the shape of an alternative field with its own journals and scholarly conferences. While this development can weaken the field as adult educators break out of the traditional boundary of their discipline, it also provides an opportunity to strengthen the field as researchers from other disciplines are encouraged to break into adult education. The focus on the so-called knowledge economy has stimulated other disciplines, economics, sociology, organizational sciences, etc. to engage with issues that would have traditionally been seen to fall under adult education. Fourth, as in other fields of education, there is a general shift away from more pure fields and disciplines and a move to organize the knowledge-generation process around cross-cutting themes such as gender and immigration that are approached from an interdisciplinary or multidisciplinary stand. In this environment, adult-education scholars increasingly develop multiple alliances housed in different academic fields.

Tensions Within the Field of Study

Since adult education embarked on expanding its knowledge base, two issues have continued to cause tension: its relationship to other disciplines and link between practice and theory.

The Black Book was organized around the understanding that:

Adult education develops a unique body of knowledge suited to its purposes through two methods of procedures:

1. Experiences gained from coping with problems of practice lead to the formulation of principles or generalizations that provide guides for future practice.

2. Knowledge that has been developed by other disciplines is borrowed and reformulated for use in adult education (Jensen, 1964, p. 105).

The Black Book allocates a chapter each to scrutinize how adult education can borrow and adopt knowledge, theory, and research traditions from the disciplines of sociology, social psychology, psychology, history, and organization and administration. As the field matured, the position presented in the Black Book began to be questioned. Instead of relying on other disciplines, the trend, particularly in the United States, was to primarily rely on adult-education literature (Boshier and Pickard, 1979). Building too closely on other disciplines was seen by some as a threat to the development of an adult-education knowledge base (Boyd and Apps, 1980; Kranjc, 1987). Some went as far as Plecas and Sork (1986), who argued against copying scholars in other disciplines and for adult-education scholars to remain focused on research that is closely related to well-established definitions of adult education. However, while warning adult educators to be cautious in their borrowing, it was generally recognized also within the U.S. adult-education community that much could be learned from other disciplines (Peters, 1991). Outside the United States, the push toward a clearly defined field of adult education was, with a few exceptions like the former Yugoslavia, less strong. Here, the dominant position has been that other disciplines can provide the conceptual apparatus for a better understanding of the structure, the functioning, and problems of adult education as scholars worked to strengthen research on the education of adults rather than building a distinct field of study. A good example of this can be found in the German series *Handbuch der Erwachsenenbildung*, in which the first volume appeared in 1974. Of special interest are vol. 3, *Anthropologie und Psychologie des Erwachsenen* (Zdarzil and Olechowski, 1976) and vol. 6, *Sociologie der Erwachsenenbildung* (Eggers and Steinbacher, 1977).

The second issue in the field of study stems from the fact that knowledge production in adult education has overwhelmingly been shaped by a stress on practicality. Consequently, the dominant view has been that theory is deemed useful only to the extent that it improves practice. Using this criterion, there has been a constant criticism of the limited relevance of the research enterprise to the practice of adult education. There are very varied views on the cause and remedy of the problem. One camp of adult-education scholars has argued that research has been influenced too much by the rituals of science and not enough by the needs of the learners, while others take a diametrically opposite position seeing the lack of influence as being a consequence of research having concentrated too much on applied problems (Cevero, 1991, p. 26). Sork and Cafarella (1989) suggest that the gap, which has been present since the outset of adult education becoming

a field of study, was widening rather than shrinking. This could be an outcome of the calls, during the late 1970s, for the field to become more theoretically sophisticated so that it might gain more respect in the scholarly world. In a response to this call, university departments of adult education began recruiting new faculty, into adult education, who often had less connection to the field of practice than the outgoing faculty.

Concern about the usefulness of adult education research is flourishing even today. However, not only practitioners in the field but also policymakers voice their disappointment. Thus, it is interesting to note that the criticism of adult-education research for a lack of usefulness is a dominant theme in the national reports from developing as well as developed countries prepared for the 2009 UNESCO CONFINTEA meeting. Developing countries point to the need for research to more directly support initiatives focusing on reducing poverty, addressing HIV, and strengthening women's role, while developing countries talk about the need for knowledge to support evidence-informed policy agendas. The European summary report to CONFINTEA speaks of the need "for a research interface to promote the use of research results in policy development and implementation" (Keogh, 2009, p. 10). The Arabic Summary report notes the lack of research dealing with literacy (Yousif, 2009), while the report from Latin America (Torres, 2009) speaks of the lack of dissemination of adult-education research results outside academic circles. While we have to remember that the national reports have been produced by governments, in many cases in cooperation with the adult-education community, they reflect a special understanding of the relationship between research and practice and policy.

Concluding Comment

As evident from this wide-ranging over view of theories, policies, practices, institutions, and scholarship in adult education and learning, the field is very broad and does not allow itself to be neatly organized within strict boundaries. While scholars are engaged in heated debates on what constitutes the field of adult education and/or how the scholarly field should evolve, adult learning has become a way of life for one-third to 50% the population in the industrialized world and is increasingly spreading in the developing world. When responding to these challenges, practitioners, policymakers, as well social activists can fall back on a rich history of practice and scholarship in adult education.

See also: Adult Basic Education – A Challenge for Vocational Based Learning; Adult Education and Civil Society; Adult Education and Nation Building; Adult

Learning and Instruction: Transformative-Learning Perspectives; Adult Learning in a Biographic Perspective; Adult Learning, Instruction and Programme Planning: Insights from Freire; Adult Learning; Adult Literacy Education; Barriers to Participation in Adult Education; Characteristics of Adult Learning; Citizenship and Immigrant Education; Class Analysis in Adult Education; Continuing Professional Education: Multiple Stakeholders and Agendas; Financing of Adult and Lifelong Learning; Gender Analysis; Informal Learning: A Contested Concept; Labor Education; Lifelong Learning; Modernization Processes and the Changing Function of Adult Learning; Museums as Sites of Adult Learning; Organizational Learning; Overview of Lifelong Learning Policies and Systems; Participation in Adult Learning; Popular Adult Education; Program Planning; Provision of Prior Learning Assessment; Race and Ethnicity in the Field of Adult Education; Rewriting the History of Adult Education: The Search for Narrative Structures; The Age of Learning: Seniors Learning; The Political Economy of Adult Education; Trends in Workplace Learning Research; University Adult Continuing Education: The Extra-Mural Tradition Revisited; Wider Benefits of Adult Education; Workplace-Learning Frameworks.

Bibliography

Adamson, W. L. (1980). *Hegemony and Revolution: A Study of Antonio Gramsci's Political and Cultural Theory*. Berkeley, CA: University of California Press.

Be'langer, P. and Valdivieso, S. (eds.) (1997). *The Emergence of a Learning Society. Who Participates in Adult Learning?* Oxford: Pergamon Press.

Boggs, C. (1976). *Gramsci's Marxism*. London: Pluto Press.

Boshier, R. and Pickard, L. (1979). Citation patterns of articles published in adult education 1968–1977. *Adult Education* **30**(1), 34–51.

Boyd, R. D. and Apps, J. W. (1980). *Redefining the Discipline of Adult Education*. San Francisco, CA: Jossey-Bass.

Bryson, L. (1936). *Adult Education*. New York: American Book.

Carnoy, M. (1995). Foreword: How should we study adult education. In Torres, C. A. (ed.) *The Politics of Nonformal Education in Latin America*, pp 9–16. New York: Praeger.

Carré, P. (2000). Motivation in adult education: From engagement to performance. *Proceedings of the 41st Annual Adult Education Research Conference*, Vancouver, University of British Columbia.

Cevero, R. M. (1991). Changing relationships between theory and practice. In Peters, J. M. and Jarvis, P. (eds.) *Adult Education: Evolution and Achievements in a Developing Field of Study*, pp 19–41. San Francisco, CA: Jossey-Bass.

Darkenwald, G. and Merriam, S. (1982). *Adult Education: Foundations of Practice*. New York: Harper and Row.

Desjardins, R., Rubenson, K., and Milana, M. (2006). *Unequal Chances to Participate in Adult Learning: International Perspectives*. Paris: UNESCO IIEP Fundamentals of Educational Planning Series.

Duke, C. (1994). Research in adult education – Current trends and future agenda. In Mauch, W. (ed.) *World Trends in Adult Education Research*, pp 7–12. Hamburg: UNESCO Institute of Education.

Eggers, P. E. and Steinbacher, F. J. (eds.) (1977). *Soziologie der Erwachsenenbildung*. Stuttgart: W Kohlhammer.

European Commission (2000). *A Memorandum on Lifelong Learning*. Luxembourg: Office for Official Publications of the European Commission.

Hake, B. (1994). Adult education research trends in the Western European countries. In Mauch, W. (ed.) *World Trends in Adult Education Research*, pp 124–153. Hamburg: UNESCO Institute of Education.

Houle, C. O. (1972). *The Design of Education*. Madison, WI: University of Wisconsin Press.

Houle, C. O. (1991). Foreword. In Peters, J. M. and Jarvis, P. (eds.) *Adult Education: Evolution and Achievements in a Developing Field of Study*, pp 13–17. San Francisco, CA: Jossey-Bass.

Jensen, G. (1964). How adult education borrows and reformulates knowledge of other disciplines. In Jensen, G., Liveright, A. A., and Hallebeck, W. (eds.) *Adult Education: Outlines of an Emerging Field of University Studies*, pp 105–111. Washington, DC: American Association for Adult and Continuing Education.

Jensen, G., Liveright, A. A., and Hallebeck, W. (eds.) (1964). *Adult Education: Outlines of an Emerging Field of University Studies*. Washington, DC: American Association for Adult and Continuing Education.

Keogh, H. (2009). The state and development of adult learning and education in Europe, North America and Israel. *Regional Synthesis Report*. http://www.unesco.org/en/confinteavi/preparatoryconferences/europe-and-north-america/HelenKeogh (accessed October 2009).

Kidd, J. R. and Titmus, C. J. (1989). Introduction. In Titmus, C. J. (ed.) *Lifelong Education for Adults. An International Handbook*, pp 23–39. Oxford: Pergamon.

Knowles, M. (1970). *The Modern Practice of Adult Education Andragogy Versus Pedagogy*. Chicago, IL: Association Press.

Kranjc, A. (1987). Research in adult education: Major areas of theory and inquiry. In Duke, C. (ed.) *Adult Education: International Perspectives from China*, pp 86–99. London: Croom Helm.

Merriam, S. and Brockett, R. (1997). *The Profession and Practice of Adult Education*. San Francisco, CA: Jossey-Bass.

Milton, J., Watkins, K. E., Studdard, S. S., and Michele Burch, M. (2003). The ever widening gyre: Factors affecting change in adult education graduate programs in the United States. *Adult Education Quarterly* **54**(1), 23–41.

OECD (2003). *Beyond Rhetoric: Adult Learning Policies and Practices*. Paris: OECD.

OECD (2005). *Promoting Adult Learning*. Paris: OECD.

Peters, J. M. (1991). Advancing the study of adult education: A summary perspective. In Peters, J. M. and Jarvis, P. (eds.) *Adult Education: Evolution and Achievements in a Developing Field of Study*, pp 421–445. San Francisco, CA: Jossey-Bass.

Peters, J. M. and Jarvis, P. (eds.) (1991). *Adult Education: Evolution and Achievements in a Developing Field of Study*. San Francisco, CA: Jossey-Bass.

Plecas, D. B. and Sork, T. J. (1986). Adult education: Curing the ills of an undisciplined discipline. *Adult Education* **37**(1), 48–62.

Rubenson, K. (2006). The Nordic model of lifelong learning. *Compare: A Journal of Comparative Education* **36**(3), 327–341.

Rubenson, K. and Desjardins, R. (2009). The impact of welfare state regimes on barriers to participation in adult education. A bounded agency model. *Adult Education Quarterly* **59**(3), 187–207.

Selman, G. and Dampier, P. (1991). *Adult Education in Canada*. Toronto: Thompson Educational.

Sork, T. J. and Cafarella, R. S. (1989). Planning programs for adults. In Merriam, S. M. and Cunningham, P. M. (eds.) *Handbook of Adult and Continuing Education*, pp 233–245. San Francisco, CA: Jossey-Bass.

Torres, R. M. (2009). Youth and adult education and learning in Latin America and the Caribbean: Trends, issues and challenges. *Regional Synthesis Report*. http://www.unesco.org/en/confinteavi/rightnavigation/download (accessed October 2009).

UNESCO (1976). *Recommendations on the Development of Adult Education*. Paris: UNESCO.

Usher, R., Bryant, I., and Johnston, R. (1997). *Adult Learning and the Postmodern Challenge: Learning Beyond Limits*. London: Routledge.

Verner, C. (1962). *Adult Education Theory and Method: A Conceptual Scheme for the Identification and Classification of Processes*. Washington, DC: Adult Education Association of the USA.

Verner, C. (1964). Definition of terms. In Jensen, G., Liveright, A. A., and Hallebeck, W. (eds.) *Adult Education: Outlines of an Emerging Field of University Studies*, pp 27–39. Washington, DC: American Association for Adult and Continuing Education.

Yousif, A. A. (2009). The state and development of adult learning and education in the Arab States. *Regional Synthesis Report.* http://www.unesco.org/en/confinteavi/rightnavigation/download/ (accessed October 2009).

Zdarzil, H. and Olechowski, R. (eds.) (1976). *Anthropologie und Psychologie des Erwachsenen.* Stuttgart: W Kohlhammer.

Further Reading

Brown, P., Green, A., and Lauder, H. (2001). *High Skills: Globalization, Competitiveness and Skill Formation.* Oxford: Oxford University Press.

Tuijnman, A. C. (1996). Preface. In Tuijnman, A. C. (ed.) *International Encyclopedia of Adult Education and Training*, pp 15–21. Oxford: Pergamon.

Rewriting the History of Adult Education: The Search for Narrative Structures

B J Hake, University of Leiden, Leiden, The Netherlands

Introduction

In collections of university libraries worldwide, one can locate relatively small sections of volumes pertinent to the history of adult education. Such volumes may include monographs and edited volumes with reference to the broad picture of the history of adult education and specific periods in the development of adult education, studies of particular institutions and organizations at national and local levels, biographies of important individuals, and the celebration of specific institutions in jubilee volumes. Essentially, these volumes will relate to the history of the country where the library is located. A much smaller number of volumes will relate to the history of adult education in other countries, while comparative histories will indeed be relatively scarce items. Even rarer will be volumes in foreign languages about the history of adult education in other countries.

Irrespective of their geographical scope or the period covered, the core question with regard to all histories of adult education involves the structure of the historical narratives which endeavor to tell the story of the development of the institutions and practices regarded as constituting adult education. There are two key issues with regard to the structure of historical narratives, namely: (1) the circumscription of the field of study in terms of the social and cultural phenomena recognized as comprising adult education, and, (2) the delineation of important eras or formative periods in the development of adult education.

Circumscription of the Area of Study

The definitions of adult education used in historical narratives raise fundamental questions with regard to the phenomena which are included in or excluded from historical studies of adult education. National histories tend to be constructed in terms of some sense of an adult education movement which is regarded as a clearly definable social system comprising the individuals, institutions, and associations which have been responsible for the development of adult education through time. This perspective views adult education as a field of readily recognizable activities which constitute the national system of institutional providers which emerged within a sequential process of historical development. These historical narratives take three major forms. First, they may trace the emergence and development of organizations and practices in the form of institutional histories at national, regional, and local levels. Second, they may be organized around significant individuals who are regarded as the great innovators and reformers in adult education. Third, they may narrate the development of successive periods of philanthropic initiatives, intervention by governments, legislation, and public funding of the provision of adult education. Such narratives are constructed in terms of institutional success which tends to result in an unproblematic narrative of the development of well-known institutions or practices. In this manner, historical studies tend to comprise the selective construction of a lineage for the growth of remembered institutional forms of adult education. These selective historical narratives are often recorded in terms of those forms of adult education which constitute the national tradition of adult education practices. Consciously or unconsciously, these selective accounts of successful and enduring institutions actively exclude the unremembered, the inconvenient, and the historically embarrassing.

Historical narratives of adult education as the story of successful formal institutions, however, actively exclude a vast range of social and cultural phenomena in the more diverse spheres of nonformal and informal adult education. Although historical research must necessarily devote considerable attention to the detailed study of the institutions, significant historical actors, and the development of public policy, historical accounts of the development of adult education must necessarily lead out to the general history of society. Such an approach must lead away from the specific and historically bounded contexts of institutional history into the broader economic, political, social, and cultural history. One of the most striking features of the literature on the history of adult education, for example, is the widespread evidence of the significant contribution made by social, political, and cultural movements to the development of adult education practices. It is necessary, therefore, to identify historical studies which analyze the historical relationships between social movements and the development of adult education in terms of the broader patterns of economic, social, political, and cultural change beyond the institutional realms of adult education.

The broader and more diverse range of social and cultural phenomena identified here as the legitimate object of study for the historian of adult education can be best understood in terms of the social organization of communication and learning. The term social organization refers here to the complex range of institutions, social movements, and groups which were involved in the historically specific development of adult education. This opens up the field of historical description and analysis of adult education practices in terms of the social organization of communication and learning in which adults were either organized by others or organized themselves for the purposes of disseminating and acquiring knowledge, skills, and sensitivities. Some of these institutions, movements, and groups will be recognized immediately as adult education, while others were embedded in the economic, political, or cultural dimensions of social life. Reconstruction of the ideas, institutions, and practices associated with adult education has, thus, to be pursued in terms of the social relationships involved in the social organization of communication and learning. The historical development of adult education institutions and practices is a socially structured process within societies, and this is a question of dominance and dependence in the history of social, political, economic, and cultural relationships. Innovation is sometimes undertaken by dominant social groups, but it may also be carried out by alternative or oppositional social groups and movements. This results in a more inclusive understanding of the range of nonformal and informal adult education at a distance from adult education institutions.

Periods in the History of Adult Education

Historical narratives are characterized by the marked consistency with which they relate the development of adult educational institutions and practices in terms of a number of specific eras or formative historical periods. The standard institutional histories tend to be formulated in terms of the notion of eras which describe periods of major changes in the institutional development of adult education. Such eras can also be regarded as formative periods of high levels of activity in the development of adult education institutions and practices. In terms of evidence-based empirical indices of activity, such formative periods are characterized, first, by high rates of innovation associated with the development of new institutions and practices; second, the significant expansion in the numbers of adults involved in organized learning activities; third, the opening up of participation in organized learning to new social groups or publics; and, fourth, significant levels of interest in developments taking place in other countries. The latter phenomenon was expressed in reports of visits, translations of foreign texts, and articles in contemporary journals. Formative periods were interspersed, however, with periods with a low conjuncture in

terms of innovation and change. This indicates the need to recognize the historical reality of breaks and shifts in historical development rather than the gradual unbroken line of the development of institutions and practices.

European and Anglo-Saxon literatures, for example, tend to reconstruct the history of adult education in terms of four significant formative periods.

The first of these periods was associated with the Protestant Reformation in northwestern and Central Europe during the second half of the sixteenth century and the first half of the seventeenth century. Development of the organization of adult learning activities in this period was influenced by the invention of the printing press, the translation of the Bible into the vernacular, Bible study groups, and high levels of adult literacy. A reading public emerged which gave rise to the demand for books, new literary forms such as devotional books, books of manners, and the first encyclopedias of knowledge. This was associated with new forms for the distribution of the printed word by colporteurs, booksellers, circulating libraries, and reading circles. In the Catholic areas of Southern Europe, however, the Counter Reformation was marked by the Baroque rejection of the promotion of literacy among the general population and the emphasis upon visual imagery rather than the written word. This geographical division between Northern and Southern Europe was expressed in very different dynamics in the development of adult education. These dynamics subsequently exerted their influence in the different strands of European expansion and colonialism in other continents. They continue to exert their influence in contemporary problems of illiteracy in many countries throughout the world.

From the mid-eighteenth century onward, a second formative period in the development of organized adult education throughout Europe and in the American colonies can be identified. The so-called Enlightenment movement, which marked the start of the European modernization process, was in effect a transnational social and cultural movement which gave priority to education, for both children and adults, in the improvement of society together with an emphasis upon virtue and individual moral behavior in the service of the common good. Historical research provides evidence of the activities of the state and voluntary societies and associations in the development of elementary education; the advancement and diffusion of knowledge; encouragement of the rational improvement of commerce, manufactures, and agriculture; the stimulation of literature, poetry, and drama; the organization of lectures and scientific demonstrations; circulating and lending libraries. The first adult schools were established in this period. The development of an active publishing trade and the further growth and diversification of the reading public was expressed in the periodical press, newspapers, and the growth of a political press.

One of the most manifest consequences of this period throughout Europe and the American colonies was the development of radical political movements, often organized in the form of corresponding societies. These movements demanded democratic rights and freedom of speech on behalf of both the commercial middle class and the artisan class in opposition to the closed oligarchies of dominant regimes. Such radical groups and their adult education activities were frequently repressed through the prohibition of the printing and selling of books and pamphlets in the vernacular. Banned books in French, such as the *Encyclopaedia* by Diderot and d'Alembert, were printed in The Netherlands and smuggled to France, while books in the Greek language were banned by the Ottoman authorities and were secretly imported from the printing presses of Budapest. This phenomenon of underground adult learning has remained a significant dimension of adult education in later periods of repression. The long-term repercussions of the French Revolution in 1789, which in itself fueled radical movements throughout Europe, resulted in the emergence of nation-states in the early nineteenth century. The cultivation of national identity led to the emphasis upon the development of national systems of elementary education and the organization of improving educational activities for adults. This was associated with the need to exert more rigorous control upon the self-organized learning undertaken by the common man, and the need to instruct adults in their rights and duties as responsible citizens of the new nation-states. In the longer term, this formative period, throughout Europe, experienced its nemesis in the revolutions of 1848 and their subsequent repression throughout Europe. This resulted in the emigration of many radicals together with the active export of many forms of self-organized adult education, from German in particular, to the other European countries and the United States.

The period between the 1870s and 1930s has been designated in the literature as a third important formative period. This period was characterized by industrialization and urbanization which contributed to the emergence of the organized working class, a militant women's movement, and the struggle for the right to vote. This resulted, on the one hand, in the development of independent adult educational activities organized by socialist, communist, and anarchist political parties, together with the trade unions and the women's movement. The period witnessed a significant expansion of independent working-class forms of provision such as the workingmen's associations, Workers' Educational Association, workers' houses, workers' book clubs, workers' travel associations, Lenin and Marx houses, and the diverse range of educational initiatives associated with the Second Communist International. On the other hand, there was a range of educational responses to this challenge by conservative and liberal parties, together with the hierarchies of the Catholic and Protestant churches. This resulted in the development of new institutional forms for the provision of adult education such as university extension, university settlements or co-called Toynbee work, the arts and crafts movement, folk houses, popular universities, public libraries, together with the folk high schools in Scandinavia, and other forms of residential education elsewhere. These forms of adult education provision were largely intended to provide educational solutions to the social question of the emergent working class, and they promoted reformist solutions to widespread concerns with urban housing, family life, working conditions, sanitation and health, prostitution, and alcohol abuse. Inherent to this conflict between adult education sponsored by independent working class and middle class was the issue of educating citizens to make use of the extension of the right to vote following World War I. Civic education became a key theme in adult education provision as was clearly demonstrated in the institutionalization of University Extension in the English-speaking world and the development of adult education institutions throughout Europe. These institutions placed the emphasis upon liberal adult education and also focused upon new didactic methods, such as reformist pedagogy in Weimar Germany and elsewhere.

This period also witnessed the development of concern of well-intentioned employers with new forms for the dissemination of scientific and technological knowledge to their employees. From the 1851 Great Exhibition onward, there had been efforts to bring employers and workers together in continuing education, learning in the workplace, and putative forms of vocational education and training. On the one hand, employers sought to establish industrial museums, perhaps badly named, which were intended to make new technological knowledge and production methods available to the working population by way of public demonstrations and short courses. Universities became involved in this process with the development of University Extension services devoted to the needs of agriculture and industry. On the other hand, elementary forms of vocational education and training developed with an emphasis upon technical drawing so that skilled workers could gain insights into the working of new machinery and production processes. At the same time, there was a growing concern with the changing employment patterns of women's participation in paid work. Initiatives by the women's movement in the 1890s were enhanced by the experience of World War I when women took the places in factories of men who were at the front. This often resulted in vigorous debates about the occupations which were appropriate to women and their needs for vocational training beyond the traditional domestic spheres of caring, cooking, sewing, and nursing. Following the Civil War in Finland, for example, there were attempts to retrain women as electricians and plumbers rather than as weavers and seamstresses.

Of particular significance later in this period were the consequences of the Russian Revolution in 1917, the end of World War I, the national independence movements following the peace treaties, and the rise of Fascism and National Socialism during the 1930s. The first All-Soviet conference on adult education was held in 1918 and the keynote address was given by Lenin, who did not fail to name the enemies of the revolution. The carnage caused by World War I resulted in significant interest worldwide in the role of adult education in the promotion of peace and international solidarity. The 1920s witnessed the establishment of numerous international associations, the first world conferences on adult education, and the establishment of international institutions such as the International Peoples' College in Ellsinore. The peace settlements of Versailles and Trianon broke up the territories of the Tsarist Russian, Austro-Hungarian, and Ottoman empires and granted national independence to many countries in the Baltic region, Central Europe, and the Balkans. In these newly independent nations, adult education became a battleground during the 1920s and 1930s between democratic and nationalist political factions. Fascist and National Socialist regimes were responsible during the 1920s and 1930s for the reorganization of adult education in the service of the state in Portugal, Germany, Italy, and Spain, together with other countries in Central Europe and the Balkans. This latter development had fundamental consequences for the organization of adult learning throughout Europe, which included the development of settlements and work camps for the ideological socialization of movement adherents, in particular, the emphasis upon youth movements, together with the so-called re-socialization of recalcitrant radicals such as intellectuals, social democrats, and communists. The first concentration camps established in Germany in 1933 were intended to re-socialize the recalcitrant through hard labor. At the same time, many refugees took their reformist pedagogy with them to other countries and became innovative forces within other adult education systems.

The period between the late 1950s and the present day can be regarded as the fourth and significantly complex formative period which has fundamentally reshaped the organization of adult educational institutions and practices, especially in the global context. On the one hand, the end of World War II led, in the longer term, to the emergence of national independence movements in the remnants of the British and French empires in Africa and Asia. This process of contested decolonization involved the recognition of a new role for adult education in nation building and economic development in the Third World which was driven by United Nations Educational, Scientific and Cultural Organization (UNESCO) and its institutes. A series of world conferences, namely Ellsinore (1949), Montreal (1960), Tokyo (1972), Paris (1985), and Hamburg (1997) focused on the role of adult education in postcolonial nations. The emphasis upon the importance of literacy for development gave rise to the repression of emancipation movements in many countries in South and Central America. On the other hand, the end of World War II gave rise in Europe to the Soviet hegemony in the Baltic, Balkan, and Central European countries. Adult education was put to work there in the service of the communist revolution and priority, especially in terms of the access of adults to higher education, was given to party members, women, the military, workers, and farmers.

In Western Europe, and elsewhere in the English-speaking world, the late 1960s and the 1970s were marked by the development of compensatory educational opportunities for adults. This involved second-chance and second-way adult education, with an emphasis upon outreach work to the nonparticipants in adult education, which was associated with the development of nonformal and informal community-based forms of adult learning. In addition to the rapid expansion of evening and day institutes for adults during this period, there was a major expansion of distance learning for adults and in particular the establishment of open universities worldwide. Important policy concepts at international and national levels during this period referred to lifelong, permanent, and recurrent education in terms of the redistribution of educational opportunities throughout the life span.

From the mid-1980s onward, however, this largely social-democratic-driven reform agenda to expand educational opportunities for adults was displaced in Europe, indeed worldwide, by the resurgence of neoliberal ideologies. There emerged a renewal of interest in vocational education and training for adults as the core learning message of the global economy. The resurgent interest in lifelong learning has been largely informed by the need to ensure the competitiveness of national economies in the global market, employability of the workforce, the integration of immigrants, demographic change, and the graying of populations in postindustrial societies. This has resulted worldwide in policy narratives which talk in terms of a learning for earning ideology, which is focused on developing the competences required by individuals in order to survive in volatile economic markets. Traditional priorities in adult education, such as the promotion of citizenship and social capital, have been increasingly marginalized. The individualization of learning has increasingly replaced the collective acquisition of knowledge, skills, and attitudes via social movements, community education, and regional development. Individual survival, rather than collective learning to improve the quality of life of communities, now dominates lifelong learning policies. Key policy issues now emphasize individual learning rather than the political economy of promoting structures of opportunity for disadvantaged groups in society.

On the one hand, learning in the workplace has now become the dominant understanding of the development of adult education in the early twenty-first century. The retreat of the state, as the motor of the welfare state and the public responsibility for the redistribution of educational opportunities for adults, has led to the withdrawal of subsidies for many traditional forms of adult education and the privatization of many forms of provision, while the emphasis has shifted toward individual responsibility for investments in adult learning. This now often results in the negation of the very real educational needs of the indigenous unskilled proletariat who is left to fend for itself, or who is encouraged to participate in the commercial learning marketplace and Internet. On the other hand, global mass migration has more recently contributed to the core question of the integration of immigrants and the challenge of Islam as the educational issue in multicultural societies. A largely unresearched area of this multicultural context is the role of the mosque as a learning environment for immigrants in Western societies.

Conclusion

The larger question raised here is the degree to which histories written from Anglo-Saxon perspectives is relevant to the larger canvas of the global dimension of the development of adult education. This raises the almost un-investigated area of the dynamics of empires, colonialism, and postcolonialism in the worldwide development of adult education. The available standard works on the history of adult education have been largely written in terms of selective national histories, which in some small measure examine the colonial tradition of European expansion. Postcolonial understandings of the development of adult education are only now emerging as narratives of resistance in the old empires together with the processes of decolonization, national independence, and indigenous identities. There are many more such examples of adults learning in difficult circumstances, whether above ground or underground, whether in adult education institutes, on the barricades, or in prison. Indeed, the phenomenon of underground adult education, often organized by the learners themselves in the face of oppressive forces remains a recurrent, but inadequately researched, theme in the history of adult education in most countries.

Historical description and explanations of the development of the social phenomena commonly known as adult education need to be more firmly rooted in the conscious use of theories and concepts from the social sciences and cultural studies. This is not an argument for the deconstruction and marginalization of the reform discourses which have dominated historical narratives about the development of institutions and practices associated with adult education in most countries. It is a critique of the strong element of celebration, the search for genealogies, and the construction of lineages in historical narratives about adult educational institutions and practices. The history of adult education is not real history when its narratives produce collections of the valued national antiques of institutionalized adult education from the past. It is necessary to recognize the complex levels at which critical historical analysis and interpretation can enter the debate and reconstruct dominant narratives. If the history of adult education is about the pioneers and their reputations, it is also about the forgotten and the defeated, even the uncomfortable and inconvenient reminders of the past. If it is about social reformers and formal institutional provision, it is also about social and cultural movements and their contributions to the social organization of nonformal and informal learning. If it is about the latter, it is also about ideologies and struggles between social groups to control communication and learning in the public sphere. If it is about ideologies and struggles in the public sphere, it is also about the formation of publics, popular expectations, and responses. If it is about the latter, it is also about the experiences of the autodidact and the learning biographies of resistance. All these aspects have to be provided with a theoretical perspective in order to achieve more insightful understandings of the construction of historical narratives. The history of adult education in its broader social and cultural contexts still has to be written. This will be the history of the individual and collective learning activities undertaken by adults in order to survive in difficult times and struggles to change society.

Further Reading

Dobbs, A. E. (1919). *Education and Social Movements, 1700–1850*. London: Longmans, Green.

Friedenthal-Hasse, M., Hake, B. J., and Marriott, S. (eds.) (1991). *British–Dutch–German Relationships in Adult Education 1880–1930: Studies in the Theory and History of Cross-Cultural Communication in adult education*. Leeds: Leeds Studies in Continuing Education.

Hake, B. J. and Marriott, S. (eds.) (1992). *Adult Education between Cultures: Encounters and Identities in European Adult Education since 1890*. Leeds: Leeds Studies in Continuing Education.

Hake, B. J. and Steele, T. (eds.) (1997). *Intellectuals, Activists and Reformers: Studies of Cultural, Social and Educational Reform Movements 1890–1930*. Leeds: Leeds Studies in Continuing Education.

Hake, B. J., Steele, T., and Tiana, A. (eds.) (1996). *Masters, Missionaries and Militants: Studies of Social Movements and Popular Adult Education 1890–1939*. Leeds: Leeds Studies in Continuing Education.

Hake, B. J., van Gent, B., and Katus, J. (eds.) (2004). *Adult Education and Globalisation: Past and Present*. Frankfurt: Peter Lang.

Harrison, J. F. C. (1961). *Learning and Living 1790–1960: A Study in the History of the English Adult Education Movement*. London: Routledge/Kegan Paul.

Knowles, M. S. (1977). *A History of the Adult Education Movement in the United States*. Huntington: Holt, Rinehart and Winston.

Marriott, S. and Hake, B. J. (eds.) (1994). *Cultural and Intercultural Experiences in European Adult Education: Essays on Popular and Higher Education since 1890.* Leeds: Leeds Studies in Continuing Education.

Morgan, W. J. (2003). *Communists on Education and Culture 1848–1948.* Basingstoke: Palgrave Macmillan.

Paulston, R. G. (ed.) (1980). *Other Dreams, Other Schools: Folk Colleges in Social and Ethnic Movements.* Pittsburgh, PA: University of Pittsburgh.

Pole, T. (1814). *A History of the Origin and Progress of Adult Schools.* Bristol: Mc Dowall Schools.

Schama, S. (1977). *Patriots and Liberators: Revolution in The Netherlands, 1780–1813.* New York: Knopf.

Simon, B. (ed.) (1990). *The Search for Enlightenment: The Working Class and Adult Education in the Twentieth Century.* London: Lawrence and Wishart.

Steele, T. (2008). *Knowledge is Power! The Rise and Fall of European Popular Educational Movements.* Frankfurt: Peter Lang.

Thompson, E. P. (1963). *The Making of the English Working-Class.* London: Gollancz.

Williams, R. (1981). *Problems in Materialism and Culture.* Oxford: Oxford UP.

Lifelong Learning

J Field, University of Stirling, Stirling, UK

Lifelong learning has become a dominant theme of education and training polices across the advanced industrial nations. Besides a wide range of national governments, it is endorsed by a wide range of intergovernmental policy actors, including the Organisation for Economic Co-operation and Development (OECD), the European Commission (EC), the United Nations Educational, Social and Cultural Organisation (UNESCO), the World Bank and the International Labour Organisation (ILO) (Schemmann, 2007). For governments, lifelong learning is an overarching policy framework which offers solutions to a number of common economic and social challenges; globalization and competitiveness often dominate the policy discourse, but promoting lifelong learning is also seen as relevant to social cohesion, demographic change, active citizenship, migrant assimilation, and public health.

Lifelong learning therefore has broad application across a variety of policy domains. It is also widely discussed by educational professionals and by academic researchers. Some claim that lifelong learning is such a broad concept that it has virtually no practical value (Gustavsson, 1995: 92). While its meanings are many and varied, they usually emphasize learning as a ubiquitous process, which takes place throughout the lifespan, and across a variety of life contexts. The recent focus among policymakers, educationalists, and researchers on the ability to learn continuously after the phase of initial education, and across a variety of contexts of which educational institutions are one among many, distinguishes the debate over lifelong learning from more conventional policy discussions of education and training as levers across a range of economic and social policy domains.

From Social Optimism to Economic Survival?

In recent years, lifelong learning has moved steadily toward the center of the policy stage. International governmental bodies have played a particularly significant role in popularizing lifelong learning as a policy concept. While the term was in occasional use before the mid-1990s, it received huge impetus when the European Commission declared 1996 to be the European Year of Lifelong Learning, an idea first floated in the Commission's White Paper on competitiveness, employment, and growth (Commission of the European Communities, 1994). This context neatly exemplifies the way in which it is economic concerns that dominate

policymakers' interest in lifelong learning. Particularly in the older industrial nations, policymakers argue that successful adjustment to a knowledge economy and society requires a highly skilled, knowledgeable, and flexible workforce as a key to sustained national and corporate competitive advantage; individuals equally need to invest continuously in their own competence in order to maintain their employability in an ever-changing labor market. This reflects and is expressed through a policy discourse that is centered on a human-capital approach to social inclusion and economic growth (Borg and Mayo, 2005; Coffield, 1999; Gustavsson, 1995).

This strong economic bias distinguishes the current debate over lifelong learning from earlier policy attempts to promote learning in adult life. Superficially, the idea of lifelong learning closely resembles notions of lifelong education, which were widely discussed in the 1970s. The idea of lifelong education was promoted particularly actively by UNESCO, who in 1972 published *Learning to Be*, a report by an international expert panel chaired by Edgar Faure, a former politician who had served in France as Minister of Education and Prime Minister (Faure, 1972). Faure's report was essentially humanistic in nature, arguing in favor of wider access to higher levels of education and greater support for and recognition of informal and non-formal learning in order to encourage personal fulfilment and development. Faure's report was enormously influential in stimulating debate, and in infusing that debate with an optimistic view of educational innovation and reform (Knoll, 1998). Its core ideas were taken up by the OECD, which developed a parallel debate over recurrent education, the aim of which was intended to provide governments with practicable means of realizing the overarching goal of lifelong education (OECD, 1973).

In practical terms, the activities undertaken by UNESCO and OECD mainly helped focus policy attention on the educational needs of those who had benefited least from the front-loaded approach to initial education. In industrial nations, this often involved developing educational entitlements for workers, with laws on paid educational leave in a number of countries. In some, there was a broad entitlement to leave for general purposes (as in Sweden, and in state-level laws on *Bildungsurlaub* in Germany); in other cases, educational leave was guaranteed for specific purposes, such as vocational training under the French law on *conge de formation* or British laws on health and safety and workplace representation. Many more countries experienced a growth of adult basic education, with particularly impressive innovations in adult literacy provision and women's basic education.

By the 1990s, a concern with personal development, or worker participation as public policy goals, had not disappeared altogether, but was found far less frequently. Much more common has been a primary concern with lifelong learning as a means of underpinning economic competitiveness and growth. In a globalized economy, where material resources are more or less ubiquitous, skills and knowledge are said to be the only sustainable sources of competitive advantage (Commission of the European Communities, 1994; Reich, 1993; Thurow, 1994). Insofar as policymakers also share an interest in equity and social cohesion, lifelong learning's importance is often valued primarily as a means of re-insertion of vulnerable individuals or inactive workers back into the labor market, leading in turn to improved income and security for individuals from disadvantaged backgrounds.

The current debate over lifelong learning is therefore distinctive in a number of ways. It is characterized by the breadth, and sometimes vagueness, with which the concept is used; it is derived more from the policy domain than from the educational field; and its dominant usage tends to be primarily economic. Yet, more positively, the concept can also be taken to emphasize and recognize the many ways in which people build up new skills and capacities throughout the lifespan and across different life spheres, including workplaces, communities, homes, and voluntary associations. It gives a central place to people's learning, as opposed to education, teaching, and institutions. To use what has become a common abbreviation, current policy concerns are with education that is lifelong, and also life-wide. For these reasons, it has often become more or less synonymous with adult learning; however, it has powerful implications for all phases of the lifespan.

Initial Education as a Platform for Learning through Life

Initial education, including early-years development, is important in its own right. From a lifelong perspective, though, it is additionally important because it provides a platform for learning later in life. A number of commentators argue that family and neighborhood influences in the early years are particularly significant in determining patterns of learning across the lifespan. From this perspective, high-quality education during the earlier years is important primarily because of its role in providing the abilities and motivation to engage effectively in learning later in life (Hargreaves, 2004; Gillies, 2005; OECD, 2004). Sociologically, many of the factors that are associated with adult well-being are already present in the early years.

One recent longitudinal analysis of adult learning in Wales demonstrated that most of the factors that affected the probabilities of participation in adult life were present by the time that the child entered primary school for the first time (Gorard et al., 1999).

Education and well-being have often been associated. The idea that education can promote individual well-being indirectly, by improving earnings and promoting social mobility, is an old one; so are notions of education helping to promote the good society by contributing to economic growth and equality of opportunity. Recent debates about the wider benefits of learning have added a new dimension to the relationship, linking education to other facets of individual and collective well-being, such as health (including mental health), security from crime, and political tolerance (Schuller et al., 2004). Through strengthening self-identity, learning is also said to help people develop a sense of authorship over their own biographies and take responsibility for their life choices (Côté, 2004).

Theoretical Perspectives

The 1970s debate over lifelong education was a broad one. While OECD's work on recurrent education was primarily concerned with the balance of resource distribution as between secondary and tertiary education, combined with an interest in worker participation in enterprise management, the work of UNESCO was profoundly influenced by the radical educational thinkers of the 1960s, along with the concerns of liberation theology and Third World development. The dominant voices in the 1990s debate, by contrast, came primarily from writers on globalization and economic change, and were almost entirely based in the economically advanced nations of the West. In a global knowledge economy, these new growth theorists argued, sustainable competitive advantage could only come from an ability to innovate continuously, and in turn this required a highly skilled and flexible workforce (e.g. Porter, 1990; Reich, 1993). Neo-Schumpeterian concerns with innovation as a basis for economic growth came to be aligned with human-capital perspectives on skills development, as well as with an interest in regional and national innovation capacities. More organizationally focused analyses have tended to emphasize the importance of organizational learning and knowledge management as strategic responses to complexity and change (Smith and Sadler-Smith, 2006).

The dominant theories of lifelong learning, then, tend to be concerned with developing workers' abilities to innovate and respond to change, and therefore contribute to sustained economic growth. Many governments, particularly those led by social democratic or Christian democratic parties, also see lifelong learning as a means of promoting equity and inclusion. Again, this is associated with a strong focus on employability as an important active measure to promote social cohesion, and equity concerns are therefore closely related to economic goals. Finally, this dominant view takes a capitalist economic order as a given; lifelong learning is not seen as a way of changing society, but at most as a way of including the least advantaged in the existing order. Particularly in its most recent phase, which may be conveniently marked by the European Commission's *Memorandum* on lifelong learning of 2000, it is a highly pragmatic concept (Schreiber-Barsch and Zeuner, 2007: 693; Commission of the European Communities, 2000). However, there are also significant critical voices, albeit from a range of differing perspectives.

Some take a broadly radical, anti-globalization stance. Thus the Maltese writers Carmel Borg and Peter Mayo suggest that the primary economic focus of dominant theories is tied to a neoliberal agenda for welfare reform (Borg and Mayo, 2005). Others have asked whether the whole concept is not associated with Western interests, and question whether, at least in its current manifestations, lifelong learning presents opportunities for or is a distraction from adult basic education as a force for development and democratization in the majority of the world (Torres, 2003). Certainly, the current policy climate tends to assume that individual workers must assume at least partial responsibility for ensuring their own employability and invest in new skills in order to maintain their labor-market value. However, this is often accompanied by incentive regimes, which seek to encourage workers to invest in new competences and improve existing skills; in some cases, workers' own organizations have promoted skills improvements as a way of protecting collective security (Payne, 2005). It is also possible to see welfare regimes as themselves bureaucratic and unresponsive to diverse needs; even in adult education, devolution and autonomy may be viewed as a form of privatization, but some will also experience it as emancipatory. In other words, there is no necessary connection between an emphasis on continuous learning and the dismantling of the welfare state, but radical perspectives do draw attention to both global and local inequalities that are material and structural, and which may be perpetuated by current lifelong learning policies.

Feminist writers have also made a significant contribution to critical debates over lifelong learning. From a feminist perspective, the radical expansion of post-compulsory education since the 1960s has brought rather ambivalent consequences. On the one hand, considerable growth in women's access to higher education has formed part of the remarkable transformation in the role of work in women's biographical trajectories (Spano, 2002). Like many radical writers, feminists tend to be sharply critical of policies and forms of provision that are driven primarily by market forces, though they go beyond the majority of radicals in identifying clear and practicable ways in which education and training might better meet the needs of women (Gouthro, 2005; Burke and Jackson, 2007).

From a feminist perspective, the invisibility of gender in a patriarchal society masks the fact that women face particular barriers to participation in learning, and much provision fails to address the diversities of women's identities; working-class women in particular are trapped in a cycle of low-paid and low-status jobs, whose skill content is barely acknowledged in public discourse about a learning society (Fenwick, 2004; Jackson, 2003). Gouthro goes rather far, suggesting that the language and ideas of lifelong learning represent a major incursion of public policy into the private sphere, as the identification of the homeplace as a site of learning is little more than a colonization of part of the lifeworld that has particular resonance for women (Gouthro, 2005).

A third alternative body of theory derives from post-structuralist and post-modernist writing. In particular, a number of writers have drawn on the thinking of Michel Foucault, the French philosopher/historian, to frame their analyses of power and knowledge and the construction of the learning citizen. Foucault's influence can be particularly seen in studies which treat knowledge as a social practice, governed by relations of power that may be expressed through various classificatory schema and their institutional manifestations. This might be seen as a relatively superficial reading of Foucault's work, and it has been supplemented more recently by studies that take Foucault's radical decentering of the human subject as their starting point. Here, instead of studying learners as agents, the focus is on studying the specific practices that constitute learning, the discourses produced by and producing these practices, and the different subject positions that are made available through these discourses and practices. These subject positions usually include the other, and discourses of nonparticipation and nonlearning are therefore analyzed as processes of othering, so that practices and discourses of lifelong learning always constitute subject positions that are excluded from the dominant framing (Fejes, 2006; Nicoll, 2006).

Finally, a number of writers have explored connections between lifelong learning and sociological theories of reflexive modernization. Ulrich Beck and Anthony Giddens both take human agency as the core of their accounts of late modernity (Beck, 1992; Giddens, 1991). There are distinct parallels between theories of reflexive modernization and core elements of the debate over lifelong learning. Beck and Giddens lead us to explore the socio-cultural forces that are shaping the demand for continuous learning, rather than seeing lifelong learning as an expression of economic forces alone. Their work also draws attention to learning and change in everyday life; people may well be confronting experiences of globalization and technological change, but they are also required to take an active approach to their own biographies, including the ways in which they negotiate intimate relationships and construct identity and social resources (Alheit, 1990; Field, 2006: 68–73).

Institutional Structures for Lifelong Learning

Lifelong learning is a highly complex area for policy, yet its current prominence is largely due to the interest of policy-makers. This paradoxical position reflects the challenges that current economic, social, cultural, and political changes pose to the policy community, particularly in the Western nations, which therefore require new approaches to governance (Field, 2006: 29–43). While policymakers are still able to resort to direct intervention of the traditional kinds, the most important actors in lifelong learning are usually non-governmental – primarily enterprises and individuals, but also trade unions, families, voluntary associations, and neighborhoods. Even within government, lifelong learning policies span the interests of a range of ministries, and a variety of layers from local and regional to national and supra-national. Lifelong learning therefore poses serious challenges of coordination of a range of actors of different kinds, besides bringing risks of unintended consequences. It also poses challenges to many of the existing institutions, particularly those providing opportunities in adult learning.

Although the current debate over lifelong learning has only been underway since the mid-1990s, governments have not had to write policies on a clean sheet of paper. Rather, they have sought to modernize and systematize existing patterns of provision of adult learning, and review existing institutional structures, with a view to raising levels of participation and attainment, usually right across the life-span but with a strong concentration on learning in and for working life. Comparative researchers have identified a number of variations in post-compulsory education and training structures, in spite of the convergent pressures of globalizing economic forces and the modernization of education systems. Particular attention has been paid to the roles of three distinct components of the lifelong learning systems:

- systems of transition between initial education and the labor market;
- higher education systems; and
- arrangements for adult education and training.

These components have attracted attention from policy analysts as well as academic researchers (see, e.g., the OECD's thematic reviews (OECD, 2005)).

The three institutional dimensions of national lifelong learning systems differ significantly from each other. The most complex, from both a policy and an analytical perspective, is the adult learning system, which involves a variety of actors and stakeholders, including a wide range of non-government organizations as well as individual citizens. Youth transition systems are only slightly less complex, as well as institutions, which may or may not be publicly funded; the key stakeholders generally include employers

and sometimes trade unions, as well as varying degrees of state provision and regulation. Some national studies note that military service may also affect youth transition processes (e.g., Tsai, 1998), and schools are also often influential actors in their own right. Initial education systems at first seem relatively unproblematic from a policy perspective; the major players are usually publicly funded schools and the state itself (though policy implementation is often influenced by teachers, particularly where the latter are able to exercise a significant degree of professional autonomy). However, initial education is often less straightforward than it first appears; particularly in early years, nongovernmental providers are often involved in nursery-level education, and families and communities exercise significant influence over children's cultural capital and social capital.

Green *et al.* (2006) identify three distinct regional models of lifelong learning and the knowledge economy. Two of these – the Anglo-Saxon, neoliberal model, and the continental European, social market model – are relatively well established, and are clearly based on conventional social policy models of welfare regimes. Green and his colleagues add a third, Nordic model, which combines high levels of social cohesion with strong support for economic competitiveness. The Nordic model has recently been subjected to particular scrutiny because of its perceived relative success in combining comparatively equal participation with high overall participation in adult learning (Tuijnman, 2003; Rubenson, 2006; Milana and Desjardins, 2007). Overall participation rates in all the Nordic countries are consistently close to or over 50% of the population of working age (OECD, 2000). Further, Nordic participation rates are high both for job-related adult education and training and for non-job-related learning (Eurobarometer, 2003).

The roots of this pattern have been traced back to the 1960s, when governments and the social partners identified adult education as a distinct and significant field of policy, linked closely to labor market policy, which itself was geared primarily to securing full employment and industrial consensus (Rubenson, 2006; Milana and Desjardins, 2007). Typically, the Nordic countries have a wide range of providing institutions, including well-established non-statutory providers (such as trade unions) and community-based providers accountable to local government. Rather than seeking to restructure the institutional system, public policy instruments since the 1960s in the Nordic nations have increasingly included targeted-funding measures aimed at engaging disadvantaged groups in the adult education system (Rubenson, 2006).

These measures have had some success in terms of overall participation. Nevertheless, despite high overall participation, and relatively high participation by disadvantaged groups, Milana and Desjardins (2007) note in a systematic review of international survey data that the same broad distribution is found in the Nordic countries as in other nations. The least likely to participate are older workers, those with lower skills levels, unemployed people, migrant workers, and those with weak initial educational qualifications. Nevertheless, on the basis of data from the International Adult Literacy Survey and a survey conducted by the EC in 2003, published by Eurobarometer, they conclude that the Nordic nations have created popular adult education systems that have led to "the attenuation of differences among these otherwise disadvantaged groups", particularly older adults of working age and less-educated workers (Milana and Desjardins, 2007: 3). They further analyze Eurobarometer data to show that although adults in the Nordic countries reported similar constraints on participation as did respondents in other European Union (EU) member states, the average incidence of the constraints was generally lower in the Nordic countries, and adults in the Nordic countries were more likely to participate even if they faced these constraints (Milana and Desjardins, 2007: 6). Interestingly, this was true for dispositional barriers as well as for more material and institutional constraints.

Milana and Desjardins conclude that public policy has been particularly significant in producing high levels of overall participation, first by maintaining a strong public adult education system, and second by adopting special targeting measures to ensure that an open and broad system of provision is not simply colonized by the already well educated (Milana and Desjardins, 2007: 14–15). In addition, Nordic economies are typically characterized by forms of organizational networking that are likely to promote informal learning. Peter Maskell and his colleagues have demonstrated that high levels of informal exchange of information, techniques, and skills are critical to the competitiveness of Nordic enterprises, particularly those who are affected by high labor costs and low levels of technological development and must therefore compete on grounds of quality and added value (Maskell *et al.*, 1998).

Supplementing various studies of national policy, Michael Schemmann has conducted a detailed systematic analysis of the policies developed by inter and supranational government bodies such as the World Bank, UNESCO, EC, and OECD (Schemmann, 2007). Of these, the EC has been most influential in practice, since it is responsible for implementing policies directly, while UNESCO and the OECD exercise a more indirect influence. Nevertheless, Schemmann traces a number of common themes, as well as marked differences, across these four bodies; above all, he believes that they have established a global lifelong learning discourse with a number of shared reference points. In turn, of course, these common themes reflect the dominance of a neoliberal policy agenda at national level, with governments seeking similar solutions to similar problems. This includes a marked trend toward employer involvement with delivery, in order to promote responsiveness to economic demands, and the adoption of active approaches to labor-market training, particularly through welfare-to-work measures.

Schemmann also notes a pronounced tendency for international governmental bodies to seek to influence national policy by compiling comparative indicators and promoting policy borrowing and transfer, trends that he finds typical of the new governance that is being applied to complex policy areas like lifelong learning (Schemmann, 2007: 246). Both the OECD and the EC publish benchmarking data, compiled on the basis of selected indicators of educational activity; the OECD's publications usually attract high levels of media coverage. In 2003, the EC set its member states the target, by 2010, of at least 12.5% participation in learning by adults aged 25–64, though the Commission has few powers to enforce such targets other than by publicizing the results. The EC has also been charged by the European Parliament with developing a European-qualifications framework covering all areas of lifelong learning. Such developments have led some commentators to question whether there are tendencies toward an international standardization process in adult learning, particularly within the EU (Schreiber-Barsch and Zeuner, 2007: 699–700).

Conclusions

Since the mid-1990s, ideas of lifelong learning have been widely debated in policy and research circles. The idea itself rose to prominence in the mid-1990s when it was embraced by a number of international policy bodies and by several countries. While there were often exaggerated claims both for the novelty of the policies, and for the likely contributions they would make to a whole plethora of economic and social challenges, these policies did indeed mark a shift in policy focus, away from instruction toward learning and away from childhood and youth toward learning through the life span. This shift reflected policymakers' preoccupations with the consequences of globalization and rapid economic and technological change, as well as business leaders' recognition of the contribution of upskilling to competitive strategies. However, it also reflected wider sociocultural factors which were also leading to a new emphasis on continuous learning as a way of coping with the demands of everyday life in a risk society.

Conceptually, the idea of lifelong learning appears neatly to parallel influential sociological conceptions of institutionalized reflexivity and risk. The task of lifelong learning, it has been argued, is therefore to enable people to regain a degree of control over their existence, and develop a learning elective biography:

> When flexibility constitutes the crucial capacity that work organizations and the unpredictability of life demands, having a stable identity can be a disadvantage. . . Questions such as 'Who am I?' and 'Whom do I want to be?' can become quite haunting existential questions (Glastra *et al.*, 2004: 294).

Others, however, view such a concern with promoting flexibility as potentially damaging and negative to the individual and community, and at worst as collusion with the excesses of globalized capitalism.

Policies for lifelong learning have tended to concentrate on learning in and for working life. Yet, particularly when compared with the innovations of the 1970s debate, most governments have notably shied away from the challenging and difficult issue of policies aimed at increasing the skills and knowledge content of jobs, especially in sectors and regions that rely on low relative labor costs as a basis for competition. Some attention has been paid to the implications for initial schooling as a preparation for learning in later life, as well as to the development of parenting skills, usually for mothers, with a view to raising their capacity for supporting their own children's learning (Gillies, 2005). Relatively little attention has so far been paid to support for learning in later life, even in countries like Scotland where population aging presents acute social and economic challenges. Patterns of participation in adult learning, even among people of working age, tend to mirror existing educational and socioeconomic inequalities. There is therefore a risk that market-led approaches to lifelong learning will simply accentuate and help to entrench the social hierarchy, as the knowledge-poor lag ever further behind in the shift to a knowledge economy. While no policy models have successfully combined uplifts in overall adult participation with a marked impact on inequality, the Nordic societies have been relatively successful in moderating the impact of existing patterns of disadvantage.

Lifelong learning is, then, a rather ambiguous concept which has been used for a range of policy purposes, mainly economic in nature. Yet, it is at heart extremely simple and – from a normative point of view – potentially rather attractive. The vision of a society where people have broad opportunities to learn across and throughout their lives is an attractive one for many educationalists – particularly those with a background in adult education. More to the point, the broad social and economic trends that have brought lifelong learning to centerstage are not short-term ones. At least in the medium term, then, the debate is likely to continue.

Bibliography

Alheit, P. (1990). *Alltag und Biographie: Studien zur gesellschaftlichen Konstitution biographischer Perspektiven*. Bremen: Universität Bremen.

Beck, U. (1992). Risk Society. London: Sage.

Borg, C. and Mayo, P. (2005). The EU memorandum on lifelong learning: Old wine in new bottles? *Globalisation, Societies and Education* 3, 257–278.

Burke, P. J. and Jackson, S. (2007). *Reconceptualising Lifelong Learning: Feminist Interventions*. London: Routledge.

Coffield, F. (1999). Introduction: Lifelong learning as a new form of social control? In Coffield, F. (ed.) *Why's the Beer Always Stronger up North? Studies of Lifelong Learning in Europe*, pp 1–12. Bristol: Policy Press.

Commission of the European Communities (1994). *Competitiveness, Employment, Growth*. Luxembourg: Office for Official Publications.

Commission of the European Communities (2000). *Commission Staff Working Paper: A Memorandum on Lifelong Learning*. Brussels: Commission of the European Communities.

Côté, J. (2004). Identity capital, social capital and the wider benefits of learning. *Wider Benefits of Learning Research Centre Conference*. London, 15–16, 2004.

Faure, E. (1972). *Learning to Be: The World of Education Today and Tomorrow*. Paris: UNESCO.

Fejes, A. (2006). *Constructing the Adult Learner: A Governmentality Analysis*. Linköping: Linköpings Universitet.

Fenwick, T. (2004). What happens to the girls? Gender, work and learning in Canada's 'new economy'. *Gender and Education* **16**, 169–185.

Field, J. (2006). *Lifelong Learning and the New Educational Order*, 2nd edn. Stoke on Trent: Trentham.

Giddens, A. (1991). *Modernity and Self-Identity: Self and Society in the Late Modern Age*. Cambridge: Polity Press.

Gillies, V. (2005). Meeting parents' needs? Discourses of 'support' and 'inclusion' in family policy. *Critical Social Policy* **25**(1), 70–90.

Glastra, F., Hake, B., and Schedler, P. (2004). Lifelong learning as transitional learning. *Adult Education Quarterly* **54**(4), 291–307.

Gorard, S., Rees, G., and Fevre, R. (1999). Two dimensions of time: The changing social context of lifelong learning. *Studies in the Education of Adults* **31**(1), 35–48.

Gouthro, P. A. (2005). A critical feminist analysis of the homeplace as a learning site: Expanding the discourse of lifelong learning to consider adult women learners. *International Journal of Lifelong Education* **24**(1), 5–19.

Green, A., Preston, J., and Janmaat, J. G. (2006). *Education, Equality and Social Cohesion: A Comparative Analysis*. Basingstoke: Palgrave Macmillan.

Gustavsson, B. (1995). Lifelong learning reconsidered. In Klasson, M., Manninon, J., Tøsse, S., and Wahlgren, B. (eds.) *Social Change and Adult Education Research*, pp 89–110. Linköping: Linköping University.

Hargreaves, D. (2004). *Learning for Life: The Foundations of Lifelong Learning*. Bristol: Policy Press.

Jackson, S. (2003). Lifelong earning: Working-class women and lifelong learning. *Gender and Education* **15**, 365–376.

Knoll, J. (1998). 'Lebenslanges Lernen' und internationale Bildungspolitik – Zur Genese eines Begriffs und dessen nationale Operationalisierungen. In Brödel, R. (ed.) *Lebenslanges Lernen – Lebensbegleitende Bildung*, pp 35–50. Neuwied: Luchterhand.

Maskell, P., Eskelinen, H., Hannibalsson, I., Malmberg, A., and Vatne, E. (1998). *Competitiveness, Localised Learning and Regional Development: Specialisation and Prosperity in Small Open Economies*. London: Routledge.

Milana, M. and Desjardins, R. (2007). Enablers and constrainers to participation: Has policy in Nordic countries reached its limit for raising participation in adult learning among certain groups? *Second Nordic Conference on Adult Learning*. Linköping University, 17–19, April 2007.

Nicoll, K. (2006). *Flexibility and Lifelong Learning: Examining the Rhetoric of Education*. London: Routledge.

OECD (Organisation for Economic Co-operation and Development) (1973). *Recurrent Education: A Strategy for Lifelong Learning*. Paris: OECD.

OECD (Organisation for Economic Co-operation and Development) (2000). *Thematic Review on Adult Learning: Sweden*. Paris: OECD.

OECD (Organisation for Economic Co-operation and Development) (2004). *Completing the Foundation for Lifelong Learning: An OECD Survey of Upper Secondary Schools*. Paris: OECD.

OECD (Organisation for Economic Co-operation and Development) (2005). *Promoting Adult Learning*. Paris: OECD.

Payne, J. (2005). What progress is Norway making with lifelong learning? A study of the Norwegian competence reform. *SKOPE Research Paper 55*. Oxford and Warwick Universities.

Porter, M. (1990). *The Competitive Advantage of Nations*. New York: Free Press.

Reich, R. (1993). *The Work of Nations: Preparing Ourselves for Twenty-First Century Capitalism*. London: Simon and Schuster.

Rubenson, K. (2006). The Nordic model of lifelong learning. *Compare* **36**, 327–341.

Schemmann, M. (2007). *Internationale Weiterbildungspolitik und Globalisierung*. Bielefeld: W. Bertelsmann Verlag.

Schreiber-Barsch, S. and Zeuner, C. (2007). International–supranational–transnational? Lebenslanges Lernen im Spannungsfeld von Bildungsakteuren und Interessen. *Zeitschrift für Pädagogik* **53**, 686–703.

Schuller, T., Preston, J., Hammond, C., Bassett-Grundy, A., and Bynner, J. (2004). *The Benefits of Learning: The Impact of Education on Health, Family Life and Social Capital*. London: RoutledgeFalmer.

Smith, P. and Sadler-Smith, E. (2006). *Learning in Organizations: Complexities and Diversities*. Basingstoke: Palgrave Macmillan.

Spano, A. (2002). Female identities in late modernity. In Chamberlayne, P., Rustin, M., and Wengraf, T. (eds.) *Biography and Social Exclusion in Europe: Experiences and Life Journeys*, pp 151–173. Bristol: Policy Press.

Thurow, L. (1994). New game, new rules, new strategies. *Journal of the Royal Society of Arts* **142**, 50–53.

Torres, R. M. (2003). *Lifelong Learning: A New Momentum and a New Opportunity for Adult Basic Learning and Education (ABLE) in the South*. Bonn: Institute for International Co-operation of the German Adult Education Association.

Tsai, S. L. (1988). The transition from school to work in Taiwan. In Shavit, Y. and Müller, W. (eds.) *From School to Work*, pp 443–470. Oxford: Clarendon Press.

Tuijnman, A. C. (2003). The Nordic model of lifelong learning. *International Journal of Educational Research* **39**, 283–291.

Further Reading

Walther, A. (2006). Regimes of youth transitions. *Young* **14**, 119–139.

ADULT LEARNING, INSTRUCTION, AND PROGRAM PLANNING

Adult Learning

Adult Learning: Philosophical Issues

The Adult Development of Cognition and Learning

Characteristics of Adult Learning

Adult Learning and Instruction: Transformative-Learning Perspectives

Adult Learning in a Biographic Perspective

Adult Learning, Instruction and Programme Planning:
Insights from Freire

Workplace-Learning Frameworks

Organizational Learning

Informal Learning: A Contested Concept

Program Planning

Adult Learning

S B Merriam, University of Georgia, Athens, GA, USA

Adult learning is a phenomenon at once deceptively simple, yet enormously complex. It is simple because we know that learning "is of the essence of everyday living and of conscious experience; it is the process of transforming that experience into knowledge, skills, attitudes, values, and beliefs" (Jarvis, 1992: 11). However, it is also complex because there is no one definition, model, or theory that explains how adults learn, why adults learn, or how best to facilitate the process. Yet the learning of adults is the key theme that unites the otherwise widely disparate field of adult education. Whether in community-based literacy classes, training sessions in corporate settings, or continuing professional education seminars, practitioners share the common goal of facilitating adult learning. Rather than a single definition or description of adult learning, what we have is a colorful mosaic of theories, models, sets of principles, and explanations that, when combined, form the knowledge base of adult learning.

Until the mid-twentieth century, what we knew about adult learning was embedded in studies by behavioral and cognitive psychologists, studies that focused on problem solving, information processing, memory, intelligence, and motivation. Much of this research was conducted in laboratory settings, and if adults were included, what was of interest was how advancing age affected the learning activity. Thorndike *et al.'s* (1928) *Adult Learning* published in 1928 is an example of this early research. This book reports the results of adults being tested in a laboratory under timed conditions on various learning and memory tasks. The authors concluded that adults aged between 25 and 45 could learn "at nearly the same rate" as 20-year-olds (p. 178). Research in the 1940s found that when time pressure is removed, adults up to age 70 did as well as younger people.

Adult learning from a psychological, and in particular a behaviorist perspective shaped adult learning research and theory building in North America until the late 1960s when other traditions and European influences broadened inquiry. We now know quite a bit about the individual adult learner, how context shapes adult learning, and how noncognitive factors play a role in adult learning. This article is thus organized into three sections, in a loosely chronological order, reflecting our growing understanding of adult learning. The first part of this article explores the foundational adult learning theories of andragogy, self-directed learning, and transformational learning. A second strand of theory building represents a shift in the focus of learning from the individual to the context in which learning takes place. The third section of this article presents the most recent additions to our understanding of adult learning. These perspectives go beyond the cognitive and include the role of emotions, body, and spirit in learning.

The Individual Adult Learner

By the mid-twentieth century, adult education was a recognized field of practice with its own professional associations, journals, and conferences. Rather than extrapolating from research with children or research that placed adults under the same conditions as children, adult educators began to consider how learning in adulthood could be distinguished from learning in childhood. Humanistic psychology provided the philosophical underpinnings for three theories of adult learning, which have become foundational to the field of adult education – andragogy, self-directed learning, and transformational learning.

Andragogy

The European concept of andragogy was introduced by Knowles (1968) as "a new label and a new technology" distinguishing adult learning from children's learning or pedagogy (p. 351). Probably the best-known set of principles or assumptions to guide adult learning practice, andragogy actually tells us more about the characteristics of adult learners than about the nature of learning itself. Knowles originally presented the following four characteristics or assumptions about adult learners:

1. As a person matures, his or her self-concept moves from that of a dependent personality toward one of a self-directing human being.
2. An adult accumulates a growing reservoir of experience, which is a rich resource for learning.
3. The readiness of an adult to learn is closely related to the developmental tasks of his or her social role.
4. There is a change in time perspective as people mature – from future application of knowledge to immediacy of application. Thus, an adult is more problem centered than subject centered in learning. (Knowles, 1980: 44–45).

In later publications, Knowles also suggested a fifth and sixth assumption:

5. The most potent motivations are internal rather than external (Knowles *et al.*, 1984: 12).
6. Adults need to know why they need to learn something (Knowles, 1984: 12).

Working from these assumptions, Knowles (1980) proposed a program-planning model for designing, implementing, and evaluating educational activities with adults. For example, with regard to the first assumption that as adults mature they become more independent and self-directing, Knowles suggested that the classroom environment be one of adultness, both physically and psychologically. Adults who plan and direct their family, work, and community lives can also participate in their own learning by assisting in diagnosing their learning needs, planning and implementing learning activities, and evaluating those experiences.

At first heralded as the explanation of adult learning, andragogy underwent intense examination by educators of both adults and children. It was recognized, for example, that some children and adolescents are independent, self-directed learners while some adults are highly dependent on a teacher for structure and guidance. Further, adults may be externally motivated to learn as when an employer requires attendance at a training program, and some children may be motivated by curiosity or the internal pleasure of learning. By 1980, Knowles had acknowledged that the dichotomy between andragogy and pedagogy was not as stark as originally drawn. A clear indication of his rethinking is represented in the subtitles of the 1970 and 1980 editions of *The Modern Practice of Adult Education*. The 1970 subtitle is *Andragogy Versus Pedagogy*, whereas the 1980 subtitle is *From Pedagogy to Andragogy*. He came to believe that there was a continuum ranging from teacher-directed (pedagogy) on the one end, to student-directed learning (andragogy) on the other, and that both approaches are appropriate with children and adults, depending on the situation.

Andragogy has been most severely critiqued for its assumption that the individual adult learner is autonomous and in control of his or her learning. Lacking is any recognition that both the learner and the learning that takes place are shaped by a person's history and culture in conjunction with the institutional context where it occurs. Despite these critiques, practitioners who work with adult learners can intuitively connect with Knowles' characteristics of adult learners and can see how they translate into concrete suggestions for program planning, instruction, and evaluation. More than 40 years after it was first proposed in North America, andragogy enjoys widespread recognition as one understanding of adult learning and a tested guide to working with adults in practice.

Self-Directed Learning

Appearing in North America about the same time that Knowles introduced andragogy, the concept of self-directed learning (SDL) also helped distinguish adult learners from children. The major impetus for this model of adult learning came from Tough's (1971) research with Canadian adult learners. He found that 90% of the participants in his study had engaged in an average of 100 h of self-planned learning projects in the previous year and that this learning was deeply embedded in their everyday lives. The uncovering and documenting of SDL – learning that is widespread, that occurs as a part of adults' everyday life, and that is systematic yet does not depend on an instructor or a classroom – has been a major contribution toward understanding and defining adult learning.

More than 35 years of research in North America and Europe on SDL has verified its widespread presence among adults, documented the process by which it occurs, and developed assessment tools to measure the extent of individual self-directedness. Of these foci, the process of SDL speaks most directly to adult learning. How one actually moves through an SDL experience has generated a number of models of the process. The earliest models proposed by Tough (1971) and Knowles (1975) are the most linear, moving from diagnosing needs to identifying resources and instructional formats, to evaluating outcomes. Models developed in the late 1980s and 1990s are less linear and more interactive in which not only the learner, but the context of the learning and the nature of the learning itself are also considered. In the Danis (1992) model, for example, learning strategies, phases of the learning process, the content, the learner, and the environmental factors in the context must all be taken into account in mapping the process of SDL. The Spear and Mocker (1984) model considers the opportunities for learning found in one's environment, past or new knowledge, and chance occurrences. These opportunities cluster into the "organizing circumstance" which in turn, structures the SDL activity, and the "circumstances created during one episode become the circumstances for the next" (p. 5).

Yet another application of SDL is in instruction in formal educational settings. The most popular is the Grow (1991) model. He presents a matrix showing how four types of learners and four types of facilitators intersect with appropriate instructional methods. For example, a dependent learner (one who is not at all self-directed) is a good match with an authority or expert, and lecture and drill are appropriate instructional strategies. At the other extreme would be a highly self-directed learner, matched with a facilitator or delegator and instruction would be embedded in independent projects and discussions.

As with andragogy, SDL has proven to be a mainstay of adult learning theory. Recent applications of SDL include its role in lifelong learning and continuing professional education, how SDL can be acknowledged and incorporated into the workplace, and how being self-directed is one criterion for success in online learning environments (Merriam *et al.*, 2007).

Transformational Learning

The third contribution to adult learning that helped define what is different about learning in adulthood is transformational learning. Rather than focusing on the learner as andragogy and, to a large extent, SDL do, transformational learning is about the cognitive process of meaning making. It is particularly an adult learning theory because transformational learning is dependent on adult life experiences and a more mature level of cognitive functioning than found in childhood. The essence of transformational learning is that through sudden or dramatic experiences, people are changed in ways that they themselves and others can recognize.

Mezirow (2000) is considered the primary architect of transformational learning, although he readily acknowledges being influenced by the Brazilian educator, Paulo Freire. Freire (1970) emphasized the need for this type of learning to deal with oppression and to bring about social change. Mezirow (2000) focuses more on the process of individual transformation, a process that is personally empowering. Learning in adulthood is not just adding on to what we already know, although that is part of the story. It is also, according to Mezirow (1996: 162), "the process of using a prior interpretation to construe a new or a revised interpretation of the meaning of one's experience in order to guide future action." In short, learning is also making sense of our experiences. Learning can result in a change in one of our beliefs or attitudes, or it can be a change in our entire perspective. A perspective transformation is key to transformational learning.

Mezirow (2000) delineated a 10-step transformational learning process that is initiated by a disorienting dilemma – a life experience that cannot be accommodated by one's present worldview. This leads the adult to examine and critically reflect on the assumptions and beliefs that have guided meaning making in the past, but now are no longer adequate. From an examination of current beliefs, the learner moves to exploring new ways of dealing with the dilemma, often in conjunction with others confronting a similar crisis. It is in dialog with others that the learner tests out new assumptions, understandings, and perspectives. A plan of action is then formulated and put into motion. The new or transformed perspective is more inclusive and accommodating than the previous perspective.

Since the 1990s, transformational learning has moved center stage in terms of the volume of research and writing. Transformational learning conferences occurring every 2 years, with the most recent in 2007, have also contributed to the burgeoning knowledge base about this type of learning. Further, connections between transformational learning and adult development (Merriam and Clark, 2006), and transformational learning and spirituality (Tolliver and Tisdell, 2006), have expanded our understanding of adult learning and the meaning-making process.

In summary, andragogy, SDL, and transformational learning have come to define much of adult learning today. Both andragogy and SDL were instrumental in distinguishing adult learning from childhood learning at a time when the field of adult education was defining itself. They remain dominant in the real world of practice, perhaps because of their humanistic foundations and the fact that they capture what is popularly and intuitively understood about adult learning. Transformational learning, though powerful and emancipatory when it occurs, is more difficult to plan for, implement, and assess.

The Context of Adult Learning

Andragogy, SDL, and especially transformative learning theory focus on the individual learner; indeed, each has been critiqued for not recognizing how the context where this learning occurs also shapes the learning. Attention to context became prominent in the later decades of the twentieth century and remains central to understanding adult learning today. One perspective that attends to context draws from critical social science and related perspectives such as Marxism, critical theory, multiculturalism, critical race theory, queer theory, and feminist theory. What this literature has in common is the relentless questioning of power relations embedded in the structures of society. The focus is on the context of learning, not the individual learner. Through questioning and critique, the *status quo* is challenged, leading hopefully to social change.

More congruent with educational psychology is a second perspective that also shifts the focus from the individual to the context where learning takes place. Emerging from cognitive psychology and known loosely as situated cognition or contextual learning, learning cannot be understood as simply an individual, internal cognitive process; rather, learning is what is constructed by the interaction of people in a particular situation with particular tools or artifacts (including technology, language, signs, and symbols). Research (Lave, 1988; Lave and Wenger, 1991) has demonstrated that the context in which learning takes place is crucial to the nature of the learning, as are the tools in that setting, and the social interaction with others. Understanding human cognition means examining it in situations of authentic activity in which actual cognitive processes are required, rather than the simulated ones typical of school. Lave's (1988) experiments with grocery shoppers is a good example of the difference. Comparison pricing was found to be considerably more accurate in the activity of shopping (98% error-free) than in doing identical calculations on a paper-and-pencil test in the classroom (59% error-free).

The notion of situated cognition resonates well with what we already know about adult learning. Fenwick (2003) points out that one cannot separate the learning process from the situation in which it takes place. Knowledge is constructed in the context; it is "part of the very process of *participation* in the immediate situation" (Fenwick, 2003: 25; italics in the original). Learning takes place when people interact with the community (including its history and cultural values and assumptions), "the tools at hand," and the activity itself (Fenwick, 2003: 25). For example, in a recent study of Korean older adults in an intermediate computer literacy course, questions were asked about the cultural context of the course, the social-interaction patterns of the participants, the tools of the setting, and how learning is constructed through the interaction of these elements (Kim, 2008).

Locating learning in the real-life experiences of adults has long been promoted as a good adult education practice. Schon (1987, 1996), for example, is noted for promoting contextually based reflective practice. Knowledge gained in school is not enough to make a reflective practitioner. One must also engage in the actual practice. Others recommend apprenticeships, internships, and practicums where one can learn through modeling, coaching, and trial and error.

An important component of situated cognition is entering into relationships with other learners, thereby becoming a member of a learning community. This learning community can be considered a community of practice (Lave and Wenger, 1991; Wenger, 1998). Communities of practice are groups of people who share insights and ideas and who help each other solve problems and develop a common practice. All people belong to communities of practice, whether through formal learning environments, civic organizations, or family structures. While most communities of practice do not have a name, they are quite familiar to us. We know who belongs. The concepts of practice are both explicit and tacit. It includes the language, documents, images, symbols, roles, procedures, regulations, subtle cues, rules of thumb, sensitivities, embodied understandings, underlying assumptions, and shared worldviews that are crucial to the success of the community. In a study of a community of practice of Wiccans, an earth-based faith group, it was discovered that learning was embedded in the rites and rituals of their practice; learning in practice was experiential, combined formal and intuitive knowledge, and was spread across the group (Merriam, *et al.*, 2003).

Communities of practice as a learning theory has extended the work on situated cognition. Situated cognition

posits that learning is context bound, tool dependent, and socially interactive. These factors suggest looking at this type of learning from the perspective of a bounded system. A family, a classroom, a profession, an online community, a town, and a corporation can all be thought of as a community of practice, or a learning community. This approach contextualizes learning, uncoupling it from a preoccupation with the individual learner.

Emotions, Body, and Spirit in Adult Learning

The mind/body split so ingrained in Western notions of learning has dominated adult learning. In addition, learning has become so connected with schooling that the activity of learning is almost always framed from a rational, cognitive perspective. We learn through processing information in the brain. By the time we are adults, learning that is valued, formal, and systematic is devoid of anything emotional or physical. However, some of the most recent research and theory building in adult learning are based on the premise that knowledge construction and learning can be through pathways other than those that depend on the mind. Scholars are now trying to explain and legitimize the role played by emotions, body, and spirit in learning.

Emotions and Somatic Knowing

Knowledge construction is more than a cognitive process of meaning making. In fact, there is little cognitive about this – rather, we know through our emotions and our physical body. Dirkx (2001) argues that learning itself is inherently an imaginative, emotional act and that significant learning is inconceivable without emotion and feelings. It is through emotions that deeply personal, meaningful connections are made so that really significant learning can take place. These connections are of two kinds. First, there is the connection to one's own inner experiences; "emotions are gateways to the unconscious and our emotional, feeling selves" (p. 69); second, "emotions and feelings can connect to the shared ideas within the world as well and are reflected in big words or concepts, such as Truth, Power, Justice, and Love" (p. 69). We learn to understand or make meaning of our experience through engagement with these emotions and the images they evoke.

Somatic or embodied learning is closely related to emotional responses in learning. In somatic knowing, we can learn through our bodies, as we do when we connect physical manifestations of stress to our psychological situation. Pert (1997) in fact argues that since receptors are found in the body's nerves of all kinds, it would then follow that emotions could be stored and mediated by parts of the body other than just the brain. "These recent discoveries are important for appreciating how memories are stored not only in the brain, but in a *psychosomatic network* extending into the body" (p. 141). In fact, the interconnectedness of body, brain, and emotions is itself receiving attention through the neuroscience of learning (Johnson and Taylor, 2006).

It is clear that a false dichotomy has been created by the Western philosophical bias that dissects the whole person into mind and body, limiting knowledge construction to what goes on in one's mind. Even physiologically, the mind, body, and emotions cannot be separated. Certainly, in our own real-life experiences of living and learning, we involve our emotions and our body at least as much as our intellect.

Spirituality and Learning

Part of the difficulty in considering spirituality in learning has been definitional. There is little consensus about the boundaries of its meaning; the most writers can do is to define it as they are using the term. All agree that spirituality is not the same as religion, which is an organized community of faith; rather, spirituality is more about one's own beliefs and experience of a higher power or higher purpose. Spirituality is "about how we construct meaning, and what we individually and communally experience and attend to and honor as sacred in our lives" (Tisdell, 2003: 29).

Spirituality is connected to adult learning through the construct of meaning making. Aktouf (1992: 415) argues that "the human being is, by definition and necessity, a being whose destiny is meaning, intentions, and projects, a subject whose being is meaning and which has need of meaning." We are inveterate meaning makers. Tisdell (1999) makes several points about the relationship between spirituality, meaning making, and adult learning. First, educators should recognize that a search for or an acknowledgement of the spiritual in the lives of adult learners "is connected to how we create meaning in our relationships with others. It is in our living and loving. It is also connected with how we understand a higher power or a transcendent being" (p. 93). Second, adults come into our classroom with this agenda (meaning making), whether or not it is articulated. Third, meaning making is knowledge construction that uses images and symbols, "which often emanate from the deepest core of our being and can be accessed and manifested through art, music, or other creative work" (p. 93).

Those writing from this more holistic perspective on learning are not about promoting a particular form of embodied or spiritual learning. Rather, they are "committed to learning that makes a difference in learners' lives and increases their sense of knowing the content of the course in their heads, their hearts, their souls, and their entire being—that has meaning to them and makes a difference in the world" (Tolliver and Tisdell, 2006: 45). Journal writing, poetry, storytelling, myths, symbols, images, and even dreams can be used in an adult learning environment to foster a more holistic learning experience. Indeed, an entire volume of *New Directions for Adult and Continuing Education* is devoted to 'Artistic ways of knowing' (Lawrence, 2005). In this volume, authors speak to the use of art, music, poetry, photography, and drama to "extend the boundaries of how we come to know" (p. 3).

Summary

Learning in adulthood defies a simple explanation, and it is highly unlikely that there will ever be a single theory or explanation that encompasses all that we know now about adult learning. There is a substantial body of research and literature dating back to the early decades of the twentieth century where adult learning was conceived of as problem solving, memory, and information processing. From that foundation, adult educators began to differentiate adult learning from pre-adult learning, a move that led to a focus on the adult learners themselves. Andragogy, SDL, and, more recently, transformational learning are the major distinguishing aspects of adult learning today.

In addition, our understanding of adult learning has been expanded to include consideration of the larger sociocultural and political context in which it takes place, and how the context itself both shapes and is an integral part of the learning transaction. The analytical tools of situated cognition and critical perspectives have allowed us to uncover how context shapes learning, as well as to critically assess and challenge the disparities in adult education and learning in particular social contexts. Finally, an even more holistic conception of adult learning acknowledges the role of emotions, body, and spirit in learning. These as well as other approaches to adult learning will continue to be investigated, contributing to our understanding of the complex nature of learning in adulthood.

Bibliography

Aktouf, O. (1992). Management and theories of organizations in the 1990s: Toward a critical radical humanism? *Academy of Management Review* **17**(3), 407–431.

Danis, C. (1992). A unifying framework for data-based research into adult self-directed learning. In Long, H. B. and associates (ed.) *Self-Directed Learning: Applications and Research*, pp 47–72. Norman, OK: University of Oklahoma.

Dirkx, J. M. (2001). The power of feelings: Emotion, imagination, and the construction of meaning in adult learning. In Merriam, S. B. (ed.) *The New Update on Adult Learning Theory.* New Directions for Adult and Continuing Education, No. 89, pp 63–72. San Francisco, CA: Jossey-Bass.

Fenwick, T. (2003). *Learning through Experience: Troubling Orthodoxies and Intersecting Questions.* Malabar, FL: Krieger.

Freire, P. (1970). *Pedagogy of the Oppressed.* New York: Seabury Press.

Grow, G. (1991). Teaching learners to be self-directed: A stage approach. *Adult Education Quarterly* **41**(3), 125–149.

Jarvis, P. (1992). *Paradoxes of Learning: On Becoming an Individual in Society*. San Francisco, CA: Jossey-Bass.

Johnson, S. and Taylor, K. (eds.) (2006). *The Neuroscience of Adult Learning*. San Francisco, CA: Jossey-Bass.

Kim, Y. S. (2008). *Situated Learning in a Korean OlderAdults' Computer Classroom*. Uupublished Doctoral Dissertation. University of Georgia, Athens, Georgia.

Knowles, M. S. (1968). Andragogy, not pedagogy. *Adult Leadership* **16**(10), 350–352, 386.

Knowles, M. S. (1975). *Self-Directed Learning*. New York: Association Press.

Knowles, M. S. (1980). *The Modern Practice of Adult Education: From Pedagogy to Andragogy*, 2nd edn. New York: Cambridge Books.

Knowles, M. S. (1984). The Adult Learner: A Neglected Species, 3rd edn. Houston, TX: Gulf.

Knowles, M. S. and associates (1984). *Andragogy in Action: Applying Modern Principles of Adult Learning*. San Francisco, CA: Jossey-Bass.

Lave, J. (1988). *Cognition in Practice: Mind, Mathematics, and Culture in Everyday Life*. Cambridge: Cambridge University Press.

Lave, J. and Wenger, E. (1991). *Situated Learning: Legitimate Peripheral Participation*. Cambridge: Cambridge University Press.

Lawrence, R. L. (ed.) (2005). *Artistic Ways of Knowing: Expanded Opportunities for Teaching and Learning*. San Francisco, CA: Jossey-Bass.

Merriam, S. B. and Clark, M. C. (2006). Learning and development: The connection in adulthood. In Hoare, C. (ed.) *Handbook of Adult Development and Learning*, pp 27–51. London: Oxford University Press.

Merriam, S. B., Caffarella, R. S., and Baumgartner, L. M. (2007). *Learning in Adulthood*, 3rd edn. San Francisco, CA: Jossey-Bass.

Merriam, S. B., Courtenay, B., and Baumgartner, L. (2003). On becoming a witch: Learning in a marginalized community of practice. *Adult Education Quarterly* **53**(3), 170–188.

Mezirow, J. (1996). Contemporary paradigms of learning. *Adult Education Quarterly* **46**(3), 158–172.

Mezirow, J. (2000). Learning to think like an adult: Core concepts of transformation theory. In Mezirow, J. and associates (ed.) *Learning as Transformation*, pp 3–34. San Francisco, CA: Jossey-Bass.

Pert, C. B. (1997). *Molecules of Emotion: Why You Feel the Way You Feel*. New York: Scribner.

Schon, D. A. (1987). *Educating the Reflective Practitioner*. San Francisco, CA: Jossey-Bass.

Schon, D. A. (1996). From technical rationality to reflection-in-action. In Edwards, R., Hanson, A., and Raggatt, P. (eds.) *Boundaries of Adult Learning*. London: Routledge.

Spear, G. E. and Mocker, D. W. (1984). The organizing circumstance: Environmental determinants in self-directed learning. *Adult Education Quarterly* **35**(1), 1–10.

Thorndike, E. L., Bregman, E. O., Tilton, J. W., and Woodyard, E. (1928). *Adult Learning*. New York: Macmillan.

Tisdell, E. J. (1999). The spiritual dimension of adult development. In Clark, M. C. and Caffarella, R. S. (eds.) *An Update on Adult Development Theory: New Ways of Thinking about the Life Course*. San Francisco, CA: Jossey-Bass.

Tisdell, E. J. (2003). *Exploring Spirituality and Culture in Adult and Higher Education*. San Francisco, CA: Jossey-Bass.

Tolliver, D. E. and Tisdell, E. J. (2006). Engaging spirituality in the transformative higher education classroom. In Taylor, E. W. (ed.) *Teaching for Change: Fostering Transformative Learning in the Classroom. New Directions for Adult and Continuing Education, No 109*, pp 37–48. San Francisco, CA: Jossey-Bass.

Tough, A. (1971). *The Adult's Learning Projects: A Fresh Approach to Theory and Practice in Adult Learning*. Toronto, ON: Ontario Institute for Studies in Education.

Wenger, E. (1998). *Communities of Practice: Learning, Meaning, and Identity*. Cambridge: Cambridge University Press.

Further Reading

Brookfield, S. (1986). *Understanding and Facilitating Adult Learning*. San Francisco, CA: Jossey-Bass.

English, L. M., Fenwick, T. J., and Parsons, J. (2003). *Spirituality of Adult Education and Training*. Malabar, FL: Krieger.

Illeris, K. (2004). *Adult Education and Adult Learning*. Malabar, FL: Krieger.

Jarvis, P. (2006). *Towards a Comprehensive Theory of Human Learning*. London/New York: Routledge/Falmer.

Merriam, S. B. (ed.) (2008). *Third Update on Adult Learning Theory*. New Directions for Adult and Continuing Education, No. 119. San Francisco, CA: Jossey-Bass.

Merriam, S. B. and associates (2007). *Non-Western Perspectives on Learning and Knowing*. Malabar, FL: Krieger.

Adult Learning: Philosophical Issues

D Beckett, The University of Melbourne, Melbourne, VIC, Australia

Experience and Andragogy

If a single concept marks out the learning of adults from the learning of children, it is experience. The pursuit and accumulation of learning, and its refinement, by adults, is usually underpinned by some assumptions about the integrity and persistence of experience. If an individual has lived longer (i.e., has passed through childhood), they are regarded, initially, as more adept at identifying what they have learned, in the past, and what they want to learn in the future. Moreover, adult individuals are also assumed to have insights into how they learn best now, and in the past, and expect to learn, in the future.

Experience, closely connected to the life span of individuals, is therefore a fruitful way into a review of the main philosophical issues involved in adults' learning. There are clearly, also, intimate conceptual links from this singular life span across into the parallel area of life-long learning, which will emerge below. The immediate task is to set out how the fruitfulness of a single concept (experience) should be distinguished from the singularity of its manifestation, that is, in individuals, all of whom experience experience differently. As Candy puts it, the assumption that experiences are only located in individuals is "so deeply entrenched in the ethos of adult education as to be thought 'obvious' or 'self-evident' and to thus be beyond question" (1987: cited in Usher *et al.*, 1997: 93).

What is so special about adults' experiences, as adults? Distinguishing between children's and adults' learning was crisply and famously done by Knowles (1970), who was not a philosopher but gave significant shape to the field of practice called adult education, at least in North America. His andragogy (not androgogy) theorized adults' learning through the explicit utilization of experience. Adults learn best, according to Knowles, when they

> learn how to take responsibility for their own learning through self-directed inquiry, how to learn collaboratively with the help of colleagues rather than compete with them, and, especially, how to learn by analyzing one's own experience...[This] is the essence of the human relations laboratory. (Knowles, 1970: 45)

By contrast, Knowles' pedagogy marked out children's learning, in which instruction continued to be central, due to the limited and naive nature of youthful experience. Later, Knowles modified this crisp distinction in favor of more experientially inclusive learning for individuals of any age.

So if we take experience as the point of entry to theorizations of adult learning, we can readily locate it within humanist scholarship, more generally. Knowles quite explicitly drew upon the psychologists, Carl Rogers and Abraham Maslow, but philosophers can agree that advocating experience as the bedrock concept for adult learning immediately looks Deweyan, and educators in general have been drawing on his vast publications well before andragogy surfaced in the 1970s and 1980s (Dewey, 1938). Of course, Dewey mainly had school-based education in his sights, but his advocacy of organic, holistic learning (and teaching) has attracted many adult educators.

However, before we go on, getting some idea of where nonschool education occurs is important in understanding the impact of Deweyan (and Knowlesian) experience. There is no single sector of the education industry in which one could find adults' learning (unlike schooling, where children mainly and compulsorily learn). We can immediately identify formal organizations and institutions, such as vocational colleges and universities, but adult learning occurs informally, in daily life: at paid work (in employment), unpaid work (in the home and in community settings), public discourse (mass media including infotainment), and political advocacy (e.g., the green agenda). There is, then, an amorphous and distributional quality about adult learning, which a simple reliance on experience under-recognizes. We will return to that inherent contextual messiness shortly.

Shaping Foundations

Giving shape to the messiness of theorizations of adult learning has been splendidly done by Elias and Merriam (2005) over the past three decades. They list and describe various main philosophical foundations of adult education: liberal, progressive, behaviorist, humanistic, radical and critical, analytic, and postmodern. It is worth noting that Knowles provided the foreword to the first edition in 1980, beginning with the claim that "[d]uring the entire time I have been in the field of adult education, which is almost half a century, I have heard it being criticized for not having a philosophical foundation (xi)." Elias and Merriam do not attempt to provide such a foundation, but instead provide an accessible overview of several main writers in the various approaches which are frequently drawn upon to underpin policies and practices in adult education. As expected, these various approaches are generically educational, so giving shape to the messiness of adults' education is assumed, rightly, to be a subset of these.

Experience – that is to say, how adult learning is best conceptualized – fares differently within each of these foundations or approaches, as Elias and Merriam (2005) show. Liberal writers draw upon the classical Greeks, the values of medieval schooling, and the character formation thought to evolve from the contemplative study of an intellectual canon: literally the classics. By contrast, progressivists, such as William James and John Dewey, engage the relationship of subjective experience to the worlds of work, democracy, and of sociality, generally, with change as the driving force.

Behaviorism is well known through the work of Pavlov, Watson, and Skinner, where experiences are manifest as modified behavior, achievements of outcomes, and reinforcement (or not) of these. Humanism has been already introduced, above, through the Knowlesian contribution to adult education, but its heritage is much broader and deeper: Heidegger, Sartre, Camus, Marcel, and Buber, in European scholarship, and Dewey, in North America, for example. In adult education specifically, Brookfield, Mezirow, and Jarvis have each shaped richer contributions to theory, policy, and practices from within this tradition (yet none would claim to be philosophers).

Radical or critical adult education takes sociopolitical stances on learning, and advances it in the spirit of ideologs such as Marxism, some feminisms, anarchism, critical theory, environmentalism, and so on. Holt, Goodman, Illich, and mainly Freire are significant contributors here.

Analytic philosophy is represented by Lawson and Paterson, who have made influential early contributions in the United Kingdom (about the same time as Knowles, in the USA) drawing upon the London School of philosophy of education, well known through the work of R.S. Peters and Paul Hirst, for example (Curran *et al.*, 2003).

Elias and Merriam (2005), draw attention, finally, to postmodern approaches, which "offer. . . a trenchant critique of the entire enterprise of adult education," (p. 14) in that a host of scholars in a vast range of fields, across the arts and social sciences, have interrogated the modernist assumptions of unilateral and monocultural progress, in human affairs in general. Postmodern perspectives in adult education were evidenced in the second paragraph of this article you are now reading: Usher *et al.* (1997: ch 5 passim) refuse to take experience as a given (bedrock) phenomenon. We may ask, in the spirit of postmodernity: Whose experience? In what contexts? By whom is it perceived? These are three interrogations of the modernist experiential narrative which was our point of entry, and in asking these sorts of questions, postmodernists seek to expose the various constructions of learning, learners, and of teachers, from which adult education can, itself, be interrogated.

Experience is, then, manifest diversely and intersubjectively (among, not merely between, each other). It follows that all constructions are relational: they build upon, and between, varieties of subjectivities. Postmodernity works the relationality of experiences even harder than that. Identities and practices are themselves constituted in and by the networks and nodes by which humans associate. We live, move, and have our being through such associations; and postmodern perspectives in philosophy of education, and in adult learning, in particular, are serious about diverse and locally devised interrogations of problems, issues, and challenges.

Embracing Diversity

So Elias and Merriam do us a fine service in mapping the main foundations of adult education, and introducing persisting and influential bodies of scholarship to practitioners and other theoreticians. Overall, we can agree that there is no one-size-fits-all philosophy of adult education, nor is there one best approach to adult learning. In their chapter in a well-received book covering all of adult education and training, Fenwick and Tennant (2004: ch 5), set out to understand adult learning, by making three assumptions:

> First, no one theory of learning or of facilitating learning trumps the others. There is no generic essentialised "adult learner". . . . Second, learning is not a mental process occurring in a vacuum. The context of a person's life – with its unique cultural, political, physical, and social dynamics – influences what learning experiences are encountered and how they are engaged. Furthermore, "context". . .is active and dynamic. Third, the "learner" is not an object separable from the "educator" in teaching-learning situations. The positionality of the educator (whether the expert, coach, liberator, observer, arbiter, commentator, guide, decoder) affects how learners perceive, feel, behave, and remember. (Fenwick and Tennant, 2004: 55.)

Drilling down even more sensitively into adults' experiences often requires a phenomenological approach. Here, bringing one's awareness of one's consciousness to the surface, and articulating it, is essential to the realization of a sense of personhood (Stanage, 1987). This Husserlian approach holds much potential for adult education in, for example, nurses' leadership of antenatal classes, where utterly personal expectations, and real experiences, of pain, can be trawled.

When faced with the messiness of theories, we can conclude so far that a postmodern spirit, rather than embrace a singular postmodernism, enables an eclectic and particularistic approach to central philosophical issues (subjectivities and their construction in and around sociopolitical associations), that themselves revolve around adult learning's traditional focus on the integrity and persistence of experience.

Now we return to the messiness of contexts. Sensitivity to diversity of contexts of adult learning is essential, but is difficult when formal and informal adult learning may well work against each other, and frequently do. An apprenticeship requires on-the-job assimilation of masterful skill (the informal) and typically also 1 or 2 days a week in a vocational college (the formal), over several years. Yet these experiences may not dovetail. Similarly, one of the main criticisms of traditional university teaching (formalized learning) at least in the West has been its disdain for those experiences brought to the lecture hall and tutorials, not just by school leavers, but also by mature age or further education students (informal learning).

Know-How at Work

The formality of what philosophers call propositional knowledge – necessary though it is for a worthwhile education – is now regarded as insufficient for genuinely lifelong learning, in particular, for enhancing a graduate's employability across the life span beyond the compulsory years of schooling. How, for example, a university or a vocational college, engages students' informal learning, which is inevitably and desirably experiential, raises fundamental issues of teaching, program design, and assessment for that institution. Ryle's (1949) important distinction between knowing that X (where X is a proposition) and knowing how X (where X is an experience) has become problematic for many educators as lifelong-learning policy discourses traverse experience as a human phenomenon, trawling it for meaning.

Know-how is emerging as a fruitful site of analysis in its own right. For example, Polanyi (1966) picked up the tacit (inarticulable) significance of knowing how: we know more than we can say. Decades on, we are now more willing to acknowledge that powerful adult learning resides in what have hitherto been low-status experiences, often called intuition, common sense, women's ways of knowing, and nous. The epistemological significance of these is now under evaluation, especially in the light of Deweyan accounts of how learning processes, such as reflection, both enhance, and are constitutive, of action. This is in the global context of adult learning at and for work, which has emerged as a major new component in the new world of free trade, rampant consumerism, and market-driven organizational changes, with the collapse of Communism in the 1980s. As Boud and Garrick (1999) put it:

Learning at work has become one of the most exciting areas of development in the dual field of management and education...Modern [sic] organisations ignore learning at the cost of their present and future success...learning has moved from the periphery...to the lifeblood that sustains them. (Boud and Garrick, 1999: 1)

Significant philosophical issues are raised by the vocationalization of adult learning, to which we now turn.

Livelihoods, Competencies, and the New Model Worker

Adults learning at and from work undergo experiences only some of which are educative, and only some of which are of enterprise, or strategic, significance. So what, then, is worthwhile workplace learning? And how can it be recognized? A good deal of attention has been given to the calibration of such learning, in various competence structures in most developed economies, and in many developing economies. The extent to which any vocational or workplace competencies can capture the really worthwhile is highly debatable, but so also is the debate – what is really worthwhile? Making a livelihood is essential: how does learning contribute to that? Only in the past couple of decades has this question achieved such prominence. After all, any educational significance that learning at and for work may have has often not been the main motive governments and organizations have in embracing competencies. Learning is not the main activity of most organizations and enterprises. Industrial, labor market, and productivity considerations are important motivators to be weighed among the educational and philosophical, here.

What helps to shape such debates is the acknowledgment of an epistemological and ethical tension. At one polarity, is a reliance on behaviorism issues in low-level checklisting of skills performed, without regard for the rich practical judgments often implied by such performances, and invites reductive, outcomes-driven accounts of human learning. Teaching and training, on this behavioral approach, consist of modifying behavior by repetition, motivators, and incentives which may have little to do with intrinsic satisfactions. An organization, or national government, can run entire learning programs on this approach.

The other polarity is humanist, which assumes the whole person is the worker, not merely a set of hands, but ascribes to the workplace the expectations of fulfillment attributable to human life in general, accompanied by the vocational self-direction to achieve these fulfillments. Again, an entire organization or national government can run entire learning programs on this approach. National generic or key competencies can be identified, often without regard for contextual sensitivities, against which varieties of more or less reductive performance evidence can be assembled, and, in some more enlightened case, some Aristotelian-influenced practical judgments can be inferred.

More commonly, controversies accrue around the fluidity and admixture of behavioral and humanist assumptions in particular contexts. Does the so-called new model worker (ideally self-directedly flexible, well-rounded, creative) get caught up in the ideology of individual success to the detriment of her or his integrity as a person? Usher and Edwards (1994) argue, following Foucault, that "the exercise of modern disciplinary power is exemplified in the panopticon" (p. 101), which was the nineteenth-century circular prison designed as cells radiating spoke-like, from a hub, with the guards in the hub, such that surveillance was always assumed, by the prisoners, even if the hub was unstaffed.

Usher and Edwards critique the new model workplace, and the competencies that calibrate the work, if workers are learning to be complicit in their own organizational or professional surveillance. This raises substantial ethical and epistemological issues for adult learning, provoked by the very shape and structure of accountabilities for worthwhile vocational learning. Although these issues arise at national, organizational, and enterprise level, they are best resolved locally and in particular cases, with due recognition of contextual sensitivities from those with the experiences that matter most. In this way, a postmodern spirit is played out in judgments of worthwhile adult learning.

Knowing That, Knowing How..., and Knowing Why

Epistemology and ethics are only part of the adult learning story. The already amorphous and distributional quality of adult learning is exacerbated by the immediacy of the self-direction which Knowles' traditional andragogy highlights. Adults learn best when they see the point of it.

Vocationalization within adult learning (as part of a globalizing lifelong-learning policy scenario), such as has just been discussed, impels us to consider the extent to which adults learn best when they can see its direction: this is to know why X... (where X is a reason, purpose, or goal).

As we have seen above, translating this across formal and informal contexts is complex: individuals will have a variety of motivations, often in any one day, and often derived from sociocultural allegiances. Through work, home, community, and national institutions, individual adults locate their sense of what is worth achieving – not only for themselves as individuals, but also for their sense of their shared self-hood. What kind of worker, partner, parent, or citizen do I, or rather, we, want to be? Once the arena for learning is broadened out, we can locate ourselves as distributed among and between diverse allegiances. This lateral dimension complements the linear dimension – the journey of the individual across the life span.

In this way, we can add to the traditional Rylean analysis, a teleological perspective: we learn, from each other, what it is to know why we have particular goals and motives. These might come from our employment (such as a corporate vision or strategy), or from our home or community allegiances (such as spiritual or activist values), or from national imperatives (policy discourses which attract or repel).

On this tripartite analysis, worthwhile adult learning is constituted, coextensively, by know-what, know-how, and know-why. This adds to propositional knowledge the significance of sensitivity to our own learning experiences (knowing how X...), and also adds the directionality of this learning, or the teleological dimension (knowing why X...). This analysis locates the individual as an intersubjectivity among not only other individuals, but also as relationships of associations and allegiances, in groups of diverse sociocultural significance.

Adult learning, analyzed this way, is a wide and deep phenomenon, with astonishingly diverse manifestations, only some of which fit with traditional assumptions of the learner as an individual, or subjective self, enrolled in formal studies in an educational institution. On the contrary, this analysis requires philosophical enquiry into diverse contexts where, almost case by case, particularistic approaches can be tailored to prospects of successful learning. So we need to look closely at educative practices, from which adults can learn.

Practices and Identities

The practice turn in education has taken much attention in recent years (Hogan, 2008), and not just with adults. However, here we are advancing an experiential analysis of adults' learning in particular contexts of practice, so it is important to bear in mind some actual learning activities which could be and often are assembled into programs and practices for groups of adults, both formally and informally:

- problem solving/workshopping; learning-to-learn/double-loop questioning; critical thinking/evaluation exercises;
- negotiation/collaboration/interactivity/interpersonal skill formation via groupwork;
- literacy and numeracy through real-life excursions/reporting;
- case studies/informal presentations;
- simulations/role playing;
- journaling;
- work placements – real on-the-job learning/training with episodes of expert instruction/guidance (coaching);
- peer-group instruction/guidance (debriefing/consulting/mentoring);

- audio–visual presentations and resultant groupwork;
- project-based team activities.

Diversity is not self-justifying. Here, the purposes in assembling diverse activities within particular contexts expose adults to diverse ways of learning – experiences – from which they build their own capacity for self-direction.

Implicit in this very Deweyan concept of organic growth is both self-direction and self-identity. Identities, or subjectivities, are constructed and reconstructed, in practices – such as in classrooms, anywhere in the world. The way, then, to clarify important aspects of experience for adult learning, given the amorphous and distributed nature of those experiences, is to pay close attention to the practical – even as a philosophy. In the policy context of lifelong learning, Leicester *et al.* (2007) argues for practical diversity in this way:

> Our notion of "practical philosophy," in encouraging attention to the diversity of voices and experiences in the real world, also has this political tendency [that is, to be more inclusive of the interests of all people]. Postmodernist epistemology recognises that knowledge is validly constructed from the intersubjective agreement in the experiences of oppressed groups and not just from that of the educated group (the group which writes papers) which has tended to exclude these voices hitherto. However...we are also suggesting that practical philosophy, recognising that meaning is rooted in the (complex and context-dependent) uses of a word, has implications for conceptual analysis regardless of any political commitments or implications. (Leicester, 2007: 263)

Both Leicester's constructive practical philosophy and the author's listing of a range of learning activities (listed at the beginning of this section) have in common an experientially diverse approach to the practice turn. Most important in this is that both imply a richer and hitherto model of agency. Adult learning is underpinned by assumptions of the integrity and persistence of human experience, as we noted at the outset, but in this era of lifelong learning, individuals are assumed, and indeed required to exercise, in their very self-direction, and to advance their self-identity, sophisticated autonomy, which assumes agency. It is in this sense that Schon's (1987) reflective practitioner gets a new lease of life: socially located, amidst the intersubjective messiness of daily work life, and fully agentive. The revitalization of Aristotle's phronesis in clinical medical practice is a case in point (Montgomery, 2006).

The Project of the Self: Always Work In Progress

If, as has been argued above, and building upon a Rylean analysis, a tripartite, more intersubjective, more social notion of adult experience is required, then agency itself needs to be rethought. If adults – and, indeed, all humans – learn not just individually, but powerfully from each other, then agency as expressed in what can be called the project of the self, needs recasting. Self-direction becomes self-management, but less of me, and more of us.

The vocationalization of higher education has been rightly criticized if it merely reduces adults' learning to employability. Such reduction of the head to the hands preserves a Cartesian dualism at the very time adult and lifelong learning is taking the organic and holistic approach that was argued by Dewey and many others in adult education across the twentieth century. Reductive attempts to produce the new model worker – utterly flexible, compliant, and creative – deserve criticism when, as often occurs, competencies and shallow skill-talk drive the educational and policy discourse. It may be that a character-driven capabilities approach (following Nussbaum) is a more defensible formulation of the project of the self.

However, what is interesting beneath all this is the need to revitalize agentive practices: these are opportunities for adult learners to make decisions and judgments in particular contexts which meet the particular purposes of those contexts. Practice-based learning activities immerse participants in intersubjective relationships with various forms of association (e.g., a team, mentorship). Moreover, they can take skill acquisition seriously – beyond behavioristic training, and often meld with broad organizational development initiatives, and can do this inclusively – with the respect for constructively diverse experiences, which Leicester claims for them, above.

In addition, the embodied nature of adult learning is crucial. Rather than leave materiality of the learning to the doing of the hands (which preserves a Cartesian dualism), some current research is bringing to prominence the whole person with a due regard for how what we find ourselves doing expresses not merely our learning, but our identities as well (O'Loughlin, 2006).

Thus, agency and identity are intertwined in deliberately providing a (strategic, purposeful) diversity of learning activities for particular formal and informal contexts. Intersubjectivity requires the selection of social, reflective (both public and private), and personal experiences of the most profound kind. In this way, the practice turn demonstrates what a new approach to agency might look like when adults gather to learn. Over time, and explicitly heading toward assessment tasks, or some other agreed outcomes, the intention is to grow self-direction and self-identity. Choices – decisions – are negotiated, and in these ways, human decision-making capacity is shown to be valued.

Beckett and Hager (2002), argued for the centrality of practical judgments, as a relational way of advancing a new epistemology of practice, one which decenters the traditional Cartesian and even Platonic epistemology.

Educators have traditionally assumed that coming to know something is to arrive at a state of the mind as evidenced in accounts of what is cognitively the case – this is about whether the propositions are in place there. Yet adults learn best when their experiences are taken seriously, so a tripartite Rylean epistemology should supplement the traditional account. The low status of the tacit, intuitive, reflective, phenomenological, embodied, and the socially efficacious leaves much human experience out of the educational vision, wherever it is, but especially for adults.

By taking seriously the holistic nature of particular everyday experiences, such as those of the workplace and the pedagogically diverse classroom, adult educators, whether they are practitioners (who have real expertise in inclusive learning strategies) or researchers (who have interests in relational practices), can find philosophically rich ways through the messiness of adult learning.

Bibliography

Beckett, D. and Hager, P. (2002). *Routledge International Studies in the Philosophy of Education 14: Life, Work and Learning: Practice in Postmodernity*. London: Routledge.

Boud, D. and Garrick, J. (eds.) (1999). *Understanding Learning at Work*. London: Routledge.

Curran, R., Robertson, S., and Hager, P. (2003). The analytic movement. In Curran, R. (ed.) *A Companion to the Philosophy of Education*, pp 176–191. Oxford: Blackwell Publishing.

Dewey, J. (1938). *Experience and Education*. New York: Macmillan.

Elias, J. L. and Merriam, S. B. (2005). *Philosophical Foundations of Adult Education*, 3rd edn. (orig. pub., 1980). Malabar, FL: Krieger Publishing.

Fenwick, T. and Tennant, M. (2004). Understanding adult learning. In Foley, G. (ed.) *Dimensions of Adult Learning: Adult Education and Training in a Global Era*, pp 55–73. Sydney: Allen and Unwin.

Hogan, P. (ed.) (2008). Philosophical perspectives on educational practice in the 21st century. *Studies in Philosophy and Education* **27** 2–3.

Knowles, M. (1970). *The Modern Practice of Adult Education: Andragogy versus Pedagogy*. New York: Association Press.

Leicester, M., Twelvetrees, R., and Bowbrick, P. (2007). Philosophical perspectives on lifelong learning: Insights from education, engineering and economics. In Aspin, D. (ed.) *Lifelong Learning Book Series 11: Philosophical Perspectives on Lifelong Learning*, pp 258–274. Dordrecht: Springer.

Montgomery, K. (2006). *How Doctors Think: Clinical Judgment and the Practice of Medicine*. New York: Oxford University Press.

O'Loughlin, M. (2006). *Embodiment and Education: Exploring Creatural Existence*. Dordrecht: Springer.

Polanyi, M. (1966). *The Tacit Dimension*. New York: Doubleday.

Ryle, G. (1949). *The Concept of Mind*. London: Hutchinson.

Schon, D. (1987). *Educating the Reflective Practitioner: Toward a New Design for Teaching and Learning in the Professions*. San Francisco, CA: Jossey-Bass Publishers.

Stanage, S. (1987). *Adult Education and Phenomenological Research: New Directions for Theory, Practice, and Research*. Malabar, FL: Krieger Publishing.

Usher, R., Bryant, I., and Johnston, R. (1997). *Adult Education and the Postmodern Challenge: Learning Beyond the Limits*. London: Routledge.

Usher, R. and Edwards, R. (1994). *Postmodernism and Education*. London: Routledge.

Further Reading

Archer, M. (2000). *Being Human: The Problem of Agency*. Cambridge, UK: Cambridge University Press.

Bagnall, R. (1999). *Discovering Radical Contingency: Building a Postmodern Agenda in Adult Education*. New York: Peter Lang.

Beckett, D. (2004). Embodied competence and generic skill: The emergence of inferential understanding. *Educational Philosophy and Theory* **36**(5), 497–509.

Belenky, M., Clinchy, B., Goldberger, N., and Tarule, J. (1986). *Women's Ways of Knowing: The Development of the Self, Voice and Mind*. New York: Basic Books.

Bright, B. (ed.) (1989). *Theory and Practice in the Study of Adult Education: The Epistemological Debate*. London: Routledge.

Brockett, R. (ed.) (1988). *Ethical Issues in Adult Education*. New York: Teachers' College Press.

Brookfield, S. (1986). *Understanding and Facilitating Adult Learning*. San Francisco, CA: Jossey-Bass.

Hager, P. and Halliday, J. (2006). *Lifelong Learning Book Series 7: Recovering Informal Learning: Wisdom, Judgement and Community*. Dordrecht: Springer.

Jarvis, P. (1997). *Ethics and Education for Adults in a Late Modern Society*. Leicester: National Institute of Adult Continuing Education (England and Wales).

Morris, G. and Beckett, D. (2004). Performing identities: A new focus on embodied adult learning. In Kell, P., Singh, M., and Shore, S. (eds.) *Adult Education @21st Century: Global Futures in Practice and Theory*, pp 121–136. New York: Peter Lang Publishing.

Mulcahy, D. (2000). Body matters in vocational education: The case of the competently-trained. *International Journal of Lifelong Education* **19**(6), 506–524.

Van Manen, M. (1990). *Researching Lived Experience: Human Science for an Action Sensitive Pedagogy*. Albany, NY: State University of New York Press.

Welton, M. (ed.) (1995). *In Defense of the Lifeworld: Critical Perspectives on Adult Learning*. Albany, NY: State University of New York Press.

The Adult Development of Cognition and Learning

E A L Stine-Morrow and J M Parisi, University of Illinois at Urbana–Champaign, Champaign, IL, USA

Introduction

Cognition in adult development arises out of the dynamic interplay of (1) gains in knowledge-based systems, expertise, and skill and (2) losses in speed of processing, working memory (WM) capacity, and inhibitory control processes. These changes have important effects on the nature of learning and entail that strategies in instruction be developmentally sensitive throughout the life span. At the same time, education early in the life span shapes these lifelong trajectories, while education and engagement in work and leisure through adulthood play an important role in engendering and maintaining competencies. Our goal in this article is to examine this interaction between the adult development of cognition and education. In the following sections, we examine the nature of cognition through adulthood and consider implications for learning. We also discuss recent research suggesting lifelong plasticity in neural networks, so that education is intimately tied with successful aging.

Theories of Life-Span Development

We review learning and cognition in adulthood and aging against the backdrop of a long history in psychology and education in which adulthood has been viewed merely as the culmination of what was achieved in childhood followed by a biologically driven decline. To the contrary, contemporary theories and empirical findings suggest that there are dynamic changes in cognition, motivation, and regulatory heuristics throughout the life span.

Multidirectionality in Cognition and Intellectual Function

While there are a number of competing theories for mechanisms that underlie age-related changes in cognition, there is broad agreement that age effects on cognition can be characterized at a coarse level as the result of two competing forces. On the one hand, the senescence process drives a decline in mental mechanics, the capacity to control attention and perform basic mental computations with accuracy and speed. On the other hand, there is accumulating evidence that the brain has immense potential for plasticity into late life; therefore, experience-based articulation of knowledge systems, skill, and expertise offers potential for growth. These divergent trajectories have also been characterized in terms of fluid versus crystallized abilities, derived from the factor structure of typical tests of intellectual ability. Fluid ability is manifested in tasks that require the encoding and transformation of information and detecting underlying relationships (e.g., block design, digit symbol, inductive reasoning, and spatial orientation). Crystallized ability, or pragmatics, depends on the acquisition of culture (e.g., vocabulary, semantic memory, and world knowledge).

Beyond that first cut, there are various theories characterizing the specific nature of declines in mechanics with age. The slowing hypothesis suggests that aging brings a systematic decrease in the speed with which mental operations can be performed. The WM hypothesis posits that aging is associated with a decline in the capacity to perform basic processing operations and store their products (as might be required, e.g., as one listens to a lecture and tries to construct an understanding of what is currently being discussed and integrate it with what has come before). According to the inhibition deficit hypothesis, aging brings a decreased effectiveness in suppressing irrelevant or no-longer-relevant information, thus reducing the functional capacity of WM. Another recent variant on the WM hypothesis is the effortfulness hypothesis, which identifies sensory loss as a critical contributor to age-related deficits in mental mechanics, not simply because they diminish the quality of information coming into the cognitive system, but also because central resources are strained by effort allocated to interpret the muddy input.

At the same time, aging may bring growth in a variety of capacities. Unlike declines, which come for free as a consequence of the senescence process, growth appears to arise out of dedicated engagement with particular types of experience. Initial conceptualizations of life-span growth focused on the normative development of capacities that could be scaled within a cultural context, for example, vocabulary and areas of common knowledge (e.g., why does bread rise? Who wrote Huckleberry Finn?), termed crystallized ability. In fact, vocabulary and some aspects of verbal ability are often found to increase or show stability through adulthood, with some evidence suggesting that such growth depends on habitual engagement with literacy-based activities. More recent conceptualizations acknowledge that normative growth of knowledge within certain cultural contexts early in the life span arises out of age-graded curricula in which there can be considerable commonality in the types of experiences to which children are exposed. However, relative to childhood, experiences in adulthood are more diverse and, rather than arising out of common school curricula, are tied to occupational and leisure activities. The particularized knowledge and skill systems that develop during adulthood are key achievements during this period and are intimately tied to selective allocation of resources to particular activities. Skill systems can be maintained well into late life, with recent evidence highlighting an important role for deliberate practice.

These two dimensions of intellectual function interact in interesting ways. First, because knowledge growth and skill development require attentional control, expansion of crystallized ability, particularized knowledge, and expertise ultimately depend on fluid abilities to some extent. Consequently, early in the life span, fluid and crystallized abilities grow apace with each other. In midlife to early old age, however, these trajectories diverge; knowledge and skill can continue their upward trajectories, but at a shallower slope as it takes a greater investment in attention to achieve the same gains, relative to earlier in the life span. On the other hand, to the extent that an individual has already invested in creating knowledge structures and skill systems (regardless of age), subsequent growth in those areas can be accomplished more easily. In part, this is because of a greater efficiency in processing information when existing knowledge can support learning. Another factor that contributes to knowledge-driven learning is that knowledge can support attentional control (i.e., effective allocation of effort).

Selectivity

A hallmark of adult development is increased selectivity, the focus of effort on a subset of available options. While the earlier part of the life span is a period in which effort is allocated to hone a diverse repertoire of skills and to expand social networks, movement through adulthood brings a motivational shift toward selectivity. There are two developmental forces that drive this.

First, the decline in mental mechanics limits the resources available to promote growth; therefore, selective focus of effort will increase the likelihood that selected domains will thrive. This strategy of selective optimization is distinctively an adult skill, with evidence suggesting that well-being in later life is enhanced by mindful selection of domains to which effort will be allocated toward growth, with the acknowledgment that this will entail loss in unselected domains. Expertise and knowledge systems may enhance selectivity by enabling more efficient focus on the most relevant features of a situation.

Selectivity is also thought to be driven by a changing perspective on the temporal horizon across the life span. Time is perceived to be open ended in youth, with unlimited – and unknowable – possibilities for experience. This expansive temporal horizon engenders concerns with information acquisition, skill development, and enrichment of social networks as a strategy for preparing for an uncertain future. With movement through the life span, the temporal horizon comes into view. Time is not limitless

and choices have consequences that may squander that limited resource. This salience of the temporal horizon may increase attention to emotional concerns and decrease motivation toward purely cognitive goals. This theory has been used to explain, for example, why social networks typically decrease in size but become more emotionally satisfying. One implication of this socioemotional selectivity theory for learning is that cognition itself may be used most reliably in service of emotional goals; therefore, learning is expected to be relatively enhanced in later life if it is well integrated with the socioemotional system.

Self-Regulation

Another theme that emerges in adult developmental theory is the extent to which aging brings a change in the ability to engage processing resources for learning. While adult education textbooks often proclaim that adult learning is self-directed, the ability to self-initiate and self-direct learning may well depend on the level of existing knowledge and skill in the domain. In fact, one theory of cognitive aging holds that it becomes more difficult to self-initiate processing and that age-related difficulties in learning can be ameliorated to a large extent by the availability of environmental supports to guide processing.

Beliefs about one's capacity to accomplish cognitive and intellectual tasks appear to play a critical role in learning throughout the life span, but these may be particularly important in later adulthood and old age. Two related constructs that have received a lot of attention in the literature are self-efficacy and perceived control, each of which appears to be domain specific (e.g., one can conceive of being able to master health-related behaviors, but be undone by a cognitive task like filing a tax form). Self-efficacy is the confidence that one can execute the behavior or process necessary to achieve the desired outcome; perceived control is a multidimensional construct defining beliefs about the locus of control for achieving desired outcomes, with internal control reflecting beliefs of personal efficacy in achieving outcomes, and external control (chance or power others) reflecting beliefs that control of achievement rests with other sources. Relative to younger adults, older adults are sometimes found to have reduced levels of self-efficacy and may be more likely to believe that there are other people who will be able to control cognitive outcomes. To some extent, certain effects of aging are beyond our control; therefore, such beliefs may arise, in part, from an overgeneralization of a veridical perception. Another factor that may contribute to these beliefs is negative aging stereotypes, which can be internalized, and thus reduce effort to cognitive performance. In any case, such beliefs can become self-fulfilling prophecies. In fact, individual differences in self-efficacy and control beliefs can often account, in part, for age differences in cognitive performance, effects that are themselves sometimes mediated by strategy utilization.

Learning through Adulthood

Memory and Aging

Memory is among the first cognitive domains to be studied through adulthood and it remains a complex and vibrant literature. Memory is often conceptualized as involving three stages: encoding of information into a relatively durable trace, retention, and retrieval of the information into consciousness. Memory failure is among the most prevalent of aging stereotypes, and with aging, many adults complain about a difficulty with memory. In fact, age differences in memory performance can depend, to a large degree, on the task conditions, the materials, and the educational levels of the samples compared. Semantic memory (e.g., the meanings of words) and retrieval of well-learned information can show great resilience throughout the life span. By contrast, episodic memory, the ability to associate information with a particular learning context, may show pronounced age differences under some circumstances.

Deficits have been attributed, in part, to the demands that effective encoding places on mental mechanics and attentional control. Normatively, in an episodic memory task, older adults may be less likely to encode information in a way that is organized, elaborate, and distinctive. Critically, older learners have a more difficult time forming new arbitrary associations. Fairly modest interventions (e.g., instruction in organizational strategies) can improve memory performance. Interestingly, even though memory training can improve performance into very late life, training gains are typically greater among the young, suggesting that it is ultimately age-graded declines in mental mechanics that limit how well these strategies can be implemented.

Age changes in the effectiveness of episodic memory can also be attributed to retrieval. For example, age deficits in memory performance are often exaggerated in free recall relative to recognition or cued recall, a difference that presumably resides in the reduced demands to generate the information. In recognition, older adults are more likely to rely on familiarity rather than direct recollection.

Difficulty with name retrieval is one of the more common memory complaints. Aging does bring more tip-of-the-tongue experiences, in which an individual knows the word he/she wants to say but is unable to retrieve any of the phonological information. This is most likely to happen for relatively rare words or for infrequently encountered names. Happily, these are most typically resolved, even among older adults.

Learning from Text

Learning from text is often conceptualized as involving distinct processing systems that operate in concert to construct different facets of the language representation. At the surface level, individual lexical items (words) are encoded from the orthographic or acoustic signal and their meanings are activated. The semantic representation can be described in terms of integrated ideas (or propositions) that establish relationships among concepts described by the text, a representation called the textbase. Knowledge plays a role in facilitating integration, enabling elaborative inference, and evoking a simulation of the situation suggested by the text. Consistent with the divergent age trajectories of mechanics and knowledge-based processes, age deficits are more likely for the resource-consuming aspects of language processing.

Understanding words

Vocabulary often shows an increase with age, particularly among those who are regularly exposed to text; therefore, word recognition and word-level comprehension appear to be highly resilient in reading. Visual-processing declines can impact reading rate, especially if the font is small or hard to decode. In speech processing, declines in auditory processing can make spoken word recognition more demanding; therefore, more acoustic information is needed to understand individual words. Such effects may not merely disrupt encoding of the surface form, but also tax WM resources that would otherwise be used to construct a representation of the text's meaning. For example, elders with normal and impaired hearing listening to a word list interrupted periodically to report the last word presented may show negligible differences; however, if asked to report the last three words, the hearing-impaired elders will show deficits. The explanation for such a provocative finding is that the hearing-impaired elders overcome a sensory loss at some attentional cost so as to exert a toll on semantic and elaborative processes that enhance memory. Presumably, the same mechanisms operate in ordinary language processing. At the same time, there is evidence that older adults can take differential advantage of context in the recognition of both spoken and written words, especially in noisy environments. One area of difficulty that older adults may have in word processing is in deriving the meaning of novel words from context, with research showing that older adults are likely to infer more generalized and imprecise meanings relative to the young, a difference that can be largely accounted for in terms of declines in mental mechanics.

Textbase processing

Older adults typically show poorer memory for the content expressed directly by the text. Processes used to construct the textbase (e.g., to instantiate and integrate concepts in the text, essentially an associative memory task) are among the most resource-consuming of those required in learning from text and are, hence, the most vulnerable to aging. When reading is self-paced, older adults require more time for effective propositional encoding (e.g., as indexed by effective reading time, the time allocated per idea unit recalled). In listening, when the pace is controlled by the speaker, older adults may have particular difficulty in understanding and retaining the information, especially as informational density is increased or in noisy environments. Older adults appear to have no difficulty drawing anaphoric inference (i.e., correctly identifying the referent when the pronoun is used to refer to a noun that was introduced earlier) over short distances, but may find it difficult when the pronoun and referent are separated by intervening text. Thus, the general impression from this literature is that the semantic (textbase) representation is more fragmented and less distinctive as a function of aging.

There is an important exception to age declines in text memory that appears to derive from socioemotional selectivity. That is, memory for text may be very good if it is consonant with emotional goals or if the task is embedded in a social context. For example, it has been reported that emotional content in narratives (e.g., characters' emotional reactions) is well retained among older readers relative to emotion-neutral information. It has also been reported that age differences in narrative memory may be minimized if there is a social goal (e.g., tell a story to a child) as opposed to an information-acquisition goal (e.g., recall the text to an experimenter).

Situation model

Aside from deriving ideas directly from the text, learning from the text also involves elaboration on these ideas based on existing knowledge. Some theories focus on the perceptual quality of this level of representation, which gives rise to a perceptual simulation of the events described by the text. Therefore, for example, in narrative understanding, readers track goals and emotional reactions of characters as well as their movement through space and time. Behavioral methods to study this level of representation include probe recognition for objects in the narrative, as well as reading time, both of which show subtle effects of situation model processing. Readers are slower to verify the existence (in the narrative world) of objects that are spatially distant from the protagonist relative to those that are nearby. Readers also slow down when new characters are introduced, or when there is a spatial discontinuity (e.g., the locus of narrative events shifts from the village to the castle) or a temporal discontinuity (e.g., The next day...). When the text describes a goal to be achieved (e.g., Susan intends to buy her mother a purse for her birthday), the goal is activated in memory until it is achieved; therefore, concepts related to the goal are more quickly verified as long as the goal is open (e.g., purse will be more quickly verified if Susan can find the purse when she goes to the store relative to a condition in which she could not find one). To the extent that these paradigms have been used to explore adult age differences in situation model processing, there has been very little evidence of developmental differences in situation construction and updating; if anything, attentional allocation to situation construction may increase with aging. This is important because it suggests that the experiential aspects of reading and language understanding

(i.e., the phenomenal experience of entering the world described by the discourse) are resilient or even enhanced through adulthood. In addition, to the extent that perceptual simulation is required to understand expository or procedural text (e.g., how the heart works or how to put together a grill), the preservation of situation model processing may enable authentic learning from text – even if measures of explicit recall might suggest otherwise.

Older adults may particularly rely on the situation model to support textbase processing. For example, in ambiguous text (e.g., "The strength and flexibility of this equipment is remarkable. Not everyone is capable of using it even though most try at one point or another..."), older readers take differential advantage of titles (e.g., driving a car) that disambiguate the meaning to facilitate processing. Since the title renders the situation instantly transparent, both younger and older adults are more efficient in reading when it is available; however, older adults show this effect to a larger degree.

To the extent that the hallmark of situation model processing is an integration of textbase content with knowledge, one might expect that older adults would be particularly adept at inferential processing; however, this is not always the case. While older adults are more likely to draw elaborative inferences (e.g., in recall, to annotate their recollections with personal experiences or related information learned in another context), if inference is constrained so that it requires retrieval of textbase content, age deficits are the norm.

Discourse structures and context

Beyond sentence processing, different genres of text have characteristic forms. For example, narratives typically begin by introducing a setting and characters and proceed to describe a series of episodes in which goals or problems are introduced to be resolved, and so on. Expository texts have certain characteristic forms of argumentation (e.g., problem–solution and thesis–evidence). Older readers generally appear to track these larger discourse structures in the same way as the young. Adult readers have also been shown to benefit from explicit instruction in discourse forms to enhance memory and understanding.

Cognitive Reserve: Lifelong Effects of Education

Differential Developmental Trajectories as a Function of Education

A growing body of evidence suggests that there is a relationship between early educational experiences and cognitive development in adulthood. Numerous studies linking education and cognition have found that greater educational attainment is associated with higher levels of cognitive performance and lower risk for the development of Alzheimer's disease. Although the mechanisms for education–cognition relationships remain unclear, four plausible explanations have been suggested, which may be operative individually or interactively. First, educational level may be a marker for innate levels of vitality or for capacities that are developed very early in the life span, such that those who are initially more able are also more likely to succeed in the educational system. Second, educational experiences early in the life span may expand neural networks, so as to create a lifelong cognitive reserve that enables relatively high levels of cognitive functioning even as the senescence process winnows neural connections later in life. Third, early educational experiences may be related to cognition through their association with socioeconomic status; therefore, it is socioeconomic advantage that enables lifelong conditions (e.g., nutrition, leisure that affords regular exercise, and medical care) that promote health and, thereby, successful cognitive aging. Finally, educational attainment may afford self-regulatory skill that promotes lifelong mental stimulation. Since educational experiences often lead to occupational, professional, and leisure experiences that provide intellectual challenge in domains in which one is invested, it may be that lifelong patterns of mental stimulation promote neural health, thereby engendering cognitive vitality. It is this latter possibility that is particularly exciting, and an important thrust of recent research in psychology, cognitive neuroscience, and education.

Cognitive and Neural Plasticity

In fact, there is growing evidence from animal models and human research that exposure to stimulating environments promotes neural growth and cognitive vitality. Studies that have administered cognitive training or practice sessions have revealed that the cognitive abilities of older adults show considerable plasticity. For example, the Advanced Cognitive Training for Independent and Vital Elderly (ACTIVE) trial is a randomized clinical trial to examine the effectiveness and durability of cognitive interventions on basic cognitive processes (memory, reasoning, and speed of processing). Results to date indicate that, in spite of the fact that each intervention has targeted a domain tapping into mental mechanics, training effects are ability specific (e.g., increased speed of processing does not transfer to better reasoning or memory). Interestingly, these effects have been shown to be durable up to 5 years. Such data not only provide evidence for the modifiability of cognitive abilities into late life, but also demonstrate that training effects may be highly selective.

On the other hand, certain conditions appear to enhance executive control (e.g., the ability to switch between two tasks) that may ultimately have the potential to affect a relatively wide array of activities. For example, aerobic exercise can increase executive function throughout adulthood. Recent evidence suggests that language processing may impact this control function as well, with several recent demonstrations of enhanced executive function among fluent bilinguals who habitually manage two language systems.

There may be limits to plasticity very late in the life span, with some training studies showing reduced effects with increasing age. Such findings highlight the dynamic nature of change during adulthood, and also imply that cognitive vitality past the age of 85 or 90 years may depend on the cognitive reserve established up to that point.

Neuroimaging studies offer further insight into how the brain is shaped by learning and experience, in particular, showing effects that are specific to experience. For example, adults with long-term experience in navigation show enhanced neural development in brain regions thought to be responsible for spatial processing (posterior hippocampus). Experimental studies in which individuals are randomly assigned to receive training in a particular skill (e.g., juggling and videogames) show distinctive patterns of change in neural structure and function (e.g., among jugglers, bilateral expansion of mediotemporal and left posterior parietal areas, thought to be responsible for visual storage and processing).

At the same time, older adults may show compensatory patterns of resource allocation and neural recruitment. In a number of different task domains, neuroimaging data have provided evidence that older adults show reduced hemispheric asymmetry in activation patterns, demonstrating expanded recruitment of brain regions from both hemispheres. Older adults, especially those with relatively better performance, are likely to show greater activation of the prefrontal cortex, suggesting that successful cognitive performance may increasingly require executive attentional control with age. Interestingly, recent research also suggests that increased frontal recruitment with aging may be exaggerated among those with relatively high levels of education, providing some support for the self-regulatory account of education–cognition relationships.

Conclusion

This article has discussed the dynamic interplay between cognitive development and educational experiences throughout the life span, so that trajectories of adult cognitive development must shape educational practices and educational practices can promote cognitive vitality. Within this framework, education throughout the life span becomes a public health issue.

Sociologists have distinguished between age-segregated and age-integrated social structures. In age-segregated structures, permissible social roles are tightly tied to chronological age (e.g., education during youth and work during midlife). Within developed countries, advances in medicine and health practices have stimulated a worldwide shift in demographics toward older populations, such that age segregation is no longer a tenable model. Life is simply too long now: effective work cannot rest on temporally removed education, and intellectual engagement is critical to vitality at every stage of the life span.

Further Reading

Baltes, P. B. (1997). On the incomplete architecture of human ontogeny: Selection, optimization, and compensation as foundation of developmental theory. *American Psychologist* **52**, 366–380.

Barnes, D. E., Tager, I. B., Satariano, W. A., and Yaffe, K. (2004). The relationship between literacy and cognition in well-educated elders. *Journal of Gerontology: Medical Sciences* **59A**, 390–395.

Beier, M. E. and Ackerman, P. L. (2005). Age, ability, and the role of prior knowledge on the acquisition of new domain knowledge: Promising results in a real-world learning environment. *Psychology and Aging* **20**, 341–355.

Bialystok, E., Craik, F. I. M., and Freedman, M. (2007). Bilingualism as a protection against the onset of symptoms of dementia. *Neuropsychologia* **45**, 459–464.

Carstensen, L. L., Mikels, J. A., and Mather, M. (2006). Aging and the intersection of cognition, motivation, and emotion. In Birren, J. E. and Schaie, K. W. (eds.) *Handbook of the Psychology of Aging,* 6th edn., pp 343–362. New York: Academic Press.

Johnson, R. E. (2003). Aging and the remembering of text. *Developmental Review* **23**, 261–346.

Kramer, A. F., Bherer, L., Colcombe, S. J., Dong, W., and Greenough, W. T. (2004). Environmental influences on cognitive and brain plasticity during aging. *Journal of Gerontology: Medical Sciences* **59A**, 940–957.

Krampe, R. T. and Charness, N. (2006). Aging and expertise. In Ericsson, K. A., Charness, N., Feltovich, P. J., and Hoffman, R. R. (eds.) *The Cambridge Handbook of Expertise and Expert Performance*, pp 723–742. New York: Cambridge University Press.

Lachman, M. E. (2004). Development in midlife. *Annual Review of Psychology* **55**, 305–331.

Lachman, M. E. (2006). Perceived control over aging-related declines: Adaptive beliefs and behaviors. *Current Directions in Psychological Science* **15**, 282–286.

Meyer, B. J. F. and Pollard, C. K. (2006). Applied learning and aging: A closer look at reading. In Birren, J. E. and Schaie, K. W. (eds.) *Handbook of the Psychology of Aging,* 6th edn., pp 233–260. New York: Elsevier.

Riley, M. W. and Riley, J. W. Jr. (2000). Age integration: Conceptual and historical background. *Gerontologist* **40**, 266–270.

Scarmeas, N. and Stern, Y. (2003). Cognitive reserve and lifestyle. *Journal of Clinical and Experimental Neuropsychology* **25**, 625–633.

Stine-Morrow, E. A. L. (2007). The Dumbledore hypothesis of cognitive aging. *Current Directions in Psychological Science* **16**, 300–304.

Stine-Morrow, E. A. L., Miller, L. M. S., and Hertzog, C. (2006). Aging and self-regulated language processing. *Psychological Bulletin* **132**, 582–606.

Thornton, R. and Light, L. L. (2006). Language comprehension and production in normal aging. In Birren, J. E. and Schaie, K. W. (eds.) *Handbook of the Psychology of Aging,* 6th edn., pp 261–287. New York: Academic Press.

Characteristics of Adult Learning

K Illeris, Danish University of Education, Copenhagen, Denmark

The slogan of lifelong learning basically involves the simple message that learning can and should be a lifelong occupation. This poses the fundamental question of whether the processes of learning are the same irrespective of age. In the traditional psychology of learning, there are no age-conditioned differences. Learning was considered to be a common phenomenon in which researchers endeavored to discover the decisive and basic learning mechanisms, and research and tests were often performed to observe animals and humans in constructed laboratory situations.

Many scholars and researchers have claimed that adult's learning, as a psychological function, is basically similar to children's learning. This was, for instance, the underlying assumption behind the massive resistance to American Malcolm Knowles' launching of a separate discipline of andragogy, dealing with adult education and learning, and at the same time limiting pedagogy to the area of children's upbringing and schooling (e.g., Knowles, 1970; Hartree, 1984; Davonport, 1993). More recently, Alan Rogers, from Britain, in connection with his description of adults' learning, has deliberately maintained, "that there is nothing distinctive about the kind of learning undertaken by adults" (Rogers, 2003: 7). However, this position is only valid in relation to some very basic features of learning. As soon as the question is examined a little deeper or related to concrete learning courses or events, there are obviously substantial life-age differences, partly because some biological capacities of learning only mature gradually during childhood and youth, and partly because learning is also a social and an emotional process, and people's social and emotional situations change with their age (Illeris, 2004, 2007).

In the following section, some of the most important fundamental features of learning that are independent of life age are outlined; the special features of adult learning are discussed subsequently.

Some Fundamental Features of Learning

Human learning is a very complex matter that has been understood and conceptualized in many ways. However, for a structural analysis, three kinds of fundamental features can be pointed out: (1) the basic processes and dimensions of learning, (2) the different types of learning, and (3) the types of barriers to learning (Illeris, 2007).

Basic Processes and Dimensions of Learning

A fundamental aspect of learning is that it always includes two integrated but very different processes: the external interaction process between the learner and the social, cultural, and material environment; and the internal psychological process of elaboration and acquisition in which new impulses are connected with the results of prior learning.

The criteria of the interaction process are of a social and societal character, that is, they are determined by time and place. The individual interacts with an environment that includes other people, a specific culture, technology, etc., which are characterized by their time and society. In the late-modern globalized world, this is blended into a giant and rapidly changing hodgepodge that offers almost unlimited possibilities for learning.

No matter how dominant and imperative the interaction process has become, in learning there is also always a process of individual acquisition in which the impulses from the interaction are incorporated. As discussed by scholars such as Piaget (1952) and Ausuble (1968), the core of this process is that the new impressions are connected with the results of prior learning in a way that influences both. Thus, the outcome of the individual acquisition process is always dependent on what has already been acquired, and ultimately the criteria of this process are of a biological nature and determined by the extensive, but not infinite, possibilities of the human brain and central nervous system to cope with, structure, retain, and create meaning out of impressions as perceived by our senses (cf. e.g., Solms and Turnbull, 2002).

Learning, thinking, remembering, understanding, and similar functions are not just cognitive or content matters, although they have generally been conceived of as such by traditional learning psychology. Whether the frame of reference is common sense, Freudian psychology, modern management, or brand new results of brain research, there is much evidence that all such functions are also inseparably connected with emotions and motivation. The Austrian-American psychologist Hans Furth (1987), by combining the findings and theories of Piaget and Freud, has unravelled how cognition and emotions during the preschool years gradually separate out as distinctive but never isolated functions. The Portuguese-American neurologist Antonio Damasio (1994) has explained how cognition and emotion work in our brain and what disastrous consequences there are when the connections between the two are cut by damage to the brain, even when neither of the functions in themselves has been affected. Thus, the acquisition process necessarily always has both a cognitive and an emotional side or, more broadly speaking, a content and an incentive side.

Consequently, all learning always includes three dimensions: the content dimension of knowledge, understandings, skills, abilities, attitudes, and the like; the incentive dimension of emotions, feelings, motivation, and volition; and the social dimension of interaction, communication, and cooperation – all of which are embedded in a societally situated context. The learning processes and dimensions are illustrated in **Figure 1**.

Different Types of Learning

Another fundamental aspect of learning has to do with the different character and scope of different types of learning processes. A very basic distinction was made by the well-known Swiss biologist and psychologist Jean Piaget (1896–1980) when he distinguished between assimilation and accommodation as two essentially different ways of learning (Piaget, 1952; Flavell, 1963). Later, other researchers found that each of these can be further differentiated into two, so that altogether four basic learning types emerge (Illeris, 2007).

As already mentioned, the acquisition process implies a linking between new impulses and the results of prior learning. These results cannot be thought of as merely an unstructured mass of knowledge, emotions, abilities, etc. One of Piaget's most fundamental assumptions was that to learn something means to mentally structure something,

that is, to incorporate it in a mental scheme, and it is the difference in which this incorporation takes place that constitutes the learning types. From modern brain research we know that such schemes have the character of dispositions to reactivate specific electrochemical circuits between brain cells that represent the content and incentives in question (Damasio, 1994). When a scheme or pattern is established, it happens by the type of learning called cumulation, a kind of mechanical process, establishing an isolated formation characterized by a form of automation that means that it can only be recalled and applied in situations mentally similar to the learning context. This is, for instance, how learning by conditioning functions.

The most common type of learning is, assimilation, or learning by addition, meaning that the new impulse is linked to a scheme or pattern already established in such a manner that it is relatively easy to recall and apply when one is mentally oriented toward the field in question.

Sometimes situations occur where we receive impulses that are difficult to immediately relate to any existing scheme or pattern. This can then take place by accommodation or transcendent learning, implying that one breaks down (parts of) an existing scheme or pattern and transforms it so that the new situation can be linked in. Thus, one both relinquishes and reconstructs something, a process that can be experienced as something demanding and even painful. The result can be recalled and applied in many different, relevant contexts.

Finally, there is also a far-reaching type of learning, which the American adult educator Jack Mezirow termed as transformation, and involves simultaneous restructuring in all three learning dimensions. This very demanding type of learning implies changes in the organization of the learner's self or identity and typically occurs as the result of a crisis-like situation caused by challenges experienced as urgent and unavoidable (e.g., Rogers, 1951; Engeström, 1987; Mezirow, 1991).

It is important that none of the learning types can be said to be better or more valuable than the others, as the more complex types of learning always presuppose that other and more basic learning has provided the preconditions that make them possible.

Barriers Toward Learning

Finally, as the third basic area of learning, it is important to deal with the different types of barriers that can prevent, reduce, or distort possible learning (Illeris, 2007).

In the content dimension, barriers will typically be about something that is not acquired, grasped, or taken in as intended. This may be generally termed mislearning, implying that the impulse or message does not come through, for instance, because of insufficient involvement or concentration, a lack of necessary prior learning, or due

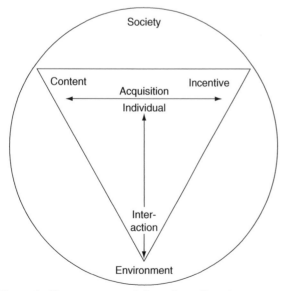

Figure 1   The processes and dimensions of learning. Adapted from Illeris, K. (2007) *How We Learn: An Introduction to Human Learning in Schools and Beyond*. London: Routledge).

to inadequate communication or teaching. The barriers to learning may also be rooted mainly in the incentive dimension. If so, it will typically be a case of some kind of mental defense. In our late-modern society, such defense mechanisms are no longer primarily the result of personal inhibitions as described by Freud a century ago, but are rather a general and necessary societally rooted defense against the overwhelming number and complexity of impulses and influences. Such defense either rejects or distorts the majority of impulses, preferably those that we dislike or are less interested in, but often those that we might profit from but do not immediately categorize as worth dealing with. Many also create learning defenses against the radically increased number of changes, the feeling of powerlessness experienced when authorities encroach on our life conditions, or the demands for change of identity, which the changing conditions impose on us.

Finally, nonlearning may be rooted mainly in the interaction dimension and have the nature of mental resistance. This can be inappropriate and annoying in many situations, but nevertheless constitutes symptoms of strong personal forces and engagement, which can lead to very important accommodative or transformative learning.

Adult Learning

In order to see what the characteristic of adult learning is, it may be useful to start by pointing out some basic features of children's learning.

Differences in Relation to Children's Way of Learning

In general, learning in childhood could be described as a continuous campaign to capture the world. The child is born into an unknown world and learning is about acquiring this world and learning to deal with it. In this connection, two learning-related features are prominent, especially for the small child: First, children's learning is comprehensive and uncensored. The child learns everything within her grasp, throws herself into everything, and is limited only by her biological development and the nature of her surroundings. Second, the child places utter confidence in the adults around her. She has only those adults and the ways in which they behave to refer to, without any possibility of evaluating or choosing what she is presented with. The child must, for example, learn the language these adults speak and practice the culture they practice.

Throughout childhood, the child's capturing of its surroundings is fundamentally uncensored and trusting as she endeavors, in an unlimited and indiscriminate way, to make use of the opportunities that present themselves. Of course, late-modern society has led to growing complexity and

even confusion of this situation as older children receive a lot of impressions from their pals and especially from the mass media, which go far beyond the borders of their own environment. But still the open and confident approach must be recognized as the starting point.

In contrast to this stands learning during adulthood. Being an adult essentially means that an individual is able and willing to assume responsibility for his or her own life and actions. Formally, our society ascribes such adulthood to individuals when they attain the age of 18 years. In reality, it is a gradual process that takes place throughout the period of youth, which as we see it today, may last well into the 20s or be entirely incomplete if the formation of a relatively stable identity is chosen as the criterion for its completion at the mental level (which is the classical description of this transition provided by Erikson, 1968).

As concerns learning, being an adult also means, in principle, that the individual accepts responsibility for his or her own learning, that is, more or less consciously sorts information and decides what he or she wants and does not want to learn. The situation in today's complicated modern society is after all such that the volume of what may be learned far exceeds the ability of any single individual, and this is true not only concerning content in a narrow sense, but it also applies to the views and attitudes, perceptions, communications options, behavioral patterns, lifestyle, etc. that may be chosen. Thus, a sorting of input must be made.

As a general conclusion it is, however, important to maintain that in contrast to children's uncensored and confident learning, adult learning is basically selective and self-directed, or to put it in more concrete terms:

- adults learn what they want to learn and what is meaningful for them to learn;
- adults draw on the resources they already have in their learning;
- adults take as much responsibility for their learning as they want to take (if they are allowed to); and
- adults are not very inclined to learn something they are not interested in, or in which they cannot see the meaning or importance. At any rate, typically, they only learn it partially, in a distorted way or with a lack of motivation that makes what is learned extremely vulnerable to oblivion and difficult to apply in situations not subjectively related to the learning context (Illeris, 2007).

In the following section, the nature of adult learning is discussed in relation to the three dimensions and other basic features of learning described earlier.

Adult Learning in the Content Dimension

For many years, it was a general understanding among learning theorists that humans acquire their full cognitive learning capacity at about the age of 11–13, when they, as described in Jean Piaget's theory of learning stages, reach the so-called formal operational level, which makes logical–deductive thinking possible as a supplement to the forms of thinking and learning acquired at earlier stages (see, e.g., Flavell, 1963).

However, during the 1980s, this understanding began to be questioned from several quarters. On the one hand, it was pointed out that not all adults are actually able to think formally and operationally in the logical sense inherent in Piaget's definition. Empirical research pointed out that in England, it was actually less than 30%, but at the same time it was confirmed that at the beginning of puberty, a decisive development takes place in the possibilities for learning and thinking in abstract terms, so that, all in all, distinguishing a new cognitive phase was justified (Shayer and Adey, 1981). On the other hand, it has been maintained that, at a later age, significant new cognitive possibilities that extend beyond the formally operative may develop (e.g., Commons *et al.*, 1984). British-American adult education researcher Stephen Brookfield summarized this criticism by pointing out four possibilities for learning that are only developed in the course of adulthood: the capacity for dialectical thinking, the capacity for applying practical logic, the capacity for realizing how one may know what one knows (metacognition), and the capacity for critical reflection (Brookfield, 2000).

Recent brain research seems to indirectly support Brookfield's claims. Whereas it is a well-established understanding that the brain matures psychologically and neurologically for formal logical thinking in early puberty, evidence has been found that the brain centers of the frontal lobe that conduct functions such as rational planning, prioritization, and making well-founded choices, do not mature until the late teenage years (Gogtay *et al.*, 2004). This finding seems to provide some clarification of the differences between the capacity of formal logical and practical logical thinking and learning as well as between ordinary cognition and metacognition in adolescence and early adulthood.

At any rate, the general conclusion of all this must be that during puberty and youth, a physiological and neurological maturing process takes place that makes possible new forms of abstract and stringent thinking and learning, so that an individual becomes able to operate context-independently with coherent concept systems and manage a balanced and goal-directed behavior. Teenagers' determination to find out how things are structured and to use such understanding in relation to their own situation could be seen as a cognitive developmental bridge signifying the difference between children's and adults' ways of learning.

It is thus at one and the same time the longing for independence and the longing for coherent understanding of how they themselves and their environment function and why things are the way they are, which in the content dimension separate adult learning from childhood learning. Up through the period of youth, individuals themselves increasingly assume responsibility for their own learning and nonlearning, make choices and rejections, and in this context understand what they are dealing with and their own roles and possibilities. However, all this has been enormously complicated by the duality of late modernity between, on the one hand, the apparently limitless degrees of freedom and reams of information, and on the other hand, far-reaching indirect pressure for control from parents, teachers, youth cultures, mass media, and formal conditions and possibilities. The transition from child to adult has thus, in the area of learning, become an extended, ambiguous, and complicated process, with blurred outlines and unclear conditions and goals.

Finally, it should be added that the possibility of transformative learning as well as the general defense systems in relation to learning seem to be developed along with the described cognitive development during the teenage years, and that the full development of the body and thereby the possibilities for bodily skills is also a process that is not fulfilled until about the age of 20 years.

Adult Learning in the Incentive Dimension

Learning in the incentive dimension is fundamentally aimed at helping the learner to control and direct emotions, feelings, motivation, and volition and thereby maintain an appropriate mental balance in relation to the complexity of life. In late-modern society, this process is concentrated on the development and maintenance of a self-understanding or identity that can secure the experience of being oneself, that is, of being the same person across the diversity of situations and challenges we meet and deal with. It is mainly in this dimension that the selective regulation and the defense mechanisms of adult learning are directed, which, in everyday life, is a mainly unconscious process and only taken up consciously in case of more important decisions. The identity, which, as mentioned, is developed during the teenage years, functions as the superior director of all this. On the more concrete level, adults typically have a range of life projects, subprojects, interests, and preferences to which the direction and regulation are related.

Most adults have a family project that concerns creating and being part of a family; a work project that concerns a personally and financially satisfying job; perhaps a leisure-time project concerning a special interest or a hobby; and sometimes a fulfillment or conviction project that may be religious or political in nature. All these projects result in many even more specific activities and attitudes that in this connection, serve as the measure for all the conscious as well as unconscious decisions about what to learn, with which kind of motivation and investment to learn, and what not to learn or not to invest so much in that the learning process becomes demanding (which usually implies a weak and superficial kind of learning).

When dealing with adult learning, it is very important to realize that adults have and practice these conscious and unconscious ways of being selective in relation to their own learning. This is why and how adults, as stated before, "are not very inclined to learn something they are not interested in, or in which they cannot see the meaning or importance." In contemporary adult education and lifelong learning, authorities and teachers very often do not sufficiently understand and respect these fundamental conditions of adult learning and many human and financial resources are wasted on programs and courses with limited or no possibilities of success (cf. Illeris, 2004).

Adult Learning in the Interaction Dimension

The general aim of learning in the interaction dimension is integration. Humans want and need to be integrated in their social environment, to communicate and collaborate with others, and this is a fundamental part of existence. But for adults, this side of life is highly selective: we have strong social preferences, and there are also communities which we do not want to be a part of. As to learning, this ambiguous attitude implies that the basic nature of our learning in the interaction dimension varies in relation to different learning spaces. In present society, five main types of spaces of adult learning can be pointed out.

Everyday life is the general and basic learning space in which a lot of learning takes place, as we are moving around and not participating in any specifically defined activities. This kind of learning is therefore mainly informal, multifarious, personal, and related to the cultures and subcultures in which the person is integrated, and it constitutes the general socialization and many patterns, norms, attitudes, general understandings, etc.

Workplaces have formed another very important learning space for adults ever since work was separated from everyday life. Here, of course, several professional qualifications are trained, but a lot of general learning takes place more or less incidentally as an inseparable part of work activities and communication (Marsick and Watkins, 1990). However, this learning is fundamentally different from general learning in everyday life, because it is marked by basic workplace conditions such as effectiveness, profit-orientation, and, not least, job stability. On the other hand, workplace learning may also include more formalized learning, which is usually accepted as relevant and meaningful, at least if the learner has a positive identification with the job. It is worth noting that even such goal-directed workplace learning is often restricted by the immediate needs of production or service and

therefore tends to lack theoretical understanding and overview (Illeris *et al.*, 2004).

Special interests or convictions are the basis of another type of learning spaces including, for example, communities, associations, hobbies, and grassroots movements. Learning here may be understood as a goal-directed kind of everyday learning in which incidental and informal features are replaced by a clear motivation and resolution, which generally make this type of learning space very effective.

Schools and other educational institutions form the type of learning space which society has established to secure a lot of learning that is today considered to be necessary for all of us to maintain the material and structural level we have reached. Originally, this type of learning space was mainly set up for children and youth, but it is significant for late modernity that such institutions are now also established for adults and the slogan of lifelong learning covers a massive upgrading of such learning. However, it is important to realize that school learning is by nature formal, rational, and externally directed. Although it is officially aimed at goals outside the educational system, it is usually experienced as directed by internal measures such as the school subjects and exams. Although adult schooling is not compulsory, many adults are brought into situations where they more or less have to undertake such formal learning. Low-skilled workers often oppose or are very ambivalent about going back to school as they have for so many years experienced that they are no good at school learning (Illeris, 2003, 2006).

Finally, it must be mentioned that computers and the Internet have opened a new learning space of rapidly growing importance, not least for adults. Computer learning has its own characteristics, advantages, and disadvantages. Net-based learning is very flexible, because it can be practiced independently of time and to some extent also of place. It also seems to have an advantage in that it forces the learner to express oneself in writing and thereby to make points, understandings, and opinions more clear than generally needed in face-to-face conversation. The disadvantage is the lack of direct social contact, but this can to some extent be eliminated by frequent classes or meetings, during a Net-based course, of some duration. Yet, so far we know very little about the transfer of Net-based learning onto the different spaces of reality.

As most adults today are involved in all or most of the main described types of learning spaces, the transitions and transfer of learning between them become increasingly essential and complex. The transition and transfer between school and education on the one side and workplaces and everyday learning on the other side forms a challenge to contemporary adult learning. Net-based learning may relate to either of these sides, whereas interest-based learning has a kind of independent position from which transfer can often be made to any other learning space.

Conclusion

Learning in late-modern society is a very complex and at the same time very important issue, and the slogan of lifelong learning strongly indicates that this also includes adult learning. However, adult learning is very different from children's learning and much of the traditional learning theory and teaching practice does not apply very well to adults. Whereas childhood naturally is time for learning and development, adulthood traditionally has been the age for applying the acquired competencies. Today, this situation has changed, and learning in adulthood has become a necessary demand. This causes many challenges and expenses, but also new possibilities of a rich and expanding adult life.

It must be remembered and respected that in free and democratic societies, adults have the right to direct their own learning. Therefore, the typical patterns and processes of childhood learning cannot just be overtaken, and the idea of lifelong learning can only be practiced successfully if sustainable ways to meet the needs of the adult learners can be developed and practiced.

Bibliography

Ausuble, D. P. (1968). *Educational Psychology: A Cognitive View*. New York: Holt, Rinehart and Winston.

Brookfield, S. D. (2000). Adult cognition as a dimension of lifelong learning. In Field, J. and Leicester, M. (eds.) *Lifelong Learning: Education across the Lifespan*, pp 89–101. London: RoutledgeFalmer.

Commons, M. L., Richards, F. A., and Armon, C. (eds.) (1984). *Beyond Formal Operations: Late Adolescent and Adult Cognitive Development*. New York: Praeger.

Damasio, A. R. (1994). *Descartes' Error: Emotion, Reason and the Human Brain*. New York: Grosset/Putnam.

Davonport, J. (1993). Is there any way out of the andragogy morass? In Thorpe, M., Edwards, R., and Hanson, A. (eds.) *Culture and Process of Adult Learning*, pp 109–117. (first publ. in 1987). London: Routledge.

Engeström, Y. (1987). *Learning by Expanding: An Activity-Theoretical Approach to Developmental Research*. Helsinki: Orienta-Kunsultit.

Erikson, E. H. (1968). *Identity, Youth and Crises*. New York: Norton.

Flavell, J. H. (1963). *The Developmental Psychology of Jean Piaget*. New York: Van Nostrand.

Furth, H. G. (1987). *Knowledge as Desire*. New York: Columbia University Press.

Gogtay, N., Giedd, J. N., Lusk, L., *et al.* (2004). Dynamic mapping of human cortical development during childhood through early adulthood. *Proceedings of the National Academy of Sciences of the United States of America* **101**(21), 8174–8179.

Hartree, A. (1984). Malcolm Knowles' theory of andragogy: A critique. *International Journal of Lifelong Education* **3**(3), 203–210.

Illeris, K. (2003). Adult education as experienced by the learners. *International Journal of Lifelong Education* **22**(1), 13–23.

Illeris, K. (2004). *Adult Education and Adult Learning*. Malabar, FL: Krieger.

Illeris, K. (2006). Lifelong learning and the low-skilled. *International Journal of Lifelong Education* **25**(1), 15–28.

Illeris, K. (2007). *How We Learn: An Introduction to Human Learning in Schools and Beyond*. London: Routledge.

Illeris, K., *et al.* (2004). *Learning in Working Life*. Copenhagen: Roskilde University Press.

Knowles, M. S. (1970). *The Modern Practice of Adult Education: Andragogy versus Pedagogy*. New York: Associated Press.

Marsick, V. J. and Watkins, K. E. (1990). *Informal and Incidental Learning in the Workplace*. London: Routledge.

Piaget, J. (1952). *The Origins of Intelligence in Children* (first publ. in 1936). New York: International Universities Press.

Rogers, A. (2003). *What Is the Difference? A New Critique of Adult Learning and Teaching*. Leicester: NIACE.

Rogers, C. R. (1951). *Client-Centered Therapy*. Boston, MA: Houghton-Mifflin.

Shayer, M. and Adey, P. (1981). *Towards a Science of Science Teaching*. London: Heinemann Educational.

Solms, M. and Turnbull, O. (2002). *The Brain and the Inner World*. New York: Other Press.

Further Reading

Jarvis, P. and Parker, S. (eds.) (2005). *Human Learning: An Holistic Approach*. Abingdon: Routledge.

Merriam, S. B., Caffarella, R. S., and Baumgartner, L. M. (2007). *Learning in Adulthood: A Comprehensive Guide,* 3rd edn. San Francisco, CA: Jossey-Bass.

Sutherland, P. and Crowther, J. (eds.) (2006). *Lifelong Learning: Concepts and Contexts*. Abingdon: Routledge.

Adult Learning and Instruction: Transformative-Learning Perspectives

P Cranton, Penn State University at Harrisburg, Middletown, PA, USA

Although adult education practice has a long history, the area only became recognized as a field of study and theoretical development in the 1930s. Lindemann's (1926) book was the first to have adult education in the title; he described adult education as cooperative, nonauthoritarian, and informal. Around the same time, the first adult education professional association was established, and we saw the beginning of the quest to understand adult learning as a distinctive process and efforts to develop teaching methods unique to working with adults. Transformative learning theory (first labeled in the mid-1970s and more fully developed by the 1990s) is described as the first comprehensive theory of adult learning.

Characteristics of Adult Learning

Throughout the 1970s and 1980s, considerable effort was put into describing adult learning as a distinctive process – different from children's learning in important ways. Tough (1979) conducted his classic survey in which he discovered that over 90% of adults engage in sustained independent learning projects. Cross (1981) and others worked to determine why adults participated (or not) in educational programs. Brundage and MacKeracher (1980) outlined the characteristics of adult learning and what those characteristics meant for program planning. Knowles (1975) presented his foundational work on adults as self-directed learners – a point of view which continues to influence our understanding of how adults learn.

At least seven broad themes can be drawn from the research and theory from those two decades – themes which are still relied upon today by adult educators in many and diverse settings: (1) Adult learning is often described as voluntary. Individuals choose to become involved in informal and formal activities in order to develop personally or respond to a professional or practical need. (2) Based on Knowles' influential work, adult learning is usually described as self-directed. Knowles (1975, 1980) saw self-directed learning as a process by which people identify their learning needs, set goals, choose how to learn, gather materials, and evaluate their progress; however, many other definitions and conceptualizations developed over time (e.g., see Candy, 1991). (3) Adult learning is seen as practical or experiential in nature. This notion can be traced back to Dewey (1938) who, though not an adult educator himself, had a lasting and profound impact on the way we think about adult learning. (4) Adults are portrayed as preferring collaborative and participatory learning, largely due to the early influence of humanism on adult education practice (via the client-centered approach of Rogers (1961) and then Knowles who was a student of Rogers). (5) Adults bring rich experiences and resources to their learning – one of Knowles' (1980) defining characteristics of adult learning. (6) Since adults have often been away from formal schooling for some years (though this is less true today) and may have had negative early experiences with school, they are seen as reentering learning with anxiety and low self-esteem. (7) Adults have a variety of learning styles and preferences. One of the most influential theorists in this area has been Kolb (1984) who delineated the converger, diverger, assimilator, and accommodator learning styles.

In the 1990s and early 2000s, the trend in adult education toward critical theory, postmodernism, and poststructuralism has led researchers and theorists away from what is now seen to be overly simplistic and even stereotypical understandings of adult learning. Nevertheless, this foundational work permeates adult-education practice and continues to influence our theory development and research. Transformative learning is voluntary and under the direction of the learner, based on making meaning out of experience, collaborative (especially through dialog or discourse), and empowering.

Instruction for Adult Learning

Early adult education had social change as its goal (Lindemann, 1926). The Higherlander Folk School in the United States and the Antigonish Movement in Canada are examples of approaches to working with adult learners to promote social action. Freire (1970), following in the radical tradition of adult education, proposed that dialogic and problem-posing strategies replace the banking model of education in which information was transmitted to the learner. However, in the 1970s and 1980s, humanistic approaches to teaching adults dominated the field and still maintain a strong influence on how we think about instruction for adult learning today.

Just as adult learning is seen to be distinct from children's learning, teaching adults is seen to be different from teaching children. Knowles (1980) distinguished between pedagogy and andragogy, first describing them as being diametrically opposed and later modifying his view to place them on a continuum. Essentially, pedagogy was seen to be more teacher-centered and andragogy more learner-centered. How-to books on teaching adults abound. Following Knowles' lead, most of these books take a humanist approach to teaching adults. Elias and Merriam (2005) outline six basic assumptions underlying humanism:

1. human nature is naturally good;
2. human beings strive for freedom and autonomy;
3. the individuality and uniqueness of each person is valued;
4. working toward self-actualization is an innate human goal;
5. each person perceives the world in his or her own way; and
6. people are responsible for developing their potential to the fullest.

Teaching from a humanist perspective puts the educator in the role of a facilitator rather than a provider of information. She creates the conditions in which learning can occur and trusts the learner to take responsibility for learning. This sets up a student-centered environment in which the growth of the whole person (the development of self-actualizing persons) is a goal. Learning is a personal process; motivation is intrinsic. Yet, self-development and learning do not occur in isolation. Humanist educators value collaboration and group work over competitive endeavors, or put another way, connected knowing over separate knowing (Belenky and Stanton, 2000).

Moving into the 1990s and 2000s, humanist approaches to teaching adults remain strong, especially in practice, but are being challenged primarily as a result of the increasing popularity of critical theory as a foundation of adult education. Brookfield (2005) calls on us to unmask power, challenge ideologies, and radicalize criticality. Although ideology critique originated in the 1970s in the Frankfurt School of Critical Social Theory, it is more recently that it has been brought to bear on teaching adults. Ideologies are values, beliefs, and assumptions that have been uncritically assimilated and believed to be true without question. They appear in our social norms and expectations and in the way we use language.

Teaching for transformation stands in both perspectives. It is humanist in its goals of self-development and freedom from constraints and oppression, and it is critical in its goal of ideology critique. Brookfield (2000) writes that an "act of learning can be called transformative only if it involves a fundamental questioning and reordering of how one things or acts. If something is transformed, it is different from what it was before at a very basic level" (p. 139). Newman (2006) writes about teaching rebelliousness, defiance, and action. He describes critical learning (transformative learning) as both a personal endeavor and a political act. It helps us see "through ourselves" and "through others," as we become "less susceptible to hegemonic control" (p. 239). Newman rejects the teaching of what he calls domesticated critical thinking and proposes that we teach people how to resist (pp. 9–10).

Transformative Learning: Overview of the Theory

Transformative learning theory had its beginning in 1975 when Mezirow conducted a study of 83 women returning to college in 12 reentry programs. He described a process of personal-perspective transformation that included ten phases:

1. experiencing a disorienting dilemma,
2. undergoing self-examination,
3. conducting a critical assessment of internalized assumptions and feeling a sense of alienation from traditional social expectations,
4. relating discontent to the similar experiences of others,
5. exploring options for new ways of acting,
6. building competence and confidence in new roles,
7. planning a course of action,
8. acquiring the knowledge and skills for implementing a new course of action,
9. trying out new roles and assessing them, and
10. reintegrating into society with the new perspective.

It was Mezirow's 1991 book, *Transformative Dimensions of Adult Learning*, that brought the theory to the forefront of the adult-education literature. Since then, Mezirow and others in the field have continued to elaborate on and provide alternative explanations of transformative learning. Here, an overview of the basic theory from Mezirow's (1991, 2000, 2003) perspective is provided, and then in the following section, other theorists' points of view are presented. The author's own writing is drawn upon (Cranton, 2006) in this discussion.

Transformative learning is a process by which previously uncritically assimilated frames of reference (assumptions, expectations, and habits of mind) are questioned and revised to make them more open, permeable, and better justified. Experiences are seen through the lens of our frames of reference, which include distortions, prejudices, stereotypes, and unexamined beliefs. When we encounter a perspective that is different from the one we hold, we may be provoked into critically questioning our current thinking. This can happen as a product of a single event or as a gradual cumulative process. The learning only becomes transformative when we make a deep shift in how we see ourselves and/or the world around us and act on the revised perspective.

Several types of meaning structures come into play in this process. A frame of reference is a meaning perspective, the structure of assumptions and beliefs that provide a lens through which we make meaning of our experiences. A frame of references has two dimensions: a habit of mind, which is composed of broad, generalized, predispositions for interpreting experience; and a point of view, which is comprised of sets of immediate, specific expectations and beliefs that shape a specific interpretation (Mezirow, 2000).

Mezirow (2003) sees discourse as central to transformative learning. Discourse is defined as a form of dialog that involves the assessment of beliefs, feelings, and values. The ideal conditions of discourse are that participants have accurate and complete information, are free from coercion, are able to weigh evidence, are open to alternative perspectives, are able to engage in critical reflection, have an equal opportunity to participate, and are able to accept informed consensus as valid.

Habits of minds can be of different types. Originally, Mezirow (1991) wrote about epistemic perspectives, those that have to do with knowledge and the way we acquire knowledge; sociolinguistic perspectives, related to social norms, cultural expectations, and the way we use language; and psychological perspectives, which have to do with how we see ourselves – self-concept, needs, inhibitions, anxieties, and fears. Later, he added three more types of habits of mind: philosophical, which can be based on a worldview, philosophy or religious doctrine; esthetic, including values, attitudes, tastes, and standards about beauty; and moral–ethical, which incorporates conscience and morality (Mezirow, 2000).

Beliefs, assumptions, values, and habits of mind can be undeveloped or unquestioned. We absorb the way we think about ourselves and the world around us from our family, community, peers, and from the social world we live in. In each of the types of habits of mind, unexamined perspectives are insidious and often do not even appear as questionable. We may become aware of unexamined perspectives through a disorienting dilemma – an experience which contradicts our assumptions. As discussed in the last section of this article, educators may consciously create learning experiences that are potentially transformative.

Critical reflection and critical self-reflection are central to transformative learning. Critical reflection involves objective reframing of the assumptions of others, and critical self-reflection involves the subjective reframing of our own assumptions. Reflection alone is not enough to label learning as transformative. It must lead to revised frames of reference upon which individuals act.

Perspectives on Transformative Learning

Mezirow's theory of transformative learning was criticized on several grounds: for its failure to address social change (Collard and Law, 1989), the neglect of power issues (Hart, 1990), the disregard for the cultural context of learning (Clark and Wilson, 1991), the overemphasis on rational thought (Dirkx, 1997), and the prominence of separate or autonomous learning (Belenky and Stanton, 2000). These critiques and others that followed, along with Mezirow's call for people to contribute to and elaborate on the theory, led to the development of a variety of perspectives on transformative learning.

Connected Knowing and Transformative Learning

Relational or connected learning and knowing are often associated with women's ways of learning (e.g., see Hayes and Flannery, 2000). Belenky and Stanton (2000) use connected knowing as a basis for adding to transformative learning theory. They describe six developmental stages of knowing for women: silenced, received knowers, subjective knowers, separate knowers, connected knowers, and constructivist knowers. They suggest that Mezirow's approach to transformative learning places separate knowing (following lines of reasoning and looking for flaws in logic) in a central role and argue that connected knowing also serves well to describe transformation. Connected knowers suspend judgment and struggle to understand others' points of view from their perspective. They look for strengths, not weaknesses in another person's point of view. The goal is to see holistically rather than analytically.

Social Change as Transformative Learning

Social reform has long been a goal of adult education, and those critics who see Mezirow as neglecting the social change aspect of transformation suggest that social reform needs to precede individual transformation. Mezirow (2000) distinguishes between educational tasks (helping people become aware of oppressive structures and learn how to change them) and political tasks (forcing economic change). It is his goal to help individuals learn how to create social change rather than to create social change himself. Others see this differently.

Brookfield (2003) proposes that the purpose of transformative learning is ideology critique, a process that helps "people uncover and challenge dominant ideology and then learn how to organize social relations according to noncapitalist logic" (p. 224). He holds that transformation includes not only the individual's structural change, but also structural change in the social world. Similarly,

Newman (1994) emphasizes that we should study not the oppressed, but oppression itself. Writers and theorists who advocate social change as a goal of transformative learning (and adult education as a whole) do not dismiss individual learning and transformation, but see it as the educator's goal to address the social context within which individuals live and learn.

Group and Organizational Transformation

The idea that groups and organizations could transform in a collective way began with the notion of a learning organization in which organizations are perceived as living entities that can learn. Watkins and Marsick (1993), in their now-classic work on learning organizations, made the link to transformative learning. Yorks and Marsick (2000) have continued with this line of thinking, basing their work on action learning and collaborative inquiry. Action learning involves teams working on real problems within the organization, and collaborative inquiry consists of repeated episodes of reflection and action in a group context. In this way, organizations transform in relation to the nature of the environment, the vision or mission of the organization, products and services of the organization, management styles and procedures, organizational structure, and individual organization members' perception of their roles.

Groups other than organizations are also seen to have the capability to transform. Kasl and Elias (2000) suggest that individuals, groups, and organizations all share common characteristics and that there can be a group mind. In this approach to transformation, frames of reference are transcended rather than analyzed through critical reflection, and transformative learning becomes an expansion of consciousness that is collective as well as individual. The notion of group transformation does not supplant individual transformation, but simply adds another possible dimension to it.

Intuition, Imagination, and Soul in Transformative Learning

One of the most popular elaborations on Mezirow's cognitive and rational approach to transformative learning is the addition of intuition, imagination, and nurturing soul. Many of the new writers in the field are drawn to this way of understanding transformation as can be seen in the large proportion of paper presentations and experiential sessions, at the International Transformative Learning Conference (Wiessner *et al.*, 2003), that are based on artistic, creative, and imaginative points of view.

This perspective began with the work of Boyd (Boyd, 1991; Boyd and Myers, 1988) who used Jungian psychology to explain transformative learning. Rather than reflection, they described discernment as the central process in transformation. In this view, transformation is a personal inner journey of individuation — learning through the psychic structures that make up the self.

It is Dirkx's (1997, 2001) writing that has carried this approach forward into the current literature on transformative learning, providing a theoretical foundation for the many people who use drama, art, music, images, poetry, and symbols to promote transformation in their practice. In Dirkx's view, transformative learning involves personal, spiritual, emotional, and imaginative ways of knowing — the way of mythos rather than logos. Mythos is a facet of knowing that we see in symbols, images, stories, and myths. We experience soul through art, music, and film; it is that magic moment that transcends rationality and gives depth, power, mystery, and deep meaning to learning. In nurturing soul, we pay attention to the small, everyday occurrences in life, understand and appreciate images, and honor the complex, multifaceted nature of learning.

The extrarational perspective on transformative learning can exist side by side with the rational perspective. When Dirkx and Mezirow discussed their approaches at the 2005 International Transformative Learning Conference, they agreed that their perspectives are "similar with respect to [their] mutual concern for transforming frames of reference that have either lost their meaning or usefulness or have in some way become dysfunctional. [They] are both interested in fostering enhanced awareness and consciousness of one's being in the world" (Dirkx *et al.*, 2006: 137).

Ecological View

Some theorists broaden the scope of transformative learning to span individual, relational, group, institutional, societal, and global perspectives (O'sullivan, 2003). The Transformative Learning Centre at the Ontario Institute for Studies in Education promotes this point of view as does the Holma College of Integral Studies in Sweden (Gunnlaugson, 2003). Transformative learning is a deep, structural shift in the basic premises of thoughts, feelings, and actions. It dramatically and permanently alters our way of being in the world and involves not only our understanding of ourselves but also our relationship with all of humanity and the natural world. Through transformative learning, we strive for a planetary community, learn to love life in all forms, and move out to universal horizons. Gunnlaugson proposes that we need to consider "our collective evolutionary destiny from the vantage point of the history of planet Earth" (p. 324).

Teaching for Transformation

Less has been written about how to teach in such a way as to promote transformative learning than has been written about the learning process. It is proposed that there are three fundamental aspects to teaching for transformation: empowering learners, fostering critical reflection and self-knowledge, and supporting learners (Cranton, 2006).

Empowering Learners

Empowerment is both a product of and a precondition of transformative learning. As Mezirow (2000) says, "Hungry, homeless, desperate, threatened, sick, or frightened adults are less likely be able to participate in discourse to help us better understand the meaning of our own experience" (pp. 16–17). Those educators hoping to promote transformative learning need to be conscious of helping learners feel empowered. There are at least three aspects to consider: (1) exercising power responsibly, (2) encouraging discourse, and (3) involving learners in decision making.

As Brookfield (2006) reminds us, teachers have power, and we cannot deny its existence or think we can give it away. Exercising power responsibly and consciously serves to create learner empowerment – power is to be shared and acknowledged among those present in the teaching environment. A variety of practical strategies can be used, for example, avoiding being in the position of providing right answers, making sure that there is equal access to all resources, including self-evaluation in graded courses, involving students in managing the learning environment, and being open and explicit about what is happening and why.

If discourse or dialog is central to transformative learning, helping learners be empowered needs to include this element of the process, especially as equal participation in discourse may not occur naturally. Educators need to find provocative ways to stimulate dialog from different perspectives, encourage learners to take on different roles in the dialog, be careful not to regulate the discussion or dismiss learners' contributions, and provide time for reflection.

Involving learners in decision making, a strategy which harks back to Knowles' and others' advocating self-directed learning, enhances feelings of empowerment. Educators can use participatory planning in which learners decide on some or all of the topics, provide choices of methods to be used in the learning, encourage self-evaluation, ask learners for their perceptions of the experience, and keep the decision-making process open and explicit.

Fostering Critical Self-Reflection and Self-Knowledge

The most an educator can do is to set up an environment and conditions in which learners are able to engage in critical reflection and critical self-reflection. Entering into this process is voluntary; to approach it otherwise is

ethically questionable. A variety of ways are suggested to create such an environment, all of which are based on the goal of opening up new perspectives, challenging existing assumptions, or presenting information from a different point of view (Cranton, 2006).

Asking questions is the most basic strategy for fostering reflection. Educators can ask learners to help them see what assumptions they are making and to challenge the premises underlying their assumptions. Questions can center on the content of individuals' beliefs, how they came to hold those beliefs, and why they value what they value (content, process, and premise-reflection questions, as suggested by Mezirow (1991)).

Journals are often suggested as a means of promoting critical reflection, but guidelines need to be given to learners to prevent the journal from being a simple log of what happened. Progoff's (1992) extensive work on journal writing is helpful. He suggests a variety of formats including writing a life history; engaging in a dialog with a person in the writer's life or a historical figure; incorporating metaphors, dreams, and images; and writing from the perspective of another person.

Experiential learning through practicums, field trips, service learning, job shadowing, and any other real-life experience that can be incorporated into a course can stimulate critical reflection if the learner encounters perspectives that are different from those he or she holds. To further the possibility of critical reflection, the educator can hold discussions before and after the experience, suggest students write about the experience, encourage critical questioning among students, and emphasize any discrepancies between learners' prior experience and the new experience.

Art-based activities promote imaginative and intuitive transformative experiences. Learners can either engage in the creation of art or they can view art. Some strategies the educator can consider are: creating collages as a group; encouraging students to make art as a project in a course; using film, fiction, and photography to present alternative points of view on an issue; or going to an art gallery or concert as a group.

Supporting Transformative Learning

In transformative learning, people are letting go of assumptions, beliefs, and perspectives that they may have held for a lifetime. Scott (1997) writes about the grieving involved in letting go of our way of seeing the world. The educator who fosters transformative learning has a moral responsibility to provide and arrange for support. He or she needs to establish relationships with learners and be conscious of what is happening in their lives when they engage in transformative learning.

This is not to say that the educator is solely responsible. Encouraging learners to support each other by helping to establish a cohesive group and setting up learner networks (formal or informal, with or without technology) are helpful strategies. However, it is also important to be there when an individual learner comes to the educator for advice and support. Even after a course is over, there are occasions when someone needs assistance in deciding how to act based on a transformative learning experience or simply needs to talk about his or her experience.

Summary

Since Mezirow (1975) first proposed his notion of perspective transformation more than three decades ago, transformative learning theory has developed into a comprehensive theory of adult learning. In recent years, with the addition of several alternative perspectives, it has become a holistic and integrated way of understanding how adults experience deep shifts in perspective. In this article, transformative learning theory has been set in the larger context of adult education. The original theory as presented by Mezirow (1991, 2000) is described and the major ways in which other theorists have elaborated on his work are presented. It concludes with a discussion of how educators can facilitate and promote transformative learning.

Bibliography

Belenky, M. and Stanton, A. (2000). Inequality, development, and connected knowing. In Mezirow, J. and associates (eds.) *Learning as Transformation: Critical Perspectives on a Theory in Progress*, pp 71–102. San Francisco, CA: Jossey-Bass.

Boyd, R. D. (1991). *Personal Transformation in Small Groups: A Jungian Perspective*. London: Routledge.

Boyd, R. D. and Myers, J. B. (1988). Transformative education. *International Journal of Lifelong Education* 7, 261–284.

Brookfield, S. (2000). Transformative learning as ideology critique. In Mezirow, J. and associates (eds.) *Learning as Transformation: Critical Perspectives on a Theory in Progress*, pp 125–150. San Francisco, CA: Jossey-Bass.

Brookfield, S. (2003). The praxis of transformative education: African American feminist conceptualizations. *Journal of Transformative Education* 1(3), 212–226.

Brookfield, S. (2005). *The Power of Critical Theory: Liberating Adult Learning and Teaching*. San Francisco, CA: Jossey-Bass.

Brookfield, S. (2006). Authenticity and power. In Cranton, P. (ed.) *Authenticity in Teaching. New Directions for Adult and Continuing Education, No. 111*, pp 5–16. San Francisco, CA: Jossey-Bass.

Brundage, D. and MacKeracher, D. (1980). *Adult Learning Principles and Their Application to Program Planning*. Toronto, ON: Ontario Institute for Studies in Education.

Candy, P. (1991). *Self-Direction for Lifelong Learning*. San Francisco, CA: Jossey-Bass.

Clark, M. C. and Wilson, A. L. (1991). Context and rationality in Mezirow's theory of transformational learning. *Adult Education Quarterly* 42(2), 75–91.

Collard, S. and Law, M. (1989). The limits of perspective transformation: A critique of Mezirow's theory. *Adult Education Quarterly* 39, 99–107.

Cranton, P. (2006). *Understanding and Promoting Transformative Learning: A Guide for Educators of Adults*, 2nd edn. San Francisco, CA: Jossey-Bass.

Cross, P. (1981). *Adults as Learners*. San Francisco, CA: Jossey-Bass.

Dewey, J. (1938). *Experience and Education*. New York: Coller Books.

Dirkx, J. M. (1997). Nurturing soul in adult education. In Cranton, P. (ed.) *Transformative Learning in Action: Insights from Practice. New Directions for Adult and Continuing Education, No. 74*, pp 79–88. San Francisco, CA: Jossey-Bass.

Dirkx, J. M. (2001). The power of feelings: Emotion, imagination, and the construction of meaning in adult learning. In Merriam, S. (ed.) *The New Update on Adult Learning Theory. New Directions for Adult and Continuing Education, No. 89*, pp 63–72. San Francisco, CA: Jossey-Bass.

Dirkx, J. M., Mezirow, J., and Cranton, P. (2006). Musings and reflections on the meaning, context, and process of transformative learning: A dialogue between John M. Dirkx and Jack Mezirow. *Journal of Transformative Education* 4(2), 123–139.

Elias, J. and Merriam, S. (2005). *Philosophical Foundations of Adult Education*, 3rd edn. Malabar, FL: Krieger.

Freire, P. (1970). *Pedagogy of the Oppressed*. New York: Herder and Herder.

Gunnlaugson, O. (2003). Toward an integral education for the ecozoic era: A case study in transforming the global learning community of Holma College of Integral Studies. *Journal of Transformative Education* 2(4), 313–335.

Hart, M. (1990). Critical theory and beyond: Further perspectives on emancipatory education. *Adult Education Quarterly* 40, 125–138.

Hayes, E. and Flannery, D. (2000). *Women as Learners: The Significance of Gender in Adult Learning*. San Francisco, CA: Jossey-Bass.

Kasl, E. and Elias, D. (2000). Creating new habits of mind in small groups. In Mezirow, J. and associates (eds.) *Learning as Transformation: Critical Perspectives on a Theory in Progress*, pp 229–252. San Francisco, CA: Jossey-Bass.

Knowles, M. (1975). *Self-Directed Learning: A Guide for Learners and Teachers*. Chicago, IL: Follett.

Knowles, M. (1980). *The Modern Practice of Adult Education: From Pedagogy to Andragogy*. New York: Cambridge.

Kolb, D. A. (1984). *Experiential Learning: Experience as the Source of Learning and Development*. Englewood Cliffs, NJ: Prentice Hall.

Lindemann, E. C. (1926). *The Meaning of Adult Education*. New York: New Republic.

Mezirow, J. (1975). *Education for Perspective Transformation: Women's Reentry Programs in Community Colleges*. New York: Center for Adult Education, Teachers College, Columbia University.

Mezirow, J. (1991). *Transformative Dimensions of Adult Learning*. San Francisco, CA: Jossey-Bass.

Mezirow, J. (2000). Learning to think like an adult. In Mezirow, J. and associates (ed.) *Learning as Transformation: Critical Perspectives on a Theory in Progress*, pp 3–34. San Francisco, CA: Jossey-Bass.

Mezirow, J. (2003). Transformative learning as discourse. *Journal of Transformative Education* 1(1), 58–63.

Newman, M. (1994). *Defining the Enemy: Adult Education in Social Action*. Sydney: Victor Stewart.

Newman, M. (2006). *Teaching Defiance: Stories and Strategies for Activist Educators*. San Francisco, CA: Jossey-Bass.

O'sullivan, E. (2003). The ecological terrain of transformative learning: A vision statement. In Wiessner, C. A., Meyer, S. R., Pfhal, N., and Neaman, P. (eds.) *Transformative Learning in Action: Building Bridges across Contexts and Disciplines. Proceedings of the Fifth International Conference on Transformative Learning*, pp 336–340. New York: Teachers College, Columbia University.

Progoff, I. (1992). *At a Journal Workshop: Writing to Access the Power of the Unconscious and Evoke Creative Ability*. New York: Penguin Putnam.

Rogers, C. R. (1961). *On Becoming a Person: A Therapist's View of Psychotherapy*. Boston: Houghton Mifflin.

Scott, S. (1997). The grieving soul in the transformation process. In Cranton, P. (ed.) *Transformative Learning in Action: Insights from Practice. New Directions for Adult and Continuing Education, No. 74*, pp 41–50. San Francisco, CA: Jossey-Bass.

Tough, A. (1979). *The Adult's Learning Projects: A Fresh Approach to Theory and Practice*. Toronto, ON: Ontario Institute for Studies in Education.

Watkins, K. and Marsick, V. (1993). *Scultping the Learning Organization: Lessons in the Art and Sciences of Systemic Change*. San Francisco, CA: Jossey-Bass.

Wiessner, C. A., Meyer, S. R., Pfhal, N., and Neaman, P. (eds.) (2003). *Transformative Learning in Action: Building Bridges Across Contexts and Disciplines. Proceedings of the Fifth International Conference on Transformative Learning.* New York: Teachers College, Columbia University.

Yorks, L. and Marsick, V. (2000). Organizational learning and transformation. In Mezirow, J. and associates (eds.) *Learning as Transformation: Critical Perspectives on a Theory in Progress*, pp 253–284. San Francisco, CA: Jossey-Bass.

Adult Learning in a Biographic Perspective

L West, Canterbury Christ Church University, Canterbury, UK

Glossary

Auto/biographical – Being aware of the extent to which we use other's stories to make sense of our own biographies as well as how we use our own to make sense of others' lives and experiences.
Biographic perspectives – Using other people's lives as a basis for understanding processes of learning, and so on.
Lifewide and lifelong learning – The idea that learning, in and across all dimensions of experience, past and present, can interconnect. Learning, in these terms, may be conceived as a psychological orientation to experience, the tendency to be relatively open to new experience, or, at another extreme, to fear and resist it. This can be rooted in early experience and the quality of our interactions with others.
Narratives – These are important in a biographic perspective. We experience our lives through some conception of past, present, and future. Such frames help bring some coherence to the fragments of experience. Biographic researchers often pay great attention to the qualities of people's narratives.
Poststructuralist – The emphasis here is on what is seen to be the pervasive power of language and power–knowledge formations to shape how we think and make sense of the world, including of ourselves.
Psychosocial – An interdisciplinary perspective in studies of adult learning, which is not only sensitive to how society and culture can structure the way we think and feel about the world, but also how our psychologies have a life of their own. There is an interest in how psychoanalytic insights can contribute to an understanding of inner and outer dynamics in people's encounters with learning.

Introduction

This article focuses on the biographic perspective and how this can illuminate the nature and processes of adult learning in unique ways. It draws on a rich body of international research and scholarship, over two decades and more, which constitutes, in fact, a major turn to biography and life history in the study of adult learning.

This is part of a broader trend across the social sciences (West *et al.*, 2007). The trend is partly a reaction against forms of research (such as behaviorism) which tended to marginalize the perspectives and subjective experiences of learners themselves or reduced learning to overly abstract entities. It has also been a reaction to theories of learning that neglected the role of meaning making and the importance of agency in human development.

The label biographic is used, for present purposes, to encompass a family of research and scholarship, which can be known in varying ways; examples are narrative or auto/biographical research, which may have common yet distinct meanings. Terms like biography or life history can be used interchangeably and may also be understood in differing ways. In Denmark, for instance (West *et al.*, 2007), a distinction is made between biography as the told life, and a life history, in which the researcher brings his or her interpretations and theoretical insights into play. In this article, biographic perspective is used inclusively to encompass different members of the family, while remembering that each can have distinct as well as related characteristics.

Some History

Feminism and oral history have been important in the emergence of biographic perspectives on adult learning, especially in North America and parts of Europe. In continental Europe, however, influences vary: in Denmark, for instance, critical theory has played an important part in the development of biographical perspectives into learning processes, alongside psychoanalysis and feminism. For many biographical researchers, the biographic perspective, methodologically, reaches back to the Chicago School of sociologists and social psychologists of the 1920s. The Chicago School developed the notion of symbolic interactionism to capture the dynamic, malleable, constructed, and also learned quality of human identity and social formation. Symbolic interactionism treated the things that members of society do as being performed by them as actors, rather than as if done by something called the system itself. The social order, in short, is dynamically learned through and from the interactions of its members. This finds renewed resonance in contemporary ideas about the role of reflexivity or biographical learning being of central importance in the contemporary world.

Second-wave feminism in the 1960s was also important in the development of the biographic perspective in adult learning, particularly in the United Kingdom, North America, and also in the French-speaking world (Dybbroe and Ollagnier, 2003). Feminism was concerned with the pervasive influence of gender in people's learning lives in positioning both women and men in particular ways. Feminism and feminist research were committed to the idea of giving voice to women previously hidden in educational research. An early biographic focus, unsurprisingly, was on women's experiences of education (Merrill and West, 2009). Writers and researchers were often mature women students themselves and brought gender and the personal directly into accounts of learning as part of a wider political project.

The biographical perspective has slowly increased in importance in the literature of adult learning and education. By the early 1990s, the proportion of papers at the Standing Conference of University Teachers and Researchers in the Education of Adults (SCUTREA, which is Britain's preeminent professional network for researchers in the field of adult and lifelong learning), concerned with life stories, narratives, transformations of selves, and struggles over identity, was increasing. In 1988, only two papers had used a biographical or narrative perspective – broadly defined – as a method; however, this was to become a mainstream preoccupation in the 1990s. There was evidence of a similar trend in the increased number of papers devoted to biographic perspectives in meetings such as the North American Adult Education Research Conference (AERC). The trend has continued (West et al., 2007).

Notwithstanding, there has been resistance to the perspective too. Among researchers, for instance, who considered that such work lacked observational rigor and objectivity in its preoccupation with internal experience and meaning-making processes. For some historians, the perspective has been criticized for being overly obsessed with the detail of learners' lives, and insufficiently focused on big educational and social questions around, for instance, the nature of educational opportunity in a capitalist economic order. From a poststructuralist perspective, the preoccupation with learners' stories, as a basis for understanding adult learning, risks neglecting the way in which stories – of learning, but of lives more widely – are penetrated by powerful discourses that individuals may barely be aware of. The biographic perspective, in this view, carries the danger of neglecting how we are storied as well as storytellers in learning lives (Merrill and West, 2009).

Mapping the Field

Nonetheless, there is a rich range of biographic scholarship providing, as suggested, not only many unique insights into processes of adult learning, but also some

new theoretical developments and challenges to received wisdom. Researchers have focused not only on learning in traditional contexts, such as higher and adult education, but also on learning and identity building in professional and workplace settings as well as other diverse locations for informal learning. These include learning in families, community development settings, trade union engagements, relationships, and even cyberspace. Researchers are busy exploring the impact of learning on health and its place in therapeutic processes. The biographical perspective is being used to examine the relationship between learning, class, ethnicity, and gender. Researchers have also addressed many criticisms, which include the capacity of people in biographic research to be aware, reflexively, of how they may be positioned by dominant social structures and or discourses (Frosh et al., 2005).

Biographic perspectives developed strongly in the Francophone and German-speaking as well as the Anglo-Saxon world. In French-speaking communities, the literature reaches back to the work of a preceding generation, such as Paulo Freire, Bertrand Schwarz, and Jack Mezirow. The biographic perspective here adopted critical approaches to recognize the adult learner on the basis of his or her life trajectory and personal story. He or she was conceptualized as an authentic knower, deserving respect for her/his learning efforts and her/his relationship to knowledge. There has been a fundamental challenge to the banking concept of learning and a celebration of human agency, not least in questioning a deeply patriarchal social order, through biographic forms of enquiry (Dybbroe and Ollagnier, 2003).

Pineau (2000) has explored the link between life history, autobiography, and self-directed learning. He has worked with homeless people and used the biographic perspective to build a fuller understanding of learning paths in such contexts. Guy de Villers, a psychoanalyst as well as an educator, has recently edited a book on the boundaries between life history and therapy, which is a source of major debate in the French-speaking life history networks in adult education and, for that matter, more widely (Niewiadomski and de Villers, 2002). For Pierre Dominicé, the biographic perspective has an educational function in its own right and can be used to analyze and better understand the experiences of learners. He stresses, through his concept of educational biography, how the biographic perspective potentially has great occupational importance in helping people understand their professional work and interactions with others: as adult educators and trainers, for instance (Dominicé, 2000).

Learning: Lifewide and Lifelong

At the heart of the biographic perspective, as noted, is a shift in focus from an exclusive preoccupation with education in formal settings to learning in many and diverse places: formal, nonformal, and informal, and toward an engagement with the interplay between these different dimensions of learning. There has been movement from the idea of a distinct field of adult education, in defined settings, to a more diverse terrain of learning in many locations. Adult education as a field tended to be preoccupied with postcompulsory education and with particular categories of learners and learning. By contrast, the biographical perspective encompasses processes of knowing and skills acquisition, affective transformation, and experiential learning beyond the walls of schools, colleges, and universities. It includes informal, tacit, and emotional learning, alongside cognitive processes and encounters with more formal bodies of knowledge. It covers learning in intensely intimate as well as more public space, and the connections between these. Formal learning is but one part, if important, of a complex tapestry.

The biographic perspective has helped to reveal some of the complex interplay between formal, nonformal, or informal processes of learning. Conventional distinctions between public and private experience, or learning in schools and families, or between structured and everyday learning, tend to unravel. This has been illuminated, for instance, in studies of professional learning (West, 2001; Olesen, 2007). Linden West has focused on family physicians learning and working in difficult and demanding innercity contexts. Thus West is concerned to understand how informal processes of learning may interact with more formal aspects of a doctor's training as well as the culture and subcultures of the profession. He notes a continuing neglect, for instance, in medical culture of learning about self and emotionality in doctor's professional training and how doctors can come to feel emotionally on the edge when working in difficult social contexts. Disturbance in others – including mental illness – can come to disturb a doctor and incidents of stress, alcoholism, mental health problems, as well as suicide have been increasing among doctors. The sample of doctors in the biographic study, which lasted for 4 years, emphasized the importance of supportive relationships as well as of self-knowledge and cultural learning alongside scientific knowledge when working in multicultural, innercity environments. The study documented the subtle interplay of learning in personal life with professional practice, and how the particular subcultures of the doctor's surgery and interactions with colleagues can be vital in creating space to learn from difficult experiences with patients. Learning, in such a biographic perspective, is understood more holistically.

A New Paradigm of Learning?

The biographic perspective, in fact, may have helped forge a new paradigm of learning (Alheit and Dausien, 2007).

Learning, viewed biographically, seems conceptually close, for instance, to the idea of reflexivity, which has become a central preoccupation of mainstream social science. This is set within a postmodern awareness of the uncertainty and rapidity of social and technological change. Here is the territory in which the self becomes a reflexive project. The globalizing tendencies of the present have been regarded as ushering in profound changes in social life and personal experience, which require constant efforts to construct and sustain the self through narratives of self-identity, in a kind of perpetual process of learning.

Biographies themselves, from such perspectives, in their unpredictability, become essential, often profound sites for learning. The capacity to compose a biography and develop reflexivity (or what Peter Alheit calls biographicity; Alheit and Dausien, 2007) is considered to be a survival necessity in a more individualized, perpetually changing, paradoxical, risk-inducing culture. This is a culture, it is argued, of new opportunities, but those that coexist with biographical fragility: in a world that fuels the necessity and/or desire to compose ourselves in new and distinct ways while generating intense anxieties about our capacity to cope. Ours is a period that offers enticing opportunities to live more autonomous lives while generating doubt about the sustainability or even desirability of such a project.

People, it is suggested, are confronted with new knowledge and the need to make choices (e.g., about what we eat or in response to illness) almost everyday, without reference to undisputed sources of authority. Science, often considered the means by which we can seek guidance, is itself a site of dispute and contestation. This is a liquid, shifting world in which we have to learn to learn, in the sense of needing to be open to new and diverse possibilities, rather than rely on a past consumption of fixed bodies of knowledge, also remembering that many of the economic, social, and familial scripts which historically shaped people's lives have weakened. Existentially, we are more on our own and inherit a world of diverse competing versions of how we should live or be. Learning becomes, in these terms, a biographical necessity. On the other hand, we can retreat into a kind of antilearning: into fundamentalism in which we seek complete answers in a body of doctrine, yet close ourselves off to the complexities of experience and their potential as a source for learning, including from the other and otherness.

Peter Alheit and Bettina Dausien identify some distinct learning imperatives in such a world. First, the need to learn from biographical crises: the processes of individualism referred to above bring considerable risk of crises-ridden biographical development. The experience of the modern world, they suggest, can turn personal meaningfulness into a problem of principle. People may have to negotiate periods of unemployment alongside employment; returning to school alongside participation in the labor market, as well as constant questions about who they are and might want to be in situations where relationships, at work or in private life, may be transient. Adult learning, in such a context, moves closer to therapeutic processes. Meaning, in Alheit and Dausien's perspective, is less and less guaranteed by an unquestioning participation of individuals in culture and society. Generating meaning, and meaningful lives, has become the province of subjects who may feel, structurally, thrown into the deep end. Learning, of necessity, takes on a quasitherapeutic dimension, as does the work of many educators.

Another dimension of adult learning is brought into sharper relief by the biographic perspective: the importance of composing life stories and of telling stories more generally. As intergenerational continuities weaken, it becomes more important to find ways to work out how we might want to live our lives, and on what terms, including which values to choose. Stories are critically important to this end. The biographic perspective, forged out of experiences in the women's movement, has constantly emphasized the importance of finding voice in struggles to learn, for agency and meaningfulness.

The biographic perspective may also problematize overly rigid notions of developmental stages in learning and human life. A well-known variant is the midlife crisis, which draws on Jungian ideas of how men, of certain ages, once competitive career-building pressures have abated, may seek more feminine, artistic, and expressive forms of learning. However, when predictable linear trajectories of school–work–retirement break down, the notion of quasifixed stages becomes questionable. Desire for and resistance to learning across the lifecycle may become much more complex and variable as we are forced, for instance, to relearn or radically change our identities in unexpected, undesired ways.

An Interdisciplinary Imperative

The biographical perspective has also engendered new forms of interdisciplinary, psychosocial understanding of learning and learners. These new developments seek to transcend old style disputes between structuralist sociology and essentialist psychology in the literature of adult learning. Adult learning was conceived, on the one hand, as a largely internal psychological process, dependent on dispositions, inherent motivations, and objectively measurable intelligence. The social and historical could largely be excluded from the frame (Tennant, 1997). On the other hand, there was great resistance to such ideas, especially in more radical and oppositional theories of adult learning. In the British tradition, for instance, there was criticism of what was seen to be a mainly North American tendency to overly psychologize the human

subject and learning processes, and to reduce sociocultural forms of oppression to matters of individual pathology (Tennant, 1997). On the other hand, more radical, structural perspectives on adult learning have lacked any convincing theory of how the sociocultural translates into diverse internal states and why some people, more so than others, in objectively similar situations, are able to transcend oppression and become life spacers.

There is a considerable momentum in the biographic research family to bridge the conceptual gap, as defined above. There are a number of psychosocial studies – often drawing on psychoanalytic ideas – which explore the interplay of inner and outer worlds, psyche, and society: of learning in families or in working contexts, for example (West, 2007; Weber, 2007). Psyche is perceived to be a product of our intersubjective experiences, which are shaped, in turn, by the structuring and discursive processes within a given society, such as of class, race, or gender. However, psyche is no longer reduced, as in an overly structuralist sociology, to a kind of epiphenomenal or determined status: the inner world has a dynamic and power all of its own. If culture and society shape even in the most intimate of spaces – through poverty or the gendered distribution of emotional labor – such processes are mediated through the intimate relationships in which we are embedded. They can encourage relative emotional openness or closedness to experience and others. If curiosity, desire, and wholehearted engagement with the world are repressed or profoundly inhibited, because of our most significant others, then learning, in a psychological sense, easily becomes something to be avoided rather than embraced.

Such processes have been mapped, biographically, in studies of young mothers in parenting projects, like Sure Start in the United Kingdom (similar to Head Start in the United States) (West, 2007). One project was designed to support young single mothers who lived on a run-down public housing estate, suffering badly from deindustrialization, demoralization, and poverty. The particular project provided the base for a university and a community arts collaboration to utilize the visual arts to stimulate creativity and build confidence among hard-pressed single young mothers. The project was located in a youth center and the disaffected young mothers were to be recruited through outreach. The arts, it was hoped, would boost participants' confidence, planning and parenting skills, as well as broaden horizons. The young mothers would be encouraged to progress toward structured educational achievement or into work.

One particular case study chronicles, in detail, how a young woman, Gina, could retreat defiantly to the edge of any group of learners. This was part of a pattern in a life riddled with abuse, hard drugs, and ridicule. Yet, providing a creative artistic space, in the context of the strong relationships that Gina forged with tutors and youth workers over time, gradually enabled her to take some risks. Her messy feelings about her pregnancy, for instance, were projected into a sculpture, made of chicken wire and plaster of Paris, which became a narrative of her pregnancy. She was able to work on the story artistically and, to an extent, transform her relationship to the experience and to her life more widely, through new narrative understanding. Her progress depended on the quality of interactions between people (the social context) and the extent to which she felt encouraged and able to play, imagine, think, and perceive herself differently, as a learner, mother, and person, and to relate to her toddler in new ways. There was as shift in her internal psychological drama, as new characters and symbolic objects, in the language of psychoanalysis, entered the stage. We are witnesses, in work of this kind, to how experience can stifle the desire to learn, and can psychologically close us down to new possibilities. However, new transitional spaces for learning and people coming alongside and tolerating our ambivalence – with sufficient self-knowledge, patience, and love, in a non-narcissistic sense – can reinvigorate creativity and the capacity to learn anew.

Other biographical researchers have used psychosocial ideas to explore learning processes from a gender perspective. Weber (2007), for example, focuses on gender and the learning processes of adult men training for work in the caring professions. Drawing on what she terms critical psychodynamic theory, she reveals learning in the workplace as a gendered battlefield where learning subjects' basic orientations can manifest themselves along gendered lines. These processes are partly theorized with reference to classic psychoanalytic insights into male struggles with intimacy. However, this is not to neglect culture, language, or material conditions. In this view, gender is inherent in social structures, stemming from historic divisions of labor, and is reproduced or changed within the scope of the accessible choices that people can make. Yet, in understanding reproduction and change processes, Weber observes that girls tend to identify with and separate from a model of their own gender while boys' paths to autonomy involve separation from a first intimacy. These patterns of early interaction are reinforced by language as symbolic representation, all of which serves to define what she calls gendered subjectivity. (Weber, building on the work of others, distinguishes gender subjectivity – the processes by which a person becomes a psychological subject – and gender identity, which refers to sexuality and cultural conceptions of gender.) Gendered subjectivity can find expression in what can be the differing responses of men and women to new kinds of training opportunities in which learning a capacity to care for others is required. Men, mirroring earlier patterns, tend to achieve this by experiencing and demonstrating degrees of autonomy first, whereas women tend to seek intimacy as a prerequisite of autonomy.

Weber stresses that these distinctions are far from absolute, but there are patterns nonetheless. We are given glimpses, through such biographical research, of the defended as well as social subject at the heart of learning.

Adult and Lifelong Learning: A Reconfiguration?

Finally, the biographic perspective can challenge received wisdom on adult learning in another, quite basic sense. The work of Knowles (1984) and others helped build the case for an academic discipline focused, distinctly, on adult learning. Knowles was reacting to the derivation of theories of adult learning from an understanding of how animals (especially rodents and pigeons) behaved, followed by observations of children. Adults and their experiences were neglected. The attempt to refocus research and scholarship, and the emergence of the associated idea of andragogy, Knowles argued, was premised on notions of a more dynamic culture of learning than pedagogy allowed. Learners should be actively involved in diagnosing their learning needs, in planning their experiences, and in developing a suitable learning environment.

Yet, from a biographic perspective, the continuities between early and adult experience are also important. The study of learning, as noted above, can reveal how past and present often intertwine. Even very confident people can feel helpless and overcome in new and demanding situations, such as entering a new course in higher or adult education. Such moments may link back to earlier feelings of inadequacy or failure, as past and present elide. Melanie Klein, a psychoanalyst, termed this memory in feeling, expressed in bodily and emotional states, rather than conscious thought. Such embodied memory can be especially intense for those taught, from earliest times, that they are of little consequence, are inadequate, or authority cannot be trusted. A range of psychological defenses may come into play, including withdrawal and denial of needs (that something may be important or desirable). There can be constant glimpses of defensiveness in adult learner narratives: early experience is never simply transcended and past and present can constantly elide (West, 2007).

Conclusion: The Biographic Perspective

It is suggested that learning, from a biographic perspective, is seen as more of a piece: social and psychological; informal and formal; and lifewide and lifelong, forged in a dynamic interplay of past and present and even future (without a sense of a future, the past cannot really be embraced). The biographical perspective, in fact, encompasses an idea of learning that echoes the humanistic and imaginative spirit associated with Wright Mills (1970) in his work on biography. Biography, he argued, was situated at a meeting point between historical imperatives, social structures, and the inner worlds of human beings. His interest was in notions of human agency and how people, even in the most oppressive of situations, can find the resources, individually and collectively, to build better worlds. We could add learn their way to better worlds: a process requiring an eclectic, interdisciplinary understanding of people in their resilience and also vulnerabilities. Moreover, the biographic perspective encourages us to engage with ourselves when engaging with others and their learning: in making sense of the other, we draw on our own experience, and in making sense of self, we can make more sense of another. This has been termed the auto/biographic perspective in adult learning. Turning to biography challenges many and varied boundaries.

See also: Adult Learning; Barriers to Participation in Adult Education; Characteristics of Adult Learning; Community Based Adult Education; Gender Analysis; Health and Adult Learning; Informal Learning: A Contested Concept; Lifelong Learning; Rewriting the History of Adult Education: The Search for Narrative Structures.

Bibliography

Alheit, P. and Dausien, B. (2007). Lifelong learning and biography: A competitive dynamic. In West, L., Alheit, P., Andersen, A. S., and Merrill, B. (eds.) *Using Biographical and Life History Methods in the Study of Adult and Lifelong Learning: European Perspectives*, pp 57–70. Frankfurt: Peter Lang/ESREA.

Dominicé, P. (2000). *Learning from Our Lives: Using Educational Biographies with Adults*. San Francisco, CA: Jossey-Bass.

Dybbroe, B. and Ollagnier, E. (eds.) (2003). *Challenging Gender in Lifelong Learning: European Perspectives*. Roskilde: University Press.

Frosh, S., Phoenix, A., and Pattman, R. (2005). Struggling towards manhood: Narratives of homophobia and fathering. *British Journal of Psychotherapy* **22**(1), 37–56.

Knowles, M. (1984). *The Adult Learner, a Neglected Species*. Houston, TX: Gulf.

Merrill, B. and West, L. (2009). *Using Biographical Methods in Social Science*. London: Sage.

Mills, C. W. (1970). *The Sociological Imagination*. London: Penguin.

Niewiadomski, C. and de Villers, G. (eds.) (2002). *Souci et soin de soi: Liens et frontières entre histoire de vie, psychothérapie et psychanalyse*. Paris: L'Harmattan.

Olesen, H. S. (2007). Professional identities, subjectivity and learning: Be(coming) a general practitioner. In West, L., Alheit, P., Anderson, A., and Merrill, B. (eds.) *Using Biographical and Life History Methods in the Study of Adult and Lifelong Learning: European Perspectives*, pp 125–141. Frankfurt: Peter Lang/ESREA.

Pineau, G. (2000). *Temporalités en Formation*. Paris: Anthropos.

Tennant, M. (1997). *Psychology and Adult Learning*. London: Routledge.

Weber, K. (2007). Gender, the knowledge economy and every day life. In West, L., Alheit, P., Anderson, A., and Merrill, B. (eds.) *Using Biographical and Life History Methods in the Study of Adult and Lifelong Learning: European Perspectives*. Frankfurt: Peter Lang/ESREA.

West, L. (2001). *Doctors on the Edge; General Practitioners, Health and Learning in the Inner City*. London: FABooks.

West, L. (2007). An auto/biographical imagination: The radical challenge of families and their learning. In West, L., Alheit, P., Anderson, A. S., and Merrill, B. (eds.) *Using Biographical and Life History Methods in the Study of Adult and Lifelong Learning: European Perspectives*, pp 221–240. New York: Peter Lang/ESREA.

West, L., Alheit, P., Anderson, A., and Merrill, B. (eds.) (2007). *Using Biographical and Life History Methods in the Study of Adult and Lifelong Learning: European Perspectives*. Frankfurt: Peter Lang/ESREA.

Further Reading

Bauman, Z. (2000). *Liquid Modernity*. Bristol: Policy Press.

Bron, A., Kurantowicz, E., Salling Olesen, H., and West, L. (eds.) (2005). *Old and New Worlds of Adult Learning*. Wroclaw: Wydawnictwo Naukowe.

Chamberlayne, P., Bornat, J., and Apitzsch, U. (2004). *Biographical Methods and Professional Practice*. Bristol: Policy Press.

Chamberlayne, P., Bornat, J., and Wengraf, T. (2000). *The Turn to Biographical Methods in the Social Sciences*. London: Routledge.

Field, J. (2000). *Lifelong Learning and the New Educational Order*. Stoke-on-Trent: Trentham Books.

Goodson, I. and Sykes, P. (2001). *Life History Research in Education Settings: Learning from Lives*. Buckingham: Open University Press.

Hodkinson, P., Hodkinson, H., Evans, K., *et al.* (2004). The significance of individual biography in workplace learning. *Studies in the Education of Adults* **36**(1), 6–24.

Hunt, C. and West, L. (2006). Learning in a border country: Using psychodynamic perspectives in teaching and research. *Studies in the Education of Adults* **38**(2), 160–177.

McClaren, A. (1985). *Ambitions and Realisations – Women in Adult Education*. London: Peter Owen.

Merrill, B. (1999). *Gender, Change and Identity: Mature Women Students in Universities*. Aldershot: Ashgate.

Plummer, K. (2001). *Documents of Life*. London: Sage.

Schuller, T., Preston, J., and Hammond, C. (2007). Mixing methods to measure learning benefits. In West, L., Alheit, P., Anderson, A. S., and Merrill, B. (eds.) *The Uses of Biographical and Life History Approaches in the Study of Adult and Lifelong Learning: European Perspectives*, pp 251–273. New York: Peter Lang.

Stanley, L. (1992). *The Auto/Biographical I*. Manchester: Manchester University Press.

West, L. (1996). *Beyond Fragments; Adults, Motivation and Higher Education*. London: Taylor and Francis.

West, L., Miller, N., O'Reilly, D., and Allen, R. (eds.) (2001). *Travellers' Tales: From Adult Education to Lifelong Learning . . . and Beyond. Proceedings of the 31st SCUTREA Conference Proceedings*, London: UEL.

Relevant Websites

http://www.canterbury.ac.uk – Canterbury Christ Church University.

http://www.esrea.org – European Society for Research on the Education of Adults (ESTREA).

http://www.learninglives.org – Learning Lives: Learning, Identity and Agency in the Life Course.

http://www.scutrea.ac.uk – Standing Conference on University Teaching and Research in the Education of Adults (SCUTREA).

Adult Learning, Instruction and Programme Planning: Insights from Freire

P Mayo, University of Malta, Msida, Malta

Introduction

Paulo Freire (1921–97) was one of the most influential educationists of the twentieth century. It is from a Freirean perspective that this article on adult learning, instruction, and program planning is written.

Argentinean scholar Daniel Schugurensky says, with reference to adult education, that: "in Latin America, Paulo Freire constitutes a watershed. There is before and after Freire" (Schugurensky, 1998: 344). Several years earlier, another Argentinean scholar, Carlos Alberto Torres, remarked: "We can stay with Freire or against Freire, but not without Freire" (Torres, 1982: 94). In addition, although Freire was undoubtedly one of the most heralded educators of the twentieth century, who inevitably has his detractors, his influence extends beyond the field of education to be felt in a variety of areas, including sociology, political theory, development studies, theology, philosophy, cultural studies, anthropology, language studies, and communications.

Paulo Freire suffered imprisonment and exile for his efforts in planning what was perceived as being a subversive approach to literacy in Brazil in the early 1960s. Freire subsequently worked, as a person in exile, in Chile, Massachusetts, and Geneva. During his 16-year period of exile, he was frequently called upon by revolutionary governments to assist them in developing and evaluating educational projects. He also engaged in projects with a variety of groups in different parts of the world. After his return to Brazil from exile, which, on his own admission, he had to relearn, he entered the complex domain of municipal educational administration in São Paulo, one of the world's largest cities.

Freire was most prolific as a published writer, with many of his works having been translated into English and other languages. Freire's better-known work, *Pedagogy of the Oppressed*, is regarded by many to be exemplary in the way it provides reflections on his many worlds of social action in a process that also involves constant recourse to theory, with Freire drawing on many sources in this regard, including Marxism, phenomenology, Christian personalism, liberation theology, and postcolonialism.

Praxis

Knowledge of the Community

Freire's pedagogy emerged from the Latin American tradition of popular education which incorporates a strong degree of nonformal education. Nonformal education is not *laissez faire* pedagogy, but includes a certain degree of planning and organization. In the classic Freirean approach, the entire process of planning involves an intimate knowledge of the community in which the learning is to take place. The team of educators and project organizers, and other project participants, were allowed to mix with community members in a variety of settings, including their most informal settings, listen to their speech patterns and concerns, as well as identify some of the thematic complexes of the community itself. This approach was repeated and reinvented by Freire within the context of public educational administration when he served as educational secretary in the municipal government of São Paulo in his native, Brazil (O'Cadiz *et al.*, 1998).

Codification

Once the information was gathered, the team worked together and consulted community members, besides other persons connected with the locality, to draw up a plan of action that focused on the reality gleaned from the research carried out in the locality. Important aspects of this reality were thus codified in the form of pictures, subjects for discussion, plays, generative themes, and other pedagogical approaches. The material connected with the participants' framework of relevance, but was codified in such a way that it allowed the participants to gain some critical distance from the matter being discussed. This process of gaining critical distance is referred to as praxis. Praxis is a key concept in the Freirean approach to education.

Praxis has a long history dating back to the time of the ancient Greeks and at least Aristotle. It involves reflection upon action for transformative learning and action. This is how Freire defines praxis in *Pedagogy of the Oppressed*:

> But human activity consists of action and reflection: it is praxis, it is transformation of the world. (Freire, 1970a/ 1993: 125)

Exile as Praxis

Freire goes on to say that the whole process involved needs to be enlightened through theory. It is praxis that lies at the heart of Paulo Freire's notion of critical literacy. Freire and other intellectuals, with whom he has conversed in talking books, conceive of different learning situations in their life as forms of praxis. This applies to adult learning in its broadest contexts including learning from life situations – informal learning. These situations are viewed as moments when people can gain critical distance from the context they know to perceive it in a more critical light. For instance, Freire and the Chilean Antonio Faundez considered exile a form of praxis (Freire and Faundez, 1989). Freire also makes statements to this effect in a book with Betto and Freire (1986). He refers to the period of exile as one that provided a profoundly pedagogical experience, thus echoing Frei Betto, who also presented, in the same discussion, his 4-year experience of imprisonment under the military dictatorship as one that had a strong and important pedagogical dimension. Freire's period of exile is presented as a time during which he gained distance from Brazil and began to understand himself and Brazil better. It was a case of obtaining distance from what he had carried out in Brazil to prepare himself better to continue being active outside his context.

Antithesis of Praxis: Empty Theorizing and Mindless Activism

Freire relates the whole process of action and reflection to theory and practice (ibid.). Freire's work underscores the point that action on its own, isolated from reflection, constitutes mindless activism. Likewise, reflection on its own, divorced from action, constitutes empty theorizing. It is for this reason that Freire, in keeping with the Marxist tradition, regards one's material surroundings as the basis for the development of one's consciousness. In the words of Marx and Engels, "Consciousness is, therefore, from the beginning a social product, and remains so as long as men (sic.) exist at all" (Marx and Engels, 1970: 51). The notion of praxis that lies at the heart of Freire's pedagogical approach and which informs learning contexts developed on Freirean lines is akin to Marx and Engels' notion of revolutionizing practice as expressed in the *Theses on Feuerbach*.

Dialectical Relations

The action–reflection–transformative action process is not sequential, but dialectical (Allman, 1999, 2001). In the introduction to the special issue of *Convergence* dedicated to Freire, Allman *et al.* (1998) state:

> Dialectical thinkers understand the internal relations among all phenomena. In the case of human beings or groups, this is a social relation which could be harmonious but which, thus far in history, normally has been antagonistic, resulting in various social relations that Freire collectively refers to as the oppressor-oppressed relation (e.g., class relations, gender, race, colonial, etc.) The antagonism is often so great that nothing short of

abolishing the dialectical relation will improve the situation. When there are no longer the two opposing groups, the possibility emerges of human beings uniting in love, with a commitment to social justice and to care for all of our social and natural world (Allman *et al.*, 1998: 10).

Teacher Student and Student Teachers

Learners can be assisted in this process of praxis, of coming to understand their reality in a more critical light, through a process of what Freire calls authentic dialog and participatory learning, as well as collective learning. The educator learns from the learners in the same way that the latter learn from her or him, the roles of educator and learner becoming almost interchangeable. In what has become a classic formulation, Freire wrote about the teacher student and students teachers. The educator is therefore regarded as a person who, while engaging in dialog with the learners, is also being taught by them. The learners, for their part, are also teaching while being taught (Freire, 1970a/1993: 80). In a dialog with Ira Shor, Freire states that:

> Liberatory education is fundamentally a situation where the teacher and the students *both* have to be learners, *both* have to be cognitive subjects, in spite of their being different. This for me is the first test of liberating education, for teachers and students both to be critical agents in the act of knowing. (Shor and Freire, 1987: 33)

Learner as Subject

The educator would therefore transcend the boundaries of his/her social location to understand and act in solidarity with the learners, no longer perceived as other. In adopting a Freirean approach, one would regard educators and learners as subjects in a humanizing relationship. Solidarity is the hallmark of this pedagogical relationship. The learner's reality constitutes an integral part of the subject matter that, therefore, becomes a mediator between the two subjects in question, that is, the educator and learner. Freire goes on to state that the dialogical process of education marks "the sealing together of the teacher and the students in the joint act of knowing and re-knowing the object" (Shor and Freire, 1987: 100). Borrowing from this conversation between Freire and Shor, one can argue that anything that the educator already knows is relearned when studied again with the learners, a point confirmed by Freire in the same conversation (ibid.).

Learners and Educators Not Equal

However, and here comes the apparent contradiction, a Freirean approach to learning based on dialog is one wherein educators and learners are not on an equal footing.

Obviously, we also have to underscore that while we recognize that we have to learn from our students . . . this does not mean that teachers and students are the same. . .there is a difference between the educator and the student. (Freire, 1985: 177)

Much depends on the specific situation in which the adult learning process occurs; however, it would be amiss to celebrate learner voices uncritically since they are never innocent (Aronowitz and Giroux, 1991: 130–131). They contain various manifestations of the oppressor consciousness which ought to be challenged. Dialog, as conceived by Freire, also involves educators allowing themselves to be challenged and to constantly undergo self-reflection and scrutiny to confront the oppressor consciousness within. In short, both educator and learner need to address their contradictions in an ongoing process of gaining greater coherence. The educator needs to help create the conditions whereby the learners develop the confidence necessary to challenge him or her where necessary in a situation of mutual respect and trust. This is part of the humility which, according to Freire, all critical educators must show.

Directive Approach

The directive nature of the educational process is affirmed (see, e.g., the discussion with Moacir Gadotti and Sergio Guimarães published in Brazil in 1989 – Gadotti et al., 1995: 50). Guarding against the perceived danger of a *laissez faire* pedagogy, resulting from a misconception of his particular notion of dialog, Freire emphasizes this directivity in the conversation with Ira Shor and elsewhere: "At the moment the teacher begins the dialogue, he or she knows a great deal, first in terms of knowledge and second in terms of the horizon that he or she wants to get to. The starting point is what the teacher knows about the object and where the teacher wants to go with it" (Shor and Freire, 1987: 103).

Freire makes it clear that he believes that the educators' pedagogical action is guided by a particular political vision and theoretical understanding. Freire, after all, considers education to be a political act, there being no such thing as a neutral education, with educators having to answer the question "for whom and on whose behalf they are working" (Freire, 1985: 180). Freire once stated that the learning experience entails a process of research and curiosity with all the elements involved – teacher, student, knowing object, methods, and techniques – providing direction (Fabbri and Gomes, 1995: 96). He argues that it is for this reason that every form of educational practice is directive, but not necessarily manipulative, and that every educational practice cannot be neutral; a directive practice cannot be neutral – no one is neutral when facing an objective to be reached (Fabbri and Gomes, 1995).

Authority and Authoritarianism

Educators therefore have a directive role; they need to exercise their authority, an authority derived from their competence as pedagogs. Freire, however, draws an important distinction between authority and authoritarianism. It is imperative that the authority derived from one's pedagogical competence does not degenerate into authoritarianism: ". . .the democratic teacher never, never transforms authority into authoritarianism" (Shor and Freire, 1987: 91; on this, also see Horton and Freire, 1990: 181). This authoritarianism would render the difference that exists between educator and learner antagonistic (Gadotti et al., 1995: 50). The educator exercises what Ira Shor calls democratic authority (Shor, 1992: 156–158).

What we have, therefore, in Freire's nuanced concept of dialog is a paradox rather than a contradiction. Freire provides a complex notion of learning and instruction, based on dialog. Freire (1974) feels that the traditional educator regards the knowledge he or she possesses, often captured in the lesson plan, as complete. The Freirean-inspired educator regards knowledge as dynamic, an object of co-investigation and unveiling that necessitates the participation of co-knowing subjects – the learners. The process of knowing involved, with respect to the object of knowledge, is considered by both educator and learner as incomplete (see Allman, 2001).

Tact and Prudence

Freire has even advocated tact and prudence when engaging in a dialogical approach, conceding that people who have been conditioned by many years of exposure to banking education do not immediately do away with this conditioning to embrace dialog. They often resist attempts at dialog, perhaps even misconstruing a dialogical approach for lack of competence on the educator's part. Freire concedes that some instruction is necessary at times. It is for this reason that he once stated that an educator can alternate between traditional and progressive teaching. It is as though he seems to be saying that, in such difficult circumstances, dialog should be introduced only gradually (see Horton and Freire, 1990: 160). Elements of the old pedagogy can coexist with the new in an overall context that, however, privileges democratic relations.

Given the strong relationship between knowledge and the learner's existential situation in Freire's approach, one assumes that the participant has a repository to draw on. This repository consists of one's life experience. The participant is therefore encouraged to draw on this experience in order to arrive at new knowledge and at a new awareness. In drawing on this experience, one is able to relate to the codified material. The educator enables this process to occur not by depositing knowledge, but by engaging the learner's critical faculties. Rather than being a dispenser of knowledge, the educator poses questions and problematizes issues. In this problem-posing education, the pedagogy applied is primarily not that of the answer, but that of the question (Bruss and Macedo, 1985).

Collective Dimensions of Learning

In adopting a democratic, dialogical approach, the circle or learning setting serves as a microcosm, indicating the potential that can exist within contexts characterized by democratic social relations. Furthermore, knowledge itself is democratized and is therefore not presented any longer as the preserve of a privileged minority. In addition, the knowledge disseminated is in itself democratic in that its starting point is the life experienced by the participants and it serves their interest. Finally, it is group knowledge that emerges from this experience that emphasizes the collective dimensions of learning and of action for social change. Freire argued that one engages in the task of becoming more fully human not on one's own (it is not an individualistic endeavor), but in solidarity with others (Freire, 1970a/1993: 85–86). This having been said, one eventually moves beyond the here and now to gain a greater level of awareness. "Educands' concrete localization is the point of departure for the knowledge they create of the world" (Freire, 1994: 85). It is just the point of departure; for the here and now represents only the starting point of an ongoing adult learning process and not the endpoint. Remaining within the here and now constitutes, according to Freire, a case of populism or *basismo*. In remaining there and not moving beyond (through co-investigation of the object of inquiry), one would be engaging in basism, the romanticization (or mythification) of the vernacular (see Freire, 1994: 84).

It is this aspect of a Freire-inspired theory of instruction, learning, and curriculum planning that renders it quite different from the more liberal notion of learning through dialog which, often, erroneously passes off as Freirean.

The insights we derive from Freire, with regard to program planning, learning, and instruction in adult education, are described in the following section.

Planning Together

One should not enter the community and impose a program on its members, but should, on the contrary, engage with a team of researchers, preferably including people with different disciplinary backgrounds and certainly including both educators and potential project participants (the adult learners), in studying the community, where the learning setting is to be developed, at close hand. This process of study or research comprises informal meetings with community members. The planning of materials occurs on the basis of the insights and information gleaned from the research.

Learning and Instruction

Learning Based on Action and Reflection

The approach throughout is one based on praxis involving critical reflection on the area of action, which also involves recourse to theory, but which entails an authentic notion of dialog in which the subject of enquiry is the focus of collective co-investigation. The research leads to insights which are to form the basis of the codified learning material whereby the educator enables the learners to gain critical distance from the community they know to be able to perceive it in a different, hopefully more critical, light. The same applies to the adult educator herself or himself who also gains critical distance from the object of co-investigation and can come to perceive it in a more critical light. We have seen how even exile is viewed by Freire and co-authors, engaged in dialog with him, as a form of praxis, of gaining critical distance.

Adult educators working with migrants in this ever-growing context for adult education can take a leaf out of Freire's book. One of the challenges for critical pedagogical work with migrants, to emerge from this Freirean insight, is that of enabling the migrants to read not only the world they now inhabit as immigrants, but also the world they left through a process of obtaining critical distance from their context of origin. This can hopefully lead to a greater understanding of the politics of their own dislocation.

Dynamic Knowledge

Through this process of praxis, based on reflection on action, knowledge is conceived as dynamic rather than static. The approach to learning is directive since learning is conceived as a political act. The roles of adult educator and adult learner are almost interchangeable, as all learn from each other, but this is not to say that the adult learner and adult educator are on an equal footing. The latter must have a certain amount of authority which should not be allowed to degenerate into authoritarianism lest the spirit of genuine dialog be destroyed.

Starting with the Learners' Existential Realities

Only through dialog does the group collectively learn to unveil the contradictions that underlie the reality on which it is focusing. Adult educators are encouraged to show tact when promoting dialogical relations and there are moments when they temper dialog with a certain degree of instruction, especially on consideration that people exposed to banking education for years do not embrace dialog easily. The starting point of co-investigation is the learner's existential reality which is, however, not the be all and end all of the learning process, lest one be guilty of populism or *basismo*. Adult educators must demonstrate the humility necessary to be disposed to relearn that which they think they already know through their dialogic interactions with the rest of the learning group or community.

Bibliography

Allman, P. (1999). *Revolutionary Social Transformation: Democratic Hopes, Political Possibilities and Critical Education*. Westport, CT: Bergin and Garvey.
Allman, P. (2001). *Critical Education against Global Capitalism. Karl Marx and Revolutionary Critical Education*. Westport, CT: Bergin and Garvey.
Allman, P., Mayo, P., Cavanagh, C., Lean Heng, C., and Haddad, S. (1998). Introduction. ''...the creation of a world in which it will be easier to love'' *Convergence* **XX1**(1 and 2), 9–16.
Aronowitz, S. and Giroux, H. (1991). *Postmodern Education*. Minneapolis, MN: University of Minnesota Press.
Betto, F. and Freire, P. (1986). *Una Scuola Chiamata Vita*. Bologna: E.M.I.
Bruss, N. and Macedo, D. (1985). Toward a pedagogy of the question: Conversations with Paulo Freire. *Journal of Education* **167**, 7–21.
Fabbri, F. and Gomes, A. M. (1995). La mia pedagogia: Paulo Freire risponde a professori e studenti bolognesi. In Gadotti, M., Freire, P., Guimarães, S., Bellanova, B., and Telleri, F. (eds.) *Pedagogia: dialogo e conflitto*, pp 92–103. Torino: Società Editrice Internazionale.
Freire, P. (1970a/1993). *Pedagogy of the Oppressed*, 30th anniversary edn. New York: Continuum.
Freire, P. (1974). *Authority versus Authoritarianism. Audiotape, in Series: Thinking with Paulo Freire*. Sydney, NSW: Australian Council of Churches.
Freire, P. (1985). *The Politics of Education*. South Hadley, MA: Bergin and Garvey.
Freire, P. (1994). *Pedagogy of Hope*. New York: Continuum.
Freire, P. and Faundez, A. (1989). *Learning to Question. A Pedagogy of Liberation*. Geneva: World Council of Churches.
Gadotti, M., Freire, P., and Guimarães, S. (1995). *Pedagogia: dialogo e conflitto*. (Bellanova, B. and Telleri, F. (eds.)). Torino: Società Editrice Internazionale.
Horton, M. and Freire, P. (1990). *We Make the Road by Walking. Conversations on Education and Social Change*. Philadelphia, PA: Temple University Press.
Marx, K. and Engels, F. (1970). *The German Ideology*. Arthur, C. J. (ed.). London: Lawrence and Wishart.
O'Cadiz, P., Wong, P. L., and Torres, C. A. (1997). *Education and Democracy. Paulo Freire, Social Movements and Educational Reform in São Paulo*. Boulder, CO: Westview Press.
Schugurensky, D. (1996). Paulo Freire: From pedagogy of the oppressed to pedagogy of hope. In Reno, H. and Witte, M. (eds.) *37th Annual AERC Proceedings*. Tampa: University of Florida.
Shor, I. (1992). *Empowering Education. Critical Teaching for Social Change*. Chicago, IL: The University of Chicago Press.
Shor, I. and Freire, P. (1987). *Pedagogy for Liberation Dialogues on Transforming Education*. South Hadley, MA: Bergin and Garvey.
Torres, C. A. (1982). From the pedagogy of the oppressed to a Luta Continua – the political pedagogy of Paulo Freire. *Education with Production* **2**, 76–97.

Further Reading

Darder, A. (2002). *Reinventing Paulo Freire. A Pedagogy of Love*. Boulder, CO: Westview Press.
Gadotti, M. (1994). *Reading Paulo Freire. His Life and Work*. Albany, NY: SUNY Press.
Gadotti, M. (1996). *Pedagogy of Praxis. A Dialectical Philosophy of Education*. Albany, NY: SUNY Press.
Kidd, R. and Kumar, K. (1981). Co-opting Freire: A critical analysis of pseudo-Freirean adult education. *Economic and Political Weekly* **XVI** (1–2), 27–36.
Kirkwood, G. and Kirkwood, C. (1989). *Living Adult Education: Freire in Scotland*. Milton Keynes, UK: Open University Press.
Marx, K. and Engels, F. (1978). *The Marx–Engels Reader*. (Tucker, R. (ed.)). New York: W.W. Norton.
Mayo, P. (2004). *Liberating Praxis. Paulo Freire's Legacy for Radical Education and Politics*. Westport, CT: Praeger.
Roberts, P. (2000). *Education, Literacy, and Humanization Exploring the Work of Paulo Freire*. Westport, CT: Bergin and Garvey.
Saul, A. M. (1995). Municipal educational policy in the city of São Paulo, Brazil (1988–1991). In Torres, C. A. (ed.) *Education and Social Change in Latin America*, pp 155–162. Melbourne, VIC: James Nicholas Publishers.
Shor, I. (1999). What is critical literacy? *Journal for Pedagogy, Pluralism and Practice* **4**(1). http://www.lesley.edu/journals/jppp/intro.html (accessed May 2009).
Steiner, S., Krank, M., McLaren, P., and Bahruth, R. (eds.) (2000). *Freirean Pedagogy, Praxis, and Possibilities. Projects for the New Millennium*. New York: Falmer.
Stromquist, N. (1997). *Literacy for Citizenship; Gender and Grassroots Dynamics in Brazil*. Albany, NY: SUNY Press.
Taylor, P. V. (1993). *The Texts of Paulo Freire*. Buckingham, UK: Open University Press.
Telleri, F. (ed.) (2002). *Il Metodo Paulo Freire. Nuove technologie e sviluppo sostenibile*. Bologna: CLUEB.
Torres, C. A. (1993). From the pedagogy of the oppressed to a Luta Continua – the political pedagogy of Paulo Freire. In McLaren, P. and Leonard, P. (eds.) *Paulo Freire: A Critical Encounter*, pp 119–145. London: Routledge.
Torres, C. A. (1994). Paulo Freire as secretary of education in the municipality of São Paulo. *Comparative Education Review* **38**, 181–214.

Workplace-Learning Frameworks

S Billett, Griffith University, Brisbane, QLD, Australia

Glossary

Duality – Two related phenomena who enjoy some degree of interdependence (i.e., the opposite of a dualism.

Educational purposes – The kinds of goals, aims, and objectives to which educational efforts should be directed.

Integrating experiences – Drawing on and reconciling experiences from different settings to assist secure the contributions from both settings and thereby.

Learning environments – Social and/or physical spaces that afford experiences and activities, that by degree invite and are supportive of individuals' learning.

Personal epistemologies – The bases by which individuals initiate, direct, monitor, and evaluate their processes of thinking and acting, and learning, not the least through how they construe and construct what they experience.

Rich or robust learning – Learning that is not restricted in its applicability to the circumstances of its generation.

Socially rich environment – Social settings that provide close guidance, by expert or more experienced social partners as well as opportunities to observe and imitate the performances of more expert counterparts.

Emerging and Growing Interest in Workplace Learning

There is a growing interest in workplace learning. This seems set to continue as the securing of skills throughout working life becomes, globally, an important priority for governments, industry, and workers themselves. Currently, workplace experiences are acknowledged as playing important roles in preparing for working life. These include assisting individuals identify preferred occupations, experiencing and understanding the world of work, and most commonly, contributing to the initial preparation of their skills for paid work. Yet now, and in their own right, these experiences are seen to offer an effective means for maintaining skill currency right across working lives, meeting enterprises' special needs, and maintaining the effectiveness of older workers. Together, these represent important social and economic purposes and in ways that are often tightly intertwined.

In effect, recently, workplaces have moved from being seen as providing experiences to support learning in educational institutions, to providing important social and economic purposes. These are associated with developing further and maintaining occupational competence, enterprise-specific skills, government economic imperatives for a competitive economy, including assisting workers resist redundancy, enhancing learning occurring in educational institutions and individuals' needs to develop and maintain skilfulness. Such an array of expanded purposes warrants adequate frameworks for understanding about how these kinds of learning might be provided for through workplace experiences.

There has also been a growth in scholarship about learning through work providing conceptual and procedural accounts of adults' learning in and throughout working life. These developments can inform both the kinds of pragmatic and strategic concerns outlined above, as well as those about learning in general, and how learning can be supported through activities in workplace settings. These include understanding the central role of the negotiations between the personal and social contributions to that learning. It is through a consideration of such purposes and these conceptual and procedural developments that frameworks for considering, organizing, promoting, and evaluating adults' learning through work can be best advanced.

Such frameworks need to be informed by a consideration of the purposes for this learning, conceptions of the processes of learning through work, and in what ways these experiences might be better ordered to secure particular kinds of learning for these purposes. This includes identifying what kinds of practices have demonstrated efficacy in supporting learning and the potential to guide workplace experiences toward particular outcomes. Moreover, there are perennial issues about the worth and legitimacy of the purposes, circumstances, and processes of workplaces as learning environments. Rather than accepting their worth, contributions and legitimacy in terms of a site for learning that predates educational institutions as we know them today, workplaces are seen as being inferior and subordinate to those institutions.

In advancing bases for a framework for workplace learning, this article first outlines some purposes for and conceptions of learning through work. Then, it discusses procedural and conceptual developments that shape and reshape workplace-learning frameworks. It concludes by offering some parameters for such a framework principally comprising a duality between what the workplace affords learners in terms of opportunities and support, and how individuals engage with these affordances as they learn through their experiences.

Purposes of Learning Through Workplace Experiences

There are three broad categories of purposes for the provision of workplace-learning experiences. The first is contributing to educational processes about preparation for work and working life. This includes assisting individuals understand the requirements for working life and to identify which occupation they are suited to and interested in. For those in the structured program of occupational preparation in schools, universities, and college, workplace experiences are also used to practice, augment, and extend learning secured in educational institutions. Second, for many entering work or occupations, there is no available or accessible education provision. Hence, workplaces are the only source of learning experiences, to develop the capacities for performing that work. Third, as foreshadowed, beyond initial preparation, there are growing imperatives of governments, employers, and workers themselves to maintain skills throughout working life in order to resist redundancy, make effective work transitions as occupational requirements change, and contribute to the workplace's continuity and development and to the economic prosperity of their communities. Added to these are growing concerns about older workers and others who are marginalized groups (e.g., disabled, nonnative speakers, etc.) who often need to maintain their employment viability with limited assistance from their employers.

The prospect for realizing these purposes through learning in workplaces was granted legitimacy and buoyed by the situated-cognition movement of the late 1980s and early 1990s (Brown *et al.*, 1989; Collins *et al.*, 1989). This movement emphasized the particular contributions to learning from the settings in which practice occurred and evidence that strategic as well as situationally specific learning can be realized through such experiences (Raizen, 1991). Yet, the key motivation behind this research was to improve experiences in educational institutions (Resnick, 1987), by understanding processes of transfer from one setting or activity to another. Considerations of situationally distinct goals for practice and contributions for learning through practice offered an explanation for the paucity of the transfer of learning from educational institutions to circumstances and practices beyond educational

institutions (Newman *et al.*, 1984, 1989). Indeed, research into the situated nature of learning often looked to workplaces as sites of authentic practices and how learning arose through participation in work activities. However, more recent accounts have now focused on the learning potential of workplaces, and include not just a consideration of their physical and social settings, but also on those who engage in and learn through work.

Occupation preparation for both the professions and trades has long engaged students in extensive periods of occupational practice in workplaces. Concerns about postschool pathways and transitions are also now leading to schools providing workplace experiences to assist students understand the world of work beyond schools. Moreover, concerns about the transition from university and the applicability of what is learned there to practice in employment is motivating universities in a growing number of countries to engage their students in professional experiences, and finding ways of integrating these experiences with those within higher education programs. Although long exercised in teacher, nurse, and medical education, these kinds of experiences are now being extended across university programs preparing graduates for professional occupations. The cooperative education movement of North America is a longstanding response to this education concern. Yet, even so, genuine efforts to integrate the learning experiences, such as these, are until now the exception, yet are important for securing rich learning from the contributions of both settings.

Therefore, the purposes for considering workplaces as learning environments in their own right and as making distinct and legitimate contributions to educational institutions' programs and curriculum stand as important bases for understanding and appraising workplace learning.

Conceptions of Workplaces as Learning Environments

To understand workplaces as worthwhile places to learn in, it is necessary to capture their qualities, demonstrate their legitimacy, and advance ways in which their contributions can be fully engaged. Certainly, there has been long-held acceptance of the value of learning through practice and through workplaces. Plato describes the process of learning to become artisans and artists as that occurring through association, imitation, and practice, starting with play, within the family of artists and artisans and in the circumstances of practice. As Lodge (1947) notes "... at first, the imitation would be playful and childish, carried out with such toy tools as a child could handle. Later it would become more deliberately purposive. Practice produced technical proficiency in detail and the growing boy would act first as his father's 'helper', then as his associate, and would eventually himself become the head of a family, and the centre from which further training in the family craft would radiate" (Lodge, 1947: 17). Yet, far earlier, similar processes were used in ancient Babylonia (Bennett, 1938). Subsequently, traditions of learning through practice for occupational purposes extended well into the medieval times, buoyed by the practices and power of guilds (Deissinger, 2002). Indeed, most of the buildings, structures, and artifacts from these times, and at which we now marvel, were the product of learning through work practice. The skills for constructing the great European cathedrals progressed in similar ways to those which Plato described in Hellenic times (Gimpel, 1961).

Therefore, long before education institutions were created for these purposes, generations of skilled artisans across Europe and elsewhere learned their skilled work through work-related learning experiences alone. Indeed, it was the impact of the decline of the guilds and the erosion of work-based experiences in some European countries that created the need for specific educational institutions. However, despite the growth of educational institutions for such purposes, experience of practice has been sustained to this day in the trades and the professions. Indeed, they are now being enacted more widely across countries and educational sectors. Yet, there is often a parsimonious acknowledgement of the quality of learning processes and outcomes that arise through these practice experiences. Typically, they are still seen as experiencing practice, rather than important sites for learning and as being less desirable and potent than learning through participation in educational institutions. Even in programs for the trades and professions, these experiences are often seen as primarily to apply or practice what has been learned in educational institutions. For instance, rarely are these components explicitly integrated into the curriculum or assessed, in ways that are commensurate with their contribution to student learning.

So, despite these traditions and now-emerging imperatives for workplace-learning experiences, their status still stands as being inferior, rather than different from what is provided and experienced in educational institutions. A significant barrier is legitimating learning through practice in an era where strong associations between teaching and learning have become embedded through universal compulsory and lengthy education, and in which teaching is seen as the way in which important learning is best mediated. While those who have learned occupational practice invariably report the importance of learning through practice, it still lacks the broader legitimacy, standing, and credibility of certified learning through participation in educational institutions. This seems to be the case across all education sectors, including those whose purpose is to develop specific vocational

knowledge (i.e., schools, colleges, and universities). Indeed, institutions express concern that their academic standing may be jeopardized through the inclusion of work-based experiences. In addition, there are fears that some educational norms, such as a liberal and critical education are being threatened by such inclusions (Boud *et al.*, 2001). Not surprisingly, in the discourses of educational institutions and practice, teaching is privileged over learning. Therefore, as (Marsick and Watkins, 1990) identified earlier, the absence of written curriculum, qualified teachers, and experiences purposely focused on individuals' learning, may lead to workplace experiences as being inevitably inferior.

However, such claims do not stand scrutiny. As studies from anthropology have found, robust (i.e., transferable) learning can arise as much through experiences outside of those organized and enacted in educational institutions, as in other settings (Rogoff and Gauvain, 1984). Indeed, anthropological literatures have provided helpful accounts of this kind of learning and evidence of their efficacy (Lave, 1990; Pelissier, 1991; Rogoff, 1990; Rogoff and Lave, 1984). So, experiences in educational institutions are not necessarily better at developing these kinds of knowledge. More likely, it is the kinds and combinations of activities and interactions that are afforded learners and how they engage with them that are central to the development of this knowledge, and not where these experiences occur. These then suggest a need to understand and appraise workplace learning through a consideration of both personal and social contributions to the processes and outcomes of that learning.

It seems that frameworks for understanding learning through work in contemporary times are well-served by a long tradition of learning through practice. These accounts also characterize workplaces as environments for learning, not just for experiencing and trialing and refining knowledge learned elsewhere. They refer to contributions such as activities, interactions, artifacts, and others as being pedagogic and purposive for learning, thereby offering frames for pedagogies and curriculum models for the workplace. Importantly, rather than didactic and school-like accounts of supporting learning, indirect forms of guidance and highly active roles for learners emerge as key qualities of these learning environments. The organization of learning through activities and interactions, and the active process of observation and rehearsal stand as central elements of the workplace curriculum and pedagogic practices as identified in these accounts.

Therefore, much of a first generation of recent research was directed at understanding how workplace experiences might improve learning experiences in educational institutions (i.e., schools, colleges, and universities). However, building on these accounts, a second generation of research is now giving more attention to the particular attributes of sites and circumstances of practice (e.g., work and workplaces) as places to both participate and learn. For instance, theoretical and procedural considerations of the pedagogic qualities of different kinds of work (Colin, 2004; Nerland and Jensen, 2006), learning through errors (Bauer and Mulder, 2007), the active role of the learner (Billett, 2006b), their subjectivity and sense of self (Somerville and Abrahamsson, 2003), and the complex entanglements between personal interests and capacities and those of the workplace (Fenwick, 2004) have arisen from quite different traditions than mainstream education.

Conceptual and Procedural Advances

Conceptual advances associated with learning through work are aligned to those associated with the processes of learning more generally. Central among these are the greater emphasis on learning, instead of teaching, as is consistent with the growing purchase of constructivism, and the acknowledgement of situational contributions, in ways analogous to social constructivism. The former indicates acceptance of an expansive and active role for the learners, and positions them as being central mediators of what they experience and how and what they learn, thereby emphasizing personal epistemologies. Here, central to individuals' participation, mediation, and learning is their agency, capacity, and subjectivity. These are central to how they construe and construct their knowledge. The later acknowledges how the tasks, activities, and settings in which learners participate afford particular kinds of contributions, which in terms of workplace learning can be understood as pedagogic qualities of work settings. Both of these emphasize participation in work and learning as a dualistic conception comprising the contributions of social setting and the person. These advances are now discussed briefly in turn.

Self and Agency of Learners

The need for learners to be actively engaged in the process of learning is widely accepted within many, and probably most, contemporary theories and concepts of learning. This includes how they construe, construct, and interact with what they experience. However, this is particularly salient to considerations of learning through work and in workplaces. In provisions for learning offered through educational institutions, the teacher has a key mediating role in assisting the learner and guiding his/ her development. However, while a range of guidance is available in work settings, including close guidance by more expert others, although usually on an intermittent basis, learners will necessarily mediate much of their own learning (Fuller and Unwin, 2003). This is also likely to be true of provisions that seek to integrate that learning in

both the educational and workplace setting, such as in apprenticeships, and now increasingly for professional preparation. This is because it is the learners who will have experiences in both kinds of settings and others' role are to assist them maximize their learning through integrating the contributions of both kinds of experiences.

So, the interests, intentions, and direction of learners come to the fore here and their agency will shape the potential to realize rich outcomes through these experiences. Moreover, the self and subjectivities as driving their learning in setting and securing rich learning outcomes will not be limited to workplace-learning experiences of this kind. A key basis for ongoing learning throughout working life will likely be directed by what motivates, directs, and focuses individuals' efforts at learning through work. For instance and in particular, it seems for older workers, semiskilled, those of color or with a disability, personal agency will be central in managing their learning through work, as the evidence suggests these workers are those least likely to be afforded workplace support for their learning.

To this end, there needs to be a greater decentering of the focus of learning through work from the physical and social attributes of the setting to accommodate the contributions of learners to workplaces as learning environments. Helpful accounts of personal epistemologies and learner agency have been generated in recent work (Hodkinson and Hodkinson, 2004). Many of these emphasize the relations and negotiations between individual workers' and their workplaces' (i.e., the personal and the situated) contributions to learning workplace practices, techniques, norms, etc. Such accounts illuminate how individuals likely elect to respond to governmental imperatives and employer requests to learn continually throughout working life. For instance, they advise governments and employers that their ambitions for lifelong workplace learning are unlikely to be realized unless more consideration is given to the needs, interests, and personal trajectories of those who they are exhorting to learn. Consequently, frameworks for workplace learning need to include considerations of the salience of personal epistemologies and the need to develop these for learning throughout working life, and in ways consistent with accommodating individuals' occupational trajectories. Yet, these epistemologies comprise more than personal strategies; they are central to and shaped by individuals' subjectivities and sense of self. This means that engaging the learners' interest is more than a nicety; it becomes an important imperative for efforts aligned with lifelong learning.

Pedagogic Qualities of Workplaces

Earlier socially orientated accounts of the contributions to learning of physical and social settings, such as communities of practice (Lave and Wenger, 1991) and activity systems (Engestrom, 1993), advanced the pedagogic qualities of workplaces in terms of shared premises for participation and learning, and social system that shape participation and learning. However, recent accounts of the social contributions to learning through work have provided more elaborated accounts of the pedagogic qualities and potential of workplace settings. Some of these detail the pedagogic qualities of particular kinds of work and workplaces, while others provide more detailed considerations of the artifacts and practices in workplaces that contribute to learning, including the kinds and qualities of interactions, that lead authors to refer to their epistemic qualities. These are helpful as they lend finesse and refine earlier accounts. This then permits more comprehensive and detailed accounts of how the contributions of workplace settings can work to shape learning and how these might best be exploited to achieve particular kinds of learning outcomes.

Moreover, as considerations of workplace as learning environments have matured, the range of procedural responses has also grown. What is distinct about these provisions is that they center on the provision of workplace as learning experiences in their own right and not to augment or extend learning from other sources (i.e., educational programs). These include learning from work errors – how both qualities of workplace environments and workers' personal dispositions shape the prospect of learning purposively through workplace errors (Bauer and Mulder, 2007), learning projects (Poell, 2006), critical reflections through work experiences (van Woerkom, 2003), guided learning in the workplace (Billett, 2001), expanding learning opportunities (Fuller and Unwin, 2004), and the development of a workplace curriculum (Billett, 2006a). In different ways, these kinds of approaches open up considerations for the means by which workplace pedagogies can be developed, which stand as a key premise for framing workplace learning.

Yet, there are important conceptual and procedural goals still to be secured. For instance, much conceptual developments is premised on learners being in socially rich circumstances that provide models, guidance, etc. However, many workers are physically and socially isolated and therefore do not engage in or learn through these kinds of socially rich environments. Therefore, much needs to be known about learning in these relatively socially weak environments. Contemporary and emerging occupational and workplace practice is such that workers may be only afforded access to particular kinds of workplace experiences, those related to their occupation alone, and possibly not those that are sufficient for the comprehensive development of the workplace. So, understanding further how these kinds of knowledge can be developed stand as important goals. Then, there is the need to learn symbolic forms of knowledge and those that are not

opaque (Bresnahan *et al.*, 2002; Zuboff, 1988) or easy to learn, thereby requiring intentional pedagogic practices that can make this knowledge accessible and comprehensible. Moreover, a key concern about learning through practice is that uncritically accepting practices of the past and present may not assist the learning requirements for the future. More needs to be done to assist improving the equity of the affordances of opportunity, considering how workplace-learning opportunities are asymmetrically distributed on the basis of age, gender, language, and educational-achievement levels. Hence, there has to be a critical and questioning element to a framework that advances learning through work. Therefore, frameworks supporting and extending learning through work, need to constantly and critically examine the kinds and processes of learning that arise through participation in work and how these forms of learning can be aligned with the array of purposes to which they are directed (e.g., rich occupational knowledge).

Workplace-Learning Frameworks

At a macro level, frameworks for organizing adult learning in workplaces or pedagogies for the workplace have commonalities with those for other settings, albeit manifested in conceptions of epistemology, curriculum, and pedagogy in ways that reflect the particular kinds of social practices that comprise workplaces. These are premised on a set of practices that support learning that predates those of schooling. Overall, the commonalities include considerations of what is provided by the setting to support learning (i.e., its affordances) and how individuals elect to engage with, participate, and mediate in what is afforded them by the setting. These framing considerations are equally applicable for adults' learning across a range of social institutions (e.g., universities, colleges, communities, and workplaces). In curriculum terms, each of these has purposes (i.e., intentions for learning), enactments (e.g., means of supporting that learning), individuals who can support learning (e.g., teachers and coworkers), and learners (e.g., students and workers) that mediate how and what they learn through what they experience in these settings. Yet, there are some distinctions in the particular kinds of experiences, workplaces, and educational institutions afford, ways in which learners identify themselves and elect to participate in learning and for what purposes. The premises of workplace curriculum and pedagogy will be founded on practices being enacted in workplaces (the provisions of goods or services) as directed toward learning occupational knowledge as per the workplace's particular requirements. This may be distinct from the stated aim of educational institutions – intentional learning for an occupation. The identity and bases for participation by workers, some of who will be guiding the work and learning of others (e.g., more experienced workers), is likely to be distinct from those who see themselves as teachers and students in educational institutions, and feature a strongly agentic role for learners. Yet, these are largely minor distinctions, thereby holding that learning through work can be informed, legitimated, and understood and appraised through orthodox curriculum concepts and pedagogic practices, and that there are also distinct features and characteristics that can be accounted for in these frameworks.

Therefore, in all, a framework for understanding learning through work can be founded on the dualities of what the workplace affords to those employed within them and how those individuals elect to engage with what is afforded them. Learning through practice, through errors, and by processes of observation and imitation, practice, and the direct guidance of experienced coworkers all stand as key elements of that framework. Besides, the kinds of work practices, and personal values and bases of identity, shape these dualities and the relations between them. In addition, the purposes of learning and the desired outcomes of that learning also stand as important foundations for making judgments about the value of that learning and how it might best be enhanced. These enhancements may well be realized through work activities or require particular and targeted intervention as perhaps increasingly, components of work-related knowledge become inaccessible and need to be made explicit.

Bibliography

Bauer, J. and Mulder, R. H. (2007). Modelling learning from errors in daily work. *Learning in Health and Social Care* **6**, 121–133.

Bennett, C. A. (1938). The ancestry of vocational education. In Lee, E. A. (ed.) *Objectives and Problems of Vocational Education,* 2nd edn., pp 1–19. New York: McGraw-Hill Book.

Billett, S. (2001). *Learning in the Workplace: Strategies for Effective Practice*. Sydney: Allen and Unwin.

Billett, S. (2006a). Constituting the workplace curriculum. *Journal of Curriculum Studies* **38**(1), 31–48.

Billett, S. (2006b). Relational interdependence between social and individual agency in work and working life. *Mind, Culture and Activity* **13**(1), 53–69.

Boud, D., Solomon, N., and Symes, C. (2001). New practices for new times. In Boud, D. and Solomon, N. (eds.) *Work-Based Learning: A New Higher Education?* pp 3–17. Buckingham: Open University Press.

Bresnahan, T. F., Brynjolsson, E., and Hitt, L. (2002). Information technology, workplace organisation and the demand for labor: Firm-level evidence. *Quarterly Journal of Economics* **117**(1), 339–376.

Brown, J. S., Collins, A., and Duguid, P. (1989). Situated cognition and the culture of learning. *Educational Researcher* **18**(1), 32–34.

Colin, K. (2004). Workplace's learning and life. *International Journal of Lifelong Learning* **4**(1), 24–38.

Collins, A., Brown, J. S., and Newman, S. E. (1989). Cognitive apprenticeship: Teaching the crafts of reading, writing and mathematics. In Resnick, L. B. (ed.) *Knowledge, Learning and Instruction, Essays in Honour of Robert Glaser*, pp 453–494. Hillsdale, NJ: Erlbaum.

Deissinger, T. (2002). Apprenticeship systems in England and Germany: Decline and survival. *Paper Presented at the Towards a History of Vocational Education and Training (VET) in Europe in a Comparative Perspective*, Florence.

Engestrom, Y. (1993). Development studies of work as a testbench of activity theory: The case of primary care medical practice. In Chaiklin, S. and Lave, J. (eds.) *Understanding Practice: Perspectives on Activity and Context*, pp 64–103. Cambridge, UK: Cambridge University Press.

Fenwick, T. (2004). Learning in portfolio work: Anchored innovation in and mobile identity. *Studies in Continuing Education* **26**(2), 229–246.

Fuller, A. and Unwin, A. (2003). Fostering workplace learning: Looking through the lens of apprenticeships. *European Educational Research Journal* **2**(1), 41–55.

Fuller, A. and Unwin, L. (2004). Expansive learning environments: Integrating organisational and personal development. In Rainbird, H., Fuller, A., and Munroe, A. (eds.) *Workplace Learning in Context*, pp 126–144. London: Routledge.

Gimpel, J. (1961). *The Cathedral Builders*. New York: Grove Press.

Hodkinson, P. H. and Hodkinson, H. (2004). The significance of individuals' dispositions in the workplace learning: A case study of two teachers. *Journal of Education and Work* **17**(2), 167–182.

Lave, J. (1990). The culture of acquisition and the practice of understanding. In Stigler, J. W., Shweder, R. A., and Herdt, G. (eds.) *Cultural Psychology*, pp 259–286. Cambridge, UK: Cambridge University Press.

Lave, J. and Wenger, E. (1991). *Situated Learning – Legitimate Peripheral Participation*. Cambridge, UK: Cambridge University Press.

Lodge, R. C. (1947). *Plato's Theory of Education*. London: Kegan Paul, Trench, Trubner.

Marsick, V. J. and Watkins, K. (1990). *Informal and Incidental Learning in the Workplace*. London: Routledge.

Nerland, M. and Jensen, K. (2006). Insourcing the management of knowledge and occupational control: An analysis of computer engineers in Norway. *International Journal of Lifelong Education* **26**(3), 263–278.

Newman, D., Griffin, P., and Cole, M. (1984). Social constraints in laboratory and classroom task. In Rogoff, B. and Lave, J. (eds.) *Everyday Cognition: Its Development in Social Context*, pp 172–193. Cambridge, MA: Harvard University Press.

Newman, D., Griffin, P., and Cole, M. (1989). *The Construction Zone: Working for Cognitive Change in Schools*. Cambridge, UK: Cambridge University Press.

Pelissier, C. (1991). The anthropology of teaching and learning. *Annual Review of Anthropology* **20**, 75–95.

Poell, R. (2006). Organising learning projects whilst improving work: Strategies for employees, managers and HRD specialists. In Streumer, J. N. (ed.) *Work-Related Learning*, pp 71–94. Dordrecht: Springer.

Raizen, S. A. (1991). *Learning and Work: The Research Base. Vocational Education and Training for Youth: Towards Coherent Policy and Practice*. Paris: OECD.

Resnick, L. (1987). Learning in school and out. *Educational Researcher* **16**(9), 13–20.

Rogoff, B. (1990). *Apprenticeship in Thinking – Cognitive Development in Social Context*. New York: Oxford University Press.

Rogoff, B. and Gauvain, M. (1984). The cognitive consequences of specific experiences – weaving versus schooling among the Navajo. *Journal of Cross-Cultural Psychology* **15**(4), 453–475.

Rogoff, B. and Lave, J. (eds.) (1984). *Everyday Cognition: Its Development in Social Context*. Cambridge, MA: Harvard University Press.

Somerville, M. and Abrahamsson, L. (2003). Trainers and learners constructing a community of practice: Masculine work cultures and learning safety in the mining industry. *Studies in the Education of Adults* **35**(1), 19–34.

van Woerkom, M. (2003). *Critical Reflection at Work*. Enschede: Twente University.

Zuboff, S. (1988). *In the Age of the Smart Machine: The Future of Work and Power*. New York: Basic Books.

Organizational Learning

P-E Ellström, Linköping University, Linköping, Sweden

Although organizational learning has been a subject of research within management and organizational studies at least since the early 1960s, interest in this concept has grown considerably since the late 1980s. Important driving forces for this development have been the globalization and growing corporate competition, and thereby, an increasing interest in finding alternatives to established forms of organization. This development was mirrored not least in the movement to abandon traditional Tayloristic and bureaucratic models of work organization in favor of allegedly more flexible and integrated work systems, that is, what has been characterized as high-commitment work systems. The performance of these types of new work systems is assumed to critically depend on their capacity to create favorable conditions for organizational learning.

Today the concept of organizational learning has become established not only within economic and management disciplines, but also within behavioral and social science disciplines such as psychology, education, and sociology. Considering empirical research on organizational learning, it is clear that there is and has been a predominance of studies within private companies. This is the case in spite of the fact that many of the early studies by researchers such as Argyris, Cyert, and March were also carried out in governmental agencies and educational institutions. However, over the last decade there has been an increase in the number of studies of organizational learning in, for example, schools, military organizations, public administration, political organizations, and unions. Considering education specifically, the interest in organizational learning is presently clearly visible in at least three areas of educational research: school development and innovative schools, human resource development (HRD), and workplace learning.

The Field of Organizational Learning

The field of organizational learning is characterized by an increasing diversity and specialization. In order to map key topics within the field of organizational learning, Easterby-Smith and Lyles (2003) distinguish between four subfields within the general field of organizational learning: organizational learning, the learning organization, organizational knowledge, and knowledge management. The first of these four subfields, organizational learning, refers to descriptive and explanatory studies of learning processes of and within organizations. That is, studies of organizational learning largely from an academic knowledge interest, aiming at an understanding and critique of what is.

In contrast to this, the learning organization subfield is characterized by more practical and normative knowledge interests. A learning organization is viewed as an ideal type of organization (or a vision of an organization), which has the capacity not only to facilitate the learning of its members, but also to transform this learning into continuous organizational renewal. The literature within this subfield focuses on how to create and improve the learning capacity of an organization through different types of intervention. One of the most well-known contributions to this subfield is the book on learning organizations by Peter Senge in 1990.

Turning to the remaining two subfields, the subfield called organizational knowledge refers to attempts to understand the nature of knowledge and processes of knowledge production within and between organizations. Within this subfield, there are studies of not only what has become known as knowledge work, but also studies of knowledge creation and the sharing and integration of organizational knowledge and competence. A key contribution to this subfield is the book by Nonaka and Takeuchi (1995) on knowledge creation through transformations of tacit and explicit knowledge. The subfield of knowledge management has a focus on issues related to the use of information and communication technology (ICT) to facilitate and support the acquisition, storage, sharing, retrieval, and utilization of knowledge in order to improve organizational performance.

As underlined by Easterby-Smith and Lyles (2003), it is not possible to make clearcut distinctions between these four subfields of organizational learning. For example, a critical study of processes of organizational learning within an alleged learning organization would belong to the subfield of organizational learning. Furthermore, studies of organizational learning interventions could belong both to the subfield of organizational learning and that of the learning organization depending on which knowledge interest predominates. As will be clear in the next section, it is also difficult to make clear-cut distinctions between the two subfields of organizational learning and organizational knowledge. In fact, in recent years, these two subfields have tended to merge.

Dimensions of Organizational Learning

In spite of the large number of studies on organizational learning that have been published during recent years, there is little consensus on how to define the concept of organizational learning. It is also, to say the least, a very difficult task to try to formulate a definition that could adequately cover the many meanings of organizational learning that can be found in the literature. On a general level, however, it is possible to distinguish a number of dimensions along which many definitions vary. In the text below, three such dimensions are dealt with.

Levels of Analysis

A first dimension is what is considered as the proper level of analysis, and thus, as the locus of learning. Many definitions and studies of organizational learning focus on an individual level of analysis, that is, on the learning by individuals in an organizational context (Huber, 1991; Simon, 1991). A main argument behind this approach is that basic concepts in the literature on organizational learning, for example, the concept of memory, only apply to individual subjects. In line with this, it is assumed that organizational learning is mediated through individual learning, conceived as an interplay between processes of cognition and action. Furthermore, organizational learning is assumed to imply individual learning, but not vice versa. Thus, individual learning is viewed as a necessary, but not sufficient condition for organizational learning. In relation to this view, questions arise concerning what it means when an organization learns, and how to understand the links between individual and organizational learning.

Other definitions of organizational learning focus on a collective subject, that is, on the group (the team) or the organization as the locus of learning. The basic assumption is that the group or the organization is more than a collection of individuals, and thus, that learning at a collective level is different from and not only the sum of each individual's learning. For example, Senge (1990), in his book on the learning organization, argues that the team is the fundamental level of learning in an organization. It is typically argued that the learning process of a group closely parallels that of an individual and that it can be described as cycles of cognition, action, feedback, and reflection (Edmondson, 2002).

When it comes to studies that focus on the organization as the proper level of learning, the notion of learning is typically used in a more metaphorical sense. That is, groups or organizations are assumed to learn in a way analogous to individual learning, and concepts found in theories of individual learning are extended to the group or organizational level (Hedberg, 1981). This approach has raised criticism of anthropomorphism. However, some would argue that this criticism is irrelevant, and that the notion of learning should be understood as something qualitatively different when applied to a collective entity like an organization compared to individuals. More specifically, it has been argued that organizational learning should be interpreted from a cultural rather than from a cognitive perspective, and that the notion of organizational culture would be useful for conceptualizing the collective aspects of organizational learning, and thereby, for understanding learning at an organizational level (Cook and Yanow, 1993). Accordingly, learning is assumed to be embedded in collective assumptions and interpretative systems, routines, technologies, and cultural practices. This view comes close to what below is called a sociocultural approach to organizational learning.

A fourth level of analysis is the level of inter-organizational learning. Much research on organizational learning has concerned learning within or of organizations, where the organization has often been treated as a self-contained system with fixed boundaries that operates to a large extent independently of other organizations in the environment. Today, there is a growing interest in new forms of organization at an inter-organizational level. Networks, clusters, innovation systems, and partnerships are a few such examples. Other examples include multinational corporations and joint ventures. A number of new issues of organizational learning are raised at this level of analysis, for example, issues concerning learning and innovation, or learning under conditions of competition and cooperation. At the same time, many of the issues dealt with above are also highly relevant to this level of analysis. Presently, there are few systematic studies of learning processes and outcomes at an inter-organizational level of learning.

Although there are a lot of studies that treat organizational learning as a process that should be analyzed and studied on one or the other of the four different system levels distinguished above, there are also studies that emphasize organizational learning as an interplay between different system levels or as a multilevel process. The latter position is taken, for example, by Crossan *et al.* (1999) in an article that emphasizes that a theory of organizational learning needs to consider the individual, group, and organizational levels. The latter authors also develop a framework including four subprocesses of organizational learning that link the individual, group, and organizational levels.

Organizational Learning as Change and/or Stability

According to many definitions, organizational learning is defined as an experienced-based process of change. It is sometimes also stated or implied that organizational learning means improvements of the actions or the performance of the learning subject, whether this is an individual, a group, or an organization. However, this kind of definition raises a number of issues that need to be addressed. First, observations of changes and adaptations to environmental events do not automatically mean that these changes are the result of a learning process. On the contrary, changes in actions and improved performance may occur for a number of reasons that have little or nothing to do with learning, for example, situational factors that trigger certain changes in behavior. Second, learning processes are not always, for a number of reasons, mirrored in observable behavior. There may, for example, be situational factors such as a lack of sufficient resources or adequate tools that constrain behavior. In line with this, some scholars have defined organizational learning in terms of changes in potential behaviors rather than actual behaviors (Huber, 1991).

Third, observed changes in action may not be positively related to the performance of the individual, the group, or the organization. On the contrary, we may, in some instances, talk about negative learning in the sense that the learning outcomes may for some reason be undesirable, or in fact, negatively related to performance. That might happen if, for example, the members of a team acquire a form of learned helplessness and an accompanying lack of self-confidence. Thus, the learning process may under some conditions unintentionally result in a deterioration of individual or organizational performance. Furthermore, learning processes, whether they result in positive or negative outcomes from a performance perspective, are in many cases neither conscious nor intentional. Thus, processes of learning, change, and improvement in performance may be totally different processes that need to be clearly distinguished both conceptually and empirically.

While recognizing that learning and change may be two different processes, many researchers have defined levels of learning in terms of the character of the individual and/or organizational changes that are implied by the concept of learning. For this purpose, distinctions have been made between: (a) changes that occur within a given framework, for example, within a given set of beliefs or values or within a given organizational structure or situation, and (b) changes that represent a break with and something that goes beyond the given (Ellström, 2001). Perhaps the most well-known version of this distinction is the one made by Argyris and Schön (1978) between single-loop and double-loop learning. More recently, related and in some respects parallel distinctions have been proposed between first- and second-order learning; adaptive (reproductive) and developmental (innovative) learning; incremental and radical learning. While the former type of learning in each pair has a focus on improving or refining existing procedures or capabilities, the latter type of learning has a focus on the more radical change of institutionalized practices and the development of new capabilities.

Learning as refinement of existing structures and processes may be viewed as a way of reproducing or stabilizing an organization or a social system over time. In a sense, then, reproduction and change (transformation) of a social

system may be viewed as two sides of the same coin. In line with this, arguments have been raised to the effect that it is important to find a balance between radical and incremental change or between the exploration of new alternatives and the exploitation of existing knowledge and technologies, and that the returns to fast learning and change are not all positive (March, 1991). Others would take a further step, and argue – from a cultural perspective – that organizational learning is not just about change, but also about organizational stability and the maintenance and preservation of an organization's activities and cultural practices (Cook and Yanow, 1993). Thus, organizational learning could be seen as a means for cultural reproduction as well as a means for transformation.

Content and Processes of Organizational Learning

The third dimension distinguished here concerns the content and processes of organizational learning. While content refers to what is learned (e.g., knowledge), the process of learning refers to how learning takes place. For present purposes, the following three main approaches may be distinguished with respect to the content (outcomes) and processes of organizational learning: the cognitive-behavioral approach, the sociocultural approach, and the knowledge-creating approach (cf. Paavola et al., 2004).

The cognitive–behavioral approach – an approach strongly anchored in the work of James March and his associates (e.g., March, 1991; March and Olsen, 1976) – has had a strong influence on theory and research on organizational learning for several decades. A basic assumption underlying this approach is that organizational learning is about the development and change of routines through the accumulation of experience. The key term routine includes rules, norms, procedures, strategies, and technologies that are assumed to guide actual behavior in and of organizations and their subunits. In some studies, the notion of routine is treated as explicitly formulated prescriptions. Other studies apply a broader definition and view routines as distributed procedural knowledge (knowing-how), skills, or habits. Still others broaden the view of the products of organizational learning to also include declarative knowledge (knowing-that) and mental models at the individual level, and at the organizational level interpretative systems or shared mental models and frameworks (Kim, 1993; Hedberg, 1981). Organizational learning is conceived of as a process where routines, beliefs, and actions adapt incrementally to past experience through feedback from organizational actions and their outcomes in relation to targets. Specifically, March and Olsen (1976) depict organizational learning as a cycle comprising four stages, including individual beliefs, individual action, organizational action, and environmental outcomes (responses).

The sociocultural (or situated) approach to organizational learning focuses on culture as a core concept. Rather than conceiving learning as a process of knowledge acquisition through experienced-based changes in cognition or action, there is a focus on learning as participation in work practices and activities. Furthermore, what is learned is assumed to be in a fundamental sense connected to the conditions under which it is learned, that is, it is in this sense situated. In line with this, a main tenet is that learning cannot be separated from working and other social practices where it is assumed to take place or be used (Brown and Duguid, 1991). On the contrary, learning is defined as a matter of participation in practices, and indeed, as an aspect of "legitimate peripheral participation" in "communities of practice" (Lave and Wenger, 1991). In line with this focus on participation, learning about practice is less central than learning to become a practitioner. Thus, processes of identity formation are viewed as important aspects of learning. Furthermore, learning and processes or activities (knowing) rather than content or products (knowledge) are emphasized. The sociocultural approach has received considerable attention in recent years as an alternative to the cognitive–behavioral approach, which has been criticized for a decontextualized view of knowledge, and for separating individual and organizational learning. However, critics of the sociocultural approach have, to some extent, reversed these arguments. Thus, it has been criticized for a tendency to reduce learning to an aspect of participation, thereby making it impossible to analytically separate learning and other organizational processes.

The knowledge-creating approach is based on the view that the production, transformation, and utilization of knowledge are fundamental for understanding organizational learning (Paavola *et al.*, 2004). Learning is viewed as an interplay between intra- and inter-individual (social) processes of knowledge creation. The content of learning is knowledge or competence and mechanisms (processes) of learning are typically conceptualized as cyclical processes of problem-solving and knowledge transformation. Perhaps the most well-known framework within this approach is the model proposed by Nonaka and Takeuchi (1995). This model assumes that knowledge creation could be understood as a cyclical process of knowledge conversion based on the interaction between tacit and explicit knowledge. Four modes of knowledge conversion are distinguished: socialization, externalization, combination, and internalization. Another example of a model within this approach is the model of expansive (innovative) learning proposed by Engeström (1999). This model, based on activity theory, views learning as a cycle of epistemic or learning actions starting with the questioning of prevailing practices in an organization. The learning cycle proceeds through an analysis of the existing situation and the creation, testing, and implementation of a conceptual model of a new idea that is assumed to explain and provide a solution to the problematic situation that initiated the learning process. This model has also been used as an intervention method for facilitating innovative learning in organizations. A third example is the knowledge evolution cycle proposed by Zollo and Winter (2002) based on the evolutionary process of variation, selection, replication, and retention. Underlying this model is a distinction between three learning mechanisms called experience accumulation, knowledge articulation, and knowledge codification.

Conditions and Practices of Organizational Learning

Although organizational learning is sometimes viewed as a natural, continuous process of adaptation in response to internal or external events – processes that may not be conscious or intentional – there is much evidence that indicates that processes of learning are easily interrupted by different kinds of barriers or constraining factors. A conclusion drawn from such observations is that organizational learning needs to be consciously facilitated and supported by consciously planned interventions. Thus, it is assumed that organizations need to learn to learn. This could mean to learn to carry out processes of deliberative inquiry and reflection, and thereby, develop new routines, new knowledge, or new ways of handling a certain organizational problem or task. In accordance with such an interventionist view of organizational learning, a wide range of organizational learning interventions have been developed based on different conceptions of learning. Examples of organizational learning interventions include: project-based learning and action learning interventions based on notions of reflective practice; process consultation; dialogue meetings; open space technology; and different types of learning laboratories (Dierks *et al.*, 2001; Easterby-Smith and Lyles, 2003).

Most organizational learning interventions are, implicitly or explicitly, based on assumptions concerning factors that are likely to constrain or facilitate organizational learning. The purpose of the intervention is of course to attempt to create favorable conditions for learning. What then, does available research tell us about conditions for organizational learning? What factors are assumed to constrain or facilitate learning? One answer to this question is the influential theoretical model proposed by March and Olsen (1976). These authors distinguish between different types of interruptions or blockages that result in restricted or incomplete learning cycles. Others distinguish between conditions related to structural factors, subjective and cultural factors, and factors related to leadership. Among structural factors, many writers underline the importance of the characteristics of the tasks that the organization is attempting to handle (e.g., task complexity and frequency). Other studies emphasize that centralized and hierarchical structures, as well as too high a degree of formalization and standardization of work processes, are likely to impede learning; in particular, when such structural conditions are combined with limited opportunities for organizational members to participate in organizational decision making. However, there are radically different views concerning the meaning and consequences of these factors for organizational learning.

Although many organizations are structured by gender, there are a few studies of gender aspects in relation to organizational learning. Rather, organizational learning has been studied as a gender-neutral process. This is the case in spite of the significance of gender in relation to other organizational processes. Considering this research, it is quite likely that organizational demographics with respect to gender – as well as in other respects – would be significant for processes of organizational learning. For example, organizations dominated by men could be expected to provide different conditions for learning compared to organizations dominated by women (Berthoin Antal *et al.*, 2001).

It is also possible to identify a number of factors with respect to subjective and cultural issues. In the analyses proposed by Argyris and Schön (1978), and in later studies, so-called defensive routines developed by individuals for protection from threatening situations are viewed as major obstacles to learning. Many writers also focus on anxiety and fear as barriers to organizational learning, and emphasize the need to create psychological safety and trust in order to counterbalance the feelings of threat and anxiety that may be provoked by organizational learning interventions. A factor that many assume is likely to facilitate learning is the extent to which the organizational culture encourages questioning and critical reflection on what is taking place in the organization. Other characteristics of an organizational culture that are considered by many as supportive of learning would include issue orientation, openness, trust, and norms that emphasize initiative and risk-taking, tolerance toward disparate views, and tolerance for admitting errors. Although conflict is assumed by some to be an obstacle to learning, many researchers would agree on the importance of conflicts as driving forces for organizational learning. An equally important factor is how conflicts are handled and resolved as part of an organizational learning process.

A recurrent issue in the literature on organizational learning is the importance of leadership as a condition for organizational learning and, conversely, the lack of adequate leadership support as an obstacle to organizational learning. Leadership support for organizational learning includes the design of an enabling learning environment in the organization, that is, an environment which has many of the structural and cultural features mentioned above. Other important leadership tasks would include the provision of organizational resources (e.g., time) for learning and the facilitation of learning on the part of organizational members both individually and collectively, for example, by asking challenging questions, stimulating intellectual curiosity, and acting as a coach or mentor (Sadler, 2001).

Power and Politics

As observed by many writers on organizational learning, issues of power and politics in relation to organizational learning have, to a large extent, been neglected in the past. This is somewhat astonishing considering that power and politics for quite a long time have been recognized as important areas within the more general field of organizational studies. The relative neglect of these issues within the field of organizational learning is also astonishing, given that many writers in this field emphasize the importance of conflicts and contradictions as essential for learning in organizations.

However, the lack of emphasis on power and politics is not uniform across the field of organizational learning. In particular, many writers, from what was previously described as a sociocultural approach and a knowledge-creating approach to organizational learning, emphasize the importance of power relations for understanding organizational learning. In line with the practice orientation of these approaches, and the view of learning as integral to everyday work practices in organizations, it is emphasized that learning practices are embedded in and are enabled or constrained within relations of power (Contu and Willmott, 2003). Consistent with this position, it has also been argued that access (or lack of access) to specific learning practices, as well as the division of labor, and thereby, available opportunities for learning, is shaped by prevailing relations of power in the organization and in society at large. The issue, then, becomes one about who participates and who is not allowed to participate in specific learning practices. Another important issue from a political perspective concerns what is valued as knowledge, and whose knowledge and ideas are recognized in an organization. Power differences between different groups in an organization, for example, between different departments or between groups with different status may be assumed to influence whose learning is recognized and acted upon.

Other important issues that have been raised and debated from a political perspective on organizational learning relate to control and ideology in organizations. According to one position, organizational learning represents the ideology of particular power groups (e.g., the management of an organization, but also different groups of experts) and it is used to mask and legitimize the interests of these groups. In addition, organizational learning is seen as a mechanism and a methodology of control that aims to discipline members of an organization (Gherardi and Nicolini, 2001). Thus, according to this view, organizational learning is a practice for the management of meaning, and a soft means for the subjugation of employees. More specifically, the latter could mean increasing the legitimacy of the organization in the eyes of the employees as regards its goals, fundamental ideology, and power structure, and thereby, contributing to increased employee loyalty with and support for the goals and values of the business. Although there are a number of articles and books that deal with these and related issues, there is a notable lack of empirically substantiated knowledge concerning these matters.

See also: Workplace-Learning Frameworks.

Bibliography

Argyris, C. and Schön, D. A. (1978). *Organizational Learning: A Theory of Action Perspective*. Reading, MA: Addison-Wesley.
Berthoin Antal, A., Dierkes, M., Child, J., and Nonaka, I. (2001). Organizational learning and knowledge: Reflections on the dynamics of the field and challenges for the future. In Dierkes, M., Berthoin Antal, A., Child, J., and Nonaka, I. (eds.) *Handbook of Organizational Learning and Knowledge*, pp 921–939. Oxford: Oxford University Press.
Brown, J. S. and Duguid, P. (1991). Organizational learning and communities-of-practice: Toward a unified view of working, learning, and innovation. *Organization Science* **2**, 40–57.
Contu, A. and Willmott, H. (2003). Re-embedding situatedness: The importance of power relations in learning theory. *Organization Science* **14**, 283–296.
Cook, S. D. N. and Yanow, D. (1993). Culture and organizational learning. *Journal of Management Inquiry* **2**, 373–390.
Crossan, M., Lane, H., and White, R. (1999). An organizational learning framework: From intuition to institution. *Academy of Management Review* **24**, 522–537.
Dierkes, M., Berthoin Antal, A., Child, J., and Nonaka, I. (eds.) (2001). *Handbook of Organizational Learning and Knowledge*. Oxford: Oxford University Press.
Easterby-Smith, M. and Lyles, M. A. (eds.) (2003). Introduction: Watersheds of organizational learning and knowledge management. In *The Blackwell Handbook of Organizational Learning and Knowledge Management*, pp 1–15. Malden, MA: Blackwell.
Easterby-Smith, M. and Lyles, M. A. (eds.) (2003). *The Blackwell Handbook of Organizational Learning and Knowledge Management*. Malden, MA: Blackwell.
Edmondson, A. C. (2002). The local and variegated nature of learning in organizations: A group-level perspective. *Organization Science* **2**, 128–146.
Ellström, P. E. (2001). Integrating learning and work: Problems and prospects. *Human Resource Development Quarterly*, **12**, 421–435.
Engeström, Y. (1999). Innovative learning in work teams: Analyzing cycles of knowledge creation in practice. In Engeström, Y., Miettinen, R., and Punamäki, R. L. (eds.) *Perspectives on Activity Theory*, pp 19–38. New York: Cambridge University Press.
Gherardi, S. and Nicolini, D. (2001). The sociological foundations of organizational learning. In Dierks, M., Berthoin Antal, A., Child, J., and Nonaka, I. (eds.) *Handbook of Organizational Learning and Knowledge*, pp 35–60. Oxford: Oxford University Press.
Hedberg, B. L. T. (1981). How organizations learn and unlearn. In Nystrom, P. C. and Starbuck, W. H. (eds.) *Handbook of Organizational Design. Vol 1. Adapting Organizations to Their Environments*, pp 3–27. Oxford: Oxford University Press.
Huber, G. P. (1991). Organizational learning: The contributing processes and the literatures. *Organization Science* **2**, 88–115.
Kim, D. H. (1993). The link between individual and organizational learning. *Sloan Management Review* **35**, 37–50.
Lave, J. and Wenger, E. (1991). *Situated Learning: Legitimate Peripheral Participation*. Cambridge: Cambridge University Press.
March, J. G. (1991). Exploration and exploitation in organizational learning. *Organization Science* **2**, 71–87.
March, J. G. and Olsen, J. P. (1976). Organizational learning and the ambiguity of the past. In March, J. G. and Olsen, J. P. (eds.) *Ambiguity and Choice in Organizations*, pp 54–68. Oslo: Universitetsforlaget.
Nonaka, I. and Takeuchi, H. (1995). *The Knowledge-Creating Company: How Japanese Companies Create the Dynamics of Innovation*. Oxford: Oxford University Press.
Paavola, S., Lipponen, L., and Hakkarinen, K. (2004). Models of innovative knowledge communities and three metaphors of learning. *Review of Educational Research* **74**, 557–576.
Sadler, P. (2001). Leadership and organizational learning. In Dierks, M., Berthoin Antal, A., Child, J., and Nonaka, I. (eds.) *Handbook of Organizational Learning and Knowledge*, pp 415–427. Oxford: Oxford University Press.
Senge, P. M. (1990). *The Fifth Discipline: The Art and Practice of the Learning Organization*. New York: Doubleday.
Simon, H. A. (1991). Bounded rationality and organizational learning. *Organization Science* **2**, 125–134.
Zollo, M. and Winter, S. G. (2002). Deliberate learning and the evolution of dynamic capabilities. *Organization Science* **13**, 339–351.

Further Reading

Antonacopoulou, E., Jarvis, P., Andersen, V., Elkjaer, B., and Hoyrup, S. (eds.) (2006). *Learning, Working, Living. Mapping the Terrain of Working Life Learning*. New York: Palgrave Macmillan.
Cohen, M. D. and Sproull, L. S. (1996). *Organizational Learning*. Thousand Oaks, CA: Sage.
Easterby-Smith, M., Araujo, L., and Burgoyne, J. (1999). *Organizational Learning and the Learning Organization. Developments in Theory and Practice*. Thousand Oaks, CA: Sage.
Leithwood, K. and Seashore, K. L. (eds.) (1999). *Organizational Learning in Schools*. Lisse, PA: Taylor and Francis.
March, J. G. (1999). *The Pursuit of Organizational Intelligence*. Malden, MA: Blackwell.
Marsick, V. J. and Watkins, K. E. (1999). *Facilitating Learning Organizations*. Aldershot: Gower.
Moingeon, B. and Edmondson, A. C. (eds.) (1996). *Organizational Learning and Competitive Advantage*. London: Sage.

Informal Learning: A Contested Concept

P Hodkinson, University of Leeds, Leeds, UK

Although the term informal learning has been widely used for a long period of time, its precise meaning remains elusive and contested. The term is normally invoked in opposition to formal learning and/or formal education, and has, therefore, much in common with the terms nonformal learning and nonformal education. In its common sense usage, informal learning is that learning which takes place outside educational institutions, such as schools, colleges, and universities. The confusions around its meaning and usage arise from three interrelated problems. They are:

- differences between the research and political developments of the term;
- confusion and disagreement over the boundaries between formal and informal learning; and
- contrasted and contested theoretical ways of understanding all learning.

The Research Development of Informal Learning

Over the last 30 years, researchers have rediscovered the fact that much learning takes place in everyday life, without the interventions of teachers or educational institutions. The importance of everyday learning had been largely lost sight of, after the decline of behaviorism, as cognitive psychologists focused most attention on learning in schools. Reinforced by liberal humanist views of education as major root of civilization, schooling came to be seen as normally the best way for people to learn. The debates in the early 1970s focused mainly on how to make schooling better.

Scribner and Cole (1973) wrote one early seminal piece pointing out that much successful learning took place outside school. They explicitly used the term informal learning and juxtaposed it with formal learning, which was what schools were supposed to be good at. Since then, there has been much research showing informal learning in a wide range of contexts, including families, communities, and workplaces. It was not just the contexts of formal and informal learning that were different. Their processes and the nature of what was learned were also different. From this perspective, formal learning is planned and organized and assessed by teachers and others, while informal learning is incidental and ubiquitous in everyday practices. Formal learning is concerned with high status, mainly propositional knowledge, which, the argument goes, is generalizable, not

situation specific. Informal learning is concerned with low-status knowledge and skills, and much of it is assumed to be situation specific.

Within this strand of literature, most writers are either concerned with formal learning and education, or with informal learning. One result of this polarization is a sometimes vehement debate about whether formal or informal learning is more efficient. As schooling developed in the twentieth century, they were the places where Enlightenment ideals of science and rationality could be applied to learning. Schools were where learning was taken seriously, and were an improvement over simple and primitive everyday learning. On the other hand, researchers into informal learning argued that it often worked better. Thus, for example, children learn language very effectively in everyday life, compared with the ways in which at least British and American children struggle to learn a foreign language in school.

The Political Development of Nonformal Education and Nonformal Learning

Whereas recent usage of informal learning grew up in opposition to formal learning, usage of the term nonformal learning grew out of the older term, nonformal education. The first use of the term nonformal education was probably a United Nations Educational, Scientific and Cultural Organization (UNESCO) report on education in what was then termed the underdeveloped world (Hamadache, 1991). The essence of nonformal education was a central desire for empowerment, through democratization. In the 1940s, this was associated with post-World War II growth of anti- and postcolonialism. Tutors could be centrally involved, working with underprivileged groups, helping them achieve their own objectives. Thus, informal education was opposed to formal education, which was seen as elitist, and primarily concerned with social reproduction, rather than emancipation. However, for those writing about informal learning (see above), this struggle was between two different forms of formal learning.

Colley et al. (2003) argue that since 1947, a broadly nonformal educational movement has ebbed and flowed, growing in strength for short periods of time, interspersed with longer periods of the dominance of formal education. In what they term the second wave, in the 1970s, the term nonformal learning first appears. These second-wave movements were found, for example, in Brazil led by

Freire and others, and in Tanzania. This time, partly through Freire's (1972) work, the movement spread into the developed world, for example, in feminist, antiracist and working-class movements.

When nonformal learning surfaced again, from the late 1980s onward, it became more formalized, under the influence of free-market capitalism and human-capital theory. Funding in most parts of the world is increasingly focused on economic production. The formalization of much nonformal and informal learning can be seen, for example, in the growth of the competence movement, whereby the outcomes of work-related learning are specified, measured, and potentially accredited, regardless or where that learning took place. The radical and emancipatory agendas of the previous waves had been largely lost.

As these two quite different origins of the concept of informal learning converge, the usage and meaning of that concept becomes further confused. What both traditions share in common is a sense of informal learning being other than formal education. This leads directly to the next problem. Informal learning is seldom clearly defined in its own right. Almost always, it is formal learning/education which is defined, leaving informal learning as its opposite.

The Blurred Boundaries Between Formal and Informal Learning

Colley *et al.* (2003) analyzed a range of texts which had explicitly set out the differences between informal learning and formal learning. What their analysis showed was that, although there was significant overlap between them, each author defined the differences in significantly different ways. Colley and coworkers identified a list of 20 criteria, all of which had been used by at least one author. This meant that learning which would be classified as informal by one group of writers would be seen as formal by another group. More tellingly, there was no small group of criteria that were universally used by all writers. Thus for some, in the informal-education tradition, informal learning could be seen as part of, say, an adult-education course, provided that course was run upon democratic lines. For many others, informal learning only took place outside educational institutions. Similarly, many agreed that formal learning was assessed and accredited. However, others did not see, say, accredited workplace learning as formal, and much learning in schools, which most would describe as formal, is often unaccredited. Marsick and Watkins (1990) suggest that formal learning is deliberative and planned, while informal learning is incidental, which cuts right across divisions based on location and both types could be accredited, for example, within the competence movement. These boundary confusions are bad enough if the focus is on formal learning, but when informal learning is the focus, there is a further problem. This is because it is often formal learning that is defined. Informal learning is all the rest.

Further confusions arose when some authors tried to distinguish between three categories: formal, nonformal, and informal learning. Traditionally, nonformal and informal had been used almost interchangeably. More recently, as we have seen, nonformal learning has been invented as a third category, possibly as a means of resolving some of the confusions in the distinctions between formal and informal learning. However, there is even less clarity and agreement between the boundaries of informal and nonformal learning than between formal and informal. Colley *et al.* (2003) concluded that the distinctions between informal and nonformal learning were largely meaningless. However, the threefold classification used by the European Union (European Commission, 2001) has become influential in relation to policy and practice in Europe. In this classification, nonformal learning was seen as a midway point between informal and formal: learning that is not provided by an education or training institution and typically does not lead to certification, but is structured (in terms of learning objectives, learning time, or learning support). Nonformal learning was defined as intentional from the learner's perspective. That is, nonformal learning is part of what was defined as formal learning by Marsick and Watkins (1990), but could equally be seen as an attempt to divide informal learning in workplaces and communities into the purposive (nonformal) and the incidental (formal).

Colley *et al.* (2003) argued that rather than distinct types of learning, termed formal and informal, there were many attributes of informality and formality in learning, and that most if not all learning contained a mixture of both. They suggest that these various attributes of formality and informality relate to four areas: the location of learning, the purposes of learning, the processes of learning, and the content of learning. Thus, the content of learning could be, say, mainly formal – perhaps academic history, the purpose relatively informal, in that the history is being learned from a TV program, watched for interest, in which case the process would also be largely informal, as would be the location, if the TV was being watched in the home, rather than as a planned part of an educational course. Multiple other combinations are possible.

Theoretical Differences

The third source of confusion around the term informal learning arises from deeper disagreements about the nature of learning itself. A full analysis of these debates lies beyond the scope of this article, although some relevant reading has been included, for those who want more detail. In essence, two radically different ways of understanding learning each has very different implications for what we take the concept of informal learning to mean.

On the one hand, much of the research on learning from a cognitive psychological perspective implicitly adopts what Sfard (1998) terms an acquisition metaphor for learning. That is, learning is understood as the process whereby knowledge, skills, understanding, etc. are acquired by the learner. Within this intellectual tradition, there has always been a concentration on learning as a cognitive mental process, and on the nature of learning either in relation to early childhood, or within educational institutions. Thus, there is an implicit switch from what might be termed informal learning in childhood, to formal learning at school. However, even in relation to early childhood, a major emphasis has been on how tutoring or teaching (by the parent and others) can improve that learning. As tutor control is an often-cited criterion for formal learning, this way of understanding learning has traditionally neglected many informal attributes of learning.

Western policymakers often implicitly adopt an extreme and oversimplified version of learning as acquisition, which sees what is learned as a commodity, to be inserted into the heads of learners. Here, and in many of the more sophisticated versions of learning as acquisition, there is a tendency to see learning processes and learning outcomes as separate – with one leading to the other. Learning is also seen as separate from the context in which it takes place, so that a major objective of education (and also a major problem) is to facilitate the transfer of what was learning on one place (such as a school) to another (such as work). When informal learning enters the acquisition perspective, it is often as an alternative method to formal learning, whereby desired outcomes are/can be achieved. Often, it is seen as of secondary importance to formal learning.

Situated-learning theories, in their various guises, see learning differently. Here, as Sfard (1998) shows, the metaphor is not acquisition, but participation. That is, people learn through participating in practices and/or activities, including those of schooling, as well as, say, those in the family, at work, or in the local community. There has been work done on learning in education from this perspective, but arguably most of the major developments in situated learning have come from focusing on other places where people learn – perhaps, especially the workplace. Perhaps, the most radical and most significant claim of situated-learning theorists is that there is no separate process, called learning. Rather, learning happens as part of the practices of participating. Thus, in a workplace, work itself, and the various social processes involved in it, embrace learning. This sort of participatory learning is inherently social, and far from being separate from its location, is an integral part of the situation where it takes place. That is, the nature of learning varies significantly from one situation to another. Within any situation, learning processes and learning outcomes are also integrated. Furthermore, for many writers, learning is embodied, involving the practical and affective as well as cognitive. Often such learning is tacit, in the sense that people are not really conscious of learning.

It follows that situated-learning theorists naturally focus on what is often termed informal learning. This is seen as the natural and therefore most common form of learning. If formal learning is thought of as different, then it is as a minor variation, not the major learning form. Thus, when researchers write about formal education, a common thrust is that we should make it more like informal learning.

If the boundary between formal and informal learning is contested and imprecise at best, from the situated-learning perspective, there is a different boundary problem with the concept. The logical conclusion from a situated-learning position is that learning is ubiquitous in life. Not only is learning ever-present, but as there is no separation between any social practices and learning, there is no clear division between learning and life. This definition problem leads to two contrary positions in the literature. On the one hand, some writers call for a return to seeing education as the main concept for analysis, rather than learning. For them, informal learning is just too vague and broad to be meaningful. The opposite view is that we have to accept that learning is ubiquitous, and it follows that learning is everywhere and that much of it cannot be measured. Rather than worry about this imprecision, we should ask different questions about learning (including informal learning), which relate to its value and its purposes, rather than its effectiveness. At the time of writing, situated-learning theories are in ascendance over cognitive theories, but a resolution to the implications of the ubiquity of learning is not in sight. More recent work is also seeking to build back an individual perspective on learning, for example, by finding ways of blending metaphors of participation with those of construction. Most of these approaches focus on learning as broadly undifferentiated into formal and informal, implicitly or explicitly adopting a similar stance to Colley *et al.* (2003), in this respect. However, there remain a significant number of cognitive researchers who are unconvinced.

Informal Learning in Educational Courses

If we adopt the situated-learning perspective when looking at learning in classrooms, schools, and colleges, it becomes apparent that there is much informal learning in such places too. As early as 1961, Jackson pointed out that while in school, the hidden curriculum was at least as important as the official curriculum. By that, he meant that pupils learned about how to behave in school, and more seriously, being in school reinforced a sense of failure and inadequacy in many. Although he never used the term, informal learning, it can be applied to this still underestimated part of what is learned at school. His use of the term hidden is telling. Most of the literature on learning at school focuses on how well or badly the official curriculum is learned, ignoring the extensive informal learning that goes alongside it. Furthermore, the two are not separate. Some situated-learning theorists argue that learning to be a pupil in a school interferes with the learning of, say, physics. For example, pupils learn how to stay out of trouble, how to do well with minimal effort, how to pass tests rather than master a subject, and how to get on with their peers, for example, to avoid being labeled a teachers' pet. In relation to some recent research done on learning in an English college, Hodkinson and Colley (2005) analyze the complex interrelationships between formal and informal learning in three very different courses. In each case, they claim that it makes little sense to see formal and informal learning as different. To do so, risks leaving a very partial understanding of the learning taking place. In arguing this way, they are taking a situated-learning view of what learning is.

Formal Learning at Work

Billett (2002), writing mainly about learning in the workplace, also argues that formal and informal learning are not distinct from each other. In fact, he argues, all learning is formal in several respects. Writing from a situated-learning perspective, he argues that the practices and activities through which learning takes place are themselves partly formalized, through formal structures of, say a workplace. Thus, work hierarchies, rules, and procedures interpenetrate all workplace learning, which is thus structured, controlled, and deliberative – that is, formalized. Whether his argument is accepted or not, it is clear that there are increasing amounts of planned, taught (or tutored), and assessed learning in modern workplaces, for example, through performance-management schemes, or managerial requirements for specific training – in health and safety, in using new technology, etc.

Is Informal Learning Becoming More Formalized?

As informal learning attracts more and more attention from researchers, policymakers, and others, those who still believe in the clear distinction between it and formal learning face a paradox. For, the more we discover about the importance of informal learning, the more we try to specify, measure, and control it. To use the terminology of Colley *et al.* (2003) we are attaching more and more of the attributes of formal learning to it. That is, we are making informal learning more formal.

This increasing formalization can be seen in a number of places. Quantitative researchers are searching for better and more-encompassing measures of or proxies for informal learning, so that they can assess how widespread it is, who has access to it, etc. In many adult- and higher education contexts, there is a growing use of accreditation of prior experience and learning (APEL). That is, having recognized that people learn a lot informally, the drive is on to find formal evidence so that such learning can also be accredited, and can be counted toward a qualification. In the workplace-learning arena, there has been a widespread growth of competence-based qualifications. Their purpose is to record, verify, and ultimately accredit learning which has taken place during the everyday practices of work. Another example is the growth of performance-management schemes at work, where employees agree learning targets with a line manager.

For those whose tradition is the radical politics of non-formal adult education, this trend to formalize the informal is deeply worrying, even though some of these initiatives, such as APEL, may be of benefit to some disadvantaged learners. The trend brings dangers of increasing hierarchical control and increasing surveillance of workers and other relatively disadvantaged groups. Moreover, if and when it is discovered that even the most disadvantaged have lots of informal learning in their lives, this can provide an easy excuse for policymakers not to provide, say, additional access to adult-education classes, because these people have enough learning anyway.

Another set of concerns about this trend relates to whether or not it is inherently counterproductive. There are subtly different arguments here. First, if informal learning is different from formal learning, and if it is also beneficial, then there are dangers that in making it increasingly formal, some of its very advantages are lost. An extension of this line of argument is that this formalization is actually the reason for increased interest in informal learning, rather than it resulting from such interest. This raises suggestions that the focus on learning rather than education has political purposes, in focusing attention and responsibility on individuals, rather than the state. It also marginalizes older debates about the purposes of education and over what people should learn or should be encouraged to learn.

The second very similar argument comes from the line taken by Colley *et al.* (2003). They argue that the interrelationship between formal and informal attributes of learning is very important. It follows that when we choose to alter the balance between such attributes, it is necessary to think carefully about what any such changes do to the nature of the learning itself. The problem is that in most cases of increased formalization, this is not done. Rather, there are assumptions that (1) we are measuring what is already there without changing it, or (2) we can simply improve what already happens, by managing it better.

The third argument links the two. If most learning is informal, and if learning is ubiquitous in everyday activity, attempts to measure it or to accredit it may miss a larger point. It is not whether people have learned or not, or how much they have learned that matters. What matters more are important questions about the value and purposes of what is being learned, and to whom. In other words, much of the growing formalization of informal learning has technical concerns, directly relating to the needs of those in power – employers, educational institutions, governments, etc. More important are questions of value – questions of why and for what purpose, rather than what or how. Of course, value questions are always contested and contestable, and raising this question about informal learning would place the contested nature of learning at the center of the debate.

Conclusion: The Value of Contestation

Ever since the first usages of the term, informal learning has been contested, and there are two dimensions to that contestation. There are theoretical and research-driven arguments about what the concept means, what its boundaries are, and how useful it is. There are political arguments about its purposes and about who can, should, or does control it.

At a practical level, all this makes the concept of informal learning difficult to use well. Too many writers are unclear about their own uses of the term, and appear unaware that many other writers use it in different ways to them. On the other hand, the concept has such widespread usage that, at least in English, it is almost impossible to avoid it. Some of its essence can be captured in alternatives, such as everyday learning, but each such alternative brings its own definitional problems and metaphorical baggage. Writers need to use informal learning and its alternatives with care, and should make clear the sense in which they are using the term.

However, if contestation and complexity bring problems, they also bring opportunities. The debates and arguments about informal learning lie at the heart of the ongoing search for better and clearer ways to understand learning *per se*. For our understanding of learning to advance, we need to keep these contestations firmly in mind, as we work to address them and find better ways forward. The political debates about the purpose of informal learning relate directly to arguably even more important concerns for

educational researchers and practitioners. These concerns are the extent of inequality and disadvantage in education and learning, related to social class, gender, ethnicity, poverty, etc. Despite the fears from some quarters that a focus on informal learning is part of a broader move to place responsibility and blame on individual learners, such issues of social and educational inequality concern all forms of learning in all aspects of people's lives. The trick is not to focus solely either on formal education or informal learning, but to see both as often related parts of a larger picture.

Bibliography

Billett, S. (2002). Critiquing workplace learning discourses: Participation and continuity at work. *Studies in the Education of Adults* **34**(1), 56–67.

Colley, H., Hodkinson, P., and Malcolm, J. (2003). *Informality and Formality in Learning: A Report for the Learning and Skills Research Centre*. London: Learning and Skills Research Centre.

European Commission (2001). *Communication: Making a European Area of Lifelong Learning a Reality*. http://europa.eu.int/comm/education/policies/lll/life/communication/com_en.pdf (accessed June 2009).

Freire, P. (1972). *Pedagogy of the Oppressed*. Harmondsworth: Penguin.

Hamadache, A. (1991). Non-formal education: A definition of the concept and some examples. *Prospects* **21**(1), 111–124.

Hodkinson, P. and Colley, H. (2005). Formality and informality in college-based learning. In Kuenzel, K. (ed.) *International Yearbook of Adult Education 31/32, 2005: Informal Learning, Self-Education and Social Praxis*, pp 165–182. Cologne: Boehlau Verlag.

Marsick, V. and Watkins, K. (1990). *Informal and Incidental Learning in the Workplace*. London: Routledge.

Scribner, S. and Cole, M. (1973). Cognitive consequences of formal and informal education. *Science* **182**, 553–559.

Sfard, A. (1998). On two metaphors for learning and the dangers of choosing just one. *Educational Researcher* **27**(2), 4–13.

Further Reading

Beckett, D. and Hager, P. (2002). *Life, Work and Learning: Practice in Postmodernity*. London: Routledge.

Coffield, F. (ed.) (2000). *The Necessity of Informal Learning*. Bristol: Policy Press.

Foley, G. (1999). *Learning in Social Action: A Contribution to Understanding Informal Education*. New York: St Martin's Press.

Jackson, P. W. (1961). *Life in Classrooms*. New York: Holt, Rinehart and Wilson.

Jeffs, T. and Smith, M. K. (1996). *Informal Education: Conversation, Democracy and Learning*. Derby: Education Now Books with the YMCA George Williams College.

Lave, J. and Wenger, E. (1991). *Situated Learning*. Cambridge: Cambridge University Press.

Livingstone, D. (2001). Adults' informal learning: Definitions, findings, gaps and future research. *NALL Working Paper No. 21*. Toronto, ON: Centre for the Study of Education and Work, OISE/UT.

Torres, C. A. (1990). *The Politics of Nonformal Education in Latin America*. New York: Praeger.

Program Planning

A L Wilson, Cornell University, Ithaca, NY, USA
R M Cervero, University of Georgia, Athens, GA, USA

Those who study and practice adult education have tended to be more interested in questions about what and how adults learn than in questions of how to organize adult education. Yet adults intentionally decide to learn something in some sort of organized fashion that typically requires some individual or group to take on the responsibility of designing and organizing educational activities. Such educational responsibilities have been called different names – program planning, program development, curriculum and instructional design, program organizing, and program design – but regardless of the label such activities typically constitute decisions and actions about what is to be learned, how the learning is to take place, who the learners and the teachers are, and what the education is for. From the beginning of the formal organizing of the study and professional practice of adult education, there has been an interest in developing program planning theory as an aide to those organizing education for adults. As Sork and Newman (2004) note, this theoretical pursuit seems more peculiar to academics in North America than elsewhere. Nevertheless, there has been a continuing effort, both as a result of academic interest as well as practitioner inquiry, to develop principles and procedures – that is, theories and methods – for designing and implementing programs for the education of adults.

Beginning in the 1920s in the United States, such effort has produced literally hundreds of program planning theories in adult education (Sork and Buskey, 1986; Wilson and Cervero, 1997). Two observations have emerged as a result of this proliferation. First was the growing sense that amidst such variety there was actually more uniformity than was apparent which Sork and Caffarella (1989) demonstrated when they developed their generic model of program planning. Second was a sense of a growing gap between what theorists prescribed in planning theories and what practitioners actually did when planning programs (Cervero and Wilson, 1994; Sork and Caffarella, 1989). That gap is a function of many factors, chief of which is the failure of planning theorists to develop adequate theories of context and practical action (Cervero and Wilson, 2006). Our view is that theory should be able to both explain and enable practical action (Foley, 1999). Most adult education planning theory, until fairly recently, represented only one main tradition for understanding and enabling practical planning action. Yet most of that theory was limited in its understanding of what actual planning practice required and instead depended upon normative prescriptions of what planners should do, which tended to be a highly idealized form of instrumental rationality (Cervero and Wilson, 2006).

The value and utility of program planning theory lies in its ability to provide plausible accounts of actual planning practice, interpretations of what is practically possible when planning programs for adults, and politically strategic practices that foster ethically informed goals (Bernstein, 1976; Forester, 1989). The purpose of this article is to review three traditions of planning theory – conventional, deliberative, and critical – in terms of how each answers the questions of what do planners do when planning programs, what really matters when planners plan programs, and what is good planning. Addressing these questions will enable us to examine the different understandings of context and action that each tradition depends upon in order to provide its theoretical accounts and practical prescriptions. We conclude with a discussion of the challenges facing adult education planning theory and practice.

Conventional Planning Theory

As is often the case with education more generally, planning theorists in adult education have tended to think of planning ahistorically (Wilson, 2005), yet it sometimes helps to see what is now by looking at what has been. There is one tradition that has dominated historically and theoretically, and continues to dominate planning discussions. Sork and Newman (2004) call this tradition the conventional which also has been described as the classical (Cervero and Wilson, 1994). Although clearly evident since near the beginning of the twentieth century (Pinar *et al.*, 1995), conventional planning theory is best landmarked by the appearance of Ralph Tyler's basic principles of curriculum and instruction in 1949. In his book, Tyler (1949) codified the essential conventional planning logic and method: "if an educational program is to be planned . . . it is very necessary to have some conception of the goals that are being aimed at. These educational objectives become the criteria by which materials are selected, content is outlined, instructional procedures are developed and tests and examinations are prepared" (p. 3). This is Tyler's rationale: that without objectives no other planning decisions can be made and that each decision logically induces the next, hence the numbering of his four famous questions (and the beginnings of decades of debate in curriculum theory). This sequential logic driven by the definition of objectives is the underlying thought – theory – of all conventional planning theory, which Malcolm Knowles in his 1950 book *Informal Adult Education* made so clear and nearly all the adult education planning theory since has personified (Sork and Buskey, 1986; Wilson and Cervero, 1997). Conventional theorists in adult education have elaborated and refined conventional logic by adding steps such as analyzing planning contexts and administering programs but have not fundamentally altered the prescribed "sequentially and logically ordered set of tasks in which educational planners first assess learning needs, then develop learning objectives from assessed needs, next design learning content and instructional formats to meet learning objectives, and finally evaluate learning outcomes in terms of whether the objectives were achieved" (Wilson, 2005: 525). The proliferation of conventional planning theory that Sork and Buskey (1986) first identified and Sork and Caffarella (1989) codified has continued without abatement (Cervero and Wilson, 2006; Sork and Newman, 2004).

According to the conventional view, what do planners really do? Planners follow the steps. What really matters? Following the steps in order, for if they are not followed in order, then logic of the rationale breaks down and the resulting planning for education is not good. What is good program planning then? Following the sequence in the prescribed order? According to the conventional view, principally and practically the systematic process of planning always starts with objectives, proceeds through multiple design and implementations steps, and concludes with the evaluation of whether the objectives have been obtained. The efficacy of conventional theory depends upon following its internal logic. If the logic is violated, then consequences are moot. What really matters in conventional planning theory is the understanding of context and practical action that drive such theories or, perhaps more accurately, the lack thereof. These planning theories represent a form of professional scientific logic that promotes "instrumental problem solving made rigorous by the application of scientific theory and technique" (Schon, 1983: 21), or, as more commonly known today, technical rationality or instrumental reasoning. The critique of technical rationality as a limited basis for the performance of professional activities like education is now well developed. Its attempt to adopt rigorous, rational problem solving as the basis for professional practice dims in the face of the actual interactive complexities of humans and organizations that planners really have to address in order to plan. So a serious limitation of conventional planning theory is the assumption that rational planning procedures will work equally well in any circumstances and that practical action is defined by and limited to the execution of procedures. Rational planning, however, does not work the same in every situation and, indeed, can actually disguise the workings of power in certain circumstances (Cervero and

Wilson, 2006). The rational planning of conventional theory typically does not eliminate but routinely ignores the noise of context and people (Forester, 1989). So conventional planning theories provide neither a plausible account of practice nor ethical standards for practice, so they therefore provide no way of imagining the need for politically strategic planning action. Within its instrumental frame, has conventional theory provided a set of principles and procedures to which planners need to attend? Certainly it has, because planners who do not know the differences between needs assessments and instructional design, between evaluation and objectives, between administrative plans and curriculum plans will be of little use to their organizations. Not only do planners need to know these concepts and principles, they likewise need the wealth of technical methods so abundantly provided by conventional theory for conducting needs analyses and audience surveys, curricular organization and site management, evaluation and organizational analysis. Yet to rely solely on conventional planning principles and instrumental technique runs the risk of ignoring the exigencies of real people planning real educational programs in real organizational settings. To get a sense of efforts to understand and enable action in such conditions, we turn now to a related but distinct tradition called the deliberative.

Deliberative Planning Theory

If Ralph Tyler personified the logic of the conventional tradition, Joseph Schwab (1969) named its major limitations: it failed to understand the way in which people made planning decisions and the conditions in which such decisions were made. Practitioners for decades have routinely indicated that although the conventional principles and techniques are helpful, they rarely represent how actual planning decisions get made in the complex human and organizational contexts that planners work. In critiquing the procedural emphasis of conventional planning theory, particularly the requirement to always begin with objectives, proponents of the deliberative traditions (Schwab, 1969; Walker, 1971) argued that planning was best understood as a process of practical (as opposed to instrumental) reasoning. Practical reasoning as a deliberative process requires analyzing the context and then making the best judgments possible about what to do, given the restrictions and possibilities of the specific set of circumstances. Another major insight of this tradition is that planners may neither need to complete all the steps of the conventional tradition nor address them in the sequentially prescribed order. Houle's (1972, 1996) insight was that planning was better understood as decision points (rather than steps) that could occur at any time and often simultaneously undermined the preferred sequential logic of the conventional view. Despite decades of producing planning models, the only significant theoretical debate in the adult education planning literature has been about whether the steps have to be followed in order (Wilson and Cervero, 1997). Planning theory has moved steadily from a discounting of the preferred sequential enactment of planning tasks to an iterative understanding of planning human decision making within the constraints of specific contexts (see Caffarella, 2002; Sork, 2000; Sork and Newman, 2004). This theoretical move is believed to diminish the acknowledged theory–practice gap characterizing conventional theory. While promising in that the deliberative tradition does bring acting people into variable settings, "this tradition's invocation of 'deliberation' . . . is actually similar to what the conventional view holds as rational problem solving . . . . because deliberation essentially represents the decision-making aspects of implementing rationalist problem-solving steps" (Cervero and Wilson, 2006: 246).

According to this tradition, planning practice is best understood as people deliberating about the best course of action to follow given the constraints of the circumstances. This is what planners do. In addition, what matters in this view are the specifics of situational constraints, the values of the planners deliberating about what to do, and the judgments about courses of action that ultimately obtain, given the confluence of constraints and values. So good planning is defined by defensible judgments that justify action in terms of constraints and values (Schwab, 1969; Walker, 1971). Such an understanding of planning does begin to provide a plausible account of practice because it adds to the proceduralism of conventional theory the actual people who deliberate about and enact the decisions on planning as well as including the understanding that such decision making is always constrained and/or enabled by the context. Bringing people and settings into the equation is a promising advance on understanding practical action in context. Where this view is limited, however, in naming more precisely how people act in context, what defines context and how it works to constrain or enable, or whose values should matter. To see what more precision might look like in terms of practical action and context, we turn next to critical traditions.

Critical Planning Theory

Whenever people have sought to change oppressive social, political, and economic conditions, there have usually also been people who have organized education to facilitate such change. With antecedents in the nineteenth century and before, and throughout the twentieth century and beyond, there have been people who have organized adult education for settlement houses, in labor movements, at workers colleges, in civil rights movements, for anti-war movements, in anti-globalization efforts, and whenever and wherever

people have needed to learn in order to seek change. Places like Hull House, Highlander, and Antigonish, and people like Jane Addams, Myles Horton, and Moses Coady plus scores of lesser-known but no less involved people and places provide a lengthy history of educators working to redress social and political injustice. There has been very little planning theory in adult education to explain and enable this kind of educational work; indeed, it may well be that movement, union, and civil rights educators rarely even thought or think of themselves as educators. Nevertheless, there has evolved various critical theories of planning. Perhaps most prominent in terms of planning theory would be Paulo Freire. Sometimes implications for planning theory are noted in his *Pedagogy of the Oppressed* (Sork, 2000); others are explicit in naming it as planning theory (Boone *et al.*, 2002; Wilson and Cervero, 1997). Specific chapters in *Pedagogy* describe organizing and implementing strategies to foster critical transformation and social change. John Forester (1989) has developed a theory of planning based on and directed toward fostering Habermasian communicative ethics and participatory practices. Cervero and Wilson (1994, 2006) have been described as beyond the conventional (Sork and Newman, 2004: 112) because of their theory's focus on fostering democratic planning by negotiating interests in relations of power.

Planners in the critical traditions typically understand the world to be structured with inequitable power relations and seek to organize possibilities for changing those relations by using education to enhance democratic participation in the planning, implementation, and consequences of educational actions. Education is thus a political and ethical activity whose purpose is to promote social justice and emancipation through a restructuring of society's cultural, political, and economic relations – this is what really matters. Good critical planners anticipate the structural distortion caused by inequitable power relations and seek to counteract such distortion by fostering democratic participation. Critical traditions fully incorporate the insights of the conventional planning theories such as the need for a professional repertoire of technical procedures and deliberative insights concerning decision making and the influence of context. But in the critical traditions the context is described specifically as power relations and practical action as tactics to enhance participation. Thus, the value positions underlying critical planning are starkly articulated. While value positions of planners and organizations are allegedly neutralized by the deployment of rational problem solving in the conventional view (the faith in the efficacy of rationality is the value position), in the deliberative traditions values are clearly acknowledged to be a formative force in shaping decisions about planning, but no values are specified. The quest for social justice and democratic participation are the platform values for planning thought and action in the critical. Overly celebrated as well as routinely ignored, there is a wealth of historical accounts and present-day examples that exemplify the plausibility of this tradition, which indicate that its interpretative stances are practically possible, and that the traditions represent ethically informed and politically strategic visions of what should be.

Conclusion

Sork and Newman (2004) have noted that most theoretical writing about program planning has emanated from North America, and we, as they, wonder what a genderized, feminized, colorized, or other-culturalized understanding of planning might be. Until the 1990s, almost all theoretical discussion represented just one tradition – the conventional (Sork and Buskey, 1986; Sork and Caffarella, 1989). That discussion tended to debate the details but not the underlying formative assumptions and structures of thought that enabled their proliferation. Because of the dominance of the conventional tradition (and probably because of who has been writing theory), there has been little awareness of possibilities of rethinking what has been the norm. Even so, as we have indicated here, there are at least three traditions of planning theory that purport to understand and enable practical planning thought and action: the conventional, the deliberative, and the critical (Cervero and Wilson, 1994, 2006; Sork, 2000; Wilson, 2005).

There are a number of challenges we could recount by way of conclusion. Knowles (1950) argued that it was time to get beyond trial and error and make adult education planning theory more scientific, by which he invoked the instrumental problem solving of the Tyler rationale. In one of the few studies of actual planning practice, Pennington and Green (1976) demonstrated empirically the deliberative tradition's understanding of planning as contextually bound decision making; Houle (1972) had already developed a theory of adult education planning defined by decisions points. Pennington and Green (1976) asked questions which we are still asking: what do planners really do and why is there a theory–practice gap. They concluded we need better planning theory because actual planning was "superficial at best" and planners often planned by "the seat of their pants" (p. 20). But even as their investigations illustrated the insights of the deliberative tradition, Pennington and Green advocated for the conventional in order to "strengthen the operational aspects of those decisions" (p. 23). Sork and Caffarella (1989) likewise sought a "firmer foundation" for planning theory because the planning literature promoted an "idealized process" that did not take "into account the exigencies of day-to-day responsibilities of practitioners" (p. 243). They concluded that the gap between theory and practice might be widening because theory was becoming "increasingly irrelevant to practice" (p. 243). Such irrelevancy might be because planners took "shortcuts" in their

planning work and because context does influence planning practice considerably, as Pennington and Green's investigations showed. Sork (2000), in noting the selective origins of most planning theory, asked whether we could develop planning theory that would "both explain the complexities of planning and guide those involved" (p. 179). Although he remained skeptical of success of accomplishing that, he nonetheless proposed his question-based approach to planning as a way to understand and guide thought and action in planning practice. Sork and Newman (2004) again questioned the narrowness of the male, North American view on planning theory and noted the perhaps not-so-coincidental dominance of technical rationality in planning theory that tries to make such theory more scientific. They invoke Malcolm Knowles's injunction about andragogy to argue that "it may be more accurate to say that program development can be thought of as *either* an art or a science, but might more productively be considered a bit of both" (p. 97; original emphasis).

The greatest challenge to planning theory remains the continuing "split between what theorists prescribe and practitioners do" (Wilson, 2005: 528). It is, no doubt, the case that there are those who are responsible for developing programs for adults do so by the seat of their pants, as Pennington and Green once characterized much adult education planning. Even so, there are many experienced practitioners who are well aware of the political, ethical, and technical dilemmas and opportunities that face them daily. Because of the dominance of the conventional theory, too many theorists continue to recommend rationalist problem-solving sequences as the only response set to the practical choices practitioners must routinely make. The consequence is the continuing theory–practice gap: "The practical, empirical, and theoretical question remains: how to integrate the technical, political and ethical dimensions of planning practice in order to better understand and act in the contexts planners actually work in" (Wilson, 2005: 528; see Caffarella, 2002; Cervero and Wilson, 1994, 2006; Sork, 2000, for integrating efforts). The gap continues because we have yet to develop the theoretical understandings of human action in context that represents plausible accounts of practice that provide politically strategic practices that foster ethically informed goals. We believe planning theories should explain and enable action and have described three related but different traditions by discussing them in terms of how they understand practical action in context.

In closing, we would like to make the following points. Each tradition contributes to creating the theory–practice gap by how they understand practical action in context while each also contributes to resolving that tension. The conventional creates the widest gap because of its rationalist assumptions and its contention that rationality neutralizes the effects of context. Yet its bountiful supply of technical planning procedures is crucial to actual planning practice although procedures cannot be mistaken for practice itself as if often the case. The deliberative promisingly attempts to understand the unavoidable interaction of people and context yet its view of practical reasoning is but a variant on technical rationality. The critical gets closer to providing an understanding of practical action in context with its view of a world saturated with power relations and planners as politically strategic and ethically charged organizers. It is closer but not exhaustive. Clearly planning theory needs more empirical investigations of actual planning in many different settings if we are to further develop the insights and injunctions of the three traditions. While there has been a plethora of theoretical modeling and an abundance of technical prescriptions, there has been relatively few investigations of actual planning practice. While the discipline of adult education has emphasized adult learning, it has depended upon an assumed professional ethos of the planner as technical facilitator of planning processes. There is certainly merit to this conception but it is quite limited as the deliberative and critical traditions would suggest. Clearly planners represent and take sides when planning programs and we need to learn more about which sides we should take and how best to take them.

Bibliography

Bernstein, R. (1976). *The Restructuring of Social and Political Theory*. Philadelphia, PA: University of Pennsylvania Press.

Boone, E., Safrit, R., and Jones, J. (2002). *Developing Programs in Adult Education*. Prospect Heights, IL: Waveland.

Caffarella, R. (2002). *Planning Programs for Adult Learners: A Practical Guide for Educators, Trainers, and Staff Developers*. San Francisco, CA: Jossey-Bass.

Cervero, R. M. and Wilson, A. L. (1994). *Planning Responsibly for Adult Education: A Guide to Negotiating Power and Interests*. San Francisco, CA: Jossey-Bass.

Cervero, R. M. and Wilson, A. L. (2006). *Working the Planning Table: Negotiating Democratically for Adult, Continuing, and Workplace Education*. San Francisco, CA: Jossey-Bass.

Foley, G. (1999). *Learning in Social Action: A Contribution to Understanding Informal Education*. London: Zed.

Forester, J. (1989). *Planning in the Face of Power*. Berkeley, CA: University of California Press.

Houle, C. (1972). *The Design of Education*. San Francisco, CA: Jossey-Bass.

Houle, C. (1996). *The Design of Education*, 2nd edn. San Francisco, CA: Jossey-Bass.

Knowles, M. (1950). *Informal Adult Education*. New York: AAAE.

Pennington, F. and Green, J. (1976). Comparative analysis of program development processes in six professions. *Adult Education Quarterly* **27**, 13–23.

Pinar, W., Reynolds, W., Slatterly, P., and Taubman, P. (1995). *Understanding Curriculum: An Introduction to the Study of Historical and Contemporary Curriculum Discourses*. New York: Peter Lang.

Schon, D. (1983). *The Reflective Practitioner*. New York: Basic Books.

Schwab, J. (1969). The practical: A language for curriculum. *School Review* **78**(1), 1–24.

Sork, T. (2000). Planning educational programs. In Wilson, A. L. and Hayes, E. R. (eds.) *Handbook of Adult and Continuing Education*, pp 171–190. San Francisco, CA: Jossey-Bass.

Sork, T. and Buskey, J. (1986). A descriptive and evaluative analysis of planning literature, 1950–1983. *Adult Education Quarterly* **36**, 86–96.

Sork, T. and Caffarella, R. (1989). Program planning for adults. In Merriam, S. and Cunningham, P. (eds.) *Handbook of Adult and Continuing Education*, pp 233–245. San Francisco, CA: Jossey-Bass.

Sork, T. and Newman, M. (2004). Program development in adult education and training. In Foley, G. (ed.) *Dimensions of Adult Learning*, pp 96–117. Maidenhead: Open University Press.

Tyler, R. (1949). *Basic Principles of Curriculum and Instruction*. Chicago, IL: University of Chicago Press.

Walker, D. (1971). A naturalistic model for curriculum development. *School Review* **80**(1), 51–65.

Wilson, A. L. (2005). Program planning. In English, L. M. (ed.) *International Encyclopedia of Adult Education*, pp 524–529. Houndsmill: Palgrave Macmillan.

Wilson, A. L. and Cervero, R. M. (1997). The song remains the same: The selective tradition of technical rationality in adult education program planning. *International Journal of Lifelong Education* **16**(7), 84–108.

DOMAINS PROVISIONS AND PARTICIPATION

Adult Basic Education – A Challenge for Vocational Based Learning

Adult Literacy Education

Citizenship and Immigrant Education

Labor Education

Popular Adult Education

University Adult Continuing Education: The Extra-Mural Tradition Revisited

Community Based Adult Education

Continuing Professional Education: Multiple Stakeholders and Agendas

Displaced Workers, Unemployed and Vocational Education and Training

Museums as Sites of Adult Learning

Learning Cities and Regions

The Age of Learning: Seniors Learning

HIV Education for Low-Literate People: Transforming Students and Communities through Paulo Freire's Praxis and the Pedagogy of Action

Overview of Lifelong Learning Policies and Systems

Financing of Adult and Lifelong Learning

Provision of Prior Learning Assessment

Portfolio Assessment

Participation in Adult Learning

Barriers to Participation in Adult Education

Adult Basic Education – A Challenge for Vocational Based Learning

R Höghielm, Stockholm University, Stockholm, Sweden

Two recent European Community policy documents on adult education raise the need for a changing role of adult basic and vocational based learning (VBL) in the context of the evolving knowledge society and knowledge economy (EC, 2006, 2007). Further, the Council of Europe has, in 2009, adopted a new strategic framework for cooperation among European Union (EU) member states to reform their education and training systems so as to better prepare people to find jobs and to help businesses find the staff they need to succeed and innovate in the face of global competition. Similar discussions can be found, for example, in the USA, Canada, and Mexico, where one is looking for a closer connection between traditional adult basic education (ABE) and workplace learning. In this article, we analyze the new demands from society on ABE. While the discussion primarily draws on what is taking place in Sweden, the underlying issues and potential developments are of universal interest.

National Developments in ABE

During the 1960s, ABE was primarily an equality issue in developed countries. However, the emergence of a knowledge economy – with its demand of a more qualified workforce – has affected the role of ABE.

Looking at the development of ABE in the USA, it should be noted that it is an umbrella term used to describe a range of educational services for adults – from basic literacy (including English as a foreign language) and numeracy to high school equivalency (general educational development (GED))/adult diploma programs (ADPs). The program is federal – originating from the Economic Opportunity Act (20 August 1964), which created the first ABE program as a state grant. During the 1960s and 1970s, several studies focused on the ability of the program to fulfill its goals (see, e.g., Firoza, 1966 and the classical study by Mezirow et al., 1975). Thereafter, the program dropped into the background. However, with changes taking place in the economy and the demand for a better-qualified workforce, it once again came into the focus of policy-makers and the Adult Education Act was repealed and replaced with the Workforce Investment Act, in 1998. In this change, the focus gradually moved from literacy to vocational education and training (VET).

In Australia, where ABE has its roots in the British-extension movement, the program has traditionally been quite broad – encompassing literacy, numeracy, communication skills, basic science, humanities, and social sciences up to the equivalent of year 10 of compulsory schooling. Further, it includes survival skills linked to personal health, social action, problem solving, and conflict resolution. With vocational training and skills formation having become the Australian government's highest priority, there is now a strong focus on using ABE to upgrade the skills of the existing workforce. This has resulted in an emphasis on narrower vocational training over the traditionally broader ABE. Australian adult educators have strong reservations with regard to the narrow focus on job skills and the vocational/nonvocational distinction underlying recent policies.

In Finland, the 1975 Adult Education Committee argued for an ABE characterized by a close connection between liberal adult education and vocational education. It is worth noting that, at the time, over 60% of the workforce in Finland lacked a vocational education. During the following decades, a number of reforms were undertaken by the Finnish government to implement the Committee's intentions and preserve the tradition of a close connection between general adult education and vocational education.

Two things stand out from this brief overview. First, it is evident that changing skill requirements have raised demands for ABE to be more closely aligned with VET. Second, different models are being developed where one is characterized by a narrow focus on training, which – as with the Finnish example – tries to combine liberal and vocational traditions. To further explore this tension, I take a closer look at the development of ABE in Sweden with a focus on the link between labor-market demands and the nature of ABE.

The Link Between Education and Work in the Original Swedish Model of Komvux

While the early groundwork for establishing comprehensive schools was being laid, the issue of the older generation – who in their youth did not have the opportunity to continue beyond 6 or 7 years of education – was raised. The school reforms of the 1950s and early 1960s led to a rapid expansion of the Swedish educational system. The result of this expansion was an ever-widening gap between the older generation – who received a minimal education – and the new generation – who benefited from 9 years of compulsory education and increasingly chose to continue on to secondary school. As a consequence, the argument that the people who paid for the increase in primary and secondary education should have their share of the growing educational resources grew stronger. However, it was not only the rights and demands of the older generation but also contemporary human capital ideology that were behind the introduction of a municipal adult education (Komvux), which would offer education equivalent to that offered by primary and schools with the purpose of providing a platform for future studies or working life.

When looking at the target group of the new municipal ABE, it is important to note that the 1967 adult education reform had its roots in an elitist concept of equality. The basic idea informing this strategy was that everyone should have an equal right to an education irrespective of social background, gender, or place of residence, and the mandate for ABE was to offer it to those who aspired to it and were able to benefit from such an education. Traditional evening-class students served as models for the target group of the newly introduced municipal adult education. These students belonged to the so-called pool of talent – they had a high level of aspiration, were motivated to study, and were often successful in their self-tuition. This was a very different target group than what has been traditionally associated with ABE. Looking at the link to labor markets, it is evident that what was being offered was an adapted form of what was regularly offered in comprehensive and secondary education and that no adjustments were made to make the program specifically vocation oriented. The economic benefit was seen coming from having more people with a solid basic education that would allow them to pursue postsecondary studies. The only direct reference to employment was that Komvux courses were mainly available as part-time studies so as to avoid production losses.

Komvux Economic Crises and Changing Demands on Competence Development

During the economic crises of the early 1990s, the debate on Komvux shifted from a focus on education discourse to its role in a labor-market strategy. The response was to introduce the Adult Education Initiative (Sweden Government Bill 1995/97: 222). It was not introduced as an educational bill, but rather as a cornerstone in a bill titled 'Special strategies introduced in order to half unemployment by year 2000.' The adult education initiative (AEI) was a massive 5-year program for adult education in which

all municipalities participated. The project comprised some 110 000 new educational places per year for adults, mainly in municipal adult education. Over the 5 years, it aimed to reach 550 000 adults – roughly 15% of the labor force. The AEI signaled a fundamental broadening of the Swedish tradition of active labor-market policy. Instead of expanding traditional labor-market training programs, the AEI attempted to raise the general level of education in unemployed adults. Another goal of the AEI was that it would act as a vehicle for reforming the adult-education sector both in terms of content and working methods. Over the 5-year period, adult education was reformed and developed so as to better meet the challenges that the individual, working life, and society would face in the new millennium.

Two things stand out in the AEI strategy: the first is the use of general education as a labor-market strategy; and the second is that the content and teaching methods of ABE in Sweden more directly began to be considered in the context of labor-market needs. Further, it is worth noting that, in view of the apparent danger of having a growing cadre of unemployed facing increasing obstacles in getting back into the labor market, the AEI contained several measures aimed at helping to reach adults who traditionally do not participate in adult education and training. A special education grant was introduced at the same time as the AEI, which was primarily intended for unemployed persons who had not completed a 3-year upper secondary program. Further, in order to reach persons with little or no experience of adult education and help them to start studying, more targeted recruitment and information activities were put in place. In a broader international perspective, the AEI that was replicated in other Nordic countries is of interest, as it illustrates an ABE strategy that combines an economic agenda with strong equality ambitions.

The new demand for continuing VET also set off a broad debate in Sweden – as in other countries – on how to develop new models of ABE that would be appropriate in the emergent knowledge economy.

New Forms of VBL in Formal Adult Education

Many providers of VET in EU countries are using a system in which theoretical and practical activities are mixed. A criticism has been that they are too often organized from a school perspective, focusing on how students' workplace activities match theoretical courses provided by the school. The transition from knowledge produced at school to the work situation has been recognized as a major problem. However, as discussed in several recent studies, this is a misconception. In this context, it is of interest to look a bit closer at the empirical findings from the so-called People Project funded by the European Social Fund, where unemployed adults participated in VET courses at the adult secondary school level. An alternative pedagogy was developed based on the idea that the foundation of a vocation is rooted in vocational culture, vocational praxis, and vocational knowledge. Traditional school-based VET does not recognize dimensions that are linked to each other like a Chinese box, see **Figure 1**.

The study reveals that when organizing VBL, it is preferable to consider this picture. This conclusion is based on the fact that the People Project was very successful in two respects – first, because the unemployed participants managed to find jobs, and, second, because the training provided a foundation for lifelong learning (Höghielm, 2005).

The root of the problem of traditional vocational education within the school system is the existence of two different cultures, each with its own logic. Within school culture, subjects should be organized in a sequencing way – from the simple to the complex – and based on this logic, skills are supposed to be generated from basic to more specific. Working life has a different logic, with a number of occupations at the same workplace constituting a community of practice.

Figure 2 shows how the two different logics emanate from the two cultures and cause problems for the participant. In this context, the vocational adult teacher can be regarded as a broker, developing new connections across communities of practice, facilitating coordination and opening possibilities for new meanings. Vocational adult-educational students are in a unique position to act as mediators, bringing insights from work experience to school and vice versa. The vocational adult teacher has an important role in encouraging the development of this process.

The figure shows the sequential logic of school subjects illustrated as ladders, while working life has a more coherent structure – where acquiring vocational knowledge is characterized as a movement from the periphery toward the center. The concept of VBL relies on the idea of situated learning – a well-known concept since the beginning of the 1990s (Lave and Wenger, 1991; Wenger, 1998). Lave and Wenger have managed to phrase, in an attractive way, an old idea that has always been present within VET – going back to medieval times when the apprentice system was established in Europe. They also elucidated how modern educational systems and VET, in particular, have an ongoing discussion on the difference between practice and theory. Thus, the VBL concept has a sociocultural approach going back to the ideas of Vygotsky (1987).

Traditional VET programs have a school perspective – implying students' workplace experiences can be organized to fit in school activities. VBL has a reversed perspective, that is, programs are organized in such a way that students' workplace experiences guide when theoretical school subjects are supposed to enter. This different way of organizing

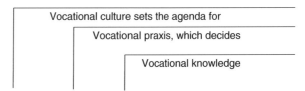

Figure 1   The Chinese Box of VET.

VET adult programs will also facilitate the vocational adult participant's boundary crossing between school and work (Tuomi-Grön and Engeström, 2003). Further on, vocational based adult learning can be a more powerful tool for organizing VET compared to a more traditional, organized, apprentice-based education. Applying the VBL concept implies that adult students must spend half of their time at a workplace, visited by teachers.

Concerning the demand on the European workforce to increase competitiveness and the ongoing demographic change within the EU, research of the kind discussed here suggests a need to develop a new way of organizing VET – which makes it necessary to relinquish the predominant, but obsolete, approach. By using a VBL approach, there will be a quicker and more obvious connection between practice and theory. The concept has similarities to the professional education of nurses and medical doctors practiced at the McMaster University medical school in Canada since 1967. Between 2005 and 2007, a major European Science Foundation (ESF) project in Sweden used the experiences from the municipality of Söderhamn, and VBL was applied in 29 municipalities. The study also involved 275 companies, 197 teachers, and a large number of principals (Höghielm, 2005, 2009).

Future Directions of ABE

ABE – as it is being practiced and organized around the world today – is still heavily influenced by how it was originally set up in the 1960s. While there is an impetus in most countries for greater skills-oriented training, these programs have not adapted to the changing realities. First, demographics have changed and educational attainment has risen dramatically in the population. Second, educational attainment plays an increasingly important role for entering the labor market. Third, there is a rising demand for continuing VET. Fourth, there has been – as discussed above – a shift in the very understanding of VET and a movement to think of vocational education in terms of VBL. Consequently, there are growing demands for a major overhaul of ABE as we have known it.

Starting from the latter, one can think of a form of ABE that takes the individual and his/her vocational background as its point of departure. Traditionally, adult education theory has been considered as a basic guideline for

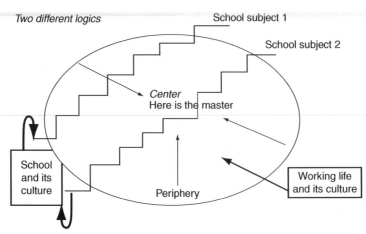

Two different logics

School subject 1

School subject 2

Center
Here is the master

School
and its
culture

Periphery

Working life
and its culture

Figure 2   The relation between the two different logics emanated from school culture and working-life culture.

educational planners and trainers wanting to pursue a reflective approach to adult learning. Based on recent research on VBL, this seems to be too narrow a perspective if the ambition is to include the learner in the process of reflection. Instead of a general curriculum, there is a need for an individual study plan for each participant. In developing this plan, one has to take into account how the individual has been trained in order to manage both previous and new-found knowledge through a validating process that takes into account both general and personal skills from a VBL perspective. (For an interesting discussion of different models of validation see OECD (2005) report Promoting Adult Learning.) The purpose of this form of ABE is to allow participants to have the opportunity to develop specific skills linked to civil and working life as well as for pursuing their own educational/vocational project. The dialog with others makes the learner test out new assumptions, understandings, and perspectives (see Mezirow, 2000). This form of VBL would avoid the dilemma of the narrowness of the skills-driven training that is being promoted in some countries as well as the general education lacking vocational connections that can be found in other countries. A development in the direction of VBL can take place within a network organization. The location of such an activity would not be built around a traditional adult-education school such as Komvux, but could be a flexible learning center such as Centre for Flexible Learning (CFL) Söderhamn (Ekelöf, 2009). This form of structure has an opportunity to meet the dual and interconnected needs for a de-schooling version and a schooling-up version of ABE. Examples of this form of organization of ABE can be drawn from different regions in Sweden where municipalities have organized themselves into flexible learning centers. The slogan in these contexts is flexibility or flexible learning – where providers organize learning centers or networks and plan and implement teaching with the primary purpose of supporting student communication and learning (Holmberg, 2004).

Such a development could suggest a return in ABE to the andragogical ideals that were in the foreground of the initial ABE debate.

See also: Adult Learning and Instruction: Transformative-Learning Perspectives; Adult Literacy Education; Organizational Learning; Provision of Prior Learning Assessment; Workplace-Learning Frameworks.

Bibliography

EC (European Commission) (2006). Communication from the Commission. Adult learning: It is never too late to learn. Brussels. http://eurlex.europa.eu/LexUriServ/LexUriServ.do?uri=COM:2006:0614:FIN:EN:PDF (accessed August 2009).

EC (European Commission) (2007). Action Plan on Adult Learning. It is always a good time to learn. Brussels. http://ec.europa.eu/education/policies/adult/com558_en.pdf (accessed August 2009).

Ekelöf, E. (ed.) (2009). *Yrkesutbildning – en framtida arena för vuxnas lärande. Anföranden och dokumentation från en konferens vid Stockholms universitet 28 – 29 oktober 2008* (Vocational education and training – a future arena for adult's learning. Contributions in Swedish and English at a conference October 28–29, Stockholm University, 2008.) Ljusdal: ab romi tryckeri.

Firoza, A. (ed.) (1966). Adult Education Association of the U.S.A. Adult basic education study 1965–1966. ERIC # ED023032.

Höghielm, R. (2005). *Yrkesbaserat lärande. Erfarenheter från PEOPLE delprojekt i Söderhamn 2002 till 2005.* (Vocational based learning. Experiences from PEOPLE subproject in Söderhamn 2002 to 2005.) CFL Söderhamn. Ljudal: ab romi tryck. http://www.ntglar.se (accessed August 2009).

Höghielm, R. (2009). En ny yrkesutbioldning i skärningspunkten mellan två kulturer. (Vocational education and training a crossroad of two cultures.) In Ekelöf, E. (ed.) Yrkesutbildning – en framtida arena för vuxnas lärande. Anföranden och dokumentation från en konferens vid Stockholms universitet 28–29 oktober 2008, pp 59–76. (Vocational education and training – a future arena for adult's learning. Contributions in Swedish and English at a conference October 28–29, Stockholm University, 2008.) Ljusdal: ab romi tryckeri.

Holmberg, C. (2004). På den studerandes villkor – flexibelt lärande. Sid. i. *Utsikter och Insikter. En antologi om flexibelt lärande i vuxenutbildningen (2004)*, pp 67–81. (On the participant's conditions – flexible learning. In perspectives and insights. An Antologi about flexible learning in adult education, pp 67–81.). Nationellt centrum för flexibelt lärande; Rapport 5: 2004.

Lave, J. and Wenger, E. (1991). *Situated Learning. Legitimate Peripheral Participation*. Cambridge: Cambridge University Press.

Mezirow, J. (2000). Learning to think like an adult: Core concepts of transformation theory. In Mezirow, J., Kegan, R., Belenkey, M. F., *et al.* (eds.) *Learning as Transformation*, pp 3–33. San Francisco, CA: Jossey-Bass.

Mezirow, J., Darkenwald, G. G., and Knox, A. (1975). *Last Gamble on Education: Dynamics of Adult Basic Education*. Washington, DC: Adult Association of the USA.

OECD (2005). Promoting Adult Learning. http://www.oecd.org/edu/adultlearning (accessed August 2009).

Sweden Government Bill (1995/97). 222.

Tuomi-Grön, T. and Engeström, Y. (eds.) (2003). *Between School and Work. New Perspectives on Transfer and Boundary-Crossing*. Pergamon: Earli, European Association for Learning and Instruction.

Vygotsky, L. S. (1987). *Mind in Society*. Cambridge, MA: Harvard University Press.

Wenger, E. (1998). *Communities of Practice. Learning, Meaning and Identity*. Cambridge: Cambridge University Press.

Further Reading

Bron, A. and Scemmann, M. (eds.) (2003). *Knowledge Society, Information Society and Adult Education. Buchum Studies in International Adult Education,* vol. 3. Munster: LitVerlag.

Cole, M., Engström, Y., and Vasquez, O. (2004). *Mind, Culture and Activity: Seminal Papers from the Laboratory of Comparative Human Cognition*. Cambridge: Cambridge University Press.

EAEA (European Association for Education of Adults) (2009). *Adult education in the world*. http://www.eaea.org/se/index.php?k=12086 (accessed August 2009).

Engeström, Y. (1999). Activity theory and individual and social transformation. In Engeström, Y., Miettinen, R., and Punamäki, R. -L. (eds.) *Perspectives on Activity Theory*, pp 19–38. Cambridge: Cambridge University Press.

Engeström, Y. (2005). Cultural History Activity Theory. http://www.edu.helsinki.fi/activity/pages/chatanddwr/chat (accessed August 2009).

Gordon, H. R. D. (2003). *The History and Growth of Vocational Education in America*. Long Grove, IL: Waveland Press.

Lasonen, J. and Young, M. (eds.) (1997). *Stategies for Achieving Parity of Esteem in European Upper Secondary Education.* European Commission Leonardo da Vinci Programme: Surveys and Analyses. *Post-16 Strategies Project*. Jyväskylä: Institute for Educational Research, University of Jyväskylä.

Manninen, J., Burman, A., Koivunen, A., *et al.* (2007). *Environments that Support Learning. An Introduction to Learning Environments Approach. Finnish National Board of Education*. Vammala: Vammalan Kirjapaino Oy.

Nijhof, W. J. and Streumer, J. N. (eds.) (1998). *Key Qualification in Work and Education.* Dordrecht: Kluwer Academic Publisher.

Schutze, H. G. and Istance, D. (1987). *Recurrent Education Revisited. Modes of Participation and Financing: Report Prepared for CERI and OECD*. Stockholm: Almqvist and Wiksell Internationell.

Tuijman, A. and van der Kamp, M. (1992). *Learning Across the Lifespan. Theories, Research, Policies*. Oxford: Pergamon Press.

Relevant Website

http://www.esrea.org – ESREA (European Society for the Research on the Education of Adults).

Adult Literacy Education

L Tett, University of Edinburgh, Edinburgh, UK
R St.Clair, University of Glasgow, Glasgow, UK

The last few years have seen growing interest in the field of adult literacy education, also known as adult basic education and adult literacy and numeracy, with increased attention at national and international levels. This has been partly inspired by the International Adult Literacy Survey of the mid-1990s (and the less influential Adult Literacy and Life Skills Survey (ALL) of the following decade), which allowed adults' skills to be compared across countries for the first time. This coincided with the move toward an information economy, allegedly making information management skills such as literacy the bedrock for success. At the same time notions of human capital (where education is the fundamental key to prosperity) were gaining favor with agencies such as the World Bank and UNESCO (Wickens and Sandlin, 2007) so adult literacy education became seen as a central and critical educational sector.

Adult literacy education is marked by a high level of diversity in terms of structure, delivery, and philosophy and performs different roles in different parts of the world, whether industrialized Europe or a developing country. It can take place in church basements, further education colleges, universities, community settings, workplaces, and libraries. It can be delivered by professionally qualified staff, or staff who are qualified in other forms of teaching or unqualified volunteers. Learners can be employed or unemployed, men or women, refugees or indigenous people, full time students, or people who study part-time. Each of these presents a unique context for literacy education, and it is important not to generalize across settings without taking great care.

What Is Adult Literacy?

There are a number of ways of conceptualizing what is meant by adult literacy. These definitions contain assumptions that matter to the focus of education because they imply different understandings of learning (Papen, 2005). Three concepts have been particularly influential: the functional, critical, and liberal concepts of literacy (**Table 1**).

Functional Literacy

In this view literacy is seen as a skill that is required for a broad range of activities associated with the individual's participation in society. There is an assumed correlation between individual skills and the overall performance of the nation in terms of modernization and economic productivity. This is particularly so in the OECD (1997, 2000), where a focus on improving literacy skills as the key to unlocking the benefits of globalization is dominant. Literacy is conceived as a set of neutral, technical skills with little to do with culture and society. Its assumed benefits are believed to include enabling access to information, developing thinking, and improving the individual's chances of finding employment and income. Reflecting this view, the ALL assessed skills against a suitable minimum for meeting the demands of daily work and life (UNESCO, 2005). The functional model emphasizes individual deficits and sees literacy as a set of discrete skills believed to be universal and transferable to all kinds of situations that require the use of written language (Barton, 1994).

Critical Literacy

The concept of critical literacy is associated with the Brazilian educator Paulo Freire and refers to the potential of literacy for not only reading the word but also reading the world (Friere and Macedo, 1987). It moves away from the functional model, toward a pedagogy intended to allow participants to understand their world in terms of justice and injustice, power and oppression, and how to transform it. Contrary to the functional model, primary purpose of critical literacy is not to help the individual to move up the existing social ladder, but to build a radical critique of the dominant culture and the existing power relationships between social groups (Shor, 1993). This model is often linked to democratic citizenship and the role that education plays in supporting people's participation in society (Crowther and Tett, 2001). People need the ability not only to decode the literal meanings of texts, but also to read between the lines and to engage in a critical discussion of the positions a text supports.

Liberal Tradition of Literacy

The third view of literacy is informed by a humanist view of education that emphasizes personal development and individual goals. It argues for the right of all citizens to education and goes beyond the functional-skills approach to include areas such as creative writing and access to

Table 1   Three views of literacy education

	Functional	*Critical*	*Liberal*
Reason for literacy education	Skills Survival/ work	Understanding Empowerment	Tools Development of person
Participant group	(Potential) workers	Marginalized groups	Everybody

literature (Papen, 2005). Participants in programs are not limited to the working population but include older people or those who are not part of the workforce.

These different definitions present competing ideologies of literacy with associated assumptions, values, and standards that need to be questioned. However, in much of the world there is an unquestioning emphasis on the functional, vocational approach such as Welfare to Work in the US (Sandlin & Cervero, 2003), resulting in a discourse of literacy as a technical skill and vocational competence.

Social-Practice and Skills Models of Literacy

In addition to diverging perspectives on the purpose of adult literacy education, there are a number of theoretical positions on how people actually use literacies. A functional-skills-based approach focuses attention on the autonomy of the text and the meanings it carries. It searches for universal features of adult literacy and other semiotic sign systems. It leads to narrow definitions of reading, writing, and calculating, and ignores aspects of learning that cannot be dealt with at the individual or cognitive level. It excludes many issues that are important for understanding learner responses. All too often it can support a deficit view of literacy, where those with limited literacy engagement are seen to be lacking in some way, whether in ability or in education.

One approach has moved away from the individually focused cognitive skills model to include the social practices associated with number, reading, and writing (Hamilton *et al.*, 2006). In this view literacy is not seen as a purely individual activity – instead, it sees literacy and numeracy as being historically and socially situated and part of wider cultural and media engagement. The focus of the social-practices approach shifts away from literacy as something learners lack toward the many different ways that people engage with literacy. Social-practices approaches recognize difference and diversity, and challenge how these differences are valued within our society.

Street (1995) describes this as a shift from seeing literacy as an autonomous gift to be given to people to an ideological view of literacy that places it in the wider

context of institutional purposes and power relationships. From this perspective adult literacy is part of a range of social practices that are observable in events or moments and are patterned by social institutions and power relationships. Attention is focused on the cultural practices within which written and spoken words are embedded. Not just reading but also speaking and writing, as well as the use of new technologies, become central to the definition of literacy. The social-practices view requires that connections are made between the classroom and the community in which learners lead their lives; with a notion of situated learning; between learning and institutional power; and between print literacy and other media.

There is not just one social-practices theory of adult literacy, numeracy, and language, but a number of different versions. The social-practice approach that has characterized the new literacy studies (NLS) draws mainly on ideas and methodologies from sociology, sociolinguistics, and anthropology rather than the more psychological approach of active problem-solving theory rooted in the work of Vygotsky and others. The NLS involves looking beyond formal educational settings to informal learning, and to the other official settings in which literacies play a key role. Learning does not just take place in classrooms but in everyday life, with meanings, values, and purposes located within a broader literacy framework than the texts themselves.

There are two important principles underlying the implementation of a social-practice approach to literacy. First, a two-way dialog and movement between formal learning and the everyday world is essential. Everyday, situated cultures and practices cannot simply be acknowledged and imported into classroom settings. The boundaries between in and out of education must be blurred so that contexts become permeable.

Second, active learning is assumed by this approach. It characterizes the process of becoming literate as one of taking hold of the tools of writing and language. This has important implications for relationships within the learning process and for reflective and questioning activity on the part of both learners and teachers (Hamilton *et al.*, 2006). The ways in which teachers and learners participate in decision making and the governance of the organization in which learning takes place are crucial, whether through management committees, consultative bodies, and research and development activities. Citizenship is modeled and enacted within such arenas.

Reconciling the Skills and Social-Practices Perspectives

The social-practices approach recognizes the importance of learners' motivations, goals, and purposes; every literacy task is done for a reason and in specific contexts, hence the challenge to concepts of universal sets of literacy skills.

Skills and knowledge acquisition are, however, intrinsic to learners' purposes and enhance many different aspects of their lives. For example, improving skills for employment may not appear to serve social practices, but skills that are gained in the pursuit of employment or promotion can be applied in other domains of people's lives, such as helping children with homework, managing the household, or pursuing further learning. Both enhancing skills and recognizing their role within learners' lives are important and both aspects should be developed in good teaching.

How far might it be possible to reconcile the functional-skills approach and the social-practices approach within policy and practice? Could social practices be seen as encompassing and extending the narrower focus of skills? The idea of two opposing broad approaches is an over-simplification and there are other ways of characterizing the guiding philosophies people bring to literacy, particularly in everyday cultural settings (see Barton *et al.*, 2000). Freebody and Lo Bianco suggest (1997: 26) that effective literacy tuition draws on a repertoire of resources that allow learners to: break the code; actively interpret the meaning of the text; use texts functionally; analyse texts critically. This is a dynamic process as represented in **Figure 1** that is an attempt to acknowledge that both skills and critical practices are enmeshed in working with texts.

In the middle circle is the process of actually understanding the words as they are written on the page, and interpreting the meaning. The outer ring represents the social uses of that meaning, which can range from functional to critical. A literacy process that is missing any of these components can be considered as only a partial engagement with the text.

Research in the US is also providing new insights on the interrelations between skills and practices. The 5-year Longitudinal Study of Adult Learning (LSAL) in Portland, Oregon has revealed that both program participation and

self-study have positive, time-specific effects on literacy practices (Reder, 2008). The research showed that self-study was prevalent among adults of all literacy levels as a means of basic skills development, whether or not they also participated in classes. Self-study appears to act as a bridge between periods of program participation and to facilitate persistence. The mixed mode of learning identified by LSAL seems to bridge social-practices and skills-based approaches. It suggests that learners use a range of resources to enhance the social practices associated with literacy, and that programs are one resource, with the specific role of providing skills to underpin the practices. As we suggest with the diagram above, skills and practices form a self-reinforcing cycle of engagement with literacy and literacy education.

The broad mode of participation suggested by LSAL brings together social-practice and skills approaches. On the one hand, it recognizes that learning involves learners actively using resources as well as programs delivering services. On the other, it indicates that literacy programs appear to have the most direct and immediate impact on literacy practices, underlining the role of skills enhancement.

The Role of Adult Literacy Education

Throughout the world, adult literacy education fulfills a variety of roles. For those in industrialized countries, one common perception is that adult literacy learners are people who have not fully benefited from compulsory education. There are a number of possible reasons, ranging from sociological explanations concerning the tendency of schools to push out certain learners to psychological rationales involving learning difficulties. Overall, the common factor is the view that adult literacy education has an ameliorative role, improving literacy engagement and compensating, to some degree, for the failure of initial schooling (St. Clair and Priestman, 1997).

The ameliorative view assumes that learners have had an opportunity to learn literacy practices, and that this opportunity has not been effective. This can lead to a deficit view of learners, where they are assumed to have some kind of problem that has led to reduced literacy abilities.

One of the reasons that adult literacy education has experienced such variability in funding and policy interest is that it can be viewed as an optional form of provision within the ameliorative perspective. After all, if people have already had a chance to learn about literacy surely giving them a second chance is an act of generosity? It follows that the most effective argument for supporting literacy education is often a moral one. This can lead to a panic about literacy education (or more often illiteracy) with dramatically increased funding followed by gradual withdrawal of support until the next moral panic (Quigley, 1997). Ameliorative perspectives can be unhelpful for the general health and stability of the field.

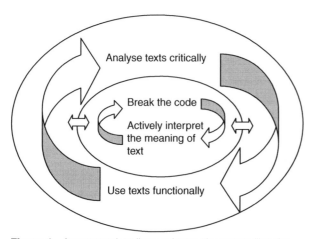

Figure 1   An approach to literacy instruction reconciling the skills and practices approaches.

Despite the dominance of some version of an ameliorative perspective in the industrialized world, there are two other roles that literacy education can play. Each of these roles is particularly relevant to groups with little access to mainstream education. The first is an adaptive role, where individuals from one language and literacy community enter another. This might include economic migrants or refugees, as well as people who have been displaced from one job or life situation into another with different demands, such as older adults attending college for the first time or farm workers following seasonal crops.

In the United States many literacy programs are going beyond people with English as their first language and working to develop initial language skills with speakers of other languages. This is particularly evident in Texas, where more than half the population are Spanish speaking. In the United Kingdom, some adult literacy agencies are working with substantial numbers of refugees to provide initial English language instruction.

Many of these learners will have well-developed literacy and numeracy practices in their first language – in the case of Texas many learners have an excellent Mexican secondary school education, and in the UK refugees are frequently academics, doctors, engineers, and other highly educated professionals. The provision of language education alongside literacy education in programs is generally not widely acknowledged. This can place unpredictable and occasionally unrealistic demands on instructors, resources, and learners themselves. The emphasis on the ameliorative role of literacy education can obscure the adaptive application of literacy learning, perhaps resulting in less appropriate services for this group of learners.

The final role of adult literacy education is foundational. Many countries throughout the world do not have the universally accessible, and generally compulsory, primary education found in the industrialized nations. While UNESCO (2005) has committed itself strongly to literacy as the core of education for all, many people around the world do not gain access to any form of literacy education until later in life. The gross enrolment rate in primary school is below 60% in some African countries, and the age of the child at enrolment may be considerably higher than usual for primary school (UNESCO, 2005). In addition, there is a degree of gender imbalance in school attendance in around 40% of countries, though this is generally reducing quite rapidly (UNESCO, 2005).

For learners in countries without universal access to schooling the ameliorative approach, with its assumption that the conventions and application of education are understood, is inappropriate. New adult learners in this context will be entering classes with little understanding of the nuances and expectations of education, and often will be motivated by economic or instrumental concerns about the care of their family.

There is also a danger of well-meaning aid agencies establishing projects that inadvertently create situations of neo-colonialism, where Western models of literacy education are applied to situations very different from the Western countries. This can easily come to be seen as the most valuable form of learning, displacing local approaches to text and traditional forms of numeracy. An example is drilling learners in rows, teaching literacy practices that then fall into disuse because of irrelevance (Wickens and Sandlin, 2007), or the use of English in post-Colonial settings (Robinson, 2007).

Given the different roles that adult literacy education can fill, some care must be taken when thinking about each situation. It is more complex than assuming that every literacy learner has somehow missed out on elementary schooling, and it is critical to avoid seeing learners as having some deficit.

Accountability and Assessment

There has been a general increase in the resources committed to adult literacy education throughout the world over the last two decades. It remains unclear how long this will last, or what the final results will be, but it has profoundly affected the conceptualization and delivery of literacy education. These changes have resulted in more attention being paid to the outcomes of literacy education. Historically, literacy programs for adults have rarely been strongly concerned with measuring the progress of learners, or indeed the efficiency and effectiveness of the agencies delivering the programs. This is no longer the case in the industrialized countries, resulting in profound transformations of the field.

In thinking about assessment and accountability, it helps to be clear about the two central ideas. Assessment is measurement of learner progress through standardized tests, individual progress reports, or some combination of these and other methods. Accountability is the requirement for programs to demonstrate that they are having a positive impact on the literacy use of learners. There is some confusion around these concepts because assessment data are often taken to be a straightforward measure of effectiveness. In this case, the best strategy for the program is to recruit only very competent learners, meaning they can easily show learners leaving the program with strong results. The issue of assessment leading recruitment and instruction has been tackled very rarely – all too often programs produce what they are asked to measure, potentially at the cost of meaningful learning (Merrifield, 1998).

One recent study (St. Clair and Belzer, 2007) looked at the accountability and assessment systems tied into adult literacy education in the United States, Scotland, and England (the latter have separate educational systems). The study suggested that there are two important dimensions to national accountability and assessment systems.

Table 2 Alignment and standardization in three national literacy systems

	Weak alignment	Strong alignment
Strong standardization	United States	England
Weak standardization		Scotland

The first is the degree of standardization in the system, meaning the extent to which tests, curricula, and methods are shared among all the programs surveyed. The second is the degree of alignment, meaning the extent to which philosophy, ideas, and approach to literacy are shared among the programs. It is possible to have one without the other, or to have both strong standardization and strong alignment (**Table 2**).

In the United States legislation of the late 1990s required the creation of a national reporting system, which collates results from across the country. To allow this to happen, a standard reporting approach has been developed, defining the preferred instruments and desired achievement while still allowing the state governments some latitude. This is a weakly aligned but strongly standardized system. In England, the adult literacy system has been standardized in outcomes in a way similar to the US, but in addition the curriculum and tests have been centralized to reflect a single approach to literacy education. This system is both standardized and aligned. In Scotland, there is strong alignment around the social-practices model of literacy discussed earlier, but very little standardization – programs are encouraged to develop their own approaches and resources.

Each of these approaches has its strengths and weaknesses. With high standardization, it is all too easy for programs and instructors to feel limited in responding to local circumstances, whereas low standardization can lead to uncertainty about the quality of the services learners are receiving. A single hierarchy of tests and exams and a requirement that learners demonstrate a certain amount of progress for a certain investment of time and money is not compatible with a social-practices view of literacy. High alignment is most effective where there is genuine commitment to a particular conception of literacy education, and that may be hard to maintain across a national system over any length of time. Despite recognition of the importance of locally tailored programs maintaining effective, learner-led practice may prove to be a significant challenge for literacy educators in the future.

Changes in the Literacy Education Workforce

The last few years have also seen a move toward professionalization of literacy instruction in the industrialized countries. This development, which is supported by many instructors and administrators, is generally accompanied by pressure for adult literacy education to more closely resemble the established educational professions – school teaching in particular. This suggests that a specific qualification for teaching adult literacy may be developed, and that there would be some attention given to providing professional development for core staff. While professionalization would fit well with the agenda of accountability and quality control, it would also raise a number of problems.

One implication of any move to a professionalized workforce would be the loss of volunteers, who currently perform a central role in many systems. If they and part-time workers were expected to undergo substantial training before being able to work with learners, there is a danger that it would be more difficult to recruit. There is also the question of what workers should be taught – if they are only provided with a basic introduction to the field, it is unclear that they would be necessarily be able to deliver better-quality instruction. There is a real possibility that a straightforward, standardized curriculum would be developed for delivery by semi-trained staff, reducing the diversity of practices in the field.

Conclusion

Adult literacy education takes place in a wide range of settings where learners engage in a variety of ways with texts of all kinds. It is critical for effective instruction that both the method and the content of instruction recognize this diversity and that deficit approaches, where the learner is assumed to have something wrong with them, are avoided. Instead, a variety of outcomes of literacy instruction should be valued.

The recent structural changes in the field throughout the world have been substantial, with issues to do with accountability and professionalization rising up the agenda. These changes have tended to move adult literacy education closer to school-based education. At the same time, the importance of having a system that is highly aligned around values and ideology is being more widely recognized, perhaps as a response to the trend for managerialism. Finally, there is real interest in bringing skills and social-practices perspectives together to create a more nuanced understanding of teaching and learning that enables literacy education to be more closely aligned to the practices used in people's everyday lives.

See also: Adult Basic Education – A Challenge for Vocational Based Learning; Lifelong Learning.

Bibliography

Barton, D. (1994). *Literacy: An Introduction to the Ecology of Written Language*. Oxford, UK: Blackwell.
Barton, D., Hamilton, M., and Ivanic, R. (eds.) (2000). *Situated Literacies: Reading and Writing in Context*. New York: Routledge.

Crowther, J. and Tett, L. (2001). Democracy as a way of life: Literacy as citizenship. In Crowther, J., Hamilton, M., and Tett, L. (eds.) *Powerful Literacies*, pp 108–118. Leicester: NIACE.

Freebody, P. and Lo Bianco, J. (1997). *Australian Literacies Part II: What a National Policy on Literacy Should Say*. Canberra: Language Australia.

Friere, P. and Macedo, D. (1987). *Reading the Word and the World*. London: Routledge/Kegan Paul.

Hamilton, M., Hillier, Y., and Tett, L. (2006). Introduction: Social practice of adult literacy, numeracy and language. In Tett, L., Hamilton, M., and Hillier, Y. (eds.) (2006) *Adult Literacy, Numeracy and Language: Policy, Practice and Research*, pp 1–18. Maidenhead: Open University Press.

Merrifield, J. (1998). *Contested Ground: Performance Accountability in Adult Basic Education*. Cambridge, MA: National Center for the Study of Adult Learning and Literacy.

Papen, U. (2005). *Adult Literacy as a Social Practice*. New York: Routledge.

Quigley, B. A. (1997). *Rethinking Literacy Education: The Critical Need for Practice-Based Change*. San Francisco, CA: Jossey-Bass.

Reder, S. (2008). *Dropping Out and Moving on: Life, Literacy and Development among School Dropouts*. Cambridge, MA: Harvard University Press.

Robinson, C. (2006). Context of key language in four adult learning programs. *International Journal of Educational Development* **27**, 541–551.

Sandlin, J. A. and Cervero, R. M. (2003). Contradictions and compromise: The curriculum-in-use as negotiated ideology in two welfare-to-work classes. *International Journal of Lifelong Education* **22**(3), 149–165.

Shor, I. (1993). Education is politics: Paulo Freire's critical pedagogy. In McLaren, P. and Leonard, P. (eds.) *Paulo Freire: A Critical Encounter*, pp 169–176. New York: Routledge.

St. Clair, R. and Belzer, A. (2007). National accountability systems. In Campbell, P. (ed.) *Accountability in Adult Basic Education*, pp 159–206. Edmonton, AB: Grass Roots Press.

St. Clair, R. and Priestman, S. (1997). What's the good of adult education? *North West Philosophy of Education Conference*. Vancouver: December.

Street, B. (1995). *Social Literacies: Critical Approaches to Literacy in Development, Ethnography and Education*. London: Longman.

UNESCO (2005). *Education for All: Literacy for Life*. Paris: UNESCO.

Wickens, C. M. and Sandlin, J. A. (2007). Literacy for what? Literacy for whom? The politics of literacy education and neocolonialism in UNESCO and World Bank sponsored literacy programs. *Adult Education Quarterly* **57**(4), 275–292.

Further Reading

Belzer, A. and St. Clair, R. (2003). *Information Series Number 391: Opportunities and Limits: An Update on Adult Literacy Education*. Columbus, OH: The State University of Ohio Center on Education and Training for Employment.

Binkley, M., Matheson, N., and Williams, T. (1997). *Working Paper No. 97-33: Adult Literacy: An International Perspective*. Washington, DC: US Department of Education, National Center for Educational Statistics.

Freire, P. (1972). *Pedagogy of the Oppressed*. Harmondsworth: Penguin.

Graff, H. J. (1995). *The Labyrinths of Literacy*. Pittsburgh, PA: University of Pittsburgh.

OECD (1997). *Education Policy Analysis*. Paris: OECD.

OECD (2000). *Literacy in the Information Age*. Paris: OECD.

Stephens, S. (2000). A critical discussion of the 'new literacy studies'. *British Journal of Educational Studies* **48**(1), 10–23.

Tett, L., Hamilton, M., and Hillier, Y. (2006). *Adult Literacy, Numeracy and Language: Policy, Practice and Research*. Maidenhead: Open University Press.

Relevant Websites

http://www.literacy.lancs.ac.uk – Lancaster Literacy Research Centre, Research and Practice in Adult Literacy (RaPAL).

http://www.ncsall.net – National Center for the Study of Adult Literacy and Learning (United States).

http://www.literacytrust.org.uk – National Literacy Trust (United Kingdom).

http://www.nrdc.org.uk – National Research and Development Centre (United Kingdom).

http://www.unesco.org – United Nations Educational, Scientific and Cultural Organization.

http://go.worldbank.org – World Bank on Education for All.

Citizenship and Immigrant Education

D Schugurensky, University of Toronto, Toronto, ON, Canada

Glossary

Citizenship – The status of being a citizen; membership in a community; the quality of an individual's response to membership in a community.

CONFINTEA(Conférence internationale sur l'éducation des adultes (International Conference on Adult Education) – A series of international meetings, which takes place every 12 years since 1949, organized by United Nations Educational, Scientific and Cultural Organization (UNESCO).

Immigrate – To enter and usually become established; to come into a country of which one is not a native for permanent residence.

Jus sanguinis – Latin for right of blood, a social policy by which citizenship is determined by having an ancestor who is a national or citizen of the state.

Jus soli – Latin for right of the soil, a right by which citizenship can be recognized to any individual born in the territory of the related state.

Naturalization – The acquisition of citizenship by individuals who were not citizens of that country at the moment of birth.

UNESCO (United Nations Educational, Scientific and Cultural Organization) – A specialized United Nations agency founded in 1945.

Introduction

In the field of adult education, it is possible to identify two separate areas of research, theory, and practice that are often related: citizenship education and immigrant education. Generally speaking, citizenship education aims at preparing individuals to become citizens in a particular political community. Typically, citizenship-education initiatives focus on the teaching of citizens' rights and duties, as well as the legal system and the functioning of government institutions. In some cases, it also includes the nurturing of critical analysis of social reality and engagement in civic and political activities. Immigrant education aims at enhancing the integration of new immigrants in the economic, social, cultural, and political life of the receiving countries through a variety of services and programs. These include programs such as second-language acquisition, special language courses for immigrant professionals, entry-level job-skills development, entrepreneurial training, financial literacy (from basic banking to investment classes), and information about local culture, laws, and regulations. Services include employment counseling and job-search strategies, settlement assistance, and access to computers.

In many countries, citizenship education and immigrant education are offered to children, youth, and adults by a variety of governmental agencies, nonprofit organizations, private institutions, and community groups. The intersection between citizenship education and immigrant education can be found in the area of citizenship education for immigrants. This area focuses on preparing newcomers to become citizens in the host country. By and large, the size and importance of this area in a given country is directly correlated to the size and history of immigration. In other words, those countries with higher immigration rates and with longer traditions as recipient societies are more likely to have established programs and pedagogical materials on citizenship education for immigrants and to devote significant human and material resources to this area. In the past, the main impetus behind those initiatives was an interest to quickly assimilate immigrants into the prevailing culture and values of the host society, and particularly to incorporate them as soon as possible into the labor market. More recently, some countries established immigration policies and programs aiming at balancing the integration of immigrants into the host society and the respect for the immigrants' cultural identity, that is, promoting simultaneously, both unity and diversity.

Before addressing general trends related to adult citizenship education and immigration education, it is useful to discuss some conceptual and historical issues related to citizenship and to immigration.

Citizenship

As noted above, citizenship education includes all those educational programs and initiatives that have as their main purpose preparing individuals to become citizens. Although at first glance this seems like a straightforward proposition, it is pertinent to ask: What does it mean to become a citizen? There is no easy answer to this question because citizenship is a dynamic, contextual, contested, and multidimensional concept. It is dynamic because its meaning, characteristics, and scope have changed throughout history. For instance, in a not-so-distant past, there were many countries that excluded slaves, women, nonwhites, and illiterates from citizenship. It is contextual because, even in the same historical moment, citizenship is a term that has interpretations and applications in different societies. Indeed, at any historical moment, many countries have applied – and still do – different criteria to determine who is a citizen and who is not, who can become a citizens and who cannot, what the traits of a good citizen are, and so on. Moreover, citizenship is a contested term because, even in the same time and space, in the same nation-state, and there are profound disagreements about what citizenship is and what it should be. In each society, different groups have different perspectives on the criteria for inclusion and exclusion, and different ideas about the qualities of good citizenship.

The term citizenship is also multidimensional because it encompasses four different dimensions that are frequently conflated: status, identity, civic virtues, and agency. Status relates to issues of membership to a particular political community. Identity relates to issues of feelings of belonging and loyalty to that political community. Civic virtues refer to the dispositions, values, and behaviors that are expected from citizens, and agency refers to the capacity to act as a citizen, that is, to engage actively in civic and political life with the possibility of making a difference. Since these four dimensions influence the approaches adopted by adult-citizenship-education programs, it is pertinent to elaborate on them.

In the most common understanding of the term, citizenship is a status bestowed on those who are full members of a community, which means that those who possess the status of citizens are equal with respect to the rights and duties endowed by it (Marshall, 1949). In modern times, that community is the nation-state, to the extent that citizenship is often equated with nationality. Noncitizens are usually known as foreign aliens. However, at this moment it is also possible to be a citizen of a supranational political entity like the European Community. Citizenship as status distinguishes between citizens, who are full members of a particular political community, and thus can have a passport, are eligible to vote and to be elected, and so on, and noncitizens (or aliens), who have limited rights or no rights at all. Today, citizenship status is usually granted by birthplace (*jus soli*), descent (*jus sanguinis*), or naturalization, although in the past it was often granted and denied on the basis of factors like class, gender, or race. For instance, in many countries it was not until the first half of the twentieth century (in some even later) that women were recognized as full citizens with equal rights. Even in the twenty-first century, some population groups are denied certain rights. For instance, only a few countries allow gay couples the same right to marriage that is granted to the heterosexual population, and although the Universal Declaration of Human Rights states that everyone has a right to a nationality, today

there are more than 15 million stateless people who have no citizenship status in any state, either because they never acquired it in their birth country or because they lost it. In considering the notion of citizenship as status it is pertinent to distinguish between formal and real citizenship: formal equality is largely irrelevant if it is contradicted on a daily basis by economic, social, political, and cultural inequalities. For this reason, any discussion on citizenship as status that is also concerned with real membership in a particular political community must consider the dynamics of inclusion and exclusion of that community.

Identity relates to feelings of belonging that a person has toward a community. This feeling as a full member of a community is independent of the formal citizen status of that person. The distinction between status and identity can be found everywhere, but it is more clear in multiethnic, multilingual, multicultural, and multireligious states, and particularly in nation-states that are multination states (Dean, 2004; Kymlicka, 2001; Wilkinson and Hebert, 1999). In these cases, identity is rooted in factors like a common history, language, religion, values, traditions, and culture, which seldom coincide with the artificial territory of a nation-state. This should not be surprising, because nation-states are imagined communities whose boundaries change over time due to invasions, wars, annexations, conquests, and separations (Anderson, 1983). Hence, it is not surprising that some cultural and linguistic minorities as well as aboriginal groups may not feel part of the nation-state in which they are legal citizens. In the same vein, immigrant communities may hold a legal citizenship status in two or more nation-states but feel allegiance to only one of them. Moreover, there are cases of immigrants who are eligible for citizenship in their host country but do not take it in order to keep a feeling of belonging to their home country, even if they never return to it. Another example of a mismatch between status and identity can be observed among people with internationalist inclinations who are legal citizens of nation-states but define themselves as citizens of the world, even if planetary citizenship is not a legal condition.

Civic virtues refer to the values, attitudes, and behaviors that are expected of good citizens. However, there is no universal agreement on the ideal of a good citizen. For some groups, the main civic virtues of a good citizen are patriotism, obedience, honor, diligence, and religiosity. Others emphasize compassion, respect, tolerance, honesty, solidarity, and individual responsibility, and others relate civic virtues to a critical analysis of social reality, interest for the common good, community participation, and political engagement. All these and many other civic virtues could be chosen, organized, and ranked according to the moral preferences of those who create the list. Moreover, the ideal of good citizen promoted by the state varies according to historical, ideological, and political contexts. For instance, the model of good citizen and the virtues cultivated by the Nazi regime were different from the model and the virtues promoted in Germany in the nineteenth century or today.

Agency refers to the state of being in action or affecting change; thus, the dimension of citizenship as agency invokes the idea of citizens as social actors. The exercise of citizenship, individual or collective, does not occur in a vacuum, but in concrete social relations mediated by power. Indeed, social circumstances determine to a large extent what citizens can do or feel allowed to do, but at the same time, citizens have some degree of agency to change those circumstances and make history. Hence, the notion of citizenship as agency recognizes that social action – which varies both in the intensity and orientation of citizen actions – occurs in a context marked by a constant interplay of limits and possibilities, domination and autonomy, and control structures and liberating forces. Although the literature often refers to passive and active citizenship, in real life these constitute end points of a continuum rather than dichotomous categories.

Immigration

While human migration has existed throughout human history, immigration is the movement of people from one nation-state to another, and involves long-term permanent residence (and eventually citizenship) in the host country. Although short-term visitors are not considered immigrants, seasonal labor migration is often considered as a special form of immigration.

According to estimates from the United Nations, in 2005, the total number of migrants amounted to 190 million people, to which can be added an undetermined number of undocumented or irregular migrants, currently estimated as 30 million people. Typically, migration is driven by two simultaneous dynamics. On the one hand, push factors such as economic, political, or social problems in the country of origin; on the other, pull factors such as economic, social, and cultural opportunities in the destination country. Globally, the large majority of migrants flow from South to North, that is, from Latin America, Asia, and Africa to Europe and North America, but in recent decades, there has been an increase of South–South migration (often due to political instability or generalized violence) and even North–South migration, usually older people who seek retirement in countries with lower costs of living and better climates than their own home countries.

Many immigrants, particularly those who migrate from South to North, often face a great variety of problems, which range from emotional issues arising from leaving relatives, friends, and a known environment to issues related to legal barriers, moving expenses, uncertainty about the future, lack of familiarity with the new culture and language, difficulties in finding decent employment,

and in many cases also exploitation, discrimination, and racism. The acquisition of legal citizenship status in the host country may not necessarily translate into the enjoyment of full citizenship on the same foot as other social groups. In many instances, the discrepancy between legal and real citizenship status has more to do with language, race, gender ethnicity, country of origin, and social class than with the formality of official citizenship papers. As Banks (2004: 5) noted, "becoming a legal citizen of a nation-state does not necessarily mean that an individual will attain structural inclusion into the mainstream society and its institutes or will be perceived as a citizen by most members of the dominant group within the nation-state."

From the perspective of the host societies, particularly those that regularly receive large numbers of immigrants, challenges include providing services, educational programs, and infrastructure to the new immigrants, making an effort to understand and respect different cultures, beliefs, and practices, and creating an environment that nurtures dialog, tolerance, and fairness. Countries with high international demand for immigration tend to establish specific selection criteria and admission policies. Whereas in the past those criteria were often based (sometimes explicitly) on racial or ethnic prejudices, presently they are likely to be based on factors such as schooling, occupation, wealth, and language proficiency, usually expressed in a point system. Such system gives preference to professionals and businesspeople, and discriminates against unskilled workers. This situation creates problems in the labor market due to unmet demand for workers in certain areas of the economy (e.g., construction, agriculture, and janitorial services), which in turn provokes a growth in undocumented migration. Another issue that has increased significantly as a result of the emphasis on professional immigrants is the limited recognition of foreign credentials and work experiences by certain professional colleges. This, in turn, creates a lose–lose situation. The home country suffers brain drain after considerable investment in human-resource development, the host country misses the opportunity of brain gain by forcing immigrant professionals to earn a living delivering pizza or driving taxis, and the professional immigrants lose the possibility of developing their full potential in their chosen field by taking jobs unrelated to their training.

Moreover, countries with large and diverse immigration populations often face the double challenge of ensuring a successful social, economic, political, and cultural integration of newcomers and at the same time reducing tensions that may arise across ethnic, national, or racial lines. In the past, most of these countries (known as settlement countries) favored the strategy of forced assimilation. This strategy, usually referred to with the metaphor of a melting pot, had as its main goal that immigrant groups adopt the language, traditions, attitudes, and values of the dominant culture as fast as possible. In recent times, some settlement countries have adopted a different integration strategy through multiculturalism. Whereas assimilation approaches perceive diversity as a threat and tries to suppress ethnic identities, multiculturalism understands diversity as a resource and seeks to accommodate differences. Hence, multiculturalism tends to promote the celebration of cultural diversity and the management of such diversity through specific policies, programs, and initiatives in different levels of government. Kymlicka and Banting (2006) identify eight frequent policies that are emblematic of a multicultural approach to immigrant integration: (1) constitutional, legislative, or parliamentary affirmation of multiculturalism; (2) adoption of multiculturalism in school curricula; (3) inclusion of ethnic representation and/or sensitivity in the mandate of public media; (4) exemptions from dress codes, Sunday-closing legislation, etc.; (5) allowance of dual citizenship; (6) funding of ethnic-group organizations to support cultural activities; (7) funding of bilingual education or mother tongue instruction; and (8) affirmative action for disadvantaged immigrant groups. They point out that the first three policies celebrate multiculturalism, the middle two reduce legal constraints on diversity, and the last three represent forms of active support for immigrant communities and individuals.

Multicultural approaches have advocates and detractors. Detractors argue that multiculturalism and liberal democracy are fundamentally incompatible, and that the emphasis on diversity and difference undermines the sense of common national identity and nurtures resentment between minority and majority cultures (Sniderman and Hagendoorn, 2007). In some instances, the tension between the values and practices of immigrant groups and the prevailing values and practices of the host society have been addressed through initiatives of reasonable accommodation that generated much public controversy and political and juridical debate. Advocates argue that multiculturalism is an effective strategy to facilitate the full integration of immigrants into the host society while preserving their identity, balancing the principles of cultural distinctiveness and equality. They also argue that multiculturalism helps immigrants to keep their culture and language, reduces discrimination, enhances cross-cultural understanding, and promotes institutional change aimed at equalizing opportunities.

Citizenship and Immigrant Adult Education: Main Orientations

Citizenship and immigrant-education programs tend to address simultaneously the four dimensions of citizenship discussed above, but frequently they emphasize just one.

Those programs that focus on citizenship as status often emphasize formal membership to a particular political community, usually a nation-state. Beyond introductory content dealing with settlement challenges (e.g., language acquisition, resumé writing, and job-searching strategies), these citizenship programs concentrate on facts about national history and geography, government institutions, and the law. In some countries, the content of these programs is codified in textbooks that immigrants seeking naturalization must memorize in order to pass a citizenship test. More often than not, these textbooks tend to promote the official story of a nation's development, with limited coverage of controversial issues (Joshee and Johnson, 2007; Derwing et al., 1998). These programs also describe the rights and duties of citizens, although seldom distinguishing between formal and real membership, or encouraging a critical analysis of the status quo. In the margins, however, there are some critical programs – usually carried out by nongovernmental organizations – that contrast the official perspective with the views of peoples that suffered conquest or discrimination. These programs also question taken-for-granted rules of inclusion and exclusion, interpret the law in the context of social dynamics of power and emancipatory struggles, and emphasize the fulfillment of human rights.

Education programs emphasizing citizenship as identity have tended for a long time to stress nation building and the assimilation of minority groups to the dominant group. Often, this has meant the mainstreaming and the malestreaming of curriculum content, and the elevation of the hegemonic language, religion, and culture to the higher level of a hierarchy. The main purpose (sometimes explicit, sometimes implicit) of many of these programs was identity conversion, that is, reshaping the identity of the recent immigrants in a way that corresponds less with their old world and more with their new world. This certainly included attitudes of loyalty and allegiance to the host country, its religion, and its political leaders. For instance, one of the main textbooks for immigrant citizenship education used in Canada during the first part of the twentieth century stated that the good citizen should love God, the Empire, and Canada (Fitzpatrick, 1919). Today, in the twenty-first century, new immigrants to Canada must pass a civics test and pledge allegiance to the Queen of England in order to become Canadian citizens. Interestingly, Canadian-born people are not required to take this oath or to pass a test as a condition for citizenship, even though 60% of Canadians fail a citizenship exam similar to the one taken by immigrants (Dominion Institute, 2007). Some citizenship-education programs strive at developing a planetary consciousness and an identity as world citizens. These programs are usually known as global education, and are often connected to peace education and environmental-education approaches.

Programs that focus on civic virtues tend to emphasize the development of a set of values, attitudes, dispositions, and behaviors that are expected from good citizens. Paraphrasing the Archbishop of York, who said that the true purpose of education is to produce citizens, Eleanor Roosevelt argued that the purpose of education is to produce good citizens. However, there is no universal agreement about the values and dispositions of good citizenship. Certainly, some values have more universal appeal than others, but the set of values privileged by official-education programs change from country to country and from time to time, and range according to factors like the ideological orientation of the government in power and the prevailing beliefs in a given society. From a pedagogical perspective, citizenship-education programs that focus on civic virtues follow two main approaches. One approach consists of instilling a particular set of values and dispositions through exhortations and inducements. The other approach aims at helping learners develop their own values by examining ethical dilemmas and examining different perspectives in a democratic environment.

Finally, programs that focus on citizenship as agency tend to promote the development of an active citizenry. However, this could take different forms and directions. Westheimer and Khane (2004), for instance, identify three implicit models of active citizenship: responsible, participatory, and justice oriented. Responsible citizens are expected to avoid littering, pick up litter of others, donate blood, recycle, volunteer, pay taxes, exercise, stay out of debt, and the like. Participatory citizens are expected to take active part in the civic affairs and social life of the community, and assume leading roles in neighborhood associations, school councils, or political parties. Justice-oriented citizens are expected to be able to critically analyze structures of inequality, consider collective strategies to challenge injustice, and, whenever possible, address root causes of social problems. Although the three models are important for the development of agency among learners, justice-oriented programs arguably have more potential for building a democratic and just society, as this requires nurturing political subjects who have a critical understanding of social structures and the capacity (and willingness) to participate actively in society. This tradition of citizenship education for transformative social action is grounded in the work of many adult educators, including Jane Addams, N. F. S. Grundtvig, Moses Coady, José María Arizmendi, Paulo Freire, and Myles Horton.

Regardless of their particular orientation and foci, most adult-citizenship-education programs tend to emphasize – often in theory, sometimes also in practice – the importance of nurturing an informed, purposeful, critical, caring, and active citizenship. This requires the development of certain attributes that include knowledge on a variety of areas (from political ideologies and societal structures to government institutions and democratic governance), skills (from information seeking and analysis to conflict resolution and public speaking), attitudes (from self-confidence to respecting other people's opinions and cooperation), and practices (from participating in local associations to voice ideas and voting in municipal, provincial, and federal elections). These attributes can be learned through different programs, although those programs that include an experiential component (e.g., allowing learners to experiment with participatory democracy) tend to be more successful (Merrifield, 2001; Benn, 2000; Annette and Mayo, 2008).

Concluding Remarks: Adult-Citizenship Education in Immigrant Societies

In recent times, some countries with large-scale, continuous, and heterogeneous immigration patterns have established a variety of educational programs to promote successful integration processes and mutual understanding. These programs are usually inspired by two main approaches. The first one, known as multicultural education, focuses on familiarizing learners with different cultures in order to reduce stereotypes and ethnocentric attitudes. Multicultural education emphasizes the teaching of history, traditions, and customs of different cultures. More often than not, this is done superficially and uncritically, focusing almost exclusively on the three Fs of folklore, food, and festivities. However, occasionally multicultural education programs also encourage a deeper social analysis that includes examining dynamics of inequality, discrimination, and racism.

The other approach, known as intercultural education, is about proactive interaction among different ethnic groups. Intercultural education is not so much about acquiring knowledge about other cultures but about promoting communication, cooperation, and regular relations among groups. Although both multicultural and intercultural education programs have similar aims (e.g., promoting understanding, tolerance, and respect among different cultures), the former emphasizes the cognitive dimension whereas the latter puts more emphasis on skills and attitudes. In theory, intercultural education is a two-pronged project that includes working with both the immigrant and the nonimmigrant population. Theoretically, intercultural education is expected to assist immigrant groups in their integration process and at the same time it should help the nonimmigrant society to accept immigrants as equals, with the overall purpose of building a more democratic, inclusive, and egalitarian society premised on an intercultural and active citizenship. In practice, however, many intercultural education initiatives tend to concentrate their efforts on compensatory pedagogical interventions with minority groups rather than on projects that involve all groups in society (Rodríguez Izquierdo, 2009).

Related to this are the debates on the most appropriate pedagogical strategies to cultivate the habits of democracy in diverse societies. The most common approach is to avoid open discussions about controversial topics among participants. Many instructors fear conflict, and hence tend to implement a safe curriculum that reduces the possibility of risk. Others, however, believe that the best way to nurture civic virtues is to welcome controversial topics and hard questions, as well as to encourage participants not to get along. This implies recognizing the plurality of viewpoints among participants and facilitating a respectful dialog among them (McLaughlin, 2004; Hughes and Sears, 2004). As Dewey (1916) pointed out, one of the most effective ways to learn democratic values is to practice democracy in a democratic community.

In closing, the potential of adult education to contribute to a more democratic society is reflected in the first theme of the agenda for the future approved at the fifth International Conference of Adult Education (CONFINTEA) in Hamburg, where it was noted that the challenges of the twenty-first century "require the creativity and competence of citizens of all ages in alleviating poverty, consolidating democratic processes, strengthening and protecting human rights, promoting a culture of peace, encouraging active citizenship, strengthening the role of civil society, ensuring gender equality and equity, enhancing the empowerment of women, recognizing cultural diversity (including the use of language, and promoting justice and equality for minorities and indigenous peoples) and a new partnership between state and civil society" (CONFINTEA, 1997: 1). The agenda adds that to reinforce democracy, it is essential to strengthen learning environments, encourage citizen participation, and create contexts where a culture of equity and peace can take root.

To achieve these goals, CONFINTEA asks adult educators to make four commitments: to create greater community participation; to raise awareness about prejudice and discrimination; to encourage greater recognition, participation, and accountability of nongovernmental organizations and local community groups; and to promote a culture of peace, intercultural dialog, and human rights. Adult citizenship and immigrant-education programs can assist these efforts by addressing issues of status, identity, civic virtues, and agency. This can be pursued through a variety of pedagogical/political strategies that adapt and reinvent the contributions of twentieth-century adult education to the realities of the twenty-first century. Adult education can play an important role in improving the conditions for learning, in increasing the sharing of this learning along the lines of intercultural education, and in equalizing opportunities for learning and for meaningful participation among all members of society.

See also: Adult Learning, Instruction and Programme Planning: Insights from Freire; Barriers to Participation in Adult Education; Characteristics of Adult Learning; Participation in Adult Learning; Race and Ethnicity in the Field of Adult Education.

Bibliography

Anderson, B. (1983). *Imagined Communities: Reflections on the Origin and Spread of Nationalism*. London: Verso.

Annette, J. and Mayo, M. (eds.) (2008). *Adult Learning for Active Citizenship*. London: NIACE.

Banks, J. (2004). Democratic citizenship education in multicultural societies. In Banks, J. (ed.) *Diversity and Citizenship Education*, pp 3–15. San Francisco, CA: Jossey-Bass.

Benn, R. (2000). Including citizenship in the adult curriculum. *Paper Presented at SCUTREA, 30th Annual Conference*, 3–5 July, University of Nottingham.

CONFINTEA (1997). The agenda for the future. *Fifth International Conference on Adult Education*, Paris: UNESCO.

Dean, B. (2004). Pakistani conceptions of citizenship and their implications for democratic citizenship education. In Mundel, K. and Schugurensky, D. (eds.) *Lifelong Citizenship Learning, Participatory Democracy and Social Change*, pp 1–11. Toronto, ON: Transformative Learning Centre, OISE/UT.

Derwing, T., Kama, J., and Murray, M. (1998). Citizenship education for adult immigrants: Changes over the last ten years. *Alberta Journal of Educational Research* **44**, 383–396.

Dewey, J. (1916). *Democracy and Education*. New York: Free Press.

Dominion Institute (2007). *What Do Young Adults Know About Canadian History? 10 Year Benchmark Study*. Toronto, ON: Dominion Institute.

Fitzpatrick, A. (1919). *Handbook for New Canadians*. Toronto, ON: Ryerson Press.

Hughes, A. and Sears, A. (2004). Situated learning and anchored instruction as vehicles for social education. In Sears, A. and Wright, I. (eds.) *Challenges and Prospects for Canadian Social Studies*, pp 17–37. Vancouver: Pacific Educational Press.

Joshee, R. and Johnson, J. (2007). *Multicultural Education Policies in Canada and the United States*. Vancouver: University of British Columbia Press.

Kymlicka, W. (2001). *Politics in the Vernacular: Nationalism, Multiculturalism, and Citizenship*. New York: Oxford University Press.

Kymlicka, W. and Banting, K. (2006). Immigration, multiculturalism, and the welfare state. *Ethics and International Affairs* **20**(3), 281–304.

Marshall, T. H. (1949). Citizenship and social class. In Marshall, T. H. and Bottomore, T. (eds.) *Citizenship and Social Class*, pp 1–51. London: Pluto Press.

McLaughlin, D. (2004). Cultivating habits of democracy. Asking the hard questions. *Education Canada* **45**(1), 33–35. Toronto, ON: Canadian Education Association.

Merrifield, J. (2001). *Learning Citizenship*. London: Learning from Experience Trust.

Rodríguez Izquierdo, R. M. (2009). La investigación sobre la educación intercultural en España. *Archivos Analíticos de Políticas Educativas* **17**(4). http://epaa.asu.edu/epaa/v17n4.

Sniderman, P. and Hagendoorn, L. (2007). *When Ways of Life Collide: Multiculturalism and Its Discontents in the Netherlands*. Princeton, NJ: Princeton University Press.

Westheimer, J. and Khane, J. (2004). What kind of citizen? The politics of education for democracy. In Mundel, K. and Schugurensky, D. (eds.) *Lifelong Citizenship Learning, Participatory Democracy and Social Change*, pp 67–79. Toronto, ON: Transformative Learning Centre, OISE/UT.

Wilkinson, L. and Hebert, Y. (1999). *Citizenship Values: Towards an Analytical Framework*. Calgary, AB: Prairie Centre of Excellence for Research on Immigration and Integration, Metropolis.

Further Reading

Boggs, D. (1991). Civic education: An adult education imperative. *Adult Education Quarterly* **42**, 46–55.

Bron, A., Field, J., and Kurantowicz, E. (eds.) (1998). *Adult Education and Democratic Citizenship II*. Kracow: Impuls.

Callan, E. (1997). *Creating Citizens: Political Education and Liberal Democracy*. Oxford: Clarendon Press.

Citizenship and Immigration Canada (2005). *A Look at Canada*. Ottawa, NJ: CIC.

Coady, M. (1939). *Masters of Their Own Destiny*. New York: Harper and Brothers.

Cogan, J. and Derricott, R. (eds.) (2000). *Citizenship for the 21st Century: An International Perspective on Education*. London: Kogan Page.

Foley, G. (1999). *Learning in Social Action: A Contribution to Understanding Informal Education*. London: Zed Books.

Freire, P. (1970). *Pedagogy of the Oppressed*. New York: Continuum Publishing.

Giroux, H. A. (1980). Critical theory and rationality in citizenship education. *Curriculum Inquiry* **10**(4), 329–366.

Gutmann, A. (1987). *Democratic Education*. Princeton, NJ: Princeton University Press.

Hahn, C. (1998). *Becoming Political. Comparative Perspectives on Citizenship Education*. Albany, NY: State University of New York Press.

Ichilov, O. (ed.) (1998). *Citizenship and Citizenship Education in a Changing World*. London: Woburn Press.

Korsgaard, O. (2001). From social citizenship to active citizenship; from adult education to adult learning. *Special Issue: Citizenship, Adult Education and Lifelong Learning. Journal of World Education* **31**(1).

Krischke, P. J. (2001). *The Learning of Democracy in Latin America: Social Actors and Cultural Change*. Huntington, NY: Nova Science Publishers.

Ladson-Billings, G. (2004). Culture versus citizenship: The challenge of racialized citizenship in the United States. In Banks, J. (ed.) *Diversity and Citizenship Education*, pp 99–126. San Francisco, CA: Jossey-Bass.

McKay, S. (1993). *Agendas for Second Language Literacy*. Cambridge: Cambridge University Press.

Nie, N., Junn, J., and Stehlik-Barry, K. (1996). *Education and Democratic Citizenship in America*. Chicago, IL: The University of Chicago Press.

Oldenquist, A. (1996). *Can Democracy Be Taught? Perspectives on Education for Democracy in the United States, Central and Eastern Europe, Russia, South Africa and Japan*. Bloomington, IN: Phi Delta Kappa Educational Foundation.

Oliver, L. (1987). Popular education and adult civic education: The Third World is a different place. *Convergence* **20**(1), 40–50.

Richardson, G. and Blades, D. (eds.) (2006). *Troubling the Canon of Citizenship Education*. New York: Peter Lang.

Roosevelt, E. (1930). Good citizenship: The purpose of education. *Pictorial Review* **April**(4), 94–97.

Schudson, M. (1998). *The Good Citizen: A History of American Civic Life*. New York: Free Press.

Schugurensky, D. (2006). Adult citizenship education: An overview of the field. In Fenwick, T., Nesbit, T., and Spencer, B. (eds.) *Contexts of Adult Education: Canadian Perspectives*, pp 68–80. Toronto, ON: Thompson Educational Publishing.

Selman, G. (1998). The imaginative training for citizenship. In Scott, S., Spencer, B., and Thomas, A. (eds.) *Learning for Life: Canadian Readings in Adult Education*, pp 24–34. Toronto, ON: Thompson Educational Publishing.

Torres, C. A. (1998). *Democracy, Education, and Multiculturalism: Dilemmas of Citizenship in a Global World*. Lanham, MD: Rowman and Littlefield.

Wildemeersch, D., Stroobants, V., and Bron, M. (eds.) (2005). *Active Citizenship and Multiple Identities in Europe. A Learning Outlook*. Frankfurt: Peter Lang.

Relevant Websites

http://www.unesco.org – United Nations Educational, Scientific and Cultural Organization, CONFINTEA VI.

http://www.un.org – United Nations, International Migration.

Labor Education

K Forrester, University of Leeds, Leeds, UK

Introduction

For many hundreds of thousands of people around the world, learning through their trade union has been an important, and occasionally, pivotal experience in their development and understanding as workers and citizens. Whether as a form of occupational socialization, self-improvement, or as a vehicle of social mobility, union education has been and remains, an important albeit uneven feature of trade union activity around the world. While most studies and reports focus on worker education's engagement with the knowledge, skills, and capabilities seen as necessary to survive within late capitalist economies, other (less-documented) recent experiences can be found of the union learning necessary in the challenge to apartheid regimes (South Africa) and forms of political injustice, authoritarianism, and dictatorship (Central Africa or South Korea). In the case of post-communist countries, union members are learning once again, to create organizations that defend worker interests within the workplace.

Paradoxically, the nature and organization of this educational activity remains an under-researched and documented area, barely visible within the voluminous literature centered on labor organizations. Few people would disagree with the Croucher (2004) view that "Education is often viewed as a key instrument for effecting change in trade unions" (p. 90). Despite such sentiments, labor education remains as a minority research concern and a marginal policy focus within labor organisations themselves (see, e.g., the recent country studies in the volume *Organised Labour in the 21ˢᵗ Century* (Jose, 2002) by the International Labour Office). Other commentators interested in union engagement with neoliberal globalization, such as Novelli (2004: 165), report that while "education and learning appear crucial ... they are largely absent in the literature". To some extent, this absence is understandable (and prudent) given the formidable conceptual, organizational, and research complexities inherent in any overview of union learning activities. Labor, union, and education, for example, all remain the focus of considerable debate and contestation. Empirically and analytically capturing this education is fraught with difficulties especially in the rapidly changing nature of this provision as unions make and remake themselves in different historical settings and in response to changes in the employment relationship and wider societal context.

Despite these substantial methodological caveats, this article provides a selective flavor of the conceptual schemas and organizational variety of union education in different parts of the world. It is suggested that recent labor education initiatives can be seen as being informed by one or more of three interrelated concerns, namely, the possible contribution of education toward union renewal and revitalization strategies, the emergence of lifelong learning as a key policy focus and third, changes in regulatory regimes resulting from more intensive capital-accumulation strategies.

The first section situates the peculiarities of worker education. Unlike most other forms of knowing, union education is characterized by its contradictory nature – its simultaneous promotion of resistance and of cooperation. Analytically grasping this tension at the center of worker education has proved difficult and controversial. A brief review of the formulations and conceptual frameworks used commonly in discussions of union education is provided. In contrast to these formulations, it is suggested that in recognizing the nature and extent of worker learning, union education needs to be situated within the wider societal context. This is the focus of the second section in the article. This wider societal approach provides the analytical focus for contexturalizing particular initiatives at particular times in particular circumstances. Examples of concerns within union education are used to illustrate the argument developed in this section. The final part briefly considers the educational implications for unions within at least rhetorically, the information society, knowledge economy, or the post-industrial society.

The Peculiarities of Union Education

Trade unions are best understood as institutions that primarily mediate between their members and opposing social interests such as the state and employers. As a condition of their survival, they are required to navigate the material structural contradictions between capital and labor. In seeking to defend and further the interests of their membership, union relationships and practices are characterized simultaneously not only by struggle and conflict but also by cooperation in the maintenance of an orderly employment environment and favorable societal contexts. The effectiveness of worker "resistance to capitalism .... also makes this resistance more manageable and predictable and can even serve to suppress struggle" (Hyman, 1989: 230). It is this key contradictory characteristic of unionism that not only unlocks understandings of unionism but also provides a rich interpretative basis for framing union education. As such, it provides a start to overcoming static institutional categories commonly used in discussion of education in general. Situating union learning within this wider societal context provides the critical dimension intrinsic to this type of education.

Scholarly attempts to situate analytically, trade union education or more broadly, worker education within the general literature acknowledges the difficulties inherent in such an ambition; there is wisely a strong cautionary element. Hopkins in his international survey of workers' education, for example, warns of the historical variety and culturally contested understandings of education, workers, and trade unions: there "are grave dangers of over-simplification and confusion" (Hopkins, 1985: 8). Newman agrees and notes that "the world of union affairs, of workplaces, of industrial relations is a complicated and confusing one. No two unions, no two workplaces are the same. No issues are identical" (Newman, 1993: 11). The International Labour Office (ILO) recognizes the complexities and offers a broad understanding. "Worker's education", it suggests, "is designed to develop the workers' understanding of 'labour problems' in the broadest sense of these words" (ILO, 1976: 10). It "should always be regarded as a means to useful action. In many cases the education will make clear both the need for action and the best forms the action can take" (ILO, 1976: 10). Spencer (2002: 17–18) in his collection on labor education provided by trade unions goes further when distinguishing between tools or role courses (those preparing members for active roles in the union), issue or awareness courses (linking workplace to societal issues such as racism, union campaigns, or new management techniques) and labour studies courses (examining union contexts through historical, economic, and political perspectives). Such a taxonomy – common in the Anglo-Saxon literature – approximates to Hopkins' longer fivefold classification of the major components of the curricula of worker' education. These he sees as basic general skills; role skills; economic, social, and political background studies; technical and vocational training; and finally, cultural, scientific, and general education (Hopkins, 1985: 43). The situating of trade union education or workers' education within perspectives that focus on curricula, program design, and pedagogy (worker-centered) has contributed toward framing important discussions about the particularities of this type of learning. Implicit within many of the discussions are a number of distinguishing features that shape not only the content but also the language, values, pedagogy, relationships, objectives, and nature of the learning experienced in the education. Although not always made explicit in the written learning materials, the examination and linkages between union experience, discussion, knowing, and action in programs occur within a number of sensibilities that are powerfully shaped by notions of social justice. More recent commentators on union education have attempted to move beyond the classificatory approach and explicitly incorporate wider societal concerns within definitions and understandings of union education. Burke and her Canadian union educators, for example, identify a number of threads which "hold together the fabric of our work: community, democracy, equity, class-consciousness, organisation-building, and the greater good" (Burke et al., 2002: 3). Other commentators such as Salt et al. (2000) distinguish between transformatory and accomodatory education in their discussion of worker education and neoliberal globalization (p. 9).

These more recent attempts to adequately capture the complexities of union education have been accompanied by the exploration of understandings of education and learning. In doing so, it has been recognized that becoming a trade unionist involves much more than a consideration of formal educational categories, as any historical account of trade unionism demonstrates. An emphasis solely on curricula considerations risks privileging institutionally driven categories at the expense of cultural and material considerations. An unproblematic view of education emphasizes education as a product to be passively acquired or consumed and transferred. For some trade unions, education assumes this quality of technical rationality, as Schon (1983) puts it. By contrast, more recent approaches to understanding education such as sociocultural approaches (Lave and Wenger, 1991) and activity theory (Engestrom, 2001) stress the contexturalized, mediated, and participative processes of, in this instance, becoming a trade unionist. Livingstone and Sawchuk for example, recognize the extensive and varied circumstances and complex processes within which union learning occurs. "Studies of adult education", they argue "have often ignored the actual array of learning activities of working people and generally implied inferior learning capacity" (Livingstone and Sawchuk, 2003b: 111). Studies by these authors have focused on union activity at the local workplace in different occupational settings in Canada in the exploration and documentation of "distinctive working-class learning practices across multiple spheres of activity, including paid employment, housework, both union-based and community volunteer work as well as private learning concerned with general interests". Using a conception of learning informed by a cultural–historical perspective, the authors analytically distinguish between formal education, continuing education, and informal learning (see also Sawchuk, 2003; Livingstone and Sawchuk, 2003b).

Novelli's (2004) study of social movement learning shares a similar concern with exploring and developing expanded understandings of worker education and learning. His analysis of the public service trade union SINTRAECALI in the south west of Colombia outlines the recent successful campaigns against privatization of public utilities. Employing the notion of strategic learning, Novelli portrays the transformation of the union from a narrow corporate trade union focused on the defense of members' particular interests, to a social movement union that linked workers and local communities in the defence of public services (Novelli, 2004: 161). The union's occupation of the company's 17th-floor administrative building in Cali is conceptualized as an educational outcome which resulted from several years of "strategic learning through social action" (Novelli, 2004: 162–163). The study illustrates the benefits of questioning dominant understandings of education and of situating these understandings within a particular material and societal context.

Situating Union Education

Uncovering the significance of the learning experienced by union members or educational participants then, can be helped through the contexturalizing of the learning within the particular political, cultural, and societal circumstances at a particular time and in particular parts of the world. Stirling (2002) uses such an approach in his survey of union education in Europe. In the Nordic countries, Germany and the UK for example, the settlements with social democratic governments provide the basis for historically understanding the comparatively extensive provision, institutional and financial support for union education. In other European countries such as Belgium and Netherlands, these settlements and support have been riven by cultural, linguistic, and religious divisions resulting in marked ideological differences to the education of the rival centers. In these instances where rival confederations are characterized by their socialist, catholic, or communist perspectives, "education programs are needed to reinforce the identity of particular Confederations as against others and to transmit an ideology to leading cadres" (Stirling, 2002: 27).

Situating union education and the unions themselves within this wider political context helps in addressing issues of significance, relevance, and purpose of the learning. Ost (2002) uses the example of unions in Poland to rebuke gently, Western commentators for reaching generalizations about union development and education based on their own particular circumstances, concerns, and frameworks. As he points out, in a number of countries, the new eastern-European unions energetically campaigned for the creation of a capitalist system and played an important role in educating workers about their responsibilities and obligations as wage employees. The early years of Solidarity in Poland in the 1980s, for example, were almost exclusively concerned with large successful mobilizations around societal issues to the exclusion of workplace concerns. The success of these Solidarity activities in Poland led to other unions, for

example, in Bulgaria and Hungary, seeking to replicate this model. However, the lack of attention given to the workplace by Solidarity resulted in dramatic membership losses in the 1990s. Withdrawal by Solidarity from the governing coalition in 2001 together with a greater emphasis on old-fashioned workplace unionism (recruitment, education courses, employer agreements, and workplace representation) is expected to reverse the period of decline experienced in the 1990s.

Unions, where possible, have always engaged educationally with employability concerns such as occupational training and apprenticeships. Although such role courses have not figured significantly in Anglo-American discussions of union education due to the frequent involvement of employers and state agencies, Lopez's account of the Brazil unions' struggle and development for the Programa Integrar (the integration program) is illustrative. Occupational training is used to include wider cultural and societal concerns by the national unions in the struggle against neoliberal initiatives. Civil society involvement and alternative economic plans are pursued through the establishment of local development forums (Lopez, 2002). In other instances such as Eastern Europe, mainstream educational courses have been designed and used to effect fundamental qualitative change (Croucher, 2004: 92) within the unions themselves. Focusing on particular trade unions in Moldova, Ukraine, and Belarus, Croucher reports on educational initiatives to assist union development in the move from Soviet-style organizations to organizations able to meet new demands in new circumstances.

The continuous search by unions through negotiation, struggle, and industrial and civil conflict for a possible and politically acceptable settlement with the state and employer agencies provides a constant tension not only within unions themselves but also in the available educational opportunities. Cooper (2002) illustrates these ambiguities in her evaluation of the Development Institute for Training, Support and Education for Labour (Ditsela) from its launch in 1996 in post-apartheid South Africa. Ditsela, as she reports (Cooper, 2002: 37), was created by the congress of the South African Trade Unions (COSATU) as a solution to "rebuilding the labour movement's capacity to respond to the major changes underway in the country .... There was a strong belief that a major educational initiative was required to build COSATU's capacity to play a proactive role in the new, democratic South Africa".

In many other countries, political accommodation is not possible. In many countries, the absence of pluralistic political cultures or the existence of repressive state regimes excludes often violently, recognition and legitimization of union practices. In parts of Africa and South America, such conditions characterize a number of countries; being a trade unionist can be very dangerous. Alexander's personal evaluation of "the courage and dedication of so many educators" in confronting "the brutal application of neo-liberalism and imposed structural adjustment programmes" in Zambia and Zimbabwe over a number of decades, provides a stark reminder of circumstances in much of the world (Alexander, 2006: 595). In such volatile political contexts, union education has been continued and aided through external sympathetic agencies. The Commonwealth Trade Union Council, for example, in 2002, was involved in supporting Sierra Leone trade unionists in a civil society program with a strong focus on HIV/AIDS, campaigning against child labor in collaboration with unions in Botswana, Mozambique, Namibia, and Tanzania, and in encouraging women participation in Bangladesh. Similarly, financial support was provided to the Ghanaian trade unions educational work from the Netherlands, the Commonwealth TUC, and from the International Confederation of Free Trade Unions (ICFTU). The Trades Union Congress in Ghana has prioritized the education of members as an important part of its difficult struggle against structural adjustment policies. Training at the Labour College covers three broad areas: union organizational issues including health and safety, trade union history, and finally, special programs. In Niger, the ILO since 1999 has been supporting the two national union confederations in the provision of worker's education in the informal sector and the French trade unions are involved in the development of a health insurance project. Maruatona's study of adult education and trade union development in Botswana is situated against a background of significant constraints imposed by the state. Education he suggests, is an important vehicle in "helping address the worker's problems" (Maruatona, 1999: 476).

Whether in Africa or elsewhere, labor organizations endeavor to ensure the initiation and reproduction of union leadership together with the necessary membership skills and capacities necessary to enter or maintain participation in the labor market. The employability agenda historically remains an important educational focus. The contexts and possibilities within which such agendas are pursued, however, differ significantly. In those regions of the world with strong repressive regimes, small formal economic sectors, and small union membership, worker learning is more likely to occur through forms of popular education (Kane, 2001), social action (Folley, 1999), or through participation in nongovernmental activity as Prieto and Quinteros' (2004) study of women's organizations and trade unions collaboration in the free-trade zones of Central America illustrates.

Union Learning in the Knowledge Economy

Today, it seems trade unions everywhere are in crisis. Whether in the Northern or Southern countries, falling membership, loss of bargaining power, new management strategies, or the need for new workers in the new workplaces, labor organizations are seen as less relevant or significant than previously. Post-Fordism, post-industrial, new-information age, the knowledge economy, or post-Taylorist is but a selection of the formulations used to distinguish the new from the old. Globalization, however, is the dominant framework that usually uncritically is used theoretically to legitimate these formulations. Simply put, globalization has resulted in the international crisis of labor organizations. This was and is not a universal experience as recent struggles for basic democratic rights in, for example, South Africa, Brazil, and Korea illustrate (Kelly, 2002). However, while such deeply contested perspectives are beyond the focus of this article, there is a widespread consensus that particular worker organizations are struggling to successfully engage with the implications of the massively increased international mobility of capital.

From a trade union perspective, an important dimension to recent union revival or renewal discussion is the increased importance given to the education function. An extensive body of evidence, for example, is beginning to emerge in the UK around recent attempts to refocus trade unions as centers of learning (Healy and Engel, 2003). Learning to organize through the training and networked organization of workplace, union learning representatives (ULRs), and the creation of workplace learning centers are seen for British unions, as an important feature of engagement with the new employment agenda and with membership growth. Similarly, training for worker representation on the European Works Councils or the creation of new training academies or institutes in Australia, the USA, and Britain (Spencer, 2002) is illustrative of the increased importance being given by unions to the training function.

The rise rhetorically at least, of human resource strategies with the accompanying focus on knowledge management then, has resulted in the exploration of fresh educational developments as a means of accommodating to, or contesting with, the new circumstances. The increasing influence in employer (and international agencies such as the World Bank and International Monetary Funds) thinking and practices of human capital theory has resulted in a greater emphasis on employer–union partnership educational initiatives. Time, financial resources, and encouragement from employers are available in joint union educational initiatives that focus on strengthening employee corporate commitment, the promotion of soft social skills, and enhanced vocational training opportunities. At a regional level, there is usually an emphasis on union education that addresses more macro-, policy-informed subject areas. The educational provision of the European Trade Union Confederation, for example, has courses on foreign languages, freedom of movement of labor and work regeneration as well as more traditional union organization, recruitment, and leadership courses.

From a different perspective, there have been important recent international discussions and developments around what has been termed the new internationalism and social movement unionism (Moody, 1997; Munck, 2002). As Novelli (2004: 166) notes, "education is a key process for contestation in the struggle to develop an (alternative) movement and incorporate new allies." There is a need, she continues, to move beyond instrumental understandings of education and training toward conceptions and practices that situate research, investigation, and learning in the formulation of alternative strategies that are seen as part of a wider political project. Such sentiments historically have formed the basis of a consistent critical perspective in the understanding, discussion, and evaluation of union education and learning. The current defensiveness of trade unions internationally in the face of the neoliberal offensive not only reinforces the search for alternatives and new allies, but also increases the pressure for more instrumental educational solutions. It is likely that this contradictory dynamic will continue to shape union learning in the period ahead.

Conclusions

As most commentators recognize, analysis and understandings of union learning need to be contexturalized within the changing nature of the unions themselves and the wider societal circumstances within which unions make and remake themselves in differing historical settings and in different parts of the world. However, irrespective of the particular place or forms that this learning might take, it remains true that for many people this learning provides an important (and sometime the only) means for an understanding of, and participation in, collective activities against social, economic, and political injustices. Despite the current difficult political circumstances, the increased attention in recent years to conceptualizing and documenting the ubiquitous nature of everyday learning incurred as a trade unionist, woman worker, or street trader has enhanced the importance and resources givento education by many union organizations.

Bibliography

Burke, B., Geronuno, J., Martin, D., Thomas, B., and Wall, C. (2002). *Education for Changing Unions*. Toronto, ON: Between the Lines.

Cooper, L. (2002). Union education in the new South Africa democracy. In Spencer, B. (ed.) *Unions and Learning in a Global Economy: International and Comparative Perspectives*, pp 37–49. Toronto, ON: Thompson Educational Publishing.

Croucher, R. (2004). The importance of trade union education: A study in three countries in Eastern Europe. *European Journal of Industrial Relations* **10**(1), 90–109.

Engestrom, Y. (2001). Expansive learning at work: Toward an activity theoretical reconceptualisation. *Journal of Education and Work* **14**(1): 133–156.

Folley, G. (1999). *Learning in Social Action*. London: Zed.

Healy, J. and Engel, N. (2003). Learning to Organise. London: Congress House, TUC.

Hopkins, P. G. H. (1985). *Workers' Education: An International Perspective*. Milton Keynes: Open University Press.

Hyman, R. (1989). *The Political Economy of Industrial Relations: Theory and Practice in a Cold Climate*. Basingstoke: Macmillan.

Jose, A. V. (2002). *Organised Labour in the 21st Century*. Geneva: International Institute for Labour Studies, International Labour Office.

Kane, L. (2001). *Popular Education and Social Change in Latin America*. London: Latin America Bureau.

Kelly, J. (2002). *Union Revival – Organising around the World*. London: Congress House, TUC.

Lave, J. and Wenger, E. (1991). *Situated Learning. Legitimate Peripheral Participation*. Cambridge: Cambridge University Press.

Livingstone, D. and Sawchuk, P. (2003a). Hidden Knowledge: Organised Labor in the Information Age. Washington, DC: Rowman and Littlefield.

Livingstone, D. and Sawchuk, P. (2003b). Hidden knowledge: Working-class capacity in the "knowledge-based economy" *Studies in the Education of Adult* **37**(2), 110–122.

Lopez, A. M. (2002). *Programa Integrar* in Brazil: Union intervention in employment, development and education. In Spencer, B. (ed.) *Unions and Learning in a Global Economy: International and Comparative Perspectives*, pp 120–129. Toronto, ON: Thompson Educational Publishing.

Maruatona, T. (1999). Adult education and the empowerment of civil society: The case of trade unions in Botswana. *International Journal of Lifelong Education* **18**(6), 476–491.

Moody, K. (1997). *Workers in a Lean World: Unions in an International Economy*. London: Verso.

Munck, R. (2002). *Globalisation and Labour*. London: Zed Books.

Newman, M. (1993). *The Third Contract; Theory and Practice in Trade Union Training*. Sydney: NSW: Stuart Victor Publishing.

Novelli, M. (2004). Globalisations, social movement unionism and new internationalisms: The role of strategic learning in the transformation of the Municipal Workers Union of EMCALI. *Globalisation, Societies and Education* **2**(2), 161–190.

Ost, D. (2002). The weakness of strong social movements: Models of unionism in the eastern European context. *European Journal of Industrial Relations* **8**(1), 33–51.

Prieto, M. and Quinteros, C. (2004). Never the twain shall meet? Women's organisations and trade unions in the *maquila* industry in Central America. *Development in Practice* **14**(1 and 2), 149–157.

Salt, B., Cervero, R. M., and Herod, A. (2000). Workers' education and neoliberal globalization: An adequate response to transitional corporations? *Adult Education Quarterly* **51**(1), 9–31.

Sawchuk, P. (2003). *Adult Learning and Technology in Working-Class Life*. Cambridge: Cambridge University Press.

Schon, D. A. (1983). *The Reflective Practitioner*. New York: Basic Books.

Spencer, B. (ed.) (2002). *Unions and Learning in a Global Economy: International and Comparative Perspectives*. Toronto, ON: Thompson Educational Publishing.

Stirling, J. (2002). Trade union education in Europe:Emerging from the gloom. In Spencer, B. (ed.) *Unions and Learning in a Global Economy: International and Comparative Perspectives*, pp 26–36. Toronto: Thompson Educational Press.

Further Reading

Holland, C. and Castleton, G. (2002). Basic skills and union activity in the UK and Australia. In Spencer, B. (ed.) *Unions and Learning in a Global Economy: International and Comparative Perspectives*, pp 89–99. Toronto: Thompson Educational Press.

Sfard, A. (1998). On two metaphors for learning and the dangers of choosing the first one. *Educational Researcher* **28**(7), 4–14.

Popular Adult Education

S Tøsse, Norwegian University of Science and Technology, Trondheim, Norway

Glossary

Folkbildning – Swedish, meaning popular adult education.
Folkeop(p)lysning – Norwegian and Danish, meaning popular adult education.
Op(p)lysning – Norwegian and Danish, meaning enlightenment.

Introduction

Popular adult education is one of those slippery concepts within the field of education that is used to denote different educational aims, ideas, approaches, activities, and programs around the world. It is used more or less synonymously with other concepts; in addition, we also have to bear in mind that it is an English translation of specific national concepts with distinctive characteristics and differences of meanings. As such, popular adult education and its national linguistic synonyms are forms of educational phenomena that are socially constructed in a process of accommodation and transformation, cultural and hegemonic strife, and social movement learning in specific historical contexts. The concept is founded and shaped by the influence of individual educators and movements that have linked popular education to different aims, target groups, educational practices, and curriculum. Taking a worldwide perspective, the term popular adult education covers different trends and philosophies and is applied to so many different practices that it is hard to tell exactly what it means (Kane, 2001: 229–230; 2005: 135). The concept cannot be framed in a single and universal definition but, rather, has to be understood as an open-ended process that is continuously adapted to the concrete situations of local needs to expand people's participation into their learning and living (Han, 1995). The article starts with the different meanings and historical traditions, more deeply explores some Nordic, Latin American, and North American practices and initiatives, presents the current trends, and finally concludes with some common dimensions characterizing the popular adult education approach.

Different Meanings and Historical Traditions

In the European context, the word popular originates from the words people or folk, and popular adult education is associated with a long tradition of people's struggle for enlightenment, access to culture and knowledge, and the development of democracy. The popular concept is historically linked to the role of popular and radical movements as educative forces, for instance, the labor movement, which did not separate education from politics, but regarded education as a guide to social and political action for a better world. Knowledge was power and instrumental in the political struggle, and this struggle itself was educative. In many countries, it has been used more or less synonymously with education of the working class and loosely associated with the interests, aspirations, and struggles of ordinary people for democracy and social change (Martin, 2007). In this broad meaning, popular adult education has been the forerunner for, and almost used synonymously with, adult education (Jarvis, 1999).

In some countries, the popular education concept is also linked to the science-popularizing movement, which can be described as a charitable form of public service by university professors and industrialists in the Enlightenment tradition (Steele, 2007a, 2007b). It led to a multitude of associations for the popularization of science, as exemplified in the British and American mechanics institutes and in the Nordic countries' working men's institutes (from the 1880s) and their Norwegian successors' folk academies. Ideologically, this popular education signified political subversion, a means of class harmonization, or democratic emancipation. In the Nordic countries, these efforts of disseminating knowledge and information to the public (e.g., related to health, social questions, and policy matters) became state funded.

A specific form of the science-popularizing movement was the university extension movement spreading from England at the end of the nineteenth century to many European countries and, later, even to South America (Jarvis, 1992; Wallin, 2000), and resulted in so-called popular or folk universities devoted to the aim of bringing both university culture to the people and developing people's own culture. Van Gent (1992) has suggested the term sociocultural education for similar professionally focused training initiatives such as the people's colleges in Hungary, folk high schools in Germany and the Netherlands, folk houses and cultural centers in the Netherlands, and the German centers for *Volksbildung*. A primary aim for some of them was to provide training for people involved in popular education; however, many of these efforts failed to reach the people (Jarvis, 1992).

Although some of the above-mentioned forms were the result of personal initiatives to educate people, the concept of popular adult education is primarily linked to the social mobilization and the educational activities within social movements. Indeed, it is the social movements themselves who have coined the term and adapted it to their practices. In the literature, we even find popular adult education referred to as a separate social movement that is held together by regional or international associations and networks. It has been a world for a nonformal, out-of-school education organized by a variety of groups that have used the popular concept to defend education as a right for all people, to be designed for the people and by the people, and essentially associated to a form of pedagogical praxis that is controlled by participants. In Latin America, Africa, and Eastern Europe, the terms popular or folk education may be used instead of, or in conjunction with, community education (Tight, 1996: 65). Hamilton and Cunningham (1989: 440) regard "community development and popular education ... as compatible." They do, however, find that subtle but important distinctions can be made, indicating that these two approaches are contradictory. Community development seeks reformation, while popular education seeks transformation. Indeed, a powerful idea, especially in Latin America, has been to make the concept identical to empower oppressed people to take part in the struggle for social and political change. Accordingly, it also shares many similarities with other terms expressing the aims of education such as resistance, liberating, and emancipatory education.

A problem for the demarcation of a popular education territory is that initiatives and practices might well fall within common definitions, but are not always considered as such. This is apparent in political liberation movements in Eastern Europe, for instance, Charter 77 in the former Czechoslovakia, which demonstrated a high activity of seminars, lectures, study groups, and free theater groups (Rubenson, 1995). The fall of communism and the drive for democratization in the former Eastern block coincided with a rise of civil society activities that have a close resemblance to popular education elsewhere. Some countries such as Slovenia have implemented new forms of study circle activities based on Nordic examples (Gougoulakis and Bogataj, 2007).

Regional Differences

The article cannot pay due attention to all forms of popular initiatives, and practices in all parts of the world, but gives some examples of regional differences. One main form has originated from the ideas of the Enlightenment and Romanticism and has a strong basis in the Nordic countries. A second trend has emerged from the popular revolt against severe oppression in former colony countries or dictatorships. This form has its strongest basis in Latin America, which is the prime example here, but is spread to all parts of the world where people have been restricted the freedom to learn. A third example is popular education initiatives, which are less integrated in social movements and popular forces, but are more a result of personal initiatives and efforts of creating new mass organizations and institutions.

Nordic Popular Adult Education

The Nordic popular adult education is often referred to as a historical tradition that has emerged from the twin influence of the Enlightenment and Romanticism. The Norwegian and Danish concept *folkeop(p)lysning* is, in fact, a composition of enlightenment (*opplysning*), meaning education from above, and the word folk, which is a romantic invention. Sweden has adopted the German concept of *Bildung* and has constructed the word *folkbildning*, which indicates that enlightenment might also come from within (Korsgaard, 1997). A third, and increasingly stronger, influence through the nineteenth century, was the rise of social and democratic movements, which further developed the idea of folk as a political subject and transformed the meaning of popular education to be not only education to the people from above, but also education of the people and the creation of knowledge from below. Since the end of the nineteenth century, popular education in the Nordic countries has been identified as social movement learning within the civil society.

A characteristic of the Nordic situation is the organization of special study associations for popular adult education within movements. It can thus be understood as a popular movement itself and a specific organized activity within movements. In the institutional meaning, especially in Sweden, popular adult education embraces the study associations and the folk high schools. In charge of these, the meaning of popular adult education multiplied into a diversity of meanings which reflected the different ideologies, aims, and activities of the movements. Some made education a part of a distinctive countercultural struggle; however, this element has faded away in the course of time. Another characteristic is the ideal of education as a collective self-education based on the belief that enlightenment and culture can emerge from below, the common people, and that knowledge can be created and disseminated through dialog within groups of equal persons. A third element is the emphasis on the aim of personal development. A unique character of Nordic popular adult education is also considered to lie in the pedagogy and methodology that is put into practice in study circles (Rubenson, 1995). These are built on the principle of independence of external requirements and are characterized by self-directed learning. In principle, all studies should not be examined and should provide a zone of freedom in which participants can choose subjects according to their real interests and needs (Andersson and Tøsse, 2006). Moreover, the study circles build on the common work of the participants and their experiences, and the active strive for knowledge, and work toward a collective goal.

Popular adult education in the Nordic countries includes a wide range of topics on every degree of difficulty, but is mainly understood as nonformal and out-of school education, spare-time and hobby-related activities, and, by tradition, often nonvocational. The study circles provide an arena for deliberation and learning in an informal way. As the level of participation is high, especially in Sweden, peaking at 2.8 million participants in the 1990s – that is, a third of the total population – popular adult education may be considered as a specific public sphere that has contributed to establishing and enforcing basic elements in the Nordic model of democracy. The concept has also been used normatively as an instrument in the construction of a Nordic dimension in relation to adult education (Ehlers, 2006). Participation is therefore largely state funded on the ground that the study associations, in addition to being agents of popular movement, contribute to diversity, support culture, and create informed, active, and committed citizens (Rubenson, 1995; Larsson, 2001). The popular adult education field has, especially in Norway, been acknowledged as a part of the educational system and encouraged to focus on the needs and aspirations of people who traditionally do not participate in adult education or are not interested in formal qualifications, for instance, the elderly (Rubenson, 2006). In the recent years, however, the state subsidies have been decreasing; however, popular adult education in the Nordic countries is, as distinct from most other countries, still a state-funded as well as a self-governing area. As stated by Swedish researchers, popular adult education in Sweden is "part of the corporate state lying at the crossroad between civil society and the state … at the intersection between the system world and the life world" (Gustavsson *et al.*, 1997).

Latin America

Outside the Nordic countries, popular adult education has almost exclusively been associated with the work and pedagogy of Freire, and has been described as "one of the most original and refreshing contributions that Latin America has made to universal pedagogical thinking" (Mera, 2005). Indeed, popular education is almost conceived as a Latin American invention and mainly associated with the endeavors of social transformation in Third World countries. In the Latin American context, the term popular education, as Kane (2001: 247) observes, has been more sharply defined and the commitment to side with the oppressed is more openly spelled out. Building on Freire's work, popular education has been advocated as a political, social, and educational process with the overall aim of counteracting the dominant worldview and creating an antihegemonic culture (Kane, 2001: 8–13). Its foundation is the convictions that grassroots people can collectively achieve critical consciousness and, from this awareness, act to challenge unjust uses of power that affects their social realities.

A pedagogical principle that Freire outlined in order to actuate the process of consciousness raising or conscientization was acquiring knowledge by way of problematizing the natural, cultural, and historical reality in which one is immersed. Another basic element is his thinking about language as inherently linked to culture which may thus convey a certain culturally transmitted worldview. Accordingly, language can both question and strengthen culture (Finger, 2005). The popular education approach is therefore making sense of the world to the ordinary people by uncovering and decoding languages (words) and meanings (themes) of their own. This must come through dialog, which in the Freireian sense is a process of generating and sharing the true word and actively naming and transforming the reality of the world (Han, 1995). This fundamental view of the teaching and learning transaction as a dialog is shared by Grundtvig and many other popular education theorists. However, far stronger than most others, Freire maintained that reflection through dialog means action, and emphasized that all education is political. A major aim of popular adult education is therefore to help participants put knowledge into practice. Under dictatorship in Latin America, popular education became a way of doing political work and naturally linked to the radical left-oriented policy and participatory research in cooperation with local groups. A basic principle politically as well as pedagogically is that it must be education with the people, not on their behalf, based on people's experiences, and aiming toward empowering the ordinary people to become subjects of change.

In Latin America and Third World countries, educators inspired by the pedagogy of the oppressed often had to work among illiterate people; therefore, popular adult education is often identified with literacy and elementary education. Moreover, education with illiterate people also means drawing on popular culture and starting from the concrete, using drama, song, dance, art, and storytelling. Popular culture is here to be distinguished from elitist culture institutions and from the mass culture. One concrete example is Augosto Boal's experiments with the People's Theatre in Peru in the 1970s (Boal, 1979). Similar efforts of using theater, dance, etc., in making the subaltern classes articulators of social and political change and waking up peoples' culture of silence, have also been, more or less successfully, executed in developing countries in Africa and Asia. The popular theater has best served the popular education approach when it has managed to not only make people aware of, but also activate participants (transforming Spectators into Spect-Actors!) in, the critical analysis of what is presented and mobilize them for taking action in their own development. At worst, it has been based on a developmentalist approach whereby popular theater forms are used to communicate government policies or to impose outsiders' views of what people need (Mlama, 1991; Lange, 1995; Bates, 1996).

Basically, popular education is defined by initiatives from below and on the grassroots level, and, in Latin America, has traditionally acted against the (oppressive) state. This was not always true in Europe, and, even in Latin America, could be a public- and state-initiated project. One example is the popular education in Nicaragua. After the revolution in 1979, the Sandinistas immediately started a literacy crusade that they followed up with a popular basic education campaign in which they copied Freireian methodology and principles. Both can be characterized as a massive training of the common people and presupposed an intensive training of teacher as well. Radio and newspapers were also put to use. However, it was a state-driven and-funded project, and some of the popular educators such as Fernando Cardinal occupied posts in the ministries of education in the 1980s (Flores-Moreno, 2005). The Nicaraguan example as well as similar educational initiatives of revolutionary movements in Latin America and elsewhere do, however, question whether education that is totally absorbed by the state or a movement in order to implement a specific policy or ideology can be termed popular. It might rather be characterized as a pedagogicalization of politics (Han, 1995).

North American examples

Popular adult education is primarily a specific form of social movement learning; however, initiatives and activities can often be traced back to individual educators. In North America, the Highlander movement is a prominent example of personal initiative and influence. It all started in 1932 when Myles Horton together with Don West founded the Highlander Folk High School in one of the poorest areas in Tennessee. Highlander did not provide mass education, but worked with leaders from several organizations or communities. Horton's assumption was that the leaders would take what they learned at Highlander and work with other actual or potential leaders and, thus, let the influence of Highlander multiply over larger numbers of people (Peters and Bell, 2001). His early contribution to popular education was then to combine the aims of social movement building and leadership training.

The creation of citizenship schools in the 1950s became, however, a mass activity. By 1970, these schools had helped 100 000 African Americans to read and write (Peters and Bell, 2001). The teachers followed the same principles and ideas as Freire and, in this way, made the citizenship education similar to popular education elsewhere. With the reorganization of Highlander to the Highlander Research and Education Center, its mission became to be an important alliance of the civil rights movement; thus, it retained its popular educational approach.

Another North America example of personal initiative is the Antigonish movement in Nova Scotia led by priest, philosopher, educator, and social reformer Moses Coady (1882–1959). His program was to organize shore fishermen so that they might be able to assist in formulating policies for the industry, promote scientific and technical education, and utilize the methods of producer and consumer cooperation. His work was founded on a strong belief in education as the solution of the economic problems of the region. Moses declared that education must begin with economics and proposed cooperation as an alternative third way between capitalism and state socialism. One of his original contributions to popular adult education was the organizing of mass meetings, which inspired people to join together into small groups called study clubs or discussion circles. As with many Nordic study circles, these groups were part of the self-help movement and did not involve any teacher (Crane, 2001). Development after the war, however, was not in favor of the cooperative ideas based on self-reliance, and, as an example of popular adult education, withered away.

Current Trends

Following Kane (2001), we may identify three currents of thought. One is concentrating on democracy, citizenship, new spaces, and social actors. This trend is intertwined with mainstream pedagogy and makes popular adult education part of the social capital formation that is initiated by social movements and may be seen as occupying and expanding the public space within civil society. This is evidently the case in Northern Europe, which has witnessed a process of convergence between the popular and the general education. In addition, in Latin America, we may see a pronounced permeability and interchange between the discursive configurations of popular and adult education. There is a feeling among some educators that the historical relevance of popular education has been lost and there is a growing willingness to make links with public and traditional schooling. As a consequence, the political aspect is de-emphasized and more importance is given to the quality of education, access, participation, citizenship training, and new social issues (Kane, 2005; Ruiz, 2006). A second trend is focusing on class and structural change while remaining sensitive to issues of identity and difference. This trend tries to maintain its political vision and commitment. An example is the Popular Education Forum for Scotland, which calls attention to the need for reinvigorating the questions of equality and justice and linking popular education to the political efforts of stimulating a democratic renewal (Martin, 2007). A third trend is less concerned with theory and ideology and more with throwing itself into the struggle and grassroots work. This trend is linked to new social movements that have transformed the popular education discourse from class and structure to ethnicity, race, gender, ecology, and environment. It has adopted a community, practical, and participatory democracy approach of which the participatory budget of Porto Alegre in Brazil serves as a prime example and inspiration (Myers, 2007). New forms of popular education now seem to take place on a global scale with the help of the Internet as is demonstrated by the work of new social movements, the World Social Forum, and Attac which use the World Wide Web in organizing meetings and activities, spreading information, and educating the people. The Internet not only opens up access to expert knowledge for everyone, but also gives the popular forces new possibilities to take part in the oppositional social movement debates of a global call for action against poverty and injustice (Preece, 2006).

In recent years, popular adult education has developed areas of specialism, that is, for specific groups or for specific matters. From the early 1980s, feminists from different countries have gathered under the umbrella term of feminist popular education and formed an international network. A central aim of this is to support the struggles of women in oppressed communities, rather than women in general, and the work is therefore closely related to other nonformal, community, or radical educational practices. The feminists have also linked social justice issues more broadly to the whole person, that is, to embodied learning, which refers to practices that engage the body, mind, spirit, and emotion (Walters and Manicom, 1996; Stromquist, 2004).

Common Dimensions

Despite the regional differences and the different currents of thought, there are at least three dimensions, which, taken together, can give a core meaning of the term. These dimensions are all bounded to a normative philosophy, but the strength of the concept is just that it is based on some few, simple yet powerful ideas: of political commitment in favor of the oppressed, of enabling ordinary people to become subjects of change, of recognizing many types of knowledge, and a methodology that allows these different knowledge to be shared (Kane, 2001: 230).

First, popular adult education has a political–ideological dimension that is linked to a social commitment. The critical approach seems to be at the heart of the popular education approach, and, in dictatorships and oppressive countries, popular education has a specific role of unmasking and challenging unequal relations of power in order to change them. Change is defined as progressive in the interests of a fairer and more egalitarian society, and, in this way, it works in the interest of democracy. However, education and politics are not two sides of the same coin as Myles Horton reminded us. He drew a line between the two, which corresponded to the distinction between education and organizing. If popular education is subordinated to the command of a political goal and ideology, it will turn into propaganda and indoctrination and take the form of political instrumentalism and pseudoschooling (Han, 1995).

Second, popular adult education has a pedagogical–participatory dimension since it tries to recruit and organize people for collective learning and action while, at the same time, maintaining education as a voluntary activity and free from external demands. This requires an educational methodology that radically calls into question the authoritarian teacher-centered practice and transmission of knowledge characteristic of traditional pedagogy (Han, 1995). The popular pedagogy is based on active participation of the learners, dialogical teaching, and sharing of experiences between the learners in such a way that all participants acquire knowledge and take part in a collective learning process. Indeed, the knowledge base of popular education comes primarily from the experiences of the people involved. The method is critical and problematizing, rather than one that produces answers. This education believes in and trusts ordinary people, and is based on the belief that people are capable of understanding and working to improve the conditions of their lives (St. Clair, 2005: 50). Ideally, it is education of equals characterized by a horizontal relationship between teacher and learner.

Third, popular adult education has an action-oriented dimension. Action usually means concrete forms of grassroots activities, which may change power relations. However, critical learning, which corresponds to this education, is also a political act in itself (Newman, 2005) and a critical consciousness is a precondition for action and social change. According to Freire, reflection cannot be separated from action. In Nordic countries, study circles will hardly lead to social and political action; however, it is supposed that they contribute to foster the prerequisite for democratic action (Larsson, 2001). The transformative potential of Nordic popular adult education is not associated with its affiliation to political radicalism, as is assumed in oppressive and developing countries; rather, it comes from the democratic and participatory characteristics of its pedagogy.

Conclusion

Popular adult education is a nonformal type of education that has emerged from the educational work of social movements and may be seen as a paradigm shift to escape from the instrumentalization, systematization, and institutionalization of traditional schooling. It also questions the system of examination in the traditional mode of education, which incessantly serves to reproduce social injustice and its legitimization. The idea of popular education has been formulated as an educational movement to challenge the monopoly of the dominant school mode of education and is capable of presenting alternatives (Han, 1995). Defined in terms of aims, popular adult education may be seen as a specific response in the pursuit of social transformation and change as well as contributing to personal development. Defined in terms of pedagogy and methodology, it is education founded on the principles of voluntarism, institutional independence, dialogical teaching, active participation and the sharing of experiences, and working toward a collective goal. In the Latin American context, popular education represents a critical approach to adult education, which has both a pedagogical aspect of consciousness raising intended to foster a critical awareness of reality, and a political aspect of organizing people for collective action and putting them together for real social change (Han, 1995). In the Northern European context, popular adult education is more about fostering people's participation in order to stimulate personal as well as social development. The meaning of the term will, however, vary with the social context as the concept is an open-ended process that continues to adapt to individual interests and needs, to the popular and collective struggle to expand one's freedom, to the pursuit of popular values and cultures, and to the sharing and acquirement of knowledge and culture.

See also: Adult Education and Civil Society; Community Based Adult Education.

Bibliography

Andersson, E. and Tøsse, S. (2006). The study associations in Sweden and Norway. A comparative investigation. *Paper to the NFPF's 34 Congress. Örebro, Sweden, 9–11 March.*

Bates, R. A. (1996). Popular theater: A useful process for adult educators. *Adult Education Quarterly* **46**(4), 224–236.

Boal, A. (1979). *Theater of the Oppressed.* London: Pluto Press.

Crane, J. M. (2001). Moses Coady and Antigonish. In Jarvis, P. (ed.) *Twentieth Century Thinkers in Adult and Continuing Education,* pp 223–241. London: Kogan Page.

Ehlers, S. (2006). The decline and fall of "folkeoplysning and adult education": Nordic policy-making during the transition from adult education to adult learning. In Sprogøe, J. and Wither-Jensen, T. (eds.) *Identity, Education and Citizenship – Multiple Interrelations,* pp 339–354. Frankfurt am Main: Peter Lang.

Finger, M. (2005). Conscientization. In English, L. M. (ed.) *International Encyclopedia of Adult Education,* pp 145–148. Basingstoke: Palgrave Macmillan.

Flores-Moreno, C. (2005). Popular education and popular schools in Latin America. In Crowther, J., Galloway, V., and Martin, I. (eds.) *Popular Education: Engaging the Academy,* pp 169–180. Leicester: NIACE.

Gougoulakis, P. and Bogataj, N. (2007). Study circles in Sweden and Slovenia – learning for civic paticipation. In Adam, F. (ed.) *Social Capital and Governance: Old and New Members of EU in Comparison,* pp 203–236. Münster: Lit Verlag.

Gustavsson, B., Larsson, S., and Rubenson, K. (1997). Civil society and Swedish popular adult education. *SCUTREA Conference Proceedings.* Leeds: SCUTREA.

Hamilton, E. and Cunningham, P. M. (1989). Community-based adult education. In Merriam, S. B. and Cunningham, P. M. (eds.) *Handbook of Adult and Continuing Education,* pp 439–451. San Francisco, CA: Jossey-Bass.

Han, S. (1995). *An Exploratory Study of the Ideas and Ideologies of Popular Adult Education: Implications for Understanding Korean Minjung Education Movement.* Unpublished Doctoral Dissertation. State University of New York at Buffalo.

Jarvis, P. (ed.) (1992). *Perspectives on Adult Education and Training in Europe.* Leicester: NIACE.

Jarvis, P. (1999). *International Dictionary of Adult end Continuing Education.* London: Routledge.

Kane, L. (2001). *Popular Education and Social Change in Latin America.* London: Latin America Bureau.

Kane, L. (2005). Popular education seen "from afar" *Adult Education and Development* **64**, 131–140.

Korsgaard, O. (1997). *Kampen om Lyset (The Struggle for Enlightenment).* København: Gyldendal.

Lange, S. (1995). *From Nation-Building to Popular Culture: The Modernization of Performance in Tanzania. CMI Report 1995: 1* Bergen: Chr. Michelsen Institute.

Larsson, S. (2001). Seven aspects of democracy as related to study circles. *International Journal of Lifelong Education* **20**(3), 199–217.

Martin, I. (2007). Introductory essay. In Crowther, J., Martin, I., and Shaw, M. (eds.) *Popular Education and Social Movements in Scotland Today,* pp 1–25. Leicester: NIACE.

Mera, C. Z. (2005). Latin America and adult education. In English, L. M. (ed.) *International Encyclopedia of Adult Education,* pp 345–348. Basingstoke: Palgrave Macmillan.

Mlama, P. M. (1991). *Culture and Development. The Popular Theatre Approach in Africa.* Uppsala: The Scandinavian Institute of African Studies.

Myers, J. P. (2007). Citizenship education practices of politically active teachers in Porto Alegre, Brazil and Toronto, Canada. *Comparative Education Review* **51**(1), 1–24.

Newman, M. (2005). Popular teaching, popular learning and popular action. In Crowther, J., Galloway, V., and Martin, I. (eds.) *Popular Education: Popular Education: Engaging the Academy,* pp 22–31. Leicester: NIACE.

Peters, J. M. and Bell, B. (2001). Horton of highlanders. In Jarvis, P. (ed.) *Twentieth Century Thinkers in Adult and Continuing Education,* pp 242–257. London: Kogan Page.

Preece, J. (2006). Beyond the learning society: The learning world? *International Journal of Lifelong Education* **25**(3), 307–320.

Rubenson, K. (1995). *Swedish Popular Adult Education: Some Comparative Remarks.* (English translation of article in Bergstedt, B. and Larsson, S. (eds.) *Om folkbildningens innebörder).* Linköping: Mimer.

Rubenson, K. (2006). The Nordic model of lifelong learning. *Compare* **36**(3), 327–341.

Ruiz, M. (2006). Research in popular and adult education in Latin America. In Merriam, S. H., Courtenay, B. C., and Cervero, R. (eds.) *Global Issues and Adult Education,* pp 412–421. San Francisco, CA: Jossey-Bass.

St.Clair, R. (2005). University faculty and popular education in the United States. In Crowther, J., Galloway, V., and Martin, I. (eds.) *Popular Education: Engaging the Academy,* pp 43–53. Leicester: NIACE.

Steele, T. (2007a). With "real feeling and just sense". Rehistoricising popular education. In Crowther, J., Martin, I., and Shaw, M. (eds.) *Popular Education and Social Movements in Scotland Today*, pp 95–105. Leicester: NIACE.

Steele, T. (2007b). *Knowledge is Power! The Rise and Fall of European Popular Educational Movements.* 1848–1939. Oxford: Peter Lang AG International Academic Publishers.

Stromquist, N. P. (2004). The educational nature of feminist action. In Foley, G. (ed.) *Dimensions of Adult Learning*, pp 35–52. Milton Keynes: Open University Press.

Tight, M. (1996). *Key Concepts in Adult Education and Training.* London: Routledge.

Van Gent, B. (1992). Netherlands. In Jarvis, P. (ed.) *Perspectives on Adult Education and Training in Europe*, pp 19–33. Leicester: NIACE.

Wallin, K. E. (2000). *Folkbildning på export? (Popular Adult Education on Exportation).* Stockholm: Pedagogiska institutionen, Stockholms universitet.

Walters, S. and Manicom, L. (eds.) (1996). *Gender in Popular Education.* London: Zed Books.

Hurtado, C. N. (2005). Contribution to the Latin America debate on the present and future relevance of popular education. *Adult Education and Development* **64**, 101–112.

Kane, L. (2000). Popular education and the landless people's movement in Brazil (MST). *Studies in the Education of Adults* **32**(1), 36–50.

Leis, P. (2005). Reflections on popular education. *Adult Education and Development* **64**, 113–125.

Mignon, J.-M. (2008). Popular education in France. *Lifelong Learning in Europe* **XIII**(2), 103–110.

Peters, J. M. and Bell, B. (2001). Horton of highlanders. In Jarvis, P. (ed.) *Twentieth Century Thinkers in Adult and Continuing Education*, pp 242–257. London: Kogan Page.

Rivero, J. (2005). Key contributions of the popular education movement. *Adult Education and Development* **64**, 93–100.

Welton, M. R. (1995). Amateurs out to change the world: A retrospective on community development. *Convergence* **xxviii**(2), 49–61.

Yoo, Sung-Sang (2006). Popular Education in Asia: A Comparative Study of Freirian Legacies in Popular Education of the Philippines and South Korea. Unpublished Doctoral Dissertation, University of California, Los Angeles.

Further Reading

Åberg, P. (2008). *Translating Popular Education. Civil Society Cooperation between Sweden and Estonia. Stockholm Studies in Politics 124.* Doctoral Dissertations 24. http://su.diva-portal.org/smash/record.jsf?pid=diva2:198245 (accessed May 2009).

Carrillo, A. T. (2007). Paulo Freire and Educación popular. *Adult Education and Development* **69**, 27–42.

Foley, G. (1998). Clearing the theoretical ground: Elements in a theory of popular education. *International Review of Education* **44**(1–2), 139–153.

Grace, A. P. (1995). The Gospel according to father Jimmy. *Convergence* **xxviii**(2), 63–77.

Relevant Websites

http://www.cpepr.info – Center for Popular Education and Participatory Research.
http://www.highlandercenter.org – Highlander Research and Education Center.
http://www.peopleseducation.org – Institute for People's Education and Action.
http://www.poped.org – Open Source Web Development for Social Change.http://www.pepe.org – pepe.org.
http://www.infed.org – The Encyclopaedia of Informal Education.
http://www.popednews.org – The Popular Education News.
http://www.trapese.org – Trapese: Popular Education Collective.
http://www.cpe.uts.edu.au – University of Technology, Sydney.

University Adult Continuing Education: The Extra-Mural Tradition Revisited

M Slowey, Dublin City University, Dublin, Republic of Ireland

Introduction

The expansion of higher education across Organisation for Economic Co-Operation and Development (OECD) countries at the end of the twentieth century represented one of the most significant aspects of change in higher education in recent times. Taking 1995 as a baseline, student enrolments increased dramatically across the higher education sectors of 21 member states (OECD, 2005). The growth was largely driven by young school leavers where, on average, participation rates of the population aged 18–24 years increased by 70%, and young adults, aged 25–29 years, where levels of participation increased by almost 50% (OECD, 2005). However, in some countries, significant numbers of older students also entered higher education (OECD, 2005) – a pattern reflecting what some analysts considered to be the basis of a lifelong learning model (OECD, 1999).

While the trends in relation to participation in higher education in the developing countries outside the OECD vary, they also reflect expansion in general. The scale is enormous – a study of middle-income countries involved in the United Nations Educational, Scientific and Cultural Organization (UNESCO) World Education Indicators (WEI) program showed that far more students entered and graduated from these countries than in the 30 OECD member states combined (UNESCO, 2007). (Countries participating in the UNESCO WEI program are Argentina, Brazil, China, Egypt, India Indonesia, Jamaica, Jordan, Malaysia, Paraguay, Peru, Philippines, Russian Federation, Sri Lanka, Thailand, Tunisia, Uruguay, and Zimbabwe.)

In 2006, for example, China had more tertiary graduates (2.4 million) than the top three OECD countries combined – United States (1.4 million), Japan (0.6 million), and France (0.3 million). Overall, however, the proportion of young people gaining a higher educational qualification in the WEI countries (19.7%) was about half that of the OECD group.

In exploring the topic of university adult continuing education (ACE) and looking behind these headline participation figures, three factors need to be taken into consideration. First, one of the key comparative indicators of the levels of participation is the age participation rate (APR). This measures the proportion of the population of the typical school-leaving age which progress to higher education. By definition, this refers to young people, and only rarely are such measures used to explore levels of participation by adults in higher education. Second, much of the expansion in higher education over the last two decades took place in non-university institutions such as polytechnics, community colleges, further education colleges, and the like. The statistics, therefore, generally refer not only to universities, but also, more generally, to participation across all types of higher education institutions. Third, international statistics usually refer to full-time undergraduate entrants, whereas mature students are more likely to be found on part-time, distance, post-experience, and non-credit programs.

The term university ACE is open to different interpretations reflected, since the 1980s or so, in the shifting policy discourse at national and international levels (Duke, 1992; Bourgeois et al., 1999; Davies, 1995; Osborne and Thomas, 2003). A benchmark international study of adult participation in higher education undertaken by the OECD 20 years ago distinguished between four categories of the adult student in higher education (OECD, 1987):

1. students who enter or re-enter higher education as adults in order to pursue mainstream studies leading to a full first degree or diploma (delayers, deferrers, or second chancers, i.e., those who are admitted on credentials gained by means of work experience or second-chance educational routes);
2. adults who reenter to update their professional knowledge, or seek to acquire additional qualifications, in order to change occupation or advance in their career (refreshers and recyclers);
3. those without previous experience in higher education who enroll for professional purposes, especially in courses of short duration; and
4. adults with, or without, previous experience in higher education, who enroll for courses with the explicit purpose of personal fulfillment (personal developers).

In a follow-up study nearly 15 years later, another categorization, based on a combination of three criteria associated with (a) entry routes, (b) modes of study, and (c) nature of program attended, was developed (Wolter, 2000).

This resulted in a six-fold classification.

1. those who take a vocational route to the achievement of the high school leaving examination (the second educational route);
2. special admission examinations (the third educational route);

3. students with high school leaving qualifications who undertake vocational training or work experience before moving on to higher education (the double qualification route);

4. students studying on a part-time or distance-mode basis;

5. graduates who return to higher education for continuing professional development courses (often of short duration); and

6. older adults taking continuing education courses largely for personal development purposes.

Building upon this work, and developing it further for analytic purposes, five different conceptions of university ACE can be identified in the international literature at the end of the first decade of the twenty-first century:

• The first conceptualization focuses on the age of the learner – namely, mature students, defined in most countries as those aged somewhere between 21 and 25 years above when entering higher education) as opposed to young, recently matriculated high school graduates.

• The second focuses on the mode of study – predominantly part-time or distance, as opposed to full-time or on campus.

• The third focuses on the type of program undertaken – for example, professional updating or retraining and noncredit or community courses, as opposed to undergraduate degree qualifications.

• The fourth focuses on the life course stage, or predominant motivation of the learner – for example, second chance or postexperience, as opposed to direct progression from initial school education.

• The fifth conceptualization focuses on the mode of organization of provision for adult learners – through specialist institutions (such as open universities) or centers with a dedicated mission to meet the needs of adults (of which the extramural tradition, considered below, is the classic example) as opposed to widening access for adults to mainstream provision.

Global Trends in Lifelong Learning and University Adult Education

The widely debated concept of lifelong learning (Coffield, 2000; Bagnall, 2000) figured prominently in national and international educational policy discourse for three decades, with some more limited resonances in higher education (Field, 2006; Scott, 1995, 1997; Tavistock Institute, 2002; Watson and Taylor, 1998; Rubenson, 2006). In Europe, in a research exercise conducted as part of the major higher education reform agenda across all the

member states of the European Union – termed the Bologna process – 54% of respondents indicated that their university had a lifelong learning strategy; a further 25% said that one was in preparation, while 19% indicated that they did not have one; and 2% did not reply (Davies and Feutrie, 2008). Within this shifting discourse, one focus of attention relates to access by adults to higher education – and the statistics do point to generally increasing levels of participation by those aged over 21 years in higher education. This trend, for example, was highlighted in a joint report from the American Council of Education and the European Universities Association (Green *et al.*, 2002). In the United States, on a head-count basis (which includes part-time students), approximately 40% of all undergraduates were over 25 years of age, while, in Canada, 31% were over 24 years of age.

The reasons behind this growth in the numbers of adults in higher education in some countries are complex – ranging from demographic trends through to the emphasis on the development of the knowledge society (Schuetze and Slowey, 2003). In many developed countries, demographic projections of a substantial decline in the numbers of young people coming through from schools fuelled concerns about skill shortages and recruitment problems for higher education. Human capital theories had also become highly influential among policymakers and politicians, sparking a renewed emphasis on the continuous need for updating and retraining of the workforce and focusing attention on the extent to which university systems, structures, and staff were, in fact, prepared to meet the projected demand from employers and the professions. Additionally, for institutions of higher education, continuing professional/vocational education was being viewed as a potential source of new revenue – increasingly important as a result of funding pressures from the neo-libero public policy agenda.

Over and above all of these factors, and interacting with them in complex ways, is the issue of equality of opportunity and access to higher education. In most countries, the social class composition of higher education remains unrepresentative of the population at large; women students have grown as a proportion, but are concentrated in particular disciplinary areas; and the limited information available on participation by those from ethnic minority groups shows variable patterns in different countries.

Also important are internal changes of a qualitative nature, such as more flexible provision, new approaches to teaching and learning, and an increasing emphasis upon quality assurance and the evaluation and certification of learning. The forms of knowledge creation and dissemination, the greater access to information sources, the use of new media and new channels of communication, the development of complex partnerships with employers, and the growing marketization of education are all factors that have a major impact on where, what, how, and why tertiary/post-secondary students learn.

In fact, many of the features associated with the policy emphasis on lifelong learning in higher education can be traced back to a wide-ranging reform agenda of Western higher education systems. For the better part of half a century, this agenda has included an emphasis on the student experience, especially at the undergraduate level; enhancing teaching quality; developing partnerships with employers and other external agencies; strategic planning at an institutional level; and expanding interdisciplinary teaching and research.

International Patterns of Adult Participation in Higher Education

While higher education systems in developed societies are subject to common economic, social, and demographic pressures, resulting in increasing levels of participation by adults, evidence from an international comparative study of ten countries suggests that the differentials between countries appear remarkably persistent over time.

Schuetze and Slowey (2000) developed a threefold typology along a continuum relating to the levels of adult participation in higher education.

- First, countries with relatively high levels of participation by adult learners and demonstrating a relatively high degree of flexibility in relation to entry criteria and study patterns; this category included Sweden and the United States.
- Second, countries with significant, but lower, proportions of adult learners across the system as a whole, and in which adult students were frequently located in open universities or dedicated centers of adult or continuing education within mainstream institutions; this category included Australia, Canada, New Zealand, and the UK.
- Third, countries at the other end of the continuum with very low levels of adult participation in higher education; this category included Austria, Germany, Ireland, and Japan.

Analyses of the same ten countries over a 10-year period indicated that, while overall levels of adult participation in higher education had increased, the relative levels of participation between countries remained largely the same.

This analysis suggests that, while trends toward convergence can be discerned as a result of globalization, the forms taken by contemporary university ACE continue to be largely determined by the higher education traditions from which they spring.

Historical Patterns of University ACE

In order to understand current patterns of university ACE, it is necessary to have a broad appreciation of the historical traditions from which they emerge.

In relation to university ACE, three major traditions can be identified.

1. First, the extramural model of bringing university education to the adult population. The origins of this model can be formally traced back to the 1870s in the ancient British universities, and led to the development of dedicated adult education departments. These departments were unusual in being multidisciplinary, and devoted to the delivery of university programs which were specifically tailored to meet the needs of adult students. This extramural approach provided a conceptual model which, for complex historical reasons, has had a widespread international influence, in particular in Commonwealth countries.
2. Second, traditions of university ACE which are connected to the ideal of service by the university to local and regional social and economic communities. A significant example of this tradition arises from the land-grant universities in the USA, which included a particular mission to support community and rural development from the start.
3. Third, traditions where educational provision to adults, as a distinctive group, was not seen as a significant function for universities. This is particularly evident where the university traditions emphasized research, and ACE allocated to other agencies and specialist institutions, such as open universities or vocational organizations (e.g., Germany).

The complexity and variability of patterns is demonstrated in the findings of a comparative study of continuing education in universities across 30 countries. This showed that:

> . . .activity with ostensibly different purposes, including continuing professional development, second chance education, education for leisure and social development, U3A and technology transfer, are all within the remit of continuing education. Increasingly, continuing education within universities has become blurred with other aspects of flexibility including part-time education, summer universities, open and distance education, accreditation of prior learning and work-based learning. (Osborne and Thomas, 2003: 20)

In terms of theoretical writing on university adult education, and the practice in many countries throughout the world (particularly Commonwealth members), the extramural tradition was, for much of the twentieth century, a particularly influential model. In order to better understand contemporary variations, therefore, it is useful to have a familiarity with the origins of the values and objectives underpinning this approach to university adult education.

Background to the Emergence of the Extramural Model of University ACE

The movement for university extension, such as the *folk-universitet* in some Scandanivian countries, formed part of the widespread growth of interest in university ACE in the nineteenth century. The extramural model which emerged from the ancient universities of Oxford and Cambridge in England is of particular interest as it was influential both in terms of time scale (several centuries) and geography (throughout the Commonwealth and in many English-speaking countries).

Some of the earliest university lectures for the general adult population can be traced to those given by Francis Hutcheson, Professor of moral philosophy at the University of Glasgow in the 1720s (Hamilton and Slowey, 2005). It was James Stuart – another academic who also had spent time at Glasgow University – who is credited with articulating the idea of university extramural (beyond the walls) provision in Cambridge University (Fieldhouse, 1996). In 1873, the University of Cambridge agreed to organize, formally, programs and lectures in various centers, and Oxford also undertook to provide a number of programs through extension centers. Shortly afterwards, the University of London established the London Society for the Extension of University Teaching (Jones, 2008). The work grew in fits and starts, but quite rapidly overall; thus, by 1902, Oxford and Cambridge had established well over 900 centers with more than 20 000 adult student learners attending.

However, from the outset, the activists were concerned to attract a broader cross section of the population and, in particular, students from working-class backgrounds – an objective which remained strong throughout much of the twentieth century. The challenges included low levels of literacy, relatively high costs, and, perhaps most notable of all, the cultural gulf between establishment, upper-class culture, as embodied in universities, and working-class culture.

What would be termed today quality assurance was also a persistent problem. How could the university ensure that its extension programs were of a standard appropriate for university-level provision? In an attempt to facilitate and sustain more focused study, both Oxford and Cambridge introduced residential summer meetings for adult learners. Despite all the problems, university extension was a significant force in the later years of nineteenth century in Britain and, consequently, also shaped aspects of the higher education systems of many countries.

Another aspect of this tradition related to the strengthening of links between universities and broader social movements – for example, the Workers' Educational Association in the UK, which reflected a broadly liberal ideological stance, exemplified the influential early leaders of university ACE such as Temple, Tawney, Lindsay, and Cole. Nottingham University was the first formally to establish a department of extramural studies, in 1920–21. Within a decade of World War II, most of the major British universities had developed such departments.

In 1947, the extramural departments came together to form the Universities Council for Adult Education (UCAE). This continues as a significant policy body in university ACE through to the present time (2009), albeit with changes in title, to the University Association for ACE (UACE) and, recently, to the Universities Association for Lifelong Learning (UALL). Many other countries developed equivalent bodies, notably the University Continuing Education Association (UCEA) in the United States, which grew out of the National UCEA – one of the oldest college and university associations in the USA, founded in 1915.

From the beginning, UCAE asserted that liberal studies, although the core concern of extramural departments, should be complemented by vocational, professional, and technical course provisions to address the changing needs of the postwar society. The resulting pattern of provision was a combination of shorter liberal studies programs (sometimes indistinct from WEA provision), attracting predominately middle-class students, and professionally orientated provision, much of it for the growing numbers of employees in the welfare state.

Internationally, in many university systems based around the Anglo-American model, large centers or departments developed over this period. Such departments often held unique positions in the university: on the one hand, they were part of the mainstream university structure, with representation on Senates, professorial appointments, and the like; on the other hand, however, they were also, in many important respects, separate and different, and more connected to their local communities.

Structural Tensions – Inside or Outside the Walls?

Structural tension – being partly inside, and partly outside, mainstream university structures and processes – is a distinguishing feature of the centers, institutes, and departments which have grown out of the extramural tradition.

To begin with, they are often separately funded, and, importantly, have the opportunity to generate their own direct fee income; their students are adults and part time, not standard age and full time; their teaching is often off-campus and at nonstandard times; and they are multidisciplinary rather than having a single-subject focus as conventional mainstream academic departments do.

At a rather different level, it is also interesting to note that not only did they include, in their number, leading public intellectuals – such as E.P. Thompson, Richard Hoggart, and Raymond Williams – but also gave birth to, or were the key catalysts for, the development of new interdisciplinary areas of research and teaching, later to become major parts of mainstream university provision – for example, cultural studies, women's studies, industrial studies, and applied social studies.

Typical examples of the forms of provision of extra-mural departments and centers for adult education over the last three decades or so include:

- liberal studies of the traditional kind, characterized by intellectual effort on the part of the student, and the attainment of a standard appropriate for university study;
- continuing education programs designed to support a change of career or life course;
- the development of part-time courses for credit leading to university awards;
- role education for groups whose common element was their role in society – often including work with the public sector and nongovernmental organizations (NGOs);
- industrial education at all levels from management to the shop floor;
- social purpose, community education, and outreach;
- project research work;
- training for those engaged in the education of adults – increasingly at the postgraduate level such as masters and doctoral programs;
- research in adult education as an academic discipline; and
- acting as a seedbed for innovative programs – frequently regarded, for one reason or another, as high risk by the parent university.

In relation to the last point, there has been a growing recognition in many countries that universities should undertake more innovative and pioneering work to open up new fields of study and attract new learners where the provision, once established, might be handed over to other agencies. This, for example, includes access provision and third-arm activities such as work with local communities, employers, or other groups.

With the rapid expansion of higher education over recent decades, the overall shape changed as many countries developed some form of binary structure. In the UK, this distinction was abolished in the early 1990s. One consequence was that financial support for adult university education was mainstreamed across the entire system, so that part-time students, and the courses on which they were enrolled, had to be accredited as equivalent to at least the first year of undergraduate study.

This created considerable turbulence in the system, with many adult learners withdrawing. On the one hand, it had the potential to bring adult learners into the mainstream of the university system; for the first time, adults could study for and, if successful, gain university awards through university ACE. In one sense, this could be seen as something of a coming of age for ACE. On the other hand, and to quite an extent, this eroded the autonomy and flexibility of university ACE, and was regarded by some as undermining the student-led, democratic culture of the ACE tradition. It also reflected an international trend, also seen, for example, in the shifting focus of the folk universities of the Nordic countries which, while originally not aimed at qualifications, "...are now increasingly involved in preparing students for professional life or upgrading previous qualifications" (Fagerlind and Stromqvist, 2004: 258).

Global Trends in University ACE – Convergence or Divergence?

As has been shown here, the forms which university ACE takes vary considerably over time, are integrally connected with the traditions from which they spring, and are subject to the broader global changes impacting national university systems. The case of the extramural tradition considered above illustrates common challenges faced. In essence, these boil down to the issue of the mainstream versus the dedicated provision for adult learners. How this balance tips is influenced by broad social and economic factors, mediated through university strategies at particular times.

In reviewing the current situation of university ACE, five broad international trends can be identified.

First, much of the recent growth in higher education has taken place in institutions other than universities. In some countries, adult students are predominantly located in these institutions which, typically, have a particular mission to work in collaboration with local and regional communities, and to strengthen links with employers. While these trends can be seen more generally (typically characterized as moving from knowing what to knowing how (Barnett, 1992, 2005)), their impact on newer and nonuniversity institutions tends to be strongest. On the plus side, it is very often the elements of flexibility and relevance that are of greatest interest to many adults. On the other hand, however, the growing emphasis on international university league tables – such as the Shanghai and the Times Higher Education rankings – serves to reinforce differentiation and hierarchical positioning of research-intensive, elite universities compared to the broader spectrum of higher education institutions.

In practice, in many countries, adult students tend to find it easier to gain access to nonuniversity institutions, and to be less well represented in the highest-status universities. Whether this matters or not – as long as learning needs are met and successful outcomes achieved – is the subject of ongoing debate.

Second, the use of new learning technologies and new modes of delivery are widespread in the broader field of continuing education for adults. However, their impact on mainstream university provision remains variable. Therefore, the utilization of new learning technologies does not (yet) appear to have resulted in an anticipated blurring of boundaries between full-time and part-time students in most countries. At the undergraduate level, the resourcing and organizational model of most university systems remains orientated toward the traditional, full-time student. However, perhaps this might change in the future as the patterns of study of young students alter, as they increasingly combine study with significant employment commitments, and as higher education comes to be viewed as an activity to be pursued over the life course (Slowey and Watson, 2003). At the professional masters' level, the pattern may be somewhat different. Some countries – for example, many member states of the European Union, through the Bologna process – have seen the growth of modular programs at the postgraduate level, which are designed to connect with the world of work and continuing professional development.

Third, core values associated with the extramural tradition of seeking to widen access to university learning to the wider public do indeed appear somewhat beleaguered along with being somewhat marginalized in relation to the broader field of research on higher education. Aspects of university ACE are also increasingly connected with the growing commercialization of higher education as evidenced, for example, through the inclusion of higher education under the World Trade Organization General Agreement on Trade and Services (GATS). As some universities in the richer countries seek to develop provision in the continuing education market as a global economic initiative, this undoubtedly carries potential implications for capacity and sustainability of universities in developing countries (e.g., UNESCO, 2005, 2008). Furthermore, within and between nation states, the arena of lifelong learning is one which is particularly subject to the growth of the private sector and both profit and nonprofit higher education providers (Peters, 2001; Marginson, 2007).

Fourth, in contrast to the structural and ideological issues which arise in relation to universities engaging in direct provision of adult education, activities such as the training of adult education professionals, doctoral education, and research in the field of adult education are all areas that sit relatively comfortably within the university environment – frequently as a special section or unit within faculties of education (Hinzen and Przybylska,

2004). Given the continuing international policy emphasis on lifelong learning, and interdisciplinary research, these are all areas which have the potential to form an important part of the future development of university ACE , and specialist research journals with a focus on adult and lifelong learning represent a flourishing area of publication (Jarvis, 2006).

Fifth, in organizational terms, long-standing structural tensions between university ACE and parent institutions continue to be observed in the twenty-first century – albeit in rather different forms. It is possible to detect on-going debates about the role of units, centers, or departments which operate at the interface between the higher education institution and external stakeholders such as local communities, employers, trade unions, and the like. This inside/outside – sometimes marginal – positioning continues to offer independence and creative space (Taylor *et al.*, 2002). The price to be paid for this independence, however, may involve exposure to institutional policies which can vary over time.

Whether or not contemporary developments will see a new flowering of university ACE and lifelong learning and will usher in a new era in which universities engage dynamically and imaginatively with the whole community remains to be seen. Without doubt, the environment is a volatile and unstable one, and there is much to strive for in the context of university ACE and the broader area of educational and training policies relating to adults.

Bibliography

Bagnall, R. G. (2000). Lifelong education and the limitations of economic determinism. *International Journal of Lifelong Education* **19**, 20–35.

Barnett, R. (1992). *The Idea of Higher Education*. Buckingham: SRHE/Open University Press.

Barnett, R. (2005). *Reshaping the University: New Relationships between Research, Scholarship and Teaching*. Maidenhead/New York: SRHE/Open University Press.

Bourgeois, E., Duke, C., Guyot, J. L., and Merrill, B. (1999). *The Adult University*. Buckingham: SRHE/Open University Press.

Coffield, F. (ed.) (2000). *Differing Visions of the Learning Society*. Bristol: Policy Press.

Davies, P. (ed.) (1995). *Adults in Higher Education: International Perspectives in Access and Participation*. London: Jessica Kingsley.

Davies, P. and Feutrie, M. (2008). University lifelong learning to lifelong learning universities. *Bologna Handbook: No 8, June 2008*. Berlin: Raabe and the European Universities Association.

Duke, C. (1992). *The Learning University*. Buckingham: SRHE/Open University Press.

Fagerlind, I. and Stromqvist, G. (eds.) (2004). *Reforming Higher Education in the Nordic Countries*. Paris: International Institute for Educational Planning.

Field, J. (2006). *Lifelong Learning and the New Educational Order*, 2nd edition, Stock on Trent: Trentham Books.

Fieldhouse, R. (1996). *A History of Modern British Adult Education*. Leicester: National Institute of Adult Continuing Education.

Green, M., Eckel, P., and Barblan, A. (2002). *The Brave New (and Smaller) World of Higher Education: A Transatlantic View*. Washington, DC: The American Council on Education and the European Universities Association.

Hamilton, R. and Slowey, M. (2005). *The Story of DACE: The Department of Adult Continuing Education of Glasgow University.* Glasgow: DACE University of Glasgow.

Hinzen, H. and Przybylska, E. (eds.) (2004). *Training of Adult Educators in Institutions of Higher Education: A Focus on Central, Eastern and South Eastern Europe.* Bonn: Institute for International Cooperation of the German Adult Education Association.

Jarvis, P. (ed.) (2006). *From Adult Education to the Learning Society: 21 Years from the International Journal of Lifelong Education (Education Heritage Series).* London: Routledge.

Jones, C. K. (2008). *The People's University: 150 years of the University of London and Its External Students.* London: University of London.

Marginson, S. (2007). Going Global: trends in higher education and research in the APEC region. *APEC HRDWG Symposium on Education Policy Challenges,* Brisbane. http://www.cshe.unimelb.edu.au/people/staff_pages/Marginson/Marginson.html (accessed May 2009).

OECD (1987). *Adults in Higher Education.* Paris: Centre for Educational Research and Innovation/OECD.

OECD (1999). *Education Policy Analysis.* Paris: OECD.

OECD (2005). *OECD Thematic Review of Tertiary Education: Comparative Indicators on Tertiary Education* http://www.oecd.org/dataoecd/56/63/35940816 (accessed May 2009).

Osborne, M. and Thomas, E. (eds.) (2003). *Lifelong Learning in a Changing Continent.* Leicester: National Institute of Adult Continuing Education.

Peters, M. (2001). *Neoliberalism, Postmodernity and the Reform of Education in New Zealand.* Auckland: University of Auckland Mcmillan Brown Lecture Series.

Rubenson, K. (2006). The Nordic model of lifelong learning. *Compare – A Journal of Comparative Education* **36**, 327–341.

Schuetze, H. G. and Slowey, M. (eds.) (2000). *Higher Education and Lifelong Learners: International Perspectives on Change.* London: RoutledgeFalmer.

Schuetze, H. G. and Slowey, M. (2003). Participation and Exclusion – a comparative analysis of non-traditional and lifelong learners in systems of mass higher education. *Higher Education* **44**, 309–327.

Scott, P. (1995). *The Meanings of Mass Higher Education.* Buckingham: Society for Research into Higher Education/Open University Press.

Scott, P. (1997). The Postmodern University? In Smith, A. and Webster, F. (eds.) *The Postmodern University? Contested Visions of Higher Education in Society*, pp 36–47. Buckingham: SRHE/Open University Press.

Slowey, M. and Watson, D. (eds.) (2003). *Higher Education and the Lifecourse.* Maidenhead: SRHE/ Open University Press.

Tavistock Institute (2002). *Review of Current Pedagogic Research and Practice in the Fields of Post-Compulsory Education and Lifelong Learning.* Exeter: Economic and Social Research Council Teaching and Learning Research Programme.

Taylor, R., Barr, J., and Steele, T. (2002). *For a Radical Higher Education: After Postmodernism.* Buckingham: SRHE/Open University Press.

UNESCO (2005). *Implications of WTO/GATS on Higher Education in Asia and the Pacific, UNESCO Forum Occasional Paper Series Paper No.8.* Paris: UNESCO.

UNESCO (2007). *Education Counts: Benchmarking Progress in 19 WEI Countries.* Paris: UNESCO Institute for Statistics.

UNESCO (2008). *UNESCO Forum on Higher Education Research and Knowledge.* www.unesco.org/education/researchforum.

Watson, D. and Taylor, R. (1998). *Lifelong Learning and the University: A Post-Dearing Agenda.* London: Falmer.

Wolter, A. (2000). Germany: Non-traditional students in German Higher Education: Situation, profiles, policies and perspectives. In Schuetze, H. G. and Slowey, M. (eds.) *Higher Education and Lifelong Learners*, pp 48–66. New York: Routledge Falmer.

Further Reading

Bron, A. and Agelii, K. (2000). Non-traditional students in higher education in Sweden: From recurrent education to lifelong learning. In Schuetze, H. G. and Slowey, M. (eds.) *Higher Education and Lifelong Learners: International Perspectives on Change*, pp 83–100. New York: Routledge Falmer.

Cropley, A. J. and Knapper, C. K. (1983). Higher education and the promotion of lifelong learning. *Studies in Higher Education* **8**(1), 15–21.

Duke, C. (2004). Values, discourse and politics: An Australian Comparative Perspective. In Tapper, T. and Palfreyman, D. (eds.) *Understanding Mass Higher Education: Comparative Perspectives on Access.* London: RoutledgeFalmer.

El-Khawas, E. (1999). The "new" competition: Serving the learning society in an electronic age. *Higher Education Management* **11**(2), 7–17.

European Commission (1995). *Teaching and Learning: Towards the Learning Society.* Luxembourg: Office for Official Publications of the European Union.

Fuller, A. (2007). Mid-life 'transitions' to higher education: Developing a multi-level explanation of increasing participation. *Special Issue: Studies in the Education of Adults* **39**(2), 217–235.

Goldman, L. (1995). *Dons and Workers: Oxford Adult Education since 1850.* Oxford: Oxford University Press.

Gorard, S. and Rees, G. (2002). *Creating a Learning Society? Learning Careers and Their Relevance for Policies of Lifelong Learning.* Bristol: Policy Press.

Halsey, A. H. (1992). An International Comparison of Access to Higher Education. In Phillips, D. (ed.) *Lessons of Cross-National Comparison in Education*, pp 11–36. Wallingford: Triangle Books.

Horn, L. J. and Carroll, C. D. (1996). *Nontraditional Undergraduates: Trends in Enrolment from 1986 to 1992 and Persistence and Attainment Among 1989–90 Beginning Postsecondary Students (Report No. NCES 97-578).* Washington, DC: NCES.

International Journal of Lifelong Learning (2000). *Special issue: Lifelong Learning* **19**(1).

McLean, S. (2008). Extending resources, fostering progress, or meeting needs? University extension and continuing education in Western Canada. *British Journal of Sociology* **29**(1), 91–103.

OECD (1996). *Lifelong Learning for All.* Paris: OECD.

OECD (1997). *Literacy Skills for the Knowledge Society.* Paris: OECD.

OECD (1998). *Redefining Tertiary Education.* Paris: OECD.

OECD (2005). *Promoting Adult Learning.* Paris: OECD.

Ordorika, I. (2006). *Commitment to Society: Contemporary Challenges for Public Research Universities.* Key Note Paper. Paris: UNESCO Global Forum of Higher Education.

Osborne, M., Gallacher, J., and Crossan, B. (eds.) (2007). *Researching Widening Access to Lifelong Learning: Issues and Approaches in International Research.* London: Routledge.

Rubenson, K. and Schuetze, H. G. (2000). Lifelong learning for the knowledge society: Demand, supply and policy dilemmas. In Rubenson, K. and Schuetze, H. G. (eds.) *Transition to the Knowledge Society: Policies and Strategies for Individual Participation and Learning*, pp 355–376. Vancouver: UBC (Institute for European Studies).

Schuetze, H. G. and Istance, D. (1987). *Recurrent Education Revisited – Modes of Participation and Financing.* Stockholm: Almquist and Wicksel International.

Schuller, T. and Burns, A. (1999). Using 'social capital' to compare performance in continuing education. In Coffield, F. (ed.) *'Why's the Beer Always Srtonger Up North'? Studies in Lifelong Learning in Europe*, pp 53–61. Bristol: Economic and Social Research Council/Policy Press.

Tapper, T. Palfreyman, D. (eds.) (2004). *Understanding Mass Higher Education: Comparative Perspectives on Access.* London: RoutledgeFalmer.

UNESCO (1992). *Learning to Be: The World of Education Today and Tomorrow: The 'Faure' Report.* Paris: UNESCO.

UNESCO (1996). *Learning: The Treasure Within: The "Delors" Report.* Paris: UNESCO.

Wagner, A. (1999). Lifelong Learning in the University: A New Imperative. In Hirsch, W. Z. and Weber, L. E. (eds.) *Challenges Facing Higher Education at the Millennium*, pp 134–152. New York: American Council on Education/Oryx Press.

Walters, S. (2005). South Africa's Learning Cape Aspirations: The idea of a learning region and the use of indicators in a middle income country. In Duke, C., Osbourne, M., and Wilson, B. (eds.). *Rebalancing the Social and Economic. Learning, Partnership and Place.* Leicester: National Institute of Adult Continuing Education.

Relevant Websites

http://www.acheinc.org – ACHE (Association for Continuing Higher Education).

http://www.bc.edu – Boston College, CIHE (Center for International Higher Education).

http://cauce-aepuc.ca – Canadian Association for University Continuing Education (CAUCE).

http://www.esrea.org – ESREA (European Society for Research on the Education of Adults).

http://ec.europa.eu/education/index_en.htm – European Commission Education & training.

http://www.EUCEN.org – European Universities Continuing Education Network.

http://www.icae.org – ICAE (International Council for Adult Education).

http://www.oise.utoronto.ca – OISE University of Toronto, Canadian Association for the Study of Adult Education.

http://www.oecd.org – Organisation for Economic Co-operation and Development.

http://www.srhe.ac.uk – SRHE (Society for Research into Higher Education).

http://www.scutrea.ac.uk – Standing Conference on University Teaching and Research in the Education of Adults.

http://www.adulterc.org – The Adult Education Research Conference (AERC).

http://www.unesco.org – UNESCO.org, IAU Scholarly Publications.

http://portal.unesco.org – UNESCO.org: Scientific and Cultural Organization, United Nations Educational.

http://www.uall.ac.uk – Universities Association for Lifelong Learning (UALL).

http://www.ucea.edu – University Continuing Education Association.

Community Based Adult Education

B Connolly, National University of Ireland, Maynooth, Republic of Ireland

Glossary

Consciousness raising – An increasing of concerned awareness especially of some social or political issue.

Empowerment – The promotion of self-actualization or influence.

Praxis – In the context of community education, praxis connotes the synergy of activism and reflection, in order to bring about a more just and equal society.

Really useful knowledge – This concept was developed in the nineteenth century to critique dominant forms of knowledge, and to contribute to changing all forms of domination while simultaneously promoting democracy and social amelioration. Really useful knowledge underpins the reflection in praxis.

Really useful methods – These include ways of working with learners to enhance democracy, participation, and equality. These methods underpin the activism in praxis.

Introduction

Any discussion on community education must take into account that perspectives vary from context to place. Community education may be seen as an extension of a pragmatic education service designed to target hard-to-reach people, and integrate them into the mainstream, through employment, further education, or rehabilitation. It may be interpreted as a dimension of community development empowering powerless people to address their own educational and social needs. It also may be perceived as an adjunct to civil society, in which citizenship and participation are enhanced and strengthened. It may be named and understood in different ways too. Terms such as nonformal adult education, outreach, extra-mural, liberal adult education, locally based adult education, lifelong learning, training, and informal adult education are also used as synonyms for community education in different circumstances. Further, community education, positioned within the meanings of community, may be construed as a caring process, with a big emphasis on relationship and interpersonal connection, with the attendant focus on processes and methods shaped to enhance these caring qualities. This article discusses these myriad dimensions, in the context of exploring differing perspectives and contexts. The historical foundations are discussed before looking at the different facets of community education. A wide breadth of concrete examples of community education is then considered in the context of inherent differences and ambiguities. Finally, the discussion is appraised to establish common ground for deepening critical democracy in these changing times.

Historical Foundations

The story of community education is somewhat elusive, but this section outlines that story to provide a backdrop to its scope and some concrete examples on the ground. Lynn Tett documented the development of community education in Scotland, identifying the recommendations of the Alexander Report as the milestones of the current practice of community education. These recommendations led to the Community Education Service, to examine nonvocational adult education. The recommendations were strongly influenced by the understanding that adult education should help address social disadvantage endured by several groups, such as lone parents, unemployed people, early school leavers, and minority ethnic groups. Further, the report recommended that community education ought to nurture a pluralist democracy, by managing the tensions between state policies and community politics. These landmarks were congruent with the historical sources of adult education for working-class people. Crowther (1999) traces the lineage of community education with the radical working-class organizations of the eighteenth and early nineteenth centuries. This source was hard fought, and wrested from the grip of the mainstream schooling and education. In Denmark, Grundtvig founded the folk high schools with the explicit objective of providing space for learning for citizenship. The legacy of the folk high schools included a strong linkage with social movements, particularly with the cooperative movement, contributing to the foundations for the welfare society in the Nordic regions. Further, the model is one of nonformal education, elevating the value of education *per se* (Smith, 2007).

In Northern Ireland, the part that community education played in the development of the peace process is yet to be assessed fully, but Lovett's earlier work in England was influential at practical as well as theoretical levels when he moved back to Northern Ireland. In Lovett (1971) he reflected on his early community-based practice, maintaining that adult and community education must be much more than the provision of classes, in that it must also be integral to the whole community and must also be a communal activity.

In the Irish Republic, women's community education developed within a setting of difficulties, from the isolation of new suburbs, high unemployment, and emigration, coupled with the destructive war in Northern Ireland and the improvement of the status of women. The literature on the sphere is sparse due to the growth in a nonformal, nonacademic manner, probably unique in education initiatives in that it was created, fostered, and supported by noneducationalists (Connolly, 2003). Slowey noted the early days of adult education in the community, especially the adult education organized and conducted by women on the ground, (Slowey, 1985). Bassett, *et al.* (1989), made the case for adult education and emancipation, emanating from the work of Irish National Association of Adult Education (AONTAS), when it became more apparent that adult education was changing enormously through the phenomenon of the women's community-education growth and development. By the time the author did a small study looking at her own experience of women's community education, it was clear that women's community education was totally different from the traditional provision of night classes in empty-ish schools or universities, based on liberal studies and leisure courses, in three specific aspects: the processes and methods, which she named really useful methods, relating this concept to Thompson's really useful knowledge, which underpinned the content, in addition to the total learning environment. Women's community education offered programs of nonformal and formal adult education, but it also provided the space for informal learning, plus, vitally, childcare within caring, supportive settings (Connolly, 1989). That is, community education, whether supported by educational institutions, sponsored by communities, or arising from difficult life worlds, provides a way of responding to oppression and discrimination, particularly by building the capacity of the learners, in their own personal development and, crucially, in their communal and social development.

Thus, these historical foundations locates community education within the milieu of community concerns, including the very difficult, deep divisions in Northern Ireland, or the almost intractable issues around suburban isolation, early school leaving, drug addiction, environmental concerns, and unemployment.

While this historical overview is scant, and elides numerous milestones, it serves the purpose of illuminating the rootedness of community education in the social agenda of liberation, problem solving, and self-determination.

The next section looks more closely at the facets of community education that help to illuminate the flexibility and resourcefulness that enables it to respond to the breadth of issues.

Facets of Community Education

This section endeavors to explore the facets of community education and to discuss the implications. The understandings of the term community is discussed in greater depth later on, but as a marker, community in this context is used in the sense of the physical location in which people live, that is, place, or in the sense of the community of interest, the social network of people who share a common interest, such as the Irish in the USA. Or community may be applied to the group of practitioners, a quasi-functional meaning, such as the community of educators, social workers, doctors, or the like. The principles of community education, identified by AONTAS (2004), the national adult learning association, in Ireland, include the rootedness of community education in social justice and the process of empowerment, which aims to build the capacity of local people to respond to educational and structural disadvantage and to participate in decision making and policy creation (AONTAS 2004: 18). That is, AONTAS aligns its perspective with the ideological positioning of working toward addressing the causes of disadvantage and inequality. On the other hand, Smith (2009) draws a thumbnail definition – education for the community within the community. He views that community is not just the place, or context of the education program – building the community is also a central concern. Thus, the overlap between AONTAS and Smith is this core concern with community. Implied in building community is the process of working on relationships between members of the community, in order to enhance their lived experience.

Thompson delineates the ways of working in community education as specific and purposeful. She includes formal education, that is, adult education with credentials; informal adult education that occurs within social networks, such as the breaks between classes; and nonformal adult education, with no credentials. She holds that the processes work with people's life experience and it connects issues, ideas, and understanding to political action. These processes also foster practical skills, which help people to overcome alienation, as well as increase their capacity for employment and participation. Finally, she contends that community education helps to build self-esteem as well as enables people to understand others' perspectives (Thompson, 2002: 9–11). That is, Thompson builds the ground in community education between the person and the communal, the individual and the social. By including credentials, she sides conclusively with the contention that community education can embrace the full range of education, from basic literacy and numeracy to certificates, diplomas, and degrees.

Community education may also straddle the divide between institutionally sourced adult education and the kind of education that arises from the people themselves. McGivney (2000) in her study of outreach adult education for marginal groups, for example, unemployed men, traces the factors which underpinned its success. These factors included the ways of working with the learners, relationships, and methods, the response to community issues and support for community groups. Outreach in this sense comprised the provision of programs from universities or other education providers, but the processes and methods are not those of institution-centered provision; rather they are responsive and relevant to the learners' lives. McGivney's research echoes closely with the experience in Ireland, with women's community education.

Figure 1 endeavors to capture the facets of community education, including the contradictions and ambiguities. It revolves around the centrality of the learners, a key component of community education, not just in terms of the processes and methods, but also in terms of meaning, experience, and responsiveness.

These myriad facets demonstrate the breadth of community education, and these dimensions are reflected in concrete examples on the ground. The next section discusses cases of community education in specific exemplary contexts.

International Examples

A rudimentary review of community education reveals concrete examples in many contexts throughout the globe. This section provides a summary of these examples, in order to illuminate the ways in which societies engage with community education.

Community education is found in contexts as diverse as a middle-class, affluent city in the USA to a rural childbirth project in Kenya. These diverse examples include content-centered education, with the focus on information and resources; process-centered, with the focus on participative creative methods; or a combination of both,

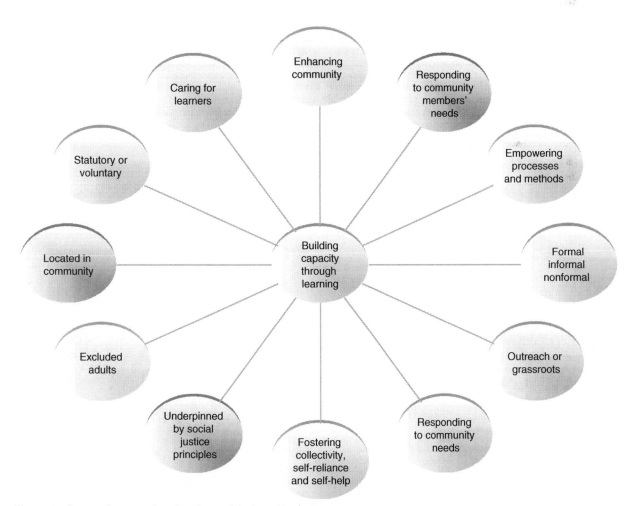

Figure 1   Facets of community education and the breadth of scope.

depending on the circumstances. They are also practiced in groups, in e-learning and in one-to-ones, employing basic resources on the one hand, and technology on the other, by a variety of educators, from peers to outsider professionals.

United Nations Educational, Scientific and Cultural Organization (UNESCO) has been at the forefront of the harnessing of community education for community, cultural, social, and personal development. The aim of meeting the learning needs of adults as well as children and youth, by 2015, is addressed through programs and targets on adult literacy, gender, and equality, human immunodeficiency virus/acquired immuno-deficiency syndrome (HIV/AIDS) education, and so on. This commitment to the use of community education as the means of addressing extremely difficult issues is evident in the examples outlined below.

In terms of the approach, the Australian agency, the Public Interest Advocacy Centre focuses on the use of information as the medium for community education. They supply a series of information leaflets, what Thompson (1996) terms really useful knowledge in their human rights community education. These information fact sheets are designed to reach out to people on the ground with background and strategies on civil, political, and human rights. The audience/learners include people from new communities, people who have come to Australia as refugee and asylum seekers, and other vulnerable people. They can access the information even from distant places, through the website.

In contrast, the indigenous community is the subject of another concrete example of community education, this time in Canada, in the Kehewin Community Education Centre. The overall objectives include the raising of awareness about the culture and practices of the Native Americans, in order to enhance the lives of both Native and non-Native communities. They undertake this through dance, theater as well as education. That is, the knowledge base is drawn from the traditional wisdom and practices within the Native community, and the learners are engaged in face-to-face creative processes.

The Grassroots Alliance for Community Education (GRACE), with its headquarters in the USA, works as a nongovernmental organization (NGO) in Africa, in a number of countries, with the objective of building the capacity of local people to take control over their own lives, by improving household health and welfare. Their processes include peer-educator training, which enables members of communities to relate to one another in an educational way, forming networks with local organizations. The agency trains local people, who use their knowledge to improve the health and welfare of families and households. Their interventions range from HIV/AIDS awareness, and consciousness raising about the illegality of female genital mutilation (FGM), to work with traditional birth attendants. That is, GRACE works in specific African countries, at once removed from the grassroots, empowering local educators in order to gradually change traditional beliefs which endanger lives. Africa is also the source for the materials that many community educators have worked with for over 20 years, *Training for Transformation* (Hope and Timmel, 1985). These resources were inspired by the work of Freire, and are balanced between the really useful knowledge of social analysis on the one hand, with the creative methods and processes that have characterized community education ever since. These texts were located firmly in the grassroots of community participation, and this work parallels the educational initiatives in Latin America.

In Latin America, popular education fulfills the role of community education for adults, that is, education for grassroots, fundamental social change. Freire's work is evident in popular education and social movements, hinged on participative processes together with political and social analysis. For example, Gadotti (1992) shows the role of participation in popular consciousness raising, and also in the strengthening of community control over the state. This role for popular education/community education is a key conduit in bringing democracy to the continent with its troubled relationship with the USA. Interestingly, the GATEWAY project in the Washington DC area uses the community-education approach to enable recent immigrants from Latin America to the USA connect with people who have experienced multiple barriers such as lack of education and low income, using the full span of community-education-method processes to motivate and empower the learners on the issues around HIV/AIDS. That is, the purposeful intervention of community education is designed to sensitively address traditional beliefs in new communities in order to enable them to stay safe and healthy, through small group or one-to-one educational settings. The use of community education in the USA ranges from the life–and-death issue of health and welfare, to community problem solving.

With regard to problem solving, when community education was reviewed on the Internet, one of the first references to community education led the author to the Government of Wisconsin website. The Wisconsin Department of Public Instruction outlines its perspective, with a set of principles which underpins its version of community education. These principles include the principles of self-determination, self-help, social inclusiveness, and formal and informal learning, in order to meet the needs of local people, provided as close as possible to those who want it. This focus on self-determination and self-help also features in a community-education initiative in South East Asia, which straddles the Wisconsin principles, but with an environmental dimension that protects the earth's resources for the benefit of humanity, that is, macro–micro integration. Further, while many community-educational objectives include the sensitive challenge to traditional beliefs, especially with regard to health, child-birth, and FGM, the Southeast Asia regional initiatives for community empowerment (SEARICE), promotes traditional knowledge of farming communities to protect them from the recent trends in agricultural production, with the attendant limiting of genetic diversity, and the copyrighting of seeds. The processes used in this community empowerment focus on information, lobbying, and advocacy. In contrast to the Wisconsin model, whereby the principles denote that community is a self-contained entity, a sub-set of the state, but autonomous and self-regulating rather than state controlled or supported, SEARICE sees the community as an integral dimension of the state – and the planet – but which needs to empower itself against the onslaught of the market. That is, the environmental concerns are held by the community, a huge burden in both the micro-sense of making a living, and also in the macro-sense of saving the planet.

On the other hand, the Scottish government locates the responsibility for community education firmly with the state, defining it as informal learning and social development, to strengthen communities by improving the capacity and knowledge of the community members. Further, it has prioritized community learning with the commitment not only to raise the educational attainments of adults, particularly literacy and numeracy, but also to support young people and to promote involvement with the planning and delivery of local services. Thus, the term community education is applied to the hands-on version of the Scottish government, to enhance democracy and participation, while the Wisconsin principles imply a hands-off approach, promoting self-sufficiency and independence. The Scottish Executive overtly locates community education within the social justice agenda, while Wisconsin government perceives community education as enhancing the community, improving services, and facilities, and applying not just to adults, and also schooling for children.

This overview of examples of community education on the ground, while superficial, illuminates the breadth of the field. It also shows the differences and contradictions, indicating the problem of delineation. The next section discusses these differences in order to establish the common ground in community education.

Contradictions and Ambiguities

Specific cases of community education have underlying contradictions, indicating the ideological understandings that underpin the practice. Tett (2002) discusses these inconsistencies with her discussion on the advantages and disadvantages of the hands-on state promotion of community education, with her reflections on the experience in Scotland. The key difficulty in the implementation of government policy is the high expectations of community education to solve deep structural inequalities. This imposes unrealistic burdens on community educators and the communities they serve. Community educators are faced with a deep ambiguity. On the one hand, they are left with the responsibility for driving change at the most grass-roots levels, sometimes underfunded and undervalued, in comparison to other educational institutions. On the other hand, they remain quite invisible in the overall perception, seen as facilitators of change rather than actors and agents. Further, Tett contends, community educators cannot attain the same professional standards for their work that other educators can, because their role is diffuse, unspecified, and undefined (Tett, 2002: 12). This is all the more the case when the educators are members of the communities, subject to the barriers that the other members endure. The task of addressing social inequality is contingent on the re-distribution of power and resources, underpinned by the clarity of vision of the just society. Teaching egalitarianism also needs access to the body of knowledge that illuminates the causes of inequality, what Thompson (1996) calls really useful knowledge, that is, knowledge that enables people to understand the social forces that shape society. As the case studies show, sometimes the knowledge is traditional and honored, while at other times, traditional knowledge is dangerous, especially with regard to gendered health and welfare. Thus, access to really useful knowledge is problematic, and can be controlled according to the beliefs of the animators.

Moreover, with such high expectations of community education, the responsibility for fundamental change is also problematic. When the responsibility for justice-based change is left with the most powerless, it has very little prospect for success. For political leaders, advocating and supporting community education does convey the appearance of concern with addressing inequity, but in effect, the *status quo* prevails.

Further, in relation to the continuum between the local and the global, the globalized influences of economic and cultural capital impinge in an incalculable way on the individual, the community, and community educator. That is, the needs which communities identify, for example, drug misuse, unemployment, or environmental degradation or appropriation may have sources completely outside the control of the local level. The solutions to these issues reside at the global level; yet, there is an expectation that community education can armor people against them, say, by drug education, community enterprise, or ecological activism, on the one hand, or animate the people to act against them. Community education advocates indicate that local people, if they corral resources, if they network with like-minded groups, and if they develop leadership, can work to overcome the deep structural divisions of race and ethnicity. As a principle, the vision of the inclusive society is commendable; yet, the causes of divided communities are not just endemic racism, ageism, and other discriminations, destructive as they are, but also globalized economic and cultural trends.

Thus, community education reaches difficult-to-reach people and communities, but not just that: it reaches difficult issues and trends, and as such, bears the burden of high expectations that it can actually resolve quite intractable social problems, as well as deal very effectively with other social issues. This raises the question about the nature of community, in which the community education operates. The next section discusses the connotations of community in this context.

Community Connotations

The term community is ambiguous and loose. Mayo (1994) contends that it is notorious for its shiftiness; yet, it is very useful for application to smaller sub-sets of society and to collectivities and communal dynamics. Williams (1976), in his discussion on the meanings and connotations of the term, traced the usage, originally referring to the common people, that is, peasants rather than people of rank. However, the connotation changed eventually to meanings closer to current usage, that is, the sharing of common characteristics and identity, and underpinned by relationship. Further, when the word is used, it conveys warm and persuasive sentiments. Thompson (2002) agrees with Williams that community has a feel-good factor associated with it that is difficult to undermine or challenge. She regards that community as a concept provides the space for security and common understandings. But she adds that community is frequently applied to others, that is, to poorer people, ethnic groups, and so on.

Toennies (1957) provided the discussion on *Gemeinschaft* and *Gesellschaft* which helped to develop insight into the characteristics of smaller social groups and looser associative relationships. These characteristics, though drawing on the contrasting traditional rural society versus urban industrialized society, nevertheless, enable the appreciation of experience of the postmodern city, and the large, isolated suburban enclaves in which huge populations endeavor to find common ground with the neighbors and common identities with like-minded people, to overcome alienation and loneliness.

The term community can also convey a more caring dimension than the larger institutional or social entity. Thus, in finding commonality, human relationships and constructions move into the central position, together with the sense of having some level of control over the immediate milieu. Harvey (1989) contends that different classes construct their sense of territory and community in radically different ways. He gives the example that middle classes can focus on tone, that is, control the status of the locality by ensuring that undesirable residents or developments are kept out. On the other hand, working classes protect relationships, characterizing the quality of the community in terms of good, supportive, and present neighbors. Harvey is obviously concerned with class, primarily, but additional analysis shows that there are other differences including gender, race, and ethnicity. For example, Irish travelers refer to themselves as a community, with a strong emphasis on kinship, custom, and tradition, with a distinct culture that differentiates them from the rest of the populations. This is not static of course, but the influences from modern Irish society are mediated through the filter of the culture, rendering them encultured so that any new phenomenon takes on a distinct traveler flavor.

However, the term is very useful in community education, as it conveys its small-scale nature; the close relationships, including those of caring, inclusion, and supporting; its flexibility and shifting nature, particularly with regard to its responsiveness; the closeness of its provision to the learners and their contexts; and the ways in which it overcomes the estranging language that was more typical, such as outreach and extra-mural, liberal adult education, locally based adult education, or more critically orientated versions, such as emancipatory, popular, or empowering education.

Government of Ireland (2000) evaluates these characteristics, and endeavors to encompass the scope of community education by acknowledging that it reaches large numbers of people, often in disadvantaged settings. Community education also pioneers new ways of working with learning groups, in nonhierarchical processes. Finally, the lived experience of the learners provides the starting point for the learning. Thus, community education is framed as educational, in terms of processes and methods; communal, in terms of groups, both learning groups and community groups; and egalitarian, in terms of organization and responding to the needs of disadvantaged communities.

Conclusion

This article endeavored to capture the dimensions and facets of community education, not only delineating it, but also illuminating the demands and stresses that shape the practice on the ground. While the origins have a diffuse lineage, from the concern with workers' rights, to the desire to strengthen civil society, community education is subjected to a series of dialectical pulls and pushes, which ensures the dynamic, process-oriented development of the field.

Community education evolved with this complex, dynamic interaction of grass roots organic growth, and statutory or pioneering animation. However, regardless of the provision, the ownership of the process remains with the participants. The community-centered approach ensures that learners participate freely, and the subjective experience of the participants is considered vital and transformative. Community education is located within the community and of the community.

Egalitarianism, which is very complex in itself, enables the learners to raise their consciousness about their own lives as well as the lives of other, engaged in the analysis of inequality. Freire's (1972) praxis connects the learning with activism, in a continuous cycle. The content of really useful knowledge (Thompson, 1996) contributes to the potential for societal transformation.

Bibliography

AONTAS (2004). *Community Education*. Dublin: AONTAS.

Bassett, M., Brady, B., Fleming, T., and Inglis, T. (1989). *For Adults Only: A Case for Adult Education in Ireland*. Dublin: AONTAS.

Connolly, B. (2003). Women's community education: Listening to the voices. In *The Adult Learner, the Journal of Adult and Community Education in Ireland*. 2003 Dublin: AONTAS.

Connolly, B. (1989). *Women's Studies in Lucan Daytime Classes 1985–1989: An Evaluation*. Unpublished Thesis.

Crowther, J. (1999). Popular education and the struggle for democracy. In Crowther, J., Martin, I., and Shaw, M. (eds.) *Popular Education and Social Movements in Scotland Today*. Leicester: NIACE.

Freire, P. (1972). *The Pedagogy of the Oppressed*. Harmondsworth: Penguin.

Gadotti, M. (1992). Latin America: Popular education and the state. In Poster, C. and Zimmer, J. (eds.) *Community Education in the Third World*. Taylor and Francis.

Government of Ireland (2000). *Learning for Life: White Paper in Adult Education*. Dublin: Government Publications.

Harvey, D. (1989). *The Urban Experience*. Oxford: Blackwell.

Hope, A. and Timmel, S. (1985). *Training for Transformation: A Handbook for Community Workers*. Gweru Zimbabwe: Mambo Press.

Lovett, T. (1971). Community adult education. In Westwood, S. and Thomas, S. E. (eds.) *The Politics of Adult Education*. Leicester: NIACE.

Mayo, M. (1994). *Communities and Caring: The Mixed Economy of Welfare*. Basingstoke: Macmillan.

McGivney, V. (2000). *Working with Excluded Groups: Guidance on Good Practice for Providers and Policy Makers in Work*. Leicester: NIACE.

Slowey, M. (1985). Education for domestication or liberation: Women's involvement in adult education. In Cullen, M. (ed.) *Girls Don't Do Honours*. Dublin: WEB.

Smith, M. K. (2009). http://www.infed.org/community/b-comed.htm, accessed (6th March 2009).

Smith, M. K. (1999, 2007). 'N. F. S. Grundtvig, folk high schools and popular education', *the Encyclopaedia of Informal Education*. http://www.infed.org/thinkers/et-grund.htm, accessed (6th March 2009).

Tett, L. (2002). *Community Education, Lifelong Learning and Social Inclusion*. Edinburgh: Dunedin Academic Press.

Thompson, J. (2002). *Community Education and Neighbourhood Renewal*. Leicester: NIACE.

Thompson, J. (1996). Really useful knowledge: Linking theory and practice. In Connolly, B., Fleming, T., McCormack, D., and Ryan, A. (eds.) *Radical Learning for Liberation*. Maynooth: MACE.

Toennies, F. (1957). *Community and Society*. Lansing: Michigan State University Press.

Williams, R. (1976). *Keywords*. London: Croom Helm.

Further Reading

Allman, P. (1999). *Revolutionary Social Transformation: Democratic Hopes, Political Possibilities and Critical Education*. Westport, CT: Bergin and Garvey.

Apple, M. (1996). *Cultural Politics and Education*. New York: Teachers College Press.

Barr, J. (2008). *The Stranger Within: On the Idea of an Educated Public*. Rotterdam: Sense Publishers.

Coare, P. and Johnson, R. (eds.) (2003). *Adult Learning, Citizenship and Community Voices: Exploring Community-Based Practice*. Leicester: NIACE.

Craig, G. and Mayo, M. (eds.) (1995). *Community Empowerment: A Reader in Participation and Development*. New Jersey: Zed Books.

Crowther, J., Martin, I., and Shaw, M. (1999). *Popular Education and Social Movements in Scotland Today*. Leicester: NIACE.

Duke, C. (2004). *Learning Communities: Signposts from International Experience*. Leicester: NIACE.

Giroux, H. (1992). *Border Crossings: Cultural Workers and the Politics of Education*. London: Routledge.

Habermas, J. (2004). *After Habermas: New Perspectives on the Public Sphere*. In Crossly, N. and Roberts, J. M. (ed.). Oxford: Blackwell.

Horton, M. and Freire, P. (1990). *We Make the Road by Walking: Conversions on Education and Social Change*. In Bell, B., Gaventa, J., and Peters, J. (eds.). Philadelphia, PA: Temple University Press.

Hooks, B. (2000). *Feminism is for Everyone: Passionate Politics*. London: Pluto Press.

Hooks, B. (2003). *Teaching Community: A Pedagogy of Hope*. New York: Routledge.

Mayo, P. (2004). *Liberating Praxis: Paulo Freire's Legacy for Radical Education and Politics*. Rotterdam: Sense Publishers.

Mayo, P. (1999). *Gramsci, Freire, and Adult Education: Possibilities for Transformative Action*. London: Zed Book.

Marx, K. and Engels, F. (1978). The Marx-Engels Reader. In Tucker, R. (ed.). New York: Norton.

Poster, C. and Zimmer, J. (eds.) (1992). *Community Education in the Third World*. Taylor and Francis.

Scottish Executive (2003). *Working and Learning together to Build Stronger Communities. Working Draft Community Learning and Development. Scottish Executive, Edinburgh*. http://www.infed.org/archives/gov_uk/working_together.htm, (accessed June 2009).

SED (1975). *Adult Education: The Challenge of Change*. Edinburgh: HMSO.

Tett, L. (2007). 'Working in and with Civil Society'. In Connolly, B., Fleming, T., McCormack, D., and Ryan, A. (eds.) *Radical Learning for Liberation 2*. Maynooth: MACE.

Tight, M. (2002). *Key Concepts in Adult Education and Training*, 2nd edn. London: Routledge.

Williams, S. (1994). *The Oxfam Gender Training Manual*. Oxford: Oxfam Publications.

Relevant Websites

http://www.infed.org – Encyclopaedia of informal education.

http://www.graceusa.org – Grassroots Alliance for Community Education.

http://www.telusplanet.net – Kehewin Community Education Centre.

http://gateway.nlm.nih.gov – NLM Gateway, A Service of US National Institutes of Health.

http://www.piac.asn.au – Public Interest Advocacy Centre.

http://www.perfectfit.org – Rage and Hope.

http://www.searice.org.ph – Southeast Asia Regional Initiatives for Community Empowerment.

http://www.unesco.org – UNESCO.

http://dpi.state.wi.us/fscp/ceprin.html – Wisconsin Department of Public Instruction.

Continuing Professional Education: Multiple Stakeholders and Agendas

R M Cervero, The University of Georgia, Athens, GA, USA

B J Daley, University of Wisconsin – Milwaukee, Milwaukee, WI, USA

The leaders of professions and the public have always assumed that professionals would maintain their competence by continuing to learn throughout their careers through reading, discussions with colleagues, and educational programs. Since the 1960s, one of these educational forms, formal educational programs, has increased dramatically. Most professions now embrace the importance of lifelong professional education. In the rapid growth of continuing education (CE), educational leaders have generally relied for guidance and models on the distinctive knowledge base and structure of their own profession. However, many observers (Houle, 1980; Cervero, 1988; Brennan, 1990) noted the similarities of the CE efforts of individual professions in terms of goals, processes, and structures. Thus, the concept of continuing professional education (CPE) began to be used in the late 1960s. Various terms are used throughout the world referring to this concept, including continuing professional development, staff development, and professional learning. The rationale for this movement is that the understanding of similarities across the professions would yield a fresh exchange of ideas, practices, and solutions to common problems.

As with any educational system, CPE has many stakeholders with multiple agendas. The purpose of this article is to chart the expansion of CPE and three agendas that are shaping its present and future: professional and social, institutional, and educational agendas. Although the growth of CPE is a worldwide phenomenon, the most articulated systems exist in the nations of the Global North, such as Canada, Europe, Australia, and the United States. As such, CE and training have been addressed in global contexts such as the World Trade Organization and the General Agreement on Tariffs and Trade (GATT) (Lenn and Campos, 1997). This article accordingly focuses on the development of CE efforts in these regions of the world.

Systems of CE for the Professions

A central feature of societies in the twentieth century was the professionalization of their workforces. One estimate is that nearly 25% of the American workforce, for example, is classified as professionals (Cervero, 1988). These professionals include teachers, physicians, clergy, lawyers, social workers, nurses, business managers, psychologists, and accountants. Educational systems have been a key feature of this professionalization project (Larson, 1977). An incredible amount of resources, financial and human, is used to support 3–6 years of professionals' initial education. Until recently, however, little systematic thought was given to what happens for the following 40 years of professional practice. Many leaders in the professions believed that these years of preservice professional education, along with some refreshers, were sufficient for a lifetime of work. However, with the rapid social changes, the explosion of research-based knowledge, the growing emphasis of evidenced-based practice, and spiraling technological innovations, many of these leaders now understand the need to continually prepare people for 40 years of professional practice through CE (Houle, 1980). Beginning in the 1960s, we started to see embryonic evidence for systems of CPE. Perhaps the first clear signal of this new view was the publication in 1962 of a conceptual scheme for the lifelong education of physicians (Dryer, 1962). The 1970s saw the beginning of what is now a widespread use of CPE as a basis for relicensure and recertification (Cervero and Azzaretto, 1990). By the 1980s, organized and comprehensive programs of CPE were developed in engineering, accounting, law, medicine, pharmacy, veterinary medicine, social work, librarianship, architecture, nursing home administration, nursing, management, public school education, and many other professions (Cervero, 1988). During this decade, many professions also developed their systems of accreditation for providers of CPE.

At the present time, the picture of an instructor updating large groups of professionals about the most recent theories and findings is easily recognizable as the predominant form of CE. We do not yet have a similarly recognizable picture of a system of CE in any profession. The major reason for this lack of a unifying picture is that the professions are in a transitional stage, experimenting with many different purposes, forms, and institutional locations for the delivery of CE. These systems, as such, are incredibly primitive and can be characterized as: devoted mainly to updating practitioners about the newest developments, transmitted in a didactic fashion by a pluralistic group of providers that does not work together in any coordinated fashion.

Relatively speaking, systems of CE are in their infancy. By way of analogy, CPE is in the same state of development as preservice education was at the beginning of the twentieth century. It is unlikely that anyone in 1910 would have predicted the structure of medical education today. Likewise, systems of CPE are likely to grow through this transitional period to achieve an equivalent coherence, size, and stature as the preservice stage of professional education. While these systems of CPE are in a grand historical transition (Young, 1998), it is quite unclear what form they will take in the future.

Social and Professional Agendas

Within every profession, there are segments using knowledge for different social purposes. As Schon (1983: 345) argues, professionals' "special knowledge is embedded in evaluative frames which bear the stamp of human values and interests." It is not surprising that the professions have conflicting values about their role in society because professions are "loose amalgamations of segments pursuing different objectives in different manners and more or less held together under a common name at a particular period of history" (Bucher and Strauss, 1961: 326). For example, many social workers deliver services by means of individual casework. However, within the profession, some argue that casework is a form of conservative politics that reinforces institutions, processes, and ideologies that are destructive to human well-being (Galper, 1975). In this view, social work is considered conservative because its basic assumption is that nothing is wrong with societal arrangements, but rather with individuals who need to adjust to the status quo. The existence of internal dissension and value conflict is not new. For example, Perrucci (1973) found 18 radical movement organizations in 12 professions, including medicine, engineering, law, and psychology. These movements share the perspective that the professionals' role is to ask for whom and for what ends their expertise should be used. As professionals' knowledge can serve conflicting social purposes, CPE likewise can and does serve many different purposes.

CPE is being used more frequently to regulate professional practice. One of the major changes of the past 20 years has been the incorporation of CE into accountability systems for professional practice. As regulatory bodies struggled to develop accountability mechanisms, participation in CE was often the method of choice. However, these new requirements have been critiqued for "promoting the appearance of accountability but [doing] little or nothing to address the underlying issue of competence" (Queeney, 2000). In spite of this lack of demonstrable connection between CE and competent practice, the use of professionals' participation in CE to regulate their practice has not abated for the past two decades. Perhaps the most obvious example is the growth of state use of CE as a basis for relicensure. What started in the 1970s is now widespread such that every profession uses some form of mandatory CE. The number of states requiring CE for relicensure has risen consistently for the past two decades. More professions are likely to follow the example of the Royal College of Physicians and Surgeons of Canada who have developed the Maintenance of Competence Program for recertification. This system allows physicians to use activities such as participation in audits of practice and a personal learning portfolio, which is a database of items of new learning recorded during the past year.

Institutional Agendas

Institutions develop the second part of the agenda, shaping present and future systems of CPE. Many different kinds of institutions have a stake in the growth of CPE systems, and each of these different institutions may have different goals and different methods by which CPE is provided. In discussing institutional agendas for CPE, four components are considered:

1. multiple goals,
2. multiple providers,
3. multiple modes of delivery, and
4. Collaboration among providers and professions.

Often the primary factor in determining the institutional agenda is the goals of the organization in which CPE is provided. Institutions tend to view CPE in different ways and most often these views are linked to the overall mission, vision, and values of the institution. For example, some institutions may view CPE as a method of employee development. Within these institutions it is believed that an educated and well-trained workforce is essential to the services provided by the institution. Healthcare, for example, most often focuses on employee development as a way to provide high-quality client care. The view here is that education assists employees to provide services that clients need. Thus, education or CPE is an essential link in the provision of institutional service.

Other institutions may see the provision of CPE as a method by which they can generate revenue. CPE is big business, especially in those states, countries, or territories that require CPE for recertification or relicensure of professionals. Higher education and professional schools, for example, are institutions that often rely on CPE as a way to generate revenue to support the overall mission of the institution. In these institutions, CPE is offered to large populations of professionals (often alumni) within the institutions' service area rather than to employees from one institution. As such, the revenue generated from day-long conference, multiday conferences, or short courses returns to the more centrally managed CPE unit within the university or school.

The providers of CPE include the workplace, professional association, higher education, and for-profit companies. The workplace is by far the largest provider of training and education for professionals and often this is accomplished through human resource development (HRD). Yet, each of these different providers offers unique CPE programs for specific audiences.

Dirkx and Austin (2005) help us understand the integrated nature of the multiple providers in CPE and the multiple goals of these providers. In their model of theoretical orientations in continuing professional development (Dirkx and Austin, 2005), they propose that the aims of professional development (based on Habermas, 1972) can range from technical, to practical, to emancipatory. Within the technical domain instrumental action, the scientific method and the hard sciences are addressed. In contrast, within the practical domain communicative action or human interest is most often the focus. Finally, the emancipatory domain focuses more on power and understanding our actions through self-reflection and self-knowledge.

In addition, Dirkx and Austin indicate that the goals of professional development are met in four primary contexts: HRD, CPE, faculty development, and staff development. Basically, these contexts represent the various areas in which professional development is most often provided. For example, HRD is usually provided as training in the workplace; CPE is most often provided through professional associations and higher education; faculty development is accomplished within colleges and universities; and staff development is associated with schools. What is evident in the Dirkx and Austin (2005) model is that the contexts of HRD, CPE, faculty development, and staff development may also overlap with different types of institutions. Finally, Dirkx and Austin (2005) indicate that the focus of professional development may be individual or organizational. In their view, offerings are not exclusively individual or organizational but they tend to predominately focus on one or the other.

In analyzing developing systems of CPE, Dirkx and Austin (2005) offer a model that focuses on the multiple and overlapping providers and goals. Their model, depicted in **Figure 1**, demonstrates the complexity of currently developing systems of CPE. As Dirkx and Austin (2005) indicate, professional development can be conceptualized around "the overall aim of or purpose for professional development; the context of professional development; and the primary focus of the professional development activity" (p. 3). The model, depicted in **Figure 1**, promotes a new understanding of institutional agendas in CPE. Each cell in this model could be considered a different type of CPE offering. Dirkx and Austin indicate:

> It is possible to take any particular context and identify different kinds of professional development that represent the different cells within that overall context. For example, one kind of faculty development program (context) might seek to develop specific skills (technical aim) in the use of a particular online software, so the professors can design and delivery more independently their own online courses (focus). This might be driven either by the organization's need to develop additional revenue in budget-tight times (organizational focus), or individual professors may freely elect to develop this new expertise as part of a re-directing of their careers (individual focus) (Dirkx and Austin, 2005: 8).

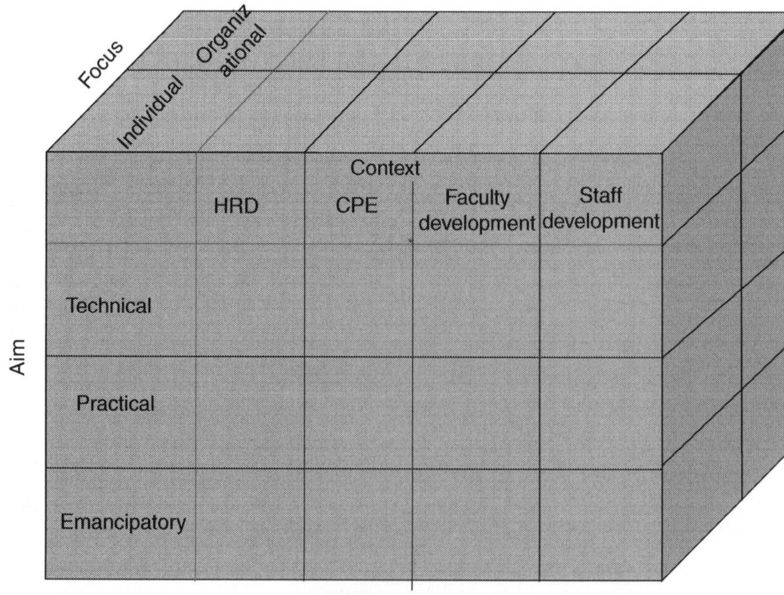

Figure 1 Dirkx/Austin model of theoretical orientations in continuing professional development. From Dirkx, J. and Austin, A. (2005). Making sense of continuing professional development: Toward an integrated vision of lifelong learning in the professions. Presented at the *Academy of Human Resource Development Continuing Professional Education Preconference*, Estes Park, CO, p. 8. 23 and 24 February, 2005, with kind permission from Dirkx and Austin.

Institutional agendas for CPE are also shaped by the multiple modes of delivery. CPE is predominately offered as limited, short-term educational programs presented in real time in a face-to-face format. These programs range from 1-day conferences, to multiday conferences, to short courses (i.e., 1–5 weeks). Most often, the mode of delivery for CPE focuses on an update of technical information so that the professional can return to their worksite with an increased understanding of new knowledge. However, increasingly distance education technologies are being incorporated into CPE programming. These technologies range from video-conferencing across multiple sites, to Internet-based courses, to Internet-based conferences, to online group discussion forums. Additionally, a relatively new form of distribution in CPE is learning objects. According to Lehman (2007) learning objects are "digital chunks of information" (p. 57). These digital chunks of information can be developed in the form of text, video, audio, or multimedia and they can be used to present case studies, new procedures, self-directed learning modules, or simulations. These smaller learning units can then be downloaded to hand-held devices making them easy to access and to share with other professionals.

Finally, collaboration among provider and professions is essential to present and future systems of CE. Collaborative arrangements among providers and across professions can not only help increase learning and understanding, but they can also help decrease the cost of providing CE. However, collaboration can raise issues within institutions and among providers. For example, providers of CPE at times feel that too much collaboration can demonstrate that their program is not needed. Once again, Dirkx and Austin (2005) offer us a way to consider collaboration. Within their model presented in **Figure 1**, areas of collaboration become evident. For example, if a healthcare employer decides that the aim of their educational programming will be technical, conducted within an HRD context at the organizational level, they may realize that they need to collaborate with universities and professional schools who can provide more emancipatory, CPE at the individual level. In this manner, different providers and different professions can analyze their own strengths and then collaborate with other providers offering different kinds of education using different methods. This type of analysis may draw on the strengths of organizations, prevent overlapping offerings, and streamline competition.

Educational Agendas

Building on professional/social agendas and institutional agendas, the educational agenda also impacts the continuing development of systems of CPE. However, for the educational agenda to be truly effective, we must include a model of learning (Cervero, 1988) at the center

of these educational agendas. As Eraut (1994) explained, behind "professional education lies a remarkable ignorance about professional learning" (p. 40).

Early models of professional learning have relied on the ideas of technical rationality (Houle, 1980), transfer of learning (Broad and Newstrom, 1992), and adoption of innovation (Rogers, 1995). In these views, knowledge for professional practice was created in one location, often a university setting, disseminated through CPE programs, and then transferred to or adopted in professional practice.

In the 1980s however, Cervero (1988) proposed a model for learning in the professions based on an understanding of how professionals "develop knowledge through practice" (p. 39). Cervero (1988) advocated that CPE providers develop a critical model of the learner that integrates the development of two forms of knowledge – technical and practical. Within this model, he incorporated components of cognitive psychology, reflective practice (Schon, 1987), and studies of expertise (Benner, 1984; Dreyfus and Dreyfus, 1985).

As systems of CPE continue to be developed, expanded models of learning will need to underlie educational offerings. Recent research (Daley, 2001a, 2001b) indicates that professionals construct a knowledge base for themselves in the context of their practice by linking concepts from new knowledge learned in education programs with their practice experiences. At this point, they actively make decisions on how to incorporate new knowledge into the context of practice based on their interpretations of the environment. What this newer research adds is an enhanced understanding of how learning in CPE occurs when professionals actively link new knowledge with the context in which they work and professional practice in which they engage.

As systems of CE continue to be developed, it is essential that education providers recognize this process of knowledge construction. Professionals do not simply take information from a learning situation and incorporate it in a practice context. They go through a much more complex process of taking in the new information, analyzing the context of their work site (including the politics and the people with whom they work), and then they decide if the new information is a good fit for their work based on the nature of their professional practice. This is a much more involved and sophisticated process than early professional learning models indicated. It requires that the educational agenda of CPE providers changes to incorporate a more active and integrated type of learning.

Additionally, an area that needs further development within professional learning is the question: How does the nature of professional practice connect to the educational agenda? We know that professionals construct a knowledge base for their practice and also know that the context of their work environment impacts the process. However, in addition, we need to understand how the nature of their professional work impacts learning. For example, do social workers learn in a fundamentally different manner than lawyers? Recent work by Donaldson (2002) indicates that individuals within different professions fundamentally think in distinctive ways. Therefore, this raises the question: Does the nature of the professional's work drive the thinking and learning process? If this is the case, then how does that shape the educational agenda of CPE in the future?

Finally, the overall purpose of learning within the professions is designed to develop expert practitioners who provide high levels of service to clients. The study of professional expertise has grown from an understanding of serial problem solving (Newell and Simon, 1972) to an understanding of the stages of career development within specific professions such as physists (Chi *et al.*, 1980), pilots (Dreyfus and Dreyfus, 1985), nurses (Benner, 1984), and physicians (Groen and Patel, 1988). These studies identified that as professionals gain experience they move from a novice to an expert practitioner. As professionals move from novice to expert, they develop the ability to think more abstractly and to see holistic patterns within their clients. They develop a sense of salience with the context that allows them to move from seeing individual issues to seeing systems and the integrated nature of professional problems. The study of expertise is now moving toward developing an understanding of the connections between learning and expertise. For example, Daley (1999) found that novice nurses tend to learn in a contingent manner, while expert nurses learn in a more constructivist manner. This type of research has implications for the educational agenda of CPE and necessitates that program planners consider the level of professional development of their audience. Finally, studies of expertise that focus on development of collective expertise across various contexts and disciplines are also needed. The idea of collective expertise within a profession or at a workplace is an area that will again shape the educational agenda of the future and will need more research.

In addition to professional learning models, evidence on the effectiveness of CPE is an important consideration in the educational agenda for CPE systems. When professionals attend CPE programs and learn new information, the question exists "Does it make a difference in the service provided to clients?" Early studies showed mixed results in response to this question, with some studies indicating little impact and other indicating great impact. To clarify this variability in the results of evaluation studies, Umble and Cervero (1996) conducted a meta-analysis of 16 studies that provided a synthesis of impact studies in CPE. A major purpose of this review was to analyze and critique the methodologies of the studies, but in addition they found that a first wave of syntheses studies existed that demonstrated a general causal connection between

CPE and impact on professional practice. Umble and Cervero (1996) found that CPE had an impact on knowledge, competence, performance and outcome.

In addition, Umble and Cervero (1996) found that a second wave of studies had begun to demonstrate a number of variables that moderate the impact. This second group of studies began identifying the types of programs that can promote performance change within the professions. Umble and Cervero (1996) indicate that as the development of CPE systems moves forward, more work is needed in understanding the impact of CPE on practice. They advocate for more experimental studies, more qualitative and mixed-methods studies, and the use of action research (Brooks and Watkins, 1994) as both a programming and evaluation methodology.

The educational agenda in current systems of CPE is thus shaped by the model of professional learning incorporated in education practice, by an understanding of the nature of expertise, and by the overall effectiveness of the impact of CPE programs. In the future, CPE systems will continue to be shaped by ongoing and expanding research in all three of these areas.

Conclusion

The task of building systems of CPE is fundamentally more complex than what faced leaders as they built the existing systems of preservice professional education. First, whereas preservice education takes place in a relatively short period of time, CE must help professionals for 30–40 years of professional practice, which is characterized not only by constant change, but also often by competing values. Second, while preservice education is predominately controlled by universities and professional schools, there are multiple institutions that offer CE, all of which stake a claim to being the most valid and effective provider. The leaders of workplaces, professional associations, universities, and governments have both a tremendous opportunity and a clear responsibility to further develop the systems of CE for the professions. As with any humanly constructed system, the building of a coordinated system of CE for any profession is a political process. While we cannot predict what these systems will look like, this process will be marked by fundamental struggles over the educational, institutional, and professional agendas and the competing interests of the multiple stakeholders for CE. As a political process, then, it is crucial that all of the stakeholders participate in a substantive way in negotiating these agendas for CE. The immediate and long-term negotiation of these struggles will define whether CE can make a demonstrable impact on the quality of professional practice.

Bibliography

Benner, P. (1984). *From Novice to Expert: Excellence and Power in Clinical Nursing Practice*. Menlo Park, CA: Addison-Wesley.

Brennan, B. (1990). *Continuing Education Promise and Performance*. Victoria, Australia: The Australian Council of Educational Research.

Broad, M. L. and Newstrom, J. W. (1992). *Transfer of Training*. MA: Addison-Wesley.

Brooks, A. and Watkins, K. (1994). The emerging power of action inquiry technologies. *New Directions in Adult and Continuing Education* **63**, 5–16.

Bucher, R. and Strauss, A. (1961). Professions in process. *American Journal of Sociology* **66**, 325–334.

Cervero, R. M. (1988). *Effective Continuing Education for Professionals*. San Francisco, CA: Jossey-Bass.

Cervero, R. M. and Azzaretto, J. F. (1990). (Eds.), *Visions for the Future of Continuing Professional Education* Athens, GA: The University of Georgia.

Chi, M. T. H., Feltovich, P. J., and Glaser, R. (1980). Categorization and representation of physics problems by experts and novices. *Cognitive Science* **5**, 121–152.

Daley, B. (1999). Novice to expert: An exploration of how professionals learn. *Adult Education Quarterly* **49**(4), 133–147.

Daley, B. (2001a). Learning in clinical nursing practice. *Journal of Holistic Nursing* **16**(1), 43–54.

Daley, B. (2001). Learning and professional practice: A study of four professions. *Adult Education Quarterly* **52**(1), 39–54.

Dirkx, J. and Austin, A. (2005). Making sense of continuing professional development: Toward an integrated vision of lifelong learning in the professions. Presented at the *Academy of Human Resource Development Continuing Professional Education Preconference*, p. 8. Estes Park, CO, 23 and 24 February, 2005, with kind permission from Dirtx and Austin.

Donaldson, J. (2002). *Learning to Think: Disciplinary Perspectives*. San Francisco, CA: Jossey-Bass.

Dreyfus, H. and Dreyfus, S. (1985). *Mind Over Machine: The Power of Human Intuition and Expertise in the Era of the Computer*. New York: Free Press.

Dryer, B. V. (1962). Lifetime learning for physicians: Principles, practices and proposals. *Journal of Medical Education* **37**(6), 1–134.

Eraut, M. (1994). *Developing Professional Knowledge and Competence*. Washington, DC: Falmer Press.

Galper, J. H. (1975). *The Politics of Social Services*. Englewood Cliffs, NJ: Prentice-Hall.

Groen, G. and Patel, V. (1988). The relationship between comprehension and reasoning in medical expertise. In Chi, M. T. H., Glaser, R., and Farr, M. J. (eds.) *The Nature of Expertise*, pp 287–312. Hillsdale, NJ: Lawrence Erlbaum.

Habermas, J. (1972). Knowledge and Human Interests. Boston, MA: Beacon Press.

Houle, C. O. (1980). *Continuing Learning in the Professions*. San Francisco, CA: Jossey-Bass.

Larson, M. S. (1977). *The Rise of Professionalism: A Sociological Analysis*. Berkley, CA: University of California Press.

Lehman, R. (2007). Learning object repositories. In Conceição, S. (ed.) Teaching Strategies in the Online Environment. *New Directions for Adult and Continuing Education*, vol. 113, pp 57–66. San Francisco, CA: Jossey-Bass.

Lenn, M. P. and Campos, L. (1997). *Globalization of the Professions and the Quality Imperative: Professional Accreditation, Certification, and Licensure*. Madison, WI: Magna Publication.

Newell, A. and Simon, H. A. (1972). *Human Problems Solving*. Englewood Cliffs, NJ: Prentice Hall.

Perrucci, R. (1973). In the service of man: Radical movements in the professions. *Sociological Review Monograph* **20**, 179–194.

Queeney, D. S. (2000). Continuing professional education. In Wilson, A. L. and Hayes, E. R. (eds.) *Handbook of Adult and Continuing Education: New Edition*, pp 375–391. San Francisco, CA: Jossey-Bass.

Rogers, E. M. (1995). *Diffusion of Innovations*. New York: MacMillian/Free Press.

Schon, D. A. (1983). *The Reflective Practitioner*. New York: Basic Books.

Schon, D. A. (1987). *Educating the Reflective Practitioner: Toward a New Design for Teaching and Learning in the Professions*. San Francisco, CA: Jossey-Bass.

Umble, K. and Cervero, R. (1996). Impact studies in continuing education for health professionals: Critique of the research syntheses. *Evaluation and the Health Professions* **19**(2), 148–174.

Young, W. H. (1998). *Continuing Professional Education in Transition: Visions for the Professions and New Strategies for Lifelong Learning*. Malabar, FL: Krieger.

Further Reading

Bereiter, C. and Scardamalia, M. (1993). *Surpassing Ourselves: An Inquiry into the Nature and Implications of Expertise*. Chicago, IL: Open Court.

Cervero, R. M. (2001). Continuing professional education in transition, 1981–2000. *International Journal of Lifelong Education* **20**(1–2), 16–30.

Cervero, R. M. and Scanlan, C. L. (eds.) (1985). Problems and prospects in continuing professional education. *New Directions for Adult and Continuing Education*, 27. San Francisco, CA: Jossey-Bass.

Daley, B. (2000). Learning in professional practice. In Mott, V. and Daley, B. (eds.) Charting a course for continuing professional education: Reframing professional practice. *New Directions in Adult and Continuing Education*, vol. 86, pp 33–42. San Francisco, CA: Jossey Bass.

Daley, B. and Jeris, L. (eds.) (2004). Boundary spanning: Expanding frames of reference for human resource development and continuing professional education. *Advances in Human Resource Development* 6(1). Thousand Oakes, CA: Sage Publications.

Moon, J. (2003). *Reflection in Learning and Professional Development: Theory and Practice*. London: Kogan.

Nowlen, P. M. (1988). *A New Approach to Continuing Education for Business and the Professions: The Performance Model*. New York: Macmillan.

Displaced Workers, Unemployed and Vocational Education and Training

B Kriechel, ROA – Maastricht University, Maastricht, The Netherlands; IZA, Bonn, Germany

Introduction

Workers with education that predestine them to occupations predominantly in declining industries are under severe pressure. There is a higher incidence of job loss in those industries, as the decline usually goes along with plant closures and firm failures. Workers cannot easily change employment out of the industry as they are bound to lose the industry-specific human capital or experience, which is usually only rewarded within the industry.

Particularly in the context of occupations that are linked closely to specific vocational education, occupational mobility is likely to be low. Vocational education is often geared to a specific occupation, teaching specific skills that are not easily transferable. It puts workers with the wrong education at risk of losing their employment. This combined with the additional difficulty of lower reemployment chances given that their education predestines them for occupations in declining industries. The choice is to change occupations, implying the loss of the occupation-specific training and experience, or to try to find employment in a declining sector.

One option is to increase the employability of workers by broadening their skills beyond the occupation-specific requirement to enable them to switch to more general positions. Another option, which is usually only taken after job loss, is to retrain displaced workers such that they can take up different occupations. Many countries offer some sort of training either to specific groups of unemployed workers, for instance, displaced workers, or generally retraining programs to all unemployed.

In this article, we concentrate on the retraining of displaced workers. The preemptive broadening of skills to increase once employability as well as to increase a worker's employment opportunities is not discussed in this context.

In the following, we first discuss the differences between unemployed workers and displaced workers. Next, the different retraining strategies that can be used to aid unemployed workers are discussed. Then we go into programs that countries offer to aid specifically displaced worker, or, in some cases, to general training programs. It will not be possible to completely cover all programs or countries; rather, we have tried to give an overview of approaches from geographically different countries, and to discuss what is known about the effectiveness of these programs.

Displaced Worker

There are considerable differences in the definition of displaced worker. The definitions vary from general layoffs (including firing for cause) to large-scale layoffs due to plant closure or reorganization only. The definition is important, especially in the context of government policies specifically aimed at displaced workers. If displaced workers are to be compensated or aided, they need to be defined properly. In addition, scientific research on displaced workers should also use at least closely related definitions of displaced workers.

Before a special survey was introduced, the Displaced Worker Supplement (DWS) to the US Current Population Survey (CPS), displaced workers were often identified as those workers being fired or unemployed in declining industries, local labor markets, or occupations. This is, however, quite a broad category. With the introduction of the DWS, the questioning used to identify displaced workers in the survey, became a focal point of a definition. According to the DWS, a worker is considered displaced if he/she filled in that he/she lost his/her job due to "a plant closing, an employer going out of business, a layoff without recall, or some similar reason." Most economists use definitions that are very close to the above wording, even if they are not using the DWS.

Displaced workers differ from unemployed workers. These workers are not unemployed for cause, or due to their own actions, but rather as a result of a plant closure or large-scale downsizing. The crucial difference between the groups is that the displaced workers undergo no selection, that is, there is no negative selection of the least-productive workers into the layoff procedure.

The group of unemployed contains a mixture of workers: those who are laid off for cause and those who became unemployed for external reasons. Thus, on average, the productivity of the pool of workers should be lower than that of a comparable group of displaced workers. This is the result of the firm selecting the least-productive workers to be laid off first. It can be shown that displaced workers will do better, in terms of wages earned after their unemployment, than unemployed workers who were not displaced.

Causes of Worker Displacement

There are several reasons that can lead to plant closures and large-scale layoffs. They can be due to new production technologies, increased foreign competition, changes in taste, and managerial errors. The first two causes can also be seen as external causes of displacement. They are the result of common technological progress, rendering some activities superfluous. Mechanization is one of the examples for the production process that leads to displacement of workers.

The cause of displacement, either through foreign competition or technological progress, actually benefits society as a whole. For example, free trade benefits all members of society, as they can buy more products more cheaply than those that are domestically produced. Opening of trade adversely affects not only import-competing companies, but also workers employed in these firms that directly compete with the foreign firms. Often, a whole range of products will be predominantly imported, rendering many workers unemployed in the present occupations. It is therefore of no surprise that society as a whole tries to redistribute some of the gain it achieves to those who are at a loss due to free trade. Similar arguments can be made for technological progress.

Losses of Displaced Workers

Displacement implies a significant burden on a worker. First of all, workers will have to find new employment, which implies that they have search costs and invest time. During the search process, they will depend on unemployment benefits or severance payments from their former employer. If they find new employment, they are often stripped of rights or protections due to seniority offering them benefits over newcomers. Empirical research has consistently shown that higher-educated workers as well as younger workers have shorter search time. However, these direct costs are, according to research into the effects of displacement, only a minor part of the displacement losses: wage drops for weekly earnings are reported to be around 10–20% on average.

In the long run, these losses can even be greater. First of all, the wage drop is not temporary – average earnings remain consistently lower compared to workers who were not displaced. In the evaluation of long-term earning development of displaced workers, negative income effects could be found even after more than a decade. Many displaced workers are not able to find long-lasting jobs. This makes them prone to dismissal in economic downturns (Eliason and Storrie, 2006).

Explanations of Wage Loss

How can the wage losses be explained? Displaced workers can often be found in companies or industries that pay above the average wage. These wage premiums can have different reasons: they can be attributed to investments in human capital, a reward for staying longer with the firm,

which is also known as deferred-compensation schemes, or it might reflect higher compensation for achieving higher hierarchical positions within a company. Displaced workers with higher-than-average labor-market pay will, after being displaced, fall back to lower wages.

Most of the economic displacement literature concentrates its attention on the human capital explanation, as there is strong empirical evidence for its importance. If the wage premium is due to an investment in human capital, it is important to understand how this is productive for the worker in a specific firm. The literature distinguishes between specific human capital and general human capital. General human capital increases the productivity of a worker in all firms and sectors, whereas specific human capital can be described as knowledge or skills that are specific for a certain firm, occupation, or industry. Wage losses that are incurred have therefore been explained by the loss of firm-specific human capital, and for those changing industries, in addition to the loss of industry-specific human capital. On average, industry switchers incur higher losses than workers who can remain within the same industry.

An alternative explanation is a wage premium that workers earn from working in high-wage industries or occupations, which can be explained by compensating wage differentials. Compensating wage differentials assumes that these wage differentials are the result of preferences of workers. Occupations or industries which are not preferred, because they are, for example, dangerous or unhealthy, warrant a higher wage. A good example is miners, who are often well paid for their work. However, it is dangerous and unhealthy work; the higher wage can be explained by these differences. If workers move from high-wage industries, which involve discomfort, to low-wage industries after displacement, it might simply involve a move to a more agreeable occupation, with lower pay.

The internal labor market with hierarchical positions can offer a further explanation for pay differences. If within a firm or sector, a worker's career can bring him/her across several hierarchical positions, it will increase not only the wage spread, but also the average pay that can be expected. If a worker moves away from such a firm with a hierarchical structure, and if he/she comes from a higher hierarchical position, he/she will have to receive a position that is at par with his/her old hierarchical position. There are firms in which higher positions are filled from within. It is therefore difficult for a worker to be able to recoup a position at the same level of his/her former hierarchical standing. Empirical research shows that higher hierarchical positions increase the chance of lower search time, hence less unemployment, along with lower wage losses. Higher hierarchical position can be seen as a form of general human capital, that is, general management skills, which can be transferred to new employment, thus diminishing wage losses (Kriechel and Pfann, 2005).

Another important aspect is that of the local labor market. Many workers who are displaced are reluctant to relocate their families to other regions. Therefore, the local labor market and the job opportunities within the local labor market will influence the opportunities that a displaced worker faces. A part of the decline in wages is due to a decline in the local labor market of the occupation a displaced worker held. Workers who restrict themselves to the regional labor market diminish the chances of finding employment at the same level and remuneration as before displacement.

Assisting Displaced Workers

The best way to aid displaced workers is by helping them cope with the job loss and moving on to new employment. Avoiding the job loss and supporting the displacing company just keeps inefficient jobs in place. It is better to move the workers to new, more productive employment opportunities and careers. The problem is, however, that many times the loss of jobs is the result of a structural shift in the employment structure of a region or country. This means that the current employment is no longer viable in the long run. A good example is coal mining in Europe. A combination of technological change, replacing coal by other energy sources, and international trade importing coal from countries in which the extraction was cheaper, made the occupation of coal miner redundant in many European countries. The occupation was often linked to a set of vocational training degrees that allowed a worker to pick up the occupation of a miner. However, once the mines were closed many of the skills were no longer needed.

Retraining is then one of the most feasible options, whose goal is to prepare the displaced workers for a new career in a different sector and occupation. Sometimes a part of the skills can be used in the new occupations; sometimes retraining means shifting the set of needed skills completely.

Retraining can be led by two forces. One is to include the existing set of skills, and try to retrain for occupations that are similar, but are not struck by the downturn; or, and that is the case in many government-sponsored retraining programs aiding unemployed, the training is predominantly demand led, offering retraining to occupations for which there is short supply, either now or in the future.

Assistance programs that offer assistance in job search or retraining to other occupations specifically to displaced workers have a long tradition in the United States. In Europe, the whole focus is on the unemployed. Given the generous welfare system, retraining is seen in Europe as a way to move unemployed workers out of a costly welfare system into productive occupations. Here, the discussion of the assistance programs is confined to the retraining programs, either devoted to displaced workers or to unemployed workers facing unemployment because of structural change.

Assistance Programs in the United States

The assistance to displaced workers can be traced back to the Manpower Development Training Act of 1962 for those displaced from work due to technology, and the Trade Adjustment Assistance (TAA) Act which targeted workers displaced through import competition. In 1974, the trade act established the current TAA program to assist workers employed by a firm that reorganizes due to increased imports or shifts in production to foreign countries. The related Alternative Trade Adjustment Assistance (ATAA) program does not provide any training, as it is devoted to older workers who are allowed to find alternative employment at lower wage while receiving a wage subsidy from the program fund. The main TAA program, however, entails allowances for job search and relocation, as well as training assistance. The training can be classroom, on the job, or customized to the needs of specific employers. The program offers compensation for the training as well as income support for the duration of the training. Many evaluation studies that are made about these programs show mixed results. Moderate gains can only be found for the short-term (Leigh, 1990; Bloom, 1990). In a longer-term evaluation, only weak evidence can be found that the training programs aimed at the displaced workers support the labor-market situation (Decker and Corson, 1995).

Assistance Programs in Countries of the European Union

Assistance programs in the countries of the European Union (EU) are usually devoted to all unemployed workers. Almost all countries have some provision for retraining unemployed workers. Here, only Austria, France, Germany, Spain, and Sweden are mentioned. The programs mentioned have experienced some form of scientific evaluation.

Austria

Training program is one of the many active labor-market programs in Austria. The aim of such a training program is a qualification enhancement of the participants. Vocational training courses result in degrees that are equivalent to apprenticeship degrees. Next to the vocational training, there is also skill training to enhance, for example, language or computer skills. While scientific evaluation is rare, a cohort study of training participants finds a positive effect of program participation of a cohort of workers on their employment stability (Zweimüller and Winter-Ebmer, 1996). In an extensive case study of a special training scheme of a large-scale downsizing in the steel industry, a special program of retraining was also evaluated (Winter-Ebmer, 2006). The scheme consisted of a combination of retraining and placement assistance, and resulted in considerable wage gains and improved employment prospects. One should be careful about the generalization of the results of this specific case.

France

France introduced specific legislation to aid displaced workers in 1987. In the *Convention de conversion*, employers are obliged to offer displaced workers retraining schemes. While the participation is voluntary for workers, they are offered to all workers with a tenure of 2 years or more, and who are 57 years or younger. Following an assessment of the worker's skills, job-search assistance is given and extra training is offered.

Germany

Germany has a long tradition of active labor-market policies. Training is one of the most important measures. The workers who are supported by the programs are unemployed as well as those who are threatened by unemployment and reentrants. Through the federal employment agencies, participants can get support to vocational training courses leading to a first professional degree. In addition, further vocational training and retraining programs are offered if deemed useful by the caseworker of the federal employment agency. Since the reforms of 2005 training vouchers that enable competition between training providers are given to eligible participants. Recent evaluations studies, using administrative data, suggest that training has positive effects on the employment probabilities and a positive effect on earnings. These evaluation studies examined the retraining of East-German workers. Both short-term training (lasting up to 6 months) and long-term training were evaluated (Lechner *et al.*, 2007).

Spain

Training schemes in Spain usually combine training with practical work experience. In an evaluation study for one region using a control group to compare the results, training programs were shown to increase the employment chances of the participants. However, average earnings were not improved compared to the unemployed who did not take part in the training program.

Sweden

In Sweden, retraining of unemployed workers is not generally devoted to displaced workers. Rather they fall under the general labor-market training programs (AMU-Arbetsmarknads utbildning) for all unemployed workers. The objective of the program is to improve job seekers' chances of finding a job. Within the AMU there is a vocational training component, which can take place in educational organizations, universities, and companies. The use of AMU is widespread, and it existed for several decades in Sweden. One of the evaluation studies could show that training participants had a significant higher chance of leaving unemployment if vocational training is followed (Richardson and van den Berg, 2001).

Evaluation of Training Programs

In the evaluation of the assistance programs, it is important to distinguish how an evaluation is made. Most programs involve some form of evaluation. However, not all include a rigorous scientific evaluation. A distinction could be made between evaluation using experiments and quasi-experiments. Scientific evaluation always implies that the success of an assistance program is evaluated using some form of comparison group. In the experimental setup, the workers are divided at random in two groups: one receives assistance, the treatment group, and the other does not receive a treatment, or a simple placebo-type treatment, the control group. In the quasi-experimental setup, a control group is constructed using external factors that influence the participation in training without affecting the variables of interest. One typical example is administrative rules that, for example, allow workers into programs based on age. Comparing workers that just are allowed into the program and those that are just not eligible allows for a comparison of similar groups.

The importance of rigorous scientific evaluations can be seen when one compares the results of informal evaluations that in most cases report positive effects of the program on employment chances and income, with programs that have scientific evaluations. Scientific evaluations in many cases report only small effects on employment chances and on income, if they find any effects at all. Particularly important in this context is to look at the scientific evaluations that have been done for several cases of firm or plant closures in the United States. While the evaluation at the end of each program concluded increased employment chances and positive effects on post-displacement income, the scientific evaluation using quasi-experimental approaches could find no effect on income, and only negligible effect on employment chances. In this light, the retraining programs proved to be ineffective, at least not more effective than simpler job-search assistance programs. These job-search assistance programs tend to be much cheaper than the more elaborate retraining programs. Based on studies that had both a scientific and nonscientific evaluation, one can thus conclude that nonscientific evaluation studies tend to overestimate the (positive) impact of their programs.

The studies evaluated above reflect only the development over the shorter term. A longer-term scientific evaluation of retraining programs in eastern Germany did find positive effects. In the program, no distinction is made between unemployed and displaced workers. The program information is matched to large-scale administrative data sets to construct control groups. In the evaluation, one can distinguish between participation in short- and long-term training, which are respectively shorter or longer than 6 months – those that enhance the skills within the own profession, and those that use retraining leading to a different vocational degree than the one held by the trainee. In the short-term, the evaluation shows negative effects on earnings and employment prospects. However, in the longer run, about a decade after the training, employment prospects and earnings are increased.

However, especially given the specific circumstances in eastern Germany, it is unclear whether the positive results would also be found in different settings and in other countries. It is crucial to consider careful and scientific evaluation studies to evaluate training programs for displaced workers. Preferably, evaluations should be continued to evaluate long-term effects. Administrative data that have become available in several countries would allow to construct both a control group and a (quasi-)experimentally determined treatment group.

Overall, scientific evaluation of retraining programs has shown that there are some improvements in employment prospects and, in some cases, in income as well. This is especially true for the programs in Europe. Some of the effects can only be found if the evaluations consider longer time frames. However, most evaluations do not take the cost of programs into account. While retraining programs are often evaluated against simpler and cheaper job-search assistance programs, they are not compared in terms of costs and benefits.

See also: Globalization and Vocational Education and Training.

Bibliography

Bloom, H. S. (1990). *Back to Work: Testing Reemployment Services for Displaced Workers*. Kalmazoo: W.E. Upjohn Institute.

Decker, P. T. and Corson, W. (1995). International trade and worker displacement: Evaluation of the Trade Adjustment Assistance program. *Industrial and Labor Relations Review* **48**, 758–774.

Eliason, M. and Storrie, D. (2006). Lasting or latent scars? Swedish evidence on the long-term effects of job displacement. *Journal of Labor Economics* **24**, 831–856.

Kriechel, B. and Pfann, G. A. (2005). The role of specific and general human capital after displacement. *Education Economics* **13**, 223–236.

Lechner, M., Miquel, R., and Wunsch, C. (2007). The curse and blessing of training the unemployed in a changing economy: The case of East Germany after unification. *German Economic Review* **8**, 468–509.

Leigh, D. E. (1990). *Does Training Work for Displaced Workers? A Survey of Existing Evidence*. Kalmazoo: W.E. Upjohn Institute.

Richardson, K. and van den Berg, G. J. (2001). The effect of vocational employment training on the individual transition rate from unemployment to work. *Swedish Economic Policy Review* **8**, 175–213.

Winter-Ebmer, R. (2006). Coping with a structural crisis: Evaluating an innovative redundancy-retraining project. *International Journal of Manpower* **27**, 700–721.

Zweimüller, J. and Winter-Ebmer, R. (1996). Manpower training programs and employment stability. *Economica* **63**, 113–130.

Further Reading

Couch, K. A. (2001). Earnings losses and unemployment of displaced workers in Germany. *Industrial and Labor Relations Review* **54**, 559–572.

Farber, H. S. (1999). Mobility and stability: The dynamics of job change in labor markets. In Ashenfelter, O. C. and Card, D. (eds.) *Handbook of Labor Economics,* vol. 3.1, pp 2439–2483. Amsterdam: Elsevier.

Fallick, B. C. (1996). A review of the recent empirical literature on displaced workers. *Industrial and Labor Relations Review* **50**, 5–15.

Gibbons, R. and Katz, L. F. (1991). Layoffs and lemons. *Journal of Labor Economics* **9**, 351–380.

Hamermesh, D. S. (1989). What do we know about worker displacement in the U.S.? *Industrial Relations* **28**, 51–60.

Heckman, J. J., Lalonde, R. J., and Smith, J. A. (1999). The economics and econometrics of active labor market programs. In Ashenfelter, O. C. and Card, D. (eds.) *Handbook of Labor Economics*, vol. 3.1, pp 1865–2097. Amsterdam: Elsevier.

Jacobson, L. (1998). Compensation programs. In Collins, S. M. (ed.) *Imports, Exports and the American Worker*, ch. 11., pp 473–537. Washington, DC: Brookings Institutions Press.

Jacobson, L. S., LaLonde, R. J., and Sullivan, D. G. (1993). Earnings losses of displaced workers. *American Economic Review* **84**, 685–709.

Kletzer, L. (1998). Job displacement. *Journal of Economic Perspectives* **12**, 115–136.

Kluve, J., Card, D., Fertig, M., *et al.* (2007). *Active Labor Market Policies in Europe – Performance and Perspectives*. Berlin: Springer.

Kuhn, P. J. (2002). *Losing Work, Moving on: International Perspectives on Worker Displacement*. Kalmazoo: W.E. Upjohn Institute.

Neal, D. (1995). Industry-specific human capital: Evidence from displaced workers. *Journal of Labor Economics* **13**, 653–677.

Stevens, A. H. (1997). Persistent effects of job displacement: The importance of multiple job losses. *Journal of Labor Economics* **15**, 165–187.

Topel, R. (1990). Specific capital and unemployment: Measuring the costs and consequences of job loss. *Carnegie Rochester Conference Series in Public Policy* **33**, 181–214.

Museums as Sites of Adult Learning

R S Grenier, University of Connecticut, Storrs, CT, USA

Hundreds of millions of people throughout the world visit museums, galleries, zoos, aquariums, nature and science centers, and historic sites. This article discusses museums as sites of adult learning. These institutions are increasingly defined by their ability to act as dynamic agents of cultural dissemination and have the capacity to expand the range of learning opportunities for adults. Adult learning theory and research in the area of museum education transform the visitor or user's experiences into learning opportunities that occur in relation to sociocultural surroundings and stimulate active and reflexive learning. Through both free-choice and organized nonformal learning visits, adults have the opportunity to experience the unknown, revisit the familiar, stimulate their curiosity, and challenge their existing beliefs.

The first section of the article explores the educational role of museums by reviewing the variety of cultural institutions defined as museums, as well as the educational missions and purposes of these organizations. The next section discusses the intersection of adult education and museum education theories and how these influence adult learning in museums. The final section reviews adult learning in museums, and attention is paid to the concepts of nonformal and free-choice learning.

Educational Role of Museums

As lifelong learning increasingly becomes more important in society, greater demands have been placed on museums to offer learning opportunities for visitors throughout their lives. The significance of museums as sites of adult learning is reflected in the definitions and missions of these institutions. Museums were once merely private collections held by aristocrats and universities; however, today, they constitute much more. The field of museum studies focuses on an array of institutions including, but not limited to, historic homes and sites, science and technology centers, aquariums, zoos, and botanical gardens, as well as the traditional art, history, and natural history museums. In general, the term museum includes both institutions with collections of exhibits, and locations without their own collections or permanent exhibitions, such as ancient remains or historic sites. These institutions function as a place of memory, where heritage is conserved, collections are maintained, and the best possible conditions are created for visitors to experience these collections. The International Council of Museums

(ICOM) defines a museum as a permanent, nonprofit institution in the service to society and the development of society. It is open to the public, and works to acquire, conserve, research, communicate, and exhibit, for purposes of study, education, and enjoyment, the material evidence of people and their environment. The American Association of Museums (AAM) offers another definition based on seven characteristics. Museums must:

1. be a legally organized not-for-profit institution or part of a not-for-profit institution or government entity;
2. be essentially educational in nature;
3. have a formally stated mission;
4. have one full-time paid professional staff member who has museum knowledge and experience and is delegated authority and allocated financial resources sufficient to operate the museum effectively;
5. present regularly scheduled programs and exhibits that use and interpret objects for the public according to accepted standards;
6. have a formal and appropriate program of documentation, care, and use of collections and/or tangible objects; and
7. have a formal and appropriate program of presentation and maintenance of exhibits.

Definitions also exist to clarify the role of education in museums. The AAM's Task Force on Museum Education, in their 1992 landmark report, offers a broad notion of museum education, which sees museums as fostering visitors' ability to be a productive member of a pluralistic society, and contributing to solutions to address the challenges of global citizenship. Hooper-Greenhill (1994) stresses the educational role of museums as central to a museum's mission and defines museum education as the creation of open relationships between museums visitors in order to increase enjoyment, motivation, and knowledge. Falk and Dierking (1995) offer further clarification by suggesting that museums provide visitors with accessible content and facilitate connections between contrasting facts and ideas. Moreover, they stress the museum's affect on visitor values and attitudes, while also promoting culture, community, and familial identity. Lastly, museum education is foundational to encouraging a visitor's confidence, interest, curiosity, and motivation to gain new knowledge, as well as to affect a visitor's thinking and worldview.

The depth and breadth of these definitions have been recognized by museum professionals and, in order to meet these demands, many museums employ educational staff or curators whose role is to direct the education, learning, and outreach functions of the museum. Several times, this is achieved within a museum education department. A museum's education department frequently works in the development of signage, exhibits, texts, community outreach, visitor services, guided and self-guided tours, visitor workshops, lectures, seminars, and speakers' bureaus. Additionally, these departments may include volunteers, guides, interpreters, and docents who work with the public to devise and deliver purposeful programming and free-choice learning experiences.

Depending on the size, expertise, and mission of the institution, museum programming may be comprised of lectures, guided tours, field trips, gallery demonstrations, costumed interpretations, teacher and public workshops, seminars and symposia, film series, classes, theater, the loaning of objects, and the development and dissemination of teaching kits and packs related to exhibitions and collections. Moreover, innovative and creative programming has emerged, including learning opportunities geared to personal and cultural development, community outreach and activism, programs for special needs visitors, collaborative programs between museums and other organizations, such as universities, libraries, and other cultural institutions, as well as virtual and mobile museums. With the advent of new forms of technology and the Internet, this last type of programming is increasing in popularity since it provides anytime, anywhere learning for visitors.

Museums have moved beyond static homepages to the creation of extensive databases for research purposes and sites and portals that provide the public with detailed content, resources, and educational material. Examples of how museums are utilizing technology for adult learning include virtual exhibitions that provide information about a thematic area determined by the museum, interactive sites that offer educational activities to support learning, and on-demand exhibits that let the user control the subjects being viewed. These multimedia forms expand the learning experience and educational programming beyond the doors of the museum.

In addition to the growing role of technology in shaping adult learning in museums, institutions have also emerged to specifically draw attention to and address the social, political, and cultural conditions around the world. Such museums extend adult learning to include the promotion of humanitarian and democratic values. For example, the International Coalition of Historic Site Museums of Conscience is a network of historic site museums throughout the world presenting and interpreting a variety of historic issues, events, and people. Its mission is to assist the public in making links between the history of the site and its contemporary implications. For example, the network includes the District Six Museum in South Africa whose mission entails ensuring the memory of forced removals in South Africa and brings visitors' attention to confronting all forms of social oppression. By focusing on social and cultural conditions, sites such as this strive to not only facilitate adult learning, but also empower visitors to challenge their understanding of history and the human condition.

Using research and scholarship to inform practice, museums are increasingly positioning themselves as places for rich learning experiences. With mission statements that highlight their key role in public learning and education, an array of physical and virtual learning opportunities, and the increase in addressing sociopolitical and cultural conditions throughout the world, the growth of adult learning in museums is evident. From highly structured programs that are identified, designed, and delivered by the institution to less formal opportunities, including incidental or free-choice learning, museums are taking a more sociocultural perspective that emphasizes visitor experiences in relation to the objects, museum context, and society.

Educational Theories

Museums have utilized research and theory in order to intentionally design and facilitate learning opportunities for adults. By introducing people to cultural, historical, and social artifacts, as well as nature and science, museums have the ability to support visitors as they become engaged with novel ideas. To accomplish this, museum educators draw from traditional educational theory, adult education principles, and museums studies research to enhance the learning experience for adult visitors. A variety of empirical and theoretical literature for examining the learning needs of adults in museums is available and the two bodies of research parallel one another, emphasizing the underlying need for a deeper understanding and commitment to adult museum visitors.

Theoretical approaches to museum education have a foundation in the broader field of education. For example, some museums support a constructivist approach to learning in their institution. Constructivism is a theory of learning focusing on the learner and the personal meanings they make based on their prior experience, knowledge, and interests. Museums utilizing a constructivist approach argue that visitors learn the most when knowledge is constructed mentally, in contexts that are physically, socially, and intellectually accessible. Thus, the needs and motivation of the visitor guide the structure of the exhibits and are essential when museum educators conceive of and facilitate learning opportunities. Other institutions utilize a sociocultural approach in museum learning research. Museums using this theoretical framework recognize that visitors' meanings are made within a social context, rather than from facts learned.

The sociocultural approach to learning in museums focuses on the interplay between individuals acting in social contexts and mediators such as tools, talk, activity structures, signs, and symbol systems found in cultural institutions.

These theoretical perspectives influence a number of museum education models. Falk and Dierking (2000) argue for an interactive experience model based on the concept of free-choice learning. Similar to situated learning, which supports encouraging the use of knowledge and strategies in a variety of settings, the Interactive Experience Model addresses the personal, social, and physical contexts of learning in museums. The personal context recognizes that: motivation and emotional cues initiate learning; personal interest facilitates learning; knowledge is constructed from prior knowledge and experience; and learning is expressed in an appropriate context. The second context, sociocultural, emphasizes learning as an individual as well as a group endeavor and the physical context addresses the notion that learning is dependent on a person's ability to place prior experiences within the context of their physical setting. These three contexts combine in an attempt to explain how, why, where, what, and with whom people learn in museums. This model aids in framing museum services, and highlights the role of educational theory in the process of exhibit development, interpretation, and programming.

Additionally, a focus on the role of prior experiences and learning is central to both the museum education and adult education fields. Experience influences adults' approaches to learning, their ability to integrate new information, and the ways in which they build concepts around new knowledge. Museums researchers are emphasizing the same ideas by addressing the prior experiences of visitors and how those experiences establish what visitors will do, talk about, and take away from their visits. Thus, museum educators are facilitating learning opportunities that recognize and underscore the role of emotions, memories, background, and personal understandings in the process of assigning reference and meaning to museum content.

The significance of understanding the adult visitor is emphasized by Sachatello-Sawyer *et al.* (2002), who categorized adult learning in museums to include six dimensions: life-changing experiences, transformed perspectives, changes in attitude, increased appreciation, exploration of relationships, and acquisition of knowledge. These levels serve to explain the forms of personal change, long-term change resulting from the learning, and the integration of new learning. They also found that adult learners in museums fell into four distinct categories: knowledge seekers, socializers, skill builders, and museum lovers. Both the forms of adult learning and the categorization of adult learners in museums mirror the work of Mezirow (1991) and Houle (1961) in the adult education literature. Mezirow describes four processes of learning: elaborating an existing point of view, establishing a new point of view, transforming

one's point of view, and, lastly, becoming aware and critically reflecting on our generalized bias of how we view groups other than our own; and Houle's typology of adult learners includes: (1) the goal oriented, (2) the activity oriented, and (3) the learning oriented.

While terminology used in the two fields may differ, this section demonstrates that the underlying theoretical frames and the parallels in how both fields characterize learning and adult learners are similar. Regardless of the scholarship, the significance of lifelong learning in museums is receiving considerable attention from researchers and is providing opportunities for furthering our understanding of adult learning theory. Moreover, the research in the two fields, as well as from visitor studies, interpretation research, and leisure and recreation studies is informing museum practice, thus increasing the likelihood of presenting museums as sites of adult learning experiences.

Adult Learning in Museums

In general, adult learners frequent museums as visitors or users of museum services that include the availability of reference and resources, cultural and community programming, and virtual offerings. These learners are diverse and create a challenge for institutions seeking ways to provide adults with education and learning opportunities. Due to their broader life experiences, established identity, abstract thinking ability, understanding of the world they live in, and unique learning expectations, it is necessary to specifically address adult learning in museums. First, the motivations and agendas that adults take to museums are important in influencing the way they experience a visit, as well as their behavior and learning. Those facilitating educational opportunities in museums take into account such motivations in order to create engaging visits. Several factors influence the decision of whether or not to visit a museum, including an opportunity to socially interact with others and with family, the sense that they are doing something worthwhile, the challenge of new experiences, feeling comfortable with their surroundings, having the chance to actively participate, and having an opportunity to learn. The combination of these factors requires museums to develop programming that incorporates the breadth and depth of visitor characteristics ranging from purposeful learning to incidental learning resulting from a leisure visit.

Although learning is not a deliberate intention of many museum visitors, they often seek out or are unconsciously drawn into an experience that encompasses learning. When visiting museums, adults tend to look for opportunities to learn more about themselves, their culture, and their heritage, and gravitate to those places where they feel most comfortable. Overall, research in the area of visitor motivation suggests that adult visitors are not only motivated to learn, but also perceive museums as sources of important information, are willing to commit to learning activities, and find such endeavors satisfying, all of which create both opportunities and challenges for the institutions.

Regardless of the motivation or intention, visits by adults to museums present both social and educational opportunities and create the possibility of purposeful and incidental learning that is the focus of much study in the fields of museum and adult education. Museums are distinct learning environments, and as such have received considerable attention by scholars. Within adult education, museums are categorized as nonformal education, while in museum studies, these learning environments are often referred to in relation to free-choice learning. Both terms provide a means for framing adult learning experiences in museums and offer similar perspectives on the role of the learner and the resources necessary to support the learning process.

Nonformal Education

Nonformal education is characterized as intentional and organized with the purpose of promoting learning to enhance an adult's quality of life (Heimlich, 1993). Ideally, it is learner centered, maintains a balance of power between the learner and the facilitator, is present-time focused, and is geared to meeting localized needs. In this same vein, learning in a nonformal context is often distinguished by activities outside the formal learning setting, with voluntary participation as opposed to mandatory participation. Within a taxonomy of adult learning, nonformal learning is identified by learners holding the objectives for learning with the means controlled by the educator or organization. In this way, nonformal education creates learning events in museums that can expand the range of opportunities for adults with practical applications to an individual's profession, personal interests, and community. Owing to the unique learning environment and resources museums offer, these institutions are constructing nonformal learning offerings ranging from senior citizen programs, programs for law enforcement officers, and restoration and preservation opportunities, to training for volunteers interested in working as docents, interpreters, and oral historians. One group of learners garnering significant attention is classroom teachers. Museums create learning opportunities for classroom teachers through in-service, continuing education and intensive, residential summer institutes. These experiences are designed and initiated by museums to provide educators with opportunities to explore museum resources, co-create curriculum with peers, and experience museum exhibits under the direction of museum staff and museum consultants specializing in k-12 curriculum and instruction.

Nonformal programming serves not only organized groups, but also those seeking personal development and educational opportunities, and individuals serving as volunteers for museums. Adults involved in museum programs are often seeking out lifelong learning opportunities and look for ways to bring together their personal interests, professional expertise, and social consciousness. Programs like the Smithsonian's Resident Associate Program are one example of museums providing a range of experiences to adult learners including structured lectures, tours, and performances that offer cultural and educational opportunities for lifelong learners.

Despite the fact that nonformal learning includes museum-derived programming, nonformal education also provides for more self-directed and informal learning opportunities. For instance, many museums are emphasizing active involvement of visitors through the use of engaging questions, involved discussion, and co-constructed workshop methods. Such experiences encourage adults to handle objects, investigate the meanings and relationships between objects and exhibits, and address their own reactions to the museum content. Although museums serve the role of nonformal education for adult learners, a good deal of visitors are informal users that include individuals, friends, and families visiting museums casually as tourists or for entertainment and social interaction. These informal experiences are at the root of another form of learning in museums, free-choice.

Free-Choice Learning

Free-choice learning (Falk and Dierking, 2000) is a nonlinear process that looks to visitors to bring their own awareness and interests to the museum experience in order to create a variety of learning outcomes. That being said, such learning opportunities are not completely unstructured since the nature and design of the exhibits form some structure to the learning experience. It is this choice and control over the learning that is central. In free-choice learning, the learner is intrinsically motivated by their desire to discover more about the world, gain information, and enhance their current understanding. More specifically, adults tend to engage in free-choice learning in museums because of one or more factors. The first factor is friendships and organizational relationships including the social connections established in civic associations, schools, and community and religious groups. These interactions strengthen a commitment to developing social networks through invitations to take part in the museum experience. The second is the visitor's family who communicates information about learning opportunities or emphasizes an interest in museums. The last factor is an adult's business and professional connections. These relationships can create the expectation of visiting a museum for professional networking, or to gain new knowledge to transfer to the work environment.

Museums are responding to free-choice learning by layering the experiences. By doing so, museums are able to present visitors with smaller segments that are more easily processed and integrated into prior experiences and learning. This limits visitors' sense of being overwhelmed and provides a chance for visitors to linger on specifics that are of most interest. Technology is also aiding museums in their facilitation of free-choice learning. Radio-frequency identification (RFID) is a method of automatic identification that relies on storing and remotely retrieving data using RFID tags. Using RFID, the Tech Museum of Innovation in San Jose, CA, began experimenting with Tech-Tags that work to link one exhibit to another within the museum, to personalize and customize the experience, and extend the museum experience beyond the visit. An RFID chip is embedded in a visitor bracelet enabling visitors to use their bracelet to activate exhibits as well as create a customized Internet record of the visit that can be explored after the leaving the museum.

In general, visitors in a free-choice environment decide whether to visit a museum, what will be viewed or done at the museum, and for how long. Essentially, free-choice is closely linked with educational leisure in that the experience is learner centered through exploration, connections to prior experiences, and control of the learning environment. Although museums are a significant source of free-choice learning for adults, it is important to note that people engage in free-choice learning through other venues including libraries, parks, radio, television and film, print media, and the Internet. When these sources are partnered with the learning opportunities of museums, what is produced is the opportunity for a robust and multidimensional form of understanding. Entities such as the Public Broadcasting Service (PBS) have used such partnerships to develop free-choice learning opportunities that bring together print media, technology, and museums to feature content and exhibits in relation to a PBS series.

Whether it is nonformal education or free-choice learning, the outcomes for adults' experiences in museums are diverse. Participation in museum-related activities contributes to the shaping of families, and other social groups, as well as expanding the personal and professional perspectives of individual adult visitors. By increasing knowledge and understanding, developing new skills and abilities, inspiring new learning and change, and stimulating lifelong learning, museums not only impact an adult's knowledge, but, often, also their attitudes, values, and beliefs.

Conclusion

Today, adult education stresses self-direction, critical reflection, experiential learning, learning to learn, distance learning, and collaborative learning. The same elements can also be associated with adult learning in museums, as is evident in this article. Museums as sites of adult learning are stimulating and offer a place where ideas originating from the media or peers can be tested, confirmed, or modified. Museums also help visitors reformulate old pieces of understanding that have lost relevance or meaning. By purposefully taking part in educational activities in museums and engaging in free-choice learning, adults have the opportunity to share in conversations, discussions, debates, and social interaction, all of which are foundational to the work of museums and the expanding role of lifelong learning in society.

See also: Informal Learning: A Contested Concept.

Bibliography

Falk, J. H. and Dierking, L. D. (eds.) (1995). *Public Institutions for Personal Learning: Establishing a Research Agenda.* Washington, DC: American Association of Museums.

Falk, J. H. and Dierking, L. D. (2000). *Learning from Museums: Visitor Experiences and the Making of Meaning.* Walnut Creek, CA: Altamira.

Hooper-Greenhill, E. (1994). *The Educational Role of Museums.* London: Routledge.

Houle, C. O. (1961). *The Inquiring Mind.* Madison, WI: University of Wisconsin Press.

Mezirow, J. (1991). *Transformative Dimensions of Adult Learning.* San Francisco, CA: Jossey-Bass.

Sachatello-Sawyer, B., Fellenz, R. A., Burton, H., *et al.* (2002). *Adult Museum Programs.* Walnut Creek, CA: Altamira.

Further Reading

Carr, D. (2003). *The Promise of Cultural Institutions.* Walnut Creek, CA: AltaMira.

Dufresne-Tassé, C., Lapointe, T., Morelli, C., and Chamberland, E. (1991). L'apprentissage de l'adulte au musée et l'instrument pour l'étudier. *Canadian Journal of Education* **16**, 280–292.

Falk, J. H. and Dierking, L. D. (eds.) (1995). *Public Institutions for Personal Learning: Establishing a Research Agenda.* Washington, DC: American Association of Museums.

Falk, J. H. and Dierking, L. D. (1997). *The Museum Experience.* Washington, DC: Whalesback Books.

Falk, J. H., Moussouri, T., and Coulson, D. (1998). The effects of visitors' agendas on museum learning. *Curator* **41**, 107–120.

Heimlich, J. E. (1993). *Nonformal Environmental Education: Toward a Working Definition (ERIC Document Reproduction Service No. ED 360 154).* Columbus, OH: Educational Resources Information Center.

Hein, G. E. (1998). *Learning in the Museum.* London: Routledge.

Hein, G. E. and Alexander, M. (1998). *Museums Places of Learning.* Washington, DC: American Association of Museums.

Hooper-Greenhill, E. (1994). *The Educational Role of Museums.* London: Routledge.

Leinhardt, G., Crowley, K., and Knutson, K. (eds.) (2002). *Learning Conversations in Museums.* Mahwah, NJ: Erlbaum.

Prentice, R., Davies, A., and Beeho, A. (1997). Seeking generic motivations for visiting and not visiting museums and like cultural attractions. *Museum Management and Curatorship* **16**, 45–70.

Roberts, L. C. (1997). *From Knowledge to Narrative.* Washington, DC: Smithsonian Institute Press.

Storr, A. V. F. (1995). *Current Practice and Potential: Research and Adult Education in Museums. Report No. IR 017 333.* (ERIC Document Reproduction Service No. ED385255) Washington, DC:

National Institute on Postsecondary Education, Libraries, and Lifelong Learning (ED/OERI).

Svedlow, A. (1997). Lifelong learning in museums: In pursuit of andragogy. *PAACE Journal of Lifelong Learning* **6**, 29–39.

Taylor, E. W. (2006). Making meaning of local nonformal education: Practitioner's perspective. *Adult Education Quarterly* **56**(4), 291–307.

Relevant Websites

http://www.aam-us.org – American Association of Museums.

http://www.gem.org.uk – Group for Education in Museums.

http://www.sitesofconscience.org – International Coalition of Sites of Conscience.

http://icom.museum – International Council of Museums.

http://www.definitionsproject.com – National Association for Interpretation.

http://www.sil.si.edu – Smithsonian Institution Libraries, Museum Studies and Reference Library.

http://www.clmg.org.uk – The Campaign for Learning through Museums and Galleries.

http://www.thetech.org – The Tech Museum of Innovation.

Learning Cities and Regions

C Duke, University of Leicester, Leicester, UK; University of Stirling, Scotland, UK; RMIT University, Melbourne, VIC, Australia

Glossary

Engaged university – A university which plans and connects its teaching and research work with the needs and communities of the locality – city or region – in which it is located.

Learning city/learning region – An administrative region that has developed the capacity to collect, analyze, and use data and experience to enhance the quality of its understanding, leading to improved practice.

Place management – Application of the recognition of the importance of the concept and reality of place for effective, integrated, and acceptable governance.

Social construct – The understanding, concept, and definition developed by a community or network of policymakers, scholars, and practitioners about a concept and/or activity which draws them together.

The Learning City and the City-Region as a Social Construct

The learning city is an ideal, rather than a description of any actual place or places. It is an aspiration for the way the city might be better managed and manage itself in a complex world characterized by terms such as global and knowledge economy. The terms learning region and city-region are used also as a way of thinking about the management of a city area or region with an evident identity, boundaries, and some form of government. It reflects a sense that city and regional governance could and should be different, and better than they presently are. Local administrations in many parts of the world have in recent years expressed the intention to be learning cities; a number of them have announced that this is what they are, will be, or are becoming. In the sense that the learning city is a social and political aspiration rather than a well-defined and understood condition with agreed characteristic measures, it is best understood as a social construct.

The learning city is a new and evolving notion. Although urban and regional studies have existed for decades, the term learning city, or city-region, emerged only in the later years of the twentieth century. There is no established definition of what it means. In terms of literature, it falls between several recognized areas of scholarship to each of which it is peripheral and ambiguous. It is best understood as heuristic, a metaphor which expresses a set of values and purposes, not an established concept in academic social science. The term is used mainly in policy arenas and among communities of practitioners who are concerned with how things can be done better.

This article explains the different ways the term is used. It then explains how it is related to issues of government rather than education. Various learning-city initiatives are referred to before considering research in the area and issues related to implementation. After a brief consideration of the important link with higher education, the article concludes by assessing the utility and the possible future of the concept.

Two Different Meanings

Although not hotly contested, the term carries different meanings and is used in different senses. Despite the word learning which locates it in the mindset of education, the richer and more fundamental sense has more to do with governance and politics than with education. Where a government authority is charged with the subject it may be a ministry of education, where it is seen as mainly related to schooling, education, and training.

In principle, there are two distinct levels of meanings to the concept of learning city or city-region. The easier-to-understand term implies an urban or regional authority that makes good provision for many people to learn. It sees learning, essentially in the forms supported by high-quality and widely accessible education and training, as crucial to economic productivity, competitiveness, and so to civic success. A UK report commissioned by the Department for Education and Employment in the late 1990s had the concept of the Educating or Learning City originating in an international conference convened by the Barcelona City Council in 1990, then focused in a report to the OECD 2 years later (Hirsch, 1992).

The policy agenda originating from this approach concerns increasing the volume and raising the quality of education, training, and learning opportunities for individuals. This may extend beyond the formal education sector, together with the less-formalized or nonformal adult and lifelong learning arena, to foster a culture of lifelong learning. Occasionally it includes museums, libraries, and other arts and cultural facilities and venues seen as part of a wider civic learning environment. It is unlikely to go beyond this although learning in and through work (work-based and workplace learning) is recognized within the education profession and policy community as a significant dimension of education and training relevant to living and working.

The second, deeper and richer, as well as more historically accurate meaning concerns the capacity of a city or region itself to learn almost as an individual person or other organism can learn, understand, and adapt its behavior. There may be a difficulty in a Western democratic and individualistic tradition about accepting the notion of learning outside the individual. The recognition has been the strongest and longer established with respect to the learning organization as an informing principle for the study of organization behavior, for consulting to management, and in management education. Subsequently, learning has been affixed to many other institutions and phenomena, from schools and universities themselves to other kinds of organizations such as hospitals and banks to events such as festivals. In a geographical and political sense, it has been applied at levels from the nation to a small locality such as a village.

A widely used term with more conceptual underpinning than many of these is the learning community, used mainly with a sense of geographical locality and also sometimes of virtual communities. Linked to this are the terms and notions of communities of interest and communities of practice (Wenger, 1998). However, these concepts lack the component of place integral to the learning city-region: the recognition that an area with its inhabitants or citizens constitutes an entity or reality, cultural, social, and historical as well as economic, political, and geographical. The term place management has acquired currency in recent years to emphasize the importance of shared location, environment, and experience as important elements in how we organize, manage, and govern ourselves.

The terms learning city, region, and city-region have stronger validity and utility in this second and larger sense. The reduction in scope and meaning in relation to education and training may appeal to local and regional authorities wishing to be part of a new wave of thinking about governance; and it may enable or assist them to reinvigorate their education sectors by using a large and ambitious term.

The larger concept has more to do with the nature of governance and the capacity of political systems at whatever level to learn from their own and others' experience and to adopt new behaviors, possibly using concepts such as double-loop learning and triple helix to focus recognition of what this means. Insofar as the concept demands introspection and reflexivity, it may be radical and unsettling, connected as it is to ideas about participation, devolution of authority, and empowerment. Perceived in this way, the learning city is about politics and government rather than about education.

Cities and Regions, Politics and Governance

In terms of fields of study, the learning city region belongs more to politics and government, geography, and urban and regional studies than to education. It is unavoidably political, having to do with the holding, sharing, and use of power rather than purely technical and organizational. Some of the terms with which it is associated have a heuristic, reformist, radical, or an ideological flavor and intent. In this sense, the idea of a learning city represents a challenge to current methods of governing and exercising authority and power. Looking at the administrative region as a place inhabited and used by different groups and communities of interest, and wishing to improve the quality of government so as to enhance the level of and capacity for learning, raises questions about participation as well as consultation in the process of government, and about the devolution of different kinds of decisions and control. The city-region may be seen as a contested space where interest groups vie for benefit and control. The style and nature of government, as well as the amount and nature of devolved authority, are called into question.

The concept of a learning region or territory can apply at all levels of government, although the main focus tends to be on the city. The term city-region is commonly used to refer not just to the metropolis, metropolitan area, or town but also to its physically, economically, and/or culturally natural territory or catchment area. A problem arises when these natural regions do not correspond with the local and regional authority boundaries, and also when the local and regional government are unstable and subject to central government intervention, with frequently changing boundaries, powers, and dispensations.

Here the idea of a learning city-region becomes entangled with another agenda: regionalization as a means of decentralizing and devolving power from the larger central state. Devolution is common in many countries; but the consequential required transfer of powers and resources does not always occur. Then a city or region may be unable to manage its resources and affairs so as to act on what it learns.

Problems occur for schools, colleges, and education systems when control and responsibility are divided among different levels of jurisdiction. They are more acute for a whole city or region. A major problem for effective learning applied to better governance is the separation and compartmentalization that is common among various functional departments, sometimes known as silos, at whatever level. This is exacerbated when there is division, and the silo walls are strong between the parts of the administration, both vertically and horizontally.

Learning City Initiatives

There have been many recent initiatives to promote and disseminate the idea and practice of a learning community and region, for example, through projects funded by the European Union (EU). Some have gone beyond discussion of the ideas and processes to practical workshops and manuals on how to go about it, and how to equip local authority staff to enable local-level community learning as a part of the process of better – more participatory, more responsive and learningful – government (Longworth, 2006; Longworth and Allwinkle, 2005). A recent example is the 2005–07 project funded by the EU through its Grundtvig program and Pascal, on Learning in Local and Regional Authorities, in which partners in six European countries identify the training that the local authority staffs need to implement the learning city concept and design a training program and workshops to meet this need.

Many countries have seen learning city and learning community initiatives over the past decade. In Australia, the State of Victoria has sponsored an initiative for several years in which eight nominated towns were enabled and supported to use this title; they undertook and publicized the initiatives mainly related to education, training, or community learning. Several of these featured in conference reports and specialized in mainly local literature. A little later the State of Victoria created the Department for Victorian Communities, renamed as the Planning and Community Development in 2007. The central purpose was to enable local communities to develop confidence and expertise as place-based learning communities and to play an active role in managing their affairs, with better integration of services between and across government portfolios.

In the United Kingdom, the Labour Administration elected in 1997 initiated devolution to Scotland and Wales and strengthened the English regions with nine regional development authorities championed by the Office of the Deputy Prime Minister (ODPM). As part of this initiative, several learning towns and learning community projects led to over 20 towns and cities defining themselves as learning cities and undertaking various initiatives; a loose community of interest and practice grew up around and anchored in these. The activity peaked early in the current decade; there is a sense that interest and energy many have slackened, perhaps from lack of clarity on what the concept and label really mean and how to go about the complex process of implementing it.

A similar sense of uncertainty affects some initiatives in Canada. In Victoria, for example, pronouncement of being a learning city was followed by hesitancy as to how to go forward, and a learning fair which proved unsuccessful, bringing the initiative to a hiatus. In Vancouver, the city resolved and pronounced similarly, setting up a working group to find ways to give expression to the concept. A steering group was led by the Superintendent of Schools and the City Librarian, reflecting a common focus in or near to the education system.

The ease of communication enabled by new information technologies globally, a tendency to compare and compete internationally, and being watchful for new initiatives mean that many countries now have local-level authorities claiming to be learning cities and regions, albeit with different emphases and meanings in different countries depending on the local traditions, culture, and conditions.

Research and Implementation

There is a lack of academic research and little strictly academic literature in the social science fields directly related to learning cities. The subject is touched upon tangentially in a number of discipline areas especially related to government, urban and area studies, and special interests within education, innovation, and organizational behavior. The main scholarly interest comes from a policy development perspective. Much of the intellectual endeavor concerns trying to improve governance and enhance practice.

The Organisation for Economic Cooperation and Development (OECD), as an economically oriented intergovernmental organization, has been prominent in developing and disseminating an understanding of the issues and dynamics. A key monograph on learning regions in the new economy was derived from five studies of city regions in Europe. It was published in 2001 (OECD, 2001) and followed by another round of case studies and an international conference in Melbourne in 2002, from which grew an international observatory on learning regions, place management, and social capital called Pascal. Pascal mirrors the learning city-region approach in being a means of dialog and exchange between policymakers, practitioners, and scholars interested as a policy community and community of practice in putting knowledge into practice, making knowledge work in this applied arena (Duke et al., 2005, 2006).

The Pascal virtual community reflects the character of the learning city as a construct, in that it includes practitioners as well as academic scholars. The latter come from many different disciplinary backgrounds. It is emphatically applied in its orientation, with the explicit purpose of fostering a dialog across professional and disciplinary boundaries. In its commitment to breaking down silos, it echoes a central issue for the learning city region about specialization and compartmentalization as an often ineffectual way of managing complexity.

Another intergovernmental organization that also has a direct governmental remit, the EU, also promotes consideration of the learning region, as well as of lifelong learning, as a means to manage and succeed economically in a competitive global environment. There is an emphasis on capacity for innovation conceived in terms of broader social issues as well as immediate economic indicators of growth. The EU has supported various activities related to learning cities and regions, some mainly of a research nature with a dissemination component, others more concerned with the development and exchange of good practice by means of networks of places and people. In thus seeking to give effect to the concept in terms of governmental and related practices, the EU mirrors some of the ideas of the learning city, trying deliberately and systematically to collect, analyze, learn from, and put into practice what is being done.

One project supported by the EU illustrates the kind of research needed to understand how cities function, and what might be implied to enhance their capacity to operate more effectively in terms of an ideal type. A 3-year research project which studied four European cities and one Australian city took the title CRITICAL as an acronym for city regions as intelligent territories, innovation, competition, and learning. Research groups in each place examined the same eight domains in each city to see how these functioned and how they compared. Domains included, for example, small and medium enterprises, cultural activities, neighborhood renewal, and city administration.

Based on these studies of different areas of city life and cities' communities, the research suggested a number of core principles on the basis of which a city functions in terms of understanding, learning, and developing in the chosen ways and directions. Crucial to the success of such a learning process appeared to be the way that governance as expressed through the city or city region administration is connected, giving and taking knowledge, and sharing reflection and planning with the different communities and arenas that comprised its complexity. The concept of communities of practice (Wenger, 1998) proved useful, as did work on the creative classes and what made cities attractive and successful places to be, attracting lively and innovative people as well as capital (Florida, 2002). Sustainability, now a significant concept for governance and management as well as in terms of the environment, was seen as an important element of learning and its wider applications.

A chronic problem at the heart of the notion of the learning city region is related to geographical scope and jurisdiction in terms of what powers are exercised at local and regional level. Thus Vancouver, a leading city within a federal system, accounts to both the national federal and the provincial government for different purposes, and is in turn divided between several city administrations. The reach of Vancouver as a learning city is restricted to just one of these administrations, although as a learning region it makes sense to think of two other levels, the greater Vancouver metropolitan area and a larger economic region, which takes in the catchment of the river valley system on which Vancouver sits. Dublin, the fast-growing capital city of the vigorous Irish Celtic Tiger economy, confronts transport and social challenges which call for a city region response for which there is no local–regional government authority. The same is true for Melbourne and other Australian cities, where the metropolitan area is divided between many small city authorities. Greater Melbourne planning falls by default to the state administration, which has competing responsibilities, and regional development bodies tend to be weak, short-lived, and are subject to the vagaries of distant federal politics.

Higher Education and the City

Given the emphasis on knowledge, including research, evaluation, and innovation that is central to the learning city, it is natural that universities in particular, and education systems more broadly, should be a subject of relevant interest. The OECD in particular has sponsored studies related to the role of higher education in regional development and therefore as a part of the learning city-region concept. (OECD, 1999, 2007). A project by the OECD launched in 2004 and completed in 2007 studied the Supporting the Contribution of Higher Education to Regional Development by means of 14 case studies in 12 countries across five continents, with a weighting in favor of Northern Europe. The project was managed jointly by two distinct parts of the OECD, the Territorial Government and the Education Divisions, thus attempting to bring together two different approaches and remits.

From the perspective of a region, higher education is important as a reservoir of expert advice and research capacity; eminent universities, like international airports, are recognized as a significant element among the characteristics of successful competitive world cities and regions. For a university, the resources, interest, and support of the city and region where it is located may be important to its prosperity as well as in terms of comfortable and productive local relations. The idea of university engagement carries with it the idea of co-production of knowledge and shared benefit. However, the idea of local–regional responsibility and accountability also discomfits some universities, which fear the loss of academic freedom and too local or parochial an identity, at the expense of their standing in the unbounded worlds of disciplinary scholarship. In this sense, the idea of the learning city region, and its active promotion by governments at different levels, has become significant to a dialog about the nature of the university in an era of mass higher education.

An Assessment of the Utility and the Likely Future of the Concept

The learning city is one of a number of terms and concepts that has been developed in an attempt to explain, understand, and in some cases to influence and shape the situation in which we live and work, in an era called global and characterized by rapid change and complexity. As a concept, it has acquired meaning, identity, and a life of its own, expressed through the pronouncements and practices of local, city, and region-level governments in many parts of the world. It exists by means of the exchange of words and ideas, and the development of language and practices, that attempt to improve the understanding and practice of administration at these different local levels more effectively and better fitted for what is seen as contemporary need and purpose.

At least in the reduced form of a place and administrative authority which provides opportunities for education, training, and different kinds of nonformal and contextualized learning, the learning city and region seems likely to retain its currency and to exercise significant influence for a considerable time. Its connection with lifelong learning, another widely used though also an ambiguous concept, now firmly established among intergovernmental and national authorities as essential at least for innovation and economic success in a competitive global economy, strengthens that probability. Even in this narrower sense, the relevance to policy and practice of the learning city may be considerable for tertiary and higher education and training, since lifelong learning is associated with the economic and social effects of changing demography, especially longevity, and the need for people to go on learning and changing.

The more fully the larger concept of learning city region is adopted, the greater may be its impact on higher education policy through the idea and practice of the engaged university, and more broadly on technical and other tertiary education. Institutions can be thought of as suppliers of highly qualified skills, and knowledge to the labor force of a regional innovation system. They may also be seen as developing and applying knowledge vital to the economic and social well-being of a region. This perception affects the content and processes of the regular curriculum; students' connection with working and community life; and the character and outcomes of the university's research activity. In these and other ways it may be seen as an integral part of a city or a region as well as of a regional innovation system. A further point along a spectrum of engagement takes the university close to the heart of planning for the region, so that its and the region's or city's long-term development are woven together in a web of interdependency.

As an idea and an agenda for regional management and development, the social construct of the learning city region connects with a complex policy agenda for mass higher education and for whole education systems. It is central to questions about the best configuration of government, devolution to subnational levels, and relations between different levels of administration in the multi-level systems. These may be federal, with significant powers belonging to the state or province, as in Australia, Canada, Germany, and the United States, or centralized but with increasing devolution, such as Spain has seen and the United Kingdom is developing.

The learning city, in the more complete sense, encourages recognition of different communities and zones of activity that cohabit the city or region. It emphasizes a need to connect and involve these, terms such as participation and empowerment as well as consultation, in order to involve and draw on their knowledge and experience in nurturing a prosperous, optimistic, competitive, and perhaps also harmonious, attractive, and sustainable social and physical environment. The concept thus calls to attention the nature of government, and the costs of dissociation, apathy, and alienation. In this stronger sense, it is about abiding issues of governance that have acquired new significance in current times.

See also: Lifelong Learning; Overview of Lifelong Learning Policies and Systems.

Bibliography

Duke, C., Osborne, M., and Wilson, B. (eds.) (2005). *Rebalancing the Social and Economic. Learning, Partnership and Place.* Leicester, UK: NIACE.

Duke, C., Doyle, L., and Wilson, B. (eds.) (2006). *Making Knowledge Work. Sustaining Learning Communities and Regions.* Leicester, UK: NIACE.

Florida, R. (2002). *The Rise of the Creative Class and How It's Transforming Work, Leisure, Community and Everyday Life.* New York: Basic Books.

Hirsch, D. (1992). *City Strategies for Lifelong Learning.* Paris: OECD.

Longworth, N. (2006). *Learning Cities, Learning Regions, Learning Communities: Lifelong Learning and Local Government.* Abingdon: Taylor and Francis.

Longworth, N. and Allwinkle, S. (2005). *The PALLACE Project: Linking Learning Cities and Regions in Europe, North America, Australasia and China.* (final report to the European Commission), Edinburgh: Napier University on line. www.pallace.net.

OECD (1999). *The Response of Higher Education Institutions to Regional Needs.* Paris: OECD.

OECD (2000). *Learning Cities and Regions in the New Economy.* Paris: OECD.

OECD (2007). *Globally Competitive, Locally Engaged – Higher Education and Regions.* Paris: OECD.

Wenger, E. (1998). *Communities of Practice. Learning, Meaning and Identity.* Cambridge: Cambridge University Press.

Further Reading

Best Value Victoria (2002). *Community Consultation Resource Guide.* Melbourne, VIC: Victorian Local Government Association (VLGA).

Bjarnason, S. and Coldstream, P. (2003). *The Idea of Engagement. Universities in Society.* London: Association of Commonwealth Universities.

Commission of the European Union (2001). *The Local and Regional Dimension of Lifelong Learning: Creating Learning Cities, Towns and Regions* (European policy paper). Brussels: EU DG Education and Culture.

Commission of the European Union (2002). *Realising a European Area of Lifelong Learning*. Brussels: EU DG Education and Culture.

Duke, C. (2004). *Learning Communities: Signposts from International Experience*. Leicester, UK: NIACE.

Faris, R. (2002). *Learning Community by Community: Preparing for a Knowledge-Based Society*. Victoria, BC: Education Canada.

Field, J. (2006). *Lifelong Learning and the New Educational Order*. Trentham Book.

Keating, J., Badenhorst, A., and Szlachetko, T. (2002). *Victoria as a Learning Region*. Melbourne, VIC: RMIT.

Longworth, N. (2003). *Lifelong Learning in Action: Transforming Education in the 21st Century*. London: Taylor and Francis.

Nyhan, B., Attwell, G., and Deitmer, L. (eds.) (2002). *Towards the Learning Region: Education and Regional Innovation in the European Union and the United States*. Thessaloniki: CEDEFOP.

Pope, J. (2006). *Indicators of Community Strength*. Melbourne, VIC: Department for Victorian Communities.

Schuller, T. (1998). Three steps towards a learning society. *Studies in the Education of Adults* **30**(1), 11–20.

Unesco (1972). *Learning to Be* (The Faure Report). Paris: Unesco.

Wain, K. (2000). The learning society: Post-modern politics. *International Journal of Lifelong Education* **19**(1), 36–53.

Yarnit, M. (2000). *Towns, Cities and Regions in the Learning Age – A Survey of Learning Communities*. London: UK Local Government Association.

Relevant Websites

info@creative.communities.org.uk – Centre for Creative Communities.

http://www.lifelonglearning.co.uk – Learning Towns and Cities UK.

http://www.ncl.ac.uk/critical/knowledgeattracts – Newcastle University; CRITICAL.

http://www.obs-pascal.com – Pascal International Observatory.

The Age of Learning: Seniors Learning

P Jarvis, University of Surrey, Guildford, UK

Older learning has become a major focus in international and national government's educational and social policies. Indeed, in support of the International Year of Older Persons, United Nations Scientific, Educational and Cultural Organization (UNESCO) and the National Institute for Adult Continuing Education in UK combined to issue a small pamphlet calling for older adults to have opportunities: to manage themselves and their quality of life; to have access to adult learning without there being an age limit to learning; for new learning; to contribute to the development of both themselves and their societies (UNESCO, nd). This article explores so many of the developments that have occurred in recent years that indicate how societies are changing in this respect. It has three main parts: the age of learning, retirement and retirement education, and organizations that promote older learning. Finally, there is a brief conclusion which makes reference to the wider benefits of learning.

The Age of Learning

The global economy has also been called the knowledge economy: products and processes have to be developed and marketed by the most efficient and effective methods. This has called for a greater investment in all forms of knowledge production and for a greater proportion of knowledge workers than ever before in humankind's history. Education has become more widely accepted as a lifelong process than ever before, despite the fact that the first book on lifelong education was written as early as 1929 (Yeaxlee, 1929). But now, it is accepted that this is an age of learning, rather than of education, and lifelong learning is a frequently employed term: it is recognized that seniors can and do continue their learning throughout the lifespan. However, it is important to recognize that they have been the driving forces of global capitalism that have generated this changed approach to learning (Jarvis, 2007; *inter alia*). It is significant to note, however, that as Stehr (1994) points out the new learning age emphasizes scientific, technological, and social scientific knowledge rather than the humanities, as Kerr *et al.* (1973) predicted. This restricted approach to knowledge meant that the broad educational program of the educated person began to appear out of date as competent professionals were sought. Now, however, a new model might be appearing within the context of lifelong learning whereby younger adults concentrate upon the sciences, technology, and the work-based subjects while liberal education

becomes a focus in the latter years of life when seniors have the time and inclination to reflect upon life itself and its meaning – if it has one. The education of elders, therefore, has assumed a totally different approach as a leisure-time pursuit which includes academic learning but which is not exclusive to it. Indeed, one other effect of globalization on the lifelong learning of elders has been the growth in educational tourism – an activity in which healthy seniors have been able to participate fully, as is seen below.

While globalization is the major cause for the development of this learning age, the focus on older learners may be seen as much as a result of demographics since we are living longer in an aging world. This is certainly the outcome of the improved standard of living that many people have enjoyed over the past century. Globalization and demographics, then, underlie the development of educational gerontology.

Education and Learning

In order to explore the idea of seniors' learning, it is necessary to unravel the complexities of definition underlying lifelong learning. The European Commission, for instance, defines it thus:

> all learning activity undertaken throughout life, with the aim of improving knowledge, skills and competences within a personal, civic, social and/or employment-related perspective. (EC, 2001: 9)

However, this definition actually conceptually confuses education and learning: learning, however, is personal and existential and transcends education. While there has been considerable debate within education about the nature of learning and a variety of different approaches and definitions have been suggested, combining them all within an all-embracing definition, learning, which is a lifelong process, may be defined as:

> the combination of processes throughout a life time whereby the whole person – body (genetic, physical and biological) and mind (knowledge, skills, attitudes, values, emotions, beliefs and senses) – experiences social situations, the perceived content of which is then transformed cognitively, emotively or practically (or through any combination) and integrated into the individual person's biography resulting in a continually changing (or more experienced) person (Jarvis, 2006: 134).

This definition emphasizes the fact that learning is not just a cognitive exercise and that our whole life experience is learned. In contrast to the existential, lifelong learning may also be seen as a social institution which is as education, as opposed to personal learning, and may be defined as:

> every opportunity made available by any social institution for, and every process by which, an individual can acquire knowledge, skills, attitudes, values, emotions, beliefs and senses within global society (Jarvis, 2007: 99).

Lifelong learning, then, is personal existential learning and recurrent education. In a sense, these two definitions also combine the more traditional ideas of informal, non-formal, and formal learning: formal learning being that which is organized within the traditional educational institution, nonformal is organized learning but does not occur within the traditional classroom setting and informal learning occurs during the processes of everyday interaction. As people age, there are fewer opportunities for them to engage in formal learning in many countries of the world, although where open universities have been founded, such as the British Open University and the Greek Open University, age is no barrier to entry to formal education and in many other countries, we are beginning to see universities and colleges open classes to older adults, as we shall see below. Additionally, there are more opportunities provided within society for nonformal learning. It is shown throughout this article that nonformal and even nonacademic learning is where the growth in education for seniors is to be found. This is to be expected since in later life, people follow their interests and attend to activities that are relevant to them – a point that Knowles (1980) stressed when he discussed the practice of andragogy.

Definitions of an Older Person

Traditionally, at the age of 65 years, a person has been deemed to have reached old age, but now we are living longer and so the question of who is old becomes a much more contentious question. Indeed, in 2004, in the UK, a 65-year-old male could expect to live a further 16.7 years, an increase of 4.4 years since 1971 whereas a female could expect to live a further 19.6 years, and increase of 3.3 years since 1971 (HMSO, 2006: 100–101). This has meant that the concept of old age is undergoing something of a re-definition with some educational gerontologists suggesting that middle age now finishes at 70 years. (This was a suggestion made by Dr Jim Fisher of Milwaukee Wisconsin University.) Nevertheless, it is still possible to treat the start of the third age in life as something between 60 and 65 years and that of the fourth age as

75 years, or as when a person loses the capacity to live independently. However, it is possible in the UK to join the University of the Third Age from the time when a person is no longer in full-time paid employment. What is clear is that people are living longer and that the span of old age is increasing quite considerably, which has resulted in some research projects now being government funded into the very old in order to prepare policies for future eventualities.

Statistics

It is impossible in a brief article like this to review the population statistics for the whole world but it is commonly accepted that the world's population is aging and Western Europe is a graying population (HMSO, 2006: 11) – it is the oldest region in the world (UNESCO, nd) – and the figures for the United Kingdom tend to confirm this. By the year 2021, it is estimated that UK will have a population of 64 729 000 people, of whom 19.67% will be 65 years and older while 9.47% will be 75 years and older. In contrast, in 1971, the population was 55 928 000 of whom 13.25% were 65 years and over and only 1.54% was 75 years and over, but in that year there were 25.49% of the population under 16 years of age compared with an estimated 17.61% in 2021 (HMSO, 2006: 10). Similar statistics can be discovered for the USA which will have an estimated population of 70 million people, 65 years and older by 2030 (McGuire *et al.*, 2005: 443), which is why these authors advocate the introduction of aging education as a national imperative. McGuire *et al.* (2005) now suggest that there are about 16 000 senior citizens centers in the USA.

However, by 2020, it is anticipated by the World Health Organization that 1 billion people worldwide will be classed as older persons, with 700 million living in developing countries: China will have 230 million, India 142 million, Indonesia 29 million, Brazil 27 million, and Pakistan 18 million. These five countries will be among the ten countries with the largest number of older people in the world. Additionally, by 2020, Japan will have 31% of it population classified as elderly and many countries will have a high proportion of its population over the age of 80 years (UNESCO, nd).

Retirement and Preretirement Education

Traditionally, the age of retirement in UK, and elsewhere in the world, has been 65 years for men and 60 years of age for women. As work has become more knowledge orientated, more women have been able to find employment and so their working lives have in some cases become similar to men's. In addition, as society has become more consumer orientated, it has become incumbent upon husbands and wives to work so that the family can enjoy the wealthy consumer lifestyle presented in the mass media and so we find that in Europe, in 2004, 70.9% of men and 55.7% of women work (HMSO, 2006: 53). However, it is now being mooted that the statutory retirement age should be later – perhaps 68 years. There are at least two reasons for this: first, pensions were planned and financed on a shorter life expectancy and age discrimination has meant that it is more difficult for employers to terminate work when an employee reaches retirement age. Indeed, it has been discovered that many people continue to work long after retirement from their job at retirement age, even to the extent of being retrained for new forms of employment.

In addition, in the UK, 23% of men and 11% of women worked over 48 h a week in 2005 (HMSO, 2006: 59). This has meant that for many people, retirement is a momentous change in lifestyle and this has been exacerbated by the fact that society has done very little to ease this status transition. Consequently, some enlightened employers have run preretirement education courses or have released their staff to attend such courses a few months or so before retirement in order to prepare for the change. Sometimes, such courses have been run by the human resources or welfare departments of employing organizations but often they have been run by colleges and other educational institutions on behalf of employers. Fundamentally, these courses are designed to help retirees consider their futures in terms of identity, health, wealth, and leisure-time pursuits. In more recent times, however, the idea of preretirement education has spread to developing countries and Ogunbameru and Bamiwuye (2004) have showed how older employees in Nigeria recognized advantages in preretirement education even though it was not widely practiced there – which indicates that preretirement education is now taking the place of instruction during the liminal period of the *rite de passage*.

Retirement is a time of major status change. In earlier times and in more primitive societies, *rites de passage* were very prevalent in social living and had three stages (van Gennap, 1960) – a ritual of separation from the former status, a period of liminality or transition, and finally a ritual of inclusion into the new status. The three stages facilitated the status change and also served to prepare the small community for the transition. It was during the transition period that those changing status were instructed into the ways of their new status before they were ritually incorporated into the new society. While the place of work has remained a more personal place, the wider society has become less personal and much more associational and flexible which means that it can adjust to minor changes, such as people retiring from work, without a great deal of tension so that it now has no need of the ritual. Hence, the ritual of inclusion has disappeared from contemporary society although the ritual of separation has still been continued and people are separated from

their place of employment and go into liminality but now retirement is an unfinished ritual because there is no rite of inclusion (Jarvis, 2001).

Stereotypes of Old Age

Old age clearly spreads over a considerable age range – from about 60 years to over 100 in some instances, so that there are certain stages of aging although studies like Sheehy's (1995) *New Passages* fail to explore them. However with the different phases, there are different images of the elderly and many of these are based on the idea of the aging body although some present pictures of the aging and poorly functioning brain through conditions such as dementia. While the study of stereotypes is beyond the scope of this article (see Featherstone and Wernick, 1995), it is important to recognzse the interconnection of body and mind which is closely related to older adult learning and that they can continue to learn and benefit greatly from the process is now beyond question. However, many people in their third age do not like being associated with the image of the fourth age which reflects the ever-increasing life span. But many advertisements, often seeking to get people to invest in retirement insurance policies, depicting happy and contented retirement are now presenting a different, younger stereotype of older persons who are able to get engaged in the world during their extended leisure time.

By contrast, in societies where old age is much more respected, for example, Islamic societies like Turkey, it might be expected that old age would be seen in a much more positive manner but this is not necessarily the case. McConatha *et al.* report that:

> Even in Turkey, a collectivist society where intergeneration contact is likely to be more common than in the United States, attitudes towards aging and old age tend to be negative. As the population of older adults grows in Turkey, it becomes increasingly important to address concerns regarding aging and the needs of older adults in order to avoid an increase in ageism. McConatha *et al.* (2004:180)

It is perhaps significant that as society becomes more individuated, younger people have fewer contacts with seniors than they did when the extended family was a more common phenomenon and so there has been an increase not only in family learning, but intergenerational learning and courses for young people to learn how to interact with older people. Lynott and Merola (2007), for instance, report that after a 5-month program of intergenerational learning in a school each year for 4 years, younger people's attitudes toward aging improved considerably. Additionally, such contacts also help older people understand more about the younger generation.

Learning and Intelligence

It was traditionally thought that intelligence increased during the early years of life but by early adulthood it had reached its peak and, thereafter slowly declined so that by old age it was impossible to learn new things: phrases such as "You can't teach an old dog new tricks" reflects this generally held traditional belief. However, learning is both an existential and an experiential phenomenon as we saw from the above definition so that for as long as we have experiences we are capable of learning and the idea of people's intelligence declining has been disputed many times since the distinction between fluid and crystallized intelligence was highlighted – the former is biologically based while the latter is experiential. Fluid intelligence is based, to some extent on memory stored in the brain and as the body slowly declines, especially as the synapses in the brain are destroyed, then the mechanism of the brain is affected and it has been suggested that fluid intelligence decreases. In contrast, crystallized intelligence is based on lifelong experience and for as long as individuals continue to remain involved in social life, through social interaction as well as through all other ways of learning, it increases. This has certainly given more credence to the idea that learning is experiential and some learning theorists (Jarvis, 1987, 2006; Kolb 1984; *inter alia*) have emphasized this in their own work. There have been many experiments in more recent times to demonstrate how seniors are still sufficiently intelligent to continue learning at advanced levels: in UK, for instance, there is a national award in adult learner's week for the senior learner of the year, and so on – the winner recently was a 98-year-old man who had just completed a masters degree! Indeed, Kliegel and Altgassen (2006: 122) have concluded from their comparative study of 45 young adults and 45 old adults that from a developmental perspective, chronological age was not a significant factor in the explanation of individual differences in learning performance, and the existence of many organizations that promote older people's learning supports this viewpoint. More recently, it has also been noted that many academics continue their teaching long past statutory retirement age even when their universities fail to support them. As Geoffrey Cantor says:

> I have joined the army of retired academic in the arts and humanities who, out of commitment to their subjects have remained research-active. But I have been disappointed how little financial support there is (Reisz, 2008: 40).

Perhaps this prolongation of academic work calls for universities to rethink their retirement policies, although it has to be conceded that they still have to prepare for the future by assisting younger academics to develop their own knowledge and skills. This, then, is an employment problem for all employing organizations. At the same time, the fact that academics can continue to do this demonstrates the fact that age is not necessarily a factor in intellectual decline. Indeed, two recent phenomena have been beginning to appear: the recognition that employers might want to retain their older workers and have to make work attractive to them, and they have to be prepared to adapt to a changing workplace (Yeatts *et al.*, 2000) and retired workers returning to new employments and even being trained for their new role.

Organizations That Promote Older Learning

As early as 1962, the Institute for Retired Professionals was founded in the USA by Hy Hirsch and sponsored by the New York School for Social Research: this was 10 years before the University of the Third Age (U3A) was established by Pierre Vellas at the University of Toulouse in France and it took another 10 years for the latter idea to spread to the United Kingdom. Despite the fact that the founder in UK, Peter Laslett was a Cambridge don, the U3A in UK has little connection with the university world. Each U3A in UK is an independent non-governmental organization (NGO), although there is a third-age trust which, in some ways, acts as a coordinating body. The diversity of U3As in UK is tremendous having 628 separate organizations affiliated to the trust and some 168 628 members as of March 2007 (as per information supplied by the third age trust). Significantly, the difference in the way these two types of U3A were founded reflects something of the difference in their approach to their activities: the ones that follow the pattern of the European continental ones are attached to universities and are much more academically orientated while those in UK tend to emphasize leisure as much as learning and it is generally recognized that only through cooperation can these diverse and independent U3As run more sophisticated academic groups, except the larger group who have sufficient members to run large and diverse programs. A small U3A, with a membership of just over 200, runs about 20 different regular-interest groups, has about eight open lectures a year, and engages in a number of social activities. There is another factor that affects the UK groups and that is the presence of the British Open University; since its foundation at about the same time as the U3As in France, it has offered formal education at a distance at undergraduate and postgraduate level to anybody and many of its students have been seniors. Indeed, for a period there was actually an older-learners-research group based at the UK Open University (Clennell, 1994: 39–46). Older people in UK seeking formal education and academic qualifications would naturally turn to the Open University and so U3As offer a wide intellectual and leisure time program with perhaps more focus of the latter than their counterparts on the continent of Europe. At the same time, this democratic and local approach to seniors' education has not been without its critics. For instance, Huang (2006) has suggested that the standard of teaching and learning in UK U3As could be improved by utilizing more university-trained teachers since its present mode of operation cannot control the level of education offered and, at the same time, the locally based democratic system might be more efficiently organized. While the accusations have some justification, there is a sense in which the present U3A activities are performing two separate roles – those of leisure and learning – roles which are undertaken in the USA by the two separate arms of the Elderhostel Institute Network. Since the organizations in UK are growing, it is clear that they are responding to local demands and so no incentive appears to exist in many local organizations to change – even though it might beneficial for them to anticipate future pressures for change at this time. In addition, it is clear that while the organization might be judged as inefficient in one sense, it is certainly democratic and is organized locally by autonomous local committees. Nevertheless, the U3A movement has spread more widely throughout Europe and beyond and has its own International Association of Universities of the Third Age (AIUTA) which has not been extremely effective in recent years although it has been in existence for many years now.

The need for research into older learners was demonstrated by the creation of Third Age Learning International Studies (TALIS) in 1990, founded by Jean Costa who was involved in Toulouse with the original founding of the University of the Third Age: TALIS was something of a breakaway from AIUTA because it wanted to concentrate on the academic study of third-age learning. From its outset, TALIS attracted scholars from all over the world, thus demonstrating the prevalence of older-adult learning.

In the USA, the development of the Institute for Retired Professionals took a totally different route: the Institute had begun under the sponsorship of the New School for Social Research in New York City but spread slowly. In 1976, however, a conference of interested parties led to these becoming known as institutes for learning in retirement. At roughly the same time (1975), in New Hampshire, another movement was born – Elderhostel and this grew extremely rapidly – offering educational travel. By 2006, it offered some 8000 programs throughout the world to about 160 000 members – its success once again reflects the significance of globalization and the wealth of the current retirees. However, it was in 1988 that 24 institutes for learning in retirement joined with Elderhostel to form the Elderhostel Institute Network. At about the same time, locally, they adopted the name Lifelong Learning Institute. The network is a voluntary association of lifelong learning institutes that are funded by Elderhostel. Lifelong learning institutes run a wide variety of teaching and learning programs and they are often sponsored by their local universities, so that they approach the type of provision made by the universities of the third age on the continent of Europe. It is significant that the cognitive-interest-motivation factor is dominant among its members, if the small-scale study conducted by Kim and Merriam (2004) is to be taken as representative. However, not all centers are sponsored in this way and some are quite independent: for instance, in a relatively large retirement community (15 000 population) it has been possible to run a college for 30 years catering for a wide variety of learning interests of the residents (Streib and Folts, 2003). In contrast, Elderhostel clearly caters for the many seniors who want to travel and learn local knowledge at the same time. It is also not insignificant that the United Nations should run a network of university departments throughout the world which is involved in educational tourism and which seeks to preserve local knowledge. Elderhostel has also spread to Canada where it is now known as Routes to Learning.

Another model that has emerged in Germany and Spain, among other places, is where universities open their classes to seniors. This certainly occurred in Germany in the 1980s and in Spain, the so-called third-age classrooms, as the Spanish government would not permit the use of the term university, began to function as early as 1978 (Socias et al., 2004) and by 1993 it was decided to open universities to seniors with the University of the Balearic Islands initiating an Open University for Seniors. Nine years after the universities opened classes to seniors, 50 universities had began to offer programs specifically for seniors and Socias et al. suggest that these programs will become more institutionalized during the twenty-first century. In Japan, there has been a similar movement but Shirasha (1995) comments on the fact that many of the academic staff working in this area are untrained.

However, the Chinese who have always had specialist universities – for example, University for Banking – have also had schools and universities for seniors – the first began in 1993 and the number grew very rapidly. (Liu Pengsheng, 1994; Li Herzhong, 1997) For instance, the TALIS conference in 2002 was held in the Wuhan University for the Aged People. It is significant that the growth of these universities reflects the fact that in the Chinese 7-year development plan of work on the aged, all cities and counties should run schools or universities for the ages (Li Zhi et al., 1997).

With this tremendous growth in elders' learning, it is significant to ask whether a new sub-discipline of adult education is not emerging and this is certainly something that concerned adult-education scholars about the time that Knowles introduced the term andragogy to American adult education. In the terminological debate of that time, humanagogy, gerogogy, and educational gerontology were among the terms being discussed. Ultimately, the idea of educational gerontology has been the one that has come to the fore since it rightly locates the study of the education of elders within the context of education *per se* and as a major element in lifelong learning, although on the continent of Europe – where the concept of andragogy has more to do with the academic study of the education of adults that the process of teaching and learning, as presented by Knowles (1980) – andragogical terminology is still utilized.

Accreditation

It is very clear that most of the above educational institutes do not offer accreditation for their courses and neither do many seniors seek it. In the UK, for instance, if they do want it, there is nothing to prevent seniors from enrolling in the Open University of in some of the university degree-course programs. This is also true for many countries where universities have an open access and a general acceptance of part-time higher education but the idea of the continental European U3As offering accreditation for some of their courses has been discussed at various times. This has not occurred everywhere in world; however, such as in many parts of the old Eastern Europe and the so-called Third World, but as the development of part-time education is almost certain to continue, the idea of older (but working) persons attending lifelong educational programs will become more common place: this might well be a precursor to the development of a more extensive senior's education movement in these countries. However, accreditation for vocational education is important and this has meant that in some countries, such as UK, government has been prepared to offer financial support for part-time vocational education but not for part-time leisure education and therefore not for the greater majority of senior's education. This reflects the emphasis placed upon the relationship between education and work in neo-liberal societies. Consequently, poorer older people are still disadvantaged in the world of education because their education is not seen to make a contribution to the neo-liberal economy.

In contrast to this approach, it is worth noting that there are other ways of measuring the value of learning: the Chinese have a scale of the value of learning (Leung *et al.*, 2006) based on Confucius' aphorisms which has five items: continuing learning, no boundaries to learning, keeping fresh in one's mind what has already been learned, people will decline if they do not continue to learn, and the harder one learns the better. There are element s here that reflect ideas in gerontology, such as the discontinuity hypothesis – that for so long as people continue to stay involved in society and continue to learn, then they will continue to develop; but, once they disconnect from the wider society the chances of decline

increase. While this Chinese approach might not be the answer to accreditation in older learning, it does suggest other ways of measuring its value.

This scale reflects in some ways the work of Cusack *et al.* (2003: 398) who have emphasized the idea of mental fitness in which they suggest that there are nine items: confidence in mental abilities, ability to set and achieve goals, willingness to take risks, optimism, creativity, mental flexibility, ability to learn new things, flexibility and ability to speak one's own mind. To enhance these in later life, is clearly a major benefit of learning.

Cusack *et al.* review three recent research programs; they note that they all have a common benefits to learning – a more positive attitude to life and increased hope. They make the point that:

> Hope plays a powerful role in life. More than a sunny disposition and a belief that everything will be fine, it means believing that you have a normal life, without fear of "losing it", and that inside you have the resources to accomplish personal goals and influence the course of your life. Hope means believing in a better future; hope means not giving in to anxiety and depression. (Cusack *et al.*, 2003: 395)

While this research as a whole is tangential to our major concern here, its findings on older learners are significant for educational gerontology and it is perhaps significant that in a survey of publications, of 4 years, of the journal *Educational Gerontology*, the number of publications on health education and there were nine papers that were specifically concerned about dementia and Alzheimer's disease. There were also a couple of papers that focused on physical fitness and one which looked at mental fitness – as the papers show, these two cannot be separated: one paper only was concerned with depression. Two papers were specifically about counseling.

Conclusion

To these studies, there is an the indication that perhaps "lifelong learning may prevent or delay the symptoms of dementia, notably Alzheimer's Disease" (Cussack *et al.*, 2003: 395). In their own studies, they demonstrate that intensive courses of study improve the level of mental fitness – but it also contributes to the improvement of the more general level of health. From their own work, they regard continuing learning as health-promoting behavior. Similar research in the United Kingdom reaches similar conclusion (Schuller *et al.*, 2002).

However, we should not assume that all older adults are longing to continue their education or that there are not barriers to it: not only do these barriers include untrained teachers but they include untrained bureaucrats who fail to assist in the developments of learning for older adults, lack of financial support for those who cannot afford to pay for their own education, lack of confidence in their own ability and so a fear of failure, and a lack of mobility and a disengagement with the wider world. Indeed, one of the major problems which advocates of older learning are confronted with is that many older people currently have negative images of their schooling and so they do not avail themselves to the benefits of nonschool learning, but as those people who have worked in the knowledge economy retire, the significance of older learning will continue to increase at every level of society.

Globalization and demographic factors have combined to make learning across the whole life span a reality and educational gerontology is not an established sub-discipline within education. The significance of its findings, such as those related to physical and mental health, have not been fully utilized by governments in education, health, or welfare programs although with the continuing aging population, it is clear that elders' learning will be seen as a major contributing factor in governmental policy. Seniors' learning has a major effect on the social capital of local towns and regions and finally, its personal benefits are beyond question.

See also: Health and Adult Learning; Participation in Adult Learning.

Bibliography

Clennell, S. (1994). Distance learning: Creativity and activity for older students. *Third Age Learning International Studies* **1994**, 39–46.

Cusack, S., Thompson, W., and Rogers, M. (2003). Mental fitness for life: Assessing the impact of an 8-Week Mental Fitness Program on healthy aging. *Educational Gerontology* 29(5), 381–391.

EC (European Commission) (2001). *Making a European Area of Lifelong Learning a Reality*. Brussels: European Commission COM(2001) 678final.

Featherstone, M. and Wernick, A. (eds.) (1995). *Images of Aging*. London: Routledge.

HMSO (HM Stationary Office) (2006). *Social Trends*. Basingstoke: Palgrave Macmillan.

Huang, C.-S. (2006). The University of the Third Age in the UK: An interpretive critical study. *Educational Gerontology* 32(10), 825–842.

Jarvis, P. (2001). *Learning in Later Life*. London: Kogan Page.

Jarvis, P. (2006). *Towards a Comprehensive Theory of Human Learning*. London: Routledge.

Jarvis, P. (2007). *Globalisation, Lifelong Learning and the Learning Society: Sociological Perspectives*. London: Routledge.

Kerr, C., Dunlop, J., Harbison, F., and Myers, C. (1973). *Industrialism and Industrial Man*, 2nd edn. Harmondsworth: Penguin.

Kim, A. and Merriam, S. (2004). Motivations for learning among older adults in a learning in Retirement Institute. *Educational Gerontology* 30(6), 441–455.

Kliegel, M. and Altgassen, M. (2006). Individual differences in learning performance: The effects of age, intelligence, and strategic task approach. *Educational Gerontology* 32(2), 111–124.

Knowles, M. (1980). *The Modern Practice of Adult Education: From Pedagogy to Andragogy* (rev. and updated). Chicago, IL: Association Press.

Kolb, D. (1984). *Experiential Learning*. Englewood Cliffs, NJ: Prentice Hall.

Leung, A., Chi, I., Chow, N., Chan, K. -S., and Chou, K. -L. (2006). Construction and validation of a Chinese value of learning scale. *Educational Gerontology* 32(10), 907–920.

Li Herzhong (1997). The University for Old People in China. *Third Age Learning International Studies* 4; *Third Age Learning International Studies* 7, 91–95.

Liu Pingsheng (1994). Creative Learning in the Chinese Schools for the Elderly. 4, 55–61.

Li Zhi, Du Zicai, and Chan Yuan (1997). The Chinese characteristics of and prospects for China's education for the aged in Wuhan. *Third Age Learning International Studies* 7, 71–77.

Lynott, P. and Merola, P. (2007). Improving the attitudes of 4th graders toward older people through a Multidimensional Intergenerational Program. *Educational Gerontology* 33(1), 63–74.

McConatha, J., Hayta, V., Rieser-Danna, L., McConatha, D., and Polat, T. (2004). Turkish and US attitudes towards aging. *Educational Gerontology* 30(3), 169–183.

McGuire, S., Klein, D., and Couper, D. (2005). Aging education: A national imperative. *Educational Gerontology* 31(6), 443–460.

Ogunbameru, O. and Bamiwuye, S. (2004). Attitudes toward retirement and pre-retirement education among Nigerian Bank workers. *Educational Gerontology* 30(5), 391–402.

Reisz, M. (2008). Senior service. *Times Higher Education*, **Feb. 21–27**, pp 38–41.

Schuller, T., Brassett-Grundy, A., Green, A., Hammond, C., and Preston, J. (2002). *Learning Continuity and Change in Adult Life*. London: Institute of Education – Centre For Research on the Wider Benefits of Learning Report No 3.

Sheey, G. (1995). *New Passages: Mapping Your Life Across Time*. Toronto, ON: Random House of Canada.

Shirasha, I. (1995). Japan, a developing country in the field of lifelong learning as well as ageing: Its new perspectives and barriers. *Third Age Learning International Studies* 5, 101–104.

Socias, C., Brage, L., and Garma, C. (2004). University programs for seniors in Spain: Analysis and perspectives. *Educational Gerontology* 30(4), 315–328.

Stehr, N. (1994). *Knowledge Societies*. London: Sage.

Streib, G. and Folts, E. (2003). A college in a retirement community. *Educational Gerontology* 29(10), 801–808.

UNESCO (nd). *Creative Learning and Active Ageing*. Hamburg: UNESCO and NIACE.

Van Gennap, A. (1960). *The Rites of Passage*. London: Routledge and Kegan Paul.

Yeatts, D., Folts, E., and Knapp, J. (2000). Older workers' adaptation to changing work place: Employment issues for the 21st century. *Educational Gerontology* 26(6), 565–582.

Yeaxlee, B. (1929). *Lifelong Education*. London: Cassell.

Further Reading

Beisgen, B. and Kraitchman, M. (2003). *Senior Centers*. New York: Springer.

Blakemore, S.-J. and Frith, U. (2005). *The Learning Brain*. Oxford: Blackwell.

Educational Gerontology (2004–2007) – Philadelphia: BrunnerRoutledge, 30–33 (1–10).

Hudson, F. (1999). *The Adult Years*. San Francisco, CA: Jossey-Bass.

Jarvis, P. (2009). *Learning to be a Person in Society*. London: Routledge.

Jewell, A. (ed.) (1999). *Spirituality and Ageing*. London: Jessica Kingsley.

Kitwood, T. (1997). *Dementia Reconsidered*. Buckingham: Open University Press.

Manheimer, R. (1999). *A Map to the End of Time*. New York: WW Norton.

Moody, H. (1998). *Aging: Concepts and Controversies*, 2nd edn. Thousand Oaks, CA: Pine Forge Press.

Peterson, D. (1983). *Facilitating Education for Older Learners*. San Francisco, CA: Jossey-Bass.

Peterson, D., Thornton, J., and Birren, J. (eds.) (1986). *Education and Aging*. Englewood Cliffs, NJ: Prentice Hall.

Schuller, T., Preston, J., Hammond, C., Brassett-Grundy, A., and Brynner, J. (2004). *The Benefits of Learning*. London: RoutledgeFalmer.

The Learning Revolution (2009). Department for Innovation, Universities and Skills Her Majesty's Government: The Stationary Office Cm 7555.

Waters, E. and Goodman, J. (1990). *Empowering Older Adults*. San Francisco, CA: Jossey-Bass.

Relevant Website

http://www.elderhostel.org – Elderhostel (downloaded 01.04.07).

HIV Education for Low-Literate People: Transforming Students and Communities through Paulo Freire's Praxis and the Pedagogy of Action

N Z Haniff, University of Michigan, Ann Arbor, MI, USA

Glossary

Activism – To become advocates of a cause related to social justice.

Consciousness – To be aware of the complex systems and ideas that drive social injustice in people's lives and the awareness that overcoming these injustices requires your own participation.

Empowerment – Ensuring that the least privileged is provided with the skills and knowledge that they can own and use to improve their lives.

Exoticism – To reduce a culture to essentialist caricatures, for example, one does not really see Africa unless one sees animals, or all Africans live in huts.

Low literacy – Population which is literate but only functionally literate.

Pedagogy – A method of teaching which facilitates the learners engagement in the teaching.

Praxis – Putting theory into action.

Introduction

This project asks some key question relating to transformation of students and communities: How young men and women can be conscientized about social injustice (race and gender) and translate that consciousness as a core principle of their own transformation as activists? How can a teacher who is a gender and human immunodeficiency virus (HIV) activist in South Africa, the Caribbean, and the United States use the nexus between privileged students and the community to develop consciousness in these communities to see themselves not as victims but as participants who can solve the problems faced by their communities if given the right tools? How can empowerment be achieved not as an academic exercise but as an act of human rights advocacy for the least literate and most marginalized?

The response to this question has been a three-course curriculum lasting a year. The first part of this curriculum is the course Pedagogy of Empowerment: Activism in Race, Gender, and Health, which educates the student about the HIV menace among African-Americans. There are four very important objectives for this class. First, the student must become fully informed about HIV and African-Americans. Second, this information provides the context for a lively discussion on race and gender. Third, the students must be theoretically grounded in both race and gender in the HIV epidemic in the African community. Finally, from this process, the students become involved in praxis through teaching the low-literate module on HIV to communities outside the university.

The module was developed in the Caribbean when the author was engaged in creating low-literacy modules to teach women about their bodies. The women in Guyana asked to be taught about HIV. At the heart of this methodology is the philosophy that people can take responsibility for themselves if given the right tools, and that literacy was not a requirement for education. This module was then taught in Guyana, St. Lucia, Grenada, Dominica, St. Vincent, and Jamaica with great success. At that time, the epidemic was beginning to emerge as a great threat in Africa, and South Africa was then on its way to becoming the country with the largest number of infections (today there are 5 million HIV-infected persons in South Africa). The author is of the opinion that this module could have had some impact in South Africa, since there were large numbers of people who were not literate and needed HIV prevention education. Through her teaching at the University of Michigan, the author intends to create cadres of student activists from among the students who took her classes and who then would learn this pedagogy and then go into these communities.

To a certain extent, many of the students would embark on a kind of peer education where they would not only teach their peers the module but any community or organized group that would listen. This perception of community engagement or community involvement is often presumed to be simply a matter of acquiring skills. Campbell and MacPhail (2002) argue that "Peer education has been described as a method in search of a theory." They then further discuss a conceptual framework of community and peer education based on the work of Paulo Freire, whose conceptualization of empowerment adds a more cognitive intellectual dimension, focusing on people's intellectual analyses. He argues that a vital precondition for positive behavior change by marginalized social groups is the development of critical consciousness. Freire's book *The Pedagogy of the Oppressed* is the theoretical text used in all of the three courses of this project.

The students must first be conscientized by examining their own education and by challenging their perception of activism, including their own privileged status. Who and what is their community? How do they define community? Do they have a community? The class itself is not structured in the traditional didactic educational style but through dialogs about race, HIV, and gender. The issues Freire raises drive the theory of their ultimate project, teaching the HIV module to their own communities. These discussions are sometimes difficult but they happen nonetheless. This is the backbone of the pedagogy of action. Freire's conceptual framework is used in all three of the courses building layers of understanding that enhance the students own critical consciousness and their own emerging awareness of the intrinsic value of this consciousness in teaching their own communities and communities outside the United States.

The reflection on conscientization and its role in teaching the module provides an important insight into the student's own inability to depart from systematic education. It is here that the concept of praxis, putting theory into action, becomes critical. The student no longer sees teaching the module as an act of charity but as an act of building democracy, allowing the silenced to have a voice and to own knowledge rather than become a receptacle of that knowledge. Here, HIV work is transformed into human rights work, making both the beneficiaries and the educators, human rights activists. The act of teaching HIV prevention is inextricably linked to empowerment of the community and their ownership of the information.

The module is oral in nature and requires very little writing, and it is resource independent, there is nothing to read, no handouts, and no literature. At the most it lasts 20 min and takes about 3 days to learn and become teachers for those who are totally illiterate and about 2 h for those who are educated. The groups must be small with no more than 10 persons. A normal session of teaching would last 3 half-day sessions lasting 2–3 h. During that time, the student will learn the module and teach it back to their peers first in English and then develop the module in their own language when it is done in South Africa. Through this methodology, thousands of people have been taught by first- and second-generation teachers.

The HIV Module

On paper the module looks like this.

Science Lesson

As this module was developed to help low-literate people teach HIV prevention, it really has no meaning as a written text. To write about this module is to write about the pedagogy of these five simple lines. It is elementary in nature – it is like looking at the alphabet – structured in such a way that the least-literate person can do it. A is for apple, H is for human, I is for ink or I is for a big long word immuno-deficiency, and V is for virus. First you begin with a story. Let us say I am in the kitchen and I am cutting cabbage and I accidentally cut my finger; what will I see? Blood. If you take a big glass and look at your blood, you will see that your blood is made up of little dots. These dots are called cells. There are two kinds of dots: red dots called red blood cells, and white dots called white blood cells. The red cells nourish your body and send oxygen throughout your body. To demonstrate this, we have to ask everyone to breathe in and out saying that we are breathing in oxygen and exhaling as it travels around our body. The white cells protect one's body. Here, we draw soldiers and explain how the white cells protect our bodies. We say, for example, if you fall and cut your knee then the white blood cells would rush to that area and form a scab, which means that it is now protecting that area from further harm, and begin the process of healing the cut. We now go to HIV (**Figure 1**).

H is for human, which means us, not dogs or cats or goats but us, humans. I stands for a big long word, immuno-deficiency, which means that all those white dots or soldiers who form a wall of protection against any disease or illness our bodies acquire, get together and fight it off so we can defeat the illness. So immuno is the white blood cells – the soldiers protecting one's body. Deficient simply means that the wall is now weakened – its not working well, something is wrong with the white blood cells.

At this point, we will show that a soldier has lost an arm or another one has lost a leg, demonstrating deficiency. The V in HIV stands for virus. The virus is explained as bacteria that have entered the body (**Figure 2**).

The Four Ways of Transmission

Here, we discuss the four ways in which one can contract HIV:

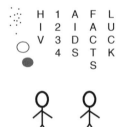

Figure 1   The immune system: The soldiers (white blood cells).

Figure 2   Immune deficiency: The soldiers (white blood cells) are compromised.

1. The first way is through sex. Depending on the audience we are speaking to, we describe sex as friction. During this time, we ask participants to put their hands together and rub them together. This is known as friction, which represents the process that facilitates the cuts and tears that can occur during sex. Since we are not able to see them, fluids, including blood from one partner, can enter the small cuts and openings in the other partner and HIV can be transmitted this way.

2. The second way is through needles. We ask them to make a cylindrical tube while joining their two hands (as a fist) together. We explain that the needle is a tube, in which blood can remain, which if it is shared can transmit blood and other fluids.

3. The third way is mother to child. Although there have been preventative measures to reduce this, we still discuss it as a way of transmission. An HIV-infected mother can give her child the virus through breast-feeding. Breast-feeding is very important because it is the best nutrition a child can receive; therefore, it is important that mothers are tested so that they can breast-feed their child without fear of transmitting any infection. The child can contract HIV from the mother in the womb, if there is any kind of disruption in the womb, before delivery. The other way a mother can transmit HIV to a child is through labor. The infection occurs when the child is being delivered. The child can exchange fluids from the mother through the child's tender skin and openings such as the eyes, mouth, and nose. This is very important from a woman's point of view, so that she knows how to protect herself and her baby during pregnancy.

4. Finally, we discuss the fourth way, namely blood transfusion. Although this is very rare too, if blood is not screened for HIV, transmission can be facilitated. In a hospital, blood transfusion is done to patients, at times, in a life-or-death situation. If that blood is not tested then the person receiving the blood can become infected that way. Nowadays, this is not such a big problem because, in most places, the blood is tested for the HIV virus.

AIDS

Next, we link HIV with AIDS. The acronym can be explicated as:

- A in AIDS stands for acquired; the word, acquired, means that something is given from one person to another person.
- I in AIDS stands for immunodeficiency, just like in HIV, and we break it into two parts. The immune part stands for immune system and the deficiency in AIDS means that one's soldiers are not only losing an arm or leg but they are dying all together. Here, we wipe out all the soldiers we draw, except one or two, explaining the

soldiers cannot fight the virus anymore, which accounts for deficiency that is now more extreme.

- D is for deficient, which means the white blood cells are defeated. Some people can fight the disease for a very long time and some cannot. If one's soldiers can no longer fight the HIV virus, then one contracts AIDS.
- S in AIDS stands for syndrome, meaning a collection of all the illnesses that the person begins to experience – diarrhea, losing weight, rashes, and many other illnesses, which can eventually cause death since the body can no longer resist infections. No one really dies of AIDS but they die from one of these illnesses, such as a cold, which can turn into pneumonia and cause death, sores that cannot heal, weight loss, or constant diarrhea.

FACTS – Prevention of HIV

FACTS are some things one can use to protect themselves, and can be defined as follows.

- F stands for faithful, which means staying faithful to oneself and to others. This is a feminist interpretation of faithful. We say the first act of faithfulness is to oneself; if life's dream involves going to school, getting into university, or being employed in a good job, then it is important to be faithful to this dream. In this way, one is faithful to oneself by making his/her life better and by making good decisions about one's priorities. If your partner wants to have sex without protection or wants you to have a child before you are ready then if you make the wrong decisions you will put your future and your life in danger. If you have one partner then you must stick with one partner as well. This might mean–
- A abstaining, having no sex until you are ready, not when your partner is ready. This is especially important when talking to young people but does not exclude adults who want this as a choice.
- C stands for using a condom or, in South Africa, condomise. If you are ready then you should use a latex condom.
- T stands for testing, which means get tested for HIV. It also means to get tested for STDs like gonorrhea and syphilis, which cause open sores on one's private parts, which can help in the transferring of HIV. Finally, S stands for 'stay away from drugs and alcohol'. These substances can cause inhibitions to be lowered, causing one to possibly make the wrong judgment. If one plans to participate in these activities, we encourage the person to always have a trusted friend who will help you make right decisions.

Then if you know a person who is HIV positive you must be a source of LUCK to them. This is a critical part of the module since it deals with stigma which is still affecting

HIV-positive people and preventing others from seeking help because of fear of rejection.

LUCK – Stigma Reduction

- L is for love; show love to the infected person. Sit with them, talk to them, if you loved them before they had HIV, you should love them after they have HIV – they are still the same person. Do not reject them or turn your back on them.
- U is for understanding. Understand what the disease is, be educated about it, and educate others about it. Know that you cannot get HIV from touching or caring for them, that you cannot get it from drinking from the same cup or sitting on the bed or toilet. You can hug them and talk to them. The virus cannot live very long outside the body and so it is important you understand all of this, the ways you cannot get HIV. Understand also what they are going through, how they must be feeling having HIV or AIDS.
- C and K are for caring and kindness. Take the time to show them love, take them to church, take them for a drive, visit with them, and help in any way you can to make their lives more comfortable and show other people they should not be rejected but accepted. Show them love understanding caring and kindness.

Today there are many drugs, herbs, and foods to help your white blood cells fight this virus. Therefore, it is important that you get tested as soon as possible. To get tested does not mean that you are going to die, but that you are going to live because now there are many ways to manage this virus than before. So know the facts and be the bearer of LUCK. And be a role model who will stand up for an HIV-positive person.

Teach-Back Methodology

Students who take The Pedagogy of Empowerment course must then teach this module to a community outside the university and have at least two people teach it back. There have been many problems with this component of the class. Many students do not have a community they can go to and are afraid to do this. Many times they teach their peers within the university. Others try to teach youth groups in their churches, often being disappointed because they cannot teach sex in the church. Students also try to teach in their high schools and find it is complicated, because the schools also cannot teach about sex unless there is a long procedure that entails getting each parent to sign off or the school board has to decide. What seem apparently easy turns out to be very complicated.

The teach-back component of this methodology is critical to its success. It is here that didactic education is most challenged. When the students in the class first learn the module, all of them must teach it back. They cannot use notes; they must look at their audience and teach the same way they were taught, that is without writing or turning their backs to the audience to write on the board. Students are so unfamiliar with this kind of presentation without notes that they intuitively want to write the acronyms out. Thus, for example, the F in FACTS they will write out facts on the board. This is strongly discouraged since for low-literate audiences this communicates that they too must write on the board. We discourage this because it slows down the story, the orality of the module, and diminishes their ability to feel empowered to teach this module. The transformation for the farmer, for example, when he/she gets up to teach is that they have taken on the role of the teacher and this act alone is empowering. That they could teach such information is, for them, the first act of egalitarianism the module facilitates. Most important, however, is the almost universal reticence to get up and teach even among the very literate. After two or three times of hearing the module, everyone thinks they can teach this, but when they are asked to do so very few actually get up. It is at this point that Freire's idea about the educational system becomes a living testimony. The hierarchy of the teacher as banker and the student as depositary is an idea so intractable in education that students become resentful and afraid when they are asked to become owners of knowledge rather than receptacles. They are often afraid and this is exactly the same when community members are asked to teach. This reticence is seen equally among the educated as well as the illiterate.

> The peasant feels inferior to the boss because the boss seems to be the only one who knows things and is able to run things. They call themselves ignorant and say the "professor" is the one who has knowledge and to whom they should listen. The criteria of knowledge imposed upon them are the conventional ones. "Why don't you" said a peasant participating in a culture circle, "explain the pictures first? That way It'll take less time and won't give us a headache" Almost never do they realize that they too, "know things." (Freire, 2002)

This process provides a pivotal teaching moment for the Pedagogy of Empowerment. It is at this point that the students examine their own education. Are they being educated for themselves or to serve their communities? Why do they have few contacts with their communities other than church and high schools? The Freirean methodology and the theory of this pedagogy become apparent for now the limits of the didactic educational system and the illiteracy of their own social justice skills are exposed.

> Only by working with the people could I achieve anything authentic on their behalf. Never had I believed that the

democratization of culture meant either its vulgarization or simply passing on to the people the prescription formulated in a teacher's office. I agreed with Mannheim that "as democratic processes become widespread it becomes more and more difficult to permit the masses to remain in a state of ignorance". Mannheim would not restrict his definition of ignorance to illiteracy, but would include the masses' lack of experience at participating and intervening in the historical process. (Freire and Macedo, 2000)

There are schools dedicated to interactions with the community, but the agenda is to teach the student to become a professional person in that community, to be a social worker, to be a clinician, a nurse, a teacher, etc. Many classes require community participation where the community provides the reality context for the student's education. The greatest beneficiary of all these 'projects' is the student ("remember you are part of a system, the field placement system which uses a variety of actors to accomplish the educational mission of the school") (Gorbman, 2002). Supervision and time for the student who is being placed to 'help' the community is done at the largesse of the community organization, which is not, as a general rule, paid to do this work, that they are getting a 'university student' to work with them is seen as payment enough (Barton et al., 2005). Many workers in these organizations feel burdened by this; often the students themselves are left to muddle through simply because teaching them requires time, which organizations under stress do not have. This does not mean that the experience is not successful for many but, as a political commentary, it is important to note that the students leave, complete their education at the university, get their degree, and become professionals.

Discussions with students who volunteer in many humanitarian and nongovernmental organizations reveal that many are often loath to consider themselves beneficiaries at all. They feel they are good people and that the Freirean methodology of the class challenges their good work. It is not that their good work is not valued, but one must be able to distinguish the difference between charity and development. This is not an easy pill to swallow for young people who are caring and want to make a difference. The difference between criticism and challenge often becomes blurred. Even though it is emphasized that they should not stop their charity work because it has intrinsic value, it is still difficult, because the intent of the challenge is to make them see how their privilege still makes them beneficiaries even when they are giving. This in part is what Freire refers to as "problem posing education." It is about reflection on action and then again action and reflection. The process of conscientization begins with problem posing education. And it is this that is at the core of the class on the pedagogy of empowerment.

Before the class on the pedagogy of empowerment, they had no idea of the level of the HIV crisis in the African-American communities. This information was shocking to them. They felt HIV was the disease of the 'other' in Africa. They raised money for Africa and felt that because they were Americans this had been addressed. It had not. At the 2008 Aids International Conference, the CDC MMWR (2008) reported the HIV epidemic was much larger in the African-American community than they had thought.

The new estimates show that MSM (men who have sex with men) of all races and ethnicities, and African-American men and women, are the groups most affected by HIV. Fifty-three percent of all new infections in 2006 occurred in MSM. African-Americans, while comprising 13% of the US population, accounted for 45% of the new HIV infections in 2006, with an annual infection rate seven times higher than whites and almost three times higher than Latinos (CDC MMWR, 2007).

This information confirms what those of us who have been working in this field for many years knew. The numbers were high but few people were paying attention on a national scale. The CDC notes that the new estimate does not represent an actual increase in the number of new HIV infections. Analyses conducted by the agency indicate the annual number of new infections has remained fairly stable over the past decade, albeit significantly higher than was originally thought (CDC MMWR, 2008).

Still the HIV epidemic has not reached a tipping point in the African-American community, and these issues were the center of many dialogs in the class. The greatest significance of this awakening was the realization "going to Africa to work on HIV" is not more important than working on HIV in the United States. The first principle of the Pedagogy of Action is that HIV in South Africa is not to be seen as a site for charity. The commitment to addressing HIV should be in the United States as well as in Africa. HIV has been exoticised as an "African disease" and the cultural politics of the racialization of disease has led to its marginalization in the United States as an African-American or American problem. This has clearly contributed to the ongoing perception that Africa is a place which must be rescued.

Preparation for the Field

Before students could embark on the culmination the Pedagogy of Action course, they had to first enroll in the class entitled 'Preparation for the Field'. This was a critical class because, once the students had been conscientized about HIV, race, gender, health, and empowerment in the United States, they had now to confront the hegemony of the United States and its image in the world. Readings and discussions about the issues, ideas, culture, and politics of the young American student engaged in communities abroad were rigorously addressed. What and where is South Africa?

What are the myths and perceptions of this African country? Is Africa a place to be exoticised or to be taken seriously as a site of cultural significance, a place of ideas and learning? What does it mean to be an American in the world today? How do South Africans see Americans? What kind of American do you want to be and present to the world?

Although the majority of the students would have taken the basic The Pedagogy of Empowerment class, a few will have applied to the 'study abroad' program and this class with those who had already taken the Pedagogy of Empowerment class will then form a cohort to bring the other students up to speed. They will also have to learn the module and teach it in the United States before they left for South Africa. The readings covered the latest information on the epidemic and its history in South Africa. The political life stories and struggles of Nelson Mandela and Bishop Desmond Tutu were required texts. The ideal number of students in this group was 10, most were undergraduates in their last 2 years and a graduate student who worked as an assistant. They ranged from engineering students to the social sciences and humanities.

A critical examination of the United States was essential in a pedagogy in which American students go into the developing world to see the world and to engage in projects. The questions they must examine were the following: Is anything or anyone better than America? If you have been told all your life that the United States is the greatest country in the world and that you are the greatest, is it possible then for you to see anyone or anywhere else as your equal? (Haniff, 2008). These questions formed the ideological basis of the preparation for the field.

The Pedagogy of Action

The Final semester is spent on the project in which the students put all these ideas into action in South Africa. The student who is now more thoughtful and reflecting is now taken into an environment that is even more radical. To teach HIV prevention, for example, in the townships in South Africa is both a frightening and exciting possibility. On the one hand, to presume that privileged American students can actually come to South Africa and teach people who speak in many different languages was a kind of arrogance or naiveté. On the other hand, it was such a challenge as to achieve it would itself be an act of supreme transformation for the student and maybe the community. Since the fall of apartheid, the universities have been developing ways to include service as a part of academic education. The tension between learning as knowledge in academia and learning as knowledge grounded in the community is at the nexus of education for all developing countries, especially in newly emerging democracies like South Africa. The Pedagogy of Action is an example of this praxis, that responsibility to one's community does not

exclude theoretical rigor or academic excellence. This is why the University of Witwatersrand and the University of Zululand were keenly interested in the Pedagogy of Action. The numbers have increased every year from 60 graduates in the HIV module the first year to a 110 the following year at the University of Zululand. At the University of Witwatersrand, students developed the module in 10 different languages, which include Sotho, Zulu, Xhosa, Yoruba, Lingala, and so on. In 2007 we met 10 of 60 students who graduated in our program in 2006 – out of their own commitment to act, they taught over 4000 people in their home villages in Kwa-Zulu Natal. This is how education can be a force for true citizenship and democracy.

Transformation

The impact of the pedagogy of action can be looked at through the evaluations conducted at various phases of the pedagogy. Evaluations of this pedagogy have been done in the Caribbean and in South Africa. The difference is that in the Caribbean evaluation represents the voices of community activists who had used the pedagogy over 4 years at the time of the evaluation (Haniff, 2004). The South Africa component was evaluated a year after the students had taught the module in their communities and reflects the voices of the teachers and not the communities who were taught. The transformation of students is expressed in their project papers where they recollect and analyze incidents pivotal to their new thinking and awareness.

The Community Activist

The early development of the module when it was taught by the author and two facilitators directly to communities did not include the capacity-building component. The sustainability of the module was left directly in the hands of the communities themselves through activists, nurses, teachers, and the outreach workers. However, this was found to have limited appeal since these activists could not go out of the communities and were not in a position to train others. They could, however, continue to teach. It was after these experiences with the module that we decided to train, for example, university students in South Africa – who were basically peers of my students who were the first-line teachers. The ideas and analyses of the impact of the pedagogy on the community as a part of the evolution of the pedagogy provide an important voice in the power of the pedagogy of action.

> Although revolutionary leaders may have to think about the people in order to understand them better, this thinking differs from that of the elite; for in thinking about the people in order to liberate (rather than dominate) them the leaders give of themselves to the thinking of the

people. One is the thinking of the master; the other is the thinking of the comrade. (Freire, 2002: 132)

It is good because going to other workshops where they give you handouts and the speaker get up then I say I have everything already so you don't pay attention, but this workshop you had to listen so you had to take in what was said. You could always jot down whatever you wanted but whatever was being said, it had to remain in your head. It also develops your listening skills, so you can listen carefully. I think that method was very good. Too many times we are given handouts and after the workshop we chuck it there and then we don't have time to go back to it and whatever knowledge was said in this workshop it remain with us because we were given the facilities to give it back and it remains with you rather than a handout.

You see when I tell people what I know they say how I know that and I am not a doctor, not even a nurse because you know what happen. Because in learning to know about health I learn to know about my own self. I learn that nobody is higher, we at the same level. I can do whatever any other person can do.

Having to go up (to teach the module first time) you always feel a little nervous, in fact in truth you always feel a little shaky. Another thing that made us able to do it like we were on one level. Like you and the facilitator came, make yourself at the same level, like we were one, but sometimes you go to workshops where you have people of different height, (class) but it is for them (the education is for them) but you are not them because you are a different class. So you feel you are not comfortable among these people, so you not open up to receive, to grasp much. But you all come and make yourself part of us, just like us so we felt much more comfortable with you so therefore we were able to grasp and to learn faster that keep people back when you go to a workshop and they rank you (look down on you) and they don't take heed of you.

The New Teachers at the University of Zululand

These are the voices of the students who were taught by the University of Michigan students in South Africa. They were not community activists but were the peers of the University of Michigan students, at the University of Zululand. These new teachers taught in their villages and field placements in the rural areas of Kwa-Zulu Natal. The module was developed by these students into Zulu and then taught to their communities using their own language.

One cannot expect positive results from an educational or political action program which fails to respect the

particular view of the world held by the people. Such a program constitutes cultural invasion, good intentions not withstanding. (Freire, 2002: 95)

Well, I already know about HIV, but what I learned was the simplest way to make HIV seem not as bad and not as complex as it is . It gives me, a teacher, like an imagination, even when I explain it to little kids. You know, kids imagine what HIV is. You don't know how to explain, but this just gives me a picture of HIV. And it's not as complex.

Also, again, I would really love, especially, foreigners or donors to make it a point that when they come to Africa, assisting people, they should empower people, not let people be in a position that they will fold their arms and just receive whatsoever. It could be information, but foreign people, they must empower people to be effective.

You are now even free to tell the whole community-you are positive. They won't, even, like, maybe hit you or do something or hate you. I mean, this program or this module has made people realize that the fact that you're HIV-positive, it doesn't mean that you are a bad person in the community. Maybe they thought you are unacceptable within the people or you are different from other people. Now people are learning to accept one another.

The Students

This is an excerpt from a student's writing on the topic 'faith', which was assigned to examine whether students really trusted that their 'low literate' audience could be empowered to teach.

The generosity of the oppressors is nourished by an unjust order, which must be maintained in order to justify that generosity. Our converts on the other hand, truly desire to transform the unjust order; but because of their background they believe that they must be the executors of the transformation. They talk about the people, but they do not trust them; and trusting the people is the indispensable precondition for revolutionary change. A real humanist must be identified more by his trust in the people, which engages them in his struggle than by a thousand actions in their favor without that trust. (Freire, 2002, 60)

A lot of things changed with a man named Timothy "Teaspoon" Zulu. On the first day of teaching, Teaspoon was the man that had said to us that he would "never wear a condom" because he was an "African man," and a real African man cannot wear a condom. As soon as I heard this, I lost any faith in him that I had in the first place, which probably was not much to begin with. How was I going to change his mind? Nevertheless, after a couple of days, he would become the most phenomenal teacher I have seen to emerge from our work using the module.

I use the term "emerge" to purposefully denote the fact that the teacher inside of him was always there, but it had now been finally given a chance to come out. Teaspoon taught the module in a way I have never seen anyone teach it before or since. He had charisma, confidence. And he knew what he was talking about. If someone would have told me on the first day that Teaspoon would be the one to get up in front of the executive board-a room full of white men, and teach them the module so perfectly that it brought tears to my eyes, I would never have believed them. When I saw Teaspoon do this, I had two feelings: pride and surprise. Pride because I was so proud of what he was accomplishing, and surprise because I had such little faith in him to begin with that I was surprised at what he accomplished. Nevertheless after the feeling of surprise had left, a little bit of faith came to take its place. Teaspoon had proven me wrong, and shown me that I should have had faith from the beginning.

Through these experiences, I have come to see that faith is not a matter of science or religion, it is a matter of choice. I can choose to have faith in the people I work with, and it will help them and me in the long run. When I met Mr. Ahmed Kathrada the other day, he said some of the most [profound words that I have ever heard: "there is no such thing as defeat if you are fighting for a just cause". I believe this means that there is absolutely no harm, but only good, in believing in people, trusting them, and putting your faith in them. It is a just cause to educate, and especially to empower, and thus no defeat may come from any endeavor to do so. In addition, I have learned from these experiences that I should not need proof to have faith in something. It is quite arrogant to not believe in something that cannot be proven, for who am I to decide what "proof" is? And I know that as a white person, I have been socially trained to be doubtful of black people and their capabilities. However, I never knew, or possibly wanted to believe, how much this social training really manifested itself in my daily life. I now see it is my responsibility to overcome this, and to have faith in people, for as Freire has so poignantly said, the person who works for the liberation of an oppressed group but continues to regard them as totally ignorant, is doing nothing but false generosity.

HIV AIDS and Impact of the Pedagogy of Action

These voices articulate the impact of the pedagogy of action. It is the immediate response to problem posing education, which is a method not only for the community but also for those in higher education. To challenge the acquisition of knowledge at the university level is particularly important for those coming from marginalized communities and those who are unconscious of the

consequences of the didactic form of education. It is an ideological position that premises education as praxis rather than education as careerist. Whose responsibility is it to transform the world and to ensure those locked out of literacy and formal education not become victims of their circumstances but rather empowered to act? It is the educated who must do this and it is the institution of education which must develop pedagogies that provide tools to equip the actors for social justice.

Many nongovernmental organizations have been struggling on the front lines with illiterate and functionally literate populations, predominantly the female. The victims of HIV are growing increasingly female and people of color. We cannot wait until these populations become literate. There have been innovative methodologies of empowerment that have addressed the immediate issues of poverty, education, and health. The Barefoot College championed by 'Bunker Roy' is one example.

> The philosophy of Mahatma Gandhi is reflected in the work style and lifestyle of the College. Traditional knowledge, village skills and practical wisdom are given greater respect than paper qualifications, and reading and writing are not seen as essential. "Just because someone cannot read or write does not mean he or she is uneducated," Roy points out. The barefoot approach clearly works, and there are now 20 such colleges in 13 states in India. Plus the college is now involved in training villages from other countries, including Afghanistan, Ethiopia, Bhutan, Senegal and Sierra Leone. "But the real achievement," says Roy," is the process rather than the result." (Milnes, 2006)

The microcredit movement, which started in Bangladesh, also wrestled with dehumanizing poverty by developing methodologies that empowered the very poor to sustain and support themselves ensuring that their integrity was not compromised by systems that undermined their autonomy. Yunus (2001), the catalyst of the Grameen Foundation, has said:

> It is not microcredit alone which will end poverty. Credit is one door through which people can escape from poverty. Many more doors and windows can be created to facilitate an easy exit. It involves conceptualizing about people differently; it involves designing a new institutional framework consistent with this new conceptualization.

The Pedagogy of Action has attempted to change not only the uneducated but more importantly the educated by teaching them the basic principles "of conceptualizing about people differently." They must first respect the uneducated and be given new eyes to see the value in traditional knowledge and practical wisdom. "Just because someone cannot read or write does not mean he or she is uneducated" (Roy). The Freirean theoretical principles used in the Pedagogy of Empowerment, and the Pedagogy of Action were developed to create a body of students who would not only become actors for good in the world but actors on the world stage where these American students must manage the hegemony of their nationality. Problem posing education as a methodology in developing 'HIV education for low-literate people' transformed both students and the communities. It is a pedagogy that has attempted to address the problematics of the privileged who must construe their responses to inequality and social injustice in their own communities and in the world.

Bibliography

Barton, H., Bell, K., and Bowles, W. (2005). Help or hindrance? Outcomes of social work student placements. *Australian Social Work* **58**(3), 301–312.

Campbell, C. and MacPhail, C. (2002). Peer education gender and the development of critical consciousness: Participatory HIV prevention by South African youth. *Social Science and Medicine* **55**(2), 331–345.

CDC MMWR (2008). Analysis provides new details on HIV incidence in U.S. populations. MMWR September, 2008 Fact Sheet.

CDC MMWR (2007). Racial/ethnic disparities in diagnoses of HIV/AIDS—33 States, 2001–2005. *MMWR Weekly* March 9, 2007.

Freire, A. M. A. and Macedo, D. (eds.) (2000). *The Paulo Freire Reader*. New York: Continuum Press.

Freire, P. (2002). *Pedagogy of the Oppressed*. New York: Continuum Press.

Haniff, N. Z. (2004). Privileging literacy: Methodologies developed and used in the Caribbean and South Africa to teach HIV prevention and catalyze community empowerment to low and non-literate populations (oral presentation). American Public Health Association, November.

Haniff, N. Z. (2008). *"Ten Thoughts" Convocation Address GIEU*. Ann Arbor, MI: University of Michigan.

Milnes, A. (2006). Community Hero: Bunker Roy. http://www.myhero.com/myhero/hero.asp?hero=bunker_roy_06 (accessed September 2009).

Yunus, M. (2001). *Banker to the Poor*. London: The University Press.

Further Reading

Farmer, P. (2008). Challenging orthodoxies: The road ahead for health and human rights. *Health and Human Rights, an International Journal* **10**(1), 5–19.

Grobman, L. M. (ed.) (2005). *What You Need to Know to Get the Most from Your Social Work Practicum*. Harrisburg, PA: White Hat Communications.

Larson, G. and Allen, H. (2006). Conscientization – the experience of Canadian social work students in Mexico. *International Social Work* **49**(4), 507–518.

London, L. (2008). What is a human – rights based approach to health and does it matter? *Health and Human Rights, an International Journal* **10**(1), 65–80.

MacPhail, C. and Campbell, C. (2001). "I think condoms are good but aai, I hate those things": Condom use among adolescents and young people in a Southern African township. *Social Science and Medicine* **52**(11), 1613–1627.

Meguid, T. (2008). Notes on the rights of a poor woman in a poor country. *Health and Human Rights an International Journal* **10**(1), 105–108.

Roy, B. (2005). Education international development. http://itc.conversationnetwork.org/shows/detail783.html (accessed September 2009).

Shevchenko, O. and Fox, R. C. (2008). "Nationals" and "expatriates": Challenges of fulfilling "sans frontiers" ("without borders") ideals in international humanitarian action. *Health and Human Rights an International Journal* **10**(1), 109–121.

UNAIDS/WHO Working Group on Global HIV/AIDS and STI Surveillance (2008). Epidemiological Fact Sheet on HIV and AIDS: Core data on epidemiology and response. http://www.who.int/globalatlas/predefinedReports/EFS2008/full/EFS2008_ZA.pdf (accessed September 2009).

Relevant Websites

http://web.mac.com – Sanjit (Bunker) Roy, Design with India.
http://hdrstats.undp.org/en/countries/country_fact_sheets/cty_fs_ZAF.html.

Overview of Lifelong Learning Policies and Systems

D-B Kwon and C H O Daeyeon, Sookmyung Women's University, Seoul, Republic of Korea

Since lifelong learning systems embodying various policies are emerging in a variety of unique contexts, they represent very different perspectives from country to country. This article reviews lifelong learning policy models proposed by Green (2000), including market-led, state-led, and social-partnership-led approaches. Different policy initiatives and/or systems can be deemed to belong to one of three different models, although they may not correspond precisely. This article depicts seven well-known policy examples according to the three models.

Three Models of Lifelong Learning Policy

During the past two decades, the significance of lifelong learning has emerged and many influential policy documents have been released to promote it throughout the world. However, policies implemented in particular contexts according to different rationales yield substantially different results. Consequently, lifelong learning policies initiated by various governmental bodies can be deemed to belong to different types; have different characteristics, emphases, and objectives; and require different kinds of interventions. To sketch out a number of different lifelong learning policies, analytical models need to be selected carefully.

Green (2000) proposes three hypothetical models of lifelong learning policy including market-led, state-led, and social-partnership-led approaches: "some policies stress the role of the market and the responsibility of the individual; some advocate the central role of the state in orchestrating and managing the learning society; others emphasize social partnership among multiple stakeholding" (p. 35). It is acknowledged that the models can be regarded as positions along a continuum.

In the market-led model, there is a belief that lifelong learning is an individual project, and, therefore, the burden of lifelong learning tends to fall on the shoulders of the individual learner. Today's global market forces individuals to take responsibility for their own learning for personal growth and development. Both employers and individuals have to make decisions about what kinds of skills and knowledge should be acquired. In this sense, learning supply through education and training can be decided based on the needs of the market, represented by employers and individuals. In the labor market, employers play a central role in providing lifelong learning for individuals at work (PARN, 2002). As the market has a

more privileged position in this model, the role of the state and civil society is relatively neglected (Rubenson, 2006). On the other hand, there are some weaknesses in this approach: market-led lifelong learning policies can lead to underinvestment, inequality, and low quality (Green, 2000).

The state-led model allows governments to invent lifelong learning systems through legislation, controlling bodies, and related policy activities. The state plays a key role as a planner; at the same time, it can be the primary source of funds and quality control for lifelong learning practice. To accomplish these, the state creates a blueprint that must meet the various long-term needs of individuals, in addition to reconciling the demands of a variety of interest groups. The state regards lifelong learning as a matter of public responsibility. Thus, it tries to create the required structural preconditions, promote well-designed arrangements between organizations and entities, and ensure policy coordination and coherence in lifelong learning (Rubenson, 2006). The state-led approach addresses equity issues for young, old, and low-skilled adults who are at risk of being routinely excluded from society. Such policies reduce social inequality and promote personal development for all. Additionally, a strong link between lifelong learning and labor market policies can be built on this model. The state has strong power to use labor markets and policies to promote human capital through lifelong learning. The state-led policies also have some disadvantages, including "a slow pace of change, less diversity and responsiveness to particular needs, misjudged plans, and bureaucratic inefficiency" (OECD, 1996, recited from Green, 2000: 39).

Another possible model is based on social partnership. This model emphasizes not only individual responsibility, but also the building of partnerships with multiple agencies involving diverse stakeholders. This implies a strengthened public–private cooperation. However, state agencies' participation and coordination are not always required in this model (Schuetze and Casey, 2006). Regardless of the state's participation, agreements or cooperation among social partners can have an impact on lifelong learning and training policies (OECD, 2003). In the 1970s, civil society developed lifelong learning systems for the purpose of reducing educational gaps in society. At that time, the volunteer sector, including nongovernmental organizations (NGOs), played an important role in promoting lifelong learning (Rubenson, 2006). As there is no doubt that civil society cannot exist alone, social partnerships with other institutions are emphasized in policy development (OECD, 2003).

The three models can illustrate the different lifelong learning policies with distinctive features. Nevertheless, it must be taken into consideration that the three models have common characteristics, which can be seen in the state-led model to some degree. The distinguishing characteristics and some policy examples of each model are summarized in **Table 1**.

More recently, Schuetze and Casey (2006: 282–283) introduced four different lifelong learning policy models: (1) an emancipatory or social justice model, which put an emphasis on equality of learning opportunity (lifelong learning for all); (2) a cultural model focusing on each individual's life; (3) an open society model in which lifelong learning is seen as an appropriate learning system (lifelong learning for all who want, and are able, to participate); and (4) a human capital model, which implies continuous work-related training and skills development for a qualified workforce (lifelong learning for employment). There exist many commonalities between Schuetze and Casey's models and those of Green. However, Schuetze and Casey classify policies according to their aims for what the policy is, while Green distinguishes the approaches according to who has the power and who is the main actor with a more holistic viewpoint toward the policy.

Policy Applications of the Three Lifelong Learning Models

This section provides some policy examples with reference to Green's three models from developed countries well known for their lifelong learning strategies.

The State-Led Model

The state-led model has many advantages insofar as it provides a certain degree of consistency and coherence in conducting policy, securing qualifications, and ensuring more equitable opportunities for individuals. Those advantages are found in the countries' initiatives that are introduced below. They vary in the details, but each shares the goal of lifelong learning for all.

Sharing financial responsibility in Japan: Kameoka Lifelong Learning Foundation

In Japan, the central and local governments have legislated strong initiatives to support lifelong learning. For a long time, governmental agencies have promoted lifelong learning by installing facilities and equipment, and by subsidizing learning events. The main responsibility for administrative support of lifelong learning tends to fall to the municipalities. Since the financial base of the municipalities is not sufficient, the National Council on Lifelong Learning proposed establishing foundations to obtain private funds at the level of the local government (Shiraishi, 1998). With this purpose, there are some foundations such as the Kameoka Lifelong Learning Foundation (KLLF).

In 1990, Kameoka City established the KLLF, giving it initial funding. This foundation operates with financial support from the municipality and the management of its initial funds. Although Kameoka City provides financial support, the KLLF is an independent institution beyond the purview of the municipal and other governmental bodies (Shiraishi, 1998). The organization is autonomous in how it conducts the bulk of events related

Table 1 Distinguishing characteristics of respective policy model

Model	Characteristics	Policy examples
State led	Law and regulation Long-term / slow change Equality / accessibility Coherence / consistency Transparency / bureaucracy Equity / control high quality Inefficiency	• Kameoka Lifelong Learning Foundation (Japan) • Ensuring equity for immigrants (Finland) • Continuing vocational education and training (France)
Market led	Market driven / demand led Rapid / short term Individual needs Individual responsibility Employability Flexibility / diversity Inequality / underinvest	• Q-Card at Fraport AG (Germany) • The Credit Bank System (South Korea)
Social partner led	Balance / partnership Stakeholders in different levels Soft regulation / mixture Negotiation Inefficiency Difficulty of cohesion	• Dual system (Germany) • The new apprenticeship program (Australia)

to lifelong learning for citizens, thus enabling it to more easily obtain financial support from other sectors.

In the case of Japan, the government played a key role in developing and funding the foundation at the initial stage, preparing the foundation to develop as an independent organization later by widening its base of financial support from private donors. This project was a part of the government's long-term plan to establish private funding for lifelong learning enterprises at the local level.

Ensuring equity for immigrants in Finland

To ensure equity for immigrants, the Finnish government has implemented many policy initiatives over the past years. As more countries join the European Union, Finland is expected to have more immigrants, and thus shares the necessity of having sound policies that seek to integrate its newcomers. In this context, the Finnish government has launched a variety of programs available to immigrants. For adult immigrants who seek employment, special programs such as language and vocational ones are provided.

Since May 1999, many special programs, for example a 6-month preparatory vocational training program, have been offered for low-skilled immigrants. The program incorporates Finnish language and customs; guidance and some courses in a student's native language; remedial instruction if necessary; support groups of students; tutors; and a personal study plan (OECD, 2005a). This effort aims to reduce unemployment among immigrants by promoting their equality within Finnish society.

The Finnish immigrant policy does have some challenges to overcome, such as inconsistencies in policy implementation, and a lack of programs specifically for low-skilled immigrants. To develop more effective policies for immigrants, the Finnish government has set out a 5-year plan for 2003–08 (Ministry of Education, 2004). The Finnish government puts much effort into pursuing equity and consistency in lifelong learning policy for immigrants. Consequently, the case of Finland focused more on immigrants as an underprivileged group. The Finnish government program examined tries to provide equity and equitable opportunities for individuals, especially for those who could be otherwise excluded from the benefits of lifelong learning.

Continuing vocational education and training in France: Social partnership regulation

France's lifelong education on continuing vocational education and training (CVT) has been in constant change and expansion for almost 40 years, thanks to the 1971 law and subsequent reforms characterized by a state-led system of social partnership regulation. This law insisted on the roles and responsibilities of the various partners in training by instituting a collective financing obligation between social partners (Green, 2000). This regulation took into consideration the promotion of equitable distribution of training costs and achieving the skills needed between social partners. In short, the creation of a huge training market could be achieved under the 1971 law in France (Colardyn, 2004).

For enterprises, the financial contribution was differed from the amount of payroll based on the number of employees. It was a very useful way to obtain equitable sharing of training costs from different enterprises. Such an equitable cost distribution encouraged greater investment in training by employers. At the same time, the state invested much effort on deciding training priorities by forming clubs of providers as well (Green, 2000). Government subsidy for training played a crucial role to overcome market failure in training. As a result, strong links were established between private and public sectors led by the regulation and public authorities.

Under the 1971 law, training became a legal right for all employees, and the responsibility for training was shared by enterprises beyond the government. In so doing, the government had better chance to look at individuals such as the young, women, and older workers. Clearly, many individuals have accessed training; a large training market has been created; and the training supply has improved (Colardyn, 2004). For instance, in the year 2000, there were nearly 42 000 training bodies, as compared to only 25 000 in 1990. The number of trainees has practically doubled in these 10 years, surpassing 12 million in 2000. Employer investment in training continues to increase (Green, 2000) and enterprises have been the major contributors since 1999. In spite of many positive results, several major critical issues can be highlighted (Colardyn, 2004): people who have had higher levels of initial education are more likely to participate in CVT; CVT chances have hardly translated into a higher level of educational attainment such as a diploma.

The Market-Led Model

There is no doubt that lifelong learning is a huge enterprise beyond a government's capacities. In addition, lifelong learning in most countries is more likely to be decentralized. Furthermore, the change of perspective from lifelong education to lifelong learning entails shifting the responsibilities for learning from the providers to the learners. This shift emphasizes the individual's role in the process of learning and deemphasizes the governmental dimension (Schuetze and Casey, 2006). Consequently, the role of employers and individuals in decision making and financing is strongly addressed. The responsibility of individuals for their own learning is emphasized to a greater degree as well. In particular, companies play a more direct and active role in promoting employees' learning in order to obtain greater global competitiveness. Workplaces that support and promote lifelong learning for employees function as good examples of the market-led approach.

Investment on employee training by Fraport AG in Germany: Qualification card

Fraport AG operates Germany's largest commercial airport with 13 000 employees. It regards personnel development as an important factor in corporate success, and has adopted a variety of strategies relating to education and training. Fraport AG introduced a new educational approach in 2000. It developed the Fraport Qualification Card (Q-Card). The Q-Card is a bonus card that the corporation loads with a virtual credit of 600 euros each year. With this card, employees can take courses provided by Fraport College and Fraport Academy. The courses at Fraport AG are not directly required for the performance of their current jobs.

Employees in Fraport AG must invest their flexitime credits from their working time accounts. The program encompasses information technology, media skills, work techniques, and business administration. Approximately 85 different training courses were offered in the first half of 2002 (Wilfried, 2003). As a cost- and time-sharing instrument for lifelong learning, the Q-Card program earned Fraport one of the initiative awards for training and further education given by the Otto Wolff Foundation (Wilfried, 2003). Responding to the demands of employees and the employer, Fraport AG created a motivational system to promote employee learning and provided a wide range of programs to meet the learning needs of employees.

The Credit Bank System in South Korea: Nonformal educational institutions

The South Korean government initiated the Credit Bank System (CBS) in 1998. This essentially allows individuals to accumulate credits from diverse institutions including colleges, universities, nonformal educational institutions, and cyber open universities. An adult student can obtain an associate or bachelor degree depending on the amount of the necessary CBS-approved credits (OECD, 2005b).

The CBS can be regarded as a precondition to realize a society of lifelong learning and open education. It has some unique features that can be discussed in the state-led model. For instance, this system has been run on a strong statutory foundation. The CBS contributes to guarantee educational equity, particularly for the under-educated. The Korean government, together with the National Center for Lifelong Education, screens the curriculum provided by all nonformal educational institutions twice a year and earned credits and/or learning experiences and activities of individuals. These efforts are to maintain and control the quality of the CBS.

On the other hand, the CBS has qualities of the market-led model as well. The CBS policies are more likely to focus on giving individuals more choices from different institutions and diverse learning programs. All types of educational institutions under the CBS need to study whether they should supply market-driven educational programs in order to meet adult learners' demands. Educational institutions that have marketing capability need to promote their credit courses by creating a variety of programs that are required to be endorsed by the government. The CBS should be utilized to sharpen adult learners' competency and employability regardless of their employment status as a way of enhancing the quality of their lives. Consequently, some features, including regulation, equity, and accessibility, which are addressed in the state-led model, are shown in CBS. However, this system still runs on the strong foundation of the market-led model. Compared with the state-led model, this case is more responsive to individual needs and tends to have more flexibility in the modes of provision.

The Social-Partnership-Led model

As most stakeholders in lifelong learning exist outside of governmental agencies, the coordination between various entities involved in policy development and implementation is crucial for overall success (OECD, 2004). However, such coordination does not fall exclusively into the domain of governmental agencies. Nevertheless, there is general agreement that using the potential of existing cooperative mechanisms is a way to build partnerships (Dace, 2003). In current lifelong learning policy and practice, cooperation among various partners has become a prominent international feature. Both cases described below created frameworks for lifelong learning in terms of encouraging cooperation among stakeholders and emphasizing the responsibilities of different partners. In this framework, various stakeholders participated in the whole process of policy development, implementation, and assessment.

Vocational education and training in Germany: The dual system

With the advent of a knowledge-based economy, Germany has recognized the importance of lifelong learning in order to pursue social cohesiveness. In particular, different types of social partnerships have been utilized to share the responsibility for lifelong learning. Among them, the dual system has been recognized as a representative example of vocational training on the social-partnership-led model. The system is called dual because vocational training takes place both in the company and in the vocational school.

Under the Vocational Training Act of 1969, the federal state sets the training regulations by which the roles, rights, and responsibilities of the different partners are determined. Representatives of employers, employees, and educators together with federal and regional state officials are positively involved in an elaborate system of social partnerships (Green, 2000). The system is financed principally by employers, a feature that distinguishes the German system from the Australian and other European models that rely heavily on government funding as well as on wage subsidies. Although the operation of vocational training schools is regulated by the state, a substantial involvement on the part of employers through very active chambers of commerce is taken into consideration as the essential feature of the social-partnership-led model (NCVER, 2001).

The German dual system of vocational training is renowned as an example of social partnership. Within such a system, companies and their social partners play a prominent role as innovators. This system emphasizes collaboration among various partners and suggests co-financing between them. As the state's full financial responsibility in lifelong learning is perceived to be limited, co-financing among stakeholders should be strongly considered. Meanwhile, the dual system itself does exhibit weaknesses, such as inefficiency, because it may take much time to negotiate among the key social partners through a very complex process (NCVER, 2001). To keep the dual system effective and efficient, the government must continue to become more flexible in how it deals with its partners.

Embracing older workers in Australia: The new apprenticeship program

The Vocational Education and Training (VET) system in Australia was created to boost the country's economy, increase employability, and develop a more skilled workforce. Under the direction of the VET, the apprenticeship program has been newly updated to combine training and employment so that people entering an occupation can receive appropriate instruction in the specific skills needed on the job (OECD, 2002). Compared to the previous apprenticeship program, the new apprenticeship program focuses more on supporting and recruiting older workers, recognizing that it is crucial to have skilled workers in the labor market and that older people still remain as key players.

The new apprenticeship program was introduced in 1998, following many reforms of the traditional apprenticeship system. The Australian government created the new apprenticeship center to promote the new program and to provide support services with employers. The government developed specific programs to ensure a more effective implementation of the new apprenticeship. These include the new apprenticeships incentives program to develop a more skilled Australian workforce and the new apprentice support services, a national network that provides support for employers and individuals across the nation. There has been a huge increase in the number of workers in the new apprenticeship program

since it was introduced, from 135 000 in 1995 (OECD, 2002) to 367 100 at the end of 2003 (NCVER, 2003).

Through the new apprenticeship program, the Australian government tries to embrace not only the need of young people to obtain skills, but also the need of older workers to be given opportunities to upgrade their skills. Moreover, the new apprenticeship program makes cooperation among various partners possible so that these partners can meet the demands of individuals and employers. On the other hand, some limitations exist, such as the lack of sufficient training plans and inadequate arrangements for monitoring the quality of training in the new apprenticeship program (NCVER, 2001).

Conclusions

In this article, several examples categorized according to a threefold system of lifelong learning policy models were examined. The KLLF in Japan, immigrant policy in Finland, and CVE in France were introduced and explored as examples of the state-led approach. The examples of the market-led approach included Fraport AG in Germany and the CBS in Korea. Germany's dual system and Australia's new apprenticeship program served as examples of the social-partner-led model. Each country examined has very different lifelong learning policies in its own unique context. In addition, every country was found to have taken various initiatives at different levels including individual, enterprise, and local and central government. Despite the diversity evident in the above examples, it is interesting to note that some clear messages regarding current and future lifelong learning policies can be discussed.

First, an economically oriented mindset has penetrated the policies of almost every country. With the advent of the knowledge-based economy, all countries seem to agree that a shortage of workers with high-level skills or a lack of adequate learning systems puts national economic competitiveness at risk. Lifelong learning systems tend to be a credible way to achieve national prosperity. In looking at the examples illustrating each model, it is found they are strongly associated with basic and upgraded skill-development strategies for individuals. At the same time, policy reports related to lifelong learning are also more likely to express concern for social inclusion, democracy, social equity, quality of life, and personal well-being (Martin, 2000).

Second, cooperation among many stakeholders seems to be an inevitable feature in terms of developing and implementing lifelong learning policies. State-led initiatives are basically the strongest and most effective way toward pursuing lifelong learning opportunities for all. While it provides relatively less accessibility of learning opportunities to individuals than the state-led approach, the market-led approach is also necessary. However, neither state-led nor market-led approaches can fully succeed without collaboration with other partners. In this sense, it is safe to say that countries try to involve relevant stakeholders and boost social partnerships between them. All the exemplary initiatives introduced show that many different parties are more likely to be involved and cooperate for the purpose of building better lifelong learning systems, regardless of the models they belong to.

The third point is related to government intervention. Today's governments face major challenges in extending lifelong learning. The government, even in the social-partner-led model, is found to play a vital role, and its intervention is unavoidable in the field of lifelong learning. Government intervention in most cases involves providing financial support, operating a qualifications system, or organizing networks for the various partners. As seen in the KLLF of Japan, municipal funding was an absolute necessity at the initial stage, allowing it to become an independent organization. The dual system in Germany and the new apprenticeship program in Australia are also evidence of the necessity of government involvement in funding and assessing evaluation. In the case of CBS, the Korean government plays a greater role in monitoring curriculum, earned credits, and learning experience of individuals to control the quality of the system.

Bibliography

Colardyn, D. (2004). Lifelong learning policies in France. *International Journal of Lifelong Education* 23(6), 545–558.

Dace, N. (2003). Towards EFA goals: Situation in Latvia and cooperation in the Baltic Sea Region. *A Paper Presented at Lifelong Learning Discourses in Europe.* Hamburg: UNESCO Institute for Education.

Green, A. (2000). Lifelong learning and the learning society: Different European models of organization. In Hodgson, A. (ed.) *Policies, Politics and the Future of Lifelong Learning*, pp 35–50. London: Kogan Page.

Martin, I. (2000). *Reconstituting the Agora: Towards an Alternative Politics of Lifelong Learning.* In Sork, T. J., Chapman, V. L., and St. Clair, R. (eds.) *Proceedings of the 41st Annual Adult Education Research Conference*, pp 255–260. Vancouver, BC: University of British Columbia.

NCVER (2001). Australian apprenticeship: Facts, fiction and future. http://www.ncver.edu.au/research/proj2/mk0006.pdf (accessed May 2009).

NCVER (2003). Australian vocational education and training statistics: Apprentices and trainees 2003. http://www.ncver.edu.au/statistics/aats/ann03/03annsum.pdf (accessed May 2009).

OECD (2002). *Mechanisms for the Co-Finance of Lifelong Learning, Presented at the Second International Seminar: Taking Stock of Experience with Co-finance Mechanisms.* London: OECD. http://www.oecd.org/dataoecd/51/27/2501342.pdf (accessed May 2009).

OECD (2003). *Beyond Rhetoric: Adult Learning Policies and Practices.* Paris: OECD.

OECD (2004). The thematic review on adult learning: United Kingdom (England). *Background Report.* Paris: OECD.

OECD (2005a). *Equity in Education, Thematic Review: Finland Country Note.* Paris: OECD.

OECD (2005b). *Promoting Adult Learning.* Paris: OECD.

PARN (The Professional Associations Research Network) (2002). Lifelong learning: Past, present and future. *Continuing Professional Development Spotlight*, 27.

Rubenson, K. (2006). The Nordic model of lifelong learning. *Compare* 36(3), 327–341.

Schuetze, H. G. and Casey, C. (2006). Models and meanings of lifelong learning: Progress and barriers on the road to a learning society. *Compare* 36(3), 279–287.

Shiraishi, Y. (1998). Alternative approaches to financing life-long learning. *Country Report.* Japan: OECD.

The Finland Ministry of Education (2004). *Education and Research 2003–2008 Development Plan.* Helsinki: Ministry of Education.

Wilfried, K. (2003). *Lifelong Learning in Germany Financing and Innovation: Report of the Federal Ministry of Education and Research (BMBF) for OECD.* http://www.bmbf.de/pub/lifelong_learning_oecd_2003.pdf (accessed May 2009).

Financing of Adult and Lifelong Learning

Å Sohlman, Ministry of Employment, Stockholm, Sweden

Adult learning is a wide-ranging phenomenon and accordingly its financing. It engages individuals, organizations, communities, and nations. It is pursued for a wide variety of purposes and in a wide variety of ways.

Theoretical foundations for principles of financing adult learning, as well as other types of activities, will be found in the literature of economics. In that literature, market failures are often highlighted as a motive for government funding of learning. However, a more fundamental concern has been social justice and distributional aspects. The market approach has been criticized for being too restrictive.

While economic principles may remain unchanged over time, political practice has to focus on the varying problem areas as they turn up, more recent adaptations to globalization, the knowledge economy, new information and communication technologies, and global warming. Therefore, in empirical practice and studies, different financing mechanisms will eventually be brought to the fore.

This article offers a few introductory comments on financiers and funding statistics. Financing principles and mechanisms are reviewed. In addition, the development of practical financing experiences in the Organization for Economic Co-Operation and Development (OECD) countries is described as an illustration to general funding problems in many countries.

Financiers and Funding Statistics

In most countries, the government is an important financier of adult learning. However, in federal states, not only will there be national governments, but also regional and local governments, each with its special financial responsibilities. Furthermore, within a government often several ministries are involved in the financing of adult learning, typically the Ministry of Education (formal learning including literacy), the Ministry of Labor (training for the unemployed), and the Ministry of Social Affairs (training for other disadvantaged groups).

Most of the public funds have traditionally been channeled to public learning institutions or sometimes to nongovernmental organizations (NGOs). The latter often receive funding from many different sources, public and private, including fees from participants. This sector includes much nonformal learning as exemplified by the folk high schools and study circles in the Scandinavian countries.

The social partners influence adult learning in different ways. An important factor can be collective agreements which regulate employee training possibilities, as in Germany and Austria. Besides that, employers, of course, engage in training their employees often purchased from private providers.

Needless to say, fundamentally, individuals remain responsible for their own education and training, not least the self-directed learning.

Some Statistics

Comparative statistics of expenditure on adult learning are not available. Not even for individual countries do complete statistics exist. (For participation in adult learning comparative statistics do exist (cf. e.g., Kailis and Pilos, 2005 for European Union (EU)-25 participation in both formal, nonformal and informal learning, and the OECD 2006 for nonformal job-related education and training). The most developed financing statistics concern labor market training and private enterprise training (OECD, 2006; EU-RA, 2004). The EU is preparing an adult education survey for 2008, including private costs for formal and nonformal adult education (SCB, 2007). Still, two financial aspects will be illustrated in this section: to what extent are individuals interested in financing their learning, and do governments fund adult training for the labor market.

Private financing

In 2003, the lifelong learning Eurobarometer charted the attitudes of individuals toward financing their own learning. The survey was directed to individuals aged 15 plus in the old EU-15, Iceland, and Norway (Ramprakash *et al.*, 2005).

Overall, 43% of the respondents were willing to pay for their own education and training. This average varied from 33% to 68%. The awareness of the importance and utility of adult learning thus greatly differs even between these European countries. Respondents in Denmark and Iceland were most prepared to invest in learning. Other countries with high figures were Germany, Sweden, and the United Kingdom. In contrast, respondents in Belgium, France, Spain, and Portugal were less willing to pay for their training.

Making a distinction between education for work-related and nonwork-related purposes, on average, there were no great differences. The same countries came out with high figures for work and nonwork training: Iceland,

Norway, and Luxemburg. In case of nonwork, Sweden and Denmark should also be added to this group. For both purposes, a middle group included Germany and Ireland (and Sweden for work purposes). Low investors in both cases were again Belgium, Spain, and Portugal.

Judging from these financial statistics, much more of a learning culture seems to exist in some countries, such as the Nordic countries of Iceland, Denmark, Norway, and Sweden, than in other countries, such as Belgium, Spain, and Portugal, with Germany, the United Kingdom, and Ireland in an intermediate position.

Public financing

For public financing of adult learning, there are OECD statistics for employment training. In 2001, the OECD (2004) concluded that the funds for adult education would, in view of their comparable small share of total education enrolments, at best equal labor market training expenditure. In the late 1990s and 2000, expenditure in support of labor market training ranged from 0.20% to nearly 1.00% of gross domestic product (GDP) in 9 of 25 countries for which data were available.

The 2007 edition of *OECD Employment Outlook* contains financial statistics for as many as 28 countries for the years 2003–05. The figures for public expenditure on training as a percentage of GDP are now spread over:

a low range 0.01–0.05;
a middle range 0.10–0.25; and
a high range 0.30–0.54.

Overall, the financing is now lower than in the 1990s. Moreover, if there are any changes over the 3 years covered in these data, they point in the direction of a lowering of expenditure.

In the low range, we find not only the Central and Eastern European countries such as Poland, the Slovak Republic, the Czech Republic, and Hungry, but also Mexico, Greece, Australia, Japan, Korea, and the United States. In the middle range are not only a number of European countries such as Luxemburg, the United Kingdom, the Netherlands, Spain, Belgium, Italy, and Ireland, but also Canada and New Zealand. On top of the list are the Nordic countries: Finland, Sweden, Norway, and Denmark. Other countries with rather high expenditures are Switzerland, Germany, Austria, France, and Portugal.

Many people seem to be interested in financing their adult learning – in some countries even a majority. Whether they do so or could be stimulated to do so we do not know. However, private interest in financing adult learning and actual government spending on training seem to go hand in hand (cf. the Nordic countries), but at a rather low expenditure level. Only a very small share of GDP is devoted to public spending on learning for the labor market.

Few aspects of the funding of adult learning are covered by statistics. This lack of financial statistics must be a drawback for the development of rational adult learning policies.

Efficiency Principles and Financing Mechanisms

In economic literature, there are two main reasons for government funding of adult learning: distribution and efficiency motives (Barr, 2001; Bohm, 1987). Arguments for governments to support a social infrastructure, including one for adult learning, have also been added (North, 1981; Rosenberg and Birdzell, 1986).

Efficiency

The efficiency, or allocation and economic growth motive, for public funding of adult learning, through individuals, institutions/organizations, or employers, is based on the idea of market failures. For a number of reasons – positive external effects, uncertainty, lack of information, and competition – individuals and firms acting on their own on markets would not achieve enough learning from a socioeconomic point of view. These market failures are often supposed to be more difficult when it comes to basic skills and less so for higher-level competences.

The government may consider financing socially profitable learning investments, that is, investments that are profitable when also social benefits are included. Privately profitable investment might be left to private investors. For tertiary education and certain adult training for the labor market, the arguments in favor of public funding are thus not so strong. Individuals and employers, to a large extent, reap the benefits from such training and should therefore bear at least part of the costs. For basic skills, the opposite is true; the main benefits of having a basically trained and trainable population and labor force are largely social.

Education and training for the unemployed, disabled, and other groups that have problems getting a foothold on the labor market can also be motivated by efficiency reasons. It may be better for society to help unemployed people to find a job. In this case, there are no opportunity costs in terms of foregone production during training.

Some arguments have also been put forward to motivate government funding of training in small- and medium-sized enterprises (SMEs). Much similar to individuals, they may not be aware of the benefits of training and existing learning opportunities and have problems financing training.

Sometimes governments also have to handle market distortions they have created themselves. Taxes introduced for financial reasons may, for example, inadvertently hamper investments in learning. Besides, the government has to carefully choose financing mechanisms not to introduce new distortions, efficiently targeting disadvantaged groups, not crowding out private investments, and avoiding fraud. Selective measures may target specific groups and be cost efficient, while general, more all-inclusive measures are more costly but leave no one out.

Distribution

The distribution motive, for one thing, is also associated with basic learning. In a democratic society, all children should have access to at least primary schooling and in modern societies secondary education is also more or less a prerequisite for citizenship. In the same vein, it can be argued that public funding of second-chance education for adults at these levels is motivated.

In addition, a democratic society should arguably aim at making cultural and humanistic values accessible to all citizens.

From a viewpoint of social justice, investing in young and old people would be valuable. From an efficiency perspective, the government had better focus funding on the learning of young people with a longer time period for reaping the benefits of training.

Infrastructure

The importance of the infrastructure for economic transactions has been highlighted, generally and also in case of learning. It includes basic laws and regulations as well as attitudes and institutions. If one is to rely on markets, there has to be market regulations and surveillance of competition fostering economic security and efficiency in adult learning markets. Information about learning opportunities has to be available. To be able to develop certificates, a national qualification framework may be necessary. Teacher training as well as research and development are also important.

This is not to say that the government itself has to provide all these services. The duty of the government is to ensure that they are available and adequately provided.

The economic literature has produced arguments for certain learning activities to be financed by the government but no exact amounts are prescribed. How to balance investments motivated by social justice, distributional, efficiency, and infrastructure effects against each other and against other types of public expenditure is a fundamentally political or even philosophical question.

Financing Mechanisms

Whatever the purpose of the spending, financing mechanisms have to be carefully chosen according to efficiency properties (OECD, 2000, 2001, 2004, 2005).

Increasing efficiency in direct public funding of institutions

Traditional public service relies on bureaucratic hierarchies, confidence, and consensus. The mechanisms that have recently been introduced in public education and training services to increase efficiency belong:

- different types of incentives, for example, in the form of output-based funding to gain more value for money;
- decentralization of financial decisions, giving more autonomy to education and training institutions that are supposed to have better knowledge about local conditions; and
- competition for government contracts or stimulation of public institutions to rely on tenders – the requirement to buy education and training services from different providers may be linked to infrastructure in terms of lists of publicly accredited institutions and programs.

Education and training institutions may also be permitted to use fees to finance their provision. This can be a way of testing individual demand for learning. For distributional reasons, however, some types of courses may be exempted from fees and some groups of individuals may have a right to tuition-free courses.

Efficiency through partnership and co-financing

Financial co-sharing arrangements can be an efficient way to investigate whether there is any private demand and willingness to pay for certain services. At the same time, the public sector can benefit from private information as to production and distribution alternatives for these activities. Examples are requirements of co-financing from individuals, employers, or municipalities for subsidies to be paid to education and training projects, and formal public private partnerships (PPPs) to finance investments.

Voluntary co-financing schemes can also be introduced mainly to raise private funds for learning, then normally requiring a subsidy element. There may be three-party versions – government/employer/individual – or two-party versions – government/employer or government/individual. Examples are individual development accounts (IDAs) and individual learning accounts (ILAs) with matched contributions by individuals, employers, and the government and publicly supported train-or-pay systems for employers.

Employers can also be stimulated to create sector- or branch-specific funds to finance common training. Such pooling of employer resources for training can be of special interest to SMEs and also an efficient way to handle poaching (in addition, or as an alternative, to pay back clauses in employment contracts).

Parafiscal funds are compulsory measures to raise funds and may, for example, be created by payroll levies on employers, eventually combined with public funding; they are an alternative to taxes. Some part of the funds may be used by the employer himself and some collectively (such as the levy/grant schemes). An additional purpose for such funds may be to raise awareness as well as to stimulate employer interest in training.

Individuals

For individuals, two types of learning costs are involved: direct costs and costs of living. Public incentives for individuals to train – to make up for market failures and handle distributional problems – take many different forms in addition to co-financing schemes:

- *Individual drawing rights, entitlements, or training vouchers.* In these cases, both direct and indirect costs may be covered. These incentives can be targeted and constructed so as to stimulate competition among education and training providers. Such arrangements are often combined with an infrastructure of information, advice, and counseling services sometimes at learning centers where the individual also can have access to accreditation of prior learning, a library, and education at a distance.
- For direct training costs, tax exemption and tax brakes can be used to stimulate participation though, of course, only individuals with a taxable income can profit from such measures.
- For indirect costs, grants and loans, mixed loan–grant models, or income-contingent loans (ICLs) are often available. The ICLs mean that the repayments of the loans are related to future incomes, which reduce individual risks.
- A legal right to training leave where the costs (direct and/or indirect) are supported by the government and/ or the employer (with or without tax brakes for employers) also exists in some countries. Training leave without at least (partial) funding may not be very successful in raising participation.

Training for unemployed people is often free of charge while the individual can live off his or her unemployment benefits. Such training may be compulsory though the individual can have some choice as to actual training.

Employers

Public incentives for employers to undertake training resemble those for individuals. Vouchers, tax exemptions, tax credits, profit tax deductions, and subsidies have been used to stimulate employers to train their employees or make them benefit from training leaves. The idea is that this type of government-supported education and training should have wider purposes than the training the employer would normally be responsible for – basic skills training, non-work-related training, and general rather employer-specific training. The government may pay both training cost and wage compensation to the employers.

Aspects of the learning infrastructure that may interest the employers are easy access to information about training alternatives and flexible training providers.

Historically, government funding of adult learning has been supply oriented, that is, directed toward learning providers in various segments (e.g., further education, labor market training, and culture). Aspects of demand-led, market-oriented learning have been introduced to make the public providers more efficient and involve private providers in traditionally public education and training.

The market-oriented measures are supposed to increase efficiency through a better match between demand and supply and lower costs. Such measures, however, risk introducing segmentation and creaming in training markets reduce access to learning. In tendering, it may be difficult to balance equity, quality, and efficiency.

However, private co-financing has also been introduced to stimulate an overall growth in adult learning investments in light of shrinking public funding.

Learning markets rely on individual choice and competition. On the one hand, this means empowerment for individual actors. On the other hand, it means an alienation from an idealistic search for learning based on a public learning infrastructure.

Policy and Practice in OECD Countries

In 1996, the OECD launched the concept referred to as lifelong learning for all (OECD, 1996). It was motivated by major trends such as globalization, trade liberalization, the aging of the population, the growing ethnic and cultural diversity, the impact of information and communication technologies, and the changing nature of work. It was to address the fundamental objectives: personal development, social cohesion, and economic growth.

Closing the Gaps

A first analytical step was to try to estimate the existing gaps and the costs involved in closing them (OECD, 1996). For adults, this proved to be very difficult but a few examples were given. Scenarios for extending lifelong learning to adults with low literary proficiency, based on the literacy surveys of International Adult Literacy Survey (IALS) and available figures for training costs, were used. For Sweden, the costs were estimated to be around 4% of GDP, in the Netherlands 5%, and in Germany between 6% and 12%.

More cost calculations were produced later on (OECD, 2000). This time they were based on country reports and participation targets. The Netherlands came up with a well-documented assessment. Now closing the participation gaps for adults was estimated annually to require public costs corresponding to 0.3% of GDP. Hungry made calculations both for public and private costs. For public costs, they were estimated annually to reach the level of 2.8% of GDP and, for private cost, 7.6% of GDP.

There seemed to be something like a natural progression. When targets for initial, primary or pre-primary, secondary, and tertiary education had been reached, lifelong learning for adults might be a reasonable target. For countries that had not achieved that stage, the challenges were daunting. For the central and eastern countries, these were also newly (re)discovered needs in response to the transition to a market economy.

Financing Lifelong Learning

Later OECD (2001) publications concentrated on how to make strategies for lifelong learning for adults affordable. Different ways of reducing costs, increasing benefits, and putting incentives to work were scrutinized. Still, the OECD ministers were convinced that the targets could be reached and in 2001 they declared that more resources had to be raised (OECD, 2004).

A project Financing Lifelong Learning was started. Participating countries submitted background reports, were visited by OECD review teams that wrote country reports, and produced material for further discussion.

However, by the mid-1990s it was evident that, although formal education systems were expanding, they were not able to ensure lifelong learning for all. One important shortfall, besides provision for young children, concerned adults, in particular those with low levels of qualifications.

The recurrent education of the 1960s and 1970s had never become a widespread practice. Training markets had not developed adequately in spite of government initiatives to stimulate supply and demand for adult learning. Neither training levies or collective agreements had spurred supply nor had vouchers for individuals or levy-exemption schemes for employers, noticeably stimulated demand.

Co-Financing

Now the OECD narrowed down the perspective. Lifelong learning for adults should not be financed but co-financed (OECD, 2003b, 2004).

Fiscal pressure in the era of global competition made for less public resources and they alone could not provide the necessary funding for lifelong learning. A consequent search for new models of financing investment revolved around the issue of co-financing by individuals, governments, and employers. Various co-financing mechanisms are available for different aspects:

1. *For reducing direct costs to individuals.* ILA and IDA (with matched contributions by individuals, employers, and the government), loans and vouchers to individuals and/or employers (subsidized by the government), and tax policy (deductions, credits, tax-sheltered savings supported by the government).
2. *For reducing individual foregone earnings.* Direct income support (from the government), ILA and IDA (with matched contributions), loans to individuals (subsidized by the government), collective agreements, and time accounts (with or without subsidies by the government).
3. *For sharing risks.* ICLs to individuals (subsidized by the government).

Much of the co-financing discussion centered around ILA and IDA (OECD, 2004). A special network, the European Learning Account Partners (ELAP), prepared a catalog of recent lifelong learning co-financing initiatives (OECD, 2004). The ILA was to be used only for learning purposes, while the IDA could be used for different purposes, including education and training. There were two main arguments in favor of ILA and IDA. On the one hand, they made for three-party co-financing, and thus the possibilities to raise resources might improve. On the other hand, they fitted a desired development away from supply-driven toward demand-driven learning, a strategy with individual needs at center that might motivate poorly qualified and disadvantaged learners to participate in learning.

Besides co-sharing arrangements, another concept was also launched and much discussed at this time, a whole-of-government approach. If resources were to be used efficiently, adult learning policy had to be developed in a coordinate way and government ministries cooperate. The Swedish Adult Education Initiative was mentioned as an example of both co-financing and cooperation as these important learning projects were co-financed by different ministries (OECD, 2004).

However, the ILA never left the preparatory stadium. In the United Kingdom and the Netherlands, they were tried but abandoned. In Sweden, the government had set aside funds for their financing, but in the end no decision to introduce them was taken. In the United States of America, some states have introduced IDA, but they have not become general government policy. (A private insurance company tried to make a product out of competence insurance (OECD, 2004) but it failed.)

There were many concurring problems attached to the ILA. As they generally were supposed to have a wide coverage, they were expensive to governments and at the same time only contained marginal subsidies to individuals. Employers also seemed reluctant to invest in savings accounts that they did not fully control; and as regards less qualified individuals, would they really be interested in these accounts and stimulated by them to undertake training?

Promoting Adult Learning

Parallel to the upcoming failures of co-sharing arrangements, the OECD initiated the Thematic Review of Adult Learning. It ran over the years 1999–2004 and resulted in two publications (OECD, 2003a, 2005) with the telling titles, *Beyond Rhetoric* and *Promoting Adult Learning*. Here, we are back to basics: how to stimulate adult learning especially for the least qualified. This now seemed to be the most pressing challenge in response to globalization and new technologies, given the restrictions to public spending. Equal distribution of skills has a strong impact on overall economic performance, making the labor forced more productive.

The focal point is on:

- financial incentive mechanisms and on policies to increase the participation of low-skilled adults;
- financial constraints to participation by low-skilled adults; and
- institutional arrangements that are conducive to investment by firms and individuals.

Structural preconditions for learning – visibility of rewards, recognition of prior learning, national qualification systems, information, advice and counseling, flexible providers, and one-stop centers – are important to increase the participation of low-skilled adults.

Still, the context of policy fragmentation and the need for an integrated approach to adult learning policies, of course, have to be kept in mind. However, a more realistic aim might be advisory bodies and coordinators suggesting priorities rather than actual whole-of-government policy-making bodies.

The grand vision of lifelong learning for all, where adult learning was identified as an important missing link, was an overarching government approach to achieve everything from social cohesion and inclusion of marginalized groups, to jobs for the unemployed and continuous upgrading of the workforce, to competitiveness in response to globalization and cultural and democratic development, including a responsible reaction to global warming. For adult learning, it has turned into a more realistic, piecemeal approach. Reforms cannot advance ahead of institutional prerequisites, political support, and coherent strategies.

The lessons learned by the OECD countries have proved to be relevant to the post-communist countries in Central, Eastern and Southeast Europe (Gunny and Viertel, 2006) and are certainly also relevant to countries such as Brazil, India, China, and middle-income developing counties. Adult learning has to be tackled to reduce underemployment and informal employment (OECD, 2007).

See also: Adult Literacy Education.

Bibliography

Barr, N. (2001). *The Welfare State as the Piggy Bank: Information, Risk, Uncertainty and the Role of the State*. Oxford: Oxford University Press.

Bohm, P. (1987). *A Concise Introduction to Welfare Economics,* 2nd edn. London: Macmillan.

EU-RA, European Research Associates (2004). *Exploring the Sources on Funding for Lifelong Learning*. Brussels: European Commission, Education and Culture DG.

Gunny, M. and Viertel, E. (2006). *Designing Adult Learning Strategies*. Turin: European Training Foundation.

Kailis, E. and Pilos, S. (2005). Lifelong learning in Europe. *Statistics in Focus 2005/8*. Brussels: European Communities, Eurostat.

North, D. C. (1981). *Structure and Change in Economic History*. New York: W.W Norton.

OECD (1996). *Lifelong Learning for All*. Paris: OECD.

OECD (2000). *Where Are the Resources for Lifelong Learning?* Paris: OECD.

OECD (2001). *Economics and Finance of Lifelong Learning*. Paris: OECD.

OECD (2003a). *Beyond Rhetoric*. Paris: OECD.

OECD (2003b). *Strategies for Sustainable Investment in Adult Lifelong Learning in Education Policy Analysis 2003*. Paris: OECD.

OECD (2004). *Co-Financing Lifelong Learning: Towards a Systematic Approach*. Paris: OECD.

OECD (2005). *Promoting Adult Learning*. Paris: OECD.

OECD (2006). *Education at a Glance*. Paris: OECD.

OECD (2007). *Employment Outlook 2007*. Paris: OECD.

Ramprakash, D. and Wadolkowska, E. EU-RA, European Research Associates (2005). *Private Household Spending on Education and Training*. Brussels: European Commission, Education and Culture DG.

Rosenberg, N. and Birdzell, L. E., Jr. (1986). *How the West Grow Rich: The Economic Transformation of the Industrial World*. New York: Basic Books.

SCB (2007). *Befolkning och välfärd. Tema: utbildning. Vuxnas deltagande I utbildning*. Rapport 2007 nr 2.

Further Reading

Axelsson, R., Westerlund, O., Bjelkeby, Å., *et al.* (2005). *Vuxenutbildningens betydelse för inkomster, rörlighet och övergång till högskolestudier*. Stockholm: ITPS.

Ikei (2004). *A catalogue of recent lifelong learning initiatives 2004. Prepared in cooperation with the OECD*. http://www.oecd.org (accessed May 2009).

Kunskapslyfskommittén (2000). *Kunskapsbygget 2000 – det livslånga lärandet, SOU 2000:28*. Stockholm: Ministry of Education.

OECD (1999). *Education Policy Analysis 1999*. Paris: OECD.

OECD (2001). *Education Policy Analysis 2001*. Paris: OECD.

OECD (2006). *Boosting Jobs and Incomes. Policy Lessons from Reassessing the Jobs Strategy*. Paris: OECD.

Relevant Websites

http://www.ec.europa.eu – European Commission, Eurostat.

http://www.eu.org – EU.org, free domain names.

http://www.etf.europa.eu – ETF, Sharing Expertise in Training.

http://www.ilo.org – International Labour Organization.

http://www.oecd.org – Organization for Economic Co-operation and Development, Financing Adult learning, Home Page; Thematic Review of Adult Learning, Main Page.

http://www.worldbank.org – The World Bank.

http://www.uis.unesco.org – UNESCO Institute for Statistics.

http://www.unesco.org/uie – UNESCO, UIE.

http://www.unesco.org – United Nations Educational Scientific and Cultural Organization.

Provision of Prior Learning Assessment

P Andersson, Linköping University, Linköping, Sweden

Introduction

Prior learning assessment (PLA) is a topic that has emerged as a central aspect of the policy and practice of lifelong learning around the world. The topic is of interest in adult education as well as in higher education. It could be not only a matter of defining eligibility and widening of access to education, but also a matter of assessment for credit so that people do not study what they already know. Further, PLA is of interest in relation to work life, where it could facilitate mobility, competence development, and competence utilization. It is not necessarily always a formal assessment; more informal methods for recognition of and making learning visible (Bjørnåvold, 2000) could be seen as expressions of the idea of PLA.

The provision of PLA differs around the world. This article will not give a description of the provision of PLA in different countries. Rather, the aim of the article is to provide some general perspectives on PLA provision, independent of national context.

Different Terms and Acronyms

There are different terms used around the world to express the idea of giving recognition to prior learning: PLA is used in the United States; prior learning assessment and recognition (PLAR) in Canada; recognition of prior learning (RPL) in South Africa and Australia; accreditation of prior (experiential) learning (AP[E]L) in the UK; validation of prior learning (VPL) in the Netherlands; and *la validation des acquis* (recognition of experiential learning) in France, for example. These different terms will not be elaborated in detail here. Instead, the article starts from the general idea of PLAR to provide a discussion that is relevant for all readers, independent of national background.

The General Idea of PLAR

The general idea of PLAR covers a number of different aspects, of which the most central aspects will be discussed here.

PLA is about giving recognition to prior learning, irrespective of when, where, and how learning has taken place. The prior of prior learning does not prescribe a certain time gap between learning and assessment. It could be a matter of recent learning, but the time gap could also be wide – the basic condition here is the assumption that the individual has present knowledge or competence as a result of prior learning. Where the prior learning was acquired could have taken place in people's daily life, in the work place, or in a foreign country for example, and learning could have taken place in the context of formal education – if that learning has not received relevant recognition – or more commonly in a nonformal setting, thereby giving this learning a more formal recognition.

One limitation in the irrespectivity of where prior learning took place is that the assessment within a course, of what has been learned in that particular course, is not normally defined as PLA. Rather, a second central aspect of the idea of PLA is that it is strongly related to transfer and mobility. PLA should facilitate transfer and mobility of knowledge and of individuals. What has been learned before – prior learning – is assessed to get present recognition. In addition to this transfer in time, PLA is also often a matter of transfer in space. The knowledge that is assessed is not normally developed in the same context as where it is assessed, which lies in stark contrast to more traditional educational assessments where the main object of assessment is the knowledge developed within a certain course or educational program. In PLA, informal and nonformal learning has taken place in everyday life, work life, voluntary organizations, study circles, etc., and is (often) assessed in an educational context. Another example of transfer through PLA is that prior learning could have been formally assessed and certified in one context, but if this certification is not valid in a new context a renewed assessment might be needed, like when professional immigrants come to a new country. Of course, there are exceptions from this transfer in space. Some processes of PLA are, for example, situated in a work place, assessing knowledge that has been developed before, informally, in the same workplace context.

The History of PLA

The idea of giving recognition to prior learning is not new. It has been present in different contexts for a long time, even if these practices have not been given a name.

Although its origins are commonly traced to the post-World War II USA (Weil and McGill, 1989), when returning veterans wanted their skills recognized by universities, RPL is not a totally new phenomenon [...] Rather, it is the formalization and (re)naming of pre-existing practices concerning alternative access and admissions, mature age entry, and so on (Harris, 2006: 3).

Thus, the more explicit ideas of PLA have roots in the post-World War II era in the USA, in the context of giving recognition to the experiences of the war veterans, to help them settle back into a normal life. There are also roots in France, where "[a] law passed in 1934 concerning engineering allowed people over 35 years old with no higher education qualifications, who had worked for at least five years on activities which are normally those of engineers, to gain the official title of engineer through the preparation and presentation of a dissertation based on their work experience" (Feutrie, 2000). In the 1970s, the interest in PLA was growing in the USA, with the idea of social justice through widening access to higher education. In the 1980s ideas from the USA had been transferred to the UK, where PLA moved on to another area, the labor market and vocational training. Aiming at economic development through better competence utilization, methods for recognition of vocational competencies were developed. In France VAP was developed. Of course, the idea spread to other countries too, but the full history of PLA is beyond the scope of this article (for further descriptions see, e.g., Evans, 2000). However, two more emerging aims of PLA should be mentioned: (1) from South Africa, the utilization of PLA in a process of social change (in South Africa, RPL) as a possible tool to give recognition to prior learning and experiences among those with limited access to education during the apartheid era; (2) the identification of possibilities of PLA for developing self-knowledge and strengthening self-esteem (see, e.g., Cleary et al., 2002; Andersson, 2006).

Differing Aims and Approaches

As we see in the history described above, different aims of PLA are discerned: social justice, economic development, social change, and individual development. It should be pointed out that these different aims are parallel to aims promoted in relation to the provision of adult education. PLA should promote social justice, for example, in relation to the admission to higher education – like availability of adult education is a matter of social justice. PLA should also promote economic development, through the process of recognizing knowledge and competence, which results in better opportunities to make use of these in the work life. This is parallel to the provision of vocational education/training for adults. Further, the idea of PLA as a tool for social change, like in South Africa, is similar to ideas of popular adult education, related to social movements with the idea of changing society through literacy

and mobilization, for example. Finally, PLA for individual development is a matter of strengthening self-esteem and self-confidence, which is an important aspect of some adult education as well.

Different approaches to PLA have been typified in different ways. One categorization is between PLA adapted to the system, as compared to PLA changing (or intending to change) the system (Andersson et al., 2003, 2004). Here, system should be understood in a generative way – it could be contributions to changes of the social system as a whole, like in South Africa, or a change of the system of education or of a single course. Among other things, this puts focus on the question of power in PLA provision. If PLA is adapted to a certain system, this means that PLA is based on an established distribution of power, where the assessment is often based on norms and criteria that are rooted in this system. For example, the assessment could be based on the pre-assumption that learning takes place in organized educational processes, rather than through informal processes, which could result in the exclusion of certain knowledge from the process or recognition. The Procrustean RPL (Jones and Martin, 1997) is an example of this type of approach, assessing people as if they were all cast in the same mold.

> According to Procrustes, a ruler in Greek mythology, everyone could fit into his bed regardless of their size and shape. If anyone was too short, he placed them on the rack and stretched them. If they were too long, he would chop of their feet. (Jones and Martin, 1997: 16).

On the other hand, there are approaches that are, more or less explicitly, aimed at changing the system. Trojan horse RPL (Harris, 1999) is a category of approaches that bring new groups into a system, and by taking their experience and knowledge seriously a change of the system from within becomes possible.

There are also other ways to categorize different approaches. For example, the difference between credit-exchange and developmental models is identified (Butterworth, 1992), and another categorization consists of the technical/market, the liberal/humanist, and the critical/radical perspectives (Breier, 2005). These differing aims and approaches have turned up in different contexts during the history of PLA.

A Broad Spectrum of PLA Methods

As mentioned, PLA in a general sense could include a broad spectrum of activities, not only formal assessments but also other types of processes to give recognition to prior learning. On the one hand, some of these activities are formal and standardized, with multiple-choice tests – like scholastic aptitude tests. On the other hand, there are PLA activities that focus on the individual and particular aspects of knowledge, to give recognition to a variety of competencies – for example, in a portfolio. This broad approach to the idea of assessment and recognition of prior learning, focusing not only the assessment *per se* but also recognition in a wider sense, means that the idea covers a spectrum from divergent (exploring and descriptive) assessment to convergent (controlling and examining) assessment methods (cf. Torrance and Pryor, 1998). Another definition of divergent and convergent assessments is that divergent methods focus on what the individual knows, while convergent methods focus on if the individual knows certain (predefined) things. It should be noted that this division between convergent and divergent methods is not a dichotomy. It is rather, as in other types of assessments, a matter of a continuum, where a certain method to some extent is more or less convergent and less or more divergent. However, putting forth this divergent–convergent dimension in the context of PLA highlights the problems in terms of validity that might be the result if the irrespectivity of when, where, and how is taken seriously, unless more divergent methods than in traditional educational assessment are considered. That is to say there will be problems making valid assessments with convergent methods, if the degree of validity refers to the extent to which PLA provides a fair assessment of what has been learnt in different times, contexts, and ways.

Different Methods in Practice

The ambitions of PLA could be reached in a number of ways. Different methods are used in different contexts, and some of these methods will be exemplified here, namely portfolios, interviews, standardized tests, traditional tests, and authentic tests. These methods are, of course, not only used in PLA, but they are also often used in different PLA approaches and illustrate the broad spectrum of PLA.

The portfolio represents a group of methods used in somewhat different ways. Challis (1993) has, for example, identified the difference between the outcome-related and the self-oriented portfolios. In the portfolio, the PLA candidate brings together documentation or proofs of his/her prior learning. These could be formal documents such as grades and certificates as well as less formal documents such as a testimonial from a former employer or an NGO (nongovernmental organization) where the candidate has done voluntary work. Another part of the contents of a PLA portfolio could be examples from your prior production of goods or texts. The proofs could be brought together and assessed in relation to certain convergent learning outcomes, but they could also be more divergent and self-oriented, that is, the task of the candidate in the latter case is to prove the personal competence,

and it is the assessor who might relate the proofs to goals or criteria.

Interviews are used in PLA, for example, as a more divergent starting point to find out the potential of the candidate, particularly when the area of knowledge to be assessed is not given. The interview could result in a mapping of (possible) knowledge and competence, which might be further assessed with other methods that provide more valid proof of the knowledge in question. Depending on what knowledge area the assessment covers, interviews could also be used in more convergent PLA. For example, an oral examination could give a better picture than a written test of what an individual knows in a theoretical subject area, if the knowledge is developed in untraditional ways and without learning the traditional way of presenting it with paper and pencil.

Standardized tests are another method used in PLA. A typical example is a scholastic aptitude test. A multiple-choice aptitude test can be used in the selection of applicants, for example, for higher education. The predictive test assesses knowledge independent of where the learning has taken place. Thus, any prior learning could be important when taking such a test, even if the convergent character of the method means a limitation of what is actually made visible.

Traditional tests – tests (or other assessment methods) used in the school system – could be used to assess prior learning too. However, a problematic issue could be that these tests are adapted to an organized learning in formal education, rather than to more divergent learning experiences from other contexts, which might reduce their usefulness in PLA. It should also be noted that all educational assessments to some extent could be a matter of PLA – as an assessor you cannot know if/what the students or pupils have learned in the class or somewhere else.

Authentic tests are still another group of methods in PLA, aiming at assessing competencies in an authentic or simulated environment. The rationality of using authentic tests in PLA is that the results of prior learning that has taken place outside school are assessed there too. These authentic tests are, for example, used in the assessment of vocational competencies developed in the work place, competencies that in this way are assessed in the original context of learning.

Theories of Learning Underpinning PLA

We can see how different theories of learning explicitly or implicitly underpin some of the different approaches to PLA that are discussed above. Here the portfolio method and the authentic assessment exemplify this and will be related to different theories of learning (these theories will not be described in detail here, but will only be mentioned briefly).

Experiential learning (Kolb, 1984) is the basis of many portfolio methods in PLA. The basic idea is the learning cycle, where concrete experience, observation, abstract conceptualization, and active experimentation, etc., form a process of learning from experience. However, there is a discussion concerning how these methods value individual experiences and knowledge as compared to collective experiences and learning processes. Individual(istic) portfolio methods are thus questioned based on the assumption that informal learning in collective contexts is not valued in a fair way in these approaches.

The idea of situated learning (see, e.g., Lave and Wenger, 1991) is (at least implicitly) the basis of authentic assessment methods, where the ambition is to assess knowledge in the context of where it has been developed and thus is situated. The questions concern if these methods really become authentic and holistic, or if the result is a behavioristic and atomistic approach (the latter seems to be the case when detailed lists of required competencies are the basis of, for example, certain vocational qualifications). These (or this group of) situated learning theories also help us understand problems with PLA in relation to transfer and mobility. From a situated perspective, it is not evident that prior learning from one context could be transferred and having the same value in another context, where the demands are actually different. The differences are related to tools (language as well as material tools) and to the social systems.

The Value of PLA

What is the value of developing different PLA methods? The main value is that PLA identifies the value of knowledge (stemming from prior learning). On the one hand, the knowledge could have an exchange value. When the PLA process results in a formal documentation of knowledge or competence, the exchange value means that the candidate through this documentation, for example, could be admitted to an education/training program, could get a job and/or a higher salary. More informal assessment or recognition processes could of course have similar results as well, where prior learning is given an exchange value. Further, the exchange value of knowledge, identified in PLA, is not limited to the individual level. For example, it might have an exchange value for a company to know, and be able to show potential customers, that there is a high level of competence among its employees. On the other hand, knowledge often has a use value. Thus, PLA is identifying knowledge that is useful. When we are aware of this knowledge, it is easier to use it, to put it into action. This value is also relevant on an individual as well as on an organizational level – the value for the company is not only the exchange value but also the possible utilization of the employees' prior learning.

Critical Perspectives on PLA

The development of PLA has been discussed and criticized from different perspectives. Some of these discussions will be covered here, concerning the situation of prior learning/knowledge, the authenticity of authentic assessments, and the governing character of PLA. For a more extensive discussion, drawing on perspectives from assessment theory, the sociology of education, poststructuralism and situated knowledge/learning theory, activity, actor-network and complexity theory, and symbolic interactionism, see Andersson and Harris (2006).

PLA has been developed in a Western context, with an underpinning perspective on learning as an individual process. As mentioned briefly above in relation to the portfolio, this individualistic approach has been questioned, and not only in relation to the portfolio. The main point in this critique is that (particularly) informal learning is taking place in a collective process, which is better understood in terms of situated learning or situated knowledge (see, e.g., Michelson, 2006). A focus on assessing individuals, and individual learning outcomes, thus means that a lot of experiential learning remains invisible, in spite of the opposite ambition of PLA. The argument is against the Enlightenment epistemology and for a perspective of situated knowledge, or as Michelson (2006) puts it:

> Reinscribed within a theory of situated knowledge, RPL can become a venue for examining how each of us moves back and forth between our own particular stories and the social production that is knowledge and for challenging oppressive taxonomies of knowledge and the power relationships they enact. It can grant visibility to knowledge that is valuable for its divergence from academic ways of knowing, not only its similarity, and affirm knowledge produced outside epistemologically-sanctioned locations, through dialogue within (and, when we are lucky, between) historically-situated communities. (Michelson, 2006: 157)

Are authentic assessments really authentic? As mentioned, some PLA approaches lean on assessment methods that are situated in an authentic or simulated context. The ambition is to assess in the situation where knowledge or competence was developed and is enacted. However, it could be argued that the assessment situation to some extent is artificial rather than authentic, even if it is situated in a context where informal learning takes place, outside the school context. It is not a part of the daily practice to be formally assessed when you use your knowledge (cf. Bowden and Marton, 1998). Thus the assessment results are not necessarily more valid in this case, even if they are viewed as authentic.

Do assessments adapted to the system provide a valid measure of prior learning that has taken place outside this (school) system? This exclusion of knowledge in, for example, the Procrustean RPL has already been discussed above, and is a matter of governing of what knowledge should count. However, PLA is not only governing what knowledge counts. In a discourse analysis of policy on adult education and lifelong learning, PLA is identified as a technique for constructing and governing the adult learner (Andersson and Fejes, 2005). When learning is assessed more broadly, new knowledge about the learners is produced, which could be the basis of a more extensive governing:

> Assessment, including validation, is a technique that colonizes the human as a knowledgeable subject; he is created as a subject by being an object of knowledge production. One way of reasoning about this colonization of the entire subject is the objective of knowledge. Formal knowledge has been, and is, a way of controlling the subject. The documentation in itself is an objectification of the subject and is the starting point from where techniques of governing are set in motion. Knowledge about the subject to be governed is the basis of all governances (Foucault, 1991) and, therefore, informal knowledge has not been given the same attention. What we now see is a trend where the informal and non-formal competence/knowledge should be transformed into formal knowledge. Consequently, this knowledge will also be the foundation of governing and control. Everything you do, lifelong and lifewide, constitutes experiences that are part of the construction of the competent adult. The subject to be governed is constructed as a different subject than was previously the case. (Andersson and Fejes 2005: 610)

Conclusion

We have seen how the provision of PLA has developed in a divergent way – with differing aims, approaches, and methods, more or less adapted to, or potentially changing, the present system of education, and more or less convergent/divergent. A particular approach also means that a certain epistemological position is taken – explicitly or implicitly. Independently of approach, a process of valuing knowledge is enacted through PLA, a process that identifies the exchange and/or use value of knowledge and that includes knowledge stemming from informal and nonformal learning to a higher extent than other educational assessments. However, there are also critical perspectives on PLA. Even if new types of learning/knowledge are included, there are also processes of exclusion present in PLA. For example, PLA has been criticized for its individualistic approach, which possibly excludes knowledge that is developed and situated in collective

processes. This way of defining what knowledge that counts is one side of the coin when it comes to critique of the governing aspect of PLA – the other side is the governing of the adult learner, where PLA means that the process of assessing a broader scope of learning also means that it is governing in a more extensive way as compared to traditional educational assessment.

Bibliography

Andersson, P. (2006). 'Validation': Mobilisation and disciplination. *Journal of Adult and Continuing Education* **12**, 139–155.

Andersson, P. and Fejes, A. (2005). Recognition of prior learning as a technique for fabricating the adult learner: A genealogical analysis on Swedish adult education policy. *Journal of Education Policy* **20**, 595–613.

Andersson, P., Fejes, A., and Ahn, S-e. (2004). Recognition of prior vocational learning in Sweden. *Studies in the Education of Adults* **36**, 57–71.

Andersson, P. and Harris, J. (eds.) (2006). *Re-Theorising the Recognition of Prior Learning*. Leicester: NIACE.

Andersson, P., Sjösten, N.-Å., and Ahn, S-e. (2003). *Att värdera kunskap, erfarenhet och kompetens. Perspektiv på validering*. Stockholm: Myndigheten för skolutveckling, Forskning i fokus, nr. 9.

Bjørnåvold, J. (2000). *Making Learning Visible. Identification, Assessment and Recognition of Non-Formal Learning in Europe*. Tessaloniki: Cedefop – European Centre for the Development of Vocational Training.

Bowden, J. and Marton, F. (1998). *The University of Learning*. London: Kogan Page.

Breier, M. (2005). A disciplinary-specific approach to the recognition of prior informal experience in adult pedagogy: "rpl" as opposed to "RPL." *Studies in Continuing Education* **27**, 51–65.

Butterworth, C. (1992). More than one bite at the APEL: Contrasting models of accrediting prior learning. *Journal of Further and Higher Education* **16**, 39–51.

Challis, M. (1993). *Introducing APEL*. London: Routledge.

Cleary, P., Whittaker, R., Gallacher, J., *et al.* (2002). *Social Inclusion through APEL: The Learners' Perspective, Comparative Report*. Glasgow: Glasgow Caledonian University.

Evans, N. (ed.) (2000). *Experiential Learning around the World: Employability and the Global Economy*. London: Jessica Kingsley.

Feutrie, M. (2000). France: The story of *La Validation des Acquis* (Recognition of Experiential Learning). In Evans, N. (ed.) *Experiential Learning around the World: Employability and the Global Economy*, pp 103–107. London: Jessica Kingsley.

Foucault, M. (1991). *Discipline and Punish: The Birth of the Prison*. Harmondsworth, UK: Penguin.

Harris, J. (1999). Ways of seeing the recognition of prior learning (RPL). What contribution can such practices make to social inclusion? *Studies in the Education of Adults* **31**, 24–39.

Harris, J. (2006). Introduction and overview of chapters. In Andersson, P. and Harris, J. (eds.) *Re-Theorising the Recognition of Prior Learning*, pp 1–29. Leicester: NIACE.

Jones, M. and Martin, J. (1997). A new paradigm for recognition of prior learning (RPL). In Fleet, W. (ed.) *Issues in Recognition of Prior Learning: A Collection of Papers*, pp 11–19. Melbourne: Victoria RPL Network.

Kolb, D. A. (1984). *Experiential Learning: Experiences as the Source of Learning and Development*. Englewood Cliffs, NJ: Prentice-Hall.

Lave, J. and Wenger, E. (1991). *Situated Learning: Legitimate Peripheral Participation*. Cambridge: Cambridge University Press.

Michelson, E. (2006). Beyond Galileo's telescope: Situated knowledge and the recognition of prior learning. In Andersson, P. and Harris, J. (eds.) *Re-Theorising the Recognition of Prior Learning*, pp 141–162. Leicester: NIACE.

Torrance, H. and Pryor, J. (1998). *Investigating Formative Assessment*. Buckingham: Open University Press.

Weil, S. and McGill, I. (1989). *Making Sense of Experiential Learning: Diversity in Theory and Practice*. Buckingham: SRHE/Open University Press.

Further Reading

Fraser, W. (1995). *Learning from Experience: Empowerment or Incorporation?* Leicester: NIACE.

Harris, J. (2000). *Recognition of Prior Learning: Power, Pedagogy and Possibility*. Pretoria: HSRC.

Mandell, A. and Michelson, E. (1990). *Portfolio Development and Adult Learning: Purposes and Strategies*. Chicago, IL: CAEL.

Portfolio Assessment

V Klenowski, Queensland University of Technology, Brisbane, QLD, Australia

Glossary

E-portfolios – A digital collection of diverse evidence of an individual's achievements over time involving selection, design, and reflection for a particular purpose and presentation to one or more audiences.

Portfolio – A purposeful collection of process artefacts and products that involves selection of evidence to demonstrate achievement over time and reflection on the process and value of the learning itself.

Introduction

At a time when global uncertainty is paramount and when a new form or re-form of curriculum is emerging – with content displaced by skills and knowledge acquisition by learning – assessment, too, begins to take on a new form or re-form. The focus for assessment has shifted to that which engages and promotes learning as a process rather than an assessment that focuses solely on measuring and reporting learning as product or score. The use of the portfolio for assessment offers the potential for the process and progress – integral to learning – to be included.

Portfolio use for assessment purposes – at the individual or systems level – to support different kinds of decision, process, or action "for which assessment results are used," has expanded over recent years to include digital media. At present, portfolios are used in all phases of education from early childhood through to higher education and in diverse fields of study such as the arts, engineering, medicine, sport, and recreation. Both students and teachers make use of the portfolio for purposes ranging from improving learning, acquiring and demonstrating new knowledge and skills, to preparing professionally for employment.

This article commences with an analysis of the numerous definitions of the portfolio. An overview of the historical and contextual use of portfolios and the utility of emergent classificatory systems is offered. There has been limited conceptualization and theorizing with regard to the development and the assessment processes of the portfolio and these issues are examined. The article concludes with an examination of digital portfolios and implications for future use.

Definitions

By the early 1990s, the term portfolio had become a popular buzz word in educational contexts. It was first defined as a systematic collection of learned material (McLean, 1990). More comprehensive definitions followed (Paulson *et al.*, 1991; Linn and Baker, 1992; Herman *et al.*, 1992; Forster and Masters, 1996) with the essential features that remain constant in these definitions, including the notion of the portfolio as:

- a collection of student work;
- an opportunity for student selection of items for inclusion in the portfolio;
- active student engagement in the assessment process by demonstrating through evidence what he or she knows and can do;
- student self-assessment on progress and accomplishments; and
- reflection on the process and the value of the learning itself.

The portfolio has also been described as "expansionist" (Mabry, 1999) because of the possibility of submitting a large amount of information and a variety of modes and types of evidence for the assessment of student achievement of knowledge, skills, attributes, or competencies. In this way, the portfolio offers an alternative to more reductionist strategies such as multiple-choice-type testing where achievement is reduced to a score.

Overview

Adult Learning

In an adult learning context, portfolios have been used since the mid-1980s. In England, for example, the field of medical education recognized the value of portfolio-based learning in the professional development of general practitioners, in particular, and for the medical profession, in general. The English National Board for Nursing, Midwifery and Health Visiting developed a framework for post-registration, education, and practice which is used by members of the nursing profession to plan and implement continuing professional education. The portfolio requires record keeping and critical reflective practice and is used as a method of accreditation. The important shift in this context is toward self-directed learning as the learner assumes responsibility for planning, managing, and evaluating the learning.

Serving teachers too have made use of portfolio assessment since the late 1980s. Teachers' competences – defined as their knowledge, skills, and attributes – are performance assessed using the assessment tool of the portfolio. It is possible to assess the level of attainment, the range of skills, and/or the progression achieved. The complexity of teaching, its multifaceted nature, and the qualities of effective teaching can be captured in the portfolio (Shulman, 1998), if the selection framework offers appropriate guidance for implementation of the portfolio and for judging the evidence included.

In the context of teacher education, the use of the portfolio for the assessment of achievements of pre-service teachers has thrived (Lyons, 1998; Chetcuti, 2007). Pre-service teachers use portfolios to develop their personal philosophy of teaching, to record their learning with regard to teaching, to engage in reflection (Zeichner and Wray, 2001, Reis and Villaume, 2002, Groom and Maunonen-Eskelinen, 2006,), and to self-assess (Klenowski, 2002).

Primary and Secondary Education

Records of Achievement (RoA) – implemented in England – were an alternative to traditional forms of assessment in that profiles were used to engage students in dialog about their achievements and to record these in the form of a collection of certificates and/or work samples (Broadfoot, 1988). Arter and Spandel (1992) were the first to provide guidelines to assist in the development of portfolios for teaching and assessment purposes. These included:

- identifying the purpose of the portfolio;
- directions for selecting work samples;
- student participation;
- self-reflection in the purposeful selection of evidence;
- criteria to judge performance; and
- portfolio use to improve and to assess learning.

More specific guidelines for assessing the portfolio developed, in that, the number and nature of the selections of evidence to be included began to be specified to illustrate how the acquisition of certain abilities, understandings, and attitudes related to particular learning experiences could be demonstrated in the collection of evidence.

By the late 1990s, portfolios were beginning to be used for large-scale summative assessment purposes in Vermont (Koretz, 1998), Kentucky (Callahan, 1997), and England, Wales, and Northern Ireland in vocational qualifications programs (Wolf, 1998). Problems emerged from the lack of alignment of curriculum and pedagogy with the purposes and paradigms of educational assessment which included portfolio use. Teachers in their classroom assessment practice need to be aware of the interrelationships of the structure of the body of knowledge, the curriculum design, and key concepts being taught to make effective use of assessment evidence to understand and promote learning.

Developments in the use of portfolios for large-scale purposes revealed a mismatch of policy contexts and assessment and learning paradigms. The tensions arising from conflicting paradigms meant that the impact of portfolio use for large-scale assessment purposes was limited. Teachers found the workload associated with classroom assessment demanding, particularly while simultaneously trying to meet the competing demands of accountability pressures of summative assessment at a systems level.

Purposes

As is evident from the range of contexts in which portfolios have been used, there is not one portfolio – there are many. They have been used for: learning, teaching, assessing, appraising, promotion, and professional development. These portfolio purposes have been described in summative terms of accountability, certification, selection, promotion, appraisal, and, formatively, to support teaching and learning (Klenowski, 2002). However, as Newton has expressed, attempts to classify and simplify can confuse rather than clarify because such classifications can suggest a level of similarity in the forms and function of the assessment used. It may be more useful to consider each purpose and context for which the portfolio is used as a category in, and of, itself.

Numerous classification systems of portfolio use have emerged in the context of teacher education (Hauge, 2006). One such classification includes: a "learning portfolio" that engages pre-service teachers in "authentic enquiry" (Harland, 2005) with regard to their teaching and records progress; a "credential portfolio" for standards-based assessment of pre-service teachers' readiness for certification and a "professional portfolio" of best work samples for interview and employment (Zeichner and Wray, 2001).

In the context of professional education programs, portfolios have been classified into four types: "a dossier portfolio" of stipulated work samples for selection or promotion to a profession or program; "a training portfolio" of collected evidence – reflective of achievements gained in the program; "a reflective portfolio" of best work to showcase the extent of achievements for promotion or further study; and a "personal development portfolio" a record of personal growth and personal evaluation (Smith and Tillema, 2003).

In higher education, four modes of portfolio implementation have been classified: upon admission, during the course, on entry to the profession, and for ongoing professional development (Meeus et al., 2006). The portfolio types are categorized according to the profession-specific or learning competencies they aim to develop. It is the learning competencies of: working independently, planning, reflecting, and modifying behavior that are claimed to add value for continuing learning. The purpose of the learning-competencies portfolio is to foster a self-directed learning process. However, these authors claim that if the learning processes involved in attaining the learning competencies are assessed and the same assessor assesses both the profession-specific competencies and the learning competencies, then tensions emerge. The implications are that, in high-stakes assessment, the purpose of the portfolio must be made clear and if, indeed, progress is to be illustrated and assessed then the assessment criteria must be inclusive of this quality. The ethics of allowing the demonstration of progress in a safe and secure manner needs to be respected.

These classifications strengthen Newton's argument that such schemes need to highlight the differences between and within purposes and supports the need to tailor assessment design to assessment purpose.

Portfolio-Development Processes

Most models of portfolio development include processes such as selection, collection, reflection, and connection. The development of the portfolio involves documenting achievements, judging work samples or artifacts for inclusion, self-evaluation of achievements, analyses of learning, experiences, learning strategies, and dispositions. The portfolio is, therefore, significantly more than just a collection of artifacts or assignments. The portfolio-development processes involved are equally important and need to be recognized. They include: critical self-evaluation, interactive learning conversations, reflection on practice and/or learning, and connection to learning experience, theory, and/or practice. These processes are integral to the development of a portfolio and are common for all purposes and audiences for which the particular portfolio can be constructed.

Selection and Collection

All portfolios include a collection of selected work samples or evidence in support of claims with regard to learning and achievements. The varying portfolio purposes of learning, assessment, or employment require different evidence to be collected and selected. A key property in selecting evidence is the relevance – the more relevant it is, the more useful it is for the assessment purpose (Forster and Masters, 1996).

In designing any assessment task, "fitness for purpose" and the positive impact of assessment on teaching and learning need to be considered (Gipps, 1994). These principles apply equally to the design of the selection framework for the development and collection of evidence for

the portfolio itself. Research into the design of a content-selection framework (Simon and Forgette-Giroux, 2000) for the use of the portfolio as an assessment instrument indicates that showcasing or selecting evidence of one's best work is inadequate. For example, in the holistic assessment of a particular competency, cognitive, affective, behavioral, metacognitive, and developmental dimensions need to be identified in the selection framework with explicit examples of entries suggested. This approach maximizes the potential for the assessment of progress and the processes of learning, yet, students require directions with regard to how to use the standards-referenced and selection frameworks when making judgments concerning their own work and selecting evidence for inclusion.

Reflection and Connection

Portfolio-based learning and assessment is characterized by valuing: one's past experience and learning; autonomy; reflection in the learning process; and the connectivity among experiences, learning opportunities, and role requirements. The importance of reflection in learning is well documented in directed and self-directed contexts (Boud *et al.*, 1985; Moon, 1999). The reflective statements or commentaries included in the portfolio are intended to illustrate how students connect their learning and/or their professional experience with the theoretical understanding gained from course work, assessment tasks, critical readings, writings, and/or research. However, such reflection has proven to be a problematic process. Students need guidelines – which specify the nature, scope, purpose, and audience when writing self-reflective statements.

Clarification is also needed regarding the value of this process in its intended positive contribution to learners in supporting them to develop confidence and competence, in the tensions created between academic and professional knowledge, and between learning and understanding of the process of becoming a professional. Reflecting on that process is to be valued and supported in the pursuit of critical, learner agency and metacognitive development. However, achieving the full value of portfolio-based learning and assessment requires teachers or mentors who have particular skills (Pietroni and Millard, 1997). They work with students or colleagues in portfolio development to facilitate the important intellectual work of moving beyond description – of what has been learnt and achieved – to analysis of what further learning and education needs to occur. The importance of critical reflection in the learning process and its role in new learning is realized through portfolio use.

Assessment and Teacher Judgment

Summative assessment of the portfolio is designed to provide quality information with regard to student learning in a timely, manageable, and inexpensive manner without impacting negatively on teaching and learning. It is high stakes and occurs for certification and selection in a range of contexts. The selection or certification process can provide the individual with a statement of achievement for entry into a profession, to further education, or it can even lead to promotion. An adequate level of reliability is, therefore, required for comparability purposes. Consistency of standards, and consistent grading, must be implemented to ensure equity and fairness and to ensure quality in the overall assessment process and outcomes. Specified standards and contents frameworks aim to achieve a reasonable degree of reliability and to ensure a level of confidence in the results and comparability across institutions. The standards framework and attributes to be assessed are generally specified by awarding or professional bodies such as: teacher education (Lyons, 1998), higher education (Fry et al., 1999), and doctoral studies (Shulman et al., 2006). Professional development for continuing learning and development is also assessed using portfolios (Baume and Yorke, 2002; Orland-Barak, 2005; Jackson and Ward, 2004; Hay and Moss, 2005).

When assessing the portfolio summatively, the consistency of approach to the assessment tasks and consistency of teacher judgment in assessing the portfolio of work, using the standards framework, need to be monitored. Replicability and comparability are the key qualities (Gipps, 1994). Professional judgment in the use of criteria and standards for assessment is developed through moderation practice. Such professional collaboration helps to maintain consistent application of standards.

Holistic or analytic approaches can be adopted to assess the portfolio of work. In the latter approach, different aspects of the portfolio are assessed independently and judgments with regard to the quality of the parts are aggregated to obtain a total grade. Holistic approaches require a judgment with regard to the overall quality with attention to how the individual tasks or samples of work contribute to the whole. The multiple entries of the portfolio require the assessor to engage in iterative and cyclical processing sequences which differ to the assessment of a single work. Major threats to validity and reliability can occur when assessors omit the use of important criteria provided, "construct underrepresentation" or give particular weighting to criteria while not attending to the given criteria with equal evaluative attention, "construct-irrelevant variance" (Messick, 1995).

The use of portfolios for formative purposes to enhance learning and for professional development is well established. One of the major advantages of the portfolio for learning purposes is the opportunity it provides to monitor development and for teachers and instructors to provide feedback to the learner to fulfill a transformative function in the learning. To achieve this, there is a need for substantive conversation concerning the qualities of the learning. This implies a facilitator role for mentor or teacher. Student self-reflection – promoted through conversation – requires interactive dialog that facilitates student recognition of strengths or weaknesses in their learning. Insights regarding how to improve are an intended consequence of this process. Thus, the portfolio provides the structure and process to facilitate understanding of one's own learning or professional practice (Klenowski et al., 2006) and for increasing one's self-regulating capacity.

Research on how best to support learning in professional contexts and how to assess the rich, qualitative materials in portfolios concludes that a hermeneutic, interpretative approach is appropriate (Tigelaar et al., 2005).

The resource implications of this approach are acknowledged any method for interpreting portfolio evidence in an equitable and responsible manner will require time and substantive conversation. Professional dialog in the context of teacher education, for instance, is fundamental for realizing the potential of this form of assessment and for engaging pre-service teachers in understanding deeply the meaning of effective teaching.

The problematic nature of the use of reflective statements in portfolios for learning and professional development has been researched and is more apparent when portfolios are assessed summatively (Chetcuti et al., 2006; Orland-Barak, 2005). Students are reluctant to include authentic reflections that illustrate their areas of weakness or gaps in learning and can revert to "tactical writing" to convince the assessor of their achievements (Meeus, et al., 2006). Students will not be inclined to reveal their failures (Smith and Tillema, 2003). Such reflections incorporated in the portfolio will not be reliable or genuine.

E-Portfolios

Electronic portfolios – also referred to as e-portfolios, digital portfolios, or webfolios – were developed in the early 1990s (Barrett and Wilkerson, 2004). The term e-portfolio has been adopted as an umbrella concept (Siemens, 2004) to include webfolios as in the concept of e-learning which includes web-based training. The characteristics that distinguish the e-portfolio from the paper-based portfolio are electronic access and digitization. Webfolios are static websites that make use of links to HTML-driven sites; however, e-portfolios are dynamic. They have been defined by the EDUCAUSE National Learning Infrastructure Initiative (NLII, 2003) as:

> a digital collection of authentic and diverse evidence, drawn from a larger archive representing what a person or organisation has learned over time on which the person or organisation has reflected, and designed for presentation to one or more audiences for a particular rhetorical purpose.

This larger archive can also be considered an e-portfolio that contains multiple views of the contents constructed for a range of audiences. The multiple views relate to the purpose and the reader of the e-portfolio. For instance, the e-portfolio can be developed to demonstrate achievement, to meet formative or summative assessment requirements, or be used in searching for a job. The collection includes evidence of learning and performance, reflections or interpretations on the evidence, and representations of relationships between and among evidence, interpretations and evaluation criteria (NLII, 2003). An e-portfolio-management platform supports the learner in organizing the archive and enables connection to services that facilitate transactions and processes such as getting feedback from peers or cross-referencing of evidence with competency or professional standards.

Given the context of the knowledge society, the changing nature of the curriculum and of learning the e-portfolio offers features that address the changing needs of learners themselves (Siemans, 2004). E-portfolios are multipurpose, adaptable, interactive, transportable, and searchable (Cotterill *et al.*, 2004). The digital nature enables the adoption of a range of structures, facilitates cross-referencing, reduces administration, and allows secure access from a range of locations. Such features provide a rich learning tool for the learner to demonstrate their knowledge and understanding through evidence that can take the form of work samples, artifacts, or illustrations of development and learning including feedback from teachers, self-, and peer-assessments. The use of multiple media to facilitate, enhance, and demonstrate learning is epitomized in the e-portfolio.

At present, learning takes place in contexts that are no longer confined to the traditional, formal education settings. Learning on the job – in communities and through networks (Siemens, 2004) – is common and it is technology that has aided learning at a distance and in remote locations. With online teaching and learning becoming increasingly popular (Russell and Finger, 2005), there are important implications for teacher education and development. Teacher educators must teach pre-service teachers to be competent in the use of information and communication technologies (ICTs). It is, therefore, not surprising that the growth in the use of e-portfolios has occurred first in the contexts of teacher and higher education (Lane, 2007; Lind, 2007; Mason *et al.*, 2004).

Research has indicated that e-portfolios offer certain benefits to learners in that they provide valuable opportunities for reflective learning (Zubizarreta, 2004) and encourage students' active engagement with learning. The interactive nature of the e-portfolio assists learners to make connections between formal and informal learning experiences and among components within a subject, across subjects within a program, between field experiences, and components of programs. Young learners, at present, who have a confidence with the use of multimedia are multi-processors and are more comfortable with a hyperlinked approach to thinking, as opposed to one that is linear (Brown, 2002). For such a learner, the advantages are many as they manage personal knowledge, the growth of their learning, planning, and goal setting, and take control over their learning history (Siemens, 2004). Meta-learning (Klenowski *et al.*, 2006) is facilitated when, in this context, the learner has the opportunity to review the learning in the e-portfolio and learns about their own learning – which can then be applied to future learning. It is the identification of new insights and understandings that brings about the changes.

The Web enables the user to be both receiver and sender of broadcast, which has been described as both push *and* pull (Brown, 2002). In this new learning context, it is possible for young people to engage in their preferred way of learning because multiple intelligences are honored in this medium. Students acquire skills in multiple literacies (text, screen, and image) and learn how to navigate through multiple-media genres and complex information spaces. Unlike the formal learning environments of the previous generation, young people today are engaging in discovery learning when browsing the digital "libraries" and the information available on the Web (Brown, 2002). The skills of judgment, discernment, and synthesis become crucial.

Research – in the context of teacher education – suggests that e-portfolios can help enhance pre-service teachers' meta-abilities. These include: higher-order cognitive skills, self-knowledge, personal resilience, and management of knowledge and time. Another finding suggests that a greater sense of interconnection seems to be fostered for pre-service teachers across and between disciplines and between theory and practice. There appears to be a greater acceptance for responsibility to plan, develop, and evaluate one's own learning outcomes and achievements (Broadbent, 2005).

Some of the principles of electronic portfolios as identified by (Cotterill, 2004) are as follows. E-portfolios have significant advantages over those that are paper based, they need to be considered in a social context of human processes, they must have clarity of purpose, they should be learner-focused, integral to the learning process, support lifelong learning, continued research and evaluation is essential, and one particular view will not suit all purposes.

Some of the limitations of the e-portfolio are that they preclude the inclusion of physical objects that may have been constructed by the student and, in terms of equity, students will have different levels of information technology (IT) experience and varied access to computers and Internet while the reliability of some IT systems could present another weakness.

Conclusion

While the potential value of portfolios remains significant in addressing the varied learning needs of students and professionals a number of uncertainties still remain. Further research to guide the use of portfolios for assessment needs to be conducted. There is also a need for further development of conceptual frameworks to guide the pedagogy and assessment of the portfolio that engage students in the negotiation of these. The emergence of the e-portfolio offers exciting opportunities for promoting learning through assessment that values reflection, participation, and narrative; however, research and development will remain a priority in this creative, digital, context.

Bibliography

Arter, J. A. and Spandel, V. (1992). Using portfolios of student work in instruction and assessment. *Educational Measurement: Issues and Practice* **11**, 36–44.

Barrett, H. and Wilkerson, J. (2004). Conflicting paradigms in electronic portfolio approaches. http://electronicportfolios.com/systems/paradigms.html (accessed September 2009).

Baume, D. and Yorke, M. (2002). The reliability of assessment by portfolio on a course to develop and accredit teachers in higher education. *Studies in Higher Education* **27**, 7–25.

Boud, D., Keogh, R., and Walker, D. (eds.) (1985). *Reflection: Turning Experience into Learning*. London: Kogan Page.

Broadbent, C. (2005). Use of digital professional portfolios to enhance pre-service teachers' meta-abilities. In Cooper, M. (ed.) *Teacher Education: Local and Global*, proceedings of the Australian Teacher Education Association, pp 70–76.

Broadfoot, P. (1988). Profiles and records of achievement: A real alternative. *Educational Psychology* **8**, 291–297.

Brown, J. S. (2002). *Growing up Digital: How the Web Changes Work, Education and the Ways People Learn*. United States Distance Learning Association. http://www.usdla.org/html/journal/FEB02_Issue/article01.html (accessed September 2009).

Callahan, S. (1997). Tests worth taking? Using portfolios for accountability in kentucky. *Research in the Teaching of English* **31**(3), 295–336.

Chetcuti, D. (2007). The use of portfolios as a reflective learning tool in initial teacher education: A Maltese case study *Reflective Practice* **8**, 137–149.

Chetcuti, D., Murphy, P., and Grima, G. (2006). The formative and summative uses of a professional development portfolio: A Maltese case study. *Assessment in Education, Principles, Policy and Practice* **13**, 97–112.

Cotterill, S. (2004). Electronic portfolios for formative and summative assessment, BeSST Conference. http://www.eportfolios.ac.uk/references/?display=eportfolios (accessed September 2009).

Cotterill, S., McDonald, T., Drummond, P., and Hammond, G. (2004). Design, implementation and evaluation of a 'generic' eportfolio: The Newcastle experience. *Paper Presented at the ePortfolio 2004 Conference* in LaRochelle. http://www.eportfolios.ac.uk (accessed September 2009).

Forster, M. and Masters, G. (1996). *Portfolios*. Melbourne, VIC: Australian Council for Educational Research.

Fry, H., Ketteridge, S., and Marshall, S. (1999). *A Handbook for Teaching and Learning in Higher Education*. London: Kogan Page.

Gipps, C. (1994). *Beyond Testing: Towards a Theory of Educational Assessment*. London: Falmer.

Groom, B. and Maunonen-Eskelinen, I. (2006). The use of portfolios to develop reflective practice in teacher training: A comparative and collaborative approach between two teacher training providers in the UK and Finland. *Teaching in Higher Education* **11**, 291–300.

Harland, T. (2005). Developing a portfolio to promote authentic enquiry in teacher education. *Teaching in Higher Education* **10**, 326–337.

Hauge, T. E. (2006). Portfolios and ICT as means of professional learning in teacher education. *Studies in Educational Evaluation* **32**, 23–36.

Hay, T. and Moss, J. (2005). *Portfolios, Performance and Authenticity*. Frenchs Forest: Pearson Education Australia.

Herman, J. L., Aschbacher, P. R., and Winters, L. (1992). *A Practical Guide to Alternative Assessment*. Alexandria, VA: Association for Supervision and Curriculum Development.

Jackson, N. and Ward, R. (2004). A fresh perspective on progress files – a way of representing complex learning and achievement in higher education. *Assessment and Evaluation in Higher Education* **29**(4), 423–449.

Klenowski, V. (2002). *Developing Portfolios for Learning and Assessment: Processes and Principles*. London: RoutledgeFalmer.

Klenowski, V., Askew, S., and Carnell, E. (2006). Portfolios for learning, assessment and professional practice in higher education. *Assessment and Evaluation in Higher Education* **31**, 267–286.

Koretz, D. (1998). Large-scale portfolio assessments in the US: Evidence pertaining to the quality of measurement. *Assessment in Education: Principles, Policy and Practice* **5**(3), 309–334.

Lane, C. (2007). The power of 'e': Using ePortfolios to build online presentation skills. *Innovate* **3**(3). http://electronicportfolio.pbworks.com/f/reading03presentationskills.pdf (accessed September 2009).

Lind, V. (2007). ePortfolios in music education. *Innovate* **3**(3). http://www.innovateonline.info/index.php?view=article&id=351.

Linn, R. and Baker, E. (1992). Portfolios and accountability. *CRESST Line Fall*, 1–2.

Lyons, N. (1998). *With Portfolio in Hand: Validating the New Teacher Professionalism*. New York: Teachers College Press.

Mabry, L. (1999). *Portfolios Plus: A Critical Guide to Alternative Assessment*. Thousand Oaks, CA: Corwin.

Mason, R., Pegler, C., and Weller, M. (2004). E-portfolios: An assessment tool for online courses, *British Journal of Educational Technology* **35**, 717–727.

McLean, L. (1990). Time to replace the classroom test with authentic measurement. *Alberta Journal of Educational Research* **36**, 78–84.

Meeus, W., Van Petegem, P., and Van Looy, L. (2006). Portfolio in higher education: Time for a classificatory framework. *International Journal of Teaching and Learning in Higher Education* **17**(12), 127–135.

Messick, S. (1995). Validity of psychological assessment: Validation of inferences from persons' responses and performances as scientific enquiry into score meaning. *American Psychologist* **50**, 741–749.

Moon, J. A. (1999). *Reflection in Learning and Professional Development: Theory and Practice*. London: Kogan Page.

NLII (National Learning Infrastructure Initiative) (2003). http://www.educause.edu (accessed September 2009).

Orland-Barak, L. (2005). Portfolios as evidence of reflective practice: What remains untold. *Educational Research* **47**, 25–44.

Paulson, F. L., Paulson, P. R., and Meyer, C. (1991). What makes a portfolio a portfolio? *Educational Leadership* **48**, 60–63.

Pietroni, R. and Millard, L. (1997). Portfolio-based learning. In Pendleton, D. and Halser, J. (eds.) *Professional Development in General Practice*, pp 81–93. Oxford: Oxford University Press.

Reis, N. and Villaume, S. (2002). The benefits, tensions, and visions of portfolios as a wide-scale assessment for teacher education. *Action in Teacher Education* **23**, 10–17.

Russell, G. and Finger, G. (2007a). ICTs and tomorrow's teachers: Informing and improving the ICT undergraduate experience. In Townsend, T. and Bates, R. (eds.) *Handbook of Teacher Education: Globalization, Standards and Professionalism in Times of Change*, pp 711–724. Dordrecht: Springer.

Russell, G. and Finger, G. (2007b). Teacher education futures: Implications of teaching and learning in an online world. In Townsend, T. and Bates, R. (eds.) *Handbook of Teacher Education: Globalization, Standards and Professionalism in Times of Change*, pp 625–640. Netherlands: Springer.

Shulman, L. (1998). Teacher portfolios: A theoretical activity. In Lyons, N. (ed.) *With Portfolio in Hand: Validating the New Teacher Professionalism*, pp 23–37. New York: Teachers College Press.

Shulman, L. S., Golde, C. M., Bueschel, A. C., and Garabedian, K. J. (2006). 'Reclaiming education's doctorates: A critique and a proposal. *Educational Researcher* **35**, 25–32.

Siemans, G. (2004). ePortfolios. http://www.elearnspace.org/Articles/portfolios.htm (accessed March 2009).

Siemens, G. (2004). ePortfolios. http://www.elearnspace.org/Articles/eportfolios.htm (accessed September 2009).

Simon, M. and Forgette-Giroux, R. (2000). Impact of a content selection framework on portfolio assessment at the classroom level. *Assessment in Education: Principles, Policy and Practice* **7**, 84–101.

Smith, K. and Tillema, H. (2003). Clarifying different types of portfolio use. *Assessment and Evaluation in Higher Education* **28**, 625–648.

Tigelaar, D., Dolmans, D., Wolfhagen, I., and van der Vleuten, C. (2005). Quality issues in judging portfolios: Implications for organizing teaching portfolio assessment procedures. *Studies in Higher Education* **30**(5), 595–610.

Wolf, A. (1998). Portfolio assessment as national policy: The National Council for Vocational Qualifications and its quest for a pedagogical revolution. *Assessment in Education: Principles, Policy and Practice* **5**(3), 413–445.

Zeichner, K. and Wray, S. (2001). The teaching portfolio in US teacher education programs: What we know and what we need to know. *Teaching and Teacher Education* **17**, 613–621.

Zubizarreta, J. (2004). *The Learning Portfolio: Reflective Practice for Improving Student Learning*. Bolton, MA: Anker.

Participation in Adult Learning

R Desjardins, Danish University of Education, Copenhagen, Denmark

Introduction

Participation research is concerned primarily with three overarching questions: What is the extent of participation? Who is participating? Why are certain people or groups participating either more or less, or not at all? Traditionally, the focus has been on adult education and training (AET), rather than a broader notion of adult learning. In this article, a distinction is made between AET and informal learning where possible.

What Is the Extent of Participation?

Adult Education and Training

Participation rates based on the International Adult Literacy Survey (IALS; 1994–98) are reported in **Table 1**. **Tables 2(a)** and **2(b)** supplement with other international comparative data sources, and although the data from the alternative sources are not strictly comparable, the overall patterns are fairly consistent. In general, it can be inferred that rates vary substantially across countries, falling into four broad groups:

- close to or exceeding 50% – the Nordic countries include Denmark, Finland, Iceland, Norway, and Sweden;
- between 35% and 50% – countries of Anglo-Saxon origin such as Australia, Canada, New Zealand, the United Kingdom, and the United States as well as a few of the smaller Northern European countries such as Luxembourg, the Netherlands, and Switzerland;
- between 20% and 35% – this group features the remaining Northern European countries such as Austria, Belgium (Flanders), and Germany, some Eastern European countries such as Czech Republic and Slovenia, and some Southern European countries such as France, Italy, and Spain; and
- consistently below 20% – some Southern European countries such as Greece and Portugal, some additional Eastern European countries such as Hungary and Poland, and the only South American country where comparable data are available, Chile.

However, according to the 2003 data from the Adult Literacy and Lifeskills Survey (ALLS), Canada, Switzerland, and the United States appear to have climbed into the exceeding 50% category.

The mean number of hours per adult is also reported in **Table 1**. This combines the incidence and volume of AET and thus offers a more comprehensive measure of the total effort. Denmark, Finland, and New Zealand report an average of over 100 h of AET per adult over a 12-month period – this is equivalent to every adult aged 16–65 years spending over 2.5 working weeks in AET per year. Countries featuring high participation but low average volume display comparatively lower adult learning per capita. Switzerland, the United Kingdom, and the United States have participation rates around 35–50% but, after adjusting for low volume, countries in the 20–35% range, such as Ireland and Slovenia, surpass them in their total AET effort. The former are considered to follow an extensive model, in which a fairly low volume is provided to a large number of adults, whereas the latter are considered to follow an intensive model, where provision is concentrated on fewer people (OECD, 2003a).

Changes in AET

Many national data sources point toward a general increasing trend in AET participation over the last 25 years. This is mostly attributed to the rising concern for human capital over the last decades since increases in AET for job-related reasons account for much of the rise since the early 1980s (Boudard and Rubenson, 2003: 267). More recent trend data from the European Union Labour Force Survey (ELFS) reveal a mixed pattern – participation rates appear to have generally increased between 1995 and 2000; however, this does not hold for all countries (OECD, 2003a: 39).

Types of AET

It can be seen from the IALS data in **Table 1** that job-related AET is dominant. Personal- and social-related AET can also play a substantial role. Comparatively high rates of participation in nonjob related AET are reported in Finland, the Netherlands, and Switzerland. It is, however, difficult to distinguish between different types of AET. Often, this is assessed on the basis of individuals' reasons for participating. However, Rubenson (2001) showed that there are many reasons for participation and that these are interrelated. Further, Desjardins *et al.* (2006) demonstrated that the way in which questions are phrased has implications for interpreting the complex motivations associated with participation. Ideally, surveys should not only permit respondents to state a number of different reasons for participating, but also ask them to rank them according to importance.

Table 1   Participation in adult education and training and average number of hours of participation in the previous year, by type of training, population aged 16–65 years[a]

	Total AET			Job-related AET			Nonjob-related AET		
	Participation rate	Mean number of hours per participant	Mean number of hours per adult	Participation rate	Mean number of hours per participant	Mean number of hours per adult	Participation rate	Mean number of hours per participant	Mean number of hours per adult
International Adult Literacy Survey (IALS), 1994–98									
Australia	36.4	179.4	65.4	31.2	165.4	51.6	8.2	229.5	18.8
Belgium (Flanders)	20.9	125.4	26.2	12.5	103.7	13.0	8.1	90.7	7.3
Canada	36.9	230.8	85.2	30.0	236.1	70.9	9.9	179.9	17.8
Chile	19.5	235.7	45.9	11.2	157.0	17.5	9.2	330.1	30.3
Czech Republic	26.4	23.4	6.2	19.8	45.5	9.0	8.0	83.2	6.6
Denmark	56.9	219.3	124.7	48.6	213.6	103.9	13.0	148.5	19.2
Finland	58.4	207.8	121.3	39.6	205.5	81.3	28.6	195.9	55.9
Hungary	19.8	177.4	35.2	13.3	156.5	20.7	7.3	153.6	11.2
Ireland	23.5	262.1	61.6	17.3	262.1	45.3	6.8	98.3	6.7
Italy	22.6	192.8	43.5	16.1	133.6	21.5	7.9	282.6	22.4
Netherlands	37.9	239.8	91.0	24.9	266.0	66.3	16.7	176.8	29.6
New Zealand	47.9	222.9	106.7	39.4	223.2	87.9	12.8	176.9	22.6
Norway	47.0	190.3	89.4	42.7	167.5	71.4	6.7	322.3	21.7
Poland	14.7	151.3	22.3	9.7	119.6	11.6	5.5	165.0	9.0
Portugal	14.2	–	–	–	–	–	–	–	–
Slovenia	33.6	201.9	67.8	25.3	172.9	43.8	11.1	216.6	23.9
Sweden	50.8	–	–	–	–	–	–	–	–
Switzerland	42.1	134.7	56.7	26.6	139.9	37.3	19.7	111.2	21.9
United Kingdom	45.0	157.0	70.6	39.6	140.9	55.9	9.8	162.8	15.9
United States	40.7	131.1	53.3	36.4	128.3	46.6	6.3	114.6	7.3

[a]Adults aged 16–19 years participating in full-time studies (4 or more days per week) toward ISCED 0–3, and who are not financially supported by an employer or union are excluded. Similarly, adults aged 16–24 years in full-time studies (4 or more days per week) toward ISCED 4–7, and who are not financially supported by an employer or union are excluded.
[b]Sweden and Portugal did not ask about job-related and nonjob-related training in a comparable way, nor did they ask about training durations. Germany is excluded because the survey did not ask about adult education and training in a comparable way.
[c]Mean number of hours per adult = Mean number of hours per participant* Participation rate/100.
[d]During the past 12 months, that is since ..., did you receive any training or education including courses, private lessons, correspondence courses, workshops, on-the-job training, apprenticeship training, arts, crafts, recreation courses, or any other training or education?
–, indicates that data are not available.
Source: International Adult Literacy Survey, 1994–98; reprinted from Desjardins, R., Rubenson, K., and Milana, M. (2006). Unequal Chances to Participate in Adult Learning: International Perspectives. Paris: UNESCO.

Table 2 Participation in adult education and training in the previous year, population aged 16–65[a]

Participation rate

(a) Adult Literacy and Lifeskills Survey (ALLS), 2003[b]		(b) EU Barometer, 2003[c]	
Bermuda	47.0	Austria	39.3
Canada	49.3	Belgium	31.5
Italy	19.0	Denmark	58.5
Norway	53.3	Finland	55.9
Switzerland	56.9	France	22.8
United States	54.6	Germany	35.0
		Greece	16.7
		Iceland	69.1
		Ireland	33.6
		Italy	25.3
		Luxembourg	38.1
		Netherlands	41.0
		Norway	46.0
		Portugal	12.7
		Spain	26.5
		Sweden	53.5
		United Kingdom	41.4

[a]Adults aged 16–19 years participating in full-time studies (4 or more days per week) toward ISCED 0–3, and who are not financially supported by an employer or union are excluded. Similarly, adults aged 16–24 years in full-time studies (4 or more days per week) toward ISCED 4–7, and who are not financially supported by an employer or union are excluded.
[b]During the last 12 months... did you take any education or training? This education or training would include programs, courses, private lessons, correspondence courses, workshops, on the-job-training, apprenticeship training, arts, crafts, recreation courses, or any other training or education.
[c]Have you done any studies or training in the past 12 months? Please choose the three answers that best describe your own situation: yes, to meet new people; yes, to be less likely to lose my job/to be less likely to be forced into retirement; yes, to better enjoy my free time/retirement; yes, to be able to do my job better; yes, to obtain a certificate, diploma or qualification; yes, to be able to take greater responsibilities/increase my chances of promotion; yes, to better manage my everyday life; yes, to change the type of work I do altogether, including starting my own business (for retraining, etc.); yes, to achieve more personal satisfaction; yes, to get a job; yes, to improve my chance of getting another job, including one which would suit me more; yes, to increase my general knowledge; yes, for other reasons (spontaneous); no, I have not, but I would like to; no, I am not particularly interested, no, for other reasons (spontaneous); and don't know. Source: Adult Literacy and Lifeskills Survey, 2003; EU Barometer, 2003; reprinted from Desjardins, R., Rubenson, K., and Milana, M. (2006). *Unequal Chances to Participate in Adult Learning: International Perspectives.* Paris: UNESCO.

Definitions and Measurement

Most AET data sources focus on measuring formal provision; however, increasingly, there is an interest in nonformal and informal activities. This poses some challenges, especially in defining what counts as adult learning. Increasingly, it is difficult to distinguish adult learners from first-time students attending regular school or university. Pragmatic solutions are to consider all the learning activities of the adult population aged 25–65 years or, if possible, to consider the population aged 16–65 years, but exclude full-time students aged 16–24 years. A more sophisticated definition, if the data allow for it, is to count the studies of the following groups as participation: full-time students aged 16–24 years who are sponsored by an employer or union/association; full-time students over the age of 19 years who are enrolled in primary or secondary programs; and full-time students older than 24 years who are enrolled in postsecondary programs. The last group is significant because there can be substantial overlap between what is considered adult learning and higher education, especially in countries where the higher education system features a high degree of openness to nontraditional adult students.

Another issue is the reference period for which participation rates are based on. For example, the IALS uses a 12-month reference period, whereas the ELFS uses a 4-week period. Shorter reference periods are adequate for reporting participation rates of populations, but inadequate for an in-depth understanding of adult learning pathways, both in terms of understanding the takeup of adult learning and its interaction to the provision of opportunities.

Informal Learning

Informal learning encompasses a broad range of learning activities (Livingstone, 1999). Patterns of engagement thus depend on what is being measured. Of the nine informal learning measures in the ALLS (2003), two dominate. Learning by doing is mentioned by around 90%, while learning by watching ranges from a high of 87% in Switzerland to a low of 77% in Canada. These former measures cover a broad range of nonspecific experiences; therefore, it is difficult to interpret their significance or value. More specific informal learning activities, related to work and culture, are particularly prevalent in Switzerland and less common in Canada and the United States with Norway somewhere in between. A vast majority of the Swiss (86%) report that they read manuals or other materials compared to 55% for Canada and the United States. The Swiss more often note that they learn by being sent around their organization or attending special talks. Further, they more frequently (44%) go on guided tours at museums or galleries than Canadians, Americans, or Norwegians (30%). Comparative measures of learning through the interactive use of information technology reveal only small differences in the use of computers or the Internet, while learning with the help of video, television, and tapes varies from a high of 52% in the United States to a low of 35% in Switzerland.

Who Is Participating?

Observed differences in participation have been linked to inequalities of opportunity and living conditions; therefore, the demographic and social make-up of participation becomes an important issue.

Adult Education and Training

For a range of countries (18 Organisation for Economic Co-operation and Development (OECD) ones and two non-OECD ones), IALS data show that those who are women, older, from low socioeconomic backgrounds (as reflected in their parents' level of education), low educated, low skilled, in low-skill jobs, unemployed, or immigrants are the least likely to participate in adult learning (see **Table 3**). In many cases, people belong to more than one group at the same time, which exacerbates observed differences (see Desjardins *et al.*, 2006: 74).

Informal Learning

Some research has stressed that the law of inequality does not apply to informal learning (e.g., Livingstone, 1999). However, this depends on the measure of informal learning used. Measures that are all inclusive or very general and refer to nonspecific situations of learning by doing or learning by watching show that informal learning is more or less a universal activity (see above). In contrast, measures which are context specific and reflect learning that is likely to enable the creation of or access to resources tend to reveal a clear pattern of inequality. Rubenson *et al.* (2007) find that groups with low levels of educational attainment report a substantially lower engagement in reading or using computers to learn. There is limited research on the extent to which different forms of informal learning contribute to strengthening resources that have economic and social value.

Why Are Certain People or Groups Participating More than Others?

Determinants

Different characteristics can be used to explore and reveal patterns of participation in greater detail. As described above, this can be done by distinguishing among salient groups such as those delineated by: age, sex, social class, level of education, level of skill, and occupational, employment, and minority status. This broadens our empirical understanding of who participates. However, a determinants analysis goes a step further by including a range of factors that are thought to be relevant in explaining the observed patterns. This may include the same characteristics used to define a group; however, the difference in a determinants analysis is that there are underlying theories that link the characteristics to the observed pattern, and thus have explanatory value. Participation research has explored various explanatory factors.

Disciplinary Perspectives

Different explanations have been put forth, ranging from those rooted in psychological to sociological to economic perspectives (Tuijnman and Fägerlind, 1989). The most appealing ones have an interdisciplinary character since they are more useful for building a comprehensive understanding of adult learning participation. It is rare, however, that different disciplinary perspectives are brought together. There is no unified or comprehensive theoretical perspective guiding participation research. One downside to complex inclusive models is that they can inhibit empirical testing and limit the usefulness of results, especially with regard to specific situations or needs. For example, practitioners may specifically be interested in knowing what information is best suited for altering adult beliefs about the likely outcomes of participating. In this situation, a psychological perspective may provide the necessary depth. Ideally, a portfolio of models, which can be applicable in different contexts for different purposes, needs to be built up.

Further research requires explanatory models or theories that are disciplinary, multidisciplinary, and multilevel. Rubenson (1987) mentions three approaches to model building. The first focuses on the individual's psychological factors – the micro-level. The second emphasizes external factors and their structural conditions which influence the individual – the macro-level. The third approach looks into the interaction between individual and social forces. Each type of explanation is essential, but neither is sufficient in isolation from each other.

Explanations Based on Psychological Perspectives

While motivation can equally be a social phenomenon that is driven by external expectations which are placed on individuals – such as family, workplace, and community demands for competencies – many explanations focus solely on individual psychological factors. The psychological perspective focuses primarily on personality traits, intellectual abilities, and other behavioral dispositions that center on attitudes, expectations, intentions, and other motivational attributes.

Personality traits and abilities

Individuals have a degree of agency; therefore, cognitions, beliefs, and psychosocial capabilities feature as crucial

Table 3 Percent of adults participating in AET and adjusted odds ratios[a,b] showing the likelihood of participating in AET during the year preceding the interview, by various classification variables, 1994–98

	Australia		Canada		Chile		Czech Republic		Denmark		Finland		Hungary		Ireland		Italy	
	%	Odds	%	Odds	%	Odds	%	Odds	%	Odds	%	Odds	%	Odds	%	Odds	%	Odds
Age																		
16–25	45.5	3.6 ***	43.6	4.8 ***	24.9	3.6 ***	24.4	1.8 **	68.0	2.4 ***	69.8	1.8 ***	27.7	3.7 ***	29.0	3.5 ***	34.5	1.4 ***
26–35	41.2	1.6 **	41.9	2.2	24.6	3.5 ***	34.0	2.1 **	63.1	1.5 *	70.4	1.0 *	27.6	3.4 ***	27.2	2.1 ***	28.3	1.0 ***
36–45	40.4	1.5 ***	41.8	2.3 ***	20.7	3.3 ***	29.1	1.6 **	64.3	1.8 ***	64.9	1.0 ***	19.6	1.8	25.3	2.1 ***	25.0	1.1 *
46–55	30.6	1.2	33.4	2.0	12.0	1.9 ***	29.9	2.2 ***	55.4	1.5 **	55.1	0.9 **	15.7	1.7	18.4	1.6 *	18.0	1.1
56–65	17.9	1.0	14.7	1.0	6.9	1.0	8.8	1.0	32.0	1.0	29.7	1.0	3.4	1.0	9.1	1.0	9.3	1.0
Gender																		
Women	35.1	1.0	36.3	1.0	19.9	1.0	21.7	1.0 ***	59.2	1.0 **	62.3	1.0 **	20.5	1.0	25.0	1.0	19.1	1.0
Men	37.8	1.1	37.6	1.3	19.1	0.8 ***	31.2	1.7	54.7	0.8	54.5	0.7	19.1	0.9	22.1	0.8	26.2	1.1
Parent's education																		
Less than upper secondary	34.2	1.0 **	28.4	1.0	15.5	1.0	22.2	1.0 *	49.2	1.0 *	50.0	1.0 *	11.6	1.0	21.3	1.0	18.5	1.0
Upper secondary	41.3	1.2	42.4	1.3	33.1	1.2 *	34.2	1.3 **	59.5	1.0	65.7	1.2 **	25.1	1.2	33.4	1.0	39.2	1.0
Higher than upper secondary	47.5	1.2 ***	55.6	2.0 ***	46.5	1.5 ***	31.4	1.0	69.5	1.1 **	77.2	1.5	43.2	1.6 *	38.1	1.3	51.9	1.5
Education																		
Less than upper secondary	24.0	1.0 ***	20.7	1.0 ***	9.8	1.0 ***	17.7	1.0 ***	41.2	1.0 ***	35.9	1.0 ***	7.1	1.0 ***	14.1	1.0	9.2	1.0
Upper secondary	38.0	1.3 ***	32.2	1.0	25.5	1.7	35.8	1.6 ***	56.2	1.2 ***	63.5	1.5 **	18.2	1.3	27.7	1.2	37.5	2.0 ***
Higher than upper secondary	56.1	1.8	55.7	1.9 ***	45.2	2.5 ***	47.0	1.7	74.6	1.8	80.0	1.9 ***	47.7	4.0	44.9	1.7	51.3	2.8 ***
Prose literacy skill level																		
Level 1	14.2	1.0 ***	17.3	1.0 ***	10.6	1.0 *	12.0	1.0 *	22.7	1.0 ***	21.2	1.0 ***	8.4	1.0 ***	8.9	1.0	8.4	1.0
Level 2	26.6	1.7 ***	28.3	1.3	25.3	1.2 **	22.4	1.6 **	47.3	1.9 ***	41.7	1.3 ***	20.3	1.3	17.8	1.4	21.9	1.5 ***
Level 3	42.6	2.8 ***	43.1	2.0 ***	40.2	1.4 ***	33.1	2.0 ***	69.2	2.9 ***	68.2	2.5 ***	34.6	1.6 ***	30.0	2.2	38.6	2.1 ***
Level 4/5	60.6	4.4	52.9	2.2	47.8	1.2	41.5	2.3	77.3	2.8	82.8	3.8	46.0	1.5	48.2	3.5	44.5	2.1 ***
Employment status																		
Unemployed	28.8	1.0	29.5	1.0	19.3	1.0	19.5	1.0	53.4	1.0 ***	30.4	1.0 ***	12.6	1.0 **	9.7	1.0	16.3	1.0
Employed	43.2	1.2	41.7	1.2	22.5	0.9	33.4	1.0 *	60.4	1.0 *	69.6	2.8 *	28.7	2.1 ***	30.2	1.3	29.1	3.0 ***
Retired	9.0	0.4 ***	10.7	0.5 ***	15.3	2.0	5.1	0.3 ***	18.0	0.3 ***	16.5	0.6 ***	1.4	0.2 ***	3.5	0.4	5.4	0.4 **
Student	96.2	69.5 *	66.1	3.9 *	100.0	>99 ***	21.3	0.7 ***	89.4	16.0 ***	91.8	93.3 ***	29.5	>99 ***	50.2	27.2	100.0	>99
Homemaker	13.0	0.3 ***	23.1	0.6 ***	8.0	0.5 **	0.0	0.0	22.0	0.3	29.1	0.5 *	0.0	0.0	11.3	1.1	3.3	0.2 ***
Occupation																		
Blue collar low skill	25.6	1.0	25.5	1.0	11.5	1.0	18.7	1.0	42.3	1.0	47.8	1.0	13.3	1.0	16.9	1.0	13.1	1.0
Blue collar high skill	32.6	1.0 ***	29.4	1.2 ***	12.8	1.1 **	29.1	1.4	47.1	1.2 ***	50.1	1.2 ***	14.5	0.9 *	15.8	0.9	14.6	1.0
White collar low skill	43.7	1.6 ***	39.8	2.0 ***	29.8	2.0 ***	22.5	1.3 **	63.0	1.8 ***	68.3	1.6 ***	25.4	1.3	37.6	1.8	26.7	1.4 *
White collar high skill	55.4	1.7	53.4	1.8	49.8	3.2	45.0	2.2 ***	73.2	2.3	82.0	2.9	45.4	1.8 **	45.6	2.2	49.8	2.5 **
Immigration status																		
Foreign born	30.9	1.0 **	33.4	1.0 **	31.5	1.0	13.2	1.0	54.9	1.0 **	61.2	1.0	24.2	1.0	26.5	1.0	28.7	1.0
Native born	38.5	1.3	37.9	1.3	19.4	4.5	26.5	2.3 **	56.9	0.6	58.3	2.0	19.8	1.7	23.3	1.0	22.4	0.9

Continued

Table 3 Continued

	Netherlands		New Zealand		Norway		Poland		Slovenia		Sweden		Switzerland		United Kingdom		United States		International average	
	%	Odds	%	Odds	%	Odds	%	Odds	%	Odds	%	Odds	%	Odds	%	Odds	%	Odds	%	Odds
Age																				
16–25	48.3	2.5***	60.4	4.4***	42.8	2.8***	17.7	3.8***	43.3	2.1**	41.0	1.1	48.8	2.3***	51.5	2.7***	33.4	1.8*	41.9	2.8
26–35	45.9	2.0***	51.6	2.1**	56.2	2.1***	17.4	2.5***	45.5	1.8**	57.0	1.4	49.6	1.9**	51.2	1.5**	46.5	1.5**	43.3	1.9
36–45	40.4	1.9**	50.5	1.7*	52.5	2.0***	18.4	2.7***	38.9	1.8**	60.7	1.6	43.7	1.7**	54.3	1.7***	44.9	1.3*	40.9	1.8
46–55	30.6	1.4*	42.7	1.4	47.3	1.8***	11.3	1.8***	27.6	1.3	57.1	1.5	38.6	1.5	41.0	1.1	43.8	1.4	33.8	1.5
56–65	17.0	1.0	27.6	1.0	23.8	1.0	2.8	1.0	9.5	1.0	34.7	1.0	24.6	1.0	21.1	1.0	26.9	1.0	17.8	1.0
Gender																				
Women	36.4	1.0	46.9	1.0	46.1	1.0	13.4	1.0	32.5	1.0	52.3	1.0	40.7	1.0	44.0	1.0	40.6	1.0	36.2	1.0
Men	39.4	1.0	49.0	1.1	47.9	1.0	16.1	1.4**	34.7	1.3**	49.4	1.0	43.5	0.8*	45.9	0.9	40.8	1.0	37.2	1.0
Parent's education																				
Less than upper secondary	33.8	1.0	44.5	1.0	38.6	1.0	11.5	1.0	23.3	1.0	47.9	1.0	30.3	1.0	44.0	1.0	26.5	1.0	30.6	1.0
Upper secondary	49.5	1.4***	51.7	0.9	49.5	1.2	21.4	1.0	44.8	1.2	53.6	1.2**	47.7	1.2*	62.8	1.5	44.7	1.1	44.4	1.2
Higher than upper secondary	46.2	1.1	62.3	1.3*	58.3	1.4**	35.7	1.3	66.1	1.4	57.4	1.1	50.1	1.1	67.7	1.3	55.3	1.3**	53.3	1.3
Education																				
Less than upper secondary	26.5	1.0	37.8	1.0		1.0	8.0	1.0	12.1	1.0	35.0	1.0	20.4	1.0	34.1	1.0	14.0	1.0	21.8	1.0
Upper secondary	43.7	1.5**	51.0	1.1	44.3	1.3	21.2	2.3**	36.4	1.7**	51.8	1.4***	45.3	2.1***	53.3	1.4**	32.1	1.2	39.6	1.5
Higher than upper secondary	52.8	1.9***	64.7	1.6***	65.0	1.8***	34.3	3.0***	73.6	4.6***	67.0	1.8***	56.5	2.9***	71.0	2.0***	62.7	2.4***	58.3	2.3
Prose literacy skill level																				
Level 1	21.9	1.0	29.9	1.0	14.6	1.0	8.3	1.0	15.3	1.0	29.4	1.0	22.4	1.0	20.8	1.0	14.1	1.0	16.7	1.0

Continued

	%	OR	sig	%	OR	sig	%	OR	sig	%	OR	sig	%	OR	sig	%	OR	sig	%	OR	sig	%	OR	sig	%	OR	sig	%	OR	sig
Level 2	29.6	1.4		36.2	1.0		38.7	2.5	***	15.4	1.0		40.7	1.8	***	41.1	1.1		35.8	1.2		34.5	1.3		30.6	1.9		30.8	1.5	**
Level 3	42.2	1.7	**	55.7	1.8	***	51.5	3.0	***	23.4	1.2		61.6	2.1	***	52.2	1.4		52.0	1.8		58.0	2.6		48.3	3.0	***	46.9	2.1	***
Level 4/5	54.4	2.5	***	68.3	2.1	***	64.2	3.9	***	40.8	1.5		75.0	2.5	*	60.1	1.5	**	63.7	2.5	***	74.5	4.4		64.2	3.8	***	59.3	2.7	***
Employment status																															
Unemployed	37.8	1.0		33.5	1.0		37.6	1.0		9.4	1.0		17.1	1.0	***	44.0	1.0		33.0	1.0		30.1	1.0		26.3	1.0		27.1	1.0	
Employed	43.4	1.0		54.2	1.4		53.4	1.1		20.5	1.5		42.2	2.5	**	59.5	1.2		46.2	1.4		56.8	1.4		48.0	1.3	*	43.5	1.5	
Retired	13.1	0.6		17.7	0.7		6.7	0.2	***	2.0	0.4		5.8	0.4		16.1	0.4		20.5	1.0		8.6	0.3		12.5	0.5		10.4	0.5	
Student	65.6	6.5	*	91.8	>99	*	44.5	4.8	***	18.7	3.1		87.7	15.7		39.7	1.3		49.1	3.8		55.8	23.7		42.0	41.7	***	63.3	22.2	***
Homemaker	23.2	0.7		23.4	0.5		14.0	0.3	***	3.7	0.5		11.0	1.3		25.5	0.4		24.8	0.8		13.6	0.4		13.7	0.6		14.6	0.5	*
Occupation																															
Blue collar low skill	29.1	1.0		35.9	1.0		36.6	1.0		11.5	1.0		17.9	1.0		39.3	1.0		28.3	1.0		36.6	1.0		22.4	1.0		26.2	1.0	
Blue collar high skill	39.5	1.5		40.5	1.0		43.3	1.3		10.2	1.0		24.9	1.4		41.9	1.0		35.6	1.2		36.9	0.9		29.4	1.3		30.5	1.2	
White collar low skill	42.8	1.5	*	54.0	1.7	***	47.4	1.4	*	18.0	1.3		47.4	2.7	***	52.0	1.6		43.6	1.3		58.0	1.6		44.2	1.9	**	42.5	1.6	**
White collar high skill	47.8	1.5	*	69.2	2.6	***	63.2	1.9	***	37.6	2.3		68.0	3.5	***	68.2	2.5		56.2	1.8	**	68.9	1.7		64.9	2.3	**	58.0	2.3	**
Immigration status																															
Foreign born	45.0	1.0		46.4	1.0		41.1	1.0		3.3	1.0		23.4	1.0		37.9	1.0		27.4	1.0		45.0	1.0		30.1	1.0		33.6	1.0	
Native born	37.4	0.7		48.2	1.3		47.4	1.5	***	14.9	2.8		34.8	1.6		52.1	1.2		45.6	1.8		45.0	1.0		42.3	1.5		37.3	1.6	

a Odds ratios reflect the relative likelihood of an event occurring for a particular group compared to a reference group. An odds ratio of 1 represents equal chances of an event occurring for a particular group vis-à-vis the reference group. Coefficients with a value below 1 indicate that there is less chance of the event occurring for a particular group compared to the reference group, and coefficients greater than 1 represent increased chances. From Hosmer, D. W. and Lemeshow, S. (1989). *Applied Logistic Regression.* New York: Wiley.

b Odds are adjusted for: age, gender, parents' education, education, prose literacy skill level, employment status, occupation, immigrant status, minority language status, and size of community.

* p < 0.10, statistically significant at the 10% level.

** p < 0.05, statistically significant at the 5% level.

*** p < 0.01, statistically significant at the 1% level.

Source: International Adult Literacy Survey, 1994–98; reprinted from Desjardins, R., Rubenson, K., and Milana, M. (2006). *Unequal Chances to Participate in Adult Learning: International Perspectives. Paris: UNESCO.*

elements that can explain participation. Participatory behavior is the result of diverse interactions between individuals' beliefs, skills, capabilities, and values. Rubenson (1987) stresses the importance of self-concepts such as self-esteem and self-efficacy in predicting participation. He suggests that adults who feel good about themselves are more likely to succeed in achievement-oriented situations. Conversely, an important benefit of adult learning is improved beliefs about self-efficacy (Hammond, 2003), pointing to a cycle of recurrent learning.

Previous learning experiences are key factors predicting further learning (Tuijnman, 1989; Boudard, 2001; Desjardins, 2004). Independent of educational attainment, Tuijnman (1989) finds that cognitive ability also exerts a positive influence on the accumulation of learning experiences over the lifespan. Educational attainment reflects accumulated knowledge, skills, and other traits that are associated with the probability of continued learning.

A common trait shared by early school leavers is a lack of self-confidence with regard to learning because of bad pedagogical experiences (Illeris, 2004a). Adults with low levels of education are less likely to participate because they lack readiness both in terms of knowledge and skills as well as their motivation to learn. A low readiness to learn is a substantial dispositional barrier to participation.

Motivational orientations and reasons

Motivational orientations toward learning can be important predictors of participation. Houle (1961) proposed a typology which suggests that participants are either goal oriented (use learning to accomplish objectives), activity oriented (find meaning in the circumstances of learning), or learning oriented (seek knowledge for its own sake). Boshier (1971, 1982) and Boshier and Collins (1985) developed the Education Participation Scale (EPS) to assign motivational orientation scores to individuals which allowed for in-depth investigation into the relationships among orientations and various demographic variables and other characteristic variables. Although the amount of variance explained by sociodemographic variables was small, research by Boshier and colleagues revealed that those with low education, low occupational status, and low income were most likely to participate for social contact, social stimulation, community service, and external expectation reasons. In contrast, those with higher levels of education, occupational status, and income were more often enrolled for professional advancement and cognitive interest reasons.

These findings partly corroborate with Maslow's (1954) hierarchy of needs theory which suggested that the motivating forces behind participation are conditional on whether subordinate needs are satisfied. Individuals with lower-order needs for survival which remain to be satisfied are deficiency motivated, whereas those working toward higher-order needs are growth motivated.

Arguably, obtaining secure employment is a lower-order need and, thus, the implication by Boshier's finding that professional advancement is associated with a higher-order need is puzzling. A more broadly based measure of job-related AET reveals that most adults participate for job-related reasons, whether associated with low socio-economic status or not (e.g., OECD, 2003a; Desjardins *et al.*, 2006).

Learning for job-related reasons is linked to goals of finding a job, finding a better job, being promoted at work, keeping a job, and/or becoming more efficient in one's current job. It is a dominant reason reported (at least 60%) in recent surveys such IALS, ALLS, and the 2000 European Union Barometer, and reaches as high as 90% in Australia, Denmark, Norway, the United Kingdom, and the United States. The divide between job- and non-job-related reasons, however, is not so clear-cut (Courtney, 1992: 50), which may be a reason why attempts to link distinct motivational orientations to participation explain little variation. Further, adults may find their reasons for participating difficult to articulate and they might not always be aware of them all (Darkenwald and Merriam, 1982: 136; Rubenson, 2001). Even a temporary lack of a specific reason may be seen as a reason for participating since the activity itself can be a way to obtain or rediscover new goals that could be pursued (Courtney, 1992: 87).

Attitudes and Intentions

Research has also pointed to the importance of attitudes toward learning. Houle (1961) claimed that every adult has an underlying conviction about the nature and value of learning which influences their opinion and, hence, the decision to participate. Darkenwald and Hayes (1988) constructed the Adult Attitudes toward Continuing Education Scale (AACES) to investigate the relationships among attitudes and participation. They found that the importance attributed to learning appears to be the most decisive factor in predicting participation; however, importance in relation to what needs further attention (see below).

Explanations Based on Social Perspectives

Individualistic perspectives have had serious consequences for how inequalities in participation are understood and what measures are deemed adequate to support lifelong learning for all. Individuals face several constraints in acting independently and making their own free choices. Shortcomings to the individualistic psychological and economic perspectives can be addressed by turning to the various external (and structural) influences on participation, such as social and economic institutions (government policy, organizations, industries, markets, and classes) at a macro level, and work structures at a micro level.

Separately, life history approaches to studying participation have broadened the structuralist approach by embracing much of the criticism of the individualistically oriented theories. This is done by situating the role of individual subjective experiences and actions as well as collective ones in their wider social and cultural contexts. A discussion regarding the relationships between life situation and participation as well as institutional barriers and participation, which are an elaboration of explanations based on social perspectives, is given elsewhere in the encyclopedia.

Explanations Based on Economic Perspectives

Most, but not all, explanations based on economic perspectives have tended to be dominated by individualistic approaches to the decision to participate. A common assumption is that individuals make a rational choice to participate or not, and that this decision is based on the information they have regarding the costs and benefits of participating. However, individuals are substantially limited by the imperfect information they have regarding the costs and benefits. There are also risks inherent with realizing the benefits which rational agents may not want to undertake.

Cost limitations and credit constraints

Desjardins *et al.* (2006) underscored the point that a lack of external economic support (from employers and governments) and credit constraints, especially for disadvantaged groups, is a significant barrier to participation. Even if individuals would like to participate because the future benefits outweigh the immediate costs, they may not have the financial means to do so because of credit constraints and imperfect capital markets. When individuals are not capable of borrowing money to invest in learning, because they do not have any collateral, which would otherwise be profitable, then market failure occurs.

Financial support and incentive-to-invest factor

The long arm of the job is becoming longer and stronger in terms of financing as well as motivation. IALS data show that about two-thirds of participants receive employer support (OECD and Statistics Canada, 2000). There are indications that participation may not always be voluntary and there may be increasing pressure to participate in job-related AET (Hight, 1998; Carré, 2000). Employer-supported AET is often suggested by employers, although a large portion that is suggested by employees is also supported by the employer (Tuijnman and Hellström, 2001). Many adults also participate for job-related reasons even though they do not receive financial support from their employer, which reveals the strength of the long arm of the job. Self-financing is, on average, the second most common

source of financial support, and, in some countries, the dominant source.

Firms represent a large portion of the training market (OECD, 2003a: 51–53). The Second Continuing Vocational Training Survey (CVTS2) data show that over 70% of firms in the majority of European countries provide support for AET (European Commission, 2002). Adults who work in large firms, especially those that compete on global markets and undergo significant technological change and/or changing work practices, appear to receive more AET.

The supply of employer-supported opportunities appears to be primarily targeted at prime-age employees who are highly educated and skilled. Plausibly, employers consider adults with higher levels of education more trainable. Older workers, women, and immigrants tend to face reduced opportunities for employer-supported AET (Desjardins *et al.*, 2006). These tendencies are consistent with the overall patterns of participation (see **Table 3**).

There is much debate about whether current levels of investment in AET are adequate. The potential for underinvestment arises due to several market failures, and can be linked to both employer and employee behavior (see Desjardins *et al.*, 2006). Overall, evidence shows that an underprovision of AET is likely to occur in all OECD countries (see OECD, 2003b: 248).

Government support, the least common source of financial support, tends to benefit those who already display high rates of participation, namely younger adults, the higher educated, and those who are in white-collar, high-skill occupations, rather than vulnerable groups. This is likely due to pressures for government policies to seek increases in efficiency through the adoption of a more market-oriented approach and outcomes-based funding. This increases the likelihood that AET initiatives/programs will target those easiest to recruit and most likely to succeed. Initiatives to reach disadvantaged groups often correspond better to the demands of the advantaged (Rubenson, 1999: 116). Few countries have effective public policies and structures in place to help those who are hard to reach. The Nordic countries are among the few and, accordingly, they tend to show comparatively higher rates of participation among the low educated (see **Table 3**).

Nature of work and skill-requirements factor

Recent research suggests that industrial and occupational structures of countries are instrumental in structuring participation. This perspective moves beyond the narrow individualistic one and encompasses a social and structural perspective. The world of work places substantial demands on individuals which necessitates continuous learning and periodic upgrades of competencies, acting as a substantial motivating force for many adults.

Recent research suggests that literacy practices at work – in particular the frequency and variety of reading practices – is one of the most significant determinants of participation in job-related AET (Desjardins *et al.*, 2006). More generally, the workplace is a learning space (Illeris, 2004b: 77–89); however, opportunities to learn new things on the job vary with the characteristic and position of the job, which exacerbates inequalities in adult learning (Åberg, 2002). Workers who are already better positioned in the labor market have more opportunities and incentives to acquire and develop competencies. Further, the structure of occupations and production in a particular country are likely to bear a strong influence on the distribution of work-related adult learning.

Explanations Based on Individuals' Interactions with Social Influences

Explanatory models of participation that include social and individual forces as well as their interaction have been proposed by a number of researchers. Some of the above explanations build on these, but a brief review of the more well-known ones is provided here. These models include most of the proximal and distal variables that are hypothesized as relevant to participation and are thus useful for building a comprehensive understanding of participation. The underlying reasons why adults participate (or not) are complex, featuring dynamic and interactive feedback effects that occur at multiple levels.

McClusky (1963) presented an individual–social interactive model called the power–load–margin model. Load represents the internal and external demands placed on the individual; power represents the agency of the individual to carry the load; and margin is the ratio of load to power which signifies the likelihood to participate. By linking Maslow's (1954) hierarchy of needs model with Lewin's (1947) force field analysis model, Miller (1967) suggested that when individual needs and social forces both point to a commonly perceived demand for participation, then participation will be high. Similarly, Boshier's (1971) congruence model suggested that when actual and perceived notions of self, others, and educational environment diverge, it is less likely that adults will participate.

Rubenson's (1975) expectancy valence model made a link between an individual's expectations about the value of participating, their attitude toward participating, and the likelihood of actual participation. According to this theory, participation will occur and persist if the learning activity is consistent with the learner's needs and expectations. According to Rubenson, the outcomes will depend on class since attitude and readiness are conditioned by structural and cultural factors. A model by Pryor (1990) and Pryor and Pryor (2005), which applied Ajzen and Fishbein's theory of reasoned action to participation,

focuses on more proximal variables. He suggested that participation is determined by the intention to participate and that the intention is determined by the attitude toward learning and perceptions of social pressures to participate. The latter is a subjective norm that is based on inferences about behavioral expectations of others. According to Pryor (1990), attitude tends to dominate over the subjective norm, and attitudes toward learning are primarily driven by a set of beliefs regarding the outcomes associated with learning.

Cross (1981) developed a psychosocial interaction model called the chain-of-response model, which suggested that participation relates to a complex chain of responses made by the individual vis à vis social circumstances. Beginning with a self-evaluation and a formation of attitudes toward learning, the importance of learning and the expectations associated with it are evaluated in relation to current needs and, in turn, this is influenced by available information, available opportunities, and institutional barriers.

Variants of these and other models exist and have been tested empirically. Based on a Swedish longitudinal study, Tuijnman (1989) puts an advanced set of structural models, which include psychological, sociological, and economic variables, to rigorous empirical testing. He reported that collectively, social origins, socioeconomic status, cognitive ability, initial levels of education, attitudes toward education, and specific interests in adult learning explain no more than 10–26% of the variance in the participation variable. Boudard (2003) more or less confirmed these patterns for a range of IALS countries.

Further Research

Major research questions that need to be addressed deal with the outcomes of adult learning and how this is linked with motivations to participate. Which mechanisms are more relevant for early development compared to the possible impact of later interventions? Is later intervention merely compensatory, with little chance of making a difference? Or could there be possibility for good timing later on? A better understanding of several relationships is needed:

- Substitutes and complements to more traditional schooling contexts.
- Formal education structures and adult learning, such as the degree of stratification and vocational specificity of pathways, and the extent and distribution of AET among different countries. This requires comparative data at both the system and individual levels.
- Occupational/industrial structures and adult learning. The structure of occupations and production in a particular country are likely to bear a strong influence on the distribution of job-related adult learning.

- Market failures and inequalities in participation. Market imperfections that may relate to learning outcomes are likely to have complex implications that spill over into other policy sectors; thus, reforms should not be undertaken without careful consideration of the relevant trade-offs. More specific information is necessary to devise viable strategies to overcome market failures and hence optimize the allocation and distribution of resources invested in the total learning effort.

- Government policy, governance, and adult learning. How are government policies regarding adult learning formed and coordinated at the intersection of various stakeholders and how does this shape the provision, purpose, and content of adult learning as well as participation?

See also: Barriers to Participation in Adult Education.

Bibliography

Åberg, R. (2002). Överutbilding – ett arbetsmarknadspolitiskt problem. In Abrahamson, K., Abrahamsson, L., Björkman, T., Ellström, P-E., and Johansson, J. (eds.) *Utbildning kompetenses och arbete*, pp 41–62. Lund: Studentlitteratur.

Boshier, R. W. (1971). Motivational orientations of adult education participants: A factor analytic exploration of Houle's typology. *Adult Education* **21**(2), 3–26.

Boshier, R. W. (1982). *Education Participation Scale*. Vancouver, BC: Learning Press.

Boshier, R. W. and Collins, J. B. (1985). The Houle typology after twenty-two years: A large-scale empirical test. *Adult Education Quarterly* **35**(3), 113–130.

Boudard, E. (2001). *Literacy Proficiency, Earnings and Recurrent Training: A Ten Country Comparative Study*. Stockholm: Institute of International Education.

Boudard, E. and Rubenson, K. (2003). Revisiting major determinants of participation in adult education with a direct measure of literacy skills. *International Journal of Educational Research* **39**(3), 265–280.

Carré, P. (2000). In Motivation in adult education: From engagement to performance. In *Proceedings of the 41st Annual Adult Education Research Conference*, 66–70. Vancouver, BC: University of British Columbia.

Courtney, S. (1992). *Why Adults Learn: Towards a Theory of Participation in Adult Education*. New York: Routledge.

Cross, K. P. (1981). *Adults as Learners: Increasing Participation and Facilitating Learning*. San Francisco, CA: Jossey-Bass.

Darkenwald, G. G. and Hayes, E. R. (1988). Assessment of adult attitudes towards continuing education. *International Journal of Lifelong Education* **7**(3), 197–204.

Darkenwald, G. G. and Merriam, S. B. (1982). *Adult Education: Foundations of Practice*. New York: Harper and Row.

Desjardins, R. (2004). *Learning for Well Being: Studies Using the International Adult Literacy Survey*. Stockholm: Stockholm University.

Desjardins, R., Rubenson, K., and Milana, M. (2006). *Unequal Chances to Participate in Adult Learning: International Perspectives*. Paris: UNESCO.

European Commission (2002). *European Social Statistics: Continuing Vocational Training Survey Detailed Tables (CVTS2 – Data 1999)*. Luxembourg: European Communities.

Hammond, C. (2003). How education makes us healthy. *London Review of Education* **1**(1), 61–78.

Hight, J. E. (1998). Young worker participation in post-school education and training. *Monthly Labor Review* **121**(6), 14–21.

Hosmer, D. W. and Lemeshow, S. (1989). *Applied Logistic Regression*. New York: Wiley.

Houle, C. O. (1961). *The Inquiring Mind*. Madison, WI: University of Wisconsin Press.

Illeris, K. (2004a). *Adult Education and Adult Learning*. Copenhagen: Roskilde University Press.

Illeris, K. (2004b). *Learning in Working Life*. Copenhagen: Roskilde University Press.

Lewin, K. (1947). Frontiers in group dynamics: Concept, method and reality in social science. *Human Relations* **1**, 5–41.

Livingstone, D. W. (1999). Exploring the icebergs of adult learning: Findings of the first Canadian survey of informal learning practices. *Canadian Journal for the Study of Adult Education* **13**(2), 49–72.

Maslow, A. H. (1954). *Motivation and Personality*. New York: Harper and Row.

McClusky, H. Y. (1963). The course of the adult life span. In Hallenbeck, W. C. (ed.) *Psychology of Adults*, pp 10–20. Washington, DC: Adult Education Association.

Miller, H. L. (1967). *Participation of Adults in Education: A Force Field Analysis*. Boston, MA: Center for the Study of Liberal Education of Adults.

OECD (2003a). *Beyond Rhetoric: Adult Learning Policies and Practices*. Paris: OECD.

OECD (2003b). *Employment Outlook*. Paris: OECD.

OECD and Statistics Canada (2000). *Literacy in the Information Age: Final Report of the International Adult Literacy Survey*. Paris/Ottawa, ON: OECD/Statistics Canada.

Pryor, B. W. (1990). Predicting and explaining intentions to participate in continuing education: An application of the theory of reasoned action. *Adult Education Quarterly* **40**(3), 146–157.

Pryor, B. W. and Pryor, C. R. (2005). *The School Leader's Guide to Understanding Attitude and Influencing Behaviour: Working with Teachers, Parents, Students, and the Community*. Thousand Oaks, CA: Corwin.

Rubenson, K. (1975). *Participation in Recurrent Education*. Paris: CERI/OECD.

Rubenson, K. (1987). Participation in recurrent education: A research review. In Schuetze, H. G. and Istance, D. (eds.) *Recurrent Education Revisited: Modes of Participation and Financing*, pp 39–67. Paris: OECD/CERI.

Rubenson, K. (1999). Supply of lifelong-learning opportunities. In Tuijnman, A. and Schuller, T. (eds.) *Lifelong Learning Policy and Research: Proceedings of an International Symposium*, pp 109–120. London: Portland Press.

Rubenson, K. (2001). *Measuring Motivation and Barriers in the Adult Education and Training Survey: A Critical Review*. Hull, QC: Applied Research Branch, Human Resources Development Canada.

Rubenson, K., Desjardins, R., and Yoon, E. (2007). *Adult Learning in Canada: A Comparative Perspective*. Ottawa, ON: Statistics Canada.

Tuijnman, A. C. (1989). *Recurrent Education, Earnings, and Well-Being: A Fifty-Year Longitudinal Study of a Cohort of Swedish Men*. Stockholm: Almqvist and Wiksell.

Tuijnman, A. and Fägerlind, I. (1989). Measuring and predicting participation in lifelong education using longitudinal data. *Scandinavian Journal of Educational Research* **33**(1), 47–66.

Tuijnman, A. C. and Hellström, Z. (2001). *Curious Minds: Nordic Adult Education Compared*. Copenhagen: Nordic Council of Ministers.

Barriers to Participation in Adult Education

K Rubenson, University of British Columbia, Vancouver, BC, Canada

Introduction

A quick review of international policy documents reveals the importance of adult learning in supporting the well-being of nations and individuals. Success in realizing lifelong learning is seen as vital in promoting employment, economic development, democracy, and social cohesion. This has resulted in an urgency to develop a better understanding of why some adults participate in lifelong learning and others do not. There are two closely integrated bodies of knowledge focusing on this question, research on determinants of participation and studies of barriers to participation, that is being addressed in this article.

This article is organized into three sections staring with a brief discussion of conceptual and methodological issues. This is followed by a presentation of empirical findings, and then finally a review of theoretical.

Conceptual and Methodological Issues

Attempts to assess barriers to lifelong learning have traditionally used a classification developed by Cross (1981: 98), who sorts obstacles to participation under three headings:

- situational barriers (those arising from one's situation in life e.g., lack of time because of work, family responsibility, etc.);
- institutional barriers (practices and procedures that hinder participation e.g., fees, lack of evening courses, entrance requirements, limited course offerings, etc.); and
- dispositional barriers (attitudes and dispositions toward learning).

A fourth category has recently been added to the list. Informational barriers refer to a lack of information on education and learning offers and benefits (OECD, 2005).

While most surveys employ some version of Cross' classification, there are fundamental differences in how barriers are conceptualized, affecting who is being asked questions on barriers. One common view is that barriers are obstacles that prevent certain groups from participating. If these deterrents could be overcome, these people would participate in lifelong learning. According to this view, questions about barriers would only be addressed to nonparticipants. A different conceptualization is that

barriers are factors that lower the extent of participation but may not entirely prohibit participation. By accepting this position, it is of interest to ask participants about possible barriers that may have caused them to lower the extent of their learning activities.

Another related issue concerns whether or not those who have indicated no interest in participating should be asked about barriers to participation. Large-scale national or international surveys like the US National Higher Education Survey (NHES), the Canadian Adult Education and Training Survey, or the Organization for Economic Cooperation and Development (OECD)-led International Adult Literacy Survey pose a battery of questions on barriers only to persons who indicate that they failed to take courses/programs they wanted to take and/or had felt a need for. The logic is that barriers come into existence only when an expressed wish to participate is thwarted; the role of research then is to discover the impediment. It seems irrelevant to ask individuals not interested in participating about barriers, because without an expressed interest there can be no barriers. Consequently, surveys using this approach tend to concentrate almost exclusively on situational and institutional barriers and pay little attention to psychological impediments.

As revealed in longitudinal research on participation, there are problems with using expressed interest to decide who should answer questions on barriers. In fact, large numbers of those who at one time had indicated no interest actually came to participate while a substantial number of people who stated that they were interested never showed up. This finding reflects the broader changes that have occurred in the labor market, which among other things, forces people to participate because they are ordered to or feel pressured to undergo some form of adult education and training linked to their work. Thus, contrary to a commonly held position in research on participation and barriers, participation is not always a voluntary act.

The other major approach in large-scale surveys of barriers, found, for example, in national adult-education surveys in the Nordic countries, the UK, and in the European Union (EU) barometer on lifelong learning, treats the lack of interest as part of the cluster of barriers. Following this approach, the questions are asked by three groups of respondents: persons who have not participated, those who have considered but not participated, and those who have participated. This assures that more interest is given to dispositional barriers. Thus, in the 2001 UK National Adult Learning Survey (Fitzgerald *et al.*,

2002) respondents were asked to sort a deck of cards describing barriers containing the following dispositional impediments:

- I prefer to spend my free time doing things other than learning.
- I do not need to do any learning for the sort of work I do.
- I am not interested in doing any learning, training, or education.
- I have difficulties reading and or/writing.
- I would be worried about keeping up with other people.
- I feel I am too old to learn.
- I do not see a point in learning or education.
- I would be nervous about going back to school.

Similar lists of dispositional-oriented reasons for not participating can be found in Swedish and Norwegian national surveys.

Either approach raises ethical dilemmas. In arguing that everyone should be asked about barriers – including those without a declared interest in participating – one runs the risk of turning participation into a moral issue where it is seen as bad not to want to participate. In fact, it may be highly rational from a personal point of view not to want to engage in organized forms of adult learning. While this line of reasoning has many advocates, others would claim that it is not that straightforward. The counter argument is that if the system of adult education too strongly assumes that the adult is a conscious, self-directed individual who possesses the instruments necessary to make use of available adult education possibilities, it will rely on self-selection to recruit participants. This will, by necessity, widen rather than narrow the educational and cultural gaps in society.

In this respect, the design issue around barriers raises crucial questions about the relationship between the state and its citizens, and what understanding should inform national surveys into barriers. In this context, Sen's (1982) concept of basic capability equality: the need to take into account, among other things, differences in those abilities that are crucial for citizens to function in society, is informative. Thus, as Nussbaum (1990) discusses, people living under difficult conditions tend to accept their fate because they cannot imagine any reasonable alternative. Consequently, it would be important to recognize that some citizens may not be sufficiently able to judge the value of and conditions for participation in adult education.

Findings

The overwhelming amount of information stems from large-scale surveys but there are also some in-depth qualitative studies that provide valuable insights into the reasoning of nonparticipants.

Findings from Large-Scale Surveys

Findings may vary between studies because of differences in methodology, target group, list of barriers, and so on, but nonetheless, some groups of barriers are consistently found to be of crucial importance. Looking across various surveys, situational and institutional barriers strongly dominate. In many countries, the main reason for not participating is commonly a lack of time. According to the International Literacy Survey (OECD, 2000), around 60% identified this as the major reason for not having started a non-work-related education one had needed or wanted to take. The EU-barometer on lifelong learning, looking at situational constrains across the 15 EU states, found that family-related obstacles like "my family commitments take up too much energy" were mentioned somewhat more frequently than job-related hindrances but the pattern differed from country to country (CEDEFOB, 2003). Not surprisingly, women are more prone to refer to family responsibilities than men.

Institutional barriers are also of major importance although to a somewhat lesser degree than situational barriers. In the *International Adult Literacy Survey* (IALS), on the average, around 45% of the adult population mentioned at least one institutional constraint that prevented participation in some form of work-related studies. The figure was lower for nonwork-related studies, around 30% (OECD, 2000). Generally, among institutional barriers, financial reasons (too expensive/no money) are by far the most prevalent hindrance, particularly in North America. However, as evident from the Euro-barometer on lifelong learning, cost is also a major restraining factor in Europe. Only between 12% and 21%, depending on purpose, were willing to pay for the full cost of studying, while close to 50% would pay none of the cost (CEDEFOB, 2003: 86). Another institutional barrier that is frequently identified is a lack of appropriate courses and the scheduling of them.

It is problematic to interpret the implications of the findings on situational and institutional barriers for policy. Time is not an endless resource and people have to make choices regarding how they want to spend their spare time. This is not to deny that some, because of work and family, may have very little time left over which they can freely decide to spend. For many, mentioning lack of time is as much a statement of the value they ascribe to education and training as to the expected outcome of such an activity. Thus, it is of interest to note that several studies have shown that participants mention situational barriers to the same extent, and in some studies, even more often than nonparticipants. This is also the case with institutional barriers where in fact there is a tendency for participants to report this slightly more often as the reason for not having taken other courses they were interested in. Similarly, Jonsson and Gähler (1996) found that there were as many people with objective barriers in terms of handicaps, young children, working hours, etc., that participated in adult education as did not participate. Based on this finding, the authors conclude (p.38): "Instead of barriers, that might have to do with cost, lack of time, it is probably differences in expected rewards that can explain why some choose to participate while others remain outside."

While many would agree with Jonsson and Gähler's interpretation of situational- and institutional-barrier data, it is important not to deny that some people face major hindrances like childcare and cost that makes it very hard for them to participate. So, for example, the fact that fewer people in upper-income brackets mentioned financial reasons is an indication that the answers not only reflect the willingness to pay but also the ability to do so.

The general findings on institutional and situational barriers are more or less the same regardless of survey approach. This is not the situation with dispositional barriers. Naturally, studies that approached only those who indicated an interest in participating pay rather scant attention to psychologically oriented barriers. Consequently, it is primarily surveys that have also approached those who indicated no interest that are of interest here. Findings from studies that have employed this strategy reveal two things. First, in almost all countries, a substantial share of the population refers to dispositional barriers. In the 11 European countries that took part in the EU-barometer the percentage raising psychological barriers varied from a low of 14% in Denmark to a high of 31% in the UK (CEDEFOB, 2003). Similarly, Livingstone (1999) found that psychological factors have a major impact on Canadians' readiness to enrol in organized learning activities. Thirty-five percent stated that they did not need more education and one in five saw studying as boring. These dispositional barriers refer to perceptions like, little to gain by participating, concerns about own ability to succeed, belief that one is too old to go back to study, and in some cases bad previous experiences of schooling.

Second, comparing participants with nonparticipants, several studies indicate that the negative attitudes and dispositions toward organized adult education and training (dispositional barriers) are by far the most deterring factor (Rubenson, 2007). This would suggest that the main obstacle to participation is not situational or institutional but rather a lack of interest.

Results from Qualitative Studies

The few existing qualitative studies of barriers tend to concentrate on indifference to participating and are commonly conducted with a small group of nonparticipants. The research provides an in-depth insight into the subjective rationale for actively declining to engage in organized forms of adult education. The overall finding is that the lack of interest often reflects a subjective rationality that is constructed around the person's life context. Several studies have pointed to how a lack of stimulating employment opportunities – either in the form of unemployment with small opportunities to become employed and/or a monotonous job – discourages participation (Paldanius, 2007). For this group, nonparticipation becomes a highly rational act. It is first when participation in adult education results in better and higher paying work that it is meaningful. The following quotes from Paldanius interviews with a group of nonparticipants can exemplify the subjective rationality of this group.

> Learning for the sake of learning never, I have much more important stuff to do, for instance I can plant onions and then know that it will take so and so long time until I see the results of my actions, I have actually made something, manufactured something (Paldanius, 2007: 472).

Carlén (1999) found that automobile workers viewed work and education as separate praxis related to class identity. As wage earners, they should produce and not enter into other spheres. Forms of adult education that were unrelated to their work challenged their routine and were perceived to encompass a threat of change. Similarly Paldanius (2007) reports that a dominant view among the nonparticipants was that education was something that had to be done while waiting for the real life that begins in adulthood. By not participating in adult education, a person can avoid boredom. Further, unemployment did not seem to stimulate an interest in participating in adult education, but instead it seemed to inhibit their readiness for action.

Theoretical Perspectives

Large-scale national surveys on participation and barriers are rarely constructed on the basis of theory but are mostly descriptive. However, there are economic as well as adult-education frameworks that could guide questionnaire construction.

Economic Theories

The human-capital perspective is prominent in education and training literature, although mostly absent in adult-education-participation frameworks. The underlying assumption is that individuals maximize welfare as they conceive it. Human capital analysis has, as a starting point, that individuals decide on their education by weighing the benefits and costs of this investment (Becker, 1964, 1993). Every action has a price tag in the market and every human act can be reduced to some kind of rational economic calculus of cost and benefit. The probability of participation increases as a function of the benefit/cost ratio. Common cost variables include: tuition, materials, and transportation as well as the less-tangible value of the time invested in studying. Benefits mostly focus on future monetary gains in the form of higher salaries but might also address job security, work conditions, and in some rare cases, cultural and other nonmonetary gains (US Department of Education, 1998: 13). As evident in the findings section above, some of the results can be interpreted in the context of a human-capital perspective. Although beyond the scope of this article, it should be noted that the homo-economicus framework has been severely criticized for its strong assumption of rationality. As Dow (1998: 13) states: if we see social structures as being organic and evolutionary, with creative, nondeterministic behaviors alongside behavior conditioned by habits and institutions, then individuals cannot be modeled according to deterministic rational principles.

An interesting variation on the cost–benefit framework is case-based decision theory (Gilboa and Schmeidler, 1995; cited in US Department of Education, 1998: 14). The idea is that people remember past problems, how they resolved them, and the outcome of action. When they meet a new problem, past experiences of similar problems direct their decisions. The framework does not assume that individuals have beliefs in the absence of data (recalled cases) and therefore does not list all possible costs and benefits, as only those in the memory can be used in reaching the decision.

It is worth noting that most large-scale surveys on participation and barriers already collect many demographic and social-background variables of interest to economic cost-benefit or expected-utility frameworks (US Department of Education, 1998: 66). However, they lack measures of relative expected utility and they are relatively meager on social psychological variables like intentionality and normativity with regard to adult education. Further, they are weak on external context, for example, the situation at work or in civil society, and mainly ignore key past experiences.

Adult Education

In adult education, it is mostly theories on participation, particularly motivation for engaging in adult education, that provide the framework for understanding barriers. Cross (1980: 122–124) found many common elements in existing adult education theories on participation and barriers. According to Cross, all:

- are interactions,
- build on Kurt Lewin's field-force analysis,
- are cognitivist,
- refer to reference-group theory,
- apply the concepts of incongruence and dissonance, and
- directly or indirectly build on Maslow's model of needs hierarchy.

On the basis of her review, Cross presents the so-called chain-response model which incorporates work on learning orientations, need press theory, and expectancy-valence theory. The model takes the individual as the starting point and begins by identifying two main constructs: self-evaluation and attitude toward education. These internal factors are seen to influence the value of goals and the expectation that participation will meet goals. Valence and expectations are also affected by life transition and development tasks that confront the individual in various life-cycle phases. Opportunities and barriers and available information will then modify whether or not an individual will come to participate. This model, like almost all others reviewed by Cross, employs psychological concepts to develop an explanation of why some adults participate while others do not. Cross (1981) argues that this does not mean that societal aspects are ignored; on the contrary, all theories are interactionist, that is, they understand participation in terms of interaction between an individual and his or her environment. However, theories tend to neglect the individual's life history. Further, they do not directly address how the main constructs in the model are related to and interact with the broader structural and cultural context. However, comparative data on participation reveal some interesting national differences that bring into question the usefulness of trying to understand barriers by focusing solely on how the individual interprets the world, which most theories on barriers and participation tend to do. First, the participation research shows that there are substantial differences in participation between countries at comparable stages in the modernization process and with quite similar economies (Desjardins et al., 2006). Second, it reveals that while age, family background, educational attainment, and work-related factors are linked to inequality in participation in all countries, the level of inequality varies substantially between countries (OECD, 2000). Third, the findings suggest that patterns of inequality in adult learning mirror broader structural inequalities in society, like inequalities in income. Participation patterns in a country thus seem to reflect its particular welfare-state regime. These empirical findings suggest that we have to consider broader structural conditions and targeted policy measures, and analyze the interaction between these and the individual's conceptual apparatus. Based on these observations Rubenson and Desjardins (2009) developed, the so-called bounded-agency model that aims to take account of the interaction between structurally and individually based barriers to participation.

The Bounded-Agency Model

The bounded-agency model is premised on the assumption that the nature of welfare-state regimes can affect a person's capability to participate. In particular, the state can foster broad structural conditions relevant to participation and construct targeted policy measures that are aimed at overcoming both structurally and individually based barriers. Structural conditions play a substantial role in forming the circumstances faced by individuals and limit the feasible alternatives to choose from, and therefore they can bound individual agency. According to the model, a particular welfare-state regime can be found not only to be implicated in social structures, adult-education systems, and life chances, but also in individual consciousness. This assumption builds on Sen's (1999) concept of human capability and functioning, which stresses the importance not only of having resources available – internal (i.e., knowledge or skills such as literacy) or external (i.e., money) – but also in terms of individuals knowing about the range of possibilities of how these resources can be employed to realize things that matter to them, and knowing how to do so. In this sense, dispositional barriers can be seen as factors that restrict a person's capability and hence freedom to participate. Further, dispositional barriers can be affected and even caused by structural barriers, such as institutional and situational ones.

To illustrate this point, the authors analyze the barrier section in the EU-barometer, which suggests that adults in Nordic and non-Nordic countries experience similar barriers to participation and nearly to the same extent. With regard to the bounded-agency model, the key question becomes the extent to which structural conditions and individual dispositions afford the individual the capability and freedom necessary to overcome barriers. In nearly all cases, adults from Nordic countries were more likely to participate in adult education even though they may perceive the same barriers as their counterparts in other countries. However, as reflected in high participation rates and relatively lower levels of inequality, the Nordic welfare state seems to be comparatively effective at resolving barriers. The Nordic welfare states feature structural conditions under which a larger group of adults, as compared to non-Nordic countries, seem to value participation and hence see an expected reward. These conditions include a labor market structured around a high-skill strategy and a civil society that fosters learning for both social and personal development. In the bounded-agency model, the impact of these conditions on a person's capabilities and consciousness with regard to the beginning of adult education is referred to as the 'conditioning of values and perspective on opportunity structure'.

Conclusion

Three findings stand out in the review of barriers. First, while the policy community's concern for adult learning has resulted in the development of major national and supranational policy-driven surveys, there does not seem to be much of an interest in the scholarly community to engage with barriers. This is in sharp contrast to the 1970s and first half of the 1980s, when a considerable body of conceptually oriented work on participation was produced. However, at that time it was more an unease regarding a lack of scholarly progress in adult education than efforts to contribute to evidence-informed policy that drove the interest. Second, the findings from national and international surveys as well a review of the scholarly literature point to some limitations in the present design of the major comparative surveys that are informing the policy discourse on barriers and suggest that the existing design might result in too simplistic an account of the factors behind barriers. A main limitation with many of the present surveys is that they concentrate almost exclusively on situational and institutional barriers. Therefore, consideration needs to be given to how to strengthen assessment of dispositional barriers. To address the lack of attention to dispositional barriers and questions on future interest, some existing conceptual frameworks can provide a fruitful starting point for getting better measures on general attitude as well as intrinsic and extrinsic values of learning. The data suggest that it would be particularly important to construct better measures of factors related to the work context and link these to expected utility and intentionality. Third, there is a serious lack of comprehensive qualitative studies. It would be particularly useful for the development of evidence-informed policy as well theory generation to have access to comparative qualitative data. This would allow researchers an in-depth insight into the subjective rational for citizens reasons to decline to engage in organized forms of adult education and also to explore how individual dispositions are directly and indirectly affected by broader structures and specific adult-learning policies.

See also: Participation in Adult Learning.

Bibliography

Becker, G. (1964). *Human Capital: A Theoretical and Empirical Analysis with Special Reference to Education*. New York: Columbia University.

Carlén, M. (1999). *Kunskapslyft eller avbytarbänk?* Dissertation. Acta universitatis Gothoburgensis: Göteborg.

CEDEFOB (2003). *Lifelong Learning Citizens' Views*. Luxembourg: Office for Official Publications of the European Communities.

Cross, K. P. (1981). *Adults as Learners: Increasing Participation and Facilitating Learning*. San Francisco, CA: Jossey-Bass.

Desjardins, R., Rubenson, K., and Milana, M. (2006). *Unequal Chances to Participate in Adult Learning: International Perspectives*. Paris: UNESCO.

Dow, S. C. (1998). Rationalisation in economics: Theory, methodology and action. In Dennis, K. (ed.) *Rationality in Economics: Alternative Perspectives*, pp 5–15. Boston, MA: Kluwer Academic Publishers.

Fitzgerald, R., Taylor, R., and LaValle, I. (2002). *National Adult Learning Survey*. London: Department for Education Skills.

Jonsson, J. and Gähler, M. (1996). *Folkbildning och vuxenstudier. Rekrytering, omfattning, erfarenheter-sammanfattning* (SOU1996: 159). Fritzes: Stockholm.

Livingstone, D. W. (1999). Exploring the icebergs of adult learning: Findings of the first Canadian survey of informal learning practices. *Canadian Journal for the Study of Adult Education* **13**(2), 49–72.

Nussbaum, M. (1990). Aristotelian social democracy. In Douglass, R. B., Mara, G. M., and Richardson, H. S. (eds.) *Liberalism and the Good*, pp 203–252. New York: Routledge.

OECD (2000). *Literacy in the Information Age*. Paris: OECD.

OECD (2005). *Promoting Adult Learning*. Paris: OECD.

Paldanius, S. (2007). The rationality of reluctance and indifference toward adult education. *Proceedings of 48th Annual American Adult Education Research Conference*, pp 471–476. Minneapolis, MN: University of Minnesota.

Rubenson, K. and Desjardins, R. (2009). The impact of welfare state regimes on barriers to participation in adult education: A bounded agency model. *Adult Education Quarterly* **59**(3), 187–207.

Rubenson, K. (2007). *Determinants of Formal and Informal Canadian Adult Learning*. Ottawa: Human Resources and Skills Development Canada.

Sen, A. (1982). *Choice, Welfare and Measurement*. Cambridge, MA: MIT Press.

Sen, A. K. (1999). *Development as Freedom*. Oxford: Oxford University Press.

Further Reading

Bélanger, P. and Valdivieso, S. (eds.) (1997). *The Emergence of a Learning Society. Who Participates in Adult Learning?* Oxford: Pergamon Press.

Desjardins, R. (2004). *Learning for Well Being. Studies Using the International Adult Literacy Survey*. Stockholm: Institute of International Education, Stockholm University.

Jonstone, J. W. C. and Rivera, R. J. (1965). *Volunteers for Learning. A Study of the Educational Pursuits of American Adults*. Chicago, IL: Aldine.

MacKeracher, D., Suart, T., and Potter, J. (2006). State of the field review: Barriers to participation in adult learning. http://library.nald.ca/research/item/6105 (accessed June 2009).

Tuijnman, A. and Hellström, Z. (2001). *Curious Minds – Nordic Adult Education Compared*. Köpenhamn: Nordic Council.

US Department of Education (1998). Adult education participation decisions and barriers: Review of conceptual frameworks and empirical studies. *Working Paper No. 98-10*. National Center for Education Statistics: Office of Educational Research and Improvement.

PERSPECTIVES IN ADULT EDUCATION RESEARCH

Trends in Workplace Learning Research

Gender Analysis

Class Analysis in Adult Education

Race and Ethnicity in the Field of Adult Education

Trends in Workplace Learning Research

T Fenwick, University of Alberta, Edmonton, AB, Canada

The nature and organization of work has changed so rapidly in the past decade with the introduction of new technologies and the effects of globalization that learning has become a lightning rod, attracting all sorts of new attention outside educational debates. Change in organizational structure and culture is now a learning issue. Innovation, now considered critical for competitive positions in the knowledge economy, is linked to learning. The increasing need to integrate migrant workers, along with attendant issues of inclusion, equity, gender, and race politics in the workplace, all have infused the workplace learning agenda. Therefore it is not surprising that research in workplace learning has accelerated since the mid-1990s, expanding into a wide assortment of fields including, besides adult education, organization and management studies, human resource development, sociology of work, economics, feminist studies, and industrial relations.

Definitions and Different Perspectives

The effect of this expansion has been to both enrich the existing perspectives and methods of understanding learning in work, and to blur categories. Across different fields, definitions of terms (such as learning, skill, empowerment, critical, and workplace) are multiple and often contradictory. Work can be paid or unpaid, based in organizational action or individual reflection. Work activity and learning varies widely depending on public, private, or not-for-profit sector, or on whether we are referring to a trades-worker or manager, self-employed professional, farmer, or domestic worker. Indeed, assertions about a generic workplace are inappropriate.

In some attempts to categorize different perspectives and definitions, the term workplace learning has been limited to individual change, with organizational learning reserved for groups. This is an arbitrary and rather unhelpful division, particularly when so many perspectives of learning in work refuse to separate the individual from the collective in examining learning processes. So in this article, workplace learning will refer to relations and dynamics among individual actors and collectives, along with group practices, tools, objects, cultural discourses, histories, and environmental forces that are all entwined with the behaviors of individuals and collectives. Workplace learning in this discussion refers not to formal planned training but to informal learning, that which is embedded in everyday material action and social interaction. Learning is defined not as

the product of change but as the process of generating new knowledge in activities and contexts of work; in particular, knowledge that expands human possibilities for flexible and creative action.

Overall, workplace learning research is a relatively new field characterized by multiplicity and vibrant debate, one that resists neat categories and typologies. This will become clear through the following discussion of three topics in workplace learning research, all prominent in current debates particularly in adult education: processes of learning, issues of identity and literacy, and power and politics in learning. These topics are not comprehensive, but illustrate key issues and point to future directions in workplace learning research.

Researching Processes of Learning in and Through Work

A review conducted of workplace learning literature published in nine scholarly journals between 1999 and 2005 identified various distinct perspectives of learning process (Fenwick, 2008). These can be distinguished according to the view of the individual relative to the collective, the role of reflection, and the role of action in learning. For example, some theorists see clear distinctions between the autonomous single individual and the environment, while others do not separate individual from collective or privilege the individual human over the complex mix of tools, cultural practices, and joint action of the system. Six perspectives are summarized here with the greatest attention accorded to the final theme of co-participation and co-emergence, as this appears to be a dominant direction emerging in workplace learning research.

Individual Knowledge Acquisition

Learning used to be understood primarily as acquisition: where individuals are believed to acquire and store new concepts and skills/behaviors as if knowledge were a package that didn't change as it transferred from its source to the learner's head. Learning tends to be valued according to the extent of its contribution to the organization's performance and productivity. Learning workers are therefore understood to be acquiring intellectual capital, increasing the organization's resources and return-on-investment on training. Research tends to focus on how to harness, draw out, and use the individual's acquired knowledge. Preoccupations include transferring acquired knowledge to practice, measuring competency (reliable valid measures and competence definitions are identified as problematic), and narrowing the gap between training investment and results. While this perspective appears to have declined since about 2001, it still appears in certain human resource development and management/organization studies of learning.

Reflection and Human Development

Here the emphasis is on sense-making. Learning is viewed as individual and collective construction of (new or altered) meanings: to identify problems, emerge solutions, or engage in collective inquiry. The general base is constructivist learning, for example, through reflection, which is affected by both the individual's history and unique perspectives, and by the meanings and language shared among the collective. Two directions have emerged in the research. One focuses on developing knowledge and practice of individuals; the other focuses on developing the organization's processes and culture. In both directions, workplace learning is viewed as fundamentally driven by reflection-on-action, in the swamp of uncertain, ambiguous, and contradictory dilemmas of practice. Reflection during and after the doing supposedly transforms experience into knowledge, which can then be represented and generalized to new contexts.

In research focused on the individual, studies have examined how to promote self-directed learning capability of individuals, and illuminate the relation of work to individual developmental processes and learning styles. In research focused on the group, studies have explored the nature of group reflection, and what factors influence particular meaning constructions at work. However, researchers who are critical of sense-making ideas show the rarity in practice of group critical reflection, dialog, and inquiry. Individuals are disillusioned with such practices, and the notion fails to sufficiently account for power relations in workplaces and knowledge hierarchies – including those created by researchers. Some critics have maintained that the emphasis placed on reflection is simplistic and reductionist, overemphasizing rational thought, and understating the unpredictable social tangles of everyday practice in which people develop.

Network Utility Model

Here, learning is portrayed as individuals and teams sharing useful strategies through networks within and across organizations, often electronically enabled, primarily for purposes of improving others' performance. Learning is thus information access. The key research preoccupations are improving diffusion: capturing, managing and organizing content, removing network barriers, and generally facilitating efficient, effective information flow or knowledge transmission (just-in-time) through a network. Learning networks are reported to take different shapes related to contexts, work characteristics, interactions, actor dynamics, and strategies; interorganizational networks are the most complex and take long time-periods to develop.

Most other research explores sociocultural issues, such as barriers and enhancements to knowledge sharing. For example, individuals and teams have been found to be willing to share if sharing is valued and supported and if the organization restructures payoffs for contributing, increases efficacy perceptions, and makes employees' sense of group identity and personal responsibility more salient. Overall, sociopolitical dynamics have been found to affect network effectiveness far more than technology.

Levels of Learning

Here the organization and individual (and team) are viewed as separate, distinct levels and forms of learning. This static layer-cake depiction is similar to the network utility model, but goes beyond linear transmission of information to acknowledge practices and politics. Research focuses on what happens at different levels, how different levels affect one another, how to link the levels in practice, and how/when to balance the exploratory (knowledge-creating) with the exploitive (knowledge-diffusion) dynamics. Learning levels might be depicted as units of people (individual, group, and organization) or as phases of learning (innovation, sharing, and routinizing). The link between levels is conceptualized rather mechanistically as cross-fertilization, diffusion, pipeline-sharing, and motoring.

Communities of Practice Model

This model, based on ideas first conceived by Jean Lave and Etienne Wenger, has been widely taken up since the publication of Wenger's (1998) book *Communities of Practice*. Learning is viewed as situated participation, embodied in the joint action evident in a community of practice (CoP). Individuals learn as they participate *in situ*: by interacting with a particular community (with its history, assumptions and cultural values, rules, and patterns of relationship), the tools at hand (including objects, technology, and language), and the moment's activity (its purposes, norms, and practical challenges). Knowing and learning are defined as engaging in changing processes of human participation in a particular CoP. A CoP is any group of individuals who work together for a period – such as a sports team, a workplace department or project group, a class, or club – developing particular ways of doing and talking about things that their members come to learn through action. The objective is to become a full participant in the CoP, not to learn about the practice. The community itself defines what constitutes legitimate practice.

Research seeks to explain the adaptation and reconfiguration of practices to meet changing pressures, and identify ways to facilitate these dynamics. Community learning is found to be affected by relational stability (trust), variety (new ideas, risk), and group structure (networks, competence). Learning is constrained by time pressure, deferral, and centralization within and across projects. Billett (2001) developed a useful model of guidance (direct, indirect, and environmental) that moves workers toward fuller participation in workplace activity, and hence to more comprehensive and critical knowledge as actors in their CoP. Critics of the CoP model of learning have pointed out its weak analysis of politics and solidarities within the community, including those which determine what counts as legitimate knowledge and expertise, and what knowledge (and identities) become marginalized. The CoP does not shed much light on how innovation occurs or how to develop specialized knowledge, especially during rapid change.

Co-Participation or Co-Emergence Model

In this orientation, individual and social processes are viewed as unique but enmeshed, and deserve examination at micro and macro levels of analysis. Learning is knowledge creation through social participation in everyday work. The conception is of mutual interaction and modification between individual actors, their histories, motivations and perspectives, and the collective (including social structures, cultural norms and histories, and other actors). Radical versions expand the collective to include environmental architecture, discourses, and objects, as in actor–network theory where knowledge circulates and is translated in each interaction of one agent mobilizing another. Cultural–historical activity theory views the individual and organization in dialectical relationship, where learning is occasioned by questioning practices or contradictions of the system, and is distributed among system elements: perspectives, activities, artifacts, affected by all contributors and clients. Complexity theory treats learning as inventive/adaptive activity produced continuously through action and relations of complex systems, occasioned in particular through disturbance. Most agree that learning is prompted by particular individuals (guides or mentors), events (conflict or disturbance), leaders (e.g., encouraging inquiry, supporting improvization), or conditions (learning architecture).

Long popular in Nordic research of workplace learning but just recently emerged in North American research is cultural–historical activity theory (CHAT). Here, learning is viewed as change in a community's joint action. The community's activity is shaped by its rules and cultural norms, division of labor and power, and mediating artifacts (language, tools, and technologies) that

it uses to pursue the object – a problem at which activity is directed. Learning occurs as the collective construction and resolution of tensions or contradictions occurring within this activity system. Unlike other practice-based systemic perspectives of workplace learning, CHAT retains its Marxist influences in its recognition of the inherent contradictions in capitalist work systems based on labor exchange, and in its analysis of the historical emergence of particular practices and ideologies (see Chaiklin *et al.*, 2003).

In organizational studies and increasingly in educational study in Canada, complexity theory is also gaining acceptance as a useful way to understand how activity, knowledge, and communities emerge together in the process of workplace learning. Individual interactions and meanings form part of the workplace context itself: they are interconnected systems nested within the larger systems in which they act. As workers are influenced by symbols and actions in which they participate, they adapt and learn. As they do so, their behaviors, and thus their effects upon the systems connected with them, change. The focus is not on the components of experience (which other perspectives might describe in fragmented terms: person, experience, tools, and activity) but on the relationships binding them together. Workplace learning is thus cast as continuous invention and exploration in complex systems.

Critics suggest that such practice-based studies of workplace learning bypass questions of politics and power relations: who is excluded from the construction of knowledge in a CoP, what dysfunctional or exploitative practices are perpetuated in communities of practice, and what hierarchical relations in the workplace reproduce processes of privilege and prejudice. Issues raised include accreditation and assessment of learning when it's buried in co-participation, distinguishing desirable from undesirable knowledge development, accounting for changing notions of what is useful knowledge, and differentiating influences of particular groups in the co-participational flux (positional, generational, gendered, etc). At issue is the extent to which sociocultural learning theories including notions of communities of practice, complex adaptive systems, or even CHAT suppress or enable core questions about the politics and purposes of workplace learning.

Researching Identity and Literacy in Workplace Learning

Work communities are powerful sites of identity, practices, and knowledge systems in which individual workers' desires for recognition, competence, participation, and meaning are both generated and satisfied. Identity is ultimately a representation or mental conception that we ascribe to ourselves and others: our conception of who we are, our identity, is constituted by the power of all of the discursive practices in which we speak, which in turn speak us, so to say (Chappell *et al.*, 2003: 41).

People's sense of their own knowledge in work, and the knowledge valued by the group to which they see themselves belonging, form a critical element of their sense of identity. Further, their participation in work practices is entwined with the identities they come to inhabit within a particular community. Identity work itself involves learning. Workers figure out how to position themselves in an organization, how to perform identities that are acceptable to their immediate peers but also that allow themselves freedom and some autonomy and control. In work environments of rapid change where people must transform their practices, they understand their knowledge as more mutable and fluid; they are adopting shifting identities: they literally learn to perform different selves and knowledge in different environments. Yet at the same time, people often employ deliberate strategies to anchor their identities.

Researchers have explored how particular identities are constituted among these varied coordinates, and how learning processes are implicated in individuals' subjections, negotiations, assertions, and shifts of subjectivity (see Billett *et al.*, 2007). One case studied miners compelled to transform their work from manual labor in heavy equipment operation to computerized manipulation of equipment using joysticks in an office. At issue was the men's macho-masculine identities, which were no longer relevant. Overall, adult education researchers are interested in how people come to recognize the limitations of their current work identities, how they recognize possibilities for new identities, and what strategies they learn to cope with repressive constraints on their work identities.

Language and literacy are closely related to identity and learning: people's sense of who they are and what they know and can do at work are embedded in the language and textual practices they use. One area of workplace research examines how learning is shaped by particular written texts in changing workplace environments such as documents, policies, record-keeping forms, or employee growth plans. Such texts standardize what counts as knowledge, thus controlling the work practices and working relations of people employed. As people are pressed to learn new literacies in their work, their sense of self shifts along with their ways of conceptualizing and doing their work. Globalizing forces, such as standardization, are introducing new texts and literacies into work such as the massive form-filling required to demonstrate compliance with ISO-9000 standards, or the accent training given in call centers to make Indian workers sound American on the telephone. New literacy practices have been engendered by the shift to post-Fordist work arrangements such as self-directed teams. Workers used to hierarchical communication pipelines have had to learn how to participate productively in team meetings: how to set goals, analyze, and assess collective work through leaderless reflective team dialogs.

A concern for technological upskilling, or developing worker literacy in new technologies, has prompted many training programs as well as research to explore exactly how people learn to work with technologies. On this theme, Sawchuk (2003) studied technology learning practices of workers, integrated with everyday life and mediated by artifacts such as computer hardware and organizational settings. He presents a "working-class standpoint" that opposes even while it accepts managerial control, and often copes through subversion. Sawchuk found that for working-class people, computer technology is a "key signifier" for workers' deepest class-based desires and fears: the sense of losing control and being left behind in an inevitable techno-obsessive world, the frustrations of trying to figure out capricious computer processes, or the trials of purchasing the right computer on limited incomes. Yet working-class learning thrives in informal networks, what Sawchuk calls "solidaristic networks" (p. 123): where mutuality and group orientations within stable working-class communities produce knowledge in everyday computer learning. It is here that Sawchuk found an "enormous surplus" of knowledge production capacity as well as emancipatory potential for working-class people.

Researching Power and Politics in Workplace Learning

Calls for greater attention to research examining power relations in workplace learning have not resulted in much empirical research. In the literature review of nine journals 1999–2005 (Fenwick, 2008), only about 15% of published articles touched upon power or politics, and these were almost exclusively theoretical in nature. Five different perspectives of power appear to be represented among these. In the radical view, organizations are viewed as sites of central contradictions and ideological struggle between those who control the means of production and those whose labor and knowledge are exploited. In the discursive view power is viewed as circulating through regimes of knowledge and discursive practices. Power is not possessed by particular people or institutions, but is constantly created and readjusted through relations among people and practices, notions of what is normal and what is valuable. Workers participate in and help to sustain the very regimes that discipline and repress their identities and opportunities. In the identity politics view, power relations consolidate a dominant workplace culture whose practices and beliefs actively marginalize or even persecute individuals by virtue of their gender, race, religion, sexual orientation, or conformance to the ability-norm valued by the dominant. The micropolitics view analyses power relations as confined to individual strategies to improve their own advantage, such as gamesmanship. Finally, the community view avoids a critical analysis of structures, knowledge politics or even interpersonal politics: power is viewed as benign energy, exercised mainly in mobilizing individuals around shared vision, mutual engagement, and sense of belonging.

Adult education analyses of work tend most to feature the radical and identity politics views of power, so further discussion of these two is warranted to show their links to learning. In the radical view, workplace learning is often envisioned as radical transformation among workers: empowerment purposed towards workplace reform. Radical or emancipatory learning involves workers first in critically analyzing existing repressive conditions of work, including mechanisms in place for controlling knowledge and the means of production. Then strategies for resistance and change are generated collectively, in a learning process that builds solidarity, individual and collective agency, and workers' capacity to defend their rights. This learning process of transformation is often positioned in opposition to reproduction, where workers learn to accept and even support exploitative, hierarchical structures that subjugate them and reproduce existing (inequitable) power relations. However, some have argued that this traditional dualism may be overly simplistic, that research needs to examine how reproductive and transformative learning are entwined in everyday work and with what workers themselves want to learn.

In critical workplace learning research, adopting an identity politics view of power, issues of race, disability, sexual orientation, and religion are almost completely absent despite their growing importance in other areas of adult education. Gender, on the other hand, has received substantial attention. Studies show that women continue to confront gendered work knowledge and training structures in organizations based on patriarchal values, male-oriented communication patterns, and family-unfriendly schedules. New expectations for continuous learning related to learning organization initiatives, self-directed teams, technological upskilling and development of new literacies, all create work overload that poses particular burdens for women who still carry the double-duty bulk of domestic and childcare work at home. Women in particular are often expected to nurture the close relationships and community that organizations want, to mentor others, and to display cheerfulness (Mojab and Gorman, 2003). Yet the learning valued and supported most in organizations tends to be related to leadership development, knowledge creation, and organizational growth, in professional/managerial jobs where women continue to be underrepresented. Meanwhile, women who are new immigrants and women of color are overrepresented in precarious, contingent employment such as call centers, food service, and home-based work where there are few learning opportunities or communities offering the rich sort of participation and learning networks to help women obtain better-paying, more secure employment.

Future Directions

As is clear in this discussion of learning process, identity, and power in workplace learning research, perspectives range widely according to fundamental understandings of what constitutes knowledge, how it is constructed, how workers are connected to one another and to their environments, and how action and reflection are related. Furthermore, different researchers and educators propose very different purposes for workplace learning, and these tend to influence the way learning is understood. Some focus on individual human development, some on building solidarity and political consciousness among workers, while others are more interested in upskilling workers or changing organizational culture to increase productivity. Labor educators tend to focus on enabling workers to obtain control of their own knowledge. Management and human resource theorists tend to focus on increasing human performance. Other differences in perspective arise from the unit of analysis. Those who focus on the individual might explain processes in acquiring concepts, developing expertise or practical intelligence, or transforming beliefs. Those who focus on the system might examine social learning processes, construction of cultural narratives, or forms of knowledge production and change occurring in the group. These different perspectives are not necessarily irreconcilable, but neither do they nest neatly into one another. Clearly, workplace learning is contested terrain filled with fundamental tensions related to what knowledge counts most and who says so. No single model for workplace learning is acceptable in the face of such distinct positions.

Three emerging perspectives described in this article may become particularly important in guiding future research. One is what is here referred to as co-participation/ co-emergent views of learning in work, including cultural–historical activity theory, actor network theory, and complexity theory. These approaches work at both micro and macro levels to help analyze the workplace mix of actors, objects, and culture and how forms of knowledge emerge and become adopted in this mix. Another is the area of new textual/literacy practices engendered by globalization, and their influence on people's work identities and knowledge. The third is analysis of power relations, particularly to address issues of disability, race, religion, and sexual orientation where significant workplace stigma and discrimination has been observed but surprisingly little research has been conducted, particularly connecting these issues to workplace learning. Overall, there continues to be great need for in-depth empirical research that traces what people actually do and think in everyday work activity, and for research methods that can help illuminate the learning that unfolds in everyday work. Of all the ideas currently afloat in adult education literature addressing work issues, these trends seem most likely to influence future perspectives, program design, and pedagogical practice in workplace learning.

See also: Characteristics of Adult Learning; Economic Outcomes of Adult Education and Training; Labor Education; Workplace-Learning Frameworks.

Bibliography

Billett, S. (2001). *Learning in the Workplace: Strategies for Effective Practice.* Sydney: Allen and Unwin.

Billett, S., Fenwick, T., and Somerville, M. (eds.) (2007). *Work, Learning and Subjectivity.* New York: Springer.

Chaiklin, S., Hedegaard, M., and Jensen, U. J. (2003). *Activity Theory and Social Practice: Cultural Historical Approaches.* Langelandsgade: Aarhus Press.

Chappell, C., Rhodes, C., Solomon, N., Tennant, M., and Yates, L. (2003). *Reconstructing the Lifelong Learner: Pedagogy and Identity in Individual, Organisational and Social Change.* London: RoutledgeFalmer.

Fenwick, T. (2008). Understanding relations of individual-collective learning in work: A review of research. *Management Learning* **39**(3), 227–243.

Mojab, S. and Gorman, R. (2003). Women and consciousness in the learning organization: Emancipation or exploitation? *Adult Education Quarterly* **53**(4), 228–241.

Sawchuk, P. H. (2003). *Adult Learning and Technology in Working-Class Life.* New York: Cambridge University Press.

Wenger, E. (1998). *Communities of Practice: Learning, Meaning and Identity.* New York: Cambridge University Press.

Further Reading

Boud, D. and Garrick, J. (eds.) (1999). *Understanding Learning at Work.* London: Routledge.

Bratton, J., Mills, J. H., Pyrch, T., and Sawchuk, P. (2003). *Workplace Learning: A Critical Introduction.* Aurora, ON: Garamond Press.

Farrell, L. and Fenwick, T. (eds.) (2007). *Educating the Global Workforce.* London: Routledge.

Fenwick, T. (ed.) (2001). *Socio-Cultural Understandings of Workplace Learning.* San Francisco, CA: Jossey-Bass/Wiley.

Rainbird, H., Fuller, A., and Munro, A. (2004). *Workplace Learning in Context.* London: Taylor and Francis Group.

Symes, C. and McIntyre, J. (2002). *Working Knowledge: The New Vocationalism and Higher Education.* New York: Palgrave Macmillan.

Taylor, J. (2001). *Union Learning: Canadian Labour Education in the Twentieth Century.* Toronto: Thompson.

Gender Analysis

J Stalker, University of Waikato, Hamilton, New Zealand

Introduction

Gender analysis is a useful tool which adult educators can use in their struggles for social justice. It is a complex activity which basically represents an optimistic attempt to end disparities and disadvantages among different genders. At its most expansive, it aims to create a paradigm shift to a world of an enduring, healthy environment and global peace.

Some might argue that the field of adult education has a strong track record of undertaking gender analysis. For decades theoreticians, researchers, and practitioners have explored women's participation and nonparticipation in various forms of adult education, the preferences and learning styles of women adult learners, the shifting roles and responsibilities of women, the different possibilities and consequences of development for women, formations of women's identities, and so on. Often, these were examined in relation to men's responses in the same contexts. However, although for many decades adult educators have theorized, researched, and practiced adult education in relation to both women and men, that is not the same as conducting the complex task of a gender analysis.

Given the above, the purpose of this article is to explore the complexities and possibilities of gender analysis for adult educators. First, this article presents the concept in terms of its interwoven theoretical positionings. Second, the artciel explores it as a research process of data collection, analysis, and strategic initiatives. Third, it briefly explores some benefits which accrue to gender analysis. Fourth, it examines the challenges which face adult educators who undertake gender analysis in the future. Finally, the article concludes with a summary and invitation to adult educators to make a commitment to gender equality.

Theoretical Positionings of Gender Analysis

In the industrialized world, our current understandings of gender analysis are shaped by its several theoretical positionings across the previous decades. Strictly speaking, gender analysis would encompass analyses of men, women, trans-genders, trans-sexuals, transvestites, homosexual lesbians, bisexuals, woman-born-woman, woman-born-man, man-born-woman, and inter-sexuals. Gender, after all, is the culturally ascribed roles given to the sexual identities of women and men.

In reality, we ascribe the term gender analysis contemporarily and retrospectively to several kinds of analyses and these in turn guide our current approach to the task. Thus, below, the basic theoretical positionings, or strands, which shape adult educators' present understandings of the concept of gender analysis, are identified. Although it is tempting to present these as linear and developmental, these approaches are actually dynamic, unstable, interactive, and cyclical.

The first strand is driven by an oppositional approach and it has a long history. In this approach, analyses focus on women's situations in relation to men's situations. Such an approach rests on the evidence that women are missing from the data. As a result, its subsequent analysis and any resultant theory, research, or practice address only half the world's population. Solutions for this dilemma emphasize the notion of equality, that is, the same treatment of women and men in the hopes of creating equal outcomes.

This oppositional approach juxtaposes women with men, and positions them through their sexual identities as unique and distinctive. Those differences most often seem to be expressed dichotomously as women against men, feminism against patriarchy, powerless against the powerful.

This approach is not new, since for centuries the major religions of the world have analyzed and defined separate roles for women and men. In the wider context, as the industrialized world evolved, these definitions tended to be increasingly extrapolated and debated in terms of women's and men's relative and different economic roles as producers, reproducers, and consumers (Dimand et al., 2004).

The second strand takes a diverse approach. Basically, it challenges the oppositional positioning of women and men, and values complexities and multiplicities. It argues that women, and men, do not belong to homogeneous groups. Rather, there are multi-faceted definitions of gender and many masculinities and femininities which theoreticians, researchers, and practitioners should acknowledge. The emphasis shifts to equitable treatment and outcomes within groups of women and of men, as well as between women and men, with a view to co-creating a new, more equitable, and sustainable world.

This strand has been strengthened by three forces. In the first instance, as the postmodern discourse in academe intensified, the oppositional positioning of women and men came under close scrutiny. It became obvious that women and men were complex and not so tidily separated from each other into two groups. The rigid stereotypes and assumptions associated with each sexual identity were challenged. The clear, all embracing, distinctive divisions between the two groups were redefined as constructs with many overlaps and congruencies, influenced by context and culture. There was an awareness that women and men can make unique, yet also similar, complementary contributions. The emphasis changed to the need for both women and men to change patterns of the past.

In the second instance, women who did not see themselves in the oppositional discourse challenged it. Women from a wide variety of classes, colors, races, ethnicities, abilities, ages, and sexual orientations argued that the approach and analyses did not include the realities of their lived experiences. Rather, they suggested that the analyses were most often based in the lives of white, middle-class, heterosexual, able-bodied women. Ironically, the discourse they generated also has oppositional and diversity approaches.

Finally, it became clear that a dichotomous positioning of men against women could work to the disadvantage of women. Such a framework lent itself to straightforward comparisons between women and men. In patriarchal environments, this led too easily to a definition of men's values, abilities, and actions as the preferred norm and women's values, abilities, and actions as deficient relative to men.

In sum, the second strand has a stronger focus on gender and broader understandings of women and men. Notions of social construction, de-construction, identify formation, context, and culture merge to create a more complex, dynamic picture which is reflected in the term gender. The more static notions of reified, strongly categorized women and men are broadened to embrace wide diversity within those terms.

These two strands can be traced in the adult education literature in the publications of industrialized nations. As the selected exemplars below illustrate, the strands are simultaneously contemporary and historical. Publications in the first strand treat women as a unique phenomenon absent from our history (Hugo, 1990) and deserving of special study (Lewis, 1988; Stalker, 2005; Thompson, 1985). Often the latter publications make reference to the classic work by Belenky *et al.* (1986). Publications in the second strand reflect a view of 'woman' and 'man' as complex and diverse categories (e.g., Hayes and Colin, 1994; Graveline, 1994; Hill, 1995; Johnson-Bailey and Cervero, 1996; Luttrell, 1989; Tisdell, 1993; Walters and Manicom, 1996).

A third hybrid approach to gender analysis also exists. This is a complex strand which attempts to acknowledge the first strand's focus on women without losing the second strand's emphasis on complexity. It focuses on the category of women yet also values the differences among and within the category. It argues that the stories, experiences, and knowledge of all women are needed in order to achieve their genuine empowerment and sometimes, it includes the role of men of multiple gender identities in the analysis and locates them as potential allies.

It is difficult to undertake gender analyses from within this strand. It requires a negotiation of space and power in new ways (Medel-Anonuevo, 1997). It is a conceptually very complex task to keep a useful balance between a dichotomous approach and a diverse approach. What often happens is that theoreticians, researchers, or practitioners give a brief acknowledgment to either approach and then proceed with a strong preference for one or the other. In other words, a truly hybrid, balanced approach to gender analysis is still in the process of evolution.

This is, in part, because the hybrid strand has struggled to survive in a sharpened global context in which those in developing, majority nations deal with cruel realities. Particularly in the late twentieth century, it seemed that their poverty flourished, war raged unabated, and environmental disasters increased in number. Even in more comfortable nations, the neo-liberal agenda thrived and the negative impacts of its capitalist focus on privatization, competition and globalization were keenly felt.

Against this backdrop, adult education activists around the world came and continue to come together at international conferences to demand increased participation and decision-making power for women. Although it is sometimes referred to as the Gender agenda, the essence of their arguments often is captured by the observation that "Women hold up half the sky." This exemplifies the hybrid positioning which hints at a more diverse approach yet has a strong, irrefutably oppositional stance. It illustrates that despite its critics, oppositional positioning continues to influence our theorization, research, and practice of gender analysis. This happens for several reasons.

First, the adult education agenda has become more globalized. It now includes the voices of many who come from contexts in which the situation of women is explicitly and irrefutably horrific. Adult educators in these contexts often argue that women's (and girls') continuing, persistent, and unrelenting oppression are the result of men and their patriarchal systems. These ensure that the effects of poverty, war, environmental disasters, and neo-liberalism are most severely experienced by women. They contend that disestablishing patriarchal systems is the real key to national progress, economic development, and self-reliance.

The voices and experiences of these educators seem to be particularly powerful and poignant. The media have helped to strengthen those voices through their increased exposure of appalling violences against women worldwide. In addition, adult educators in industrialized nations, perhaps valuing diversity, seem to have a will to value the lived experiences of their majority nation colleagues and to accept their judgments about how to interpret and resolve gendered issues.

At the same time, the adult education global agenda has been shaped by the World Bank and International Monetary Fund. As the major global players for aid and development programs, they now incorporate women into many of their priorities. They and other international aid agencies see the inclusion of gender and in particular women as an efficient and effective way to increase national stability and improved, sustainable economic outputs. In other words, women are key to improving the lives of all citizens, men included. Significantly, education and adult education are identified as strategic devices to engage women and girls in these goals.

A second factor that encourages the oppositional approach to gender analysis concerns the criminalization and/or condemnation of sexual minorities. Numerous industrialized and majority nations reject the idea that multiple gender identities are possible. Many have explicit legislation that makes it illegal to either identify as, or practice as, any identity other than man or woman. Other nations are more subtle, but equally hostile to the idea. These forbidden identities can include trans-gender, trans-sexual, transvestite, homosexual lesbian, bisexual, woman-born-woman, woman-born-man, man-born-woman, and inter-sexual. Within these contexts, data collection is restricted to the categories of male and female. When international comparisons are planned, this then also impedes the research agenda of more liberal nations.

Finally, readily available historical, and also contemporary, databases are shaping the approach to gender analyses. Although these provide a logical foundation for further analyses and comparisons, they often used male–female categories. When these become the base for further research, the pattern of dichotomous positioning is entrenched and difficult to disrupt.

These databases have also kept alive the oppositional approach because, as some data have been collected for global projects, they have revealed boy's educational underachievement. Two arguments that revolve around these data further the oppositional discourse. Some argue that women's and girls' concerns have been largely solved and that boys and men must now become the priority. Others argue a preoccupation with establishing policies, practices, and funding for girls' and women's education has undermined boys' and men's achievement. Both arguments place women/girls and men/boys in competing opposition to each other.

Global publications reflected this persistent oppositional approach when women's nongovernment organizations and feminist activists organized internationally to put women, and increasingly girls, on the agenda and in their published documents (UNIFEM and UN/NGLS, 1995). The International Women's Decade (1976–85)

played an important role in this process as did policies generated at Women's World summits (e.g., 1975, Mexico City; 1985, Nairobi; and 1995, Beijing). Significant, clear resolutions and publications devoted to the advancement of women and girls were promulgated around the world (e.g., 1979, Convention for the Elimination of all Forms of Discriminatory Against Women, CEDAW) (REPEM, 1996).

Publications generated at summits not devoted entirely to women's issues also began to highlight the role of women (Scampini, 2001). Typical of their tone is a resolution included in the *1995 Copenhagen World Summit for Social Development* document. It stated specifically that social and economic developments were unlikely to be achieved in the long term if the full participation of women was not achieved.

Similarly, world summits focused specifically on education established global legislation, clear commitments, and specific goals related to women's and men's education. Key among these were *Education for All (EFA)* (launched in 1990), *CONFINTEA V* (1997 adult education global UNESCO conference), and the *Millennium Development Goals (MDG)* (signed by the United Nations in 2000). These summits committed, and continue to commit, signatory nations to many education-related goals and include the promotion of gender equality and empowerment of women and girls and more recently, men and boys. Significantly, the MDG's stated aim was to address these issues preferably by 2005, and in a worse case scenario by 2015. These tight and specific deadlines are propelling much of the current analysis.

In summary, this section has examined how gender analysis is shaped by its theoretical positionings. Clearly gender analysis is a complex concept – and made all the more muddy by the seemingly random use of the term gender. What we name concurrently and retrospectively as gender analysis can display oppositional, diverse, and/or hybrid approaches.

As the agenda of adult education becomes more globalized, sexual minorities continue to seek legal identities, and historical databases are used, the oppositional approach has re-emerged. However, simultaneously, there is a robust underlying discourse which acknowledges the complexity of gender and seeks equitable outcomes within groups of women and of men, as well as between women and men. In the end, the exposure of explicit differences between women and men, enhanced by this more complex view, creates the base for rich analyses. In the discussion which follows, the terms gender equality, women, and men will be used to represent that richer meaning.

A Research Process

It is against this vibrant, dynamic background that gender analysis is undertaken as a research process. Researchers collect, measure, manipulate, and interpret data in systematic ways to provide evidence of the comparative situation between women and men. Gender analysis reveals, interprets, revises, monitors, and evaluates in a continuous, cyclical process which moves toward gender equality. The research process is the foundation of gender analysis and is composed of three interwoven elements: data collection, data analysis, and strategic initiatives.

Data Collection and Analysis

Data collection in gender analysis can be understood through an examination of the approach, focus, and technique. In terms of approach, data are collected systematically through both quantitative and qualitative approaches.

An increasingly popular and powerful quantitative approach used in gender analysis involves the use of indicators for monitoring. This is a kind of social watch which examines the extent to which nations have achieved the goals to which they committed at international conferences. Quantitative indicators related to the goals are identified so that "concrete aspects of reality can be observed and measured" (ICAE, 2003: 12). This allows the adult educator to collect rich data on a nation's real commitment to issues like: general policies on adult learning, adult literacy and basic education, promotion of active citizenship, awareness of discrimination, culture of peach and human rights, work-related adult learning, health education, involvement of civil society in environmental and development problems (ICAE, 2003). The data expose the increase, decrease, or lack of movement in these areas. They have the added advantage of being comparable across nations and this means that they can expose the relative commitments of nations.

A qualitative approach is particularly important at two levels. First, it is useful to supplement the limited representation of reality yielded by quantitative data. It provides a more multi-dimensional and complex account of the social facts and processes within which they develop (ICAE, 2003). Second, a qualitative approach is useful to uncover the subtle, murky yet powerful historical and cultural obstacles to equality. It can reveal these barriers through the study of peoples' views of gender disparities in a wide range of areas. It can reveal respondents' assumptions and allow for a more flexible probing of their beliefs to reveal their subjective interpretations of their lived experiences.

In both the qualitative and quantitative approaches, data may be collected from already-existing databases and may also be generated by new research. It can be a snapshot of a moment, frozen in time. To give more depth to the findings, those data can then be compared to previous, baseline data, or collected continuously over time to give a longitudinal picture of the situation.

The second important element in data collection is the focus. It is concerned with the domains of investigation and the way in which the data are framed. Data can be gathered from the microlevel of day-to-day household differential responsibilities and from more complex levels of policies, programs, service delivery, and political/economic/social/cultural elements of institutions and structures. It can be gathered on an endless number of variables such as employment, unemployment, violence, health, education, housing, sanitation, safe water, nutrition, property rights, literacy, social mobility, and so on.

Whatever the domain, a priority for gender analysis is that the approach is gender sensitive, and as we might expect from the theoretical discussion above, often it is framed from women's perspectives. However, gender analysis goes beyond the mere collection of data on women to men ratios. For example, in relation to participation, a key domain of gender analysis, one might begin by examining the women to men ratios in recruitment, involvement, and completion. Although those data are revealing in and of themselves, gender analysis would also include the study of the gendered nature of access to, and control and management of resources, production, reproduction, decision making, benefits, gendered roles, responsibilities, knowledge, skills, and activities. Gender analysis thus brings a greater depth of understanding to the issue of women's inequality because it emphasizes issues of women's relative power, control, and management.

Similarly, in relation to work, research traditionally focuses on paid work. Research based in gender analysis, however, acknowledges the reality of women's lives and reframes it as an issue of the gendered division of labor in both the public/paid and private/unpaid spheres. In the same way, traditional research often presented women as the victims and passive recipients of their situations. However, gender analysis research tends to present them as agents of resistance and change despite their oppressive contexts.

The technique of collection is the third important element in the data collection process. Adult educators undertaking gender analysis strive to ensure that the process is participatory and based in sound relationships. Ideally, the rights and needs of grassroots communities drive it and data are given back to those whose lives they effect so that they increase peoples' understandings of gender discrimination and foster their agency. These civil society relationships are strengthened by healthy partnerships with other key stakeholders. These are at the local, national, and international levels and include relationships with government departments, women's offices/leaders/organizations/networks, religious/educational/media organizations, think-tanks, corporations, businesses, and academics. This participatory, relationship-based approach to collection permeates gender analysis, including the process of data analysis.

Data analysis is not a summative activity which occurs only after data collection is completed. Rather, it is ongoing process which begins at the very first steps of the collection and measurement of data. Data analysis is a process of manipulating and interpreting the collected data so that it makes sense. It highlights and prioritizes patterns, trends, and relationships and is based in the search for differences and gaps, in the first instance, between women and men but also within those groups. It tells us what exists by providing a dense, information filled picture of the situation. It helps us to understand why it happens by exposing crucial links between components of the data.

In summary, data collection and analysis are dynamic, interactive, and ongoing elements of the research process. Both are done with rigor and are shaped by a focus on gender equality.

Strategic Initiatives

Gender analysis does not stop with the collection and analysis of data. It includes the creation of strategic initiatives which are interventions to foster equality between and within groups of women and men. It is important to note that data collection and analysis are strategic initiatives in and of themselves. The very process of beginning a gender analysis is a strategy which begins to reveal barriers to women's full participation in decision making. The initial activities of collection and analysis can provide us with new understandings of our worlds and, by placing women's and men's inequalities at the center of the research process, expose oppressive attitudes, systems, and structures.

The summative outputs of gender-sensitive data collection and analysis projects are equally important in shaping strategic initiatives. Like the initial collection and analysis, they can focus on inequalities embedded in a wide range of areas from day-to-day household differential responsibilities to the policies, programs, service delivery, and political/economic/social/cultural elements of institutions and structures. Strategies can be immediate and practical, as well as sustained and long term. As in the processes of data collection and analysis, strategic initiatives seek to be participatory. Ideally, civil society and key stakeholders together create collaborative strategies aimed at gender equality.

In brief, strategic initiatives are part of a sustained, ongoing, dynamic, cyclical process of planning, implementation, monitoring, and evaluation. They are neither tidy, final, nor definitive solutions and they need to be designed with a view to the particular contexts within which they will exist. Nonetheless, there are some important strategies which are worth mentioning.

First, as an adult educator might expect, gender training is a frequently used strategy. This training gives communities, organizations, networks, and the people within them the time and space to engage with the concepts and issues of gender equality. It seeks to strengthen the capacity of women and men within the organization or network so that they can address gender inequalities. Ideally, the training is a process of both capability building and politicization. In the first instance, the objective is to build a solid information, skills and knowledge base and the self-confidence of the participants. In the second instance, the objective is to enable advocates to work collectively to claim equality at all levels.

A second example of a common strategic initiative is the reform of gender architecture, that is, the creation of structures within organizational structures to ensure that gender is a key consideration of every process, goal, and output. Often a gender unit is created to undertake a gender watch for the organization and acts in an advisory capacity to ensure that gender is mainstreamed. Gender training is frequently an important part of the unit.

A third initiative is gender-based budgeting. It uses a gender lens to assess and guide local, national, and international financial decisions about funds so that women and men can benefit equally. Such a lens reviews the allocation of funds for women-centric schemes, the incorporation of women into the decision-making processes of budget creation, the reflection of the concerns of women, and the assessment of the budget in relation to any commitments made to women and girls at international conferences.

In sum, there are many strategic initiatives which are part of the research processes of gender analysis. They must be responsive to their contexts, but there are some contemporary, exciting examples of global initiatives. It is worth noting too that essentially all initiatives seem to share the goal of gender mainstreaming. In other words, gender is irrefutably, irrevocably at the center of every consideration at every level. Women's views and their priorities are integral to every process, with the goal of achieving gender equality.

Benefits

Given the complexity of the concept and the intensity of the research process, one might well ask if the benefits which accrue to gender analysis are worth the effort. There are several responses to this. First, from an altruistic point of view, one might argue that the rights of women and men to lead full and satisfying lives is a worthwhile outcome for us all. It is a humane response to counter the asymmetric impact on women of fundamentalisms, wars, and neo-liberalism.

The second, and frequently presented, argument for gender analysis is an economic one. The basic line of reasoning is that, as 51% of the world's population, women are a largely untapped reserve of labor which nations need to support their economic objectives. It is simply a matter of investing in people. Fuller participation of women, created by the insights of gender analysis and related strategic initiatives, can remove women from unproductive labor and engage them more fully in the paid labor market. Associated with this is the notion that women, once part of the paid labor market, can then become consumers – a role which also creates more demand for the production of goods.

An associated economic argument is that gender analysis allows for a more efficient allocation of resources. By exposing inequalities across a variety of variables, nations and funding aid agencies can see how to better utilize their funds. For example, gender analysis can reveal that participation of women in educational programs is low and that is because women travel miles to collect safe water. The problem can then be redefined as an infrastructure rather than educational problem and resources directed into drilling local wells to remediate the underlying problem.

The final economic argument is a very muted one, for it suggests that women have unique knowledge, skills, and experiences which will help achieve economic objectives. A gender analysis, for example, can reveal that women have longstanding practices which can better serve economic growth than ones introduced from other contexts.

Challenges for the Future

Gender analysis has a strong potential to address the oppression between and among groups of women/girls and men/boys. However, it faces several challenges. The first challenge is to create a global gender agenda to further the struggle for equality. It would be naive to believe that uncoordinated gender analysis projects, by themselves, are effective. They cannot effectively resist or indeed defeat the globalized neo-liberal agenda which impacts more harshly on women than on men. Lacking a global gender agenda, it is questionable if gender equality can ever be achieved.

The second challenge is to engage industrialized nations in the search for gender equality. Although many have ratified conventions like CEDAW, their operationalization of that commitment is often minimal. They too often seem to see gender analysis as an activity which needs to be undertaken in the nations to which they give aid rather than in their own backyards. They seem reluctant to expose the gender inequalities which so clearly still exist in their own industrialized nations. This reluctance also subverts the global gender agenda and is a major stumbling block to the realization of gender equality.

The third challenge is to extend the existing networks and alliances in the global struggle for gender equality. Currently, the movement is driven primarily by nongovernment organizations and women. Gender is related to issues of the environment, peace, sustainability, and partnerships by gender activists with those issues are essential. In addition, men must be made accountable for women's ongoing disadvantage. This is particularly important since men continue to hold the majority of decision-making positions in the world. Although there are men who are allies in the struggle for women's equality, there are many more who, through their silences, allow women's oppression to continue.

Fortunately, adult educators are able to face these challenges with optimism. In the adult education sector, there are global organizations of women and men committed to gender analysis. They have been active for decades and have driven the global gender agenda with unfailing enthusiasm and commitment. These include the Gender Education Office (GEO) of the International Council for Adult Education, Development Alternatives with Women (DAWN) and Red de Educacion Popular entre Mujeres (REPEM). Our support for their work is a key to gender equality.

Conclusion

In conclusion, it is clear that gender analysis is neither a tidy concept nor exact research process. It is equally clear that there are individual and global benefits which accrue to gender equality. Despite the challenges, gender analysis is a useful tool to move us toward gender equality.

We know from history that the advancement toward women's equality is an uneven and precarious progress. However, the field of adult education is well located to play a key role in leading the struggle for gender equality. We have the expertise and experience to promote and undertake gender analysis. Adult education is, by definition, involved in the processes of teaching and learning so integral to that analysis. The final factor will be the extent to which the field makes an authentic, energized commitment to achieve gender equality. That is the ultimate challenge which confronts us all.

See also: Adult Education and Nation Building; Community Based Adult Education.

Bibliography

Belenky, M. F., Clinchy, B. M., Goldberger, N. R., and Tarule, J. M. (1986). *Women's Ways of Knowing.* New York: Basic Books.

Dimand, R., Forget, E., and Nyland, C. (2004). Retrospectives: Gender in classical economics. *Journal of Economic Perspectives* **18**, 229–241.

Hayes, E. and Colin, S. A. (eds.) (1994). *Special Issue: Confronting Racism and Sexism. New Directions for Adult and Continuing Education: No. 61.* San Francisco, CA: Jossey-Bass.

Hill, R. (1995). A critique of heterocentric discourse in adult education: A critical review. *Adult Education Quarterly* **45**(3), 142–158.

Hugo, J. M. (1990). Adult education history and the issue of gender: Toward a different history of adult education in America. *Adult Education Quarterly* **41**, 1–16.

ICAE (2003). Agenda for the future six years later. *ICAE Report*. Uruguay: ICAE.

Johnson-Bailey, J. and Cervero, R. (1996). An analysis of the educational narratives of reentry Black women. *Adult Education Quarterly* **46**(3), 142–157.

Lewis, L. (ed.) (1988). *Special Issue: Addressing the Needs of Returning Women. New Directions for Adult and Continuing Education. No. 39.* San Francisco, CA: Jossey-Bass.

Luttrell, W. (1989). Working-class women's ways of knowing: Effects of gender, race, and class. *Sociology of Education* **62**(1), 33–46.

Medel-Anonuevo, C. (ed.) (1997). *Negotiating and Creating Spaces of Power.* Hamburg: UIE.

REPEM (1996). *Education in Motion. Agreements on the World Conferences of the Nineties.* Uruguay: REPEM.

Scampini, A. (2001). United Nations conferences: Commitments on education and gender justice. Education in motion. In Gender Education Office (ed.) *Women's Education. Chronicles of a Process*, pp 35–51. Uruguay: International Council for Adult Education.

Stalker, J. (2005). Women's learning. In English, L. (ed.) *International Encyclopaedia of Adult Education*, pp 659–663. New York: Palgrave MacMillan.

Thompson, J. (1985). *Learning Liberation. Women's Response to Men's Education.* London: Croom Helm.

Tisdell, E. J. (1993). Interlocking systems of power, privilege, and oppression in adult higher education classes. *Adult Education Quarterly* **43**(4), 203–226.

UNIFEM and UN/NGLS (1995). *Putting Gender on the Agenda. A Guide to Participating in UN World Conferences.* New York: UNIFEM.

Veronica McGivney's recent critical survey. *Excluded Men*.

Walters, S. and Manicom, L. (1996). *Gender in Popular Education: Methods for Empowerment.* London: Zed Books.

Further Reading

Buttterwick, S. (2005). Feminist pedagogy. In English, L. (ed.) *International Encyclopaedia of Adult Education*, pp 659–663. New York: Palgrave MacMillan.

Hayes, E. and Flannery, D. D. (eds.) (2000). *Women as Learners: The Significance of Gender in Adult Learning.* San Francisco, CA: Jossey-Bass.

Imel, S. (1995). Race and gender in adult education trends and issues. *ERIC Document ED382822.*

Johnson-Bailey, J. and Cervero, R. (2000). The invisible politics of race in adult education. In Wilson, A. L. and Hayes, E. R. (eds.) *The Handbook of Adult and Continuing Education*, pp 147–160. San Francisco, CA: Jossey-Bass.

Stalker, J. (1996). The New Right and adult educators: A feminist view. *Access: Critical Perspectives on Cultural and Policy Studies in Education* **15**(2), 67–79.

Relevant Websites

http://www.awid.org – AWID.
http://www.icae.org.uy – ICAE.
http://www.ilo.org – International Labour Organization.
http://www.oecd.org – Organisation for Economic Co-operation and Development.
http://www.unifem.org – United Nations Development Fund for Women.
http://www.undp.org – United Nations Development Programme.

Class Analysis in Adult Education

T Nesbit, Simon Fraser University, Vancouver, BC, Canada

The concept of class is indispensable but elusive. Notions of class are deeply embedded within broader beliefs about society and history and preserved by the need to explain continuing inequalities in opportunities and standards of living or the social divisions that they foster. However, it remains an ambiguous concept, challenged by the lack of a generally accepted definition, new forms of social stratification, and identity and other subjective politics. Also, the political and cultural changes of recent times – accelerating globalization, the rise of neoliberalism and free-market capitalism, a shift from manufacturing to service economies, the decline of an industrial working class, increased militarization, greater concern for the environment, the promotion of individualism and consumerism, and widening disparities between rich and poor – have witnessed diminishing public interest in the concept of class. Some commentators have even gone so far as to proclaim its demise or at least that it has outlived its relevance. Yet, class stubbornly fails to disappear and remains an important analytic concept for examining the structural causes and manifestations of inequality and power.

Class, however, means different things to different people: a theoretical device for analyzing the social world; shared social conditions; or a set of particular orientations, beliefs, and life practices. Popular understandings still describe class in terms of occupation, income, wealth, education, mobility, lifestyle, taste or ownership and the power that accrues from them. Others see class less as a possession than a dynamic – a relationship made between different people and groups divided along axes of power and privilege. As class differences play out in power relations, adult education can play a critical role in forming and mediating these relations.

Generally concerned with identity and personal and social change, adult education seeks to provide the knowledge, skills, and attitudes for people to engage more fully in and shape their individual and social worlds. Yet, such worlds are not continually created anew but shaped by the past. So, adult education provides opportunities for personal mobility but within systems already marked by social inequality. Whatever its particular focus, approach, or clientele, adult education is essentially a sociopolitical endeavor with struggles for power – who has it, how they use it, and in whose interests – at its heart (Cervero *et al.*, 2001).

Adopting a class analysis of adult education does three things. First, it draws clear links between adult learners, educational institutions and processes, the social worlds of work, family, and community, and the economic systems that underpin them. Second, it makes visible the struggles of those who are variously poor, excluded, or dispossessed and the educational resources they can draw upon. Third, it highlights how educational institutions and processes function to inculcate and maintain dominant ideologies and values. As adult education is a moral and political endeavor as much as it is a technical practice, it is affected by its role in maintaining or challenging the social order. Do educational policies and practices reproduce existing relations of dominance and oppression? Alternatively, do they contribute to lasting social as well as personal change?

In general, adult education is intended to ameliorate the personal and social disadvantages created by circumstance and background. So, social divisions and the tensions they bring about are commonly seen as critical issues for adult educators. In fact, the educational approaches, structures, and activities that perpetuate the silence and invisibility of marginalized and disenfranchised groups are a regular feature of the adult education literature. This literature is permeated with regular exhortations to consider class, race, and gender as prime markers of social division. Yet, in comparison with its counterparts, the study of class has tended to be underexplored by adult education researchers. To examine why this might be so, several of the relationships between class and adult education are outlined. First, some differing perspectives on class are provided before exploring how they inform and illuminate various areas of adult education practice.

Perspectives on Class

In capitalist societies, all aspects of peoples' lives and social relations are subjected to market requirements which are then normalized and made to seem natural. People's prestige and status are related to their productive ability; society values people by how much they earn or own. Basic aspects such as where we live, how we earn a living, who our friends are, and what access we have to healthcare and education are all dependent on our ability to produce wealth and other resources. Of course, these attributes are not fixed permanently; because the distribution of resources is unequal, people strive to maintain or enhance their own share. Thus, people's struggle for access to and control of resources is dynamic. Capitalist societies are stratified into classes, hierarchies of power and privilege related to the ownership and control of various forms of capital. Capitalist systems of structured inequality continue because society portrays them as normal or inevitable: the system encourages its victims to blame themselves for their failure to be successful. In this way, dominant groups are able to maintain the status quo and the hegemony of their own ideas without facing too strong a challenge from those less powerful.

Although ideas about class have been in use since Roman times, its current articulation stems from the Industrial Revolution. By the middle of nineteenth century, Marx used class as the foundational concept for explaining social organization in terms of understanding the ownership, means, and control of work processes. He claimed that societies consisted of two main classes: the bourgeoisie (who owned and controlled the mills, mines, and factories) and the proletariat (workers with only their labor power to sell). For Marx, the relationship between these two classes is essentially unequal and exploitative. The working class generates surplus wealth but does not profit from it as much as they might because the bourgeoisie disproportionately appropriates and accumulates it. He regarded all social life as marked by the struggles and conflicts over the generation and distribution of wealth and the status attached to it. Societal transformation was only possible when workers developed class consciousness about the sources of exploitation: a sense of a shared predicament, awareness of the capitalist class as their common enemy, and a realization of their common strength and destiny (Marx and Engels, 1845/1970).

Not everyone regards class in such materialistic terms. Weber, for instance, argued that class is better defined by also including notions of culture, politics, and lifestyle. People who fall within the same economic class may nevertheless occupy different social class positions and have differing opportunities for work, income, developing skills, obtaining education, and owning property. For Weber, one's class is based more on these life chances, cultural background, status, and life outside of work than it is on one's relationship to the ownership and control of the means of production. Rather than see society as a two-class system, Weber posited a system of social stratification of many different classes that sometimes overlap. This less-deterministic approach can also be seen in the work of Bourdieu for whom a class is any grouping of individuals sharing similar conditions of existence and tendencies or dispositions. Equally important as one's location in an economic order is the possession of various forms of capital – economic, cultural, social, or symbolic – which can constellate differently in different societies. Bourdieu's concept of class thus takes into account other stratifying factors, such as gender, race, ethnicity, place of residence, and age. Finally, these class structures are not predetermined or imposed from without but subtly reproduced by people acting within preexisting contexts. Although both Weber and Bourdieu allowed more scope for human agency than did Marx, they still regarded external class structures as fundamental and quite constant. In other words, class relationships transcend the individuals who occupy the positions: people may move around (or stay put) but they still divide into exploiters and exploited.

These two broad views have shaped current understandings of class. Throughout the social upheavals of industrialization, definitions of class in Europe continued to be affected by older ideas of rank. The lower orders, laboring classes, and the middling ranks of society (such as merchants or teachers) existed alongside the aristocracy and the gentry. However, as the stratification of industrial society became more rigid, these definitions settled into the familiar classification of working, middle, and upper class. This depiction treats class as essentially static. Although it underlines the essentially economic nature of class, such a definition ignores the dynamic and shifting nature of the relationships between those who possess wealth and power and those who do not. More recently, class has come to be regarded as a relation that is constantly changing. As one major British historian puts it, "class is not a category...but rather an historical relationship between one group of people and another.... It is defined by men [*sic*] as they live their own history" (Thompson, 1971: 9–10).

Non-European countries – many still affected by the legacy of colonization – regard themselves as relatively free from the archaic categories of class distinction. For example, in the United States, one commonly hears either that class has ceased to exist or, alternatively, that everyone is middle class. Instead, the ethics of self-reliance and mobility and the ideologies of individualism, egalitarianism, and meritocratic achievement have been more powerful forces than class solidarity. Nowadays, existential rather than social factors tend to influence who people think they are. For example, it is far more common for people to define themselves as black, gay, Jewish, Latino, lesbian, or age- or mobility-challenged than to refer to themselves in terms of class. In some countries, the historical legacy of slavery and its lingering consequences have shaped a more complicated system of stratification – one kept in place by ideological as well as economic factors (Levine, 1998). Older depictions of class are now regarded as too simplistic for heterogeneous countries such as the USA. This has been further confounded by the rise of movements specifically identified with racial, women's and gay equality, environmental concerns, and various manifestations of religious, national, and ethnic rights. Nowadays, constructs such as class, race, and gender are commonly seen as interrelated and overlapping (Collins, 1993; Wood, 2002); social class is recognized as both gendered and racialized and viewed as but one part of a wider and interlocking system of oppression and domination (Rothberg, 1998).

With these different and competing notions of, and perspectives on, class, discussing it can be difficult. Wright (1979) identifies four major approaches to understanding class: a functional differentiation of positions within a society, groups unified by their common position in a hierarchy of power or authority, groups with different market capacities that result in different life chances, and a shared location in the social organization of production. However, whatever one's orientation, an attention to class and class analysis reveals several general principles. First, a class analysis focuses on materialist concepts regarding the production and reproduction of social life and the importance of human activity in shaping both material subsistence and consciousness. Second, a class analysis highlights the fundamental and dynamic relationships between economic and social structures, the ideologies that frame our world, and the ways we experience, understand, and shape the world. Third, a class analysis suggests that we cannot explain social phenomena by their surface manifestations nor by the ways that individuals experience them, but as, instead, representations of external divisions of power. Fourth, a class analysis provides a basis for explaining why people organize themselves into collective forces to resist injustice and exploitation. Finally, for those with a commitment to social justice, a focus on class also raises several important questions: How do we negotiate or internalize dominant ideologies and relations of ruling? How might alternative ones develop? How can marginalized people, silenced by social, economic, and cultural relations of power, recover their voices and the right to be heard? These questions are often central to the practice of adult education, and I now turn to exploring the relationships between it and class.

Class and Adult Education

Various forms of adult and continuing education are now firmly established as central to the smooth functioning of economic systems and societies. As concepts such as lifelong learning and the knowledge or learning society have gained prominence, various forms of adult education and training have become key vehicles for preparing people to be adaptable to economic and cultural changes in society. Prevailing educational practices tend to inculcate dominant values rather than confront them and, because most educational institutions are generally a middle-class domain, their policies and practices are weighted strongly in favor of middle-class values. So capitalist societies, in which class operates as a primary structuring of social inequality, usually ignore or bury class perspectives. As such, many adult educators are uncertain about how their work reflects underlying political structures, let alone economic systems. Observing the effects of power and privilege is far easier than determining their causes.

A number of studies explore how education can reproduce existing patterns of power. Economists Bowles and Gintis (1976) demonstrated how educational systems are part of a system of broader capitalist class relations. Their correspondence theory explains how, in general, schools reproduce the social relations that capitalist production requires. As Bowles and Gintis describe, capital requires two things: workers of specific types and relative social stability and ideological acceptance of class relations. The capitalist class thus has a broadly shared set of interests pertaining to educational systems and the capacity to promote such interests.

Some find the correspondence theory too mechanistic or reductive; it allows little agency for those involved. One less-deterministic approach suggests that education serves the interests of the privileged by structuring learners' access to and uses of various forms of social and cultural capital (Bourdieu and Passeron, 1977). Others have introduced notions of struggle and resistance into this process. For example, Willis (1977) showed how several working-class teenage boys consciously resisted and rebelled against school and classroom authority. Tellingly, however, this resistance worked better within school than outside it: when the boys left school, they remained unable to find anything but unskilled and unstimulating jobs. McLaren (1995) and Apple (1996) also show how individuals can resist and contest social and cultural oppression in educational settings. They document the complex relationships between cultural reproduction and economic reproduction and explore how class interrelates with the dynamics of race and gender in education.

These studies indicate the essential role of education in promoting and maintaining the social relations required for capitalist production. Adult education is far from immune from these trends. Although we now recognize that the relationships between educational practices and political structures are much more complex than correspondence theory suggests, adult educators who work in areas such as adult basic education, literacy, vocational and workplace education, and welfare-to-work, and other social programs will recognize how often their work, the policies about it, and the textbooks and curricula they use are still much more closely tied to employers' needs than to their adult or working-class students' interests (Boughton, 2006; D'Amico, 2004; Kincheloe, 1999; Rose, 1989).

Much of the published research on class in adult education explores the consequences or experiences of class and examines issues such as the participation, access, and attainment of different groups. In documenting how social class affects participation in adult education programs, such studies consistently underscore how far social class remains a key determinant of adult participation in organized learning. To give just one recent example, Sargent and

Aldridge (2002) indicate that upper- or middle-class adults are twice as likely to engage in some sort of learning activity than those from the working class.

However, although such studies detail how class remains a major factor affecting adult education participation, most do not really explore either the constitutive dynamics of class or how it operates in practice. From a conceptual perspective, they add little to London's classic study (London *et al.*, 1963) which explored the important contribution that adult education makes to larger society, specifically for those deemed less educated and less skilled. London and his colleagues found a strong connection between social class and people's abilities to prosper in a rapidly changing world. Class not only affected participation in adult education activities but was also closely related to other facets of social life such as jobs, vocations, and leisure pursuits. Anticipating subsequent debates about lifelong learning, London's report called for adult education and training to "become a continuing part of everyone's life" (p. 148), providing "both education for work and education for leisure" (p. 153).

Perhaps more seriously, too few published studies further class awareness or address what Allman *et al.* (2007) describe as the chasm between class as social inequality and class as a constitutive element of the world of struggle. Instead, the published studies linking class and adult education concentrate on the results rather than the causes or workings of class. This is understandable. Individuals tend to internalize the conflicts within hierarchical systems, especially those individuals without much power. Also, people usually closely experience class at the same time as other, more recognizable forms of oppression. These factors, when combined with the scarcity of class scrutiny, ensure that people do not always have readily available concepts to identify – let alone analyze – the class aspects of their experiences. So scholars prefer to focus on more obvious markers of social division and overlook class in their theoretical lexicon. Class is also difficult to discern: we can only examine it through its consequences or outcomes. And, as it is not easy to identify or operationalize on an individual level, it is much better suited to macro- rather than micro- analyses. Even when it is acknowledged, class still tends to be regarded as an individual characteristic or an entity rather than a constituent social relationship. So, the tendency of many adult education researchers to assume a strong individual orientation tends to further divert attention away from class perspectives.

Yet, sophisticated and theoretical explorations of class and adult education do exist – generally emanating from countries with a more prominent appreciation of class relationships. For example, Allman (2001), Livingstone (1999), Stromquist (1997), Thompson (2000), Walters (1997), Welton (1995), and Youngman (2000) all provide rich empirical and theoretical examinations of how adult education practices are linked to social class and the increasingly globalized nature of capitalism. Appreciating that class is understood and experienced differently around the world, Nesbit (2005) gathers several adult educators from different countries to explore how class affects adult education and to examine how the complex relationships between class, gender, and race play out in its policies, practices, and discourses. Discussions of the relationships between adult education and social class are also more noticeable on the margins of the established adult education literature. To give a flavor of such work, I now explore how class has been used to analyze several different arenas of adult education practice: approaches to learning, its role in social movements, and the related fields of higher education and working-class studies.

One distinguishing feature of adult education is its close attention to learning. In their studies of working people's intelligence and learning, both Rose (2004) and Sawchuk (2003) provide two of the best recent analyses of the interrelationships of class and adult learning. Both identify a distinctive working-class learning style that operates independently of formal training and centers around informal workplace and community networks. This learning style is collective, mutual, and solidaristic: people exchange knowledge and skills, hardware and software, and draw upon each other's different expertise to develop group resources for anyone to use. So they develop an expanding learning network – a powerful working-class resource that stands opposed to the trajectory of dominant forms of workplace and institutionalized education that individualize and commodify learning. Although most research on adult education and class focuses on how working-class people are excluded and help to exclude themselves from formal education, Rose and Sawchuk show that working-class adults can bring rich cultural resources to their learning.

Adult education deliberately seeks to link the personal with the social and much of its historical development and traditions are linked with movements for social justice and equity. A class perspective on adult education's role in social movements underscores that lasting social change comes about through people acting together to challenge inequality and oppression. For example, Altenbaugh (1990), Schied (1993), and Walters (2005) provide compelling accounts of the ways in which class affects the educational activities of those who are active in labor and workers' movements or who struggle for social justice in South Africa. As Walters shows, learning about and discussing earlier battles for social justice can provide resources and hope to those involved in current struggles. Other discussions of the role of adult learning and education in social movements are provided by Holst (2002) and Foley (1999). Basing their work on the ideas of Freire, Gramsci, and Marx, they each explore the idea that radical adult educators can help build civil society through social movements. Two aspects of their work are particularly important to a class-based appreciation of adult education. First, "learning in such situations is tacit, embedded in action and often not recognized as learning" (Foley, 1999: 3). Second, the notion of learning in and through struggle: "people's every day experience reproduces ways of thinking and acting support which support the, often oppressive, status quo, but [can also] enable people to critique and challenge the existing order" (ibid, pp. 3–4).

The related field of higher education also provides analyses of how universities treat adult learners from different class backgrounds and how such students experience university-level education (Ball, 2003; Tokarczyk, 2004). Other studies explore how curricula and pedagogy in different disciplines reflect class-based interests (Margolis, 2001), how the pedagogical status quo might be challenged and classroom practices democratized (Shor, 1996), and how class shapes the identity and teaching of educators (Malcolm, 2005). The emerging field of working-class studies has also reinvigorated discussion of the intersections of class, adult learning, and institutional practices (Roberts, 2007; Zandy, 2001). Acknowledging that working-class learners now constitute a significant proportion of students enrolled in institutions of higher education, this body of work incorporates a sensitivity to students' working-class roots while suggesting curricular and pedagogic innovations informed by an awareness of class culture.

Conclusion

Class analyses of adult education highlight the unexamined patterns of behavior through which society produces and reproduces social classes in the dynamics between educational activities and the wider cultural politics of societies. They show how capitalism is not just an economic system but rather a totalizing system of social relations. They also expose the superficiality of a variety of currently prescribed educational reforms: instrumental outcomes, the individualizing of educational opportunities, increased competition, accreditation, and commercial involvement, privatization of post-secondary institutions, a return to so-called basics, the streaming of learners into cultural or functional literacies or core competencies, the increasing pressures to work harder and longer, and the tendency to disregard or downplay social and collective notions of identity and action.

Despite overwhelming evidence to the contrary, too many still claim that the idea of class has outlived its usefulness and that focusing on it and other forms of oppression is misguided and unnecessary. Instead, educational approaches seem generally more committed to the management of inequality rather than its elimination and often encourage people to accept rather than challenge their place in society. Yet, adult educators need not be bystanders to political contexts but vital and essential members of them. A class analysis of adult education raises important and challenging questions that build upon learners' lived experiences about how inequalities play out in communities, lives, and workplaces. It also confronts any approach to confine adult education to the production and maintenance of human capital or advances the political and economic interests of the powerful at the expense of the poor. Finally, it helps adult educators and their learners resist what has been called the postmodern condition of "skepticism, uncertainty, fragmentation, nihilism, and incoherence" (Allman, 2001: 209).

Bibliography

Allman, P. (2001). *Critical Education against Global Capitalism*. New York: Bergin and Garvey.

Allman, P., McLaren, P. L., and Rikowski, G. (2007). After the box people: The labour–capital relation as class constitution and its consequences for Marxist educational theory and human resistance. In Scott, A. and Freeman-Mohr, J. (eds.) *The Lost Dream of Equality: Critical Essays on Education and Social Class*, pp 125–150. Rotterdam: Sense Publishers.

Altenbaugh, R. (1990). *Education for Struggle: The American Labor Colleges of the 1920s and 1930s*. Philadelphia, PA: Temple University Press.

Apple, M. W. (1996). *Cultural Politics and Education*. New York: Teachers College Press.

Ball, S. (2003). *Class Strategies and the Education Market*. London: Routledge Falmer.

Boughton, B. (2006). Researching workplace learning and class. *Economic and Labour Relations Review* **17**(2), 157–164.

Bourdieu, P. and Passeron, J. C. (1977). *Reproduction in Education, Society, and Culture*. Thousand Oaks, CA: Sage.

Bowles, S. and Gintis, H. (1976). *Schooling in Capitalist America*. New York: Basic Books.

Cervero, R. M. and Wilson, A. L., and associates (2001). *Power in Practice*. San Francisco, CA: Jossey-Bass.

Collins, P. H. (1993). Toward a new vision: Race, class and gender as categories of analysis and connection. *Race, Sex, and Class* **1**(1), 25–45.

D'Amico, D. (2004). Race, class, gender, and sexual orientation in adult literacy: Power, pedagogy, and programs. In Comings, J., Garner, B., and Smith, C. (eds.) *Review of Adult Learning and Literacy: Connecting Research, Policy, and Practice*, pp 17–69. Hillsdale, NJ: Erlbaum.

Foley, G. (1999). *Learning in Social Action*. London: Zed Books.

Holst, J. D. (2002). *Social Movements, Civil Society, and Radical Adult Education*. New York: Bergin and Garvey.

Kincheloe, J. L. (1999). *How Do We Tell the Workers? The Socioeconomic Foundations of Work and Vocational Education*. Boulder, CO: Westview.

Levine, R. F. (ed.) (1998). *Social Class and Stratification*. Oxford: Rowman and Littlefield.

Livingstone, D. W. (1999). *The Education–Jobs Gap*. Boulder, CO: Westview.

London, J., Wenkert, R., and Hagstrom, W. O. (1963). *Adult Education and Social Class*. Berkeley, CA: University of California, Berkeley Survey Research Center.

Malcolm, J. (2005). Class in the classroom. In Nesbit, T. (ed.) *Class Concerns: Adult Education and Social Class*, pp 45–52. San Francisco, CA: Jossey-Bass.

Margolis, E. (ed.) (2001). *The Hidden Curriculum in Higher Education*. New York: Routledge.

Marx, K. and Engels, F. (1845/1970). *The German Ideology*. Arthur, C. J. (trans. and ed.). London: Lawrence and Wishart.

McLaren, P. L. (1995). *Critical Pedagogy and Predatory Culture*. New York: Routledge.

Nesbit, T. (ed.) (2005). *Class Concerns: Adult Education and Social Class*. San Francisco, CA: Jossey-Bass.

Roberts, I. (2007). Working-class studies: Ongoing and new directions. *Sociology Compass* **1**, 191–207.

Rose, M. (1989). *Lives on the Boundary: The Struggles and Achievements of America's Underprepared*. New York: Free Press.

Rose, M. (2004). *The Mind at Work*. New York: Viking Books.

Rothberg, P. S. (ed.) (1998). *Race, Class and Gender in the United States: An Integrated Study*. New York: St. Martin's Press.

Sargent, N. and Aldridge, F. (2002). *Adult Learning and Social Division*. Leicester: National Institute of Adult Continuing Education.

Sawchuk, P. H. (2003). *Adult Learning and Technology in Working-Class Life*. New York: Cambridge University Press.

Schied, F. M. (1993). *Learning in Social Context*. DeKalb, IL: LEPS Press.

Shor, I. (1996). *When Students Have Power*. Chicago, IL: University of Chicago Press.

Stromquist, N. P. (1997). *Literacy for Citizenship*. Albany, NY: SUNY Press.

Thompson, E. P. (1971). *The Making of the English Working Class*. Oxford: Oxford University Press.

Thompson, J. (2000). *Women, Class and Education*. New York: Routledge.

Tokarczyk, M. M. (2004). Promises to keep: Working-class students and higher education. In Zweig, M. (ed.) *What's Class Got to Do With It?*, pp 161–167. Ithaca, NY: Cornell University Press.

Walters, S. (ed.) (1997). *Globalization, Adult Education and Training*. London: Zed Books.

Walters, S. (2005). Social movements, class, and adult education. In Nesbt, T. (ed.) *Class Concerns: Adult Education and Social Class*, pp 53–62. San Francisco: Jossey-Bass.

Welton, M. R. (ed.) (1995). *In Defense of the Lifeworld: Critical Perspectives on Adult Learning*. Albany, NY: SUNY Press.

Willis, P. (1977). *Learning to Labour*. Farnborough: Saxon House.

Wood, E. M. (2002). Class, race and capitalism. *Political Power and Social Theory* **15**, 275–284.

Wright, E. O. (1979). *Class Structure and Income Determination*. San Diego, CA: Academic Press.

Youngman, F. (2000). *The Political Economy of Adult Education*. London: Zed Books.

Zandy, J. (ed.) (2001). *What We Hold in Common: An Introduction to Working-Class Studies*. New York: Feminist Press at CUNY.

Further Reading

Althusser, L. (1971). Ideology and ideological state apparatuses. In Brewster, B. (ed.) *Lenin and Philosophy*, pp 170–186. London: New Left Books.

Gramsci, A. (1971). *Selections from the Prison Notebooks*. Hoare, Q. and Smith, G. N. (trans. and eds.). New York: International Publisher.

Hooks, B. (2000). *Where We Stand: Class Matters*. New York: Routledge.

Linkon, S. L. (ed.) (1999). *Teaching Working Class*. Amherst, MA: University of Massachusetts Press.

Reay, D. (2001). Finding or losing yourself? Working-class relationships to education. *Journal of Education Policy* **16**(4), 333–346.

Seabrook, J. (2002). *The No-Nonsense Guide to Class, Caste and Hierarchies*. Oxford: New Internationalist Publications.

Sennett, R. and Cobb, J. (1972). *The Hidden Injuries of Class*. New York: Vintage.

Tisdell, E. (1993). Interlocking systems of power, privilege, and oppression in adult higher education classrooms. *Adult Education Quarterly* **43**(4), 203–226.

Weber, M. (1920/1968). *Economy and Society: An Outline of Interpretive Sociology*. New York: Bedminster Press.

Wright, E. O. (ed.) (2005). *Approaches to Class Analysis*. New York: Cambridge University Press.

Youngman, F. (1986). *Adult Education and Socialist Pedagogy*. London: Croom Helm.

Race and Ethnicity in the Field of Adult Education

J Johnson-Bailey and D Drake-Clark, The University of Georgia, Athens, GA, USA

Race and ethnicity are factors that act in major ways in determining how our society functions. Whether you divide the world into South and the North, East or West, or look within national cultures with diverse peoples, race can be tied to one's social and economic status. At present, the Northern Hemisphere is the site of unprecedented economic growth, while the Southern Hemisphere struggles with hunger, malnutrition, and preventable diseases. Within the North's multicultural nations, such as the United States, Canada, and the United Kingdom, race remains a more predictable marker of wealth, class, and poverty than educational level.

While ethnicity and other terms such as multiculturalism and diversity are identifiers and qualifiers often used more broadly than the term race, these descriptors not only denote racial groups, but the cultural aspects associated with racial groups and with groups that can be distinguished by religion, language, and traditions. There is no one correct way to define ethnicity since its usage varies across the world with different connotations specifying race, national origin, and tribal and clan membership. Over time, these terms came to be used interchangeably. Although race and ethnicity are socially constructed phenomena, herein, race and ethnicity will be used to refer to both genotypic and phenotypical differences.

Quite often societal customs, traditions, and norms conceal how one race is privileged over another or how a group of people is disadvantaged because of their racial or ethnic membership. The ordering of our society around race and ethnicity does not disappear at the classroom door; it continues to operate within our educational systems. Race is not the only positionality that categorizes or impacts the social order; however, race is an important factor in the rankings that regulate societal hierarchy. The effects of how race and ethnicity are viewed in the world are embedded in our educational fabric and the field of adult education is no exception.

There are historical and contemporary understandings of race in adult education and these views have framed the practical educational responses of adult educators. Race is a social construct that has no basis in biology (Frankenberg, 1993; Gregory and Sanjek, 1994; Winant, 1994) as anthropologists and biologists have long recognized that the human form cannot be examined through visual or scientific inspection to definitively determine a person's race. It is, at best, a fleeting notion established by an arguable set of physical characteristics. Although race

is a social construct, its effects are real in terms of social power and privilege (Giroux, 1997). Race has a major role in determining how our society functions. This ordering of the world along set queues occurs because, as people are categorized as belonging to a race, those persons are accorded all the rights, privileges, and baggage that accompany the classification (McIntosh, 1995). Therefore, to be of Asian ancestry has a different meaning than to be of White ancestry. And these meanings change depending on geography. So to be White in France carries a different set of connotations than does being Asian; and to be Asian in Malaysia carries yet another set of implications.

To discuss race and ethnicity in adult education is to confine the discussion largely to the West (as in North America, the United Kingdom, and Europe) and to limit the analysis to what is referred to as the North (highly industrialized nations located primarily in Europe and North America) simply because race and ethnicity are not widely acknowledged in adult education literature in the South. The adult education literature from the South tends to bound their discussions along the lines of nationality with national and regional parameters. Therefore, the discussion herein will focus unevenly on the North due to its availability of programs where an analysis of race and ethnicity are more possible. This article first presents a discussion of how race operates in the larger society and in the educational system. This introduction is followed by the discussions of adult education in the North and South.

A Historic Perspective of the West and the North

Adult education as a field was established in the early 1920s and its primary mission was the education and the continuing education of adults. From its inception, the field held that being an educated adult allowed one to participate fully as a citizen, to contribute materially to the well-being of society, and to develop as a person capable of striving toward self-actualization. Therefore, one of the primary purposes of adult education was to teach adults throughout their lifespan so that they could lead more fulfilling and productive lives. An American example of how the field worked toward the democratization of society through the education of adults was the Highlander Folk School (now called the Highlander Research and Education Center), an organization established in 1932, whose adult education programs contributed significantly to two of the most important Western social movements of the twentieth century: the workers' rights and the Civil Rights movements.

While the stated goals of adult education have consistently been set forth as aspiring toward leveling the playing field for all adults, especially those lacking a basic education, and as desiring to empower learners so that they might engage in full citizenship, just the opposite often occurs. Since Western society is a place replete with hierarchical systems that privilege some and deny others, its academic systems are designed to reproduce the *status quo*. And as an academic discipline, adult education has also mirrored society by functioning like other areas of education. The major portion of adult education programs today in the United States, Europe, Australia, Japan, and in other heavily industrialized settings, involve continuing education, particularly continuing professional education, and human resource development programs in business and industry. Literacy, citizenship, and adult basic education programs in such settings have been largely relegated to federally and community-funded programs.

As a field, how we define race is reflected in how we write, research, and teach. For the most part, adult education literature has encompassed an implicit cultural hegemony, regardless of intentions, that centers the dominant White majority as the norm and empowers one group while disempowering others. In our major texts and publications, data on people of European descent is always present, making it therefore logical to assume that Whites have done the most or certainly have made the more significant contributions. The concealed message is that other groups have not done the same. In addition, in an educational setting, membership in a disenfranchised group translates into direct inequities: sub-standard education, tracking, and unequal opportunities for higher education. In society at large, such inequities have negative economic outcomes that construct barriers to the opportunities that are set forth as the ideals for all people in a democratic and prosperous society. Without naming it as race, or more accurately racism, in our educational arena, the underlying ideas of whiteness as superior and non-whiteness as inferior or deficient are ever present.

Other than the grassroots activist programs, which are bounded by their locale, the field of adult education in both practice and programming has been somewhat quiet on issues of race and ethnicity in that research by and about peoples of African, Asian, and Hispanic descent has been essentially absent from the adult education literature. Throughout the years, on the few occasions when race and ethnicity have been topics in the North American adult education literature, the discussion has been confined mostly to a dialog about Blacks or African Americans. Race and ethnicity in contemporary Western society are used to refer primarily to people of color; Whites are treated as if they have no race.

In examining race in the West, the conversation in the United States has been more overtly framed in racialized terms, while European and British examination of difference have been framed by discussions of class. In the 1930s and 1940s in the United States, there was a strong conversation in the literature on Blacks in adult education that was led by Alain Locke, the first Black president of the American Association for Adult Education (an organization which exists today as the American Association for Adult and Continuing Education). It was under his direction that national conferences on African American adult education issues were held in 1938, 1940, 1941, and 1942, and it was his leadership that led to the chronicling of African American adult education national efforts in the 1948 yearbook issue of *The Journal of Negro Education*. However, these efforts waned after the publication of the 1948 yearbook.

The historical documents that define North American and European Adult Education are the nine *Handbooks* published from 1934 through 2000, which provide comprehensive overviews of the field's major issues and concerns. Given the importance of these texts in the field, the ways in which race is addressed or not addressed is informative. Although race is a central location for the negotiation of power and privilege in education and in society, this topic never formed the focal point of a single chapter until the 2000 handbook. While the 1934 (Rowden, 1934) and both handbooks of 1936 (Locke, 1936a, 1936b) had chapters on adult education for Negroes, and the 1948 handbook (McCurtain, 1948) had a chapter on adult education of American Indians that offered descriptions of programs for these groups, no chapter dealt with race and ethnicity as a topic by addressing the central role that race was playing in Western society during this period of legal segregation in the United States. This absence of discussion about race and ethnicity continued in subsequent handbooks, even in the face of major social upheavals such as the Civil Rights movement and the American desegregation of public schools and other public institutions that provided adult education. The 1989 handbook returned to the trend of the 1930s and 1940s by having a chapter on racial and ethnic minorities and adult education (Briscoe and Ross, 1989). In addition to this chapter on specific racial groups, a discussion of race in the context of the social setting for adult education appeared in two handbooks (London, 1970; Rachal, 1989).

The way race has been socially constructed in the literature of North American and European adult education over the past half-century has been remarkably stable. This view is that the White race is the norm against which all other races are to be compared. This perspective, which is the colorblind perspective (it is not seen and it is not discussed) is so deeply embedded in the social fabric that there has been little discussion of adult education for Whites even though the White race has constituted the vast majority of the population for adult education. Whenever race is discussed in the handbooks, then, it is conceptualized as non-White. Of course, when one group is normative, then the others are viewed as abnormal. This leads to the obvious conclusion that separate chapters would be needed to discuss the specific educational efforts being made to address the needs of these special populations.

Starting in the 1980s, there was a renewed interest in issues of race and ethnicity in the adult education literature. These contemporary perspectives on race in adult education fall into two major categories: multiculturalism and social justice. The terms multiculturalism and cultural diversity are used interchangeably throughout adult education literature, with the latter being the more current term. However, multicultural scholars distinguish a difference between multiculturalism and cultural diversity. They explain that cultural diversity is a view of society as a collection of varied cultures whereas multiculturalism is a particular political and ethical stance toward cultural differences. Globalization, the process where goods move freely among nations without regard to national borders and national identity, is also included under the multiculturalism umbrella and routinely offers an analysis of the place of disenfranchised or indigenous cultures in the shrinking world economy. A central idea that is shared by all types of multiculturalism is that one culture is seen as dominant and therefore the educational need is to teach the importance of values and beliefs that are held by other cultures. Thus, from its inception, multicultural education has called for recognition and inclusion of the contributions of other cultures in the literature, research, and praxis. Multicultural education was first introduced in the adult education literature by Horace Kallen in 1915 and expanded on by Alain Locke in 1925. Locke, one of the few leading Black adult educators of the early 1900s, represents a segment of the field that champions the multicultural argument by making known the causes and worth of certain groups. He expressed a belief in the redemptive powers of multiculturalism and this view remains constant in the contemporary adult education literature.

The social justice perspective can be divided into two categories. One social justice outlook states that there is indeed a right and moral position that should direct our society. Proponents of this position, like contemporary noted adult educator Phyllis Cunningham, the Presidential Teaching Professor at Northern Illinois University, ask adult educators to remember and live by the mission of the field, which is to equip adults to be full participants in a democratic society. This message has remained constant since the field's inception in the early 1920s, when writings by Alain Locke suggested that adult education could equalize the wrongs of society by providing an education to an adult populace that did not receive the basics through traditional education. This position continues in current writings by many adult education scholars.

The second trend in the social justice movement is not only to state the right and moral imperative of what should occur in the field but also to add an activist component, addressing the differences between groups and highlighting how power is exercised in favor of one group and to the detriment of others. The contemporary writings in this category use this approach not only for issues of race but also for all societal hierarchies constructed to serve one group while disenfranchising another. For example, scholars of critical race theory, such as Derrick Bell, explore how the systems and structures of White supremacy that subordinate people of color have been created and are maintained in American society as well as how to change the relationship between the law and racial power. An important part of fostering diversity and multiculturalism in adult education means discussing the elements of power and privilege accorded along the positionalities of race and ethnicity and the effects of this privilege on those from such marginalized positionalities. In the last decade, another important aspect of discussing race and ethnicity has been an examination of how Whites construct their racial identity and how the social construction of Whiteness affects educational systems.

When the discourse on Whiteness or privilege occurs in the adult education literature, it usually involves the following: recognition of privilege and of under-privilege, an examination of classroom practices, examples of curriculum and/or texts that reproduce privilege, and various anecdotal examples of how privilege operates in society. A large segment of the literature in social justice deals with the interlocking nature of race, gender, and class. Even though this area of research and writing acknowledges that the power lies in the hands of a dominant White majority, it stops short of saying that the concentration of power is deliberate and that the intent is to retain the present balance of interests. Instead, the social justice literature asks for a renegotiation of the balance of power.

Several factors contributed to the return of race and ethnicity in the 1980s as a focus in the adult education literature, research, and praxis. This specific focus was a direct outgrowth of two changes in perspective that were introduced in the 1970s: Freire's work around class and adult student empowerment, and the emergence of critical theory. In addition, the influx of people of color as students and instructors affected the attention given to issues around race and ethnicity. The impact of this new presence became evident in the 1980s as race and ethnicity emerged in the literature and at research conferences, as well as in curriculum and program planning.

The field's elite measure of acceptance, refereed journals, began to show an increase in the number of articles that could be classified as directly related to race and ethnicity. In 1991, a landmark article, Needed: A multicultural perspective for adult education research, by Ross-Gordon on the subject of race and ethnicity in adult education research, appeared in *Adult Education Quarterly*, one of the field's most prestigious journals. Ross-Gordon analyzed the status of racial and ethnic research and found 15 articles on race and ethnicity published between 1985 and 1990. A subsequent article in 2001 by Johnson-Bailey in the *International Journal of Lifelong Education*, examining the period between January 1990 and December 1999, revealed that 94 articles were published on issues, concerns, or prominent historical figures pertinent to ethnic or racial groups: 20 on African Americans; ten on Native Americans; ten on Asians; nine on Hispanics; and 45 on multiculturalism or cultural diversity. Interestingly, the articles pertaining to Asians only looked at Asian groups existing within their national homelands, and without exception, the works did not focus on 'Asian-ness' as otherness.

Research conferences, which provide a unique opportunity for the exchange of ideas among colleagues, have also demonstrated a surge of interest in race and ethnicity. The proceedings of major adult education conferences reveal a developing public discussion on race and ethnicity at the Adult Education Research Conference (AERC) and Standing Conference on University Teaching and Research in the Education of Adults (SCUTREA), two of the premier conferences in the field. With a small degree of variance, approximately 3–7% of the research presented at AERC and SCUTREA in the late 1980s through 2005 focused on ethnic and racial diversity and an increasing 2–3% on social justice issues such as gender and sexual orientation.

Only one adult education conference has research on race and ethnicity as its focus and unifying theme. The African Diaspora Adult Education Research Conference (formerly the African American Research Pre-Conference) was founded 1993 and has historically been attached as a pre-conference to the larger AERC. The African Diaspora Adult Education Research Conference debuted at Pennsylvania State University in May 1993, accompanying the 34th annual AERC. The theme of that first conference, *A Link for Community Development and Empowerment*, was suggestive of the conference's perspective and is now a consistent ideology connecting the subsequent conferences to the first.

The field of adult education in the North has enjoyed two distinct time periods relevant to focusing on race and ethnicity. During the discipline's formative years, beginning in the 1920s, issues of race and ethnicity were examined in a summative fashion through descriptive writings that related what was transpiring within various communities. The second and contemporary phase of adult education began 60 years later and reflects both a more open, analytical, and a growing discussion of race and ethnicity with a definite focus on multiculturalism and social justice.

A Southern Focus of Adult Education

To speak of adult education in the Southern Hemisphere is to speak of nationality, indigenous peoples, poverty, globalization, and literacy, more so than to speak of race and ethnicity. However, race and ethnicity are tied to these issues and are especially linked to poverty and low levels of literacy in the South. Literacy and literacy initiatives dominate the Southern adult education literature, followed only by indigenous peoples' knowledge as a topic of discussion. The topic of indigenous knowledge includes honoring the oral traditions and languages of native populations amidst the emerging push to use Western languages to accommodate commerce.

The focus on literacy in the South seems driven by the global economic market as African nations, India, and China, the fastest growing and more populous world areas, are thought to lag behind industrialized nations due in part to the fact that large segments of their citizens are undereducated. So the literacy exchange is twofold, with the idea being that both sides win from the effort regardless of the impetus: for the purpose of advancing economic initiatives for the South and for the purpose of developing and advancing a labor pool for the North. However, it must be noted that when economics drives the market and dictates policies, individual nations and therefore groups of people are inevitably disenfranchised because the idea of equality and other democratic ideals are inextricably tied to governments and social movements and not to economies. The capitalistic process and the phenomenon of globalization disempower countries, their people, and any claims for rectifying any social ills that might have occurred within set national borders.

The countries that comprise the Southern Hemisphere are more homogenous populations than the North, thus minimizing the necessity to focus on race. Migration patterns show a movement of people from the South to the North. Much of the diversity in the North derives from voluntary migrations and involuntary relocation of peoples of color from the South. However, since many Southern Hemisphere countries have been subjected to colonization by Europeans and those of European descent, the presence of race-based privilege is still a factor in the South. This factor perhaps encouraged Bostwana scholar, Youngman, to ask about the role that adult education plays in the reproduction or contestation of race-ethnic domination (Wangoola and Youngman, 1996). In addition, globalization, which is driven by the Northern countries of the United States, Japan, Germany, and the United

Kingdom, is the new face of colonialism. The complex global-connectedness phenomenon, a result of globalization which deemphasizes borders, also weakens cultural ties to home and place. To this end, it is theorized that modern racism has been exported with capitalism (Wangoola and Youngman, 1996).

Although race and ethnicity are not as generally discussed in international forums as they are in the West, the United Nations Educational and Scientific Cultural Organization (UNESCO), which was established in 1945, adopted a *Declaration on Race and Racial Prejudice* in 1978. The preamble noted that racism, racial discrimination, colonialism, and apartheid continue to afflict the world in ever-changing forms and the United Nations declared a desire to play a vigorous and constructive part in implementing the program of a *Decade for Action to Combat Racism and Racial Discrimination*, as defined by the General Assembly of the United Nations at its 28th session. The ten articles of the declaration encouraged the countries of the world to eliminate discrimination, adopt policies to improve the lives of its citizens of color, and to respect cultural differences.

For the most part, any discussion of adult education in the South occurs against the backdrop of UNESCO, its conferences, and programs. For many nations in the South, adult education is a matter of redress as many Southern nations did not have free mandatory children's education and/or because of an agricultural base, experienced low participation in formal schooling as farming necessitated the involvement of all members of the family, including children. The United Nations' *Literacy Decade*, 2003–2012, emphasizes the importance of honoring indigenous knowledge as a means of promoting education. Important adult education enterprises spearheaded by UNESCO are Education for All (EFA) and International Adult Learners' Week. Adult Learners' Week was first held in the United Kingdom in 1992 and was formally endorsed by UNESCO in 1999. Since then, over 40 countries have joined in the annual participation of Adult Learners' Week. The Week's purpose is to impact policy, promote access to the existing adult education programs, and increase literacy. Another cornerstone program that addresses issues of redress is the EFA movement that began in 1990 at the World Conference in Jomtien, Thailand, setting as its universal goal, education for all children and adults and pledging a 50% reduction in the 1990 rate of illiteracy by 2000. By the 2000 World EFA Conference in Dakar, Senegal, 180 countries had signed on to promote basic education for all citizens.

The region of Southern Africa provides an opportunity to look at adult education in a Southern setting. Prior to the emancipation of many nations in Southern Africa, adult education was recognized by the 14 nations in the region as an essential and necessary part of liberation struggles. This is aptly illustrated by the underground educational plan that was laid by the Black South Africans interned at Robben Island. The literate and educated prisoners worked in secret during their lunch breaks to tutor the less literate and undereducated inmates.

Southern African nations came together to form the Southern African Development Community (SADC) in 1992. This coalition of 14 countries, which includes Botswana, South Africa, Zambia, and Mozambique, expresses the importance of educating the citizenry as a means of encouraging full participation and exercising of rights, with most countries in the pact spending 20% of their budgets on education. Given the homogeneity of its countries and the legacy of colonization, SADC members focus on indigenous knowledge as a bridge between organic knowledge and formal knowledge. The concept of knowledge from the people is particularly important in health education. The low life expectancy of the region has been compounded by the HIV/AIDS pandemic. While championing the importance of local knowledge, the adult health educators are faced with the challenge that at times religious, gender, cultural, and tribal-based behavior, practices, and traditions may conflict with modern medical practices.

Summary

In conclusion, it is noted that the North has a perspective on race and ethnicity that is bound by genotypic and phenotypical differences. However, the South's viewpoint regarding difference is based more on nationality and culture. In addition, the adult education needs of the two regions are determined more by economic forces than by the races of its people. For example, the South's focus on literacy is driven by the North's need for a readily available and cheap workforce and the South's desire to become an economic competitor. Despite this commonality, within each of the two regions, the poor and disenfranchised are the colored peoples of the area, whether they are the majority Blacks of South Africa or the African Americans or Hispanics of the United States. Further, the breakdown of national borders by globalization is replacing national adult education initiatives with corporate initiatives. The North is experiencing a tremendous growth in the human resource development sector of adult education, while literacy efforts are relegated more to the non-profit sector and to being a low priority for the underfunded public sector.

Bibliography

Briscoe, D. B. and Ross, J. M. (1989). Racial and ethnic minorities and adult education. In Merriam, S. B. and Cunningham, P. M. (eds.) *Handbook of Adult and Continuing Education*, pp 583–598. San Francisco, CA: Jossey-Bass.

Frankenberg, R. (1993). *The Social Construction of Whiteness: White Women, Race Matters*. Minneapolis, MN: University of Minnesota Press.

Giroux, H. A. (1997). Rewriting the discourse of racial identity: Towards a pedagogy and politics of whiteness. *Harvard Educational Review* **67**(2), 285–320.

Gregory, S. and Sanjek, R. (eds.) (1994). *Race*. New Brunswick, NJ: Rutgers University Press.

Locke, A. (1936a). Adult education for Negroes. In Rowden, D. (ed.) *Handbook of Adult Education in the United States, 1936*, pp 126–131. New York: George Grady Press.

Locke, A. (1936b). Lessons of Negro adult education. In Ely, M. (ed.) *Adult Education in Action*, pp 224–226. New York: George Grady Press.

London, J. (1970). The social setting for adult education. In Smith, R. M., Aker, G. F., and Kidd, J. R. (eds.) *Handbook of Adult Education*, pp 3–23. London: Macmillan.

McCurtain, R. H. (1948). Adult education of American Indians. In Ely, M. L. (ed.) *Handbook of Adult Education in the United States*, pp 65–69. New York: Teachers College Press.

McIntosh, P. (1995). White privilege and male privilege: A personal accounting of coming to see correspondences through work in women's studies. In Anderson, M. L. and Collins, P. H. (eds.) *Race, Class, and Gender*, pp 76–87. Belmont, CA: Wadsworth.

Rachal, J. R. (1989). The social context of adult and continuing education. In Merriam, S. B. and Cunningham, P. M. (eds.) *Handbook of Adult and Continuing Education*, pp 3–14. San Francisco, CA: Jossey-Bass.

Rowden, D. (1934). Adult education for Negroes. In Rowden, D. (ed.) *Handbook of Adult Education in the United States*, pp 124–130. New York: American Association for Adult Education.

Wangoola, P. and Youngman, F. (eds.) (1996). *Towards a Transformative Political Economy of Adult Education: Theoretical and Practical Challenges*. DeKalb, IL: LEPS Press.

Winant, H. (1994). *Racial Conditions: Politics, Theory, Comparisons*. Minneapolis, MN: University of Minnesota Press.

Further Reading

Cassara, B. (1994). *Adult Education in Multicultural Society*. London: Routledge.

Denton, V. L. (1993). *Booker T. Washington and the Adult Education Movement*. Gainesville, FL: University Press.

Merriam, S. B., Courtenay, B. C., and Cervero, R. M. (2006). *Global Issues and Adult Education: Perspectives from Latin America, Southern Africa, and the United States*. San Francisco, CA: Jossey-Bass.

Neufeldt, H. G. and McGee, L. (eds.) (1990). *Education of the African American Adult: An Historical Overview*. New York: Greenwood Press.

Sheared, V. and Siskel, P. (2001). *Making Space: Merging Theory and Practice*. Westport, CT: Bergin and Garvey.

ADULT LEARNING, ECONOMY, AND SOCIETY

Modernization Processes and the Changing Function of Adult Learning

H S Olesen, Roskilde University, Roskilde, Denmark

Education increasingly appears to be the natural form of learning in modern life within a contemporary Western mindset. However, learning is more than that. It is an integral aspect of human life, taking place all the time, necessarily and unnoticed. The societal functions of adult learning are accordingly multiple. The theme of this article is to look at the societal nature of adult learning and hence, the societal functions of adult education. We want to emphasize the historical dimension in the sense of linking adult education to the socioeconomic, political, and cultural context.

Adult Education and Modernization

We can distinguish three main types of adult education defined by their main content. These have developed as educational traditions in their own right, related to particular areas of learning. As such they have been described and critically analyzed elsewhere in the encyclopedia:

- Basic literacy education, such as reading and writing, with the aspect of cultural integration in the nation and state.
- Community and popular education.
- Education for work, such as continuing education and training.

Much of the recent discussion in adult education is a clash between educational cultures. On the one hand, there is a humanistic focus on personal and political self-articulation, which seems to be inherited from the traditional functions of community learning and liberal adult education. On the other hand, there is the instrumental perspective on lifelong learning for work, theoretically underpinned by human capital theory and similar frameworks of understanding. These ideological struggles refer to historical experiences, and so an understanding of the societal functions of adult learning in their contexts may bring them to bear on wider issues of contemporary society. The theoretical notion of modernization seems to be a productive backbone in understanding the multiple institutional realities, conceptual meanings, and historical changes of adult education and learning. Modernization, here, refers to the economic, social, and cultural changes which have taken place in the last 300–500 years, comprising the inclusion of

feudal dynasties and independent city republics in the melting pot of European nation-state building, as well as the imperial inclusion of cultures and countries in the Third and Fourth World that had been living separate from dynamic centers right until the great discoveries or later.

Capitalist economy has been the main motor in this modernization process, where traditional, self-sustaining local communities were included in larger societies, affecting all aspects of political, social, and cultural relations. The development of institutional (formal) education, replacing informal education and learning, is just one of these effects.

Adult education develops complementarily to this greater history of modernization and (formal) education, enabling individuals to deal with new societal realities. The very notions of adulthood and individuality result from this history, as a gradual and complex process creating the individual as a conscious agent in society has replaced the definition of adulthood by ceremonial inauguration.

There is a built-in risk in using the theoretical perspective of modernization framework. Seen from the dominant center of a global, modernized world, it may seem that adult education and learning is on hand to enable modernization, harmonize the levels of learning between generations, and live up to the accelerating needs for individuals to change. This may be a local truth of occidental modernization, where the efficiency and speed of knowledge transmission seems to be secured by institutional education. In order to avoid a narrow functionalist perspective, we must study adult education history with the perspective of discovering the multiple and infinite nature of this modernization process.

Literacy Education: Enabling Modern Societies

The original and most widespread understanding of literacy is related to reading and writing. Prototype literacy education has been engaged in making developing societies literate or in compensating for lack of adequate schooling in modern societies. If we look at it from a societal perspective, literacy is a precondition for citizenship and socioeconomic participation. In Europe, literacy has been closely related to the building of nation-states. The development of secular education activities and the emergence of literature in national languages were instrumental in the building of nation-states.

Today, literacy has become a political issue in the multicultural societies emerging in modern Europe, and in some cases, instrumental for minorities to establish home rule. However, the cultural integration of rural and urban working classes is also a condition for socioeconomic development. Today's industrial worker must be literate in order to fulfill simple work tasks because logistics and communication are built into every single task on the shop floor. Consequently, concern has moved from formal education to functional literacy – the competence to actually read and write in everyday life. New literacies are added, for example, numbers and mathematical modeling (Johansen and Wedege, 2002). Information and communication technology necessitates new reading and writing skills in order to be a competent member of society, but may also relativize the importance of traditional written language skills.

Literacy is empowering, but the acquisition of cultural techniques – whichever they are historically – also entails submission under cultural dominance. As a result of colonial modernization we can see derivates of the great colonial empires, some united by the colonial language, and all to some extent influenced and shaped by colonial rule. Brazilian Paolo Freire answered this contradiction with a notion of political literacy he called conscientization, or learning to reflect the social reality and power relations involved in it. You may see Freire's ideas as congenial with mainstream modernist pedagogy, only related to the political learning process of those who are the victims and beneficiaries of a modernization coming to them from outside. In a more analytical key, questions have been raised about peripheral modernization, that is, a specific version of modernization in countries and regions that have had a modernization process pushed and influenced, but not entirely determined by colonial rule (e.g., Brazil).

Language is a medium for the individual sensual experience, as well as, for elaborating cultural experiences historically in a wider society. Written language has contributed significantly to societalization by enabling communication and knowledge transfer across time and space, creating a fundamental tension between immediate (local, situated) and mediated human experience. When printing technology created the industrial basis of the literate modernity, it reinforced this duality. The modern experience of the world is a language-mediated experience. Digital technology is probably proclaiming a new and more radical version of the same – or possibly a qualitative new relation to reality, an extended version of sensual access.

Community Education and Popular Education: Struggles about the Societal Atmosphere

All the different types of community and popular education are based in a community of people defined by location, religion, cultural values, or political assumption, and often have a perspective of social, cultural, and political self-articulation. Most people engaged in such education probably perceive it as a free space for learning that is relatively independent of societal conditions and constraints. In a societal perspective however, adult learning is a substantial aspect of modernization itself. Community interests are very often defined by and responsive to societal change. Education preserves cultures that are threatened and overcome – and these pockets of social and cultural life that are not entirely penetrated by societal dynamics provide a productive space for self-articulation. Most typical community and popular education is probably based on resistance against some of the influences of modernization, for example, minority communities that also happened to be marginal and/or impoverished by capitalist modernization and centralization.

Independent of whether these communities see learning as explicitly political or not, learning is part of an attempt to create a public sphere of their own or set the cultural framework of understanding on a societal level. Out of closed communities or specific resistance grows – in a number of cases – a structural characteristic of modernity: the existence of civil society. Community and popular education based on specific histories of socioeconomic and cultural circumstances may – in very different and paradoxical ways – produce a general societal development. The history of independent Danish folk high schools provides a historical example. The folk high schools were based on and also contributed to a particular development of political, cultural, and social movement among Danish self-owning peasants, which in turn played a decisive role in establishing a modern democracy. In spite of the fact that the folk high school education was based on an antimodern, romantic ideology, it produced the experience of popular self-regulation and self-organization, which also in later developments contributed strongly to the specific modernization process in Denmark (Olesen, 1989). Its cultural-class compromise, uniting egalitarian and liberal principles and a basically anti-academic, informal notion of education, anticipated some of the developments of lifelong learning around the beginning of the twenty-first century.

The dialectic of local community learning and societal development is, more than anything, related to the role of work in culture and economy. Since the main driving force of modernization has been capitalist industrialization, the most important popular education activity in Europe in the previous century was of the labor movement and trade unions. Industry formed the life conditions in (urban) communities, and the labor movement in most countries organized working-class culture and its learning institutions, first as a resistance solidarity movement, then gradually as a more proactive cultural self-articulation and political movement. In some cases, community education also entails alternatives to the dominant capitalist economy – in the form of cooperative economies – prominently in the Basque country and also at a smaller scale in most developed capitalist countries.

It is obvious that labor movement education activities are in one sense a product of an active resistance against some of the effects of modernization, similar to the culture of many communities that have been marginalized or impoverished by modernization. It is a clearly partial culture defined by political and trade union action, or at least from a general class perspective. Unlike many local and minority communities, however, labor movement education activities developed a universalistic perspective, challenging individualistic liberalism with ideas about equality and solidarity. The political struggles between different types of Socialism can be seen as different versions of a universalistic aspiration – communist, social democratic, anarchist, and syndicalist – that each carry in them more or less ambitious aspirations of justice and a new level of democracy beyond capitalism. The real histories of different countries have provided a variety of working-class cultures and not just labor movement experiences, as well as some in which universalist aspirations turned into totalitarian power.

Seen in a societal perspective, popular education comes out of premodern communities, as well as urban communities generated by modernization itself. They are formed by the specific histories of modernization and they take advantage of one of the effects of modernization, namely the existence of a space for noncoerced social organization, what we in modernization theory call civil society. The societalization – from *Gemeinschaftswesen* to *Gesellschaft* in the notions of the classical sociologists – eradicates or restructures communities at the same time as modernization extends the space of relatively free cultural activity. The juridical basic rights and economic affluence in modernized parts of the world create the societal basis of this civil society. A contemporary form of popular education must have its potential base in the organization of citizenship to deal with societal issues on a level and with an outlook adequate for contemporary society as a whole. Many one-cause movements and actions have a similar profile as community action of resistance or opposition though not necessarily founded in a community.

The bourgeois public sphere as the communicative framework of a fully developed civil society corresponds largely with the nation-state and ideas of formal (state) democracy. At the same time, global capitalism has in several ways bypassed this structure. Structurally, by its international operation and concentrations of power and capital in organizations larger than many states, creating a democratic deficit. Culturally, by the media and consumer cultures which take active part in the shaping of desires, fantasies, and preferences. One may see international labor organizations and forms of organizations like World Social Forum as – very fragile – civil society responses to this situation.

Learning for Work, or Human Resource Development

In the last couple of decades, the need for work competence building has tended to prevail over traditional forms and rationales of adult education and training in developed Western societies. In traditional societies, intergenerational transfer of knowledge and competences enables the reproduction of the labor force. Modernization has brought basic school education and some specialized institutions for academic and professional education – generally serving as basic, lifelong qualifications in the initial career. In advanced capitalist societies, this mode of transfer has increasingly come under pressure. When changes in work and labor market happen faster than the generational turnover in the labor force, adult education and training come in as a mediating instrument to secure the adaptation of labor to the requirements of work life.

It has mostly been left to employers and the individual worker to take care of retraining and adult education. The consequences have typically been a general market failure (i.e., underinvestment) and a very unequal distribution of training resources. Big industrial employers have in some cases been able to secure up-skilling of their own employees, but not mobility across sectors and competence levels. In Nordic countries, training of workers became part of welfare state policies. In Denmark, with its late development of industrial economy, urban industries needed skilled workers, and rural workers needed skills and socialization for industry. A separate new strand in adult education developed to support a rapid migration from rural to urban life, from agriculture to industry. What became later known as the flexicurity model (Jørgensen and Madsen, 2007) consisted mainly of adult education and training together with relatively good unemployment benefits. This combination enabled a more proactive policy from trade unions and employees than in a number of European countries in periods of economic growth. In the period of crisis and stagflation in the 1970s, continuing education was redirected/enhanced to take care of more long-term competence development for the more vulnerable segments of the labor force (e.g., women, young people without vocational qualification, and others).

Recently, adult learning seems to have assumed a more universal or all-embracing nature in all the advanced capitalist countries. As long as the development of work takes the form of strong division of labor based on mass unskilled wage labor, societal needs remain limited to training and retraining specialists and highly skilled craftspeople. However, with the development of postindustrial forms of work organization, a need for broader adult education emerges. The societal demand for knowledge economy has changed to include not only what were mostly called soft skills (e.g., communicative and collaborative skills, quality consciousness, professional attitudes, and self-confidence) but also traditional literacy, as well as new literacies (e.g., numeracy and mathematic understanding, and computer literacy). Work-related learning seems to become broader and deeper and increasingly interferes with personal needs and identity (Olesen, 2005). Nevertheless, it is obvious in the rhetoric of lifelong learning that economic concerns and the focus on employment and work are determining factors. This can be seen as a very local view on global development. The position of most developed economies can hope to maintain their relative competitive advantage in a division of labor where they take care of knowledge-based, complex work and the service work for themselves, whereas developing countries deliver raw materials and build up low-tech industrial production.

The political consensus about lifelong learning of competences may not be so easy to maintain in this narrow key. Rather, the focus on work and human resource development may raise issues of control and the quality of work. The ideas of a knowledge-based economy have been criticized from several perspectives. One applies a wider, ecological perspective on work and learning, questioning the inward colonialism of human life without boundaries (Hochschild, 1997) and its cultural consequences (Sennett, 1998; Negt, 1984). The requirements on human flexibility and adaptation may erode the conditions of socialization and subjectivity, that is, the human resources on the whole. Another perspective emphasizes the direct political aspect of learning in which labor movements should take the opportunity to advance a politicization of work, including environmental questions, ownership, and use value of production, drawing on vanguard experiences of cooperative enterprises (e.g., The Mondragon cooperative – Antoni and Campbell, 1983), projects for conversion of production (Lucas Aerospace and others), and a vision of self-regulated work (Forrester, 2007). The dramatic emergence of the climate crisis and the fragility of the capitalist world economy underscore the need for more comprehensive perspectives on work and learning.

It seems most plausible to outline a neoliberal scenario of an individualized competence market, which will be subsumed into a global labor market. However, it also seems likely that this competence market will show an unprecedented example of market failure – and it will definitely have extreme effects in terms of inequality and the colonization of human labor. The question is whether there is another scenario in which the significance of the labor force as a subjective factor in the economy can be turned into individual and collective self-regulation of work and learning. This seems to be the open question that places the discussion about learning for work and the workers' role in the development of work as a central issue in global politics.

The resources for any alternative to neoliberal global capitalism must to some extent be found in institutional practices, embodied experiences of the past, social organizations, and experiences of trade unions and other cultural organizations. They are present in the forms and levels of education, expectations, and preferences of young people as well as adults, but they do not form a simple and coherent alternative. While the new discourses of lifelong learning are international, Anglophone, and relatively homogenous, adult-education traditions have many names: popular education, community education, *educacao popular*, *politische bildung*, liberal education, *folkeoplysning*, *folkbildning*, *formation des adultes*, *formazione popular*, *volksbildung*, and citizenship education to name a few. In adult education discussions, these many names give rise to translation problems – although the names in different languages cover more or less corresponding phenomena, they do not have the same meaning because meaning is related to societal and cultural context.

Functions of Adult Learning in Historical Context

The exploration of the historical function of adult learning may lead to an open discussion of present-day modernization. The main types of adult education form strands of historical functionality over long periods of time. Analyzing them in terms of modernization may present a simplistic scheme: literacy enables modernization by integrating ordinary people in cultural communities that are independent of time and space; popular education elevates the ability of communities to reproduce themselves to a level of cultural construction and self-articulation, eventually a level of collective self-assertion and political activism; and continuing education and training for work aligns individual competence-building cycles with an accelerated and distributed organization of societal work in global capitalism. Obviously this complex societal evolution is not a unified process – it is asynchronous and very diverse across the world. So the societal function of adult education must be studied in concrete contexts, regarding the interplay with socioeconomic, political, and cultural history. Socioeconomic modernization and the type of learning needed and enabled are mutually interrelated, but institutional developments also set general conditions of this process. When and what type of adult education contributes to modernization (the level of general schooling and the influence on school by church and class movements), and political circumstances, may form very specific conditions and challenges (e.g., the *entnazifizierung* as a project for political education in Germany after World War II, or the modernization in Spain under a long-lasting dictatorship).

Today, on a global scale, we may ask whether modernization is just one process. The discussion about peripheral modernization has been touched upon in this article. In postcolonial theory and political discussion, the emphasis on difference and multiple histories serves to demonstrate the overcoming of the modernist tale or vision of a rational evolution toward a better society. Sometimes the argument that modernization should not be seen as a continuous progress gets confused with the assumption that there was and is no modernization process at all. In a generalized discussion of global capitalism one may at the same time observe a pessimistic view of one culturally homogenized world (McDonaldization) and much more relativistic postcolonial theory of a general dissolution of the modernization process in a firework of difference. Both fail to grasp the complexity of durable social changes. Having said that, what is the role of learning in modernization processes? It can be argued and underpinned by examples that broad processes of learning and democratic participation lead to durable societal changes, whereas change processes that fail to engage the broader population remain unstable and produce conflicts in the form of imperialism and/or violent repression on macro- and micro-levels. The postcolonial discussion of education may, in the era of global capitalism, oscillate between the critical perspective of one culturally homogenized world at the end of the story (McDonaldization), and the postmodernist theory of a general dissolution of the modernization process in a firework of difference. There is a key to dynamic mediation between the two perspectives in an open-minded exploration of specific experiences and learning resources in their historical context.

It is essential to maintain that the possible futures of late- or postmodernity is a matter of social agency and hence also of learning processes taking place now. Lifelong learning implies a new discourse that brings learning beyond institutional education and into social reality. However, the lifelong learning discourse has been heavily influenced by neoliberal politics and human capital theory, and the world is relatively short of alternative ideas that can embrace the critique of educational institutions without accepting the neoliberal economic rationale. The options available are societal and subjectively relevant

conditioned by experiences and resources of the past. The author has mentioned a long-lasting influence of the popular education tradition in his own country, which formed the ideological basis for a relatively democratic and liberal provision of formal and higher education, as well as adult education. Others are to be found in Latin America, South Africa, and other particular pathways of modernization.

Modernization is still an uncompleted development even in its original centers. While it seems that globalization brings forward further homogeneity, there are also factors that tend to enable a multicentered and polyphonic global world. The fact that China has had its own almost independent cultural and social pathway, which is now – forcefully – joining global capitalism, forms an exciting experiment for the relation between human socialization and societal development. Oskar Negt calls it "the greatest social experiment in our time" (Negt, 1988/2007) in his discussion of the modernization(s) in China in the perspective of European modernization since the Renaissance. We may most productively see modernization as an infinite process that is still dependent on human efforts and choices on individual, as well as global level.

See also: Adult Education and Civil Society; Adult Literacy Education; Community Based Adult Education; Lifelong Learning; Popular Adult Education; The Political Economy of Adult Education.

Bibliography

Antoni, A. and Campbell, A. (1983). *The Co-Operative Way: Worker Co-Ops in France, Spain and Eastern Europe* vol. viii, 75 pp. London: ICOM Co-Publications.

Forrester, K. (2007). Becoming visible? Notes on work, union learning and education. In Shelly, S. and Calveley, M. (eds.) *Learning with Trade Unions: A Contemporary Agenda in Employment Relations*. Aldershot: Ashgate Publishing.

Hochschild, A. R. (1997). *The Time Bind: When Work Becomes Home and Home Becomes Work*. New York: Metropolitan.

Johansen, L. Ø. and Wedege, T. (eds.) (2002). *Numeracy for Empowerment and Democracy?* Adults Learning Mathematics Research Forum ISBN 87-7349-540-9.

Jørgensen, H. and Madsen, P. K. (eds.) (2007). *Flexicurity and Beyond: Finding a New Agenda for the European Social Model*. Copenhagen: DJØF Publishing.

Negt, O. (1984). *Lebendige Arbeit – enteignete Zeit*. New York: Campus Verlag.

Negt, O. (1988). *Modernisierung im Zeichen des Drachens. China und der Europäischen Mythos der Moderne*, 2nd edn. Frankfurt a.M. Fischer: Steidl.

Olesen, H. S. (1989). *Adult Education and Everyday Life*. Roskilde: Roskilde University.

Olesen, H. S. (2005). Work related learning, identities, and culture: New work – new genders? New genders – new work?. In Bron, A., Kurantowicz, E., Salling Olesen, H., and West, L. (eds.) *'Old' and 'New' Worlds of Adult Learning*, pp 27–41. Wroclaw: Wydawnictwo Naukowe.

Sennett, R. (1998). *The Corrosion of Character*. New York/London: Norton.

Further Reading

Elias, N. (1976). *Über den Prozess der Zivilisation* (orig. publ. (1939); 1994, The Civilizing Process. Oxford: Blackwell). Frankfurt am Main: Suhrkamp.

Feidel-Mertz, H. (1975). *Erwachsenenbildung seit 1945: Ausgangsbedingungen und Entwicklungstendenzen in der Bundesrepublik*. Köln: Kiepenheuer und Witsch.

Freire, P. (1970). *Pedagogy of the Oppressed*. New York: Seabury Press.

Negt, O. and Kluge, A. (1981). *Geschichte und Eigensinn*. Frankfurt am Main: Zweitausendeins.

Olesen, H. S. (2006). Beyond the abstractions? Adult Education research from idealism to critical social science. *International Journal of Lifelong Education* **25**(3), 241–256.

Olesen, H. S. (2006). Experience and Learning. In Billett, S., Fenwick, T., and Somerville, M. (eds.) *Work, Subjectivity and Learning*. Zürich: Springer.

Steven (2006). The fight for useful work at Lucas Aerospace. http://libcom.org/history/1976-the-fight-for-useful-work-at-lucas-aerospace (accessed June 2009).

Wallerstein, I. (2000). *The Essential Wallerstein*. New York: New Press.

The Political Economy of Adult Education

G Rees, Cardiff University, Cardiff, UK

The expansion of post-compulsory education and training has been one of the most striking recent changes in the education systems of more developed societies. Much of this expansion is accounted for by rising levels of participation among adults. Of particular interest here has been the growing prominence attached to the provision of learning opportunities for individuals throughout their working lives and, indeed, into retirement.

In part, this reflects the demographic shifts which imply an aging population – and workforce – in most of the more developed countries. Equally, there has been a fundamental political re-evaluation of adult education's role. Governments in these societies (and beyond) have been remarkably consistent in prioritizing policies for what has come to be termed lifelong learning; that is, learning throughout the life course, from preschool to old age. These policies, in turn, are based on a robust conventional wisdom – what Grubb and Lazerson (2004) have dubbed the education gospel – about the essential role of education and training in generating the high levels of skills necessary for economic competitiveness and growth in the globalized economy.

This conventional wisdom partly derives from the work of academic economists in developing human capital theory (HCT). This theory has become one of the most influential economic doctrines of the age, especially in its contemporary manifestation in theories of the knowledge-based economy (KBE). However, the central characteristic of the political economy approach is that it interrogates such economic doctrines in order to uncover their political and sociological premises. Rather than simply treating economic theories as frameworks of analysis in their own terms, political economy aims to explore the – often implicit – social assumptions on which they are based. In this case, for example, approaches to adult education derived from HCT assume that individuals are able to calculate the instrumental benefits of human capital formation; and that individuals' skills are rewarded in ways which reflect their productivity. Alternative approaches are clearly possible.

Equally, the political economy approach seeks to explain the influence which economic theories exert on policy in terms of the wider social and political context in which they are located. Here, the increasing dominance of neoliberalism during the 1980s and 1990s, orchestrated by international agencies, such as the World Bank and the Organization for Economic Co-Operation and Development (OECD), created a fruitful ideological environment for the development of the individualized and instrumental approaches to adult education which are embodied in lifelong learning strategies. While governments adopted policies which reflected national circumstances, the policy repertoire available to them was limited by the wider ideological climate.

The next section presents an account of how the current conventional wisdom views the relationships between adult education and HCT, paying particular attention to theories of the KBE. Then, the critique from political economy of this position is explained. In the final section, the significance of the ideological context of neoliberalism for state policies on adult education is reviewed.

Theories of Adult Education as Human Capital Formation

The analytical basis for the view that, in general, education has a key role in determining economic development is provided by HCT, although the versions adopted by governments to underpin their policies have involved highly simplified accounts of the academic research. HCT has a very long pedigree, but its influence on thinking about the relationships between education and economic life became especially marked during the 1960s. Here, the macroeconomic arguments that investment in education and technological change constituted the basis for national economic growth provided a rationale for the expansion of educational provision by governments, especially at the upper secondary and tertiary levels.

In the harsher economic climate of the 1970s and 1980s, the emphasis shifted to the returns (e.g., from enhanced future earnings) which would flow to the individual from his/her investment in increased human capital (e.g., through undertaking extra education and training); and the productivity gains which would accrue to employers from the resulting enhanced skills levels. State intervention became limited to ensuring that the optimal conditions for these private individual investments prevailed. By the 1990s, the intellectual terrain had shifted again, strongly influenced by the development of theories of the KBE.

Human Capital in the KBE

Theories of the KBE adapt HCT to what are construed as the essential characteristics of contemporary economic life.

On this view, the globalization of trade and investment has intensified competitive pressures, especially for those national economies which are unable to compete on the basis of low-cost production. In these economies, competitiveness can be maintained only by enhancing the productivity of capital and labor. This implies continuous innovation, developing new goods and services and more effective processes for producing, marketing and distributing them, and applying the most efficient patterns of work organization. Hence, the creation and – critically – the application in production of new forms of knowledge become the key factor in shaping the prosperity of individual enterprises and economic development more widely.

This valorization of knowledge production and innovation also has critical implications for the operation of labor markets. The KBE offers expanding opportunities for the so-called knowledge workers who have the very high-level skills required to operate in professional, managerial, scientific, and creative jobs in the upper echelons of the new occupational hierarchy. Equally, even workers who do not attain the very highest occupational levels require, at a minimum, high-quality general education and cutting-edge intermediate skills, so that they can engage actively in driving up productivity.

However, the corollary of these new occupational opportunities is the sharp decrease in unskilled or partly skilled occupations, which formerly comprised significant segments of the workforce. Some of these occupations have been relocated to the low-cost economies, reflecting patterns of globalization more widely. Others have simply disappeared because of changes in the industrial structure and transformations in product and process technologies. The implication is, therefore, that, in the KBE, employment opportunities for those individuals who do not have significant amounts of human capital are bleak.

Adult Education and the KBE

Theories of the KBE have significant consequences for how the production of human capital is conceived. Effective systems need to be in place to ensure that individuals with the requisite high-level skills are produced in sufficient numbers to meet the growing demand for knowledge workers. This implies the expansion of tertiary education, increasing the numbers of people with degrees and postgraduate qualifications. Equally, through the compulsory phases of education, everyone needs to attain high levels of general education – especially in respect of the essentials of literacy, numeracy, and science.

Moreover, theories of the KBE have specific implications for human capital formation through adult education. In an economy that is characterized by continuous innovation and the adoption of new technologies and modes of working, individuals need the forms of human capital which ensure that they are able to respond flexibly to these changing demands.

This requires the provision of opportunities for adults already in the workforce to compensate for any shortcomings in their previous education, in terms, for example, of the essential basic skills of literacy and numeracy or general vocational skills, such as communication, team working, and information and communication technology (ICT) competences. It also implies that workers are enabled to develop new knowledge and skills, as and when these become necessary. Not only are individuals expected to transfer from one job to another much more frequently than hitherto, but also new demands arise as existing occupations change in character. In these circumstances, workers need to be competent and flexible learners; learning to learn is thus an essential prerequisite.

Adult education is required to deliver effective opportunities for individual workers to acquire new knowledge and skills not only through participation in formal learning within institutions dedicated to the provision of education and training, but also through nonformal learning effected, in particular, within the workplace itself and largely instigated by employers. The workplace is also increasingly recognized as a crucial setting in which informal learning, especially through interaction with colleagues, should be facilitated.

It is, of course, important to emphasize that these theories of the KBE – as with most theories in the social sciences – are not without their critics. In the next section, some of these opposing views, drawing on political economy approaches, are explored.

Beyond Theories of Adult Education and Human Capital

Adult Education, the Social Construction of Skills and Learner Identities

In general terms, the link between human capital formation and economic development is well attested empirically. At the macroeconomic level, innumerable econometric studies demonstrate the strong positive relationship between education and national economic growth in the long term (Barro, 1997). There are also many microeconomic studies which show the returns which accrue to individuals from their investments in human capital formation.

Much of this evidence relates to school-based and tertiary education and qualifications. However, the available studies indicate that work-related adult education (and basic skills development in particular) does have positive associations with the earnings of individuals and with productivity increases (although the returns to other forms of adult education are less certain) (OECD, 1999). Accordingly, on the basis of this evidence – wholly consistent with theories of the KBE and the consequent understanding of adult education's role – both individual workers and their employers benefit from greater participation in work-related adult education (Blöndal *et al.*, 2002).

Approaches to adult education derived from HCT assume that individuals and employers recognize that increased human capital will increase productivity and that this will be rewarded in higher wages. However, as many commentators have argued, skills and the returns that accrue to them cannot be understood simply in terms of productivity. How skills are defined is the product of complex social and political processes, which are frequently as much about excluding social groups from the rewards which derive from what are defined as highly skilled occupations, as the technical requirements of production. Most notoriously, the skills attached to jobs which are characteristically done by women have not been recognized as such by employers and, indeed, male workers and their trade unions. While the knowledge and competences embodied in occupations may have changed, skills remain socially constructed. Moreover, once the notion of skill is detached from its technical content, it becomes clear that human capital may best be understood in terms of regulating access to occupations of different kinds, and, in the case of work-related adult education, to the kinds of screening which employers operate to determine what kinds of people enter more desirable jobs.

Equally, it cannot be inferred from the evidence on returns to human capital formation alone that individuals will actually participate in work-related adult education. Hence, approaches derived from HCT assume that individuals accrue human capital (e.g., by participating in work-related adult education) on the basis that future returns (e.g., through increased earnings) will outweigh the costs incurred. In reality, however, people's participation even in work-related adult education reflects more than this narrowly constructed, instrumental valuation. For many forms of work-related training, people choose to take part only in a very limited sense. Participation is experienced as compulsion by the employer; and may, in consequence, result in very little by way of new learning. Even where participation is a matter of choice, individuals' decisions are constrained by their material conditions: their financial resources, family commitments, and even where they live. Moreover, people's choices are shaped by the expectations and norms – deriving from their experiences in their families, communities, and previous educational institutions – which define their identities as learners and, therefore, potential participants in adult education of all kinds (Rees *et al.*, 2006).

Adult Education and the Demand for Skills

Theories of the KBE predict increasing demand for skills across the economy as a whole, largely through the growth of high-skills jobs. However, while there has been a significant increase in the professional, managerial, scientific, and creative occupations filled by highly skilled knowledge workers, this has not been matched by the demise of low-skilled, low-waged employment. Many more developed economies have experienced an increase in jobs at both the top and the bottom of the occupational hierarchy, with a hollowing out of occupations at the intermediate levels. To this extent, therefore, a substantial and even growing proportion of occupations do not require high levels of skill, either to enter them or to carry them out effectively.

While there may be persistent shortages of specific skills, there is no convincing evidence that there are general shortfalls in skills across the more developed economies as a whole. This is the case even in those national economies in which human capital formation has been regarded as problematic. For example, recent studies in the UK suggest that, if occupations are categorized by broad level of required skills, the only category for which there are more job openings than people qualified at the appropriate level is that where no formal qualifications are required. Conversely, the number of jobs requiring tertiary-level qualifications is far exceeded by the number of people having such qualifications (Felstead *et al.*, 2007). Evidence of this kind has led to the claim that, in many of the more developed economies, demand for skills, especially at higher levels, is being outstripped by supply.

Work-related adult education is not provided across the board in the ways prescribed in theories of the KBE. Access to such learning opportunities is not distributed evenly between different groups of workers. In general, the higher someone is in the occupational hierarchy and the greater his/her previous educational attainment, the more likely they are to benefit from the provision of work-related adult education. As **Table 1** indicates, while there are important national differences in rates of participation, this is the pattern across the more developed economies; and it reinforces the notion that significant parts of the labor market remain dominated by low-skill occupations.

Indeed, it has been argued that some economies are characterized by what Finegold and Soskice (1988) called a low-skills equilibrium. Here, employers adopt strategies geared to the production of low-cost, low-quality goods and services. These strategies are sustainable because production is primarily or wholly for local or domestic markets with little threat from cheap imports. Employers rely upon labor-intensive production systems and the mass production of low value-added goods. Therefore, they do not require workers with high skills levels. While there is little evidence to suggest that a low-skills equilibrium exists across any of the more developed economies as a whole, it is apparent that particular sectors and even regions can be dominated by low-skills, low-cost

Table 1 Participation in work-related adult education and previous education[a]

Level of education	Lower secondary	Upper secondary	Tertiary	All levels	Ratio (%) hours in training to annual hours worked
Canada	6	20	35	25	30
Denmark	22	36	54	39	63
France	9	19	33	19	49
Germany	3	10	24	12	28
Italy	1	6	12	4	5
Netherlands	5	11	13	6	21
Sweden	24	37	57	40	40
Switzerland	8	27	44	29	46
United Kingdom	7	26	46	27	19
United States	12	32	56	37	26
OECD	7	17	31	18	25

[a]Annual participation rate in nonformal, job-related education and training for 25–64-year olds (2003).
From OECD (2007). *Education at a Glance 2007*. Paris: OECD.

production, often reflecting a residue of past economic activity (OECD, 2001).

The development and application of skills are situated within the wider strategies which firms and other organizations adopt with respect to the production, marketing, and distribution of goods and services. Moreover, there is not a single strategy that provides employers with a pathway to competitiveness and profitability. Hence, simply expanding the supply of skills is insufficient, unless employers' production strategies are of a kind which ensures that extra skills can actually be applied. This has important implications for the kinds of skills development strategies adopted by governments.

In spite of these well-founded critiques, the KBE continues to provide the foundation for the very robust conventional wisdom as to how governments across the more developed countries should deal with adult education. In the next section, the role of an ideological context dominated by neoliberalism in explaining this seeming paradox is addressed.

The State and the KBE

In the official discourses of governments and international organizations, theories of the KBE provide the key justification for policies aimed at promoting higher levels of skills through lifelong learning. While the latter encompasses learning throughout the life course, adult education has been identified as an especially important mechanism for enhancing human capital formation. Hence, many national governments in the more developed countries have shifted priorities for adult education toward directly vocational provision, thereby displacing its contributions to traditional concerns such as personal fulfillment or cultural development.

So robust is this consensus on the need to gear state policies to promote high skills levels that it has become the common sense of policy on adult education across the more developed economies. Accordingly, it is important to emphasize that this current conventional wisdom is situated within a historically specific ideological and institutional context.

Neoliberalism and Lifelong Learning

For much of the twentieth century, the governments of the developed economies operated Keynesian national settlements between employers, trade unions, and government. These were based on the mass production of standardized goods and services, high wage levels, and, consequently, rising living standards as well as an emergent consumer culture. The state played a key role in regulating economic activity and in providing key welfare services. While approaches to skills development varied significantly between different national economies, HCT was interpreted as providing the rationale for increased government investment in education, especially at the upper secondary and tertiary levels, in order to keep pace with the growing technological complexity of goods and services; but adult education was not given special attention.

This Keynesian regime broke down during the 1970s, to be replaced by one based broadly on neoliberalism. On this view, in the face of new patterns of globalized economic activity and competitive pressures, markets are deemed to provide the most effective mechanisms for the organization of economic activity. The role of government is limited to ensuring the conditions within which markets can function effectively, through maintaining macro-economic stability and providing public goods (physical infrastructure, basic education, environmental protection, etc.). Only where markets manifestly fail to deliver effective outcomes should state provision play a major role, as, for example, in meeting the basic needs of the poorest members of society through income redistribution.

Therefore, although the development of high skills levels through lifelong learning is acknowledged as central to meeting the demands of global competition and the KBE, the state's role in skills formation is a restricted one. It should ensure that the supply of basic education through schools, colleges, and universities is maximally effective. However, employers can be relied upon to encourage the development of vocational skills in response to the changing patterns of demand, and to reflect the true value of such skills in wage levels.

Most importantly, the principal responsibility for human capital formation is seen to lie with the individual worker. Intervention by government should be restricted to ensuring the availability of information, removing barriers to participation, and, where the market fails, subsidizing individuals' engagement in work-related adult education. The very language of lifelong learning implies that its effectiveness in creating and preserving human capital depends upon the capacities and motivations of individuals themselves. Failure in the labor market is interpreted in terms of the decisions that people make about improving their employability through increased human capital; and increasingly, welfare payments to the unemployed and other economically inactive people are conditional on their participation in education and training.

In this way, neoliberal approaches emphasize the key importance of human capital formation. However, they prescribe particular means of achieving this, emphasizing individualized and instrumental orientations to lifelong learning and work-related adult education, more specifically.

Government Strategies for Adult Education

The work of international organizations, such as the World Bank and the OECD, has been a key influence in shaping this neoliberal agenda on lifelong learning. More specifically, such organizations have been crucial in ensuring their significance in shaping the actual roles undertaken by governments. The work of the OECD has been especially important here and illustrates this agenda very clearly (Henry et al., 2001).

From the late 1980s onward, the OECD has produced highly influential analyses of the essential role of human capital in the development of the KBE (e.g., OECD, 1989). It has also been an enthusiastic advocate of the necessary benefits of lifelong learning and, more specifically, of enhancing the human capital of adults. Moreover, it has been crucial in specifying the exact roles to be played by governments in ensuring effective provision of adult education. Workers require access to ongoing opportunities for learning of all kinds. Where firms and other organizations are unwilling to provide these opportunities, the state needs to intervene to ensure that such market failure is rectified, through, for example, providing subsidies for employer-led provision, specifying mandatory spending on training by enterprises or granting the right to be trained to employees (OECD, 2002).

However, despite the almost hegemonic influence of neoliberalism, there remain significant differences in the strategies adopted by national governments toward adult learning. At the most fundamental level, this reflects the choices made by governments. For example, as has been seen earlier, the high-skills strategy is not the only possible response to the competitive pressures of a globalized economy. One clear alternative is, in effect, to adapt the strategies of the Keynesian era to changed circumstances, through an intensification of Fordist production of goods and services, emphasizing low-cost and, to a considerable extent, low-skill methods. This kind of low-skills strategy has not been adopted explicitly by any of the governments of the more developed economies, reflecting both competitive pressures from lower-cost economies as well as the ideological influence of the neoliberal consensus on the KBE. Nevertheless, it remains the case that, in reality, a low-skills equilibrium is characteristic of substantial parts of all of these economies.

The choices which governments make, in turn, are shaped by the skills development strategies which have been characteristic of national societies in the past. For example, the enthusiasm with which the Anglo-Saxon economies (the USA, the UK, Australia, and New Zealand) have embraced market-driven approaches reflects their voluntaristic traditions, as well as an ideological willingness to accept sharp inequalities between enclaves of highly skilled knowledge work and large numbers of low-skilled and low-waged jobs. In contrast, many of the northern European governments (e.g., in Germany, the Netherlands, and the Scandinavian countries) have based their adult education strategies much more on consensus between employers, employees, and government. This reflects both their historical attachment to this form of political economy and a rooted ideological commitment to avoid the worst social inequalities of a market-driven system through state support for greater employment security and access to learning opportunities among the socially disadvantaged. In developmental states, such as Japan, Korea, and Singapore, circumstances have been different again. Here, the state has continued to play a significant role in skills development, simply to try to ensure that the supply of skills matches the demands of economies undergoing strong growth (Brown et al., 2001).

The Value of Adult Education

Despite these important differences in approach, it remains the case that the hegemonic discourse on adult education is currently dominated by instrumental orientations. Its value is seen to lie overwhelmingly in the contribution which it makes to economic life. In distributional terms, investment in human capital formation through lifelong learning is argued to benefit not only the individual workers and employers making the investments, but also the wider economy through increased productivity, thereby warranting – limited – state support. Moreover, it is the recognition of these individual and social benefits that are viewed as underpinning individuals' motivations to invest in human capital formation in the first place.

Adopting a wider frame of reference, however, suggests alternative frameworks through which the value of adult education may be judged. In the right circumstances, engagement in lifelong learning certainly offers the possibility of significant economic returns, both to the individual and to the economy more widely. However, as many commentators have argued, this by no means exhausts adult education's potential total public value. Ironically, however, realizing this total public value may require governments to reassert priorities for adult education which have declined in significance over recent decades, reviving their role as provider of a liberal general education, especially to those social groups who need an educational second chance.

See also: Economic Outcomes of Adult Education and Training; Lifelong Learning; Participation in Adult Learning; Wider Benefits of Adult Education.

Bibliography

Barro, R. J. (1997). *Determinants of Economic Growth: A Cross-Country Empirical Study*. Cambridge, MA: MIT Press.

Blöndal, S., Field, S., and Girouard, N. (2002). *Investment in Human Capital through Post-Compulsory Education and Training: Selected Efficiency and Equity Aspects. Economics Working Paper No. 333*. Paris: OECD.

Brown, P., Green, A., and Lauder, H. (2001). *High Skills: Globalization, Competitiveness, and Skill Formation*. Oxford: Oxford University Press.

Felstead, A., Gallie, D., Green, F., and Zhou, Y. (2007). *Skills at Work, 1986–2006*. Cardiff: SKOPE.

Finegold, D. and Soskice, D. (1988). The failure of training in Britain: Analysis and prescription. *Oxford Review of Economic Policy* **4**, 21–53.

Grubb, W. N. and Lazerson, M. (2004). *The Education Gospel: The Economic Power of Schooling*. Cambridge, MA: Harvard University Press.

Henry, M., Lingard, B., Rizvi, F., and Taylor, S. (2001). *The OECD, Globalisation and Education Policy*. Oxford: Pergamon.

OECD (1989). *Education and the Economy in a Changing Society*. Paris: OECD.

OECD (1999). *OECD Employment Outlook*. OECD: Paris.

OECD (2001). *Cities and Regions in the New Learning Economy*. Paris: OECD.

OECD (2002). *Beyond Rhetoric: Adult Learning Policies and Practices*. Paris: OECD.

OECD (2007). *Education at a Glance 2007*. Paris: OECD.

Rees, G., Fevre, R., Furlong, J., and Gorard, S. (2006). History, biography and place in the learning society: Towards a sociology of life-long learning. In Lauder, H., Brown, P., Dillabough, J.-A., and Halsey, A.H. (eds.) *Education, Globalization and Social Change*, pp 926–935. Oxford: Oxford University Press.

Further Reading

Becker, G. S. (1993). *Human Capital: A Theoretical and Empirical Analysis with Special Reference to Education*. Chicago, IL: University of Chicago Press.

Bélanger, P. and Valdivielso, S. (eds.) (1997). *The Emergence of Learning Societies: Who Participates in Adult Learning?* Oxford: Pergamon.

Bell, D. (1973). *The Coming of Post-Industrial Society*. New York: Basic Books.

Crouch, C., Finegold, D., and Sako, M. (1999). *Are Skills the Answer? The Political Economy of Skill Creation in Advanced Industrial Countries*. Oxford: Oxford University Press.

Dore, R. (1997). *The Diploma Disease: Education, Qualification and Development*, 2nd edn. London: Institute of Education.

Field, J. (2000). *Lifelong Learning and the New Educational Order*. Stoke-on-Trent: Trentham.

Lazear, E. P. (ed.) (2002). *Education in the Twenty-First Century*. Washington, DC: Hoover Press.

Lundvall, B.-A. (1992). *National Systems of Innovation: Towards a Theory of Innovation and Interactive Learning*. London: Pinter.

Machin, S. and Vignoles, A. (eds.) (2005). *What's the Good of Education? The Economics of Education in the UK*. Princeton, NJ: Princeton University Press.

Marginson, S. (1997). *Markets in Education*. St. Leonards, NSW: Allen and Unwin.

OECD (1998). *Human Capital Investment: An International Comparison*. Paris: OECD.

OECD (2001). *The Well-Being of Nations: The Role of Human and Social Capital*. Paris: OECD.

Prais, S. J. (1995). *Productivity, Education and Training: An International Perspective*. Cambridge: Cambridge University Press.

Reich, R. (1991). *The Work of Nations: A Blueprint for the Future*. London: Simon and Schuster.

Woolf, A. (2002). *Does Education Matter? Myths About Education and Economic Growth*. London: Penguin.

Relevant Websites

http://www.skope.ox.ac.uk – Centre for Research on Skills, Knowledge and Organizational Performance (SKOPE) (UK).

http://ioewebserver.ioe.ac.uk – Institute of Education, Centre for Research on the Wider Benefits of Learning (UK).

http://www.oecd.org – Organization for Economic Co-operation and Development, Statistics Portal.

http://ec.europa.eu – The European Commission, Eurostat.

http://www.uis.unesco.org – United Nations Educational, Scientific and Cultural Organization: Education.

Adult Education and Civil Society

J Crowther and I Martin, University of Edinburgh, Edinburgh, UK

Civil Society: The Problem of Definition

It is important to understand that the idea of civil society has been defined and deployed in different ways at different times, depending on what kind of social and political struggles were being fought, and won or lost. The meaning of civil society is part of the particular arguments and struggles of particular times. Consequently, for example, contemporary interpretations in adult education range from (literally) conservative formulations such as Robert Putnam's influential account of civil society as the source of social capital to Gramsci's radical notion of civil society as a site of struggle for moral and ideological hegemony.

Walzer (1996: 7) identifies civil society as the "sphere of uncoerced human association and also the set of relational networks ... that fill this space." Essentially, civil society, in its most widely accepted current usage, is distinct from the state (formal/representative politics) and the market (economic production, consumption, and exchange). It is generally understood to refer to those aspects of informal social and political life in which citizens come together in voluntary groups, associations, and movements to pursue their own collective interests and projects in freely chosen and relatively autonomous ways. Modern civil society organizations would therefore include, for example, trades unions and employer associations, churches and voluntary agencies, nongovernmental organizations (NGOs) and not-for-profit social enterprises, cultural and ethnic groups, and a whole range of popular campaigns, struggles, and movements. It is widely recognized that the vitality and relative autonomy of such informal and non-institutionalized political activity outside the state is an important precondition for the health of democratic politics within the state.

In reality, civil society is frequently in danger of invasion, colonization, and control by the state or the market. For instance, third way policies often seek to incorporate citizens and civic associations into particular kinds of partnership with state and market interests. Similarly, in their concern to roll back the frontiers of the state, neoliberal programs of privatization and structural adjustment may turn civil society into little more than an extension of the market or a manufactured instrument of state policy (Hodgson, 2004).

Finally, civil society is an ideal as well as an idea. Essentially, it may be said not only to embody a vision of democratic associational life, but also to represent the site of the kind of prefigurative work that is required to show that another world is possible. There is an important sense, then, in which civil society should be understood as an "intellectual space, where people in a myriad of different groups and associations can freely debate and discuss how to build the kind of world in which they want to live ... a realm of emancipations, of alternative imaginations of economic and social relations and of ideological contest" (Howell and Pearce, 2002: 2–8).

Adult Education and Civil Society Today

There are a number of distinct, but related, reasons for the remarkable revival of interest in the idea of civil society in recent years. These include: the failure and collapse of the totalitarian communist state and its command economy in Eastern Europe; fiscal crisis in social democratic welfare states and the effects of neoliberal retrenchment on public service provision; growing disillusionment with the politics of representative democracy and its characteristic democratic deficit; evidence of the increasingly important role of NGOs and other third sector agencies in both service delivery and governance; and the growth of new social movements and their demands for radical political and economic change. Edwards (2004: 13–15) distinguishes between the developmental roles of civil society in economic, social, and political terms: it compensates for market underdevelopment or failure; generates social capital and informal welfare; and is the site for the development of grassroots people power. In the context of what he calls peripheral capitalism, Youngman (2000: 209/210) sees the functions of civil society in wholly positive terms as promoting democratization and constructing alternative models of development – in both respects giving power back to ordinary people. At a more theoretical level, the work of Antonio Gramsci has been of singular importance in presenting civil society as the key site of struggle for the radical left; in addition, in terms of democratic thinking, the ideas of Jurgen Habermas have been particularly fruitful and influential. The impact of civil society on real political change is evidenced in the recent history of varied examples such as South Africa, Latin America, Poland, and Scotland.

As Welton (2001) emphasizes, there is nothing necessarily progressive, or even civil, about the idea of civil society. On the other hand, it does tend to be deployed in its current usage to focus attention on struggles for greater democracy and freedom and against injustice and oppression.

Essentially, it has been important in stimulating new thinking. For instance, on the post-Marxist left, the focus of interest on new social movements suggests that the traditional working class can no longer be regarded as the privileged agent of the emancipatory project (Mouffe, 1992). Indeed, some writers who take an interest in civil society adopt a self-consciously radical position. For instance, Powell and Geoghegan (2004: 7) argue that what they call the new face of civil society denotes "a force for democratisation in liberal democratic societies, where the poor and oppressed have found a voice through associational activities", thus making common cause in the struggle against exploitation and oppression.

There is an important sense in which civil society can be conceived as the distinctive space in which citizens come together to make democracy work (Cohen and Arato, 1992). On the one hand, this learning process may be ideologically constructed in different ways for different purposes. It is quite clear that much adult education today, particularly in the guise of lifelong learning, is primarily an instrument of state economic policy. The kind of technical rationality which drives it has nothing to do with democratic deliberation or social purpose. On the other hand, it is also important to recognize that learning in social movements has always been part of a particular kind of adult education. Indeed, some writers would argue that civil society is the natural territory of radical adult education. Welton (1995, 2001, 2005) suggests that learning, particularly the kind consistent with the emancipatory interest which lies at the heart of radical adult education, develops directly out of the communicative interaction that characterizes the groupings, associations, and movements of civil society.

Three Perspectives on Adult Education and Civil Society

The Communitarian Perspective: Learning for Membership

The key characteristic of the communitarian perspective is the focus on a decline in moral standards in civil society caused by a variety of interconnected social changes. These include permissiveness in the 1960s, the break-up of traditional family structures, a decline in social trust, the growth of a dependency culture nurtured by welfare provision, increases in violent crime, a lack of responsibility, particularly among the young and the unemployed, and the proliferation of minority rights (Etzioni, 1995). These trends were exacerbated in the 1980s with the thrust toward the unbridled pursuit of self-interest associated with neo-liberal politics and policies. Communitarianism aims to shore up the moral foundations of society by remoralizing those groups which cause social problems. Educating

people to be more responsible and active members of civil society is posed as the remedy for this situation.

The conservatism of communitarianism might have had very little appeal to many adult educators. However, its message that human relationships needed repairing and rebuilding chimed well with the emergence of social capital as a key policy concern, which has been influential in social policy and adult education. The dominant tradition of social capital refers to the norms of reciprocity and trust that appear to have been undermined by the breakdown in human relationships. Putnam's (2000) metaphor of Americans bowling alone (rather than in clubs) captured the sense of the loss of trust, cooperation, and shared activities that bind people together. Whereas communitarianism located the problem in a moral deficit in individuals, social capital relocates the deficit in the structure of people's relationships. Putnam's research (see also Putnam, 1993; Coleman, 1994) spurred the growth of a veritable social capital industry among academics. Distinctions have been made between bridging social capital (making ties between different groups), bonding social capital (developing contacts between like minded people), and linking social capital (connecting different levels of power or social status) (Kay, 2005).

The importance of trust, reciprocity, and participation in civic affairs has informed programs of community development which seek to create, enhance, and consolidate social capital in communities. In the UK, the Centre for the Wider Benefits of Learning has documented various positive social, political, and health outcomes related to the impact of adult education on social capital (Schuller et al., 2004). Participation in post-compulsory education – including adult literacy – is identified as one way of developing trust and building civic responsibility (Field, 2005; Tett et al., 2006). Furthermore, social capital can increase the likelihood of enhanced economic activity as confidence levels increase and networks of connections ease the path into work (Falk and Kilpatrick, 2000). However, too much bonding social capital among groups with negative dispositions toward education has also been put forward as an explanation for non-participation in adult education (McGivney, 2001). The bonds that tie people can, in some cases, bind them. Social capital may also contribute toward civic involvement through volunteering and people becoming more active members of their community (Schuller et al., 2004).

Arguably, social capital is an idea which is both politically expedient and highly normative. It is expedient in the sense that focusing on social relationships allows inequalities in social structure and resources to be ignored. Etzioni and Putnam take little interest in poverty and inequality as causal factors in the decline of communities and their social capital. The separation of civil society from the economy therefore leads away from politically controversial issues such as the distribution of wealth and power. It is normative in that only some types of social capital are valued, whereas others are not. For example, communities such as New Age Travellers may exhibit high levels of social capital, but are not the type of communities that governments want to support.

The focus on civil society, rather than the role of the state in reviving civil society, can let governments off the hook by transferring responsibility from statutory provision to voluntary effort (Ehrenberg, 2002). Ironically, the state's interest in encouraging participation in civic activity seems to be increasing at the same time as democratic spaces for learning seem to be diminishing. The distinction between the invited spaces of policy and the demanded spaces of communities are two distinct ways of thinking about democratic participation (Gaventa, 2006). In the former, participation is structured around the interests of top-down policy imperatives, whereas, in the latter, the spaces for participation emerge because of popular demands from below. Both present opportunities for adult education engagement, however, the context, purpose, and focus of the work provide very different challenges and prospects.

The Habermasian Perspective: Learning for Deliberation

From an adult education perspective, it could be argued that Jurgen Habermas is concerned about rescuing democracy, and the learning process embedded in it, from both the instrumentalism of capitalism (in which it becomes simply a political means to an economic end) and the relativism of postmodernism (in which universal values and purposes are deemed no longer to matter). For Habermas, who "steadfastly refuses to ditch modernity's dream of using human reason to create a more humane world" (Brookfield, 2005: 25 and 26), the central task of critical theory is to encourage people to think constructively and creatively for themselves and to enable them to follow the agreed rules of democratic discourse. These are intended to ensure that "no one may be excluded; anything may be said, questioned, or challenged; and no force may be used" (Chambers, 1996: 197).

Habermas emphasizes the democratic work that is done in civil society when he describes it as a "network of associations that institutionalizes problem-solving discourses on questions of general interest inside the framework of organised public spheres" (Habermas, 1996: 367). According to John Keane, an eminent contemporary theorist of civil society, the key distinction for Habermas is between the "logics of the political and economic systems, regulated respectively by administrative power and money, and the life-world of self-organized public spheres based on solidarity and communication" (Keane, 1988: 18). In this sense, the state and the economy are complementary domains based on distinctive systems of power, and civil

society is defined, partly, in contradistinction to them. The boundaries are often shifting and there may be a high degree of overlap and interpenetration; however, it is, nevertheless, important to maintain the distinction.

Democratic deliberation is essentially about communication, and how we use language to communicate with each other. This kind of discourse, including the rules of argumentation on which it is based, is something we have to learn. The appeal to reason in this process removes the distortions of power which would otherwise saturate and corrupt it. Democracy is constituted and sustained through a process of rational deliberation, which is conducted according to agreed rules and procedures, among equal citizens. In other words, adult learning is absolutely central to the Habermasian idea of building a democratic culture and defending the lifeworld, where people are authentically themselves, against invasion of and colonization by the steering mechanisms of the systems world of state or market. Habermas is concerned about stipulating the discursive conditions and procedures for conducting the democratic argument in the public sphere, understood as the space for deliberative democracy which civil society must keep open if it is to protect democracy. This is necessarily a continuing process, always unfinished.

There are many examples of adult education approaches which reflect this concern for democratic deliberation and organized public spheres. The Workers Educational Association in the UK is, at its best, a bearer of this tradition of social purpose and political engagement (Fieldhouse, 1996). Perhaps the obvious example of this tradition is the study circle. The term itself suggests an egalitarian relationship between members in which participation and democratic discussion focused on issues of common interest or concern are fundamental. This form of organized democratic learning is strongly associated with the Scandinavian and Nordic countries. It also has important parallels in the USA, and resonates with the principles of mutuality which informed learning in the co-operative and labor movements in the nineteenth century (Bjerkaker and Summers, 2006). Moreover, as Welton (2005) points out, the social learning that occurs in progressive movements constitutes a communicative public sphere in which new meanings can be created and debated. These movements assert the importance of the lifeworld and seek to defend it against the corrosive power of instrumental rationality associated with the political and economic systems.

What the Habermasian perspective suggests is that the task of adult education is to create the pretexts and the contexts for this kind of learning to take place within the uncoerced associations and affiliations of civil society. In order to think through what this means, Habermas (1978) distinguishes between three domains of learning, each informed by particular interests: technical learning, which concerns the manipulation of environment and control of the world we live in; practical learning, which concerns the development of interpersonal understanding and relationships; and emancipatory learning, which concerns self-understanding and critical consciousness. Each has its part to play in learning for democracy; however, clearly, Habermas's main interest lies in the emancipatory project.

It is important to emphasize that good adult learning models the process of deliberative or discursive democracy. In this sense, adult education can be said to do the prefigurative work of democracy in which key ideas and arguments are tested out and interrogated in discussion. The purpose of this kind of learning is not necessarily to reach agreement: in the end, it may well be about agreeing to disagree, and learning to live democratically with the consequences.

The Gramscian Perspective: Learning for Activism

Radical adult education from the 1970s onwards drew inspiration from the Italian Marxist Antonio Gramsci because of his work on cultural politics and the role of intellectuals in social change. While Gramsci was never precise in his definition of civil society, its relationship with the state in his work is unique. He makes the distinction between two aspects of the superstructure of society (in contrast to the economic base) in terms of civil society and the state/political society. These correspond to the exercise of two forms of power which reinforce class domination: hegemonic power (the leading and directive ideas and values in society) and the state's monopoly on legitimate coercive power. Civil society is made up of so-called private organizations like churches, trades unions, and voluntary bodies which are characterized by social relations based on autonomy and free association, whereas the state is primarily defined in relation to its coercive potential exercised through the activities of the army, judiciary, and courts. Gramsci was aware, of course, that the state was not merely coercive. More importantly, the boundaries between civil society and state are permeable, and organizations and practices can embody social relations belonging to both spheres. The connections between state and civil society in reproducing class rule are reflected in Gramsci's (1971) expanded view of the state as "political society + civil society, in other words, hegemony protected by the armour of coercion" (p. 263).

However, civil society's apparent distance from the state means it can be a powerful medium for the diffusion of the dominant hegemony. Education, for example, is provided in many countries by the state and influenced by its policies and economic priorities; however, Gramsci locates education firmly in civil society, which seems strange. The school is an important institution of social reproduction. In addition, schooling may be coercive, although adult education still has a voluntary status.

Nevertheless, the core of educational relationships is primarily open, rather than closed; critical education can serve to engage the dominant hegemony, rather than simply reproduce it. This ambivalence (produced by social relations that are partly a product of the state and partly of civil society) provides opportunities and spaces for resistance against dominant ideas, values, and priorities.

The voluntary nature of adult education means that there is potentially more space for radical education because of its freer status. It has a crucial role to play in weaning the working class away from their dependency on traditional intellectuals, by creating their own organic intellectuals, who are able to articulate their interests and galvanize class action as a necessary first step toward social transformation. In this perspective, the focus is on winning hearts and minds before a frontal assault on the state – or even to remove the necessity for it. Education is therefore the foundation of revolutionary activity (Holst, 2002).

The radical nature of this type of education means that it is seldom located in the formal adult education provision. In the UK, there is the important historical example of the Labour College movement which focused on educating revolutionary militants (Simon, 1992). In some respects, this development prefigured Gramsci's analysis of the role of education in class struggle. Holst (2004) has made visible the largely unacknowledged educational role of revolutionary political organizations in the USA, and Boughton (2005) has documented the role of the Communist Party in educating generations of militants in Australia. Allman (2001) addresses the centrality of alliance building under proletarian hegemony involving different social movements and popular forces as a key issue in critical and progressive educational work. The struggle against apartheid in South Africa is an example of the importance of alliance building across civil society in which radical educators played a significant role (von Kotze, 2005).

However, the emergence of new social movements from the 1960s onwards challenged the focus on social class as the privileged agent of change. The growth of neo-Marxist accounts of civil society and the development of postmodernist thinking also influenced various strands of radical adult education. Localized narratives of change (Usher et al., 1997) and selective change around particular issues such as the environment (Welton, 1995), rather than generalized class struggle, have either used or dispensed with Gramsci to explain the dynamics of power in civil society and what can be done.

Toward a Global Civil Society? Roles for Adult Education

The discussion so far has considered three perspectives on adult education and civil society in the context of the nation state. It is now becoming increasingly important, however, to think in trans-national and supra-national terms. Each perspective suggests a distinctive way of thinking about the possible contributions of adult education in the context of a global civil society.

It might seem premature to talk of a global civil society, but it is important to recognize the growth of non-state actors such as trans-national social movements with a global interest (Mundy and Murphy, 2006). The spread of neo-liberal globalization, global systems of production, geo-political wars, nuclear armament, environmental degradation, and the role of powerful unelected international organizations in economic affairs have led to an increasing number of civil society groups, NGOs, and social movements contesting and challenging these trends. This globalization from below has been aided by the development of information and communication technologies which have made the coordination of action and dissemination of counter-information possible on a global scale. While the influence of these groups on policy development is debatable, they do have a highly visible international presence.

In the communitarian perspective, the focus is on developing membership among nation states at an international level to promote adult education and to develop reciprocal relations between different countries. There have been various adult education initiatives which might broadly be conceived as reflecting this perspective. The International Council of Adult Education (2007), for example, is a trans-national advocacy organization which is campaigning for the right to learn and wider recognition of the role adult education can play in combating poverty, discrimination, and exclusion. In addition, United Nations Educational, Scientific, and Cultural Organization (UNESCO)'s International Conference on Adult Education (CONFINTEA) conferences target policy makers, academics, adult educators, civil society organizations, trade unions, and other interested parties to facilitate linking social capital, among other things. These events – held every 12 years – seek to promote adult education on a global scale and to embed it in various development goals and resourcing priorities of nation states and international organizations.

In the Habermasian perspective, learning in the public sphere is another arena where adult educators can make a contribution to the development of a global civil society. The World Social Forum, for example, actively contributes to what Barr (2007) calls "undiscovered public knowledge." By this, she means independent sources of knowledge rooted in people's experiences and directed at the collective social, political, and human problems they seek to address. Newman (2007) argues that a deliberative democratic process is essential for making national politicians accountable. This process demands a sustained dialog between citizens and electors, and requires particular skills: "how to critically appraise the statements of others; how to think clearly for ourselves; how to think inventively; how to participate actively in the affairs of state; and how to participate wisely" (p. 10).

In the Gramscian perspective, globalization raises issues about the growth of a trans-national capitalist class, its hegemony, and how it can be opposed (Robinson, 2005). Gramsci's own work focused on civil society in the context of nation states; therefore, we need to extrapolate and develop his concepts for the new global context. This raises questions about the type of strategy and the type of social forces necessary to create an alternative hegemony. For example, the confrontational action against the World Trade Organisation in Seattle in 1999 and against the Group of Eight (G8) in Genoa in 2001 is, in Gramsci's terms, a "war of movement" (direct frontal assaults on the state) in contrast to his view about the necessity for a "war of position" (a systematic struggle for ideological hegemony). The latter points to the need for detailed and systematic critique of the intellectual and moral authority of international institutions, such as the International Monetary Fund, World Bank, World Trade Organisation, G8/9, and the Organisation for Economic Cooperation and Development, which legitimate the hegemony of an increasingly global capitalist class.

Conclusion

The three perspectives on adult education and civil society, constructed in terms of learning for membership, deliberation, and activism, demonstrate competing meanings and distinctive practices. These are reflected in different adult education purposes, contexts, and constituencies. In the era of globalization, the struggle to define and control what civil society means and who it is for is increasingly likely to occur at an international level. Adult education has a distinctive contribution to make to the social and political contestation this will entail.

See also: Adult Learning, Instruction and Programme Planning: Insights from Freire; Class Analysis in Adult Education; Community Based Adult Education; Popular Adult Education; Wider Benefits of Adult Education.

Bibliography

Allman, P. (2001). *Critical Education against Global Capitalism*. London: Bergin and Garvey.

Barr, J. (2007). Educational research and undiscovered public knowledge. *Studies in the Education of Adults* **39**(1), 22–37.

Bjerkaker, S. and Summers, J. (2006). *Learning Democratically: Using Study Circles*. Leicester: National Institute of Adult Continuing Education.

Boughton, B. (2005). 'The workers university: Australia's Marx schools. In Crowther, J., Galloway, V., and Martin, I. (eds.) *Popular Education: Engaging the Academy – International Perspectives*, pp 100–109. Leicester: National Institute of Adult Continuing Education.

Brookfield, S. (2005). *The Power of Critical Theory: Liberating Adult Learning and Teaching*. San Francisco, CA: Jossey-Bass.

Chambers, C. (1996). *Reasonable Democracy: Jurgen Habermas and the Politics of Discourse*. Ithaca: Cornell University Press.

Cohen, J. and Arato, A. (1992). *Civil Society and Political Theory*. Cambridge, MA: MIT Press.

Coleman, J. S. (1994). *Foundations of Social Theory*. Cambridge, MA: Belknap Press.

Edwards, M. (2004). *Civil Society*. Cambridge, UK: Polity Press.

Ehrenberg, J. (2002). Equality, democracy, and community from Tocqueville to Putnam. In McLean, S., Schultz, D., and Steger, M. (eds.) *Social Capital*, pp 50–73. London and New York: New York University Press.

Etzioni, A. (1995). *The Spirit of Community*. London: Fontana Press.

Falk, I. and Kilpatrick, S. (2000). What is social capital? A study of a rural community. *Sociologia Ruralis* **1**(40), 87–110.

Field, J. (2005). *Social Capital and Lifelong Learning*. Bristol: Policy Press.

Fieldhouse, R. and Associates (1996). *A History of Modern British Adult Education*. Leicester: National Institute of Adult Continuing Education.

Gaventa, J. (2006). Finding the spaces for change: A power analysis, exploring power for change. *IDS Bulletin* **37**(6), 23–33.

Gramsci, A. (1971). *Selections from the Prison Notebooks* (translated by Hoare, Q. and Smith, G. N.). London: Lawrence and Wishart.

Habermas, J. (1978). *Knowledge and Human Interest*. London: Heinemann Educational.

Habermas, J. (1996). *Between Fact and Norms: Contributions to a Discourse Theory of Law and Democracy*. Cambridge, MA: MIT Press.

Hodgson, L. (2004). Manufactured civil society: Counting the cost. *Critical Social Policy* **79**(24), 139–164.

Holst, J. D. (2002). *Social Movements, Civil Society and Radical Adult Education*. London: Bergin and Garvey.

Holst, J. D. (2004). Globalization and education within two revolutionary organisations in the United States of America: A Gramscian analysis. *Adult Education Quarterly* **55**(1), 23–40.

Howell, J. and Pearce, J. (2002). *Civil Society and Development: A Critical Exploration*. Boulder, CO: Lynne Rienner.

International Council for Adult Education (2007). Adults' right to learn: Convergence, solidarity and action. *Adult Education and Development* **67**, 65–68.

Kay, A. (2005). Social capital, the social economy and community development. *Community Development Journal* **41**(2), 160–173.

Keane, J. (ed.) (1988). *Civil Society and the State: New European Perspectives*. London: Verso.

McGivney, V. (2001). *Fixing or Changing the Pattern?* Leicester: National Institute of Adult Continuing Education.

Mouffe, M. (ed.) (1992). *Dimensions of Radical Democracy: Pluralism, Citizenship, Democracy*. London: Verso.

Mundy, K. and Murphy, L. (2006). Transnational advocacy, global civil society? Emerging evidence from the field of education. In Lauder, H., Brown, P., Dillabough, J-A., and Halsey, A.H (eds.) *Education, Globalization and Social Change*, pp 991–1015. Oxford: Oxford University Press.

Newman, M. (2007). Adult education and the home front. *Adults Learning* **18**(7), 9–11.

Powell, F. and Geoghegan, M. (2004). *Reclaiming Civil Society or Reinventing Governance?* Dublin: A and A Farmar.

Putnam, R. (1993). *Making Democracy Work: Civic Traditions in Modern Italy*. Princeton: Princeton University Press.

Putnam, R. (2000). *Bowling Alone: The Collapse and Revival of American Community*. New York: Simon Schuster.

Robinson, W. I. (2005). Gramsci and globalisation: From nation-state to transnational hegemony. *Critical Review of International Social and Political Philosophy* **8**(4), 1–16.

Schuller, T., Brasset-Grundy, A., Green, A., Hammond, C., and Preston, J. (2004). *Wider Benefits of Learning*. London: Routledge Falmer.

Simon, B. (1992). *The Search for Enlightenment*. Leicester: National Institute of Adult Continuing Education.

Tett, L., Hall, S., Maclachlan, K., *et al.* (2006). *Evaluation of the Scottish Adult Literacy and Numeracy [ALN] Strategy*. Edinburgh: Scottish Executive Social Research.

Usher, R., Bryant, I., and Johnson, R. (1997). *Adult Education and the Postmodern Challenge*. London: Routledge.

von Kotze, A. (2005). People's education and the academy: An experience from South Africa. In Crowther, J., Galloway, V., and Martin, I. (eds.) *Popular Education:Engaging the Academy – International Perspectives*, pp 11–21. Leicester: National Institute of Adult Continuing Education.

Walzer, M. (1996). The civil society argument. In Mouffe, M. (ed.) *Dimensions of Radical Democracy:Pluralism,Citizenship,Democracy*. London: Verso.

Welton, M. (1995). *In Defense of the Lifeworld: Critical Perspectives on Adult Learning*. Albany, NY: State University of New York Press.

Welton, M. (2001). Civil society and the public sphere: Habermas's recent learning theory. *Studies in the Education of Adults* **33**(1), 20–34.

Welton, M. (2005). *Designing the Just Learning Society: A Critical Inquiry*. Leicester: National Institute of Adult Continuing Education.

Youngman, F. (2000). *The Political Economy of Adult Education and Development*. Leicester: National Institute of Adult Continuing Education/Zed Books.

Further Reading

Baron, S., Field, J., and Schuller, T. (eds.) (2000). *Social Capital:Critical Perspectives.* Oxford: Oxford University Press.

Bauman, Z. (1999). *In Search of Politics*. Cambridge: Polity Press.

Crowther, J., Martin, I., and Shaw, M. (eds.) (1999). *Popular Education and Social Movements in Scotland Today.* Leicester: National Institute of Adult Continuing Education.

Delanty, G. (2003). *Community*. London: Routledge.

Finger, M. and Asun, J. (2001). *Adult Education at the Crossroads: Learning Our Way Out*. Leicester: National Institute of Adult Continuing Education.

Held, D. (1996). *Models of Democracy*. Cambridge: Polity Press.

Hobson, B. (ed.) (2003). *Recognition Struggles and Social Movements*. Cambridge: Cambridge University Press.

Kane, L. (2001). *Popular Education and Social Change in Latin America*. London: Latin America Bureau.

Little, A. (2002). *The Politics of Community*. Edinburgh: Edinburgh University Press.

Welton, M. (2005). Civil society. In English, M. (ed.) *International Encyclopedia of Adult Education*, pp 100–106. Basingstoke, UK: Palgrave Macmillan.

Wildemeersch, D., Finger, M., and Jansen, T. (eds.) (1998). *Adult Education and Social Responsibility*. Frankfurt am Main: Peter Lang.

Wildemeersch, D., Stroobants, V., and Bron, M. (eds.) (2005). *Active Citizenship and Multiple Identities in Europe: A Learning Outlook*. Frankfurt am Main: Peter Lang.

Williamson, B. (1998). *Lifeworlds and Learning*. Leicester: National Institute of Adult Continuing Education.

Adult Education and Nation Building

S Walters, University of Western Cape, Bellville, South Africa

Introduction

The late President of Tanzania said in 1976 that, "Adult education is a highly political activity. Politicians are sometimes more aware of this fact than educators, and therefore they do not always welcome real adult education" (Nyerere, 1976). By juxtaposing adult education and nation building, the political dimensions of adult education are foregrounded.

This article privileges experiences particularly in the Southern African Development Community (SADC) concerning adult education and nation building, to act as a lens to illuminate key issues which are also relevant to other regions of the world. The discussion is framed utilizing the following three social purposes of adult education:

1. Education that enhances strategies which enable women and men to survive the harsh conditions in which they live. Examples of this include literacy, primary healthcare, and some home-craft skills.
2. Education and training geared to developing skills for people in the formal and informal sectors that describe education for economic purposes.
3. Cultural and political education which aims to encourage women and men to participate actively in society through networks of cultural organizations, social movements, political parties, and trade unions.

The article begins with a discussion of various understandings of nation building, then moves to a discussion of adult education and nation building within SADC, highlighting universally important themes. This is followed by concluding remarks and suggestions for further readings.

Nation Building

"Nation building depends upon winning popular support for rapid change," commented Lowe (1971). In the early 1970s, 20 years after the United Nations had been established, and many countries had recently gained independence from the colonial powers, there was much interest in the role of education in national development. Developing the nation-state was the primary focus of attention. Over 30 years later, a fundamental political question is whether existing plural states, which make up 90% of the current 180 or so nation-states in the world, would be able

to withstand the dual onslaught of ethnic nationalism and global economic integration (Phadnis and Ganguly, 2001).

The nation-state is a legal concept describing social groups who occupy a defined territory and are organized under common political institutions and an effective government. The state exercises sovereign powers within its borders and is recognized as sovereign by other states in the international system. A nation is therefore different from an ethnic group which can be transnational. (Phadnis and Ganguly 2001: 20) A key social construct within the nation-state is the citizen; therefore literature on adult education and citizenship (e.g., Bron and Schemmann, 2001; Korsgaard et al. 2001), can be a useful resource.

Mamdani (1996) provides a very rich analysis of the complexity of how the citizen and subject have been constructed in postcolonial states in Africa, which highlights the bifurcated state between urban and rural, between modern and customary, which is highly gendered, within one hegemonic state apparatus. Oga and Okwori (2005) illustrate the complexities of citizenship in Nigeria where people have stronger affiliation to ethnicity or religion than an imagined community of a nation-state. How citizenship is understood is therefore essential to the discussion on nation building.

Gaventa (2007), as editor of a series of texts on Claiming Citizenship: Rights, Participation and Accountability, points out that there is a growing crisis of legitimacy in the relationship between citizens and the institutions that affect their lives. In countries, both in the North and South, citizens speak of mounting disillusionment with governments, based on concerns about corruption, lack of responsiveness to the needs of the poor, and the absence of a sense of connection with elected representatives and bureaucrats. The rights and responsibilities of corporations and other global actors are being challenged, as global inequalities persist and deepen. Nation building is therefore deeply connected to notions of democracy, development, and globalization (Korsgaard, 1997; Finger, 2005). It is undoubtedly complex and contested.

The question arises then as to how far people's struggles for power, through liberation or social movements, can also be seen as part of a nation-building project Or is it a process that can only be led by a legitimate government in power? This question harks back to understandings of development and nation building (Youngman 2000). In this article, the position taken is that there are a range of actors in a society which contribute to nation building and, as Lowe suggests, winning popular support for rapid change. There can be nation building from below, through social movements, and nation building through government interventions. As Finger (2005) points out, formal education for children, is often more tied to the state machinery than adult education which has most often stayed outside of government.

We look at what adult education and nation building means in southern Africa and in doing so elaborate on some of the above points, particularly relating to struggles for democracy and development.

Adult Education and Nation Building in the SADC

Southern African Development Community (SADC)

This section is adapted from an article entitled 'Adult education in lifelong learning in southern Africa', by Walters and Watters (2001).

Political and Socioeconomic Picture of the Region

The present global economy is pushing national economies and local industries to compete in the world market. The SADC was formed in 1992 and in 2000 the protocol on trade came into force which is moving SADC toward a free-trade area. SADC grew out of the Southern African Development Co-ordination Conference (SADCC), which had had South Africa as its common political enemy while sharing with it complex historical and economic dependence. The SADCC provided the structure for the countries to organize themselves in geopolitical terms in order to maximize their political clout and minimize their economic dependence on South Africa.

SADC is comprised of 14 countries, which vary in population from the Democratic Republic of the Congo (DRC), which has 62 million, to Swaziland which has just over a million inhabitants. Another four of the countries have populations of 2 million or less: Botswana, Lesotho, Mauritius, and Namibia. Many SADC countries still rely heavily on agriculture. Only Angola, Botswana, and South Africa have less than 10% of their production coming from agriculture. Five countries, Malawi, Mozambique, DRC, Tanzania, and Zambia, obtain more than 20% of their production from agriculture. It is one of the least urbanized parts of the world and only Angola, Botswana, and South Africa have urban dwellers in the majority. Economic performance is dominated by that of South Africa, which represents more than 70% of the combined sub-regional gross domestic product (GDP).

Commonly used indicators of poverty reveal that SADC members are among the poorest countries in the world. In 2005, the average human-development index for

the region's countries was 0.54, while the SADC website reports a 2003 GDP per capita of US$1062. This compares unfavorably with the world average in 2003 of US$5822 and the average for Western Europe, for example, of US$30 449. The per capita income per person in the DRC in 2006 was only US$128 per year, which makes it one of the poorest in the world.

There are a few countries which have a relatively high GDP per capita for developing countries. The 2003 SADC figures put Mauritius at the top with US$4522 with South Africa and Botswana having above US$3000 per capita per annum. But even in these relatively well-off countries, there is major inequity between the rich and poor. The SADC Regional Human Development Report of 2000 states that 30% of SADC population live in abject poverty while 30–40% of the labor force is unemployed or ekes out a living as subsistence farmers.

The life expectancy is very low in most SADC countries, for example, Swaziland where it is just 31 years and Botswana where it is 35 years (2004 figures. The terrible human immunodeficiency virus/acquired immunodeficiency syndrome (HIV/AIDS) pandemic is pushing the life expectancy even lower. The infant-mortality rate is as high as 260 in Angola and 205 in DRC per 1000 live births. Again, this compares unfavorably with, for example, Japan at 3.2 or the United Kingdom at 5.3.

Although still experiencing difficult economic situations, most SADC countries have adopted macroeconomic and social policies aimed at improving regional human-development performance. In order to achieve this, several governments spend around 20% of their budgets on education and almost 5% on health development.

This sketch provides a picture of a region that has a very wide spread of developmental needs, including adult education. The countries of SADC are peripheral capitalist economies and the development of adult education has been shaped very directly by this, including the macro-policies of international development agencies and the socioeconomic realities within each of the countries. (See, e.g., Torres, 2004) These in turn have sometimes spurred local people on to finding alternative approaches to development.

Social Purposes of Adult Education in the SADC Region

Most of the countries of the region have experienced major political and economic upheavals in the last 50 years. During this time, all of them went through, more or less, traumatic processes of decolonization. The last five countries to gain independence were Mozambique in 1976, Angola in 1975, Zimbabwe in 1980, Namibia in 1990, and South Africa in 1994. All five of these countries experienced extended liberation struggles. All of the countries in the region went through processes of reconstruction and development toward building new nations in about the last 50 years. The approaches adopted by the different countries were shaped strongly by dominant development theories of the time which reflect particular ideologies and material interests (see, e.g., Youngman, 2000).

In order to give a sense of the fragmented and contested nature of the role of adult education in nation building, illustrations are provided, falling within the three major social purposes: survival; economic development; and political and cultural development.

Adult education for political and cultural development

As adult education is integral to social processes, it is not surprising that it gains in prominence at heightened political or economic moments through actions within the state, civil society, or the private sector. In the past, most governments have invested minimally in adult education with their emphasis on schooling. At the point of political independence, adult education became significant. For example, after the historic transition in South Africa to democratic governance in 1994, adult education was highlighted particularly in relation to redress for black people, economic development, and the growth of a democratic culture. Adult basic education was declared a presidential lead project but was to be dependent on international donors.

Another example is taken from Mozambique. The watchwords of Samora Machel, the late president of the newly independent Mozambique and head of the liberation movement, Frelimo, were "study, produce, and fight." These were taken as serious marching orders in preparation for independence and a broad, popular literacy movement emerged throughout the country (Marshall, 1990: 83). Popular education involved mobilizing human resources for creating the new Mozambique and literacy was part of the dynamizing groups set up in most villages and towns. A national directorate of literacy and adult education was set up in 1976. Since those heady days with the systematic destructive power of the apartheid state in South Africa, state-sponsored adult education all but disappeared in Mozambique between the mid-1980s to mid-1990s. Since then, according to Mario and Nandja (2006: 192), there has been a process of rediscovery and rescue of adult literacy and education, with there now being an average rate of illiteracy of about 54%, with rates in rural areas and among women being disproportionately high.

The fact that most countries in the region have undergone radical political change in the last 50 years implies that there have been high degrees of political activism and education at different times. From the 1960s, Namibians and South Africans built powerful democratic movements of citizens, both inside and outside the countries, which created alliances of socialist revolutionaries, social democrats, and social reformers. Creative informal and nonformal education was integral to these movements which involved thousands of community-based organizations which were forged into the democratic movements. (Walters 1989) There was rich learning through social and political action as people strove to build a new nation from below.

The struggles for people's democracy in the mid-1970s in places like Angola and Mozambique had been overshadowed in the following 15–20 years by civil wars spurred on by the apartheid regime and other international interests. Many of the gains hoped for in education, health, social welfare, and economic development had been decimated. In Angola alone it is reported that over 500 000 people had been killed since 1989 and 3 million people became refugees (Oduaran 2000). The DRC too has recently emerged from a devastating civil war. In the region, while people's movements for democratic social change have engendered innovative responses in some countries, in others, many millions of people are confronted with the struggle for survival from poverty, war, and disease under the most trying conditions. Not all people's movements are necessarily positive; some are mobilizing children and adults for participation in violent crime and war. Literature is not available on what educational efforts are occurring within these situations but there are no doubt activists working to bring about peace and reconciliation on the one hand and activists training new recruits for violence and war on the other (see, e.g., Thompson, 2000).

Adult education for survival

One of the greatest educational challenges facing SADC presently is the devastating HIV/AIDS pandemic. The region has the highest incidence in the world. Thousands of people are dying of the disease. It is having substantial effects on the economies as it is the working adult population which is most vulnerable. The estimation is that there were 12 million AIDS orphans in Africa at the end of 2007 and estimates are that currently the higher education population in South Africa is 22% HIV/AIDS positive.

There have been various strategies developed over the last 15 or so years to counter the pandemic. It is primarily a sexually transmitted disease which is exacerbated by poverty. Educational processes are called on which challenge deep seated cultural, religious, ethnic, gender, or class attitudes and behaviors. In many societies, there are cultural practices that propagate the spread of the virus through promiscuity. Women are most at risk as often it is men who have multiple partners. The power relations between women and men make it nearly impossible for many women to insist on safe sexual practices. Some people predict that until women are empowered and gender relations are more equal, it will be extremely difficult to stem this tide.

Educational programs are being orchestrated in some countries through the health ministries, but this is seen to be inadequate. In South Africa, departments of education, labor, welfare, and health are working together. There are over 600 nongovernmental organizations (NGOs) working to counter HIV/AIDS. Some workplaces have begun running education and counseling services for workers. There is a growing awareness that all sectors of society, working with people of all ages, must join together to educate about HIV/AIDS. At the World Aids Conference held in Durban in July 2000, 13 000 scientists, activists, educators, development workers, government officials, and health workers, all came together to share research, information, methodologies, and policies. There were discussions, debates, information, and papers disseminated on a daily basis through community and national radio, television, and newspapers. It was a massive and impressive public educational process.

The growing campaign is being interpreted and taken forward by a very wide range of interest groups with different values, for example, rurally based indigenous healers, rural and urban women's groups, youth groups, religious and community organizations, and educational institutions. They are using different approaches, from ethnocultural, to feminist, to popular, to spiritual, among others, to organize awareness-raising, skills-training, and organizational-development strategies.

The responses to HIV/AIDS provide excellent contemporary examples of adult education for survival which involve most sectors of society and which draw on multiple pedagogical, organizational, and developmental frameworks simultaneously.

Adult education for economic development

In a region with such high unemployment and levels of poverty, economic development is of paramount importance. The United Nations Department of Economic and Social Affairs states that unemployment in the region varies from Namibia at 34% (2000) to Madagascar at 4.5% (2003. An independent assessment puts the rate in Zimbabwe in 2007 at 80%. A 1998 SADC report estimates that 30–40% of the labor force of SADC are either completely unemployed or are eking out a living as subsistence farmers. The same report indicates that less than 50% of the labor force is women. In the last 20 years, numerous adult-education programs focused on skill development have been embarked on by SADC countries in both the formal and informal economies.

Within the context of globalized economies, economic development and adult education, or adult learning, have become more urgent and complex. Within the debates on globalization are debates about the importance and the role of information communication technologies (ICTs) in economic development. Africa is the most poorly

serviced continent in ICT. Africa, with 14.2% of the world's population, has only 3.4% of its Internet users. South Africa has the most users in SADC, but is fourth on the continent after Nigeria, Morocco, and Egypt. This is seen as another major barrier to Africa's development and one which will lead to even greater inequality both within the continent and between Africa and other regions.

The type of adult education for economic development that has occurred in the last 20–30 years within SADC can be differentiated again in terms of competing interests. For instance, the economic-development projects for women have often been within a modernizing frame which has not challenged the sexual division of labor or attempted to transform women's subordinate positions.

Adult education for economic development occurs most frequently in large companies in the formal sector and for employees at the middle and upper levels. This is a worldwide trend which most often favors educated men and is reflected in the SADC region as well. This is likely to continue as, within the dominant neo-liberal framework, the globalizing economies require flexible, well-educated workers. As Stromquist (1998) suggests, it also requires uneducated workers to service the professional classes and hence the low priority given to literacy in the region despite government rhetoric.

The SADC is trying to position itself in the global economy. The discussions and debates about adult and lifelong learning are shaped directly by this. A key question is what is the primary objective of economic development? Is it to be globally competitive? Which is the predominant view? Or are there alternatives as argued by Klein (2007) and others? Within SADC, these are very pertinent and hotly debated issues within organizations of state, civil society, and business. Adult education is implicated in these debates and political contestations.

Adult education within lifelong learning

The discourse of adult education is being challenged by that of lifelong learning. Lifelong learning has entered the education and development debates of the region, as elsewhere. Education policy documents in Botswana, Namibia, South Africa, for example, all refer to lifelong learning as a goal. The contestation over lifelong learning for what among and within the different sectors is ongoing (see, e.g., Walters, 2006).

The shift in the discourse of adult education to lifelong learning may signal shifts in understandings of relationships between individuals and the nation-state; between individuals and their identities as national, regional, or global citizens. Lifelong learning most commonly relates to the need for continuing education and training for global competitiveness. It may reflect the weakening of the nation-state and the increasing requirements for transnational and global relationships between the local and the global.

Conclusion

Experiences in SADC have shown how adult education gained in significance both during the struggle for and at the time of independence, with the formation of the new nation-state. Adult education was identified by social movements struggling for liberation in order to mobilize and prepare citizens for rapid change. It was also identified by new governments as necessary to mobilize and (re) shape citizens for their roles and responsibilities in the new society. The utilization of informal and nonformal adult education, within movements, helped to prefigure the new state. It was intimately connected to contestations concerning social and economic development, including notions of democracy and citizenship. Most of the SADC countries had leftist movements (i.e., Marxist, socialist, or social democratic) involved in the national revolutions. South Africa's apartheid government, in turn, played a catalytic role in the 1970s and 1980s in providing a common enemy, against which regional governments and liberation movements struggled. Solidarity among countries against apartheid was therefore an important element of citizenship of the region.

At independence, each of the governments projected adult education as an important part of their reconstruction and development of their nation state. However, few resources were invested and adult education and training has been dispersed among civil-society organizations, workplaces, and various departments in government. At the time of independence, adult education had a powerful symbolic purpose but it has not necessarily translated into systematic programs for the adult population. After the novelty and excitement of the birth of the new nation, adult education has settled back to being barely visible, but is integral to new social movements who are continuing to contest power relations in the society, and notions of citizenship, whether shaped by gender, race, class, geography, and physical ability; or specific cross-cutting issues, like health or criminality.

The discussions on adult education and nation building show that they cannot be divorced from understandings of democracy and development, within local, national, regional, and global contexts. This means that nation building is intimately linked to notions of citizenship, which, on one hand, are determined through the legal frameworks of a country. On the other hand, citizenship is often contested by social movements, political parties, or other social structures, as its interpretation reflects the power relations in the society. Nation building can therefore be driven by state structures or it can be driven from below. Adult education, whether informal, nonformal, or formal is interwoven into political, economic, and social processes, which comprise the nation-building project at particular historical moments, in specific contexts. In the twenty-first century, with nation-states losing their predominance as defining economic entities, it is hard to hold the question of the relationship between adult education and nation building for long, before questions of the specificities of the local, regional, or global shout for attention.

Bibliography

Bron, A. and Schemmann, M. (eds.) (2001). *Civil Society, Citizenship and Learning.* Germany: Lit Verslag.

Finger, M. (2005). *Globalization.* In English, L. (ed.) *International Encyclopedia of Adult Education,* 1st edn., pp 269–273. New York: Palgrave Macmillan.

Gaventa, J. (2007). Foreword. In Cornwall, A. and Schattan Coelho, V. (eds.) *Spaces for Change? The Politics of Citizen Participation in New Democratic Arenas.* Zed Books: London.

Klein, N. (2007). *The Shock Doctrine. The Rise of Disaster Capitalism.* London: Penguin Books.

Korsgaard, O. (1997). *The Impact of Globalization on Adult Education.* In Walters, S. (ed.) *Globalization, Adult Education and Training: Impacts and Issues,* pp 15–26. London: Zed Books.

Korsgaard, O., Walters, S., and Anderson, R. (eds.) (2001). *Learning for Democratic Citizenship.* Copenhagen: Association for World Education and Danish University of Education.

Lowe, J. (1971). *The Role of Adult Education.* In Lowe, J., Grant, N., and Williams, T. (eds.) *Education and Nation Building in the Third World,* pp 146–159. Edinburgh: Scottish Academic Press.

Mamdani, M. (1996). *Citizen and Subject. Contemporary Africa and the Legacy of Late Colonialism.* Princeton, NJ: Princeton University Press.

Mario, M. and Nandja, D. (2006). *Literacy in Mozambique: Education for All Challenges.* In *Adult Education and Development No 67,* pp 189–203. Germany: DVV.

Marshall, J. (1990). *Literacy, State Formation and People's Power.* Bellville: University of the Western.

Nyerere, J. K. (1976). *Adult Education and Development.* In *Adult Education and Development Journal, No 67, 2006,* pp 77–88. Germany: DVV.

Oduaran, A. (2000). Order out of chaos: Repositioning Africa for globalization through lifelong learning.

Oga, S. and Okwori, J. (2005). *A Nation in Search of Citizens: Problems of Citizenship in the Nigerian Context.* In Kabeer, N. (ed.) *Inclusive Citizenship,* pp 71–83. London: Zed Books.

Phadnis, U. and Ganguly, R. (2001). *Ethnicity and Nation-Building in South Asia.* New Delhi: Sage.

Stromquist, N. (1998). *The Confluence of Literacy, Gender and Citizenship in the Democratic Construction of South Africa. Occasional Paper.* Bellville: CACE Publications, University of Western Cape.

Thompson, J. (2000). *When Active Citizenship Becomes 'Mob Rule'.* In *Adult Learning.* England: NIACE.

Torres, R. (2004). *Lifelong Learning in the South.* Stockholm: Sida Studies No. 11.

Walters, S. (1989). *Education for Democratic Participation.* Bellville: CACE Publications, University of Western Cape.

Walters, S. (2006). Adult learning within lifelong learning: A different lens, a different light. *Journal of Education* **39**, 7–26.

Walters, S. and Watters, K. (2001). Adult education in lifelong learning in southern Africa. *International Journal for Lifelong Education* **20**(1–2).

Youngman, F. (2000). *The Political Economy of Adult Education and Development.* London: Zed Books.

Relevant Websites

http://www.internetworldstats.com – Internet World Stats.
http://www.sarua.org – Southern African Regional Universities Association (SARUA).

http://www.sadc.int – South African Development Community.
http://unstats.un.org – UN Department of Economic and Social Affairs.
http://www.weforum.org – World Economic Forum.

Health and Adult Learning

P Bélanger, UNESCO Institute for Education, Hamburg, Germany
M Robitaille, University of Quebec in Montreal, Montreal, QC, Canada

Generally absent until now from the *International Encyclopedia Education*, the theme adult learning and health is taking momentum in many countries as well as in international multilateral networks (UNESCO, 1997; US Dept. of Health, 2000; ICAE, 2001; WHO, 2005b). The growing recognition of "health as a basic human right" and the appeal for "relevant, equitable and sustainable access to health knowledge" (UNESCO, 1997), as well as the crisis of the welfare state, particularly with regard to health systems, is driving up the social demand for lifelong health education throughout life.

A new policy context is emerging linking health and lifelong learning policies. The call for Health For All, heard increasingly over the last two decades in multilateral organizations (European Commission, 2004; WHO, 2005a) finds growing legitimacy in positioning health as a key aspect of human development. In 2000, for example, the United Nations Economic and Social Council adopted a resolution recognizing the right to health, a state of physical and mental well-being, as "essential to the exercise of other rights."

However, the attainment of this overall objective and of the more specific health-related Millennium Development Goals (to reduce infant mortality, improve maternal health, and fight world pandemia such as HIV/AIDS, malaria, and tuberculosis) could be severely hampered if the increasing cost of current curative policy cannot be controlled and the productivity of the health system is not improved. Researchers and policymakers are exploring ways to solve this predicament by pursuing the Health For All objectives while paradoxically searching to curb the increasing demand for curative services. One of the key responses to this contradiction has to do with adult learning.

Two major trends are emerging linking health and adult learning. First, health promotion is increasingly acknowledged as a critical component of health policies. It refers to the documented impact that general levels of health competency and knowledge have on both the social demand for health and the cost of curative services among different strata of a population. Health literacy and health promotion thus becomes mounting issues in national health policies. A second significant tendency relates to continuing medical education of health personnel. Intensive research and development in this domain is transforming the long-existing perspective and practices within medical and paramedical professions and, as a result, may turn medical and nursing continuing education into a prototype of a much larger trend in continuing professional development (CPD) among other professions and occupations.

Health Literacy

In a time when an ever-growing part of public budgets is allocated to health services, the rapidly increasing need for healthcare tends to change the relations between health professionals and the public. In the context of a welfare state, already under pressure from neoliberal forces and now confronted by a continuously growing demand for healthcare services, the former pattern of interrelation between health professionals and patients is increasingly under time and economic pressure. Medical doctors, nurses, and therapists have less time available to spend with each of their clients who at the same time tend to question their traditional identity as patients. The tendency is, on the one hand, to reduce direct contact time by passing on more information through printed or electronic communication (pamphlet of information about the preparation of a coming surgery or treatment, instructions on direction for use of prescribed drugs, public vaccination campaign, information on preventative measures) and, on the other hand, to acknowledge ambiguity in past modes of unilateral relation between professionals and the public.

The trend toward written communication has the unexpected consequence of relying on people's capacity for initiative to be informed sufficiently and properly, and it does so without fully recognizing the impact of uneven distribution of health cultural capital. A mismatch is thus being created in these new healthcare systems between the growing complicated demand with which national health systems are confronted, and the average basic competency of the public for whom more self-gathering and treatment of information is required (Rudd *et al.*, 2004).

This unspoken transition in the mode of interaction between health professionals and people is bound to produce inequalities and puts at risk the attainment of the Health For All objective. In such a context, equitable and sustainable development of health literacy and health-related adult learning in general may become a key element of future public health and lifelong learning policy.

Of course, the association between formal education and health status is known in both developed and developing countries (Kickbusch, 2001), as well as between adult learning and socioeconomic benefit. What is new is the impact of various levels of health skills and knowledge on health condition. Health literacy represents the cognitive and social skills that determine the curiosity and ability of individuals to gain access to understand and use information in a way that will promote and maintain good health. It involves the ability to judge, sift, and act in the context of one's own life on the information provided (Kickbusch, 2001).

New inquiries on health literacy and more precisely on the direct assessment of people's health-related basic skills and knowledge are revealing a relation between levels of such competency and levels of education and income (Murray *et al.*, 2007). According to these surveys, between a third and half of all adults in postindustrial societies struggle with low levels of health literacy, a percentage much higher among the aging population. They have difficulty understanding and acting on currently available health information.

Health literacy levels tend, in many ways, to influence people's ability to benefit from healthcare and to prevent illness and avoid pandemic diseases. It affects the capacity to discriminate information printed on drugs or food labels, to search and use accessible information in order to prevent sickness. Health literacy also has an influence on the ability to navigate into the labyrinth of current healthcare services. This has to do, of course, with the capacity to read written dietary or medical advice, complete open entry forms, understand complementary professional advice given on paper, grasp the importance of danger notices found on domestic product packaging, access critical information on health and safety at home or at the workplace, and to read about disease prevention.

However, health literacy is more complex. It means not only to read messages, but also to interpret them and proceed accordingly in one's specific life context. It means to be able to draw consequences from consent forms, deal with health alerts conveyed in the media, and detect in one's own immediate environment early signs of emerging sickness. It means to have skills to interpret symptoms and be able to tell a professional one's health story or the story of a family member in order to inform him appropriately. Health competency is needed also to benefit proactively from preventive services operating increasingly through distance communication. Thus, health literacy impacts directly on the accessibility of the health system through people's capacity to get, screen, and mobilize information now mostly delivered not only in print, but also in a more diffuse way, through broader consequences of cultural and educational advantages or disadvantages throughout the life course.

Medical journals are beginning to address this issue. Uneven distribution of health competency is challenging

not only the functioning of current healthcare systems, but also its universal accessibility (Sentell and Halpin, 2006; Somnath, 2006; Paasche-Orlow *et al.*, 2006). The practice of including an adult literacy variable in health disparity research is increasing; it reduces the explanatory power of the already known variables (Nutbeam, 2000). Because health literacy significantly affects people's health and the ability of a system to provide effective quality healthcare (Institute of Medicine of the National Academies, 2004), it is of no surprise that growing awareness on the impact of heath literacy is giving new impetus to the already well-known domain of public health. Health promotion comprises efforts to enhance positive health and prevent ill health, through the overlapping spheres of health education, prevention, and health protection (Downie *et al.*, 1990), and it is often centered on lifestyle diseases. However, following the horizontal perspective developed in health literacy, health promotion tends now to be extended to the full continuum of health-related activities and tends to rely more on interactive communication and adult learning approaches (see, e.g., Davis *et al.*, 2003b, 1999).

We observe, in the last few decades, a diffuse but growing demand for health-related adult learning, either through structured activities or through supported and nonsupported self- and informal learning. Associated with shifts in attitudes and behaviors during adulthood, participation in adult learning is seen as an important element of health prevention policies (Feinstein and Hammond, 2004). A growing number of study circles in Nordic countries (Swedish National Council for Adult Education, 2005: 24–26) and already nearly one-fourth of night courses in the German adult education centers are related to health issues (Reichart and Huntemann, 2006; Nuissl and Pohl, 2004). A similar emerging trend is observed in adult literacy where some education ministries are introducing health and hygiene modules in their adult literacy programs (ICAE, 2001). Studies on informal learning in Canada indicate similar content interest (Livingstone, 1999). National health departments are developing evidence-based health education programs (Bartholomew *et al.*, 2001). They are setting up nutritional education programs, environmental sanitation training, prenatal courses, etc. Studies are made on patterns of health information handling in order to improve health education interventions (Zanchetta *et al.*, 2007; Kok *et al.*, 2004; Zorn *et al.*, 2004).

However, health literacy is more than functional; it means more than transmitting information and developing skills to be able to read pamphlets and successfully make significant appointments with physicians. It is also to be interpreted in the emerging expectation of people to participate in decision making related to their own health and to follow through on these decisions. In discourse and research on literacy in general, and also in health literacy in particular, we observe "a new introduction of humans as active agents in the construction, negotiation over, and transformation of their social worlds" (Barton *et al.*, 2000: 5). Some refer to this as a paradigm shift from pathology to empowerment (Shernoff, 1997). Hohn (2002), a well-known author in this field of health literacy, refers to "empowerment health education." The reality of health literacy is complex in another dimension. Current health literacy skills assessments tend often to ignore the multi-cultural dimension of health reality, the many social health literacies (Street, 1995), the popular knowledge, "the different medical traditions" and complementary "local ways of healing" (UNESCO, 1997: 6). In that sense, interactive and critical health literacy does not focus only on compliance, it relates to the autonomy of the subject, with the capacity of a local community to act on their health conditions, with people better equipped to overcome structural barriers to health (Nutbeam, 2000) and modify the relation between professionals and the subjects.

Aware of the important gap between the complexity of current health materials and the basic skills of the intended public (Rudd, 2004), public health agencies are looking not only on people's capacity to participate in this evolving system, but also on communication and practice of institutions and health personnel. Public health agencies tend to revise accordingly their information–education–communication (IEC) plan. Communication strategies are developed using plain-language or clear-communication approaches. In the same perspective, new continuing education programs are created to help physicians, dentists, and nurses better interact and communicate with their various patients. Some journals of continuing medical education (e.g., the American *Journal of General Internal Medicine*) are even proposing proxy measures or screening items to help professionals identify patients with limited health literacy skills.

The issue of the various levels of health literacy and more broadly of its consequence on equity, quality, and productivity of health services is making a big push for stronger investment in health-related education and adult learning, particularly in low-income communities (Rudd *et al.*, 2004). Paradoxically, the recommendation of WHO to allocate 5% of national health budgets to health promotion, prevention, and education may put a strain on the already tight public finances, but in the long term may be the best strategy to bend demand for curative services as well as reduce the cost of those services precisely among people at risk. In this new context, prescription of learning (Institute of Medicine of the National Academies, 2004; James, 2001) may well become an integral part of national health policy: prescription of lifelong learning not only among the public, but also among the professionals. Already in 1986, WHO insisted, in its Ottawa Declaration, on the necessity of a two-pronged approach: individual participation and structural change. People cannot

assume more responsibility for more aspects of their health without more protection and better opportunities to improve their health competency (Gruman, 2003).

Professional Continuing Education in the Health Sector: In Transition

Professional continuing education is in transition (Cervero, 2001), particularly in the health domain. It is one of the fastest growing areas of adult learning. The number of hours spent on continuing education activities in the course of both medical doctors and nurses' occupational careers, after their certification and licensure, tends to exceed the duration of their initial education and training (Davis *et al.*, 2003a). In many countries already, taking part in continuing education has been made obligatory for professionals and conditional to keeping their certification. Continuing medical education (CME) has become an essential effector arm in complex healthcare systems (Davis *et al.*, 1999). The demand for continuing education among health professionals is expected to grow even further. The accelerating pace of clinical and bio-pharmaceutical or medical research as well as of epidemiological studies requires doctors and other professionals to update their knowledge on indicators of disease predictability and on new practices or medication. It explains in part the growing demand for continuing education. Indeed, more than 80% of physicians as well as nurses of the coming decade have already left universities or colleges and have terminated their initial education. In fact, CME has already become in the United States alone an industry producing more than $3 billion of activities every year. CME has even become a recognized international discipline (Davis, 1998) with its scientific journals like the *Journal of Continuing Education of Health Professions*, the *Canadian Journal of Continuing Medical Education*, and the *Journal of Advanced Nursing*.

What is of particular interest in the continuing education of health professions is not its expansion, which constitutes a trend that one could observe, though at different pace, in other professional fields, together with the typical diversity of the education agencies involved.

More significant is the shift in orientation of activities within the health sector. Up to the mid-1990s, CME activities tended to take the form of obligatory or voluntary information and formal education sessions aiming at updating knowledge among field practitioners. The logic of action tended to be one of passive dissemination of information and knowledge transfer in order to keep professionals up to date with the recent developments in their field of practice (Bero *et al.*, 1998).

Particularly because CME, together with the continuing education of nurses, became an intensive area of activities involving a growing amount of financial resources, many studies have been requested to assess the acceptability and effectiveness of prevailing approaches (Thomas *et al.*, 2006; Davis *et al.*, 2003b, 2003a, 1999, 1995; Elwyn and Hocking, 2000; Brigley *et al.*, 1997; Kok *et al.*, 1997). Various aspects were scrutinized: continuing education practices, knowledge transfer, impact of various formal and nonformal strategies, contexts and conditions differently conducive to efficient linking between CME and practice, uneven circulation of clinical and scientific knowledge, as well as required alteration of initial education. Most of these assessments came to the same conclusion: formal and didactic transfer of information tends to have low educational value. They have little effect on professional practice. Attendance at passive educational events, even when reaching most practitioners through incentive, tends to have limited impact on individual practice and on the activity of health services involved.

Since then, a shift of orientation is taking place with new approaches being assessed for their impact not only on upgrading the knowledge of practitioners, but also on their daily practice as well as the operation of medical units and clinics. The aim is to make interventions relevant to the identified individual and organizational needs (Elwyn and Hocking, 2000). Some researchers have translated this change as a transition from CME to CPD (Du Boulay, 2000; Peck *et al.*, 2000). Essentially, what is going on is a shift in logic of action through which priority is given to supporting individual professionals in the ongoing development of their capacity to act, observe systematically, gather evidence, and co-produce research or at least be able to discriminate in one's context new knowledge relevant for one's practice. Then, validation and certification could be done but *a posteriori*, separated from the situated learning process.

Such approaches tend to be more tailor-made, more situated in their content and in their process, referring to both the perceived needs of professionals and local organization's demand. The input of recent scientific evidence produced by research networks remains central, but the question raised concerns the mobilization or appropriation of such external knowledge and its transfer into new capacity for action. However, such transition takes time and, even though more effective approaches have been proven, use of least-effective approaches still continues (Bloom, 2005).

A recent trend has emerged trying to create organic links between scientific institutional research, clinical observation, and practice. The aim is to connect more closely formal research agendas with questions emerging from practice, while simultaneously training field professionals on evidence-based medicine (Cusick and McCluskey, 2000), and offer advice and guidance to practitioners interested in research (Bateman and Kinmonth, 2001). This shift of orientation, bound to take place eventually among other professions, is happening earlier

among the health professions for many contextual factors. The first one, already mentioned, is the huge investment in time and money that has been made in CME. This considerable effort has urged agencies to assess its impact. The result was to look for CPD strategies that could be less focused on logic of education supply then on logic of individual and organization demand.

The very specific nature of practice in health professions and of its recent developments has also played an important catalytic role in its shift of orientation. First, the context of health service is changing. The multidisciplinary profile of today's health personnel (doctors, nurses, therapists, epidemiologists and sociologists, physical educators, dieticians, social workers, learning advisers, etc.) in clinics or hospitals, together with the increasing cooperation required from different departments (health, education, industry, sport, social affairs, etc.) raise questions about the monodisciplinary orientation of traditional CME and, more importantly, have put the focus on cooperation between these different content and agency inputs. Second, the relationships between health professionals and among health professionals and the public are changing. The health profession is relational in character; it is a profession of contact. At the core of their practice, health professionals have to relate directly with people coming from all social strata; they are working in close proximity with the general public. As such, this relational character is not new; the relation with patients has always characterized the practice of these professions. What has changed is the nature of these relations through external pressure to request more autonomy from the public, and through rising aspirations of patients to have their say and negotiate their life course, more so when it encounters health problems.

The reduction of time available in the relation between professionals and patients has tended to integrate health professions in a wider web of specialties. It has also created a demand for more capacity of initiative among a public having various levels of health literacy, with important consequences in daily practice of health professions, and therefore in CPD: necessity to acquire new relational skills and to practice new forms of cooperation with various agencies and professions. Relations between professionals are also changing to take into account social demand coming either from new social movements or simply from genuine aspirations of more literate patients eager to pilot their life, body, and soul. An interesting new phenomenon in this area is the emergence around typical sicknesses or pandemics of networks of patients and patients' relatives or peers who look for new information and review research reports in order to validate diagnoses, explore and suggest new therapies, and even discriminate, in given diagnoses, between scientific evidence and cultural bias. A good example is the role of gay movement supporting their members in their relations with health professionals more so at a time when research on AIDS was proposing various curative procedures and some interpretations of AIDS occurrence amounted to discrimination (Epstein, 1995, 2000). The same can be said about the role of the women's movement questioning the handling of breast cancer (Lantz and Booth, 1998). Becoming credible participants in the process of knowledge construction, these movements, entering a realm traditionally restricted to the medical experts (Kleinman, 2000), bring about changes in the practices of biomedical research and of health professionals; they thus become complementary agencies of CPD.

The continuing education of health professionals, having to practice in such a changing social and scientific environment and being in daily intimate relations with a public also in transition, could not remain an updating unidirectional process. Hence, the shift in orientation of CME toward contextualized CPD was somewhat predictable. Of course, CPD of physicians and other health professionals is not without ambiguity. The interest of the biopharmaceutical industry to promote their brevetted drugs may explain their quasi-predominant role in nonobligatory CME (Relman, 2001). The vast resources involved in this new market tend also to create a tension between a logic of supply in the provision of courses and self-learning kits and the emerging logic, of a more reflexive nature, aiming to integrate more closely ongoing research with the specific concern of each practitioner, clinic, or hospital department.

Conclusion

A shift is emerging in national health policies that tend to balance their historically dominant remedial and prophylactic orientation with new concerns for health promotion and consideration of the health literacy dimension in public health strategies. Similarly, professional continuing development within health professions is reframing professional practices of physicians and transforming their initial and further education career. A timid but steady transition, not unrelated to the tension between functional and empowerment-driven health literacy, is thus taking place from the prevalent health welfare organization to a health participative and learnfare system.

More rapidly developed than in many other professional fields, CME is currently undergoing important changes that may be prototypal of similar developments taking place in other professions and occupations.

These two trends in health-related adult learning are indicative of the enlarged vision of adult learning policy that is currently taking place. Adult learning policy environment has indeed to be rethought and reconstructed; it can no more exclude indirect lifelong learning policies (Bélanger and Federighi, 2000), like the learning component of health policies described in this article.

The demand for health-related learning throughout one's life course both within health professions and among the general public may very well be, after work-related adult education and training, the strongest forces driving up the demand for adult learning in decades to come.

See also: Wider Benefits of Adult Education.

Bibliography

Bartholomew, L., Parce, G., Kok, G., and Gottlieb, M. (2001). *Intervention Mapping: Designing Theory- and Evidence-Based Health Promotion Programs*. Toronto, ON: McGraw-Hill.

Barton, D., Hamilton, M., and Ivanič, R. (2000). *Situated Literacies: Reading and Writing in Context*. London: Routledge.

Bateman, H. and Kinmonth, A. L. (2001). Journeys and pathways: Exploring the role of professional development advice and educational guidance for practitioners expressing interest in research. *Medical Education* **35**(1), 49–55.

Bélanger, P. and Federighi, P. (2000). *Unlocking People's Creative Forces. A Transnational Study of Adult Learning Policies*, 274p. Hamburg: UNESCO Institute for Education.

Bero, L. A., Grilli, R., Grimshaw, J. M., *et al.* (1998). Closing the gap between research and practice: An overview of systematic reviews of interventions to promote the implementation of research findings. *British Medical Journal* **317**, 465–468.

Bloom, B. S. (2005). Effects of continuing medical education on improving physician clinical care and patient health: A review of systematic reviews. *International Journal of Technology Assessment in Health Care* **21**, 380–385.

Cervero, R. M. (2001). Continuing professional education in transition 1981–2000. *International Journal of Lifelong Education* **20**(1–2), 16–30.

Cusick, A. and McCluskey, A. (2000). Becoming an evidence-based practitioner through professional development. *Australian Occupational Therapy Journal* **47**(4), 159–170.

Davis, D., Barnes, B. E., and Fox, R. (eds.) (2003b). *Continuing Professional Development of Physicians: From Research to Practice*. Chicago, IL: American Medical Association.

Davis, D., Evans, M., Jadad, A., Perrier, L., and Rath, D. (2003a). The case for knowledge translation: Shortening the journey from evidence to effect. *British Medical Journal* **327**(7405), 33–35.

Davis, D., Thomson O'Brien, M., Freemantle, N., *et al.* (1999). Do conferences, workshops, rounds, and other traditional continuing education activities change physician behavior or health care outcomes? *Journal of the American Medical Association* **282**, 867–874.

Davis, D., Thompson, M. A., Oxman, A. D., and Haynes, B. (1995). Changing physician performance: A systematic review of the effect of continuing medical education strategies. *Journal of the American Medical Association* **274**, 700–705.

Downie, R. S., Fyfe, C., and Tannahill, A. (1999). *Health Promotion Models and Values*. Oxford: Oxford University Press.

Du Boulay, C. (2000). From CME to CPD: Getting better at getting better? *British Medical Journal* **320**(7232), 393–394.

Elwyn, G. and Hocking, P. (2000). Organisational development in general practice: Lessons from practice and professional development plans (PPDPs). *BMC Family Practice* **1**, doi:10.1186/1471-2296-1-2.

Epstein, S. (1995). The construction of lay expertise: AIDS activism and the forging of credibility in the reform of clinical trials. *Science, Technology and Human Values* **20**(4), 408–437.

European Commission (2004). *Enabling Good Health for All*. Brussels: European Commission.

Feinstein, L. and Hammond, C. (2004). The contribution of adult learning to health and social capital. *Oxford Review of Education* **30**(2), 199–223.

Gruman, J. C. (2003). The fragility of evidence: Why study health behavior now? *Paper Presented at the Bloomberg School of Public Health at John Hopkins University.* Johns Hopkins Bloomberg School of Public Health: Baltimore, MD, USA.

Hohn, M. (2002). Literacy, health, and health literacy: State policy considerations. *NCSALL/Focus on Basics* 5(C), 20–25.

Kleinman, D. L. (ed.) (2000). *Science, Technology, and Democracy.* Albany, NY: State University of New York Press.

Kok, G., Schaalma, H., Ruiter, R., Van Empelen, P., and Brug, J. (2004). Intervention mapping: A protocol for applying health psychology theory to prevention programmes. *Journal of Health Psychology* 9(1), 85–98.

Kok, G., van den Borne, B., and Mullen, P. D. (1997). Effectiveness of health education and health promotion: Meta-analyses of effect studies and determinants of effectiveness. *Patient Education and Counselling* 30, 19–27.

ICAE (2001). *Agenda for the Future. Six Years Later ICAE Report.* Montevideo: ICAE.

Institute of Medicine of the National Academies (2004). *Health Literacy: A Prescription to End Confusion.* Washington, DC: The National Academy Press.

Kickbusch, I. S. (2001). Health literacy: Addressing the health and education divide. *Health Promotion International* 16(3), 289–297.

James, K. (2001). *Prescription for Learning, Evaluation Reports.* Leicester: NIACE.

Lantz, P. M. and Booth, K. M. (1998). The social construction of the breast cancer epidemic. *Social Science and Medicine* 46(7), 907–918.

Livingstone, D. W. (1999). Exploring the icebergs of adult learning: Findings of the First Canadian Survey of informal learning practices. *Canadian Journal for the Study of Adult Education* 13(2), 49–72.

Murray, S., Rudd, R., Kirsh, I., Yamamoto, K., and Grenier, S. (2007). *Health Literacy in Canada. Initial Results from NALS.* Ottawa, ON: Canadian Council on Lifelong Learning.

Nuissl, E. and Pohl, A. (2004). *Portrait Continuing Education Germany.* Bonn: DIE.

Nutbeam, D. (2000). Health literacy as a public health goal: A challenge for contemporary health education and communication strategies into the 21st century health. *Health Promotion International* 15, 259–267.

Paasche-Orlow, M. K., Schillinger, D., Greene, S. M., and Wagner, E. H. (2006). How healthcare systems can begin to address the challenge of limited literacy. *Journal of General Internal Medicine* 21(8), 884–887.

Peck, C., McCall, M., McLaren, B., and Rotem, T. (2000). Continuing medical education and continuing professional development: International comparisons. *British Medical Journal* 320, 432–435.

Reichart, E. and Huntemann, H. (2006). *Volkshochschul-Statistik 2006.* Bonn: German Institute for Adult Education (DIE).

Rudd, R., Kirsh, I., and Yamamoto, K. (2004). *Literacy and Health in America. Public Information Report.* Princeton, NJ: Educational Testing Service.

Relman, A. S. (2001). Separating continuing medical education from pharmaceutical marketing. *Journal of the American Medical Association* 285, 2009–2012.

Swedish National Council for Adult Education (2005). *Folkbildning of the Future, Its Role and Objectives.* Stockholm: SNCAE.

Sentell, T. L. and Halpin, H. A. (2006). Importance of adult literacy in understanding health disparities. *Journal of General Internal Medicine* 21(8), 862–866.

Shernoff, M. (1997). Individual practice with gay men. In Mallon, G. P. (eds.) *Foundations of Social Work Practice with Lesbian and Gay Persons,* pp 77–103. New York: Haworth Press.

Somnath, S. (2006). Improving literacy as a means to reducing health disparities. *Journal of General Internal Medicine* 21(8), 63–98.

Thomas, D. C., Johnston, B., Dunn, K., *et al.* (2006). Continuing medical education, continuing professional development, and knowledge translation: Improving care of older patients by practicing physicians. *Journal of the American Geriatrics Society* 54(10), 1610–1618.

UNESCO (1997). Health promotion and health education for adults. *Booklets 6b of the CONFINTEA V International Conference on Adult Education in Hamburg 1997.* Hamburg: UNESCO Institute for Education.

WHO (World Health Organization) (2005b). Global health promotion scaling up for 2015 – a brief review of major impacts and developments over the past 20 years and challenges for 2015. *Unedited Working Paper from WHO Secretariat for the 6th Global Conference on Health Promotion in Bangkok, Thailand.*

WHO (World Health Organization) (2005b). *Health for All: The Policy Framework for the WHO European Region.* Copenhagen: WHO.

Zanchetta, M., Perreault, M., Kaszap, M., and Viens, C. (2007). Patterns in information strategies used by older men to understand and deal with prostate cancer: An application of the modelisation qualitative research design. *International Journal of Nursing Studies* 44(6), 961–972.

Zorn, M., Allen, M. P., and Horowitz, A. (2004). *Understanding Health Literacy and Its Barriers. Bibliography.* Washington, DC: National Institute of Health.

Further Reading

Ad Hoc Committee on Health Literacy. (1999). Health literacy: Report of the council on scientific affairs, American medical association. *Journal of the American Medical Association* 281, 552–557.

Epstein, S. (1996). *Impure Science: AIDS, Activism, and the Politics of Knowledge.* Berkeley, CA: University of California Press.

Hiramanek, N. (2005). Self directed learning and continuing medical education. *Australian Family Physician* 34(10), 879–880.

Rootman, I. and Ronson, B. (2005). Literacy and health research in Canada: Where have we been and where should we go? *Revue canadienne de santé publique* 96(Supplement 2), S62–S77.

Spiros, C. (2005). Health literacy: Concept analysis. *Journal of Advanced Nursing* 50(6), 633–640.

Tang, K.-C., Beaglehole, R., and O'Byrne, D. (2005). Policy and partnership for health promotion – addressing the determinants of health. *Bulletin of the World Health Organization* 83(2), 884.

WHO (World Health Organization) (2006). *Core Health Indicators: The Latest Data from Multiple WHO Sources.* http://www.who.int (accessed May 2009).

Globalization and Vocational Education and Training

P Loveder, National Centre for Vocational Education Research, Adelaide, SA, Australia

Introduction

Globalization has many adherents and detractors (e.g., Friedman, 2005; Bhagwati, 2004; Stiglitz, 2003), including large groups of people opposed to the effects they believe it has on traditional ways of living, especially in developing countries (Klein, 1999).

Defining globalization is a problematic task and usually involves economic, technological, sociocultural, and political contexts. As early as 1994, Friedman came up with a useful literal definition of globalization as the "process of transformation of local or regional phenomena into global ones. It can be described as a process by which the people of the world are unified into a single society and function together" (Friedman, 1994).

Since that time, understanding of globalization has become more sophisticated, such that commentators now characterize globalization as consisting of three phases:

- Phase 1: the mobility of capital.
- Phase 2: the mobility of goods and services.
- Phase 3: the mobility of people.

Each of these phases poses distinct challenges to vocational education and training (VET), in terms of adapting to changes brought about through economic restructuring, the entry and exit of skills through migration flows, and a focus on new types of skills in an increasingly knowledge-based society.

This article seeks to establish the causes for the growing interdependence of nations and the degree to which VET is being impacted by the developments within the global economy. In particular, it addresses issues around patterns of labor mobility and the development of mechanisms to facilitate this phenomenon, including international education, the growth of higher-level skills, the transparency of qualifications systems, and the transferability of skills.

Economic Restructuring

The free flow of capital and goods and services allows employers the option to relocate investment from one region of the world to another, in anticipation of greater returns. In many Western countries, the most recent examples of this are the closure of factories, with operations typically moving to China or Southeast Asia (low-cost manufacturing), and the establishment of call centers and back-room processing for financial services in India (service-sector work). Workers who are made redundant may be unable to find work in the same industry and may have to acquire new skills to regain employment. This has been the fate of many workers in the textiles, clothing, and footwear industry in some developed nations (Webber and Weller, 2001).

Finegold (2009) suggests there is a process of 'bifurcation' of skills and jobs occurring in the global labor market – where there is demand at both the 'low-end' and 'high-end' of the job market creating a form of 'barbell' market. With, presumably, most of the jobs at the low-end concentrated in developing countries, the corollary is that those at the high-end are concentrating in more developed economies that have access to pools of highly educated and skilled people. Many jobs in the middle are simply disappearing.

Further, some estimates suggest that, by 2030, up to 60% of all jobs could be automated, and new industries are beginning to emerge (such as biotechnology, renewable energy, and nanotechnology) which are all requiring new skills to be developed – and it is these (and other) industries which will provide the high-skill jobs of the future (Elliott, 2007).

At the macro level, governments worldwide have adopted different responses to the economic and social consequences of globalization. Often, assistance is provided to firms and workers in vulnerable industries to enable them to adjust – with the scale and type of assistance provided varying according to the industries affected. The political consequences of allowing adjustment to occur with or without assistance are also an influencing factor.

Another significant strategy adopted by governments is the development/enhancement of workforce skills to maintain or improve the competitiveness of industries – relative to equivalent industries in other countries. Industry bodies – including unions and employer associations – are willing supporters of government policy and initiatives in this area. Examples of these types of initiatives are occupationally linked literacy, language, and numeracy programs.

A further response (which has usually come much later) has been to develop overarching national skills strategies – examples being the Leitch Review in the United Kingdom which resulted in a national skills strategy for Britain through to 2020 and the Lisbon Strategy in the European Union. In Australia, the

National Skills Shortages Strategy (NSSS) – and, more recently, the establishment of Skills Australia – are examples of national skills planning in response to global economic factors.

Alongside the restructuring occurring as a result of more open economies has been the development of the new information and communication technologies (ICT), which have been increasingly deployed across all areas of industry and which have had a profound impact in many industries, from computer-aided design and just-in-time management of inventories, to a range of new and enhanced telecommunication services requiring workers to gain entirely new skill-sets.

During the 1990s, the term knowledge economy became a popular way of describing the economies now underpinned by the information and communications technologies. The term had originally been coined by the well-known management expert, Peter Drucker (1968), in his book, *The Age of Discontinuity.* Governments in many countries adopted the notion of a knowledge economy as an overarching goal through which to frame overall policy direction – including in the area of education and training. The European Union, for example, set itself a goal in its 2000 council meeting in Lisbon to become, by 2010, "the most competitive and dynamic knowledge-based economy in the world," with lifelong learning one of the means of realizing this goal.

An early commentary which anticipates the impact the knowledge economy will exert on people's working lives is Reich's (1991) *The Work of Nations,* in which he categorizes the workforce according to three groups: routine producers, in-person service providers, and symbolic analysts. The last category was defined as those who "solve, identify and broker problems by manipulating symbols. They simplify reality into abstract images that can be rearranged, juggled, experimented with, communicated to other specialists, and then, eventually, transformed back into reality" (p.178). Examples include engineers, lawyers, journalists, academics, and most professionals.

The VET system needs to reflect the general societal changes from an industrial society to a knowledge society as well, and be able to meet the skills needs of a changing labor market. New occupations are arising within sectors such as ICT, the services, and in new technologies such as biotechnology, and these have to be integrated as new training provisions within the VET system.

In addition, the process of economic restructuring has highlighted the disjuncture of VET systems which, in the main, have been set up primarily to deliver skills to entry-level students when, in reality, a component of the existing workforce requires re-skilling. Therefore, it is imperative to explore a range of mechanisms that provide workers, who have already completed their formal training, with the opportunity to acquire new skills (Ball *et al.*, 2001).

Movement of Skills through Migration Flows

Another facet of globalization is the mass movement of people. The United Nations (2003) estimated that some 175 million people lived outside of their country of birth at the beginning of the twenty-first century.

An aspect combined with this phenomenon has been skilled migration. Comparative data (from 2000) suggest that some 20 million highly skilled workers from developing countries (i.e., highly skilled foreign-born workers with tertiary qualifications) now live in Organisation of Economic Co-operation and Development (OECD) member countries alone; a 70% increase in merely 10 years (Beine *et al.*, 2006).

The global trend toward mass movement of skills has increased significantly following World War II. This phenomenon has seen a brain drain to receiving nations – and a perception that more developed nations have been 'poaching' the best and brightest (Grecic, 2007).

Recent theoretical literature suggests, however, that emigration prospects can raise the expected return to human capital and foster investment in education at home – although there are clearly winners and losers in this (Beine *et al.*, 2006). In fact, some economists have established that there is an overall increase in the standard of living for both donor and recipient country through the migration of skilled people.

There are a range of consequences for VET arising from labor mobility, especially in supporting migrants to work to their full capacity. This may include the need for training in language, literacy, and numeracy skills; country-specific health and safety training; and particular vocational skills training. In addition, there could be a need for more practical training on living in a new culture (Learning and Skills Council, 2007).

VET also has a role in ensuring the integration of immigrants and weak learners, and thereby contributing to social cohesion. As informal learning is the dominant form of skills acquisition in some countries and for many learners, these experiences will increasingly need to be incorporated into the more formal system of skills development – especially if these learners are to be fully effective in the modern labor market. In this respect, VET is starting to play an important role in the integration and social policies of many countries.

To ensure good learning outcomes for new migrants, educators and trainers need to be aware of alternative classroom-management strategies. These may include smaller class sizes, different types of institutional support, and placing learners from similar backgrounds together (Burgoyne and Hull, 2007). There are other considerations such as integrating education, training, and employment pathways more effectively. The main barriers to success for many migrants relate to a lack of recognition of the qualifications and experiences they bring from their former countries and restrictions on using overseas-acquired skills through regulation (Phillimore *et al.*, 2007).

International Education Markets

International education markets, according to the World Trade Organization (WTO), are defined as the cross-border trade or 'consumption abroad' of education and education-related services. This can be in the form of students attending study in a country other than their own (onshore education), through distance learning, or by undertaking courses offered in a student's own country by an education provider of a second country (offshore or transnational education). Many countries, such as the United Kingdom, America, and Australia, have been quick to grasp the potential for this – especially in the domain of higher education.

The twentieth century saw a surge in higher education; in the early twenty-first century, the idea of going abroad to study has become thinkable for ordinary students. In 2006, the most recent year for which figures are available, nearly 3 million were enrolled in higher education institutions outside their own countries – a rise of more than 50% since 2000 (Economist, 2008).

(Australia – by comparison with other OECD countries, for example – has by far the highest proportion of overseas students among its higher education intake, at 17.8%, well in excess of the OECD average of 6.9% (OECD 2008, **Table C3.1**). International education services are Australia's third largest export industry worth 12.6 billion dollars per annum (ABS, 2007).

Finegold (2009) suggests there are other benefits beyond the influx of dollars that can be generated by global education services, especially through the access to new innovation networks provided through the graduates. In fact, graduates are a major source of potential business incubation and start-up companies, especially in high-technology areas. Benefits also derive to the recipients who take home credentials that are considered world-class and which help local business.

International education has had a direct impact on patterns of mobility as well. For the qualification holder, having Western qualifications often makes migration (especially for skilled-migration purposes) to a new country much easier. Access to Western-country qualifications is also seen to benefit the growth in trade and the rise of the middle class in many countries (e.g., China and India). In countries such as Australia, international education has been a direct route to permanent residency.

The growth of international education has resulted in a range of issues, however, including how to assure quality, the accreditation process where multiple countries'

contexts need to be considered, possible diminished research capacity, and crowding out of native-born populations in the intensified efforts to recruit international students (Lim, 2007; Finegold, 2009).

The move toward internationalizing curriculum which takes into account a wider view of the world – and is aimed at preparing all students for performing professionally and socially in a global context – is becoming increasingly important both in terms of good global citizenship and plain good business! Although difficult to quantify the actual benefits, the value of international education in promoting intercultural development should not be underestimated.

Transparency and Transferability

Another element of globalization and its links to both education and the labor market has been the rush to develop a range of mechanisms to facilitate mobility. In this, the education and training sector has a major role to play.

People increasingly require skills that are portable and transferrable and which, in some circumstances, can be recognized across national borders. In fact, the development of qualifications systems that can accommodate skills and qualifications acquired in other countries are being seen as a key part of trade diplomacy. In some regions of the world (particularly Europe through the Copenhagen and Bologna processes), efforts are afoot to realign qualifications frameworks to become regional in nature.

The need then for harmonizing country-specific VET systems (such as what is currently occurring through the new European Qualifications Framework (EQF)) has significant consequences for the cultural patterns underlying both the practice, the theory, as well as the policy of VET in these countries, and in addressing incompatibility between systems (Deissinger, 2008). For example, the development of country-specific VET systems happen over a significant time span and are fashioned to meet local and national imperatives. The question of how to then balance these national needs with the wider regional or international agenda often produces conflicting goals.

A strategy for dealing with perceived incompatibility may lie in a nation-specific strategy which encourages and enables change without dumping the benefits and the functionality of the established system (Deissinger, 2008).

Another recent strategy from Europe has been the introduction of the European Credit System for Vocational Education and Training (ECVET – a device which will facilitate the transfer, validation, and recognition of learning outcomes acquired by individuals moving from one learning context to another or from one qualification system to another – in particular, during a mobility period – and who wish to obtain a qualification (European Commission, 2009).

Issues around the recognition of qualifications and transnational quality assurance strategies which require local, national, and regional approaches need to be considered. This will become increasingly pressing as the world continues to divide into major trading blocs with the erosion of traditional borders and trade barriers. These need to be balanced with other issues to do with quality assurance and ensuring training standards are maintained, however.

Innovation and the Growth of Higher-Level Skills

It has been widely argued that global economic competitiveness rests in the main on the knowledge and skills of the workforce (see, in particular, Brown *et al.*, 2001). But the link between global competitiveness and skill formation is complex – especially when other factors are taken into account, such as country context, social justice, and the role of government. In some countries, especially those in Europe, there is a far stronger role for government in driving skill formation – irrespective of global economic factors – than in others (such as the United States).

Bosworth *et al.* (2008) identified globalization as a major factor in placing pressure on less skilled jobs and driving the policy in Western nations, in particular, toward concentrating on raising education and skills levels in response. This has especially been a feature of many European countries – through the European Lisbon Strategy. This has also been the experience in Australia as well, where successive governments have targeted skill development as a way of maintaining the country's economic performance.

Several recent government reports ('Rising above the storm' from the United States, 'Race to the top' from the United Kingdom, and 'Benchmarking against the global best' from Canada) note the importance of innovation in driving growth in national productivity and competitiveness and that this plays an equally important role in achieving social-inclusion objectives (Finegold, 2009).

Globalization is perceived as a factor in stimulating growth in higher skills as the nature of production becomes more sophisticated (Curtain, 2004). This dictates that as methods of production become more complex, so the need for people with higher level technical and problem-solving skills also increases. Despite there being an accepted view that there is a strong and tangible link between university education and the process of innovation, there is anecdotal evidence that there also needs to be a pool of highly trained technical expertise at the paraprofessional level – and that this, in itself, can foster the development of entrepreneurial skills in workers; essential for success in an increasingly globalized free economy.

Changes in production, in particular, have resulted in the need for the workforce to acquire higher-level skills;

and VET clearly needs to have a focus on the development of higher skills if it is to contribute to this phenomenon. However, the nature and numbers of these higher-level skills required for the economy are difficult to determine, and can only be predicted at a highly aggregated level for a few years ahead. This clearly has implications for training-program development and in a wider national skills-planning sense.

Examples of higher-level qualifications within the rubric of VET include foundation degrees in Britain, professional degrees and Advanced VET in Scandinavia, and vocational graduate certificates and diplomas in Australia.

Conclusion

This article has attempted to demonstrate that the effect of globalization on national VET systems is substantial and complex. A range of international factors such as economic restructuring – coupled with technological development and the growth of ICT and the internationalization of education and skills development – are all playing a part in the move toward the growth of higher-level skills. To date, this has probably impacted higher education more than VET, but this is changing as work practices and occupational skill-sets become more sophisticated.

Second, the trends described in this article all have a significant professional development needs attached to them; and VET practitioners need to be provided with ample opportunity to develop skills for coping with a rapidly changing world.

Finally, it is important to note that it is not correct to attribute all structural change to the process of globalization. There are many factors – including the specific country's economic and social development as well as the prevailing economic, political, and educational institutions – fashioning structural change within the economy. Nevertheless, globalization is a substantial force, and it has direct consequences for the VET sector.

Bibliography

Ball, K., Lee, Y. -H., Phan, O., and Ra, Y. -S. (2001). *Adult Retraining and Re-Skilling in Australia and South Korea*. Adelaide: NCVER.

Beine, M., Docquier, F., and Rapoport, H. (2006). *Brain Drain and Human Capital Formation in Developing Countries – Winners and Losers*. University of Luxembourg.

Bhagwati, J. (2004). *In Defence of Globalization*. New York: Oxford University Press.

Bosworth, D., Jones, P., and Wilson, R. (2008). The transition to a highly qualified workforce. *Education Economic* **16**(2), 127–147.

Brown, P., Green, A., and Lauder, H. (2001). *High Skills: Globalisation, Competitiveness and Skill Formation*. London: Oxford University Press.

Burgoyne, U. and Hull, O. (2007). Classroom management strategies to address the needs of Sudanese refugee learners, NCVER, Adelaide.

Curtain, R. (2004). *Vocational Education and Training, Innovation and Globalisation*. Adelaide: NCVER.

Deissinger, T. (2008). Institutional and cultural determinants of national VET systems: Problems arising with the European Qualifications Framework (EQF). *Paper Presented at the Australian Vocational Education and Training Research Association Conference*, 11th, 2008, Adelaide, Australia.

Drucker, P. (1968). *The Age of Discontinuity: Guidelines to Our Changing Society*. New York: Harper & Row.

Economist (2008). The future is another country, in *The Economist,* December, 2008.

Elliott, S. (2007). Projecting the impact of computers on work in 2030. *Workshop on Research Evidence Related to Future Skill Demands,* Centre for Education, National Research Council, May 31–June 1, 2007.

European Commission (2009). *The European Credit System for Vocational Education and Training,* http://ec.europa.eu/education/ecvt/index_en.html (accessed August 2009).

Finegold, D. (2009). Skills, jobs and the global economy: A comparative perspective. *Paper Presented to the BIG SKILLS Conference,* 3–5 March, 2009, Sydney.

Friedman, T. (1994). *Cultural Identity and Global Process.* London: Sage.

Friedman, T. (2005). *The World is flat: A Brief History of the Globalized World in the Twenty-First Century.* London: Allen Lane.

Klein, N. (1999). *No Logo: Taking Aim at the Brand Bullies.* New York: Picador.

Learning and Skills Council (2007). Employer perceptions of migrant workers. *Research report, Learning Skills Council,* Coventry.

Lim, F. (2007). Quality assurance of Australian offshore education: The complexity and frameworks for understanding the problem. *Postgraduate Journal of Education Research* **8**(1), 19–36.

OECD (Organisation for Economic Co-operation and Development) (2008). *Education at a Glance: OECD Indicators 2008.* Paris: OECD.

Phillimore, J., Goodson, L., Hennesy, D., *et al.* (2007). Employability pathways: An integrated approach to recognising the skills and experiences of new migrants, National Institute of Adult Continuing Education, Leicester.

Reich, R. (1991). *The Work of Nations: Preparing Ourselves for 21st-Century Capitalism.* London: Simon & Schuster.

Stiglitz, J. (2003). *Globalization and Its Discontents.* New York: W.W. Norton.

United Nations (2002). *International Migration Report - 2002.* Sales No. ST/ESA/SER.A/220.

Webber, M. and Weller, S. (2001). *Refashioning the Rag Trade: Internationalising Australia's Textiles, Clothing and Footwear Industries.* Sydney: UNSW Press.

Further Reading

Gregic, V. (2007). The economic impact of migration flows: Sustainable development of the Western Balkans and emigration. *Paper Presented at the Annual Meeting of the International Studies Association 48th Annual Convention*, Chicago.

Moran, L. and Ryan, Y. (2004). *The Australian Quality Training Framework and Globalisation of Training Markets.* Canberra: ANTA.

NGOs and Globalization of Education

M Ahmed, Brac University, Dhaka, Bangladesh

Globalization and Education

Globalization in its generic and literal sense is the process of transformation of local or regional phenomena into global ones. It refers to the idea of the people of the world being connected and unified in multiple ways. It is not a new phenomenon, but the issue has come to the fore in recent decades with economic aspects of globalization receiving the most attention. In the economic context, it refers to the reduction and removal of barriers between national borders in order to facilitate the flow of goods, capital, services, and labor. Another dimension of globalization is cultural integration, again an ancient phenomenon, intensified by recent revolutionary changes in communication and transportation technologies.

Cultural globalization, driven in its recent manifestations by digital communication technology, has led to both a process of homogenization and an enhanced potential for promoting and appreciating cultural diversity. Effective and aggressive marketing of American and Western cultural industries has raised the specter of the global domination of Western culture at the expense of national and indigenous cultural diversity. However, the spread of communication technologies has also supported the emergence of movements in defense of local uniqueness, individuality, and identity (Croucher, 2004).

A critical aspect of cultural globalization, or the influence of the globalizing forces beyond the economic sphere, is the development of a global perspective and global interaction on education. This includes influence of globalization on educational content, objectives, and delivery of services.

A Global Perspective on Education

In the post-World War II era, under the auspices of the United Nations, a different form of globalization, in contrast to economic globalization driven by the free market principles, has developed. This other form of globalization is based on the recognition of the need for an international order to guide action on common interests of humanity. Principal tenets of this order include peaceful resolution of conflicts; common responsibility to promote and protect human rights and human dignity, justice for all, and development of the human potential everywhere; protecting and nurturing the planetary resources for the benefit of the present and future generations; and inculcating a spirit of human solidarity and responsibility.

The establishment of the United Nations itself is a manifestation of the phenomenon of globalization arising from interdependence and connectedness of peoples and nations. Globalization guided by the principle of human solidarity, since the creation of UN, has found a concrete expression in the regime of international treaties and conventions which have emerged to establish and protect human rights and promote human development. International and national NGOs and civil society organizations have played a prominent role in shaping the content of these international agreements and lobbying for the adoption and ratification of these internationally and in countries.

The Universal Declaration of Human Rights adopted in 1948 was the first global statement about the inherent dignity and equality of human beings. In adopting the declaration, the governments representing the international community accepted a set of principles and obligations covering a wide range of human endeavor, which applied to all nations universally.

The principles directly related to education are set out in the declaration's Article 26, which affirms that: (1) everyone has the right to education, (2) education shall be directed toward the full development of the human personality and to the strengthening of respect for human rights and fundamental freedoms, and (3) parents have a prior right to choose the kind of education that shall be given to their children.

The universal declaration served as the touchstone for subsequent international agreements in the form of declaration, treaties, and conventions addressing common concerns and interests of humanity, which called for collective and global action. For example, the universal declaration directly led to the negotiation and adoption of the two binding treaties in 1966, recognized as the twin pillars of global human rights standards and provisions – the International Covenant of Civil and Political Rights and the International Covenant of Economic, Social and Cultural Rights. These agreements impose a moral obligation, and many place a legal obligation, on the signatory countries to abide by these agreements. They constitute a body of legal and institutional structure of common responsibility for common good of humanity (United Nations, 2002).

Major international treaties include a provision for states to report to a treaty body on progress made and steps taken in implementing the agreements by national governments who have become signatories to these treaties. There are, for example, the Human Rights Committee and the Committee on Economic, Social and Cultural Rights, which serve as treaty bodies for the relevant agreements. Similar bodies exist for reviewing progress in countries on implementation of the Convention to End all forms of Discrimination against Women (CEDAW) and the Convention on the Rights of the Child (CRC). NGOs have often served as an effective watchdog in respect of efforts of countries to implement the agreements and adequate and objective reporting by countries to the treaty bodies. Often, NGOs and other civil society bodies have prepared alternative reports to draw public attention, form their perspective, to lack of good-faith efforts to live by the treaty obligations.

The creation of the United Nations Educational, Scientific and Cultural Organization (UNESCO) itself represents a commitment of the international community "to contribute to peace and security by promoting collaboration among the nations through education, science and culture in order to further universal respect for justice, for the rule of law and for the human rights and fundamental freedoms which are affirmed for the peoples of the world, without distinction of race, sex, language or religion, by the Charter of the United Nations" (Article 1, Constitution of UNESCO).

In the case of education, several international treaties and agreements have been adopted since 1945 by international conferences convened either by the United Nations or by UNESCO. Probably the best-known examples in the field of education are the World Declaration on Education for All, adopted by the World Conference on Education for All (EFA), held in Jomtien, Thailand, in 1990 and, as its follow-up, the World Education Forum in Dakar in 2000. A framework for EFA with specific global goals for 2015 was adopted in Dakar. The framework has served as both the guide for formulation of national plans of action and the focus of advocacy for national and international NGOs. (See below the description of advocacy activities of the Global Campaign for EFA.)

The United Nations General Assembly has from time to time adopted resolutions proclaiming an international day, year, or decade relating to education, the purpose being to focus world opinion on a particular aspect of education considered to be deserving of attention and support. Examples include International Literacy Day (September 8), World Teachers Day (October 5), International Literacy Year (1990), and United Nations Decade for Human Rights Education (1995–2004). These proclamations and events and activities related to these, on the one hand, reflect a broad international consensus on educational issues; on the other hand, these serve as the basis for advocacy and mobilization activities on educational issues by national and international NGOs and other civil society bodies.

Development in education over the years since the beginning of the process of establishing global norms and goals, starting with the proclamation of the Universal Declaration of Human Rights, has been dramatic. In the late 1940s, a little more than 50% of the world's adults were literate at a rudimentary level and less than 50% of the children had access to formal education. Today, most children go to school and the majority has access to beyond primary education. Four out of five of the adults have acquired literacy skills at least at the basic level, although women still lag significantly behind (UNESCO, 2000).

As noted, important contribution of the globalization forces in the progress achieved in education has been in articulating the norms and goals that all shared and in assessing and comparing the country situations in global league tables. NGOs and the civil society have played an important role in advocacy, awareness raising, and capacity building, and, in many instances, extending educational opportunities in creative ways to those left out from the mainstream educational services. What do all these add up to? It is reasonable to argue that the international consensus and expression of commitments, cooperation and sharing of lessons and experience, the global recognition of the right to education and the obligation to fulfill this right, and the work of NGOs in driving the messages home, have considerably strengthened the momentum for the secular trends of educational expansion that existed.

Changing Educational Paradigm in the Context of Globalization

The demands of globalization in terms of competitive market, skills and capabilities that young people must acquire, dramatic changes in knowledge dissemination possibilities, and interdependence of people and nations have altered the conventional centuries-old thinking and models about learning content, objectives, and delivery of educational services. At the same time, it has become more critical than ever that learners are aware of and that they interact effectively with the world in which they live and appreciate and claim the common heritage of human thought, action, and, creativity.

The need for change in the educational paradigm has been argued cogently in the report of the UNESCO-appointed International Commission on Education for the Twenty-first century led by Jacques Delors. The Commission identified four key purposes as the pillars of learning on which the educational systems must be built. These are:

1. learning to know,
2. learning to do,
3. learning to live together, and
4. learning to be.

These pillars refer to the imperatives of acquiring the skills of learning (to learn rather than to accumulate facts), being purposefully productive, being responsible and effective members of the human community locally and in the world, and, at the same time, being confident of one's identity (UNESCO, 1998).

The point is often made that advances in information technology and telecommunications have created unprecedented opportunities for learning for every one; that the barriers of time, distance, language, pedagogic skills, and resources can be less critical. However, this potential can be realized and transformation of learning can happen, only if the new paradigm of knowledge, education, and learning can incorporate components that are neglected in the current models. The Global Information Infrastructure Commission suggests the following key elements as essential components of the new learning paradigm (Cogburn, 1998):

- focusing on concepts and understanding, rather than accumulation of factual information;
- using a holistic and iterative approach in pedagogy, rather than a linear development of knowledge and skills;
- emphasizing on enhancing the learners' ability to manipulate symbols;
- enhancing the student's skills to acquire and utilize knowledge;
- producing an increased quantity of scientifically and technically trained persons;
- blurring the distinction between mental and physical labor;
- encouraging learners to work in teams;
- overcoming the barriers of time and space in learning; and
- developing an agile and flexible system of education.

Recognizing the global implications of local action and vice versa, educational content has been developed, frequently n higher education, and at secondary and primary levels as well, under the label of global education or international education. Global education places particular emphasis on the changes in communication and relationships among people across nations and regions. It sheds light on how major societal phenomena, such as human conflict, economic systems, human rights and social justice, human commonality and diversity, the common legacy of literature and culture, and technological revolution affect people and communities. Without denying the value of traditional branches of specialist knowledge, global education seeks to blur the boundaries between disciplines. It encourages interdisciplinary and multidisciplinary studies, which can help offer solutions of complex human problems.

The term international education, sometimes used as the substitute for global education, may mean different things, but two meanings are generally attached to the concept. The first refers to education that transcends national borders through the exchange of people, as in study abroad. The other meaning reflects a comprehensive approach to education that attempts to prepare students to be effective participants in an interconnected world.

The premise underlying the approach of global education and international education is that the understanding of society, nations, and the human condition is deepened through examination of cultures, languages, environmental situations, governments, political relations, religions, geography, and history of the world. Professionals and students particularly wishing to be engaged in international educational development are mostly the participants in international education academic programs (Cummings and McGinn, 1997).

Commodification of Education

One effect of economic globalization is that education may be treated as a marketable commodity. The traditional view of education as a public good financed largely by public funding is being challenged by the criterion of efficiency of the market. The neoliberal view – the belief that society's needs can be best met and problems can be best solved by the market with minimal government regulation and public sector involvement – has spread from the economic sphere to what have been generally regarded as public services and the domain of the public sector.

At least three elements of the neoliberal market approach may be found in the design for educational provisions:

1. attempting to make the provision of education cost efficient by designing them as marketable products;
2. standardizing the educational services and experiences as well as assessing their performance by objective and standardized testing of results; and
3. focusing on marketability of outputs.

The three elements are reflected in policies, such as cutbacks in the public sector, closing inefficient programs that do not directly meet market needs, and the use of technology, including distance learning to bring about greater efficiency, comprising courses and degrees that are packaged for delivery over the Internet by for-profit corporations (Tabb, 2007).

The intergovernmental body World Trade Organization (WTO), established in 1994, is dedicated to the goal of removing trade barriers among nations. The General Agreement on Trade in Services (GATS), a product of the WTO, is aimed at deregulating international markets in services, including education. Two key operating principles of GATS are: the most favored nation and national treatment. The former requires that all countries be treated identically with regard to import or export, while the latter enjoins countries to treat foreign companies at least as favorably as their equivalent national competitors. The purpose of these principles is the creation of an open, global market place where education and other services can be sold to the highest bidder.

GATS covers educational services which are not exclusively provided by the public sector, or those which have commercial purposes. Since education systems are rarely exclusively public and many programs are partially commercial, large parts of the education systems of countries fall under the purview of GATS.

Internationally, education is estimated to be a trillion-dollar industry. Corporations have seen the prospects of a deregulated education sector and of having a market share in the industry, to the extent education can be turned into a tradable commodity (Frase and O'sullivan, 2007).

This aspect of globalization is a direct challenge to the public good character of education. It is a crucial political and educational policy issue in many countries to decide how the balance should be struck between the public good character of education and education as a market commodity. Civil society bodies and NGOs have a role in advocacy and awareness raising in respect of molding public opinion about the political choice that must be made (Tabb, 2007).

NGOs and Globalization

There is no one widely accepted definition of the term nongovernmental organization.

The diversity of NGOs, with hugely varied goals, structures, and the driving force behind them, makes it difficult to agree on such a definition.

While NGOs vary widely, their activities often fall into two broad categories: they engage in operational activities related to delivery of services and/or they undertake advocacy activities designed to influence policies and programs. Their size and scope of activities can be limited to a local community or extend across nations. Many NGOs in developing countries receive international funding for their work in areas such as research, advocacy, relief, environment, human rights, and health and education services.

Education is an important arena of public good in which NGOs have played a prominent role both as provider of services and in undertaking advocacy. The scope and nature of their involvement in education and the impact and significance in respect of globalization of education in a particular national, subnational, and international context vary in line with the diversity of NGOs themselves. However, the overall significance of NGOs in shaping globalization of education is impressive, as will be seen below (The Commission and Non-Governmental Organisations, 2000).

Economic globalization and advances in communication and transportation technology have influenced the growth of international NGOs and global civil society institutions. Although international religious and academic networks can be traced back to the Middle Ages, international NGO activity began to spread during the middle of the nineteenth century. They multiplied since the last quarter of that century (Seary, 1996; Charnovitz, 1997). It has been argued that governments followed the lead of international NGOs in addressing international issues (Charnovitz, 1997).

In the 1980s, funding for NGOs from bilateral aid providers, such as the US Agency for International Development (USAID) and the official European donors as well as private Northern donors, grew significantly. The prevailing neoliberal and pro-market policies of US and other Northern governments promoted the reduction of the role of the state and expansion of the role of the private sector, including NGOs.

While economically the role of NGOs was to complement the provisions for public goods, politically NGOs served as building blocks of global civil society (Spiro, 1995; Mathews, 1997). Participation of NGOs in the UN system deliberations on global issues has helped the process of the formation of global civil society. It has been observed that there are often strong differences of viewpoint between Northern and Southern NGOs in these deliberations. For example, at the UN Conference on Environment and Development (UNCED) in Rio in 1994, Southern NGOs raised concerns about the debt crisis and multinational corporations contributing to environmental destruction, while Northern NGOs were more interested in commitments to preserve certain resources (Clark *et al.*, 1998). This diversity of voices representing genuine stakeholder interests added to the legitimacy and credibility of NGOs.

NGO Response to Globalized Education – Two Examples

Building Resources Across Countries

BRAC (formerly known as the Bangladesh Rural Advancement Committee, renamed in 2008 as Building Resources across Countries, but well known just by the acronym BRAC) illustrates the significant role of NGOs in national development, including the development of education. BRAC, exceptionally among Southern NGOs, has also become an international organization working in several Asian and African countries.

BRAC was established as a relief organization to assist war-displaced people in the aftermath of the Bangladesh

Liberation War. It now operates in all 64 districts of Bangladesh as well as in Afghanistan, Sri Lanka, Pakistan, Tanzania, Uganda, Southern Sudan, Sierra Leone, and Liberia. In Bangladesh, BRAC has over 7 million microfinance group members, 37 500 nonformal primary schools, and more than 70 000 health volunteers. It employs over 1 20 000 full-time and part-time staff, the majority of whom are women. Among others, BRAC operates its own bank and runs a well-known university. BRAC USA and BRAC UK have been established as affiliates both to generate funding support, especially for the international programs, as well as to operate programs aiming at the disadvantaged immigrant populations in the two countries (BRAC, 2008).

BRAC's Non-Formal Primary Education (NFPE) program provides the 5-year primary education course in 4 years to poor, rural, disadvantaged children and dropouts, who cannot access formal schooling. These one-room-one-teacher schools are for children between 8 and 14 years of age. Each school typically consists of 33 students who as a cohort are taken through the 4-year program, before another cohort is recruited. Core subjects include mathematics, social studies, and English in line with the national curriculum objectives. The schools also offer extracurricular activities. As of June 2008, 37 500 primary schools and 24 750 pre-primary schools were in operation enrolling nearly 3 million children, 65% of whom are girls. The schools have a dropout rate of less than 5%.

BRAC has set up centers for adolescent girls called Kishori Kendra that provide reading material and serve as a gathering place for adolescents where they are educated about issues sensitive to the Bangladeshi society such as reproductive health, early marriage, and women's legal rights. BRAC has also set up about a 1000 community libraries, 20% of which are equipped with computers (Smilie, 2009).

The Global Campaign for Education

The Global Campaign for Education (GCE) is a civil society movement, established originally with the initiative of Education International, the worldwide federation of teachers' organizations. Its aim is to end the global education crisis. Its mission is to hold governments to account for their promises made to provide EFA and to ensure that they act to deliver the right of children and adults to quality public education.

Since its formation in 1999, organizations and people from over 100 countries – civil society organizations, trade unions, child rights campaigners, teachers, parents, and students – have united under its auspices to demand universal education.

GCE was a strong civil society voice in the World Education Forum in Dakar 2000 in setting the EFA

agenda for 2015. The GCE's membership is open to national coalitions and international and regional organizations that advocate for EFA and subscribe to GCE's principles and goals. The main advocacy approaches and activities of GCE are summarized below.

Global action week

GCE coordinates the Global Action Week on education with all its national and international partners in April every year. Activities included the World's Biggest Lesson and Send My Friend to School. In 2008, close to 9 million people took part in the World's Biggest Lesson, including national leaders and celebrities aimed at drawing attention to the state of education and actions that must be taken.

Year-round campaign

GCE represents civil society on education at key education decision-making bodies, including the Education Fast Track Initiative Steering Committee, the EFA UNESCO-led Working Group and High Level Group. It also guides national campaigns to lobby the annual G8 and World Bank and International Monetary Fund (IMF) meetings to demand adequate long-term financing for education.

EFA class of 2015

GCA helped launch the EFA Class of 2015 at the UN high-level meeting on the Millennium Development Goals on 25 September 2008. This class brings together governments, faith leaders, corporations, civil society, and education advocates who are committed to making sure that the EFA goals become a reality by 2015.

Global advocacy

GCE encourages policy research on different aspects of the EFA agenda, what is needed to achieve EFA and rate the performance of national governments. It has produced a school report that ranks governments' efforts toward achieving EFA.

Recent Developments

There have been always winners and losers from economic globalization. Who the winners and who the losers are from the inexorable forces of globalization are determined by whether people live in the global North or in urban and developed parts of a country, whether they are skilled and educated, whether people have acquired the capacity to adjust to change and new situations easily, whether they possess assets, their gender and ethnic status, and such factors over which people have little control (Streeten, 2001).

Globalization-induced improvements in a nation's standard of living also can promote women's status and raise household income, education, nutrition, and life expectancy, while lowering birthrates. The key issues clearly are: discerning the factors which create the winners and losers; identifying the vulnerable groups affected by these factors; determining the conditions and actions that would reduce the vulnerability of people; and promoting and supporting the creation of these conditions and enabling people to engage in these actions. Enhancement of people's capabilities to discern and assess the options and make the choices can happen through effective access to education, knowledge, and information.

The quality of human resources determines success for a nation in the era of intensified globalization. The intellectual capital of a nation has become more important than natural resources and financial capital to a country's ability to compete in the global economy.

The economic crisis of 2008–9, manifested in the meltdown of the financial market, causing huge contraction of capital, decline in consumption, and increase in unemployment has posed new challenges to the legitimacy of the premises underlying economic globalization. This situation creates new opportunities for the civil society and NGOs to reinforce the international coalitions and compromises that are necessary to mitigate the negative aspects of globalization and enhance the positive effects – putting a higher premium on global human solidarity than on unimpeded global competition. Education and learning, in multiple ways and in the broadest sense, have to be regarded as a critical element in this effort.

Bibliography

BRAC (2008). *Annual Report.* Dhaka: BRAC.

Charnovitz, S. (1997). Two centuries of participation: NGOs and international governance. *Michigan Journal of International Law* **18**(2), 183–286.

Clark, A. M. (1995). Non-governmental organizations and the influence on international society. *Journal of International Affairs* **48**, 507–525.

Clark, A. M., Friedman, E. J., and Hochstetler, K. (1998). Global civil society: A comparison of NGO participation in United Nations world conferences on *World Politics*, vol. 52, No. 1, p 136.

Cogburn, D. L. (1998). Globalisation, knowledge, education, and training in the information age. *International Forum on Information and Documentation* **23**(4), 23–29.

Croucher, S. L. (1994). *Globalization and Belonging: The Politics of Identity in a Changing World.* London: Rowman & Littlefield.

Cummings, W. K. and McGinn, N. F. (eds.) (1997). *International Handbook of Education and Development: Preparing Schools, Students, and Nations for the Twenty-First Century.* Kidlington: Elsevier Science.

European Commission (2000). The commission and non-governmental organisations: Building a stronger partnership. http://ec.europa.eu/civil_society/ngo/en/communication.pdf (accessed October 2009).

Frase, T. and O'Sullivan, B. (2000). *The Future of Education under the WTO.* Madison, WI: 180/Movement for Democracy and Education Clearing House.

Potier, B. (2004). Globalization and education explored at GSE. *Harvard University Gazette,* 4 March, 2004.

Seary, B. (1996). The early history: From the Congress of Vienna to the San Francisco Conference. In Willetts, P. (ed.) *The Conscience of the World: The Influence of Non-Governmental Organizations in the UN System,* pp 15–30. London: Hurst.

Smilie, I. (2009). *Freedom from Want: The Remarkable Success Story of BRAC, the Global Grassroots Organization That's Winning the Fight against Poverty.* W. Hartford, CT: Kumarian Press.

Spiro, P. J. (1995). New global communities: Nongovernmental organizations in international decision-making institutions. *The Washington Quarterly* **18**(1), 45–56.

Streeten, P. (2001). *Globalization: Threat or Opportunity?* Copenhagen: Copenhagen Business School Press.

Tabb, W. (2007). Globalization and education as a commodity. *Clarion. Public Service Congress,* City University of New York, Summer (2007).

UNESCO (1998). Learning: The treasures within. *Report of the International Commission on Education for the 21st Century.* Paris: United Nations Educational, Scientific and Cultural Organization.

UNESCO (2000). *World Education Report 2000. The Right to Education: Towards Education for All Throughout Life.* Paris: United Nations Educational, Scientific and Cultural Organization.

United Nations (nd) United Nations Documents: Research Guide. http://www.un.org/Depts/dhl/resguide/resins.htm (accessed October 2009).

Wolf, M. (2005). *Why Globalization Works.* New Haven, CT: Yale University Press.

Further Reading

Chabbott, C. (2003). *Constructing Education for Development: International Organizations and Education for All.* New York: Routledge Falmer.

Drucker, P. F. (1997). The Global Economy and the Nation-State. *Foreign Affairs* **76**(5), 159–171.

Gordenker, L. and Weiss, T. G. (eds.) (1996). *NGOs, the UN and Global Governance.* Boulder, CO: Lynne Reinner.

Nadjam, A. (1998). Searching for NGO Effectiveness. *Development Policy Review* **16**, 305–310.

Rossello, P. (1970). Historical Note. In UNESCO/IBE *International Conferences on Public Education: Recommendations.* Paris: United Nations Educational, Scientific and Cultural Organization.

Spring, J. (2008). *Globalization of Education: An Introduction.* Oxford, UK: Taylor and Francis.

Suarez-Orozco, M. (ed.) (2007). *Learning in the Global Era: International Perspectives on Globalization of Education.* Berkeley, CA: University of California Press.

Valderama, F. (1995). *A History of UNESCO.* Paris: United Nations Educational, Scientific and Cultural Organization.

Relevant Websites

http://www.un.org – GA Resolutions, International Instruments (1946 onwards), UN Documentation: Research Guide, United Nations (UN).

http://www.campaignforeducation.org – Global Campaign for Education.

http://ec.europa.eu – The commission and non-governmental organizations: Building a stronger partnership. *Commission Discussion Paper* by Prodi and Kinnock, European Commission.

Wider Benefits of Adult Education

T Schuller, OECD, Paris, France
R Desjardins, Danish University of Education, Copenhagen, Denmark

Introduction

This article focuses on the wider benefits of adult learning, covering a mix of personal and social (external) effects. The emphasis is on the effects of adult learning on health and civic engagement. Less attention has been given to this area than to the economic benefits of adult learning, although there is a growing body of research in this area. Some reference is made to the human and personal development aspects of adult learning as these can also be considered wider benefits; however, this topic has been discussed more elaborately elsewhere in the encyclopedia.

Defining the Wider Benefits

A basic issue is the question of what changes are affected by learning interventions. The changes are not limited to the individual. Adult learners can in turn initiate changes in the wider sense, by affecting the home/family, work, and community contexts that they engage in. There is a deep-rooted belief that adult learning has the potential to create personal, economic, and social value. This value can accrue to a variety of actors: to the learner, other private interests such as a current or future employer, and/or to society at large. In short, individuals, employers, and governments invest in adult learning with an expectation that there are benefits of different kinds to be realized.

Benefits can be categorized in a number of ways: cognitive or affective; psychological or behavioral; job or leisure related; and expected or unexpected. The notion of wider benefits usually refers to a mix of external, public, and nonmonetary benefits. The term social benefits is often used to refer to a similar range of effects (Behrman and Stacey, 1997; McMahon, 1999; Wolfe and Haveman, 2001; Psacharopoulos, 2006), although it does not include private nonmonetary benefits as in the notion of wider benefits as used by some authors (e.g., Schuller *et al.*, 2001, 2004).

Benefits that do not necessarily accrue to individuals (or other private interests such as firms) who make the decisions to invest are referred to as external. They are external because they are not taken into account when deciding to invest, even if they might be expected. The presence of external benefits provides justification for public policies that foster adult learning (Desjardins *et al.*, 2006). Otherwise there may be underinvestment from the standpoint of public policy. External effects are commonly associated with public or societal effects because they tend to be nonexclusive (Lucas, 1988).

The notion of wider benefits can also encompass nonmonetary benefits which occur at both the private or public levels. Private individual-level nonmonetary benefits are valued by the individuals who take up the adult learning but these are not directly exchangeable on markets and hence have no direct monetary value. Examples include the entertainment or consumption value of learning, health and life satisfaction, and improved family life. In contrast, public benefits are those benefits to members of society other than the learners themselves. Nonmonetary examples of public benefits include crime reduction, trust, social cohesion, political stability, and a well-functioning democracy. **Table 1** highlights examples of each private–public and monetary–nonmonetary combinations. Public monetary examples include reduced health and social transfer costs. These various benefits are not independent of each other (McMahon, 1999). For example, a private monetary return can in turn lead to the private nonmonetary return of improved individuals and family health – which in turn can lead to the public monetary return of reduced public expenditures on healthcare.

Different Types and Purposes of Adult Learning

The incentive to invest (time, effort, money, and other resources) varies among the different actors, depending on the type of value and who it is that benefits; in principle, this has implications for who should (and does) pay (Becker, 1964). It also has implications for the demand structure of different types of adult learning interventions. Majority of adults participate in adult learning for job-related reasons (OECD, 2003). Nonetheless, participation for personal and social-related reasons also plays an important role, and depending on the country these can form a substantial component of overall participation rates in adult learning (Desjardins *et al.*, 2006).

The reasons for participating have an impact on the nature and supply of learning interventions, including the form and content, and this in turn has implications for the potential wider benefits. However, specific evidence on the effects of different stages and types of schooling, or different curricula and pedagogical approaches is sparse. Most studies focus on the number of years of schooling or

Table 1　Possible economic and social outcomes of learning

	Private	*Public*
Monetary	Earnings, income, and wealth Productivity	Tax revenues Social transfer costs Healthcare costs
Nonmonetary	Health status Life satisfaction	Social cohesion Trust Well-functioning democracy Political stability

From OECD (2007). *Understanding the Social Outcomes of Learning*. Paris: OECD.

highest level of educational attainment, primarily because these data are relatively cheap to collect and hence readily available in social surveys. Few studies focus on adult learning and what it is about these learning experiences that matter for wider benefits. In essence, much of the discussion of the benefits of learning at various levels has viewed education as a black box. Findings suggest that adult learning has positive effects on a wide spectrum of health and social outcomes and that these depend on individual life histories, social context, and the type of learning experience (e.g., academic, vocational, and leisure – see Feinstein *et al.* 2003).

Channels through which Adult Learning Can Affect Outcomes

Effects on Economic Positions and Resources

Adult learning can improve employability and income, which is a key pathway to realizing a range of other benefits. Adults with a record of adult education and training are less likely to be unemployed and more likely to experience wage growth (OECD, 2005: 35). This can translate into improved personal satisfaction and autonomy; personal health and security; and quality of child rearing. It can generate resources (e.g., time and money) for engaging in social, civic, and political activities, which in turn are key elements for democratic processes; solidarity and social cohesion; human rights and peace; equity, equality, and the absence of discrimination; and ecological sustainability – all important dimensions of a well-functioning society (Gilomen, 2003). Further, it can reduce inclinations toward criminal and antisocial behavior by meeting basic needs of subsistence and improving the chances for a successful life (Feinstein, 2002). The instrumental effect of education on income and wealth therefore feeds through into intrinsic benefits such as better health.

Effects on the Self

Learning can develop skill and cognition and can modify the traits and behavior patterns of adults (OECD, 2007).

Educational experiences can also serve an enlightenment function (Lauglo and Øia, 2006). They can promote tolerance of and respect for other groups (Turner, 1991), and in turn social cohesion. Many learning experiences make people aware of others around them and the complex processes involved in society (Pring, 1999), creating an interest to take part in the processes of social change. This also promotes an awareness of the value of investing in the future as well as an awareness of risks by providing an insight into the trade-offs among costs and benefits occurring at different points in time, which in turn influences a range of choices and behaviors, for example, regarding healthy lifestyles (Feinstein *et al.*, 2006). It can also develop psycho-social capabilities such as resilience that help to cope with adversity (Schoon and Bynner, 2003). Resilience has been empirically linked to a set of internal attributes (i.e., autonomy, problem-solving skills, a sense of purpose and future, and social competence), all of which are plausibly affected by continued learning (Howard *et al.*, 1999). Effects on other psychological characteristics include self-efficacy (the belief that the self can influence the world around them) and external efficacy (the belief and trust that others will respond to one's own actions).

In summary, learning experiences can lead to wider benefits by directly: shaping what people know; developing competencies, which help people use their knowledge to yield benefits for themselves and society; and cultivating values, attitudes, beliefs, and motivations that foster the potential for generating wider benefits. There is also a potential for negative effects, particularly where access to learning opportunities is unequal and where provision is injurious to self-concepts, learning, and development.

Effects on Social Position

The channels described above share the assumption that education affects outcomes by directly changing the self. A distinctly different mechanism suggests that education's impact is indirect, and operates by changing the position of the individual in the hierarchy of social relations (Verba *et al.*, 1978; Campbell, 2006; OECD, 2007). The main premise is that the relative position of individuals in a social hierarchy is largely a function of access to learning opportunities, and education's primary effect derives from its ability to locate people in this hierarchy. This can be called the positional or relative effect. For example, Campbell (2006) finds that certain social outcomes fit this model best, namely participating in politics: belonging to a party, or seeking to influence politics through lobbying. His findings imply that an across-the-board increase in adult learning participation preserving overall inequality may do little to increase political participation; or education may help people to better health by enabling them to secure access to health treatment ahead of those below them in the pecking order.

Thus, learning may benefit individuals by increasing (or preserving) their social status. However, the benefit to the wider community may be nil or even negative, so that the benefits to some are achieved at the expense of others. This is far from hypothetical: to the extent that education accentuates rather than mitigates inequality, its overall net impact on health and other outcomes may well be negative.

Effects via Context

Adult learning can also have an impact on the role of contexts. Contexts refer to family, work, or community settings, where individuals have varying but always limited or bounded agency. Adult learning may influence the structural conditions of choice and opportunity as well as the distribution of resources (especially through collective agency). Therefore, it enables people, to some extent, to choose and shape the contexts within which they live and work, and the peers they associate with. Peer effects are potentially extremely strong, to positive and negative ends.

Effects on Health

Recent studies highlight the significance of the relationship between education and health outcomes (OECD, 2007; Feinstein *et al.*, 2006). Typically, health professionals have interpreted the association more narrowly as a marker of socioeconomic status. Findings now indicate that there are sizeable differences in health for those with different levels of education and that these are partly due to the effects of education and not solely due to differences that precede or explain education, such as socioeconomic status. For example, Ross and Mirowsky's (1999) findings suggest that education has health effects at all levels of income. Using rigorous methods, Spasojevic (2003) suggests that the effect of education on health is at least as great as the effect of income. An extensive review of the evidence on the direct effects of education concluded that independent of economic position, those with more years of schooling are substantially associated with better health, well-being, and health behaviors (see Feinstein *et al.*, 2006). In some cases, the evidence is particularly robust and suggests causality.

By combining findings from the National Child Development Study in the UK with a series of insights from biographical case studies collected by the Centre for Research on the Wider Benefits of Learning, Feinstein *et al.* (2003) (also see Bynner and Hammond, 2004; Feinstein and Hammond, 2004; Bynner, 2001) provide a rare analysis of the extent and nature of the wider benefits of adult learning. They find that adults who took at least one course between the age of 33 and 42 are more likely to have given up smoking, increased their level of exercise, and increased their life satisfaction. According to the authors, such improvements can in turn lead to economic return, by reducing pressure on health services, and thus offer a return to the taxpayer and the economy more generally.

All types of courses were linked to an increase in exercise, but the marginal effects were larger for academic and leisure-related courses than vocationally oriented courses. Further, leisure courses appear to have a more important effect among adults who did not complete secondary schooling qualifications. One possible rationale for this latter observation is that the path to an increased sense of self-value and empowerment (psychological attributes that help people lead healthier lives) through learning, depends partly on previous learning experiences. Many adults, who have not completed secondary schooling, will have experienced academic difficulties and even failure; therefore, for some adults, an alternate sequencing of different types of learning may be necessary to build up a positive attitude toward learning and to avoid negative overall effects to psychological well-being. The biographical data, complemented with statistical results, strongly suggest that adult learning features as an important element in positive cycles of development and progression, and that there are cumulative effects associated with learning that occur in reinforcing sequences.

In a separate study using the British Household Panel Survey, Sabates and Feinstein (2006) estimate the effects of adult learning on the take-up of preventative health services. Using a model to predict changes in the levels of uptake of screening, they simulate the impact of whether 100 000 women were enrolled in adult learning on cervical cancer prevention. Adult learning is associated with a 2.2% point increase in the probability of utilizing screening. Using statistics on the smear tests analyzed in 2002 in the United Kingdom and the claim by health officials that cervical screening can prevent 80–90% of cancer cases in women who attend regularly, the authors estimate that about 116–134 cervical cancers would be prevented for every 100 000 women in adult learning.

Effects on Civic and Social Engagement

Adult learning can be instrumental for many in providing aptitudes that are useful for civic living and contribution. Svensson (1996: 62) found that the majority of participants in study circles (a form of adult popular education in Sweden) believes that they develop useful knowledge from participating. Civic skills acquired through nonpolitical channels, including on the job and in voluntary associations, are an important predictor of whether someone is politically engaged (Verba *et al.*, 1995; SOU, 1996: 47). Having skills motivates people by instilling a sense of agency – skills make people feel like they have something to offer in the civic and social realm. Further, adult learning that takes place in the civic realm has been linked as an important contributor to the sustenance of democracy (Larsson, 1999).

The same study that was introduced above, Feinstein *et al.* (2003), also explored the effect of adult learning on a range of civic and social outcomes. They found that adult learning has a pervasive impact on social and political attitudes, especially among adults who participate in courses that are academically oriented. The suggestion is that these types of courses are most suited for opening minds and challenging previously held beliefs. Effect sizes of academically oriented adult learning on racism and political cynicism are on the order of about –0.07 to –0.10 and –0.03 to –0.065, respectively (Preston and Feinstein, 2004: 25). Some respondents to the biographical field work indicated that learning experiences led to a greater understanding of people from different backgrounds. Even though social and political attitudes are thought to be fairly stable by mid-adulthood, adult learning was found to have normatively beneficial effects on most of the attitudes considered on a magnitude of up to 5% points, representing up to a 34% change from the baseline level predicted for those who did not participate. Overall, their findings link adult learning to increased racial tolerance, a reduction in political cynicism, a higher inclination toward democratic attitudes, and a higher level of political interest.

Bynner and Hammond (2004) report findings which suggest that participation in adult education courses is linked to higher levels of civic and political participation, including increased membership in groups and voter participation. Those who participate in one or two courses are about 34% more likely to become a member of an association and 13% more likely to begin voting compared to all those who abstained in the previous election. In contrast to its effects on attitudes, it is leisure-oriented courses that have the most significant impact on civic and social participation, especially among adults who have not completed secondary schooling. From the biographical accounts, it is those adults who are most initially isolated and lacking confidence that ascribed significant changes in their social activity to adult learning participation. In Sweden, Svensson (1996) found that at least 33% indicate that their motive for participating in study circles was to meet others.

Despite the link to increased social activity, less has been said about the effects of adult learning on the intents and purposes, or other qualitative aspects of different groups or networks (Emler and Frazer, 1999). Using the same biographical data from the Centre for Research on the Wider Benefits of Learning, Preston (2004) demonstrates that learning experiences may not only lead to an expansion of social networks, but can also cause their relocation and dissolution, albeit in such a way as to

maintain improvements in well-being. He linked adult learning to increases in self-confidence and self worth, which help to motivate individuals in removing themselves from unhealthy or even dangerous relationships.

Conclusions

The impacts of learning extend beyond those measured by increased productivity in the production of goods and services exchanged on markets. Learning in adulthood is linked to diverse items such as reductions of criminal activity, increases in social cohesion, changes in income distribution, savings in welfare and medical costs, and voter participation. Strong theoretical expectations about the wider benefits of adult learning exist, and although less abundant and generally less rigorous than the evidence on the impact of initial education (compulsory and post-compulsory schooling), there is some empirical research to support these expectations.

The measurement of noneconomic outcomes is attaining greater significance in many Organization for Economic Co-Operation and Development (OECD) countries. This trend brings with it a range of difficult methodological issues, notably in establishing robust techniques for assessing causality. A key issue is how far adult education is brought into this debate. Quantitative data on adult learning are universally weaker than that on initial schooling, and effects are therefore harder to measure using conventional approaches. Yet, extending the rationale for public and private investment in education to cover outcomes, such as improved health and stronger civic democracies, is a challenge which has much to offer.

See also: Adult Education and Civil Society; Economic Outcomes of Adult Education and Training.

Bibliography

Becker, G. S. (1964). *Human Capital: A Theoretical and Empirical Analysis with Special References to Education* (revised in 1975/1993). Chicago, IL: University of Chicago Press.

Behrman, J. R. and Stacey, N. (eds.) (1997). *The Social Benefits of Education.* Ann Arbor, MA: University of Michigan Press.

Bynner, J. and Hammond, C. (2004). The benefits of adult learning: Quantitative insights. In Schuller, T., Preston, J., Hammond, C., Brassett-Grundy, A., and Bynner, J. (eds.) *The Benefits of Learning: The Impact of Education on Health, Family Life and Social Capital,* pp 161–178. London: RoutledgeFalmer.

Bynner, J. (2001). The wider benefits gained by adults returning to higher education. In Lourenço, E. (ed.) *Wider Benefits of Learning: Understanding and Monitoring the Consequences of Adult Learning,* pp 142–149. Lisbon: For ESREA by Xàtiva.

Campbell, D. E. (2006). What is education's impact on civic and social engagement? In Desjardins, R. and Schuller, T. (eds.) *Measuring the Effects of Education on Health and Civic/Social Engagement,* pp 25–126. Paris: OECD/CERI.

Desjardins, R., Rubenson, K., and Milana, M. (2006). *Unequal Chances to Participate in Adult Learning*. Paris: UNESCO.

Emler, N. and Frazer, E. (1999). Politics: The education effect. *Oxford Review of Education* 25(1/2), 251–273.

Feinstein, L. (2002). *Quantitative Estimates of the Social Benefits of Learning, 1: Crime*. London: Centre for Research on the Wider Benefits of Learning.

Feinstein, L. (2002). *Quantitative Estimates of the Social Benefits of Learning, 2: Health (Depression and Obesity)*. London: Centre for Research on the Wider Benefits of Learning.

Feinstein, L. and Hammond, C. (2004). The contribution of adult learning to health and social capital. *Oxford Review of Education* 30(2), 199–221.

Feinstein, L., Hammond, C., Woods, L., Preston, J., and Bynner, J. (2003). *The Contribution of Adult Learning to Health and Social Capital*. London: Centre for Research on the Wider Benefits of Learning.

Feinstein, L., Sabates, R., Anderson, T. M., Sorhaindo, A., and Hammond, C. (2006). What are the effects of education on health? In Desjardins, R. and Schuller, T. (eds.) *Measuring the Effects of Education on Health and Civic/Social Engagement*, pp 171–354. Paris: CERI/OECD. http://www.oecd.org/edu/socialoutcomes/symposium (accessed May 2009).

Gilomen, H. (2003). Desired outcomes: A successful life and a well-functioning society. In Rychen, D. S. and Salganik, L. H. (eds.) *Key Competencies: For a Successful Life and a Well-Functioning Society*, pp 122–147. Cambridge, MA: Hogefe and Huber.

Howard, S., Dryden, J., and Johnson, B. (1999). Childhood resilience: Review and critique of literature. *Oxford Review of Education* 25(3), 307–323.

Larsson, S. (1999). Studiecirkeldemokratin. In Amnå, E. (ed.) *Civilsamhället*, vol. 84, pp 243–279. Stockholm: SOU.

Lauglo, J. and Øia, T. (2006). *Education and Civic Engagement among Norwegian Youths*. Oslo: Norwegian Social Research.

Lucas, R. E. (1988). On the mechanics of economic development. *Journal of Monetary Economics* 22(1), 3–42.

McMahon, W. (1998). Conceptual framework for the analysis of the social benefits of lifelong learning. *Education Economics* 6(3), 309–346.

McMahon, W. (1999). *Education and Development: Measuring the Social Benefits*. Oxford: Oxford University Press.

OECD (2003). *Beyond Rhetoric: Adult Learning Policies and Practices*. Paris: OECD.

OECD (2005). *Promoting Adult Learning*. Paris: OECD.

OECD (2007). *Understanding the Social Outcomes of Learning*. Paris: OECD.

Preston, J. (2004). A continuous effort of sociability: Learning and social capital in adult life. In Schuller, T., Preston, J., Hammond, C., Brassett-Grundy, A., and Bynner, J. (eds.) *The Benefits of Learning: The Impact of Education on Health, Family Life and Social Capital*, pp 119–136. London: RoutledgeFalmer.

Preston, J. and Feinstein, L. (2004). *Adult Education and Attitude Change*. London: Centre for Research on the Wider Benefits of Learning.

Pring, R. (1999). Politics: Relevance of the humanities. *Oxford Review of Education* 25(1/2), 71–87.

Psacharopoulos, G. (2006). The value of investment in education: Theory, evidence and policy. *Journal of Education Finance* 32(2), 113–126.

Ross, C. E. and Mirowsky, J. (1999). Refining the association between education and health: The effects of quantity, credential and selectivity. *Demography* 36(4), 445–460.

Sabates, R. and Feinstein, L. (2006). Education and the take-up of preventative health care. *Social Science and Medicine* 62, 2998–3010.

Schoon, I. and Bynner, J. (2003). Risk and resilience in the life course: Implications for interventions and social policies. *Journal of Youth Studies* 6(1), 21–31.

Schuller, T., Bynner, J., Green, A., *et al.* (2001). *Modelling and Measuring the Wider Benefits of Learning: A Synthesis*. London: Centre for Research on the Wider Benefits of Learning.

Schuller, T., Preston, J., Hammond, C., Brassett-Grundy, A., and Bynner, J. (2004). *The Benefits of Learning: The Impact of Education on Health, Family Life and Social Capital*. London: RoutledgeFalmer.

SOU (1996). *Cirkelsamhället: Studiecirklarnas Betydelse för Individ och Lokalsamhälle*. Stockholm: Fritzes/Regeringskansliet.

Spasojevic, J. (2003). *Effects of Education on Adult Health in Sweden: Results from a Natural Experiment*. New York: City University of New York.

Svensson, A. (1996). *Vilka deltar i studiecirklar? II. Rapport från en undersökning av deltagare i studieförbundens cirkelverksamhet hösten 1995*. Stockholm: Folkbildningsrådet.

Turner, J. H. (1991). *The Structure of Sociological Theory*, 5th edn. Belmont, CA: Wadsworth.

Verba, S., Nie, N. H., and Kim, J. (1978). *Participation and Political Equality: A Seven-Nation Comparison*. Chicago, IL: University of Chicago Press.

Verba, S., Schlozman, K. L., and Brady, H. E. (1995). *Voice and Equality: Civic Voluntarism in American Politics*. Cambridge, MA: Harvard University Press.

Wolfe, B. and Haveman, R. (2001). Accounting for the social and non-market benefits of education. In Helliwell, J. F. (ed.) *The Contribution of Human and Social Capital to Sustained Economic Growth and Well-Being*, pp 221–250. ch. 11, Ottawa, ON: Human Resources Development Canada and Organisation for Economic Co-operation and Development.

Further Reading

Bourdieu, P. (1990). *The Logic of Practice*. Cambridge: Polity Press.

Pryor, B. W. (1990). Predicting and explaining intentions to participate in continuing education: An application of the theory of reasoned action. *Adult Education Quarterly* 40(3), 146–157.

Rubenson, K. (1975). *Participation in Recurrent Education*. Paris: CERI/OECD.

Economic Outcomes of Adult Education and Training

A Ferrer, University of Calgary, Calgary, AB, Canada
W C Riddell, University of British Columbia, Vancouver, BC, Canada

Glossary

Active labor market policies – Policies aimed to facilitate adjustment to job loss, assist the jobless to find work, and encourage labor force participation. In addition to training and skills development, these policies include public employment services (counseling, job-search assistance, information, and placement), youth measures to aid the transition from school to work, subsidized employment, and measures for disabled workers.

On-the-job training (OJT) – Training taking place in the firm to learn procedures that are job related, but where learning is an activity separate from regular job duties.

Portability (of training) – The capacity to utilize skills and obtain returns on human capital investments obtained with a previous employer. This concept is linked to that of the specificity of training.

Selection bias – Error committed when estimating the effect of an intervention such as a training program, due to the fact that treatment and comparison groups are intrinsically different, and would have experienced different outcomes even in the absence of the intervention.

Specific training – Training that provides skills that are exclusive to a particular firm, occupation, or industry and cannot be applied elsewhere. The antonym is general training.

Introduction

Adult education and training have been focal points of labor market studies in developed economies since the 1960s. Increased attention to this topic is part of a shift toward greater emphasis on human capital in both economic and social policy in societies that are increasingly knowledge based. Several factors account for the growing interest in these issues. Technological change – especially advances in information and computer technologies – and globalization of production have resulted in a growing demand for highly skilled workers and changes in workplace skills requirements. Within specific occupations and professions, rapid changes imply a greater need for

maintaining and updating skills and knowledge about current best practice. In addition, because of demographic changes and reduced fertility in many countries, the labor force is both aging and growing more slowly than in the past. In an environment in which labor shortages may become more common, there is greater emphasis on the skills of the existing workforce. As the workforce ages, there is a growing risk that older workers who lose their jobs may not have the skills needed to become reemployed.

Skill acquisition of adult workers takes many forms. Learning by doing (acquiring skills during the course of one's regular duties), for instance, is an important source of growth in workers' skills. Here, we focus instead on the acquisition of abilities that are job related, but where learning is a separate activity from regular job activities. Within these, we distinguish between formal (learning leading to the completion of diploma or degree) and informal (seminars, interdepartmental visits, etc.) training. A second important distinction relates to who pays for training. From the institutional point of view, individuals, employers, and governments generally differ in their goals when purchasing or providing adult education and training. Government-sponsored training is often concerned with enhancing the employability of displaced or unemployed workers, disadvantaged workers with limited skills, and those at high risk of social exclusion. Recipients of publicly provided training are likely to be unemployed and to come from the bottom of the skill distribution curve. In contrast, employer-sponsored training is provided to those currently employed, as is much of the adult education and training funded by individuals. Furthermore, as many studies have shown, those who are already well educated and highly skilled are more likely to receive work-related training. Employer-sponsored training is also more likely to provide firm-specific skills, which do not raise the value of the trainee to other employers. Governments, on the other hand, prefer general skills that increase individual employability in a variety of workplaces. Finally, these types of training generally differ in their timing. Employer-sponsored training will likely be spread out over the worker's career but the duration of any particular spell may be short, whereas government-sponsored training is concentrated during spells of unemployment and is usually discontinued when the worker becomes reemployed. Thus, there are numerous reasons to distinguish between publicly financed and employer-sponsored training.

Human capital theory has long emphasized the importance of on-the-job training (OJT) and work experience for productivity and earnings. Recently, additional empirical findings have given rise to a new training literature (Acemoglu and Pischke, 1999). Leuven (2005) provides a useful survey of theoretical developments. Evaluating the impacts of adult education and training on outcomes has generated an extensive literature and a wide range of estimated impacts. In this article, we provide an overview of the methods commonly used to evaluate the outcomes of adult education and training and a summary of the results of this literature.

The principal outcomes that have been examined – especially for government-sponsored training – are individual labor market outcomes such as wages, employment, and earnings. Earnings is a useful summary measure because it captures both the price dimension – the wage rate – and the quantity dimension – hours, weeks, and years of work. For employers, the key outcome is worker productivity and thus firm profitability, although the provision of training opportunities may also influence other dimensions of performance such as innovative activity as well as recruitment and retention of employees. The impacts on earnings and productivity are key ingredients in any assessment of the costs and benefits of adult education and training.

Methodological Issues in Evaluating Outcomes

Obtaining credible estimates of the impacts of adult education and training programs is a difficult problem. In modern approaches to evaluation, the nature of the challenge is usually illustrated using the potential outcomes model (Angrist and Kreuger, 1999). Each individual in the population of interest – which in this case consists of individuals who may or may not receive training – has two potential outcomes: (1) the outcome that would be experienced if he/she receives training, and (2) the outcome that would be experienced if he/she does not receive training. One of these two potential outcomes is inherently unobservable. For each participant, we can never know what outcomes that individual would have experienced had they not participated. Similarly, for each person who does not participate we cannot know what outcomes would have been experienced had they participated. The problem is thus one of obtaining credible estimates of the counterfactual outcome – the potential outcome that cannot be observed. For participants, this means obtaining an estimate of the outcomes they would have experienced had they not participated in adult education or training.

The gold-standard approach to the evaluation problem is to use random assignment to treatment and control groups. Random assignment ensures that the treatment group that receives training and the control group that does not receive training are statistically equivalent in their pretreatment characteristics; that is, that there are no statistically significant differences in the characteristics of the two groups. Since the two groups are statistically equivalent prior to treatment, any differences in outcomes experienced by the two groups can be attributed to the causal impact of the treatment.

When random assignment is not feasible or desirable, there are a number of nonexperimental methods that can be employed, including regression-based methods, natural or quasi-experiments, instrumental variables, matching estimation, and panel data methods. Each of these methods has advantages and disadvantages, and has different data requirements. Furthermore, no one method dominates other methods in all circumstances. Determining the methodological approach to employ in a particular setting requires a detailed understanding of institutional features relating to program operation and the nature of available data. Simply put, there is no magic bullet in nonexperimental methods.

All nonexperimental methods for estimating the impacts of education and training programs use a comparison group of nonparticipants to estimate the outcomes that participants would have experienced had they not participated in the program. However, in the absence of random assignment, participants and nonparticipants will generally differ along several dimensions, some that are observed by the researcher and some that are unobserved. Because of these differences between the two groups, the outcomes experienced by the comparison group – in the absence of statistical or econometric modeling – are unlikely to provide a reliable estimate of the counterfactual. In particular, since individuals choose whether or not to apply for and/or enroll in a training program, the individuals who receive training constitute a self-selected sample and may differ in various ways from the individuals who do not apply for and/or enroll.

Employers also choose which employees receive training and which do not. Similarly, for government-sponsored training, there may be some selection by those who administer or operate the programs. Simple comparisons of participants and nonparticipants are thus likely to be subject to selection bias and do not provide credible estimates of program impacts. The various nonexperimental methods provide different ways of dealing with the selection bias problem.

In the past two decades, there have been significant advances in nonexperimental evaluation methods. Equally important have been improvements in the quality of the data available for analysis. As a consequence, recent studies using state-of-the-art techniques to assess the impacts of adult education and training generally provide more credible evidence than earlier studies.

Outcomes of Adult Education and Training

As noted previously, there are several reasons for distinguishing between government-sponsored adult education and training and private-sector-sponsored training. Although the expenditure on private-sector-sponsored training far exceeds that by governments – even in countries such as Sweden that devote considerable public expenditure to training – more is known about the outcomes of publicly supported training. This situation reflects a greater desire by governments (and taxpayers) to evaluate the impacts of their programs, as well as data challenges in assessing the impacts of employer-based training.

Government-Sponsored Ttraining

Government-sponsored training is part of the broader category of active labor market policies (ALMPs) that facilitate adjustment to change, assist the jobless to find work, and encourage labor force participation. These policies include public employment services (counseling, job search assistance, information, and placement), youth measures to aid the transition from school to work, subsidized employment, and measures for the disabled. Our focus here is on training programs, which are the most important active measure in many Organization for Economic Co-operation and Development (OECD) countries.

There is a significant amount of research assessing the labor market outcomes of government-sponsored training and other active programs. The comprehensive survey by Heckman *et al.* (1999) summarizes more than 40 studies from the US and Europe. Other useful surveys of this literature include LaLonde (1995), US Department of Labor (1995), Martin and Grubb (2001), and Kluve and Schmidt (2002). Our treatment is brief because several excellent surveys are available and there are space constraints.

Relative to other OECD countries, the US has traditionally displayed a stronger commitment to rigorous evaluation of government programs, including substantial use of randomized trials. As a consequence, the state of knowledge about the effectiveness of these programs is dominated by US evidence. However, as the recent surveys by Martin and Grubb (2001) and Kluve and Schmidt (2002) indicate, there is growing use of serious evaluations in several European countries, resulting in a rapidly expanding body of evidence on the impacts of active programs.

Several salient features emerge from reviews of the US evidence (LaLonde, 1995; US Department of Labor, 1995; Heckman *et al.*, 1999). First, the impacts on earnings of disadvantaged workers are mixed, being positive for some groups and zero or even negative for others. In this regard, it is worth noticing that training programs for displaced workers (who typically have considerable work experience and are highly motivated) have in general, a better track record than those for the disadvantaged (Jacobson *et al.*, 2005b). Other generalizations include:

- government-sponsored training significantly raises the earnings of economically disadvantaged adult women;
- the effects of these programs on disadvantaged adult men are often smaller than on women, and not always positive;
- the impacts of training on out-of-school youth are generally zero or negative;
- classroom training can be effective for adult women, but has limited success for adult men, especially those with low education; and
- best results are obtained when classroom training or OJT have a strong work experience component linked to local employers.

Greenberg *et al.* (2004) offer evidence from meta-analytic techniques on the persistence of these effects. Impacts on earnings seem to diminish over time for adult males and youth, but remain stable over time for females.

A second feature of the US evidence is that estimated impacts, even when they are positive, are generally modest in size. As noted by LaLonde, this outcome is not surprising, given the limited duration and cost of these programs:

> The best summary of the evidence about the impact of past programs is that we got what we paid for. Public sector investments in training are exceedingly modest compared to the magnitude of the skill deficiencies that policymakers are trying to address. Not surprisingly, modest investments usually yield modest gains...
> (LaLonde, 1995: 149)

A third salient feature of the US evidence is significant heterogeneity in estimated effects. Evaluation of experimental programs shows earnings effects that range from negative impacts for individuals who never worked before, to large positive impacts on economically disadvantaged female household heads or economically disadvantaged male household heads. Substantial variation in program impacts across sites is common in training programs using random assignment. Variability of estimated impacts on earnings is also evident in nonexperimental programs. However, when studies most susceptible to selection bias are removed, the qualitative evidence from nonexperimental programs is similar to that of experimental programs (Heckman *et al.*, 1999).

In Canada, the published literature on government training programs is considerably sparser – likely due to the fact that program evaluations are carried out internally by government agencies and the findings are not published in academic or policy journals (Riddell, 1991). Riddell

(1995) reviews employment and training programs that operated in the 1980s and early 1990s. Programs targeted on the economically disadvantaged had modest effects similar to those found in US studies, but impacts of programs serving clients with fewer barriers were larger. Subsequent analysis by Park *et al.* (1996) found significant gains from training programs for some groups, including women reentering the workforce and individuals trained in areas with identified skills shortages.

European programs are more focused on speeding the transition to work and reducing unemployment, especially among youths. The difference in emphasis reflects the facts that European youth are generally less economically disadvantaged than US youth, but are more likely to be unemployed for extended periods of time. A common finding of European studies is that training results in substantial gains in employment but has little impact on wages (Heckman *et al.*, 1999; Kluve and Schmidt, 2002).

In summary, government-sponsored training has a mixed record, with rising earnings of some groups (adult women and displaced workers) but having little or no impact on earnings of others (disadvantaged adult men and youths). Even when they are positive, the impacts on earnings are modest and are usually not large enough to substantially reduce poverty rates. Training does, however, have a better track record in improving the transition to employment.

Two general responses have emerged in response to the mixed performance of public training programs. One, illustrated by Carneiro and Heckman (2003), is to argue that problems associated with low skills should be addressed much earlier in the life cycle. The other, illustrated by Martin and Grubb (2001), argues that public training programs can be made more effective by improving their design. Design features that they regard as crucial include careful targeting on participants most likely to benefit from training, keeping programs small in scale, including a strong work experience component to establish links with employers, and having programs that produce a certification that is recognized in the labor market.

Private Sector Training

Private-sector training refers to forms of skill acquisition that are job related and where learning is an activity separate from regular job duties. This type of skill acquisition may include both formal and informal learning, be general or specific and either employer- or individually-sponsored. In general, employer-financed training tends to be firm specific and informal in nature. However, firms may finance the acquisition of (formal) vocational training, such as apprenticeships, that is more general in nature. Studies of work-related training focus on one or the other type of training, depending on data availability.

Methodologically, the literature surveyed here relies on nonexperimental data. The selection problems are acute, as employers are likely to select for training the most promising individuals, who may have higher-than-average earnings regardless of training. Similarly, individuals who choose to undertake training are likely to be more productive or to have unobserved characteristics, such as motivation, associated with higher wages. The papers we consider here use different methods to resolve this problem.

Interest in the training policies of firms and the skill acquisition choices of workers originated in the US during the 1980s when slow productivity growth (relative to Japan) was at the forefront of the economic agenda. However, there was little information about training in available data (Barron *et al.*, 1997). During the next decade, research produced many studies on the determinants of training and on the effects of training on wages, thanks to the availability of the National Longitudinal Survey of Youth (NLSY), which follows a representative sample of youth over the period since 1978, gathering exhaustive information about their labor market experiences. The survey asks about any type of training, other than schooling, military training, and government-sponsored training, and further categorizes it as: (1) company training or OJT, (2) apprenticeship programs, and (3) off-the-job training (OFT). The richness of information regarding skill-related characteristics contained in the survey allows for adequate measurement of the variables involved, including usually unobservable variables such as those measuring ability. In addition, the longitudinal nature of the data allows researchers to address the methodological issues regarding selection bias.

Most of the US literature is hence based on the NLSY. One of the earlier studies by Lynch (1992) focuses on a subsample of non-college-educated youth to estimate the effect on wages of weeks spent in company training, OFT, or apprenticeship training. The estimated coefficients translate into approximately 25% higher wages for an average apprenticeship of 63 weeks and 15% for an average spell of company training of 31 weeks. Using all workers in the NLSY sample, Veum (1995) finds smaller returns of 7.5% for an episode of company training, 6% for an apprenticeship, and 11% for an occurrence of OFT. In addition, he estimates that company training and OFT increase wage growth by similar magnitudes. Both these studies are confined to episodes of training lasting more than 1 month. Later, Parent (1999), using a more sophisticated methodology and not restricting the sample to long training episodes, estimates that 1 year of OFT or OJT training increases earnings between 12% and 16%.

Further issues arise within this literature. One relates to the portability of training. Lynch (1992) separates training into that received with a current employer and that received with a previous employer, finding high returns to apprenticeships and OFT received during a previous job, but no returns to company training received during a previous job. The results in Parent (1999), on the other hand, suggest that employer-based training and OFT are the most portable forms of training. Given the small fraction of individuals undertaking apprenticeships (around 1%), results regarding this form of training should be treated with caution. A second issue is who pays for private-sector training. Parent (1999) finds that workers partially pay for OJT with lower initial wages. Barron *et al.* (1999) use a different data set and find that although the initial wages seem to be smaller for workers undergoing OJT, the difference is small. The general perception in this matter is that firms pay for OJT training and reap the benefits through higher productivity of the firm.

In Canada, private-sector training has been much less analyzed and the results are nonconclusive. Parent (2003) uses the Follow-Up of the School Leavers Survey (FSLS) and finds that participation in employer-provided training raises male earnings by 10% but not significantly so for females. Results from this study also suggest that training may increase employment. Hui and Smith (2003), using the Adult Education and Training Survey (AETS), find positive effects of self/employer-financed training on employment for women. In addition, small positive effects on weekly earnings from employer-financed training are apparent for both genders, while self-financed training seems to have small negative impact on female wages. These findings seem to be contradicted by Havet's (2006) study, which uses matched employer–employee data and finds a positive impact of firm-provided training on the wages of women, but not of men.

Studies from Europe also tend to find positive effects of training on labor outcomes. In Great Britain, Greenhalgh and Stewart (1987) find positive effects of vocational training on occupational status. Booth (1993) estimates that 1 week of training raises the earnings of graduates by 1%. Both studies find significant gender differences. More recently, Blundell *et al.* (1999), use the National Child Development Study (NCDS) to study the impact of work-related training on the earnings of UK workers. They find positive returns (5–6%) for employer-provided training and also that this type of training seems transferable across employers. These findings are corroborated in a later study by Arulampalam and Booth (2001) that uses the same data.

For countries other than North America or the UK, evidence on the returns to training is less abundant. Goux and Maurin (2000) estimate wage returns to employer-provided training for France. They report around 7% higher wages among those who received training, but the estimates become insignificant when they account for firm selection of workers on the basis of posttraining mobility. Similarly, Pischke (2001) finds that, in Germany, 1 year of full-time work-related training (training during leisure time) increases wages between 3% and 4%. When he

accounts for selection based on wage growth, the returns are higher in magnitude, from 3% (males) to 6% (females), but not statistically significant. Schøene (2002) finds that employer-financed training participation is associated with 1% higher wages in Norway when controlling for selection based on seniority and job complexity (down from a 5% return in the absence of selection controls).

Overall, the returns to private-sector training seem quite high – higher, for instance, than the returns to schooling. In contrast, the incidence of training is not large, which is puzzling if there are such high returns. A leading explanation for the high returns to training is selection bias – that is, high-productivity workers are more likely to receive training and to have higher wages and/or wage growth. All papers find that addressing this selection problem is important. Estimates produced with a selection correction procedure are generally smaller than those obtained without, corroborating the heterogeneity of the returns to training. The effect of accounting for selection varies depending on the method used. In general, estimates are reduced by 40–50%. In some cases, the results are quite extreme. For instance, when selection is based on worker's mobility, since firms are less likely to train workers at high risk of leaving in the near future, the effect of training practically disappears (Goux and Maurin, 2000). A potential explanation could be that most of the benefits of training accrue to job movers and not to job stayers. Gerfin (2003) provides some evidence for this hypothesis in his study of Swiss work-related training. He shows that training undertaken during the last year generates the highest returns to individuals who changed jobs (around 5% increases in monthly earnings) versus those who stayed at the firm (1.2%). Other studies find no returns to training once selection is taken into account. For instance, Leuven and Oosterbeek (2007) find that when comparing the returns to training of Dutch workers who took training with the returns of workers who intended to undertake training but did not do so because of a random event (sickness or family circumstances), earnings differences are not statistically significant. There is also cross-country evidence from the European Community Household Panel indicating that the effect of training is significantly smaller when individual heterogeneity is accounted for (Bassanini *et al.*, 2007).

Finally, other factors may explain the correlation between high wages and training. Promotions, for instance, are a factor generally overlooked. These positively influence both pay and training. In addition, the returns to training are likely to differ by type of job, with more productive jobs (managerial/professional) requiring more training and higher pay than blue-collar jobs. Failure to account for these factors is also likely to overestimate the effect of private-sector training (Frazis and Lowenstein, 2005).

In summary, studies of informal private sector training seem to agree on the following:

- returns to training are generally positive and significant, particularly employer training and OFT;
- there are gender and ethnic differences in the returns to training, although the sign of the difference seems to be country specific; and
- there is substantial evidence that unaccounted-for factors lead to overestimating the returns to training. In general, those who undergo training seem to be those whose productivity, occupation, or other characteristics would lead them to have high wages regardless of training.

The papers examined so far in this section do not formally distinguish between formal and informal education, although it is expected that some OFT may be conducive to a degree or diploma. However, there are studies analyzing the impact of adult education and training that focus specifically on the effect of acquiring formal schooling later in life. Although the notion of adult education is country specific, it is generally accepted that formal schooling is associated with the completion of courses toward the achievement of a degree or diploma. The skills acquired with formal schooling are also more likely to be general rather than trade or profession specific.

The North American literature finds substantial returns to formal certification for older workers. Leigh and Gill (1997) and Jacobson et al. (2005a) find returns to community college in the US for workers over age 28 that are around 8% (9%) for males (females). In Canada, Zhang and Palameta (2006) use longitudinal information from the Survey of Labor and Income and Dynamics to evaluate the impact of formal schooling on earnings for individuals who have been out of school for more than a year and then enrolled in formal education. They find substantial earnings gains for those individuals who obtained a certificate (7% increase in earnings for men, 10% for females). In this study, younger workers who switch firms after obtaining a certificate gain the most from their studies, whereas workers over 35 reap higher benefits staying with the same firm. Ferrer and Menendez (2007) also find evidence for Canada of large earning effects from acquiring formal education later in life.

However, the European findings about the impact of adult formal education show that formal qualifications obtained later in life seem to have little impact on earnings. With the exception of the Blundell et al. (1999) study, which finds that all forms of work-related training leading to formal qualifications enhance earnings by 5–10%; other studies do not find such positive returns. Egerton (2000) uses 10 years of the British General Household Survey, which incorporates a rich data set of covariates including father's social class, to examine this issue. Her results show no significant difference in earnings between full-time mature students and early graduates, although she does not address selection bias. Jerkins et al. (2003) use panel data from the NCDS to analyze the impact of adult education on employment and earnings. Their findings reveal that episodes of adult education, particularly in occupational training, have positive effects on employment but a limited effect on wages, except for the least-qualified individuals. Part of the difference in results with Blundell et al. (1999) is likely due to differences in the goals of study, which lead them to consider different control groups. In Sweden, Ekström (2003) analyzed the impact of adult secondary education on annual earnings during the early 1990s, finding a negative effect for males and only weakly significant positive effects for females. Later, Albrecht et al. (2004) follow the large expansion of Swedish adult education programs during 1997 through 2002, called the Knowledge Lift, to estimate the impact on annual earnings and employment of increasing formal schooling for the low skilled. Their results show no effect of Knowledge Lift programs on earnings or employment, with the exception of an increase in the employability (but not earnings) of young men.

In summary, the literature on employer-based training finds that this type of human capital investment generally has positive effects on labor market outcomes such as wages. The magnitude of the returns varies depending on the type of training undertaken and the methodology employed. As is the case with the literature on the returns to education, careful econometric analysis is needed to take into account the possibility of selection bias arising because training is undertaken by individuals who are more productive and would have commanded higher wages regardless of training.

See also: Lifelong Learning; Participation in Adult Learning.

Bibliography

Acemoglu, D. and Pischke, J.-S. (1999). The structure of wages and investment in general training. *Journal of Political Economy* **107**(3), 539–572.

Albrecht, J., van den Berg, G. J., and Vroman, S. (2004). The knowledge lift: The Swedish adult education program that aimed to eliminate low worker skill levels. *IZA Discussion Paper No. 1503*. Institute for the Study of Labor (IZA), Bonn, Germany.

Arulampalam, W. and Booth, A. (1998). Labour market flexibility and skills acquisition: Is there a trade-off? *British Journal of Industrial Relations* **36**(4), 521–536.

Barron, J., Berger, M., and Black, D. (1997). How well do we measure training? *Journal of Labor Economics* **15**(3), 507–528.

Barron, J., Berger, M., and Black, D. (1999). Do workers pay for on-the-job training? *Journal of Human Resources* **34**(2), 235–252.

Blundell, R., Dearden, L., and Meghir, C. (1999). *Work-Related Training and Earnings*. London: Institute for Fiscal Studies.

Booth, A. (1993). Private sector training and graduate earnings. *Review of Economics and Statistics* **75**(1), 164–170.

Carneiro, P. and Heckman, J. (2003). Human capital policy. *NBER Working Paper No. 9495.* Institute for the Study of Labor (IZA), Bonn, Germany.

Egerton, M. (2000). Pay differentials between early and mature graduate men: The role of state employment. *Journal of Education and Work* **13**(3), 289–305.

Ekström, E. (2003). Earnings effects of adult secondary education in Sweden. *Working Paper Series No. 16.* IFAU – Institute for Labour Market Policy Evaluation, Uppsala, Sweden.

Ferrer, A. and Menendez, A. (2007). The returns to flexible post-secondary education: The effect of delaying school. *CLSRN Working Paper No. 7.* CLSRN, Vancouver, BC, Canada.

Frazis, H. and Lowenstein, M. (2005). Reexamining the returns to training functional form, magnitude and interpretation. *Journal of Human Resources* **XL**(2), 453–476.

Gerfin, M. (2003). Work-related training and wages – an empirical analysis for male workers in Switzerland. Mimeo, Volkswirtschaftliches Institut, Universität Bern.

Goux, D. and Maurin, E. (2000). Returns to firm provided training: Evidence from French worker–firm matched data. *Labor Economics* **7**, 1–19.

Greenberg, D. H., Michalopoulos, C., and Robins, P. K. (2004). What happens to the effects of government-funded training programs over time? *Journal of Human Resources* **39**(1), 277–293.

Greenhalgh, C. and Stewart, M. (1987). The effects and determinants of training. *Oxford Bulletin of Economics and Statistics* **49**(2), 171–190.

Havet, N. (2006). La valorisation salariale et professionnelle de la formation en entreprise diffère-t-elle selon le sexe? l'exemple canadien. *Working Paper 06-02 Groupe d'Analyse et de Théorie Économique (GATE).*

Heckman, J. J., Lalonde, R., and Smith, J. (1999). The economics and econometrics of active labor market programs. In Card, D. and Ashenfelter, O. (eds.) *Handbook of Labor Economics,* ch. 31, pp 1865–2085. Amsterdam: North Holland.

Hui, S. and Smith, J. (2003). *The Labour Market Impacts of Adult Education and Training in Canada.* Ottawa, ON: Statistics Canada.

Jacobson, L., LaLonde, R., and Sullivan, D. G. (2005a). Estimating the returns to community college schooling for displaced workers. *Journal of Econometrics* **25**(1–2), 271–304.

Jacobson, L., LaLonde, R., and Sullivan, D. G. (2005b). Is retraining displaced workers a good investment? *Economic Perspectives* **XXIX** (2), 47–66, Federal Reserve Bank of Chicago.

Jenkins, A., Vignoles, A., Wolf, A., and Galindo-Rueda, F. (2003). The determinants and labor market effects of lifelong learning. *Applied Economics* **35**, 1711–1721.

Kluve, J. and Schmidt, C. (2002). Can training and employment subsidies combat European unemployment? *Economic Policy* **35**, 409–448.

Lalonde, R. (1995). The promise of public sector-sponsored training programs. *Journal of Economic Perspectives* **9** (Spring), 149–168.

Leigh, D. and Gill, A. M. (1997). Labor market returns to community colleges: Evidence for returning adults. *Journal of Human Resources* **32**(2), 334–353.

Leuven, E. (2005). The economics of private sector training: A survey of the literature. *Journal of Economic Surveys* **19**(1), 91–111.

Leuven, E. and Oosterbeek, H. (2007). A new approach to estimate the wage returns to work-related training. *IZA Discussion Paper No. 526.* Institute for the Study of Labor (IZA), Bonn, Germany.

Lynch, L. (1992). Private-sector training and the earnings of young workers. *American Economic Review* **82**(1), 299–312.

Martin, J. P. and Grubb, D. (2001). What works and for whom: A review of OECD countries' experiences with active labour market policies. *Working Paper Series 2001: 14.* IFAU – Institute for Labour Market Policy Evaluation, Uppsala, Sweden.

Parent, D. (1999). Wages and mobility: The impact of employer-provided training. *Journal of Labor Economics* **17**(2), 298–317.

Parent, D. (2003). Employer-supported training in Canada and its impact on mobility and wages. *Empirical Economics* **28**, 431–459.

Park, N., Power, B., Riddell, W. C., and Wong, G. (1996). Special Issue (Part 1): An Assessment of the Impact of Government-Sponsored Training. *Canadian Journal of Economics* **29**(1), S93–S98.

Pischke, J. (2001). Continuous training in Germany. *Journal of Population Economics* **14**, 523–548.

Riddell, W. C. (1991). Evaluation of manpower and training programs: The North American experience. In OECD (ed). *Evaluating Labour Market and Social Programs,* pp 43–72. Paris: OECD.

Riddell, W. C. (1995). Human capital formation in Canada: Recent developments and policy responses. In Keith, G. B. and Beach, C. M. (eds.) *Labour Market Polarization and Social Policy Reform,* pp 125–172. Kingston, ON: School of Policy Studies, Queen's University.

Schøene, P. (2002). Why is the return to training so high? Mimeo, Institute for Social Research, Olso, Norway.

US Department of Labor (1995). *What's Working (and What's Not): A Summary of Research on the Economic Impacts of Employment and Training Programs.* Washington, DC: US Department of Labor.

Veum, J. (1995). Sources of training and their impact on wages. *Industrial and Labor Relations Review* **48**(4), 812–826.

Zhang, X. and Palameta, B. (2006). Participation in adult schooling and its earnings impact in Canada. *Statistics Canada, Analytical Studies Branch Series 2006. Research Paper No. 276.* Business and Labour Market Analysis Division, Ottawa, ON, Canada.

Further Reading

Angrist, J. and Kreuger, A. (1999). Empirical strategies in labor economics. In Card, D. and Ashenfelter, O. (eds.) *Handbook of Labor Economics,* pp 1277–1357. Amsterdam: North Holland.

Bassanini, A., Booth, A. L., Brunello, G., De Paola, M., and Leuven, E. (2007). Workspace training in Europe. In Brunello, G., Garibaldi, P., and Wasmer, E. (eds.) *Education and Training in Europe,* pp 141–157. Oxford: Oxford University Press.

Blundell, R., Dearden, L., Meghir, C., and Sianesi, B. (1999). Human capital investment: The returns from education and training to the individual, the firm and the economy. *Fiscal Studies* **20**(1), 1–23.

OECD (1994). *The OECD Jobs Study – Facts, Analysis, Strategies.* Paris: OECD.

OECD (2006). *Boosting Jobs and Incomes.* Paris: OECD.

Subject Index

Page numbers suffixed by t and f refer to tables and figures respectively.

A

Accommodation learning 48
Accountability
  adult literacy education 103, 104*t*
  see also Assessment strategies
Accreditation
  elder learning organizations 168
Acquired immune deficiency syndrome (AIDS) *see* HIV/AIDS
Activism-based learning 268
Activity theory, CHAT
  workplace learning 227
Addams, Jane 90
Adult basic education (ABE) 95–99
  future directions 97
  national developments 95
  Swedish educational model/Komvux 95, 96
  vocational-based learning (VBL) 96, 97*f*, 98*f*
Adult education and training (AET) 3–13
  adult basic education (ABE) 95–99, 97*f*, 98*f*
  adult learning 7
  barriers 216–221
  basic concepts 6
  Black Book 11
  characteristics 205, 206*t*
  citizenship education 106–112
  civil society 265–270
  educational sectors 7
  formal learning 302
  government-sponsored training 301
  historical background 4
  historical narratives 14–19
  human capital theory 9, 253, 259
  immigrant education 106–112
  importance 216
  informal learning 207, 208, 302
  nation building 271–276
  outcomes analyses 8, 294, 295, 295*t*, 296, 297, 299–305
  participation research 8, 205–215, 206*t*, 207*t*, 209*t*, 219, 262*t*
  political economy model 9, 259–264, 262*t*
  popular adult education 118–124, 254
  private-sector training 302
  race and ethnicity 244–249
  social class 238–243, 296
  socioeconomic modernization 253–258
  socioeconomic perspectives 9
  tension and conflict 11
  training programs 10
  value considerations 263
Adult learning 29–34
  adult basic education (ABE) 95–99, 97*f*, 98*f*
  background information 29
  barriers 216–221
  biographic perspectives 60–65
  characteristics 47–52, 48*f*, 53, 205, 206*t*
  context-based learning 31
  early education–cognition relationships 44
  formal learning 302
  funding considerations 186–191
  government-sponsored training 301
  health considerations 277–282
  historical narratives 14–19
  importance 216
  individual learning characteristics 29, 30, 31
  informal learning 207, 208, 302
  institutional models 23, 263
  instructional strategies 7, 53
  mind–body perspectives 32–33
  museums 152, 153, 154, 155
  outcomes analyses 8, 294–298, 295*t*, 299–305
  participation research 8, 205–215, 206*t*, 207*t*, 209*t*, 219, 262*t*
  philosophical perspectives 35–40
  plasticity 45
  portfolios 198
  socioeconomic modernization 253–258

transformative learning theory 53–59
see also Lifelong learning; University adult and continuing education (ACE)
Adult literacy education 100–105
  assessment and accountability systems 103, 104*t*
  background information 100
  basic concepts 100, 101*t*
  educational role 102
  functional literacy 100
  social-practices model 101, 102*f*
  workforce influences 104
Africa
  adult education 247
  community education 136
  labor education 115
  Southern African Development Community (SADC) 272, 273, 274
  see also South Africa
AIDS module 173
American Association for Adult Education (AAAE) 3
American Association of Museums (AAM) 151
Andragogy 29, 35
Angola
  socioeconomic/sociopolitical characteristics 272
  see also Africa
Antigonish movement 90, 121
Assessment strategies
  adult literacy education 103, 104*t*
  large-scale assessment portfolios 199
  learning cities and regions 161
  portfolios 198, 199, 200, 201, 203
  records of achievement, NRA 199
  summative assessment portfolios 200
Assimilation learning 48
Australia
  adult basic education (ABE) 95
  community education 136
  lifelong learning model 181*t*, 184
  vocational education and training (VET) 181*t*, 184
Austria
  displaced worker assistance programs 148
Authentic tests 194
Autobiographies, biographic perspectives 61

B

Bildung 119
Black Book 11
Boal, Augusto 120–121
Botswana
  socioeconomic/sociopolitical characteristics 272
  see also Africa
Bounded-agency model 219
BRAC (Building Resources across Countries) 291
Brazil
  nonformal education 83

C

Canada
  community education 136
  immigrant education 109
  popular adult education 121
Capitalist societies 238, 256
Cardiovascular diseases *see* Health considerations
Caribbean countries
  HIV/AIDS education 171
Chain-of-response model 214
Chicago School
  historical background 60
China
  elder learning organizations 167, 168
Citizenship education 106–112
  background information 106
  basic concepts 106, 107–108